I0138193

LET US DRAW NEAR

Let Us Draw Near

A Commentary on Hebrews

Second Edition

David McClister

Let Us Draw Near: A Commentary on Hebrews

P.O. Box 290696, Tampa, FL 33687
www.deward.com

The first edition of this commentary was published as *A Commentary on Hebrews* by Florida College Press (2010).

Cover design by Barry Wallace.

Unless otherwise noted, all Biblical quotations are the author's translation.

Printed in the United States of America.

ISBN: 978-1-947929-34-0

To Lisa

CONTENTS

PREFACE TO THE SECOND EDITION

I am happy for the occasion to provide a second edition of this work, as it has given me a much-needed opportunity to correct numerous errors of several kinds, to revise and clarify, and to update discussions with scholarship that has appeared since the first edition. Several parts of the commentary have been extensively rewritten, and a new excursus has been added. While this commentary is not new, it is, I believe, improved. Special thanks is due to Ryan Boyer, who did a close reading of the manuscript and offered invaluable help. I am also grateful to the DeWard Publishing Company for the willingness to make it available, and to several brethren in the Lord who, in many ways, have made this effort possible.

David McClister
June 2024

ABBREVIATIONS

Biblical and Apocryphal Books

Gen	Genesis
Exod	Exodus
Lev	Leviticus
Num	Numbers
Deut	Deuteronomy
Josh	Joshua
Jdg	Judges
Sam	Samuel
Kngs	Kings
Chron	Chronicles
Neh	Nehemiah
Esth	Esther
Psa	Psalm
Isa	Isaiah
Jer	Jeremiah
Ezek	Ezekiel
Dan	Daniel
Hos	Hosea
Mic	Micah
Hab	Habakkuk
Hag	Haggai
Zeph	Zephaniah
Hag	Haggai
Zech	Zechariah
Mal	Malachi
Matt	Matthew
Rom	Romans
Cor	Corinthians

Gal	Galatians
Eph	Ephesians
Phil	Philippians
Col	Colossians
Thes	Thessalonians
Tim	Timothy
Phlm	Philemon
Heb	Hebrews
Jam	James
Pet	Peter
Rev	Revelation
Macc	Maccabees
Wisd	Wisdom of Solomon
Sir	Sirach

ABR	*Australian Biblical Review*
AD	*anno domini*
AGJU	Arbeiten zur Geschichte des antiken Judentums und des Urchristentums (series)
AJP	*American Journal of Philology*
ALGHJ	Arbeiten zur Literatur und Geschichte des hellenistischen Judentums (series)
Ant.	*Antiquities of the Jews* (Josephus)
ANF	*Ante-Nicene Fathers*
AsJT	*Asbury Journal of Theology*
ASV	American Standard Version
AUSS	*Andrews University Seminary Studies*
AYB	Anchor Yale Bible (series)
AYBD	*Anchor Yale Bible Dictionary*
BBR	*Bulletin for Biblical Research*
BC	before Christ

BDAG	Danker, Frederick W., Walter Bauer, William F. Arndt, and F. Wilbur Gingrich. *Greek-English Lexicon of the New Testament and Other Early Christian Literature.* 3rd ed. Chicago: University of Chicago Press, 2000.
BDB	Brown, Francis, Samuel Rolles Driver, and Charles Augustus Briggs. *Enhanced Brown-Driver-Briggs Hebrew and English Lexicon*. Oxford: Clarendon Press, 1977.
Bib	*Biblica*
BDF	Blass, Friedrich, Albert Debrunner, and Robert Walter Funk. *A Greek Grammar of the New Testament and Other Early Christian Literature*. Chicago: University of Chicago Press, 1961.
BibSac	*Bibliotheca Sacra*
BTB	*Biblical Theology Bulletin*
BZNW	Beihefte zur Zeitschrift für die neutestamentliche Wissenschaft (series)
c.	*circa* (about)
CBQ	*Catholic Biblical Quarterly*
CE	common era
cf.	*confer* (compare)
ch, chs	chapter, chapters
CJT	*Canadian Journal of Theology*
CRINT	Compendia Rerum Iudaicarum ad Novum Testamentum (series)
CTR	*Criswell Theological Review*
CurBR	*Currents in Biblical Research*
DBI	Ryken, Leland *et al*, eds. *Dictionary of Biblical Imagery*. Downers Grove, IL: InterVarsity Press, 2000.
EBTC	Evangelical Biblical Theology Commentary (series)
ed.	editor or edition
EDNT	Balz, Horst Robert, and Gerhard Schneider, eds. *Exegetical Dictionary of the New Testament*. 3 vols. Grand Rapids: Eerdmans, 1990.
e.g.	*exempli gratia* (for example)

EJud	Neusner, Jacob, Alan J. Avery-Peck, and William Scott Green, eds. *The Encyclopedia of Judaism*. 2nd ed. 5 vols. Leiden: Brill, 2005.
esp.	especially
ESV	English Standard Version
et al	*et alia* (and others)
etc.	*et cetera* (and so on)
EvQ	*Evangelical Quarterly*
ExpTim	*Expository Times*
f, ff	following verse, following verses
fn	footnote
frag.	fragment
GKC	Kautzsch, Emil, ed. *Gesenius' Hebrew Grammar.* Translated by Arther E. Cowley. 2nd ed. Oxford: Clarendon, 1910.
GTJ	*Grace Theological Journal*
HCSB	Holman Christian Standard Bible
HTR	*Harvard Theological Review*
HvTSt	*Hervormde teologiese studies*
ICC	International Critical Commentary (series)
idem	same (author)
IDS	*In die Skriflig*
i.e.	*id est* (that is)
ISBE	Bromiley, Geoffrey W., ed. *The International Standard Bible Encyclopedia, Revised.* Grand Rapids: Eerdmans, 1979–1988.
JBL	*Journal of Biblical Literature*
JBR	*Journal of Bible and Religion*
JETS	*Journal of the Evangelical Theological Society*
JGRChJ	*Journal of Greco-Roman Christianity and Judaism*
JQR	*Jewish Quarterly Review*
JRASup	Journal of Roman Archaeology Supplements (series)

JSJ	*Journal for the Study of Judaism*
JSJSup	Journal for the Study of Judaism Supplements (series)
JSNT	*Journal for the Study of the New Testament*
JSNTSup	Journal for the Study of the New Testament Supplement Series
JSPSup	Journal for the Study of the Pseudepigrapha Supplement Series
JTS	*Journal of Theological Studies*
K&D	Keil, Carl Friedrich, and Franz Delitzsch. *Biblical Commentary on the Old Testament*. Translated by James Martin *et al*. 25 vols. Edinburgh, 1857–1878. Repr., 10 vols., Grand Rapids: Eerdmans, 1949.
KBL	Koehler, Ludwig, Walter Baumgartner, M. E. J. Richardson, and Johann Jakob Stamm. *The Hebrew and Aramaic Lexicon of the Old Testament*. 4 vols. Leiden: E.J. Brill, 1994–2000.
KJV	King James Version
ktl	*kai ta loipa* (and the rest)
LB	*Linguistica Biblica*
LCL	Loeb Classical Library
LEC	Library of Early Christianity (series)
lit.	literally
LNTS	Library of New Testament Studies (series)
Louw-Nida	Louw, Johannes P., and Eugene Albert Nida. *Greek-English Lexicon of the New Testament: Based on Semantic Domains*. 2 vols. New York: United Bible Societies, 1996.
LSJ	Liddell, Henry George, Robert Scott, Henry Stuart Jones, and Roderick McKenzie. *A Greek-English Lexicon*. 9th ed. with Supplement. Oxford: Clarendon Press, 1996.
LSTS	Library of Second Temple Studies (series)
LXX	Septuagint
m.	The Mishnah

MM	Moulton, James Hope, and George Milligan. *The Vocabulary of the Greek Testament*. London: Hodder and Stoughton, 1930.
MT	Masoretic text (Hebrew)
NAC	New American Commentary (series)
NASB	New American Standard Bible
Neot	*Neotestimentica*
NET	NET Bible
NIBCNT	New International Biblical Commentary on the New Testament (series)
NICNT	New International Commentary on the New Testament (series)
NICOT	New International Commentary on the Old Testament (series)
NIDB	Sakenfeld, Katharine Doob, ed. *The New Interpreter's Dictionary of the Bible*. 5 vols. Nashville, TN: Abingdon Press, 2006–2009.
NIDNTT	Brown, Colin, ed. *New International Dictionary of New Testament Theology*. 3 vols. Grand Rapids: Zondervan Publishing House, 1986.
NIDNTTE	Silva, Moisés, ed. *New International Dictionary of New Testament Theology and Exegesis*. 5 vols. Grand Rapids: Zondervan, 2014.
NIDOTTE	VanGemeren, Willem, ed. *New International Dictionary of Old Testament Theology & Exegesis*. 5 vols. Grand Rapids: Zondervan, 1997.
NIGTC	New International Greek Testament Commentary (series)
NIV	New International Version
NKJB	New King James Bible
NovT	*Novum Testamentum*
NT	New Testament
NTL	New Testament Library (series)
NTS	*New Testament Studies*
NPNF[1,2]	*Nicene and Post-Nicene Fathers (series 1 and 2)*

NRSV	New Revised Standard Version
NSBT	New Studies in Biblical Theology (series)
OCD	Hornblower, Simon, and Antony Spawforth, eds. *Oxford Classical Dictionary*. Edited by 3rd ed. Oxford: Oxford University Press, 2003.
OT	Old Testament
PIBA	*Proceedings of the Irish Biblical Association*
PNTC	Pillar New Testament Commentary (series)
Presb	*Presbyterion*
PRSt	*Perspectives in Religious Studies*
RB	*Revue biblique*
repr.	reprinted
ResQ	*Restoration Quarterly*
rev.	revised
RevExp	*Review and Expositor*
RSV	Revised Standard Version
SBLMS	Society of Biblical Literature Monograph Series
SJT	*Scottish Journal of Theology*
SNTSMS	Society of New Testament Studies Monograph Series
Str-B	Strack, Hermann L., and Paul Billerbeck. *A Commentary on the New Testament from the Talmud & Midrash*. Edited by Jacob N. Cerone. Translated by Andrew Bowden and Joseph Longarino. 3 vols. Bellingham, WA: Lexham Press, 2021–2022.
SWJT	*Southwestern Journal of Theology*
TDNT	Kittel, Gerhard, and Gerhard Friedrich, eds. *Theological Dictionary of the New Testament*. Translated by Geoffrey W. Bromiley. 10 vols. Grand Rapids: Eerdmans, 1964–1976.
TDOT	Botterweck, G. Johannes, Helmer Ringgren, and Heinz-Josef Fabry, eds. *Theological Dictionary of the Old Testament*. 15 vols. Grand Rapids; Cambridge, U.K.: Eerdmans, 1977–2012.
TMSJ	*The Master's Seminary Journal*

TNTC	Tyndale New Testament Commentaries (series)
trans.	translated by
TrinJ	*Trinity Journal*
TS	*Theological Studies*
TWOT	Harris, R. Laird, Gleason L. Archer Jr., and Bruce K. Waltke, eds. *Theological Wordbook of the Old Testament*. 2 vols. Chicago: Moody Press, 1999.
TynBul	*Tyndale Bulletin*
v, vv	verse, verses
viz.	*videlicet* (namely)
vol.	volume
WBC	Word Biblical Commentary (series)
WTJ	*Westminster Theological Journal*
WUNT	Wissenschaftliche Untersuchungen zum Neuen Testament (series)
ZNW	*Zeitschrift für die neutestamentliche Wissenschaft und die Kunde der älteren Kirche*

INTRODUCTION

I. Authorship

We simply do not know who wrote the document we call "Hebrews." The author of Hebrews was probably a converted Hellenistic[1] Jew. He was well-educated, as evidenced by his good literary style, he was trained in handling the Greek translation of the OT (the Septuagint), and he had training in rhetoric. He was an intensely religious man whose thought was completely immersed in the OT. Some scholars have further speculated that the author of Hebrews was acquainted with the categories of Hellenistic philosophy (especially late Platonism) and the writings of Philo of Alexandria.[2] Verbal parallels between Hebrews and Philo exist,[3] but they fall short of demonstrating a shared conceptual world, let alone Hebrews' literary dependence on Philo.[4] If anything, they suggest that

[1] *I.e.*, Greek-speaking. Since Martin Hengel's *Judaism and Hellenism: Studies in Their Encounter in Palestine during the Early Hellenistic Period*, trans. John Bowden, Vols. 1 & 2 (Philadelphia: Fortress, 1974)), drastic distinctions between "Hebrews" and "Hellenistic Jews" are generally no longer supported in modern scholarship. See also Craig C. Hill, *Hellenists and Hebrews* (Minneapolis: Augsburg Fortress, 1992). Modern scholarship is shifting more to the terminology of bicultural dialogue and exchange. Gabriella Gelardini, "Faith in Hebrews and Its Relationship to Soteriology: An Interpretation in the Context of the Concept of Fides in Roman Culture," in *So Great a Salvation: A Dialogue on the Atonement in Hebrews*, ed. Jon C. Laansma, George H. Guthrie, Cynthia Long Westfall, and Chris Keith, LNTS 516 (London; New York; Oxford; New Delhi; Sydney: T&T Clark, 2019), 249–56, at 251.

[2] For example, Sigurd Grindheim, "Direct Dependence on Philo in the Epistle to the Hebrews," *NovT* 65 (2023): 517–43; but he acknowledges that "it is not possible … to trace direct lines of influence from Philo's works to the Epistle to the Hebrews" (542).

[3] See Sigurd Grindheim, *The Letter to the Hebrews*, PNTC (Grand Rapids: Eerdmans, 2023). 11–14.

[4] Grindheim, *Letter to the Hebrews*, 14: "All the parallels between Philo and the author of Hebrews also show that there is a big distance between them. Philo's allegorical method of interpretation and his Middle Platonist worldview are alien to Hebrews." Gareth Lee Cockerill, *The Epistle to the Hebrews*, NICNT (Grand Rapids: Eerdmans, 2012), 31: "Because of their common heritage in the Hellenistic world Philo can be helpful in understanding Hebrews at the level of semantics and imagery. A brief glance, however, at Philo's worldview reveals the essential gulf between the two." See also Alan M. Fairhurst, "Hellenistic Influence in the Epistle to the Hebrews," *TynBul* 7–8 (1961): 17–27; L. D. Hurst, "How 'Pla-

the author of Hebrews had been exposed to Alexandrian ways of thinking (which were widespread in the ancient world), and may have been an Alexandrian himself. He also knew at least Timothy within Paul's circle of friends (Heb 13.23).

See the Appendix: Candidates for the Author of Hebrews.

II. Genre

The question of genre asks about what kind of writing Hebrews purports to be, and therefore, how best to read it. It has been common throughout the reception history of this document to refer to Hebrews as an epistle (letter). Technically, however, it is not a letter. Hebrews lacks the characteristic features of a Hellenistic letter[5] except for the few personal greetings at the close of the work. In Hellenistic letter-writing, the convention was to begin with the author identifying both himself and the recipient(s) of the letter. The opening lines of Paul's letters were quite typical in this regard, but Hebrews lacks this feature entirely. It was also common, especially in the letters of the apostles, to follow the greetings with a doxology (an ascription of praise to God concerning the readers). Paul's letters also provide good examples of this, but Hebrews has no doxology. Since the author of Hebrews shows every sign of being an educated person otherwise, we must assume that he knew how to write a letter by the conventions of

---

tonic' are Heb. viii.5 and ix.23f?," *JTS* 34 (1983): 156–68; Felix H. Cortez, "Creation in Hebrews," *AUSS* 53 (2105): 279–320. The case for Philonic influence was made most strongly by Ceslas Spicq, but his arguments were answered by Ronald Williamson, *Philo and the Epistle to the Hebrews*, ALGHJ 4 (Leiden: Brill, 1970), and many modern scholars believe that a Platonic approach does not do justice either to the complexity of Hellenistic thought or of Hebrews. See L. D. Hurst, *The Epistle to the Hebrews: Its Background of Thought*, SNTSMS 65 (Cambridge: Cambridge University Press, 1990), 41–2. The two authors had very different approaches to Scripture. In short, Philo lacked the sense of history in connection with the divine word that is so prevalent in Hebrews (Luke Timothy Johnson, *Hebrews: A Commentary*, NTL (Louisville: Westminster John Knox, 2012), 19–21, although he thinks of the author of Hebrews as a "Platonist"), and the allegorical approach to Scripture that pervades Philo's work is very different from the specific Christological way Hebrews read and used the OT. Also, the concept of a two-storied universe, and some of the terminology of Platonism (or Neo-Platonism), pervaded many aspects of the ancient Hellenistic world, but this did not make everyone a Platonist. Most recently, James W. Thompson (*Hebrews*, Paideia (Grand Rapids: Baker Academic, 2008)) has argued that the author of Hebrews used Platonic categories of thought in this document.

[5] For the form of ancient Hellenistic letters, see John L. White, *Light from Ancient Letters* (Philadelphia: Fortress, 1986); Stanley K. Stowers, *Letter-Writing in Greco-Roman Antiquity*, LEC (Philadelphia: Westminster, 1986); and Hans-Josef Klauck, *Ancient Letters and the New Testament: A Guide to Context and Exegesis* (Waco, TX: Baylor University Press, 2006).

his day. That Hebrews lacks these features likely means that Hebrews was not intended to be read primarily as a letter.

If Hebrews was not a letter, then what was it? Was it a book? When we think of a "book" we think of a volume of many pages (or to the ancients, a long scroll) that gives information, explores several facets of subject, or relates a story and presents its thought in a series of "chapters" (as we call them) that bring the reader to a conclusion or the resolution of a conflict. The gospels, for example, are possibly books in this sense. Luke and Acts certainly are. Hebrews is not a book in this strict sense. It certainly is one of the longer writings of the NT, and there is a case to be made for saying that Hebrews takes its readers to a definite conclusion by a series of arguments. There are clues within Hebrews itself, however, that tell us that this piece of literature was written to be approached as something other than a "book." If we continue to call Hebrews a book, it is done in the sense that it is one of the "scrolls" or "books" of the "library" that we call the NT canon.

Most modern students of Hebrews are more comfortable calling Hebrews a sermon or a tract. Generally speaking, literature in the Greco-Roman world was written to be *heard*, since the majority of people could not read.[6] Hebrews certainly has features that suggest it was originally intended for oral delivery.[7] For example, the phrase "by faith" in chapter 11 is repeated throughout the chapter in good aural, rhetorical fashion. The author repeatedly characterized his material in terms of the spoken word (*cf.* 2.5; 5.11; 6.9; 8.1; 9.5; 11.32). He also sometimes quoted a lengthy passage and then repeated certain lines from it to make particular points (*cf.* 3.7–4.9 and 10.5–9), something that is more necessary in oral presentation than in written presentation. In 12.32 the author (like many preachers) was concerned about not having enough time to say all he would like to say. And we must not overlook the elegant, rhythmical style of Hebrews (in the Greek). Its flowing style fits an oral presentation well. Moffatt claimed that the author consciously mingled meters of varying

[6] *Cf.* Col 4.16; 1 Thes 5.27; Rev 1.3. Literacy rates in the Greco-Roman world are impossible to establish with accuracy, but the usual estimates are that only 10–25 per cent of the population could read or write. The ancient literary culture was more aural than visual. See William V. Harris, *Ancient Literacy* (Cambridge: Harvard University Press, 1989); Mary Beard *et al*, *Literacy in the Roman World*, JRASup 3 (Ann Arbor: University of Michigan Press, 1991); Brian J. Wright, "Ancient Literacy in New Testament Research: Incorporating a Few More Lines of Inquiry," *TrinJ* 36 (2015): 161–89.

[7] Johnson, *Hebrews*, 10.

kinds, which would make it more pleasant to hear.[8] Such "oratorical" elements of Hebrews were addressed to the ear more than to the eye.

Several modern studies suggest that the authors of the NT documents were more skilled in the art of ancient rhetoric than we previously understood. Concerning Hebrews, some scholars have argued that the best way to make sense of the book's arrangement is in terms of classical rhetoric.[9] There is, however, disagreement about exactly what type of ancient rhetoric Hebrews actually represents, specifically whether it is a piece of deliberative rhetoric (persuasive, designed to advise concerning the future) or epideictic rhetoric (designed to praise correct action and rebuke incorrect action).[10] Beyond this there is the larger question of whether the ancients ever produced formal rhetoric in the form of letters or treatises.[11] Scholars do agree, however, that written treatises certainly could have rhetorical features, and Hebrews has several,[12] especially the use of comparison (*sunkrisis*).[13] As with anything else, however, such an approach must not be made the master to which the text must submit. It would seem unwise to say that reading Hebrews in the light of ancient rhetoric is *the* way to read it, but it would be equally improper to ignore this aspect of the work also.

Perhaps the best evidence that Hebrews is a sermon appears in Acts 13.15. Paul and Barnabas were in the synagogue at Pisidian Antioch, and the leader of the synagogue said "Brethren, if you have any word of exhortation for the people, say it." Paul then proceeded to deliver what we would call a sermon to the people gathered there. Since no one complained that Paul's action was inappropriate, we may safely conclude that a "word of exhortation" was what we call a sermon. Now in Hebrews 13.22, the author said of his own work, "But I urge you, brethren, bear with this word of exhortation." If the author was using the phrase "word of exhortation"

---

[8] James Moffatt, *A Critical and Exegetical Commentary on the Epistle to the Hebrews*, ICC (Edinburgh: T&T Clark, 1924), lvi–lxiv.

[9] A recent attempt to demonstrate this in a thorough-going way is Thompson, *Hebrews*.

[10] Craig R. Koester, "Hebrews, Rhetoric, and the Future of Humanity," *CBQ* 64 (2002): 103–23, at 105–6; Johnson, *Hebrews*, 12–15.

[11] See Jeffrey T. Reed, "The Epistle," in *Handbook of Classical Rhetoric in the Hellenistic Period (330 B.C.–A.D. 400)*, ed. Stanley E. Porter (Leiden: Brill, 1997), 171–93.

[12] See David L. Allen, *Hebrews*, NAC (Nashville: Broadman & Holman, 2010), 29.

[13] Grindheim, *Letter to the Hebrews*, 36–37; David G. Peterson, *Hebrews: An Introduction and Commentary*, TNTC 15 (Downers Grove, IL: InterVarsity Press, 2020) 4; Thompson, *Hebrews*, 12.

in a technical sense, then he meant that he had written a sermon for his readers/hearers (*cf.* 1 Tim 4.13). Wills has argued that the particular type of Jewish sermon called a "word of exhortation" had fairly regular features, and that Hebrews fits this pattern,[14] and Boyarin describes Hebrews as "a homily presumably closely related to other Jewish homilies of the time in style and to a great extent, in content as well—with a twist, of course...."[15] Also, if Hebrews was originally meant to be read as a sermon, this would explain why it lacks epistolary features.[16] Reading Hebrews as a sermon instead of a letter may at first seem like a distinction without a real difference, but approaching the document as a sermon reinforces to our minds that this was originally addressed to a group of Christians who were experiencing a real crisis in their faith, and whose first need was moral exhortation to persevere in the struggle they faced.[17] Hebrews was, in the words of R. T. France, "a sustained piece of trouble-shooting, deliberately targeted at a congregation with a specific problem."[18] As Lane describes it, Hebrews is "a sermon rooted in actual life."[19]

Yet there can be no escaping the fact, however, that Hebrews has—its oral features notwithstanding—a literary character. After all, the author

---

[14] Specifically, the pattern of authoritative exempla, conclusion, and exhortation. L. Wills, "The Form of the Sermon in Hellenistic Judaism and early Christianity," *HTR* 77 (1984): 277–99. The pioneering work on this aspect of Hebrews was by Hartwig Thyen (*Der Stil der Judisch-Hellenistischen Homilie*), who suggested that Hebrews fits the form of a Palestinian synagogue sermon. However, most scholars now question some of the basic tenets of Thyen's arguments. See also James Swetnam, "On the Literary Genre of the 'Epistle' to the Hebrews," *NovT* 11 (1969): 261–69. For a thorough-going approach to Hebrews as a synagogue homily, see Gabriella Gelardini, "Hebrews, An Ancient Synagogue Homily for *Tisha Be-Av*: Its Function, Its Basis, Its Theological Interpretation," in *Hebrews: Contemporary Methods—New Insights*, ed. Gabriella Gelardini (Atlanta: Society of Biblical Literature 2005), 107–27.

[15] Daniel Boyarin, "Midrash in Hebrews / Hebrews as Midrash," in *Hebrews in Contexts*, ed. Gabriella Gelardini and Harold W. Attridge, Ancient Judaism and Early Christianity 91 (Leiden: Brill, 2016), 15–30, at 29.

[16] Pamela M. Eisenbaum, "Locating Hebrews Within the Literary Landscape of Christian Origins," in *Hebrews: Contemporary Methods—New Insights*, ed. Gabriella Gelardini (Atlanta: Society of Biblical Literature, 2005), 213–37.

[17] See Lanier Burns, "Hermeneutical Issues and Principles in Hebrews as Exemplified in the Second Chapter," *JETS* 39 (1996): 587–607.

[18] R. T. France, "The Writer of Hebrews as a Biblical Expositor," *TynBul* 47 (1996): 245–76, at 249.

[19] William L. Lane, "Hebrews: A Sermon in Search of a Setting," *SWJT* 28 (1985): 13–18; at 18. Similarly, Johnson notes that "A mark of effective rhetoric is that it addresses the real situation of the hearers" (*Hebrews*, 33).

said to his readers that "I have written to you" (13.22). It appears to be a carefully and smoothly composed sermon that was intended to be read to its audience in lieu of the preacher's personal presence among them (Heb 12.19). As it was read to the church (*cf.* 1 Thes 5.27; Col 4.16; Rev 1.3) it surely would have sounded like a sermon, but it was a written sermon. We must remember that the last chapter of Hebrews is strikingly like the close of a normal letter, and there is no evidence that chapter 13 was simply "tacked on" to the rest of the book, *i.e.*, with no regard for how it fit with the rest of the treatise. It is, indeed, of a piece with the rest of Hebrews. Hebrews, therefore, was a sermon in the form of a piece of literature. As such it partakes of both oral and literary characteristics.

The only question that might remain is, why did the author write a sermon to his readers instead of a letter? We can only guess, but we may suggest with confidence that the choice of the sermon form had to do with the author's desire to present his exhortation effectively. Maybe the sermon form would have been heard with more seriousness than a regular letter. In light of the oral/aural and literary qualities of Hebrews, we will refer to its original recipients in the commentary as both readers and hearers.

III. Place of Origin

Where the author was when he wrote Hebrews is impossible to say. The author was so concerned about his brethren and exhorting them in their precarious situation that he left few clues concerning his own situation (not to mention that the original readers probably knew where he was, or the person who delivered the sermon informed them of this, so it did not need to be mentioned in the sermon). He expressed a wish in 13.19 that he would soon be restored to his readers, but this does not necessarily mean that he was in prison. It may simply mean that he had been away traveling and was hopeful to visit them soon (similar to Rom 15.32, except the author of Hebrews had been among his readers before). Hebrews 13.23 would suggest that the author was waiting for Timothy, who had recently been released, to meet him, in which case it would not seem that the author was in prison himself.

IV. The Recipients and Their Problem

The questions concerning the original recipients of Hebrews are nearly as difficult as the question of authorship and comprise one of the most notoriously thorny issues in all of NT scholarship. We proceed, then, only with caution and reservation. I would note, up front, that the precise identity of the original recipients is not crucial to understanding the document. Nowhere did the author tie the problem he was addressing to the ethnicity of his readers. Also, I recognize that some of the arguments below may actually tell us more about the author of Hebrews than they tell us about the original recipients. We may note, however, that the NT documents are what has been called occasional literature. That is, they were not written because of their potential general interest but because they addressed occasions or problems that had arisen. Hebrews was no exception.

The word "Hebrews" in the title of the document means, of course, Jewish Christians. "Hebrew" is, among other things, an archaic way of saying "Jew." However, the title was not an original part of the book. It was added later as a deduction based on the contents of the work. Therefore, the title of the document is not evidence for determining its original audience. Yet it was not necessarily an erroneous deduction to suppose that it was written for Jewish Christians. The message of Hebrews is so thoroughly grounded in the OT that it is sensible to assume that the majority of the first readers/hearers may likely have come from a Jewish background.[20] It is obvious from even a cursory reading of the sermon that the recipients of this treatise were Christians whom the author expected to be well-acquainted with the OT and the things of Judaism (*cf.* 5.11–14), including things such the layout of the tabernacle and the obscure character Melchizedek. Also, as Filson noted, "there is not a non-Jewish argument in Hebrews."[21] Even more, Hebrews consciously shaped an identity for Christians that is thoroughly Jewish in its features: believers are followers of the great Jewish high priest, who are encouraged to enter the most holy place with Jesus, and they are the new, or true, Israel on their way to the heavenly promised land. Perhaps more so, the original audience was people who presumably would have personally appreciated the better features of the new system of things Jesus has inaugurated. That is, it is not clear that this argument, which appears repeatedly in Hebrews, would have had much rhetorical weight for con-

---

[20] Johnson, *Hebrews*, 33: "There is certainly more internal evidence to support the position that they were Jewish rather than Gentile."

[21] Floyd V. Filson, "The Epistle to the Hebrews," *JBR* 22 (1954): 20–26, at 23.

verted Gentiles who had little or no prior exposure to Judaism before their conversion. An appeal to embrace what is better has less force for people who have had no experience with what came before. The argument would have been powerful, however, for people who had actually lived under the sacrificial system of the Law of Moses and trusted it for their relationship with God. The author presumably wrote in such a way that he thought his appeal would be convincing to his readers, and the heavy and detailed use of the OT, and the presentation of something better than the Levitical system, would, it could be argued, suggest that the original readers had some prior history in Judaism.

In fairness, we must note that nothing in the document would preclude the presence of Gentile Christians among the original recipients. We know that in the case of Paul's letters, Paul did not hesitate to make arguments from the OT to churches that were predominantly Gentile. It seems likely that Gentile Christians were taught that the Jewish Scriptures were the authoritative guide to understanding the person and work of Jesus, and that any references to those Scriptures needed to be heard accordingly (whether they had prior familiarity with those texts or not).[22] Therefore, we cannot not rule out a partially Gentile audience for Hebrews just because Hebrews appealed to the OT. But just because the audience could have been a mixed group, this does not mean that it actually was. Nothing in Hebrews indicates that there were Gentiles among the original recipients. Metaphors drawn from Hellenistic culture appear in Hebrews 12 with its imagery of athletics and training, and its discussion about legitimate sons, but otherwise we do not see the abundance of Hellenistic imagery (things like Roman triumphal processions, slavery, military imagery, *etc.*) such as we find in Paul's writings to Gentile churches. Absent, as well, are any discussions of past lives of ignorance and fleshly indulgence, inclusion of the Gentiles by God's promise, adoption of Gentiles into God's family, Jews and Gentiles together making up a new temple of God, *etc.* In light of these considerations, it is not unreasonable to suppose that Hebrews was written primarily to Christians with a Jewish background. Again, this would not exclude Gentiles among the first readers, especially if those Gentile Christians had some pre-conversion background in syna-

[22] See Christopher D. Stanley, "'Pearls Before Swine': Did Paul's Audiences Understand His Biblical Quotations?," *NovT* 41 (1999): 124–44.

gogues,[23] but it does not seem likely to me that Hebrews was written to a church in which Gentiles made up the majority.

For all their assumed familiarity with Judaism, however, the first readers of Hebrews were apparently well-conversant in Greek, at least enough to listen to the polished Greek of Hebrews, which suggests that they could have been Hellenistic Jews. The group had suffered persecution that included verbal and physical abuse and the confiscation of their property by unbelievers (10.32–34; 12.3). This latter action could indicate that some of them were wealthy and had property worth confiscating.[24] Also, Hebrews was written to Christians in some particular locale. If the document was meant for all Christians everywhere (as some have thought that the title of the book implies), the author's hope to be reunited with them (13.23) would be puzzling. Also, the author knew of specific experiences and problems among his readers (5.12–6.1; 10.32–34; 13.1–7) which likely would not have been true of Christians everywhere. The readers had been Christians for more than just a little while (10.32; 5.12) and they had been helpful to other Christians, perhaps by sending money (6.10), and these considerations reflect a specific audience as well.

The most important fact about the recipients of this sermon is that they were on the verge of falling away from the faith. In a word, they felt like quitting. Over and over again the author encouraged them to remain in the faith to which they had committed themselves. He told them "Take care, brethren, that there not be in anyone of you an evil, unbelieving heart that falls away from the living God. But encourage one another day after day, as long as it is called 'Today,' so that none of you will be hardened by the deceitfulness of sin. For we have become sharers of Christ, if we hold fast the beginning of our assurance firm until the end" (3.12–14). He feared that some of his readers would come short of entering into God's rest (4.1), that they were about to fall because of a lack of diligence and obedience (4.11). They were not holding fast to the confession they made (4.14). Not only had they failed to make adequate progress in their spiritual growth, but they had also even regressed to

[23] Peterson, *Hebrews*, 16. Acts tells us that God-fearing Gentiles and proselytes became Christians in various places.

[24] David A. deSilva, "The Epistle to the Hebrews in Social-Scientific Perspective," *ResQ* 36 (1994): 1–21, at 6. Interestingly, God-fearing Gentiles seem to have been wealthy patrons of the synagogue at Aphrodisias. See Jerome Murphy-O'Connor, "Lots of God-Fearers? '*theosebeis*' in the Aphrodisias Inscription," *RB* 99 (1992): 418–24.

the point that the author thought they were about to fall away (5.11–6.6). At one time they had been zealous and active, but now they were sluggish and ready to quit (6.10–12; 10.32–39). They needed to hold fast to their faith, quit wavering, and get back to the business of encouraging each other (10.23–25). There may have been some quarreling among them (12.14–15) as well as other forms of worldly behavior (13.4–5), and some may not have been following their leaders (13.7, 17). The author's biggest fear, however, was that they faced the wrath of God for their unfaithfulness (2.1–3; 3.15–18; 6.7–8; 10.26–31; 12.25–29).

Why were they becoming unfaithful? Whatever else the answer to that question is, opposition seems to have been part of it. As Acts reveals, opposition from outsiders quickly became the way of life of the early Christians, and this is reinforced by numerous references in other NT epistles.[25] The numerous exhortations to endurance in Hebrews seem to point to this same reality.[26] Before we can say more about the problem these Christians faced, however, we may inquire about the source of this opposition. This might tell us something about the nature of the problem.

Gentile opposition? Who was opposing the recipients of Hebrews? Gentiles could be hostile to Christians (Acts 16.16–24 and 19.23–41, 1 Thes 2.14, 1 Pet 1.16 and 4.12–16, *etc.*). Some Gentiles simply did not want Christians living in their towns because Christians were viewed as troublemakers (*cf.* Acts 17.6; 24.5, by about the middle of the first century). Of course, this was not official (*i.e.*, government-sponsored) opposition, but social opposition. Apart from the persecution in Rome in 64 AD, there is no evidence for any government-directed persecution of Christians in the first century. But antagonistic, social opposition became a fact of life for many Christians. However, if the recipients of Hebrews had been known to have previous connections with Judaism (which I think is likely), then quitting Christianity (as they were thinking about doing) might not have helped much in such an atmosphere. Gentiles would have been just as intolerant of the recipients of Hebrews for their Jewish ethnicity as they were of them for their Christian identity (and assuming that outsiders would make such distinctions). That is, Jews could be objects of scorn

[25] *Cf.* 1 Thes 1.6; 2.2, 14–16; 2 Thes 1.5–6; Gal 3.4; Phil 1.29; 1 Pet 1.6–7; 2.8; 3.14; Jam 2.6.

[26] See Scott D. Mackie, *Eschatology and Exhortation in the Epistle to the Hebrews*, WUNT 223 (Tübingen: Mohr Siebeck, 2007), 12–13.

whether they were Christians or not.[27] However, if the Jewish Christians to whom Hebrews was addressed had normally enjoyed at least the toleration of local Gentiles, and they now experienced added resistance because they were Christians, then it is possible that quitting Christianity would have allowed them to return to a somewhat normal life.

Some have surmised that there might have been a predominantly Jewish church in Alexandria, Egypt.[28] An Alexandrian destination, it is suggested, would account for the supposed "Alexandrian flavor" of Hebrews and its good Greek style (if the author was one of their number, and since Alexandrian Jews would have been more proficient in Greek). We also know that tensions could be high between Jews and the Gentile population there. Alexandria was the site of one of the worst anti-Jewish events in the first century (38 AD), when the populace rioted against Jews upon the visit of Herod Agrippa I to that city.[29] According to this line of reasoning, Hebrews could have addressed Gentile hostility against Christians in Alexandria. However, acquaintance with Alexandrian ideas was widespread in the first century (*cf.* Acts 6.9), and there is no objective evidence for an Alexandrian destination of Hebrews. The early Alexandrian church fathers thought that Hebrews was originally addressed not to Christians in their city, but to Palestinian Christians.

The only possible internal clue about the location of the audience appears in an ambiguous statement in 13.24. The author said, "those from (Greek *apo*) Italy greet you." But what exactly does this mean? The author's use of "from" could mean that some brethren from Italy,

---

[27] Gentile scorn for Jews is a well-known fact of the ancient Hellenistic world. See the statements about the Jews in pagan authors such as: Apollonius Molo, reported in Josephus, *Apion* 2.148, 236; Seneca, as reported in Augustine *De civ. D.* 6.11; Horace, *Satires* 1.9; Tacitus *Hist.* 5.4–5; Juvenal 14.105–6; Petronius *Satyr.* frag. 37. All references to Jews in ancient classical literature are collected in Menahem Stern, ed., *Greek and Latin Authors on Jews and Judaism* (Jerusalem: Israel Academy of Sciences and Humanities 1984). An overview can be found in Jerry L. Daniel, "Anti-Semitism in the Hellenistic-Roman Period," *JBL* 98 (1979): 45–65.

[28] Several of the arguments are summarized, and answered, in Gottlieb Lünemann, *Critical and Exegetical Handbook to the Epistle to the Hebrews*, trans. Maurice J. Evans, Critical and Exegetical Commentary on the New Testament (Edinburgh: T&T Clark, 1882), 43–51. See also F. F. Bruce, *The Epistle to the Hebrews*, rev. ed., NICNT (Grand Rapids: Eerdmans, 1990), 12–13.

[29] The story is recorded in Philo, *Flaccus*. The account includes a description of the plundering of Jewish property, which is similar to Heb 10.34. However, Philo said nothing about anti-Christian violence in Alexandria. On the event, see Sandra Gambetti, *The Alexandrian Riots of 38 C.E. and the Persecution of the Jews: A Historical Reconstruction*, JSJSup 135 (Leiden: Brill, 2009).

whom the recipients knew, were with the author (similar to Phil 4.21) somewhere else in the empire, and these brethren were sending their regards back to the recipients in their homeland. According to this view, then, we could paraphrase the latter part of Hebrews 13.24 thusly: "your brethren from the church there (at Rome?), who are with me now, send their regards back to you."

The problem, however, is that Hebrews 13.24 does not bear all this interpretation places upon it. The statement does not necessarily imply that Rome was the destination of the letter. If anything, it might more clearly imply that *the author was in Italy* when he wrote Hebrews. Mosser has argued that this is what the phrase would naturally mean.[30] In the right contexts, "from" could mean nearly the same thing as "in" (*cf.* Acts 10.23; 12.1; 17.13). The letter could just as easily have been addressed to some other church where these brethren from Italy had acquaintances. In fact, Hebrews 13.24 does not *necessarily* imply that these brethren from Italy were with the author. All it says is that some Christians "from Italy" were sending their regards to the recipients of Hebrews.

The significance of how we understand this little phrase is that it has a bearing on the destination of the letter. If the author was in Italy (presumably Rome; in Acts 18.2 "Italy" can be used in the sense of "Rome"), then he was not writing to the church in Rome. But if the author was not in Rome, he may have been writing to the church in Rome, but just as possibly to another place.

Those who take Hebrews 13.24 to indicate the sermon's destination as Rome argue that the persecution of 64 AD fits the picture described in Hebrews. The Roman historian Tacitus reported:

> But all human efforts, all the lavish gifts of the emperor, and the propitiations of the gods, did not banish the sinister belief that the conflagration [the burning of Rome] was the result of an order. Consequently, to get rid of the report, Nero fastened the guilt and inflicted the most exquisite tortures on a class hated for their abominations, called Christians by the populace. Christus, from whom the name had its origin, suffered

---

[30] Carl Mosser, "No Lasting City: Rome, Jerusalem and the Place of Hebrews in the History of Earliest 'Christianity,'" (PhD diss., St. Mary's College, University of St. Andrews, 2004), 157 (cited also in Allen, *Hebrews*, 63): "When manuscript subscriptions based upon the phrase in question are examined it is observed that they consistently interpret the phrase to indicate the place *from which* the epistle was written."

> the extreme penalty during the reign of Tiberius at the hands of one of our procurators, Pontius Pilatus, and a most mischievous superstition, thus checked for the moment, again broke out not only in Judaea, the first source of the evil, but even in Rome, where all things hideous and shameful from every part of the world find their centre and become popular. Accordingly, an arrest was first made of all who pleaded guilty; then, upon their information, an immense multitude was convicted, not so much of the crime of firing the city, as of hatred against mankind. Mockery of every sort was added to their deaths. Covered with the skins of beasts, they were torn by dogs and perished, or were nailed to crosses, or were doomed to the flames and burnt, to serve as a nightly illumination, when daylight had expired. Nero offered his gardens for the spectacle, and was exhibiting a show in the circus, while he mingled with the people in the dress of a charioteer or stood aloft on a car. Hence, even for criminals who deserved extreme and exemplary punishment, there arose a feeling of compassion; for it was not, as it seemed, for the public good, but to glut one man's cruelty, that they were being destroyed.[31]

A problem, however, is that we simply do not know enough about the events in Rome in 64 AD to make this connection securely. Also, Tacitus described several executions of Christians, which would seem to contradict Hebrews 12.4, and he said nothing about the property and possessions of Christians being seized as Hebrews 10.32–34 describes. If Hebrews was written late in the first century, it might be possible that the event in Rome was the persecution of the "former days" mentioned in 10.32–34, despite the differences in the descriptions between Hebrews and Tacitus, but to make that connection is to speak past the evidence, and there is no indication of persecution of Christians in Italy (outside of the famous event in 64 AD in Rome) in the latter part of the first century.[32]

---

[31] *Annals* 15.44 (*The Annals of Tacitus*, trans. Alfred John Church and William Jackson Brodribb (New York: MacMillan and Co., 1906), 304–05). The account of the fire begins in 15.38. The fire happened in July of 64 AD. The story is repeated in Suetonius, *Nero* 38 and Dio Cassius, *Roman History* 62, but without reference to the persecution of Christians.

[32] Some scholars claim to have detected an anti-Jewish bias in Roman policies (see E. Mary Smallwood, "Domitian's Attitude towards Jews and Judaism," *Classical Philology* 51 (1956): 1–13; and H. Dixon Slingerland, *Claudian Policymaking and the Early Imperial Repression of Judaism at Rome*, USF Studies in the History of Judaism 160 (Atlanta: Scholars Press, 1997)), but that is about as close as the evidence gets. But the so-called Domitianic persecution probably never happened. See Duane Warden, "Imperial Persecution and the Dating of 1 Peter and Revelation," *JETS* 34 (1991): 203–12, esp. 205–8; Leonard Thompson, *The Book of Revelation: Apocalypse and Empire* (Oxford: Oxford University Press, 1990),

Jewish opposition? Another possibility is that the oppressors were unbelieving Jews who saw Jewish Christians as heretics. That Jews, even outside of Palestine, saw Christianity in exactly these terms is amply illustrated in Acts, where it is clear that some unbelieving Jews sometimes used violence against their fellow-countrymen who had turned to Christ. This will be the perspective upon which this commentary proceeds. I do not, however, think that this perspective (specifically, opposition against Jewish Christians by unbelieving Jews) is crucial to the exegesis of the text. I present it as a (in my view) likely scenario against which we might profitably read Hebrews.

The Problem. If the source of opposition was unbelieving Jews, then it might be possible to speak with more precision about the nature of the conflict in which the original readers were caught. The Jews believed that what we might call "the religion and culture of Judaism" was the expression of covenant loyalty to God. Matters such as Sabbath-keeping, observing the kosher laws, circumcision of males, *etc.* were practiced within the context of a firm belief that God, by his grace, had entered into a special covenant with the Jews and demanded these things from them as expressions and indicators of their special status before him. By these "works" the Jews maintained their separateness from the Gentiles.[33] Jewish Christians continued to live according to the Jewish lifestyle. The evidence of Acts confirms this, and there is no evidence against it.[34] When Paul arrived in Jerusalem in Acts 21, the church there—full of converted Jews—was at peace with the surrounding Jewish society partly because the Jewish Christians there continued to live within Jewish culture. Such was the testimony of Peter himself in Acts 21.20.[35] But Jewish Christians

---

chs 6 and 7, and *idem*, "A Sociological Analysis of Tribulation in the Apocalypse of John," *Semeia* 36 (1986): 147–74, esp. 153–62.

[33] For this assessment of Judaism, see E. P. Sanders, *Paul and Palestinian Judaism: A Comparison of Patterns of Religion* (Philadelphia: Fortress, 1977) as a starting point.

[34] We hear complaints in some of the ancient Jewish literature of some Jews who either abandoned their religion for purposes of cultural assimilation or, in the opinion of the authors, adopted Hellenistic culture to the point that it constituted a compromise of their Jewishness, but this is a different issue. There is no evidence that Jews regularly ceased participating in Jewish culture upon their conversion to Christianity. *Cf.* David A. deSilva, *The Letter to the Hebrews in Social-Scientific Perspective*, Cascade Companion 15 (Eugene, OR: Cascade Books, 2012), 35: "we have no firm indication that Jewish Christians as a rule *ceased* to participate in the temple cult prior to 70 CE." (emphasis his).

[35] What made that situation so potentially volatile was that some Jews *thought* that Paul advocated, or even demanded, a complete abandonment of the Jewish lifestyle. "Concern-

had a different perspective. While they continued to live according to Jewish culture, they believed that Jesus was the Messiah of Israel, and that the messianic age had now dawned as a result of his work.

One of the things at issue between Christian Jews and unbelieving Jews was *the theological value, or interpretation, placed on Judaism.* The apostles objected to the ideas that Judaism was *the* way to be right with God, that ethnic Jews were (now) the exclusive covenanted people of God, and that one had to live according to the Torah *in order to* be in good standing with God. Instead they proclaimed rightness with God through faith in Christ Jesus (who was the ultimate object of the Jewish Bible) and that nearness to God is by membership in the new covenant people of God, the church of Jesus Christ, and *not* through God's covenant with the Jews.[36] Unbelieving Jews saw these differences as unacceptable compromises of the ancestral faith, and they not only refused to tolerate them but actively opposed them (as examples in Acts makes clear).

We should clarify that the Christian perspective was *not* that God had abandoned the Jews and his covenant with them, and had now done something different in, with, and for the church (although there were apparently some Christians who mistakenly believed such things). Such "supersessionist" ideas, which are still prominent in some modern approaches to the Bible, are not found in Hebrews, nor anywhere else in the NT. God did not abandon the Jews. Rather, God has fulfilled his promise to bring Israel to glory in the gospel concerning Jesus of Nazareth, whom Hebrews holds up as the high priest in the new covenant.

Because of the different perspectives between Jewish Christians and other Jews, a divide began to form between Judaism and Christianity during

---

ing you, they have been told that you teach defection (Greek *apostasia*) from Moses to all the Jews who are among the Gentiles, telling them not to circumcise their children nor to walk after the customs" (v 21). This, of course, was not true. Paul had no problem with someone (even himself, 1 Cor 9.20) engaging in the practices of their culture. Christianity can be practiced within any culture (Christianity's moral limits assumed, of course). The false concern was that Paul advocated, if not demanded, an abandonment of Jewish culture upon conversion to Christ, whereas what Paul actually advocated was abandonment of trusting in Jewish culture, abandonment of the belief that the cultural practices of Judaism (understood within the framework of the Jews as God's exclusive covenanted people) were what made a person right with God.

[36] As N. T. Wright puts it, there has been a redefinition of who God's people are, a redefinition of who "Israel" is. See his *Paul: Fresh Perspectives* (London: SPCK, 2005), 110–22. Although he is speaking there about Paul's gospel, the conceptual framework is the same, I believe, for the author of Hebrews.

the first century. Modern scholars have called it "the parting of the ways."[37] It actually began in the days of Jesus himself, when Jewish authorities in Jerusalem ruled that followers of Jesus would be unwelcome in synagogues (John 9.22; 12.42; 16.2), and Stephen's speech in Acts 7 served as an initial catalyst to widen the breech between Jewish Christians and other Jews. As more and more Gentiles became Christians, especially through the work of Paul, the divide accelerated even more (*cf.* Acts 21.28a). Hebrews, in its own way, actually contributed to the divide by presenting Christianity as "better" than the approach to God under the Levitical system.[38] It is possible that the original readers / hearers of Hebrews were experiencing the break firsthand and that this provides a context for understanding Hebrews.

It has been common to suggest, in light of this growing breech, that the original recipients of Hebrews had left Judaism, but now they were falling away from Christianity and contemplating a "return to Judaism."[39] However, this approach is inadequate for at least three reasons:

1) It simply does not fit the facts.[40] Specifically, it does not fit what we know about Jewish Christianity in the first century. As noted above, Jew-

[37] For an introduction to this topic, see the essays in James D. G. Dunn, ed., *Jews and Christians: The Parting of the Ways A.D. 70 to 135* (Grand Rapids: Eerdmans, 1999); *idem, The Partings of the Ways: Between Christianity and Judaism and Their Significance for the Character of Christianity*, 2nd ed. (London: SCM Press, 2006); also Jared W. Saltz, "Parting the Waves, Parting the Ways: The Identity of Christ and Christianity in the Early Church," in *Studies in Church History: Essays in Honor of Daniel W. Petty*, ed. David McClister (Temple Terrace: Florida College Press, 2020), 28–57; Richard Bauckham, "The Parting of the Ways: What Happened and Why," in Richard Bauckham, *The Jewish World around the New Testament: Collected Essays I*, ed. Jörg Frey, WUNT 233 (Tübingen: Mohr Siebeck, 2008), 175–92.

[38] Bruce Chilton and Jacob Neusner, *Judaism in the New Testament: Practices and Beliefs* (New York: Routledge 1995): 175–88.

[39] For example, Barnabas Lindars suggested that they were reverting to Judaism because they felt a continuing consciousness of sins due to the fact that Christianity has no external rite of purification ("The Rhetorical Structure of Hebrews," *NTS* 35 (1989): 382–406, at 388). He believed that the original recipients were "a strand of Christianity which required a complete break with Jewish worship" (389). A list of modern authors who take this same kind of position can be found in Mackie, *Eschatology and Exhortation in the Epistle to the Hebrews*, 13–15. Older works that take this view would include H. D. M. Spence in the *Pulpit Commentary*, and the commentaries by Moses Stuart, Franz Delitzsch, and Simon Kistemaker.

[40] The matter of Christian self-definition *vis-a-vis* Judaism did not happen uniformly or evenly. Some scholars have suggested that it was not until the fourth century AD that the divide became critical. See Adam H. Becker and Annette Yoshiko Reed, eds., *The Ways That Never Parted: Jews and Christians in Late Antiquity and the Early Middle Ages* (Philadelphia: Fortress, 2007). It clearly would be a mistake to project modern long-standing and clear-cut differences between Judaism and Christianity back onto the world of the first century.

ish Christians had never abandoned the Jewish lifestyle, and it is not likely that any Jewish Christian in the first century would have understood himself to have "quit" Judaism for Christianity. As Church has put it,

> The first readers of Hebrews were probably Christ-allegiant ethnic Judeans, who would have considered themselves to be faithful Israelites. The notion of two religions, Judaism and Christianity would have been meaningless to them, and they would not consider themselves to have abandoned one religion and adopted another. Their ongoing attraction to the temple and its ritual reflected their ongoing sense of Judean identity, and it is anachronistic to suggest that they had converted to a new religion called Christianity and were tempted to revert to their former religion.[41]

Furthermore, the divide between Christianity and Judaism was at its earliest stages. We can see it now, from our perspective two thousand years later when the divide has matured, but it is not likely that anyone in the ancient world would have characterized the relationship between Judaism and Christianity in the latter part of the first century as a "divide."[42] "Returning to Judaism" was simply not how they would have viewed the situation.

2) The idea that Hebrews' constant critique of the old system (and the corresponding insistence that the new order of things in Jesus is better) reflects a desire on the part of the readers to return to that old system is simply a kind of mirror reading of the text. Mirror-reading is when we assume that if the text says, exhorts, or emphasizes one thing, then the opposite thing must have been the problem it was addressing. When one takes this approach to Hebrews, one might see the sermon's discussion of the weakness of Judaism, and the exhortations to remain in the Christian faith, as arguments not to participate in the things of Judaism. The difficulty with this is readily apparent, however, for the same exhortation could be prompted by more than one scenario, of which this particular mirror image is only one possibility. In short, a mirror reading of Hebrews' theological critique of the old covenant and its elements is not necessarily the way to discover the problem He-

---

[41] Philip Church, "Turning Away from the Living God (Heb. 3:12): The Growth and Decline of the Relapse Theory for the Setting of Hebrews," *EvQ* 94 (2023): 1–25, at 5.

[42] Dunn, *Jews and Christians*, 368.

brews addressed.[43] Such an approach is too simplistic for the historical complexities of the situation as we know it. To put it bluntly, "there is no convincing evidence in the epistle that the community was tempted to return to Judaism."[44] Instead, the "return to Judaism" idea must be read into the epistle. Nowhere does Hebrews itself speak of, or warn its readers of, "turning back" to Judaism. The only thing to which they would have "returned" would have been unbelief in Jesus, and this is exactly the warning of Hebrews as it cautions its readers not to fall into unbelief (3.12,19) with its increasing hardness of heart and wholesale rejection of God's final word, as well as the book's exhortation to be people of faith in Jesus (ch 11).

3) Such an approach is not necessary to understand the sermon. The purpose of the author's critique of Judaism makes perfect sense if it is viewed as serving the function simply of highlighting (by way of contrast) the greatness of the new order of things in Jesus without implying that the readers were desiring to "return to Judaism." The constant references to the limitations of the old covenant served as a common point of reference and comparison which enabled the readers to appreciate even more just how much *better* the new order of things in Jesus really is. In other words, how could the author impress upon his readers just how great Christianity is (in order to convince them not to quit it)? His answer was to compare it to something his readers already knew well: Judaism. When viewed in this way, the critique of Judaism served a positive function, to demonstrate just how much more things are "better" in Jesus.[45] The author's critique of Judaism was not offered in order to convince his readers not to go back to it, but to encourage them to "press on" in their faith in Jesus, which offers a greater hope and the consummate way of dealing with our sins. Such an approach to Hebrews' critique of Judaism stays within the evidence and is consonant with the broadly typological quality of Biblical

---

[43] See John M. G. Barclay, "Mirror-reading a Polemical Letter: Galatians as a Test Case," *JSNT* 31 (1987): 73–93.

[44] James W. Thompson, "The Underlying Unity of Hebrews," *ResQ* 18 (1975): 129–36. See fn 39 above.

[45] This was the purpose of rhetorical comparison (*sunkrisis*): "Comparison (Greek *synkrisis*) was, however, a common rhetorical device designed, not for polemical purposes, but to demonstrate the greatness of the speaker's subject (Aristotle, *Rhet.* 1.9.39). Exercises in *synkrisis* were a common feature in rhetorical education. Thus the author's comparisons reflect not a polemic against Judaism but his desire to demonstrate the greatness of the Christian revelation." Thompson, *Hebrews*, 36.

theology as a whole, where God often established one thing so that his people may know the better quality of what he does later.

The problem facing the original readers of Hebrews, then, was not that they were being pressured to return to following the kosher laws, or to not working on the Sabbath, *etc.* They had never quit these things. They had not rejected Judaism (*i.e.*, the Jewish lifestyle), but Judaism was rejecting them, and this rejection caused them to feel the pressure of shame, a strong desire to erase it, and to recapture an accepted status in their culture.[46] The ancient Hellenistic world, including Jewish society, was an honor culture in which doing what was expected by one's peers, and living up to the social values of one's group, was a consideration in almost everything one said or did.[47] People were conscious of the potential of their behaviors to uphold and reinforce what was considered honorable, or to generate shame by a failure to live according to the norms, values, and expectations of their definitional group(s). Acting against those norms brought dishonor, with a corresponding damage to those peer relationships that one needed for support and a sense of identity. Uncorrected, shame ultimately brought exclusion by one's peers,[48] sometimes violently so, as Hebrews 10.32–34 attests.

A sense of identity, of belonging to an established group, was important to the ancients[49] (as it continues to be in modern cultures as well). Family and cultural ties were strong in the ancient world. Breaking them, or choosing others over them, was serious business. Among

---

[46] Norman H. Young, "'Bearing His Reproach' (Heb 13.9–14)," *NTS* 48 (2002): 243–61. David A. deSilva: "A person born into the first-century Mediterranean world, whether Gentile or Jewish, was trained from childhood to desire honor and avoid disgrace." (*The Hope of Glory: Honor Discourse and New Testament Interpretation* (Collegeville, MN: Liturgical Press, 1999), 2); and "The culture of the first-century world was built on the foundational social values of honor and shame." (*Honor, Patronage, Kinship, and Purity: Unlocking New Testament Culture*, 2nd ed. (Downers Grove, IL: IVP Academic, 2022), 11).

[47] For an introduction to honor and shame in the ancient world, see deSilva, *Honor, Patronage, Kinship, and Purity, 2nd ed.*, 11–17; *idem, The Hope of Glory*; Richard L. Rohrbaugh, "Honor," in *The Ancient Mediterranean Social World: A Sourcebook*, ed. Zeba A. Crook (Grand Rapids: Eerdmans, 2020), 63–78.

[48] The "disciplinary" procedures described in Matt 18.15–17, 1 Cor 5.11–13, and 2 Thes 3.6 are exactly the kinds of things done in the ancient honor culture to reinforce the judgment that a group member had acted contrary to the group's values.

[49] See Philip A. Harland, *Associations, Synagogues, and Congregations: Claiming a Place in Ancient Mediterranean Society* (Minneapolis: Augsburg Fortress, 2003), 86; John S. Kloppenborg, *Christ's Associations: Connecting and Belonging in the Ancient City* (New Haven: Yale University Press, 2019), 147, 215.

Jews, this sense of identity was also bound up with the belief that they were the chosen people of God. The idea of rightly belonging to the group was, then, an especially strong force within Jewish culture, because more than just social standing was at stake. The persecution the original recipients of Hebrews had experienced in their early days of following Christ (Heb 10.32–34) had been followed by continued, non-violent social rejection by their unbelieving fellow-countrymen. When Jewish Christians experienced ongoing rejection from other Jews, it caused a crisis in identity for them. Rejection by friends and family, exclusion from the synagogue, exclusion from meals with other Jews (Heb 13.9), verbal reproaches, *etc.* had stripped them of many of the identity markers by which they measured and understood themselves. The stigma of being unacceptable to their fellow Jews left them with nowhere to turn (except to each other, Heb 10.24) and confused about how they were supposed to think of themselves. Their world, and their sense of who they were, had been turned upside down.[50]

Terms that were common in ancient discussions of honor and shame[51] appear in Hebrews 2.9–10; 10.33; 11.26; 12.2; and 13.13, 18, and a situation in which the original recipients of Hebrews where being shamed seems the likely backdrop of the sermon. The scenario is not hard to imagine. deSilva argues that, since becoming Christians, these people felt that

---

[50] Although the following words were written to describe a later time, they probably capture some of the spirit of what was going on for converted Jews in the latter part of the first century as well: "One thing must be made clear: one way or another, the *Conversos* had a hard time of it, spiritually speaking, even if they encountered no overt difficulties in Christian society. The *converso* always had to expect that there would be gossip around him, and the higher he rose in society, the more hatred and envy were to be anticipated. There were cases in which the *converso* brought disgrace upon his family, and he did not always find himself in a sympathetic environment; for the most part he had to enter an alien society, devoid of friends and relatives. There were many incidents of families' being torn apart when the wife and children did not follow the father. *Conversos* also lost their social positions and standing and there were incidents of *conversos'* having to toil in their new environment to arrive at a status similar to that they had enjoyed before this. Most tragic was that many of them also became impoverished, since they had left their property and assets behind in the Jewish community and if they had been money-lenders, as Christians, this was now out of bounds." Moisés Orfali, "*Conversos* in Medieval Spain," *EJud* 4:1676–90.

[51] "Words like *glory* or *reputation* (*doxa*), *honor* (*timē*), and *praise* (*epainos*), together with their related verbal and adjectival forms, are frequent. Their antonyms, *dishonor* (*aischynē*), *reproach* (*oneidos*), *scorn* (*kataphronēsis*), *slander* (*blasphēmia*), together with the adjectives and verbs derived from these roots, are also prominent." (deSilva, *Honor, Patronage, Kinship, and Purity*, 2nd *ed.*, 17; italics his). See also Rohrbaugh, "Honor," 74–75.

they were now outcasts from the larger society and the sub-groups in which they had so long been comfortable.[52] In sociological terms, they felt marginalized, and it was this ongoing sense of rejection, displacement, and dishonor that led them to rethink their allegiance to Christ. Jewish Christians were being shamed as heretics for their allegiance to Jesus. They were paying a high social price for their faith. In this approach, the purpose of Hebrews was not so much to exhort them to endure "persecution" (in the sense of physical violence against them, although that had happened to them at least once), but to encourage them to disregard the ongoing shame of rejection at the hands of their fellow-countrymen and to understand that true honor comes from God.[53]

Living in this condition of continual dishonor in the eyes of others, along with the sense of disorientation it brought, was causing the original recipients of Hebrews to rethink their allegiance to Jesus.[54] It became impossible to be both a "good Jew" *and* a Christian. Lines were being drawn, and decisions had to be made. The original recipients of Hebrews felt themselves caught in the middle of it and were uncertain at this point in their lives as to whether they should continue in their faith in Jesus. Continuing in the Christian faith meant a life of ongoing reproach, insults, exclusion, isolation, a diminished sense of self-worth, and shame. For these Christians, in the culture in which they lived, these things seemed like more than they could bear. They were beginning to think that life would be easier for them if they just quit Christianity. If they did, they reasoned, their friends and family would accept them once again, their lives would return to some semblance of what they knew as normal, and they would regain a sense of who they were.

Other factors may have been at work as well. Dahms has argued that their motives were more innocent, due to a failure to appreciate the full significance of the work of Christ,[55] Schmidt has suggested that it was moral laxity within the church, not persecution from without, that

[52] "The Epistle to the Hebrews in Social-Scientific Perspective," 10, 20.

[53] David A. deSilva, "Despising Shame: A Cultural-Anthropological Investigation of the Epistle to the Hebrews," *JBL* 113 (1994): 439–61; at 440, 448–52. This is the perspective of his commentary, *Perseverance in Gratitude: A Social-Rhetorical Commentary on the Epistle 'to the Hebrews'* (Grand Rapids: Eerdmans, 2000).

[54] See deSilva, *The Hope of Glory*, 149.

[55] John V. Dahms, "The First Readers of Hebrews," *JETS* 20 (1977): 365–75; at 372–73.

prompted the writing of Hebrews,[56] and Thompson suggests that it was the ordinary loss of zeal that any movement experiences as it enters into its second and third generations.[57] If we date the book before 70 AD, then increased pressure to stand up and be identified as a "good Jew" in opposition to Roman oppression could possibly have been another factor.[58] I see no reason why these positions should necessarily be mutually exclusive, although I do not find them all equally plausible. The truth may well be that a combination of problems, or a complex problem, faced these people.[59] Koester is right to remind us that "The causes of decline were probably complex and may not have been fully apparent to the members of the community themselves."[60]

In summary, the problem for the original recipients of Hebrews was that continual social rejection, with perhaps a threat of renewed persecution and/or some other factors in the mix as well, was wearing them down spiritually, and they were tempted to quit. The pressures against them had created the crisis in their faith. The load was becoming heavy—some of them thought it was too heavy—and not only were they weary and ready to give up, but for some of them the constant struggle with hardship and rejection was making them frustrated, angry, and bitter against Jesus. The author of Hebrews saw this as a real dilemma in their faith. He knew where this could lead. Unless the recipients began to see, in a much greater way than they had before, the surpassing greatness of all they had in Jesus, this frustration would eventually turn into a repudiation and rejection of Jesus accompanied by contempt (see 6.4–6). The author's solution was to increase their understanding of the greatness of Christianity, because a faith that is well-informed, and mature, endures. The overall point was, if we may paraphrase it, that if they could only

---

[56] Thomas E. Schmidt, "Moral Lethargy and the Epistle to the Hebrews," *WTJ* 54 (1992): 167–73.

[57] *Hebrews*, 8–10. A review of several theories can be found in Richard W. Johnson, *Going Outside the Camp: The Sociological Function of the Levitical Critique in the Epistle to the Hebrews*, JSNTSup 209 (Sheffield: Sheffield Academic, 2001), 18–20.

[58] Young, "'Bearing His Reproach' (Heb 13.9–14)," 251.

[59] Harold W. Attridge, *The Epistle to the Hebrews: A Commentary on the Epistle to the Hebrews*, Hermeneia (Philadelphia: Fortress Press, 1989), 290. See also Mackie, *Eschatology and Exhortation*, ch. 2, "The Situation of the Recipients" (9–17).

[60] Koester, "Hebrews, Rhetoric, and the Future of Humanity," 123. See also Jared Compton, *Psalm 110 and the Logic of Hebrews*, LNTS 537 (London: Bloomsbury T&T Clark, 2015), 13–18 for a brief survey of views.

come to see just how great their situation in Jesus (in comparison to Judaism) was, they would never want to quit following him.

V. Purpose

Once we appreciate the problem the sermon was written to address, its purpose becomes clear. Hebrews presents us with a picture of Jewish Christians who were confused in their faith, weary of persecution and alienation, and were leaning toward quitting Christianity to find relief from their oppression. The sermon was written to inform their faith more perfectly and to encourage and warn them not to quit following Christ.

It is not difficult to see the relevance of this document. Many people today have the same fundamental problems, and are tempted to do the same thing, as the original readers of Hebrews. Because they have not sufficiently appreciated neither the uniqueness nor the greatness of Christianity, in difficult situations they find themselves tempted to turn their backs on Christ in order to make things easier on themselves. What is important, however, is not that our religion always pleases us or those around us, but that it pleases God (Heb 10.38; 11.5–6; 13.6, 21). Only by following Christ, even when it means we must suffer with him (Heb 13.13), can we legitimately hope for a reward in heaven or hope to avoid the wrath of God. Enduring faithfulness to Jesus, and Jesus alone, is the way to God. This is the great exhortation of Hebrews.

VI. Destination

Where were these confused, oppressed Jewish Christians who were thinking about abandoning their confession of Jesus? As we noted above, we might find the answer to this question by asking where their oppressors were. That question, however, is difficult to answer because social rejection of Christians was widespread. Two places might vie for being the most likely. As with the previous discussion about the sources of opposition, so here as well, certainty is neither possible nor necessary.

Rome? One possibility is that the epistle was written to Jewish Christians in Rome. In fact, most scholars today posit a Roman destination for Hebrews because, it is claimed, this seems to fit with what we know about early Christianity in Rome.[61] The argument runs like this: First, He-

[61] An example of a summary defense of the Roman destination is George A. Barton, "The Date of the Epistle to the Hebrews," *JBL* 57 (1938): 195–207. For reasons discussed

brews 13.24 could indicate that the recipients were in Rome. We know that there was a large Jewish population in Rome in the first century.[62] We also know that Christians eventually came to Rome and established a church there. The common theory is that they probably first preached to Jews in synagogues, and the first converts in Rome were probably Jews. It is likely (according to the theory) that the unbelieving Jews in Rome opposed the new religion violently, just as Jews had done in Pisidian Antioch (Acts 13.50), Lystra (Acts 14.19), Thessalonica (Acts 17.5–9), Berea (Acts 17.13), and Corinth (Acts 18.12–17). This violence could be the persecution of the "former days" mentioned in Hebrews 10.32–34.

Much of this has been inferred from a statement made by the Roman historian Suetonius, and partially confirmed by Luke, that the Roman emperor Claudius expelled the Jews from Rome because there was rioting over a man named Chrestus.[63] Most historians believe that the Chrestus over whom they were rioting was Christ. In the Latin language at that time, Chrestus and Christus (the Latin form of Christ) would have sounded very similar[64] and it is possible that Suetonius either did not know what the term meant, or he did not bother to see if the name of the leader of these "troublemakers" was spelled correctly. The widely accepted date for the expulsion of the Jews by Claudius is 49 AD.

It may also be possible to limit the scope of the decree of Claudius more narrowly. Suetonius' statement can be translated in two ways. It could be rendered to say "he expelled from Rome the Jews who were constantly making disturbances at the instigation of Chrestus," or as "since the Jews constantly made disturbances at the instigation of Chrestus, he expelled them from Rome."[65] The first of these translations would mean that Claudius only expelled Jews who were making trouble over Chrestus, while the second of these translations would mean that because there was trouble over Chrestus, the emperor expelled the Jews. Lane argues

---

elsewhere in the Introduction, we reject a Domitianic date (90s AD) for Hebrews, such as set forth in Donald W. Riddle, "Hebrews, First Clement, and the Persecution of Domitian," *JBL* 43 (1924): 329–48.

[62] See Karl P. Donfried and Peter Richardson, eds. *Judaism and Christianity in First-Century Rome* (Grand Rapids: Eerdmans, 1998).

[63] *Claudius* 25:4; Acts 18.2.

[64] F. F. Bruce, *New Testament History* (New York: Doubleday, 1969), 297; William L. Lane, *Hebrews 1–8*, WBC 47A ((Dallas: Word, 1991), lxv.

[65] Lane, *Hebrews 1–8*, lxiv.

that the first translation represents the more probable situation.[66] If he is correct about this, then Suetonius' statement could mean that Claudius expelled Jewish *Christians* from Rome, ostensibly because their teachings about Jesus provoked the unbelieving Jews to anger and rioting.[67]

There are, however, some serious problems with taking Suetonius' remark as constituting evidence of early disturbances in Rome related specifically to Christianity:[68] 1) It assumes that the historian confused the names Chrestus and Christus (the Latin version of "Christ"). The assumption may not be far-fetched, since Chrestus was a common name,[69] especially for slaves, in ancient times. Evidence from Tacitus seems to suggest that both spellings, with either the "e" or the "i," were in use in the first century with reference to Christians.[70] It is just as likely, however, that Suetonius got the name right (he was otherwise careful with names), and that this otherwise unknown Chrestus went around the city inciting Jews to riot (for what reason, we do not know).

Even more problematic is 2) that Suetonius seems to have "Chrestus" in Rome and personally causing the disturbances, in which case this cannot be a reference to Jesus. Furthermore, 3) Suetonius knew who "Christians" were, since he mentioned them in *Nero* 16.2. It would have been easy for him to call them "Christians" here if they were indeed the source of the trouble. 4) Luke does not say that Priscilla and Aquila had been expelled from Rome because Jews had been ordered to leave the city for rioting *over Christianity*, and it certainly would have been consistent with Luke's narrative to mention that detail. Luke's silence here is

---

[66] Lane, *Hebrews 1–8*, lxv.

[67] For other considerations, however, see A. Andrew Das, *Solving the Romans Debate* (Minneapolis: Fortress, 2007): 171–81.

[68] *Cf.* Slingerland, *Claudian Policymaking*, 151–218.

[69] The name itself is Greek, but Latinized versions of it appear in the ancient inscriptions. See Slingerland, *Claudian Policymaking*, 191 fn47.

[70] Tacitus, *Annals* 15.44: "Therefore, to dispel the rumor, Nero applied the guilt and inflicted the most peculiar punishments on those hated for their shameful acts, called Christians [*Chrestianos*, according to the oldest available manuscript] by the common people. The originator of the name was Christ (*Christus*), who during the reign of Tiberius was afflicted with punishment by the procurator Pontius Pilatus, ..." A phenomenon known as itacism led to the "e" and "i" sounding similar in pronunciation (*cf.* Tertullian, *Apology* 3: "Even when it is wrongly pronounced 'Chrestianus'"). The interchange of *e* and *i* in this word is evidenced even in Codex Sinaiticus, which spells "Christian" with an *ē* (Greek *eta*) in Acts 11.26, 26.28, and 1 Pet 4.16. It seems likely to me that the Roman author, Tacitus, would have originally written the form more familiar to him: *Chrestus*.

interesting. 5) Reading Suetonius' remark as a broad expulsion of Jews still leaves much unknown. Did Claudius expel only non-Christian Jews? Or would Jewish Christians have been included with them (since the Romans at first did not distinguish the two groups)? If only non-Christian Jews were expelled, "We seem to have here the astonishing spectacle of the Roman government in the role of protector of the Christians against the Jews."[71] Overall, this entire reconstruction of events based on Acts 18 and Suetonius is not as stable as it has often been made out to be.

There are other factors, it is argued, that point in the direction of a Roman destination for Hebrews.[72] First, Clement of Rome, in *c.* 95 AD (?; see below), cites phrases from Hebrews in his epistle to the Corinthians (the epistle is commonly called *1 Clement*). The fact that a Christian in Rome quotes Hebrews at such an early date could easily be explained on the basis that Hebrews originally went to Rome. Second, Timothy was, at one point, with Paul in Rome (Phlm 1), and thus the church at Rome would have known Timothy, who is mentioned in Hebrews 13.24 (assuming it is the same Timothy!). Third, an issue over "food" was raised in Hebrews 13.9, and such a problem existed in the church at Rome (Rom 14).

The factors in the paragraph above are not, however, conclusive. That Hebrews was known in Rome by 95 AD does not prove that Rome was the original destination of the work. It simply means that a copy of Hebrews had circulated that far, regardless of its original destination. Similarly, Timothy was known to other churches besides the one in Rome (*cf.* 1 Cor 16.10; Phil 2.19; 1 Thes 3.16; *etc.*), and concerns over meals were not confined to the church in Rome (*cf.* 1 Cor 8). While a Roman destination for Hebrews is possible, and most modern scholars have adopted it, it remains unclear how the situation addressed in Romans had changed to the one reflected in Hebrews. The problem that Christians were having as reflected in Romans (rivalry between Jews and Gentiles *within* the church) is very different from the picture in Hebrews (where the problem is coming from *outside*). Based on the problems with the information we have, it seems easier to solve the problem by looking elsewhere for the original destination of Hebrews.

---

[71] Hubert McNeill Poteat, "Rome and the Christians," *Classical Journal* 33 (1937): 134–44, at 141.

[72] Other arguments appear in E. Scott, "The Epistle to the Hebrews and Roman Christianity," *HTR* 13 (1920): 205–19; and Rodney J. Decker, "The Original Readers of Hebrews," *Journal of Ministry and Theology* 3 (1999): 20–49.

Southern Palestine? It is possible that Hebrews was originally written to Greek-speaking Jewish Christians who lived in Judea, perhaps even in Jerusalem itself (note the mention of the "city" in 13.14), who had been persecuted by the religious orthodoxy in Judea and were facing continual social pressure to abandon their Christian faith.[73] This would make sense of several things:

1) It fits well with what we know about conditions in Judea. Jerusalem certainly was home to a predominantly, if not completely, Jewish church, as Acts amply attests, and there were churches in Judea as well (Gal 1.22; 1 Thes 2.14) that most likely were predominantly Jewish. We also know that the relationship between Christians and unbelieving Jews there was sometimes tense. Jews who became Christians were regarded by the Judean religious leaders as heretics. No clearer example of this spirit could be found than Saul of Tarsus, who was eager to rid the world of Christians because he thought it pleased God to do so. The religious orthodoxy of Judea was perfectly willing to, and did, use violence to protect what they saw as the purity of Judaism (Acts 8–9, *etc.*). Their treatment of Stephen, who is specifically identified as a Hellenistic Jew, is a case in point, and this type of situation would fit Hebrews well.

We must, however, in fairness note that just because the situation inferred from the book of Hebrews matches what we know of conditions in or around Jerusalem from the book of Acts, this does not prove that Hebrews was addressed to Christians there. There is always the possibility that another church somewhere else found itself in the same situation, that Hebrews was actually written to that church,[74] and that our thesis of a Jerusalem destination is a mistake based on coincidence. For example, we know from the gospels and other sources that there was a sizable Jewish population in Galilee, and we know from Acts that there were churches there (Acts 9.31). A similar demographical situation existed in Syrian Antioch, farther to the north. For what it is worth, however, the early Alexandrian church fathers believed, as noted above, that Hebrews was addressed to Jewish Palestinian Christians (yet written by Paul!).

2) It would make good sense of the many references to the suffering of Jesus. The author of Hebrews referred often to the sufferings of Jesus (2.10–

[73] Allen proposes an even more narrowly constituted group: converted priests (Acts 6.7). Allen, *Hebrews*, 64–70.

[74] Allen supports Syrian Antioch as the destination for Hebrews. Allen, *Hebrews*, 66–68, 72–74.

18; 4.15–16; 5.8–9; 12.2–3; 13.13). Although the patient suffering of Christ is a model for all Christians everywhere (*cf.* 1 Pet 2.21), it is tenable to think that the reason for Hebrews' frequent mention of this is none other than Jesus himself suffered at the hands of the Jews in Judea, just as the recipients were experiencing (*cf.* 1 Thes 2.14). Such reminders would be especially appropriate for Christians who lived where Christ had lived and who were being persecuted by, basically, the same people who had persecuted Jesus.

3) It would fit well with the exhortations in chapters 12 and 13. Consider the comparison of Sinai and Zion in Hebrews 12. While that passage could have been understood by Jewish Christians everywhere, it would have been especially appropriate for Christians who lived in Jerusalem. The statement about Jesus suffering "outside the camp" (13.12), while it may have a figurative connotation, is clearly based on his suffering outside the city walls of Jerusalem and at the hands of the official Judaism there. The statement "here we do not have a lasting city" (13.14) would also fit well with recipients in Jerusalem who felt that they had been all but shunned from the place that was, more than anywhere else, identified with Judaism, and possibly their home.

4) External evidence. In his *Ecclesiastical History* 4.5 (written *c.* 324 AD), Eusebius said of the church in Jerusalem, "For their whole church consisted then of believing Hebrews who continued from the days of the apostles until the siege which took place at this time."[75] The siege to which he referred was the war that culminated in the destruction of the city in 70 AD. The *Clementine Homilies* 11.35 (written in the late second or early third century AD) refers to "James, who was called the brother of my Lord, and to whom was entrusted to administer the church of the Hebrews in Jerusalem,"[76] and the pseudonymous *Epistle of Clement to James* prefixed to that collection is addressed "to James, the Lord, and the bishop of bishops, who rules Jerusalem, the holy church of the Hebrews."[77] While we may dismiss the notion that James was the first to hold an "episcopacy" in Jerusalem, these documents are evidence of a tradition that the Jerusalem church was called "the church of the Hebrews." Chrysostom, in the introduction to his homilies on Hebrews (written in the latter part of the fourth century AD), also thought that this "letter" was originally sent

[75] *NPNF*[2] 1:176.

[76] *ANF* 8:291.

[77] *ANF* 8:218.

to Jerusalem.[78] While these statements are not conclusive for a Jerusalem destination for our letter, they do fit the theory.

To be fair, we should note that the theory of a Jerusalem destination for Hebrews has its problems. One is that the recipients of Hebrews had given aid to other Christians (6.10), but the Christians in Judea were proverbially poor and often in need of help from other churches (Acts 11.29; 24.17; Rom 15.25–26). Another problem is that Stephen had died for the faith (Acts 7–8), but Hebrews 12.4 says "You have not resisted as far as shedding blood in your striving against sin." However, neither of these problems are decisive. Hebrews 6.10 could refer to the generous giving in Acts 2.45 and 4.34–37 or some other effort unknown to us, and the economic situation of the Jerusalem Christians could have fluctuated. We certainly do not have a complete record of the history of the Jerusalem church. Hebrews 12.4 could mean that none of them *in that generation* had yet suffered martyrdom (although a previous generation had), or that none of them had been martyred *in the then-present situation.* Hebrews 13.7 may imply that former leaders among them *had* suffered martyrdom, which would fit either Stephen or James (or both), and which would condition the statement in 12.4.

A more serious problem for a southern Palestinian destination is the elegant Greek in which Hebrews was composed. One might expect a letter to Jerusalem Christians (or those in the immediate area) to have been written in Aramaic, the common language of the Jews in Palestine.[79] However, it is clear from the surviving evidence that many, and probably most, Judeans understood Greek.[80] The fact that we find Hellenistic (Greek-speaking) Jews in Acts 6 opens the possibility that Greek was the primary language of some Jews even in Jerusalem. We should also consider that the LXX,[81] used by the author of Hebrews, was the Bible of Hellenistic Jewish Christians, and there is every indication that Palestinian Jews read it as well as other Greek works in the Apocrypha. On

---

[78] *ANF* 8:364.

[79] As noted above, Clement of Alexandria even knew of a tradition to this effect (in Eusebius, *Ecclesiastical History* 6.14).

[80] See G. Scott Gleaves, *Did Jesus Speak Greek?: The Emerging Evidence of Greek Dominance in First-Century Palestine* (Eugene, OR: Pickwick, 2015).

[81] The common designation for the Septuagint is LXX. The Roman numeral for seventy represents the ancient tradition that the Septuagint was initially produced by 70 Jewish scholars.

the whole, the Jerusalem or southern Palestinian destination is a viable theory. However, as with the question of authorship, the scarcity of hard evidence should caution us not to be dogmatic about it.

VII. Date

As we noted above, Clement quoted from Hebrews, and therefore Hebrews was written prior to 1 Clement. However, this is not very helpful in establishing the date of Hebrews because the date of Clement's epistle has not been settled. It is commonly dated to *c.* 95 AD primarily on the basis of a single statement in chapter 1 that is interpreted to refer to persecutions under the Roman emperor Domitian. This interpretation, however, is problematic, and so the date of 1 Clement can only be "narrowed" to somewhere between 90 and 120 AD.[82]

Hebrews 13.23 mentions that Timothy "has been released." It seems to me that the likelihood is high that this is the same Timothy who was a well-known partner with the apostle Paul. To mention "Timothy" without any other qualifier suggests he was a well-known person. Of course, there could have been a person named Timothy who was well-known to the recipients of Hebrews and who was not the same person who worked with Paul, but when we couple the name in Hebrews with the fact that Paul's fellow-worker named Timothy was widely known among the early Christians, the likelihood of it being the same person is probably good. Timothy joined Paul's work in Acts 16, which can be dated to 50 AD. Since there is no record in Acts of Timothy being imprisoned, we cannot fit his release into a Pauline chronology with precision. Timothy was included in the greetings in 1 and 2 Thessalonians, and what is mentioned there suggests Timothy was free to travel at that early point in Paul's work. He was then mentioned in Romans 16.21, suggesting that he was with Paul at that time of writing, in Corinth. He was mentioned again in the introduction to 2 Corinthians (1.1), which would put Timothy in Ephesus at that point, and he was mentioned in two of Paul's "prison epistles," Philippians and Colossians, naturally suggesting he was with Paul, probably in Rome. If anything, then, this incomplete picture of Timothy's whereabouts would suggest that an imprisonment was likely later in Paul's life rather than earlier, but we cannot say this with certainty. At any rate, it seems unlikely that Timothy would

[82] Attridge, *Hebrews*, 7–8.

have been imprisoned for his work with the gospel earlier than the mid-50s AD, and it also seems unlikely that Timothy would have been active past the late first century.[83]

As discussed above, one consideration that makes the determination of Hebrews' date so difficult concerns the problem the letter's recipients faced and where it fits into what we know of the complex situation of the early Christians. Three broad situations developed for the early Christians: 1) in the earliest days of Christianity, before Paul and his helpers spread the gospel far into Gentile lands, the issue facing the Christians was opposition from unbelieving Jews who perceived that the Christians spoke against the perpetuity of the Law and against the Jerusalem temple (Acts 7.51–53).[84] 2) After the gospel spread to Gentile lands, however, Christianity faced a new problem, *viz.* Jewish opposition to Christian inclusion of Gentiles apart from the Law of Moses. This is the problem that occupied many of Paul's letters. Then, 3) as the churches came to be planted in the Gentile provinces, churches faced the problem of misunderstanding and opposition from Gentile unbelievers who saw Christians as social misfits and troublemakers. This is the scenario reflected in Revelation. Hebrews could possibly fit with 3), but it does not fit well with 2) since the question of the religious status of Gentile Christians never appears as an issue in Hebrews. It fits easily with 1). However, Jewish opposition to Christianity persisted well toward the end of the first century as "the parting of the ways" continued. The result is that Hebrews could have been written to just about any group of Christians who were experiencing opposition, at any time between the mid 50s to perhaps the early 90s AD.

It has sometimes been argued that Hebrews must have been written before the destruction of Jerusalem in 70 AD. The basis for this argument is not what Hebrews says, but what it never says: that the Jerusalem temple was gone.[85] The argument is often coupled with the assumption that the problem of the readers involved the so-called "return to Judaism." It goes something like this: the author's exhortation implies that his readers had the choice to return to Judaism, and throughout the book the author was trying hard to show his readers that Christianity is "better"

---

[83] Grindheim, *Letter to the Hebrews*, 21.

[84] See Bauckham, "Parting of the Ways," 183–89.

[85] *Cf.* Johnson, *Hebrews*, 38–39.

than Judaism. This argument would hardly have been possible in the first case, or necessary in the second case, if the practice of Judaism had already been practically wiped out in Jerusalem. If the author had wanted to show without doubt the superiority of Christianity and make a case for not "returning to Judaism," all he would have needed to do was point to the ruins of the temple. But he did not, and he did not in all likelihood (so goes the argument) because he could not. Thus, pre-war Judaism was still alive, and Jerusalem was still standing. A date of composition shortly before the destruction of Jerusalem—in the early to mid-60s AD—would therefore seem to fit well (again, according to the theory) with what we can surmise from the absence of any mention of the temple's destruction.

This argument, however, is not without its problems. First, as we have suggested, the argument relies on the questionable assumptions that these Jewish Christians had practically ceased significant participation in the Jewish lifestyle in the first place, and that they wanted to return to it in the second place. Neither of these assumptions are warranted or supported by any evidence, while there is much against them. Even given those assumptions (for the sake of argument), while the temple's destruction introduced a formidable crisis to Judaism, it certainly did not eliminate Judaism, so the temple's destruction would not have eliminated the choice of Jewish Christians to "return to Judaism." Second, the author of Hebrews argued in chapters 9–10 on the basis of the tabernacle, not the temple. In fact, Hebrews never mentions the temple, and one could argue just as well that the author's failure to mention the temple meant that it was no longer standing. In the end, the argument that Hebrews' failure to mention the destruction of Jerusalem is evidence that the temple was still standing is an argument from silence which has no evidentiary value and is not conclusive either way.

In support of a pre-70 AD date, it is sometimes argued that since the writer spoke of Jewish rituals in the present tense (as in 8.4–5), they must have still been going on at the time of writing. This argument is weak, however, because both Josephus[86] and Hebrews spoke of past Jewish institutions in the present tense, but no one would argue either that the tabernacle was still standing when Hebrews was written (or that the author

[86] *E.g., Ant.* 15.403; 18.19; the author of Hebrews speaks of the tabernacle in the present tense in 9.6–7 and 13.10. Other examples are in Craig R. Koester, *Hebrews: A New Translation with Introduction and Commentary*, AYB 36 (New Haven: Yale University Press, 2008), 53.

was unaware of its demise!), or that Josephus likewise did not think the temple was gone. Besides, the Greek present tense can have a different force than the English present tense, and it had a number of uses within the Greek language, so we must not think that whenever an author used the Greek present tense he was always speaking of (his) present time.[87] It could be used, for example, to state a truth in the form of "when this thing happens, then this thing results" (*cf.* 9.6–8) without indicating a then-present historical reality.

Some have thought that a clue might be present in 8.13, where the author said, "whatever is becoming obsolete and growing old is ready to disappear." This could be taken to mean that the destruction of Jerusalem was near, and it would fit well with a date in the mid-60s AD. Again, however, it is possible to read 8.13 as a statement of a general truth (which was relevant to the discussion in Heb 8), in which case it says nothing about the date of the sermon.

Some scholars favor the view that Hebrews was written after 70 AD. One problem with the pre-70 AD view, for these scholars, is that it would have an early Jewish Christian author criticizing the temple-based religion of the Jews while it was still active. Since this is hard for some to imagine (and is also politically incorrect in our time), they reject any such early approach to the date of Hebrews. Another consideration is that the presentation of Jesus as high priest would fit well with Jews who were struggling to understand things (or perhaps struggling under pressure to show solidarity with other Jews[88]) in the wake of the destruction of the temple.[89] In this connection it is argued that the absence of any mention of the temple in Hebrews could be understood as reflecting the fact that the temple was already gone. A late date would also fit better with the growing divide between Judaism and Christianity (and hence a more acute sense of crisis for Jewish Christians), a divide which seems to have intensified at the end of the first century.

---

[87] Recent investigations into Greek verbal aspect suggest that the present tense can be explained better in other ways. Relevant here is the discussion in Constantine R. Campbell, *Verbal Aspect, the Indicative Mood, and Narrative* (New York: Peter Lang, 2007), 35–76; see also Buist M. Fanning, *Verbal Aspect in New Testament Greek* (Oxford: Clarendon, 1990), 98–103.

[88] As Bauckham notes, Christians had a very different view of the temple and its destruction ("Parting of the Ways," 183–89).

[89] See Merrill C. Tenney, "A New Approach to the Book of Hebrews," *BibSac* 123 (1966): 230–36.

These considerations are not insignificant, but they are not decisive either. The presence of the Qumran community shows that Jews could openly criticize things like the temple or the Jerusalem leadership before 70 AD. In fact, there was at that time much on-going debate among Jews over many issues that were central to their faith. The Jews debated their relationship with the Hellenistic world around them, they debated the meaning of circumcision, they argued over definitions of purity, and many other things. These were inter-Jewish discussions in which debate was valid, and they did not result in open hostility among themselves. Also, both Stephen and Paul were believed to have spoken against the temple while it was standing (Acts 6.14; 21.28), so a pre-70 criticism of Judaism by a Christian Jew is not unthinkable. Furthermore, while there was a growing divide between Christianity and Judaism in the first century, Hebrews could fit just about anywhere within the early history of that divide.

To summarize our findings thus far we may say that Hebrews was possibly written by an author unknown to us, sometime between the mid-50s and the early-90s AD. The sermon was likely addressed to Jewish Christians (possibly including Gentile Christians with backgrounds in Judaism), possibly in or near Jerusalem, who had once been violently persecuted and who were currently being shamed by unbelieving Jews. The ongoing social pressure wearied these already-tested Jewish Christians and tempted them to abandon Christianity. The sermon exhorted these weary saints not to forsake the confession they had made and the journey they had begun, but rather to endure for the sake of the reward promised to them and to avoid the wrath of God. The details of the historical reconstruction must remain tentative,[90] but they are useful to us to the extent that they suggest an interpretive context and they can help us to see how Hebrews met a real need in an early church.

VIII. Use of the OT

Since Hebrews draws so heavily on the OT, it is appropriate to consider this feature of the book more closely. The sermon quotes the OT direct-

[90] For a survey of modern scholarship on Hebrews, see Sheila Griffith, "The Epistle to the Hebrews in Modern Interpretation," *RevExp* 102 (2005): 235–54. As Johnson notes, Hebrews "reminds us of how little we really know about the history of earliest Christianity outside the framework established by the Acts of the Apostles and the letters of Paul" (*Hebrews*, 1).

ly about thirty-five times, which is a high incidence compared to other NT writings (there are about ninety-three direct OT quotations for all of Paul's letters together). The number of quotations in Hebrews accounts for over a tenth of all the OT quotations in the NT.[91] In Hebrews, the most-quoted part of the OT is Psalms, with the Pentateuch quoted nearly as much.

Many of the quotations are drawn from the Septuagint, the Greek translation of the Hebrew Scriptures (hereafter LXX; although sometimes the citations in Hebrews do not conform exactly to any particular text known to us from antiquity; more on this below).[92] The LXX likely originated in Alexandria, Egypt around the middle of third century BC, and at first covered only the Pentateuch. The rest of the OT was probably translated over a span of several years (maybe as much as 100 years) in a somewhat piecemeal fashion by different people, some more and some less competent for the task. As a translation, it suffered from all the drawbacks and pitfalls that beset any translation (our modern English ones included). The use of the LXX by the author of Hebrews should not be seen as implying that this particular translation was inspired or that he thought it to be so. To the extent that it communicated the message of the OT in the language of its readers it was useful, just as our modern translations are. Nicole put it this way: "their [the NT writers'] willingness to make use of the Septuagint, in spite of its occasional defects, teaches the important lesson that the basic message which God purposed to deliver can be conveyed even through a translation, and that appeal can be made to a version insofar as it agrees with the original."[93]

The OT quotations in Hebrews are generally longer than the quotations in other NT documents, and the author of Hebrews often provides extended treatments of the quoted texts, which makes Hebrews unique in this regard in the NT canon. These facts suggest two things. First, the lengthy nature of the quotations might mean that the author was not

---

[91] Walter C. Kaiser, Jr., *The Uses of the Old Testament in the New* (Chicago: Moody Press, 1985), 3.

[92] For a detailed presentation of the characteristics of the quotations, see George Howard, "Hebrews and the OT Quotations," *NovT* 10 (1968): 208–16. The textual history of Hebrews indicates that scribes were constantly tempted to "correct" the quotations to conform to the LXX; Alan H. Cadwallader, "The Correction of the Text of Hebrews Towards the LXX," *NovT* 34 (1992): 257–92.

[93] Roger Nicole, "The New Testament Use of the Old Testament," in *Revelation and the Bible*, ed. Carl Henry (Grand Rapids: Baker Books, 1958), 135–51, at 143.

quoting from memory.[94] However, it would not have been unusual for an educated person in that culture to have committed long literary passages to memory. But when we couple the length of the quotations with the fact that the quotations often conform to known Septuagintal readings, the combined force of these facts could argue for the idea that the author had a Greek Bible available to him as he composed his message. The variants between Septuagintal readings and the quotations in Hebrews can be accounted for on the basis of variations among copies of the LXX, or by the author's use of particular exegetical methods (more on this below), or (more likely, I think) by the author's paraphrasing of his texts. Second, the OT quotations were crucial parts of the author's argument. It is obvious that the OT quotations were not secondary, but primary to the author's presentation. The quotations were not introduced simply to support an assertion by the author but were the bases of his arguments, and his exhortations were given in the conviction that they were the exhortations of the God himself. The whole argument of the book was carefully grounded in the Jewish Scriptures.[95]

The author of Hebrews preferred to introduce an OT quotation with a form of the Greek verb *legein* ("to say").[96] Scripture is introduced with words such as "he says" or "the Holy Spirit says" (3.7). That is, the quotations are introduced as God (deity) speaking for the church to hear.[97] This is especially clear in Hebrews 4, where the writer focuses on the word "today" from Psalm 95. The author of Hebrews believed that the Scriptures were not just historical records of what God said in the past, but that God continually addresses his people through his word.[98] For our author, the message of the OT has an abiding force to it. Hebrews agreed with Paul that the words of the Scriptures speak "for our learning, that we through patience and comfort of the Scriptures might have

---

[94] Simon Kistemaker, *The Psalm Citations in the Epistle to the Hebrews* (Amsterdam: Van Soest, 1961), 57.

[95] A survey of recent thought on this topic can be found in George H. Guthrie, "Hebrews' Use of the Old Testament: Recent Trends in Research," *CurBR* 1 (2003): 271–94.

[96] This is the preferred method of introducing a quotation in the Mishnah. Bruce M. Metzger, "The Formulas Introducing Quotations of Scripture in the NT and the Mishnah," *JBL* 70 (1951): 297–307.

[97] See Madison N. Pierce, *Divine Discourse in the Epistle to the Hebrews: The Recontextualization of Spoken Quotations of Scripture*, SNTSMS 178 (Cambridge: Cambridge University Press, 2020).

[98] See Johnson, *Hebrews*, 22–23.

hope" (Rom 15.4). The long list of examples of faith in Hebrews 11 that are drawn from the OT is ample proof.

This is a long way, however, from saying that our author thought that the OT (*i.e.*, the old covenant and its regulations) was still in force. No one could read Hebrews straightforwardly and come away with such an impression! The author of Hebrews believed that the OT pointed past itself,[99] to Jesus the Son, and he saw this message everywhere in it. The overriding idea in Hebrews is that God's word through Christ is a better and final message from him. Like the rest of the NT writers, the author of Hebrews believed that the "first covenant" spoke of its own demise (a point which quickly inflamed the passions of unbelieving Jews).[100] Hebrews thus treats the OT as authoritative, but at the same time recognizes it to be a limited and incomplete thing by itself. The authoritative message of the OT was that it was to be consummated by what the Messiah would bring.

The author of Hebrews read the OT Christocentrically. In particular, he saw that the OT found its focus and completion in *Jesus*.[101] The Jews clearly recognized messianic themes and types in their Scriptures, but the defining difference between the messianic views of the Jews and those of the Christians was that the latter believed and preached that *Jesus of Nazareth* is the Messiah of Israel. In asserting this, the author of Hebrews stood in continuity with the rest of the early church (*cf.* Acts 2.14–36; 26.22; Rom 1.1–2; 1 Pet 1.10; *etc.*) and with Jesus himself, who taught his disciples to see that the OT was all about him (*cf.* Luke 24.27; John 5.39, 46). Yet in this perspective the author also stood against the Judaism of his day. The author of Hebrews also read the OT eschatologically, that is, as finding its fulfillment "in these last days" (1.2). The importance of these two facts is perhaps difficult for us grasp. It is not uncommon for people today to think of the OT basically as a book about the Jews, with scattered references (prophecies) to Jesus and Christianity throughout it. This was not, however, the perspective of the early Christians in general nor of the author of Hebrews in particular. The

---

[99] See J. Gamble, "Symbol and Reality in the Epistle to the Hebrews," *JBL* 45 (1926): 162–70.

[100] George B. Caird, "The Exegetical Method of the Epistle to the Hebrews," *CJT* 5 (1959): 44–51.

[101] Ronald E. Clements, "The Use of the Old Testament in Hebrews," *SWJT* 28 (1985): 36–45.

early Christians saw virtually everything in the OT as pointing either to Jesus or to the new situation that resulted from his work that accomplished the plan of God.[102] The creation, the priesthood, the sacrifices, the flood, the journeys of Abraham, Melchizedek, Joshua, David, the conquest of Canaan, the Babylonian captivity, the exodus, the monarchy—and many more things—were all, to the Christians, types, illustrations, and explanations of the realities of the messianic age that had come with Jesus of Nazareth. It behooves us to recapture that kind of thinking in our own handling of the OT.

It should be clear that Hebrews was not an academic commentary on selected OT texts. It was rather an exhortation (13.22) based on sacred texts that were believed to speak authoritatively to people in the messianic age. Hebrews presented its exhortation as the exhortation of Scripture itself (preachers and teachers today should take a clue from this and avoid the proof-texting type of preaching that calls on Scripture to validate one's own ideas), and it presented that exhortation to Christians on the basis of the approach noted above, that basically everything in the OT was pointing forward to the messianic time that has arrived in Jesus, and that the OT has something to say about that time and to the people who live in it.

This last observation has caused some to question whether the author of Hebrews treated the OT fairly (and the same concern has been voiced against the NT as a whole). It is obvious that the author of Hebrews did not engage in the kind of "scientific" exegesis we practice today (but even those who claim their methods are "scientific" have much that is subjective in their treatments of Scripture!). That is, he did not begin a treatment of an OT text by establishing its historical context or by analyzing the grammar and syntax of the passage. This has led some to charge that he violated the contexts of OT passages and that his treatment of Scripture was not exegesis ("bringing out" the meaning), but eisegesis (bringing a meaning to the text). With such charges we strongly disagree. The OT texts, while originally spoken to specific people at specific times in specific circumstances, were also spoken in the broader theological context of the promise of a coming Savior. The author of Hebrews treated

[102] To be clear, however, we should realize that the early Christians learned to read the OT in light of their experience of Jesus. That is, it is not as if they knew Jesus from Scripture first. See Fredrick Holmgren, *The Old Testament and the Significance of Jesus* (Grand Rapids: Eerdmans, 1999), 13–55.

the OT with perfect respect for that larger theological context. He saw that the laws, institutions, and types of the OT were to be understood in light of the Jesus event which was the goal and consummation of all that went before it. Thus, for example, the author could call the tabernacle a "parable" in 9.9. Only when we read those old texts in light of Jesus do we discern their true meaning; he is the key to understanding them. The author of Hebrews believed that "the true significance of OT Scripture is found only with Christian hindsight."[103] Ellingworth aptly describes the author's handling of the OT this way: "Given that the OT speaks of Christ, the central task was to discover, with the help of clues provided within the OT itself, which texts spoke most directly of him, and to which aspects of his life and work they referred .... This is not, of course, the modern historical-critical approach; but neither is it a random, subjective, or arbitrary procedure. On the contrary, it was based on a careful and sensitive examination of the text as a whole."[104] That "whole" involves the fact that the OT documents were all, each in their own way, promises of things to come in Christ Jesus.[105] This Jesus-centered perspective no doubt partially accounts for the fact that the NT authors, as a group, tended to cite a broader part of the OT than the rabbis did, or different passages within the same books as the rabbis cited. In particular, the NT authors cited most from the Torah, Isaiah, and the Psalms, whereas rabbinic attention tended to focus on Leviticus.[106]

We may further notice that when the author of Hebrews appealed to some OT texts (such as Psalm 95), it was because the historical situations behind those texts were typologically parallel to the situation of his readers. Far from being verses taken out of their contexts, those

[103] France, "The Writer of Hebrews as a Biblical Expositor," 274.

[104] Paul Ellingworth, *The Epistle to the Hebrews: A Commentary on the Greek Text*, NIGTC (Grand Rapids: Eerdmans, 1993), 42.

[105] Even this was not wholly alien to Judaism, for, as Neusner explained, the Jews always read their Scriptures from a particular faith perspective. "When Judaic and Christian authorships proposed to compose their statements, they of course appealed to Scripture. But it was an appeal to serve a purpose defined not by Scripture but by the faith—the Judaic or Christian system—under construction and subject to articulation." Jacob Neusner, *Writing with Scripture* (Minneapolis: Fortress, 1989), 3. What is distinct about the Christian use of Scripture is not that they brought a faith perspective to it, but the content of that faith perspective (namely, Jesus).

[106] Gary Edward Schnittjer, "A Comparison of the Use of the Scripture in the NT and Early Rabbinic Judaism" (paper presented at the Annual Meeting of the Evangelical Theological Society, Nashville, TN, 15 November 2000).

texts were especially relevant. He said, for example, "For we also have had the gospel preached to us, just as they did" (4.2). The fact that the original readers of Hebrews were in the same *kind* of situation as those described in Psalm 95 made the author's use of that text especially appropriate. The same consideration seems to have driven some of the examples cited in Hebrews 11. The careful selection of texts that paralleled the readers' situation further argues against any idea that our author mishandled Scripture.

While the Jesus-centered *perspective* behind Hebrews' use of the OT was quite different from that of Judaism in that time, its *methods* of arguing from Scripture were not. The Jews had already come to believe that the sacred text spoke to their own day. After all, if God's inspired record of the past was not meant to speak across the ages, then what was the point? Accordingly, Jewish methods of handling Scripture were largely designed to make this relevance clear. This is not the place to enter into an extended discussion of the Jewish rabbinical exegetical methods. The student of Hebrews should understand, however, that neither the author of Hebrews nor other NT writers invented new methods of arguing from Scripture. Jews familiar with the teachings of the rabbis would have been generally accustomed to the ways Hebrews handled the sacred texts.[107] Lane[108] conveniently summarizes nine methods of handling Scripture the rabbis and Hebrews shared in common:

1) ***Dispelling confusion.*** Sometimes the rabbis quoted a text and then followed it by a comment to clear up possible confusion about its wording. An example of this occurs in Hebrews 2.8–9, which clarifies the "all things" in Psalm 8.6.

2) ***Reinforcement*** was the practice of "nailing down" an exhortation by appealing to Scripture as its ultimate source. An example of this is the quotation in Hebrews 10.37–38, which forms the basis for the exhortation of 10.26–36.

---

[107] "In terms of methods employed, the author of the Epistle to the Hebrews is thoroughly Jewish. He or she uses exegetical terminology, rules of interpretation, and expository patterns (like the midrash) that are found elsewhere in Judaism. But the *christological* interpretation of the biblical writings makes a unique contribution." Elke Tönges, "The Epistle to the Hebrews as a 'Jesus Midrash'," in *Hebrews: Contemporary Methods—New Insights*, ed. Gabriella Gelardini, Biblical Interpretation Series Volume 75 (Atlanta: Society of Biblical Literature, 2005), 89–105, at 90.

[108] *Hebrews 1–8*, cxix–cxxiv; based partly on Dan Cohn-Sherbok, "Paul and Rabbinic Exegesis," *SJT* 35 (1982): 117–32.

3) Rabbis also quoted texts and then commented on their ***implications.*** There are several examples of this in Hebrews, most notably the treatment of Jeremiah 31.31–34 in Hebrews 8.8–10.18.

4) In some arguments, rabbis would concentrate on the plain, ***straightforward sense of words.*** Hebrews does this somewhat in its treatment of the word "today" in Psalm 95.

5) There were ***seven "rules"*** (*middoth*) propounded by rabbi Hillel for use in interpreting Scripture. These were not strict, objective exegetical guidelines in the sense of grammatico-historical interpretation, and they could lead to fanciful interpretations,[109] but some of them involved common-sense types of approaches to texts and their applications.[110] Hebrews appears to have used at least two of these rules. Rule number one was called *qal wahomer*, "light and heavy," or the argument from the lesser to the greater (*argumentum a minore ad maiorem*). Jesus used this kind of reasoning (*cf.* Matt 7.11), and the author of Hebrews employed it in several passages (see 2.1–3; 3.2–6; 7.4–10; 9.13f; 10.28f; 12.9). There is a very real sense in which this kind of argument is the foundation of the presentation of Hebrews.[111] Rule number two was *gezerah shawah* (literally "similar law"), or the use of one verse to help explain another based on the fact that the verses have terms in common.[112] The author's combination of texts that mention "son" in Hebrews 1.5 and the combination of texts about God's "rest" in Hebrews 4 are examples of this method at work.

6) ***Chain quotation***, sometimes called "a string of pearls" (*ḥāraz*) took several texts that made the same point and quoted them one after another to emphasize just how strongly Scripture makes the point. A good example is Hebrews 1.5–13.[113]

---

[109] *Cf.* Richard B. Hays, *Echoes of Scripture in the Letters of Paul* (New Haven: Yale University Press, 1989), 12–13.

[110] For more detail see E. Earle Ellis, *The Old Testament in Early Christianity* (Grand Rapids: Baker Books, 1991) 87–91, and *idem*, "Biblical Interpretation in the New Testament Church," in *Mikra: Text, Translation, Reading and Interpretation of the Hebrew Bible in Ancient Judaism and Early Christianity*, ed. Martin Jan Mulder, CRINT 2.1 (Philadelphia: Fortress, 1988) 691–725; Richard N. Longenecker, *Biblical Exegesis in the Apostolic Period* (Grand Rapids: Eerdmans, 1975), 34–35.

[111] Johnson, *Hebrews*, 31–32.

[112] Not every argument based on verbal analogy was necessarily *gezerah shawah*. See Michael Chernick, "Internal Restraints on Gezerah Shawah's Application," *JQR* 80 (1990): 253–82. For a fuller description of how the method works in Hebrews, see David H. Wenkel, "Gezerah Shawah as Analogy in the Epistle to the Hebrews," *BTB* 37 (2007): 62–68.

[113] In Paul, see Rom 3.10–18.

7) ***Example lists*** were used to illustrate that an exhortation was in keeping with the practice of God's people in the past. Hebrews 11 is a prime example.[114]

8) ***Typology.*** A type is a historical person, event, or institution that serves as a pattern for a later corresponding person, event, or institution (called an antitype). Since typology deals with historical things, it differs immensely from the more subjective method of allegory (which often uses fiction to present an idea). The presence of types in Scripture argues that there is a sovereign God behind the flow of history who introduces things first by way of a type, and then in its fullness as an antitype. It also shows the wisdom of God in that he introduced spiritual concepts first in "physical" ways. Once we understand the "physical" we are prepared to appreciate the spiritual, which is the point of, or the "reality" of, the type, and which is greater than the type. The fact that types are superseded by their fulfillments accounts for the fact that the author of Hebrews sometimes wished to emphasize the difference between two parallels more than their similarities.

9) Homiletical ***midrash*** was perhaps the most commonly encountered rabbinical method. Midrash (derived from a term that means "to interpret") was a way of reading and expounding Scripture "to bring the text into the experience of the congregation. It involved making the Scriptures contemporary so that they could no longer be regarded only as a record of past events and sayings but as a living word through which God continues to address the audience directly."[115] Ellis says "the midrashic procedure (1) is oriented to Scripture, (2) adapting it to the present (3) for the purpose of instructing or edifying the current reader or hearer."[116] Its purpose was to show the relevance of a text to a current situation.[117] It was in some ways similar to what any good, conscientious preacher today does with Scripture: showing how the ancient texts fit our lives today. Much of Hebrews' use of the OT could be called an exercise in midrash.

Midrash allowed a reader of the OT to see its various stories and characters as models and patterns which correspond to things in the present.

---

[114] The list of examples of punishment in 2 Pet 2 is another NT example.

[115] Lane, *Hebrews 1–8*, cxxiv. For an explanation of the "logic" of this procedure, see Martin Pickup, "New Testament Interpretation of the Old Testament: The Theological Rationale of Midrashic Exegesis," *JETS* 51 (2008): 353–81.

[116] Ellis, *Old Testament in Early Christianity*, 92.

[117] Longenecker, *Biblical Exegesis in the Apostolic Period*, 37.

This was not an approach that claimed that everything in the OT was a prophecy that had some fulfillment in the present. Instead, it was a way of contemporizing the text by drawing attention to similarities between situations then and now. For example, Jeremiah's rejection by Israel was similar to Jesus' rejection by his people, but this does not necessarily warrant the conclusion that Jeremiah was a full-blown type of Christ. It is simply that there are some similarities between then and now that make it possible for us to use the ancient Scriptures to understand what is going on in the present.[118]

The midrashic procedure often had an effect on the way Scripture was quoted. There was a particular kind of midrashic treatment known as *pesher*. In this form, a text was quoted at length, followed by comments on the text with repeated references to specific key terms.[119] In Hebrews, texts such as 3.4–4.11, 7.1–10, 8.7–10.18 follow the pattern of *pesher*. In other cases, a text was quoted according to its meaning rather than in a strictly word-for-word fashion (a technique Ellis has called "implicit midrash").[120] An expositor could slightly rephrase the text, that is, paraphrase it, so as to make its meaning more obvious, thus helping the reader or hearer to see its relevance. We should think of this neither as their altering the text nor as a license for us to reword passages according to our fancy. It was a procedure that aimed at clarification. This no doubt accounts for those places where the author's quotation of the LXX was not verbatim.[121] He was simply using an accepted practice to help his readers see the exhortation that was already there in Scripture (see this at work in 10.5ff). In fact, the paraphrasing of primary sources was the accepted literary norm in Hellenistic times, not just among Jews.

None of this rules out the possibility that some OT texts were not subject to being contemporized because they were direct messianic prophecies. They were "direct" in the sense that they did not describe some prior reality which would serve as a type or parallel of the messianic situation. While

---

[118] See James W. Thompson, "The Hermeneutics of the Epistle to the Hebrews," *ResQ* 38 (1996): 229–37.

[119] Kistemaker, *Psalm Citations*, 65, 75. The Dead Sea text 1QpHab is perhaps the most well-known example contemporary with Hebrews.

[120] Ellis, *Old Testament in Early Christianity*, 66; see also his "Biblical Interpretation in the New Testament Church," 703.

[121] See J. C. McCullough, "The Old Testament Quotations in Hebrews," *NTS* 26 (1980): 363–79.

many, if not most, OT texts previewed the messiah and the messianic age indirectly, through typology, analogy, *etc.*, there is nothing that said every messianic "prediction" in the OT had to be of this nature. As an example, a good case can be made that Psalm 110, the key OT text in Hebrews, had no historical roots within Israel, but was a direct messianic prophecy.

To Jewish Christians, none of these methods of handling Scripture would have seemed radical, new, unorthodox, or unconventional. They were accustomed to hearing Scripture expounded in these ways from their days in the synagogues. In fact, it is Hebrews' use of these methods that helped make its exhortation so powerful to its first readers. These readers would have found the exhortation convincing precisely because it presented that exhortation from Scripture using methods they already accepted as valid.[122] Yet, as we mentioned above, it was not the methods of handling Scripture that were new in Christianity, but the perspective from which Christians read the Jewish Bible. That perspective was that the Jewish Scriptures pointed specifically to Jesus and the new order of things in him.[123] Hebrews succeeded as an exhortation not because it used Jewish methods of handling the Scriptures (as if they were somehow normative), but because it demonstrated how Jesus fulfills Psalm 110 and the rest of the Scriptures.

IX. Canonicity and Text

The inclusion of Hebrews into the NT canon was debated for a while. It was well-known that Hebrews was written in apostolic times, but this alone did not prove it worthy of inclusion in the canon (*cf.* 2 Thes 2.2). Those who were reluctant to include Hebrews into the canon were hesitant basically on two grounds. First, the epistle was of unknown authorship. Since those in post-apostolic times did not always succeed in making the important distinction between authorship and authority, apostolic authorship became an important factor to determine whether a document belonged in the canon, and those documents that could not be directly attributed to an apostle were automatically suspect. For example, Hebrews was not listed in the Muratorian Canon, a list of accepted books that dates to about 200 AD. However, the problem of anonymous

[122] This is possibly another indicator that the original recipients of Hebrews were Jewish Christians.

[123] See Tönges, "The Epistle to the Hebrews as a 'Jesus-Midrash,'" 89–105.

authorship did not prevent people from using the book, and it was quoted by 1 Clement, Polycarp, the author of 2 Clement, Justin, Irenaeus, Hippolytus, Clement of Alexandria, Origen, and others.

The second grounds for reluctance to accept Hebrews was that, for some, the document disagreed with a doctrine or practice that was held on some other basis. The Montanists were fond of Hebrews because 6.4–6 seemed to confirm their belief that repentance and restoration was not allowed for a Christian who had sinned after baptism, but anti-Montanists, who believed that a "second repentance" was allowed, consequently denied any authority to Hebrews.[124] It is clear that, in these cases, decisions about the canonicity of Hebrews were being made with the cart in front of the horse, so to speak. Doctrinal beliefs were controlling which texts were accepted rather than letting the texts dictate the doctrines to be accepted. Thus, some of the debate over Hebrews' place in the canon actually did not address the real subject at all. This entanglement in doctrinal controversies no doubt also accounts for the fact that Hebrews was accepted more readily in the eastern part of the empire than it was in the west, because the debate over the readmittance of Christians who had sinned into fellowship was settled in the negative in Rome and in the churches under its influence.

Despite the fact that Hebrews seemed to run counter to the theological views of some, the resilience of the book proved its worthiness to be included in the canon. Hebrews was found to be such a profound, insightful, and useful book that it could not be ignored.[125] So powerful was its influence that even those who rejected it on prior doctrinal grounds thought it necessary to refer to the book, even if only to register their disagreement. Thus, in their own way, they acknowledged the authority of Hebrews. Furthermore, extremist groups such as the Montanists and their opponents eventually disappeared from the scene, which allowed men a clearer look at the book and allowed Hebrews to speak more for itself. When its own voice was heard, people agreed that Hebrews was in no way inferior to those documents whose canonicity was unquestioned. By the fifth century (the third Synod of Carthage, 397 AD) Hebrews was universally recognized as having a rightful place in the Scripture of the

[124] Philip Edgcumbe Hughes, *A Commentary on the Epistle to the Hebrews*, NICNT (Grand Rapids: Eerdmans, 1977), 214–15; Moffatt, *Epistle to the Hebrews*, xvii-xviii; Grindheim, *Letter to the Hebrews*, 44.

[125] See Johnson, *Hebrews*, 3–7 for a succinct history of the reception of Hebrews.

church. Even then, however, its association with Paul lingered (although by that time many had come to doubt Pauline authorship).

Concerning the text of Hebrews, in order to simplify the discussion here and to appeal to a standardized Greek text in the commentary I will accept the decisions of the editors for the Greek text as it appears in the fifth edition of the United Bible Society's *The Greek New Testament* (which is the same text as that in the twenty-eighth edition of the Nestle-Aland *Novum Testamentum Graece*). The English text in the commentary is my own modest translation (designed more for the purpose of commentary than for smoothly flowing prose), but recourse will be made to other English versions in the course of explaining the text.

X. Structure

By "structure" we intend to ask how this piece of literature is arranged and how it presents its thoughts. Imposing a modern kind of outline on an ancient work is always an artificial matter because outlining requires interpretation (which may be incorrect), and because the author possibly did not have the same kind of outline in mind when he wrote. This does not mean that Hebrews (or any other ancient text) lacked organization, but we must understand that the ways the ancients organized their materials were sometimes different from ours, and the indicators of organization were different as well. For example, in books today we see words in italic or bold type, paragraphs offset from each other, different fonts, extra spacing when a new section starts, *etc.* We have all kinds of *visual* clues to show readers how a text has been organized. In ancient times, however, those clues were *literary*. They employed certain techniques, such as the repetition of words, to let readers (or hearers) know when a section was ending and a new one beginning. What we need to do, therefore, is become sensitive to the methods the ancients used.

As soon as we say this, however, we find that there is no agreement among students of Hebrews about the structure of this work.[126] This is somewhat surprising, because Hebrews abounds in rhetorical devices more than any other NT writing, and rhetorical or discursive[127] devic-

[126] *Cf.* Barry C. Joslin, "Can Hebrews Be Structured? An Assessment of Eight Approaches," *CurBR* 6 (2007): 99–129. Note also the brief survey of approaches in Heath, "Chiastic Structures in Hebrews," 62.

[127] For an outline of Hebrews based on discourse analysis, see Cynthia Long Westfall, *A Discourse Analysis of the Letter to the Hebrews: The Relationship between Form and Meaning*, LNTS 297 (London: T&T Clark, 2005).

es are often good clues to structure. It would seem that discerning the structure of Hebrews would be a matter of identifying those features, listing them as they occur, and deducing the author's outline from them. However, even with extensive literary analysis in recent years, scholars are nowhere near agreement as to the structure of Hebrews. This is due partly because some proposals about structure also require judgments about content, and those judgments may vary from one interpreter to the next. Also, the author of Hebrews often artfully foreshadowed discussions that occur later in his treatise,[128] and this can make drawing lines between one section and the next difficult. Generally speaking, however, proposals about the work's structure that proceed on linguistic grounds rather than doctrinal/interpretive grounds, are preferable.[129] Added to the mix is the extensive use of the OT in Hebrews, which has led some to seek for the structure there. The lack of modern consensus about the structure of the work means that discerning Hebrews' structure has not proven to be easy, and in such a case a simpler approach may have more merit. We must admit, however, that the way we outline the book may prejudice the reading of the book (by using the outline to emphasize certain features over others), and we must view a proposed outline as an interpretive, and therefore possibly biased, statement.[130]

As with the matter of genre, coming to grips with the structure of Hebrews (or any Biblical document) is just as much a part of the interpretive task as the exegesis of individual verses. The point of any such exercise is to see the interrelationship of the various parts and to identify contexts by which we may interpret individual verses. The outline presented below,[131] therefore, is the basis upon which our exegesis will proceed, but it is put forward with the acknowledgement that it must be considered provisional.

---

[128] This technique has been called "chain-link." See Bruce W. Longenecker, *Rhetoric at the Boundaries: The Art and Theology of New Testament Chain-Link Transitions* (Waco, TX: Baylor University Press, 2005).

[129] Extensive work on the overall structure of Hebrews from a linguistic basis has been done by George H. Guthrie. See his *The Structure of Hebrews: A Text-Linguistic Analysis*, Biblical Studies Library (Grand Rapids: Baker Books, 1998).

[130] See David Alan Black, "The Problem of the Literary Structure of Hebrews: An Evaluation and a Proposal," *GTJ* 7 (1986): 163–77.

[131] Many scholars are at least agreed that there are five major sections in the book. There is not, however, agreement about the divisions or contents of the five sections. For a topical approach, see George E. Rice, "Apostasy as a Motif and its Effect on the Structure of Hebrews," *AUSS* 23 (1985): 29–35.

However one decides upon the smaller details of the sermon's structure, at least one thing is clear: Hebrews oscillates between two related discussions. The first discussion of the sermon is the high priesthood of Jesus, and how it is better in every way compared to the Levitical system.[132] The second discussion, interwoven with the first, is a combination of encouragement and warning: encouragement to persevere in their faith, and warning about what will happen to them if they do not. The sermon's two discussions must be seen as complementary. Both of them served the same purpose, that is, to encourage its original hearers to remain faithful to Jesus. The point to which the discussion of Jesus' high priesthood drives is that since we have such a better situation than was available under the old covenant with its Levitical priesthood, now is not the time to be quitting, but to persevere unto the end. The implied, but unspoken, point of that discussion is that it would be absurd to quit when one has finally come into a better situation. Of course, the author emphasized that the situation under our new high priest is indeed better, because the shame and rejection the original recipients were experiencing from others surely did not seem to be a better situation than their pre-conversion lives! Looking above, and looking to the end, became the keys to endurance. The author consistently called upon them to look to the heavenly reality and its better quality, and to the end of their "journey," and not become distracted by the temporary, earthly hardships that challenged them. The second discussion makes this same point, but in the more direct method of exhortation. Therefore, through a combination of textual/doctrinal discussion and exhortation, the sermon aimed at securing the faithfulness of its audience. We would do well to note the connection and preserve it in our own preaching. Doctrines are not abstract theological ideas. They are the foundation and reasons for why Christians live as they do. Biblical preaching should look like the sermon we call Hebrews, with adequate portions of both doctrine and exhortation, each reinforcing the other.

The second discussion (the need for perseverance in the faith) is regularly recognized as five "warning passages." They appear at 2.1–4, 3.7–

---

[132] Landgraf has proposed an outline of Hebrews that follows the lead of Leviticus and that traces the general "flow" of the events of the Day of Atonement. Paul David Landgraf, "The Structure of Hebrews; A Word of Exhortation in Light of the Day of Atonement," in *A Cloud of Witnesses: The Theology of Hebrews in its Ancients Contexts*, ed. Richard Bauckham *et al*, LNTS 387 (London: T&T Clark, 2008), 19–27.

4.16, 5.11–6.19, 10.19–39, and 12.25–29. The warning passages also become more intense, more forceful, as the sermon progresses. One could argue, however, that the last "warning passage" extends from 10.19–12.29, since the discussion of Jesus' high priesthood ends at around 10.21, and all of Hebrews 11 and 12 is occupied with encouragement to faithfulness. If we view the sermon in this way, then the first part of the sermon is predominantly a discussion of the high priesthood of the exalted Jesus, but it then shifts to become a discussion of the need for perseverance in the faith.

"See to it that you do not refuse him who is speaking"

I. **First exhortation:** 1.1–2.18. The superiority of the Son and of the revelation from God that has come through him.
   - A. 1.1–2.4. God has now spoken in a final way to us in his Son, Jesus, who is superior to the angels. We must pay closer attention to the word that came in him.
   - B. 2.5–18. Exposition of Psalm 8.4–6. The superiority of Jesus is not diminished by his death. It was instead an act of humility for the benefit of Jesus' brethren.

II. **Second exhortation:** 3.1–4.13. The need for faithfulness (endurance) to obtain the promised rest.
   - A. 3.1–6. Jesus is greater than Moses. Moses was a faithful servant in God's house, but Jesus is the faithful Son over God's house.
   - B. 3.7–4.13. Exposition of Psalm 95.7–11.
     1. 3.7–19. We must not follow Israel's example of faithlessness and disobedience.
     2. 4.1–13. God's promised rest remains open for the faithful, and we must strive to enter into it.

III. **Third exhortation:** 4.14–10.39. The new, and better, order of things under the high priesthood of Jesus.
   - A. 4.14–5.10. Exhortation introducing the high priesthood of Jesus, whom God appointed to that position.
   - B. 5.11–6.20. Rebuke for failing to have grown in knowledge, and encouragement to press on to maturity.
   - C. 7.1–28. Jesus is high priest after the order of Melchizedek (exposition of Psalm 110.4).

- **D.** 8.1–10.18. The new high priest is mediator of a new covenant in which there is the forgiveness of sins.
- **E.** 8.19–10.39. Exhortation based on the fact that we have a new high priest of a new covenant in which there is forgiveness of sins.

IV. Fourth exhortation: 11.1–12.29. The need for faithfulness (endurance) to obtain what has been promised.

- **A.** 11.1–40. Some examples of faith (endurance) of OT saints.
- **B.** 12.1–13. We should endure through hardships, because these are God's discipline upon us for our good.
- **C.** 12.14–29. Further exhortation to faithfulness.

V. Fifth exhortation: 13.1–19. Our relationships with our brethren.

- **A.** 13. 1–6. Moral exhortations.
- **B.** 13.7–14. Remain steadfast in the truth and endure suffering with Christ.
- **C.** 13.15–19. Concluding exhortations.

VI. Conclusion: 13.20–25.

- **A.** 13.20–21. Prayer for the recipients of the "book."
- **B.** 13.22–24. Author's personal note.
- **C.** 13.25. Farewell.

This approach to the book of Hebrews also suggests that the contents are generally arranged chiastically, which was a common literary device in ancient texts[133] by which material was presented and then re-presented in reverse order. Thus, Hebrews proceeds as:

---

[133] See Augustine Stock, "Chiastic Awareness and Education in Antiquity," *BTB* 14 (1984): 23–27; see also P. E. Pickering, "Did the Greek Ear Detect 'Careless Verbal Repetitions'?," *Classical Quarterly* 53 (2003): 490–99.

A The superiority of Jesus and his becoming like his brethren (1.1–2.18)
  B The need for faithfulness (endurance) to obtain what is promised (3.1–4.13)
    C The new, and better, order of things under the high priesthood of Jesus (4.14–10.39)
  B′ The need for faithfulness (endurance) to obtain what is promised (11.1–12.29)
A′ Our relationship with our brethren (13.1–19)

Similarly, Geldarini[134] has suggested the following chiastic structure:

A 1.1–2.18 elevation and abasement of the Son
  B 3.1–6.20 faithlessness of fathers and sons
    C 7.1–10.18 new covenant and cult institution
  B′ 10.19–12.3 faith of sons and fathers
A′ 12.4–13.25 abasement and elevation of sons

Discerning chiastic structures in texts is complicated, and ultimately must be based on a close reading of the original text, especially in light of repetition of key terms.[135] There seems to be, however, a growing consensus that a chiastic structure underlies Hebrews.[136]

Since Hebrews' use of the OT is significant (see above), some scholars have insisted that the key to understanding the structure of Hebrews is first to notice those places where the OT is quoted at length, and then see the "outline" of the book as centering around those texts.[137] Our approach

---

[134] *Verhartet eure Herzen nicht: Der Hebraer, eine Synagogenhomilie zu Tischa be-Aw* (Leiden: Brill, 2006). Other proposals for a chiastic structure are Albert Vanhoye, *A Structured Translation of the Epistle to the Hebrews*, trans. James Swetnam (Rome: Pontifical Biblical Institute, 1964); see also Gabriella Gelardini, "From 'Linguistic Turn' and Hebrews Scholarship to *Anadiplosis Iterata*: The Enigma of a Structure," *HTR* 102 (2009): 51–73; and David M. Heath, "Chiastic Structures in Hebrews: With a Focus on 1:7–14 and 12:26–29," *Neot* 46 (2012): 61–82. George E. Rice sees chiasm in the central part of the book ("The Chiastic Structure of the Central Section of the Epistle to the Hebrews," *AUSS* 19 (1981): 243–46). Perhaps overdone is John Bligh, *Chiastic Analysis of the Epistle to the Hebrews* (Oxon: Athenaeum Press, 1966) which sees the epistle as composed of thirty-three chiastic units.

[135] See the criteria in Craig Blomberg, "The Structure of 2 Corinthians 1–7," *CTR* 4 (1989): 3–20; David J. Clark, "Criteria for Identifying Chiasm," *LB* 35 (1975): 63–72.

[136] See also Black, "The Problem of the Literary Structure of Hebrews," 175–6.

[137] See David J. MacLeod "The Literary Structure of the Book of Hebrews," *BibSac* 146 (1989): 185–97; Longenecker, *Biblical Exegesis in the Apostolic Period*, 175; Kistemaker, *Psalm Citations*, 130; France, "The Writer of Hebrews as a Biblical Expositor," 259; Compton, *Psalm*

here (following more recent scholarship) modifies this idea and suggests that the exhortations and expositions must be read together. They are so tightly interwoven in Hebrews[138] that preferring one over the other will result in an uneven reading of the book. The table below shows how we might map the relationship between our suggested outline and the major OT quotations.

Exhortation	Major OT texts
1.1–2.18	a collection of texts on "the Son" and Psalm 8.4–6
3.1–4.13	Psalm 95.7–11
4.14–10.39	Psalm 110.1,4; Jeremiah 31.31–24; Psalm 40.6–8
11.1–12.29	a collection of references to OT people of faith and Proverbs 3.11–12
13.1–19	Deuteronomy 31.6 and Psalm 118.6

The last exhortation is somewhat problematic in that it does not build upon an extended discussion of an OT text. This is likely because the main point of that exhortation did not require extensive argumentation.

Modern scholarship has agreed that whatever we may say about the arrangement of Hebrews, the exhortations (the "warning passages") are not to be considered as secondary to the expositions of OT texts. It is a fault of some theologians that they tend to focus more on the expository material in Hebrews than the hortatory material, but it is important that we understand that "exhortation is not to be viewed as superfluous to the progression of thought in Hebrews. Rather, argumentation serves exhortation."[139] The author has constructed his exhortations based on a careful selection of OT texts that were especially appropriate to the situation of his readers and the exhortation he wished to give them. In those exhortations that were based on more than one text, the texts have a common theme (such as "the Son" or "faithful endurance" or "the new order in Christ"), and the author supplemented his main texts with additional quotations along the way (such as Psa 40 in Heb 10).

---

110 and the Logic of Hebrews, esp. "Appendix: Survey of Literature on the Use of the Old Testament in Hebrews' Structure" (172–81).

[138] See Ellingworth, *Epistle to the Hebrews*, 58.

[139] John R. Walters, "The Rhetorical Arrangement of Hebrews," *AsTJ* 51 (1996): 59–70, at 60.

HEBREWS 1

1.1 God, having spoken long ago in many portions and in many ways to the fathers by means of the prophets,

Verses 1–4 are a single, elegant sentence in Greek, a kind of sentence known as a period, which is a Greek stylistic device that contains a complete thought. Some have argued that it is chiastic.[1] The author begins with the general fact of God's communication **to the** ancient Israelites, who are the **fathers** from a Jewish perspective. The term "fathers" is not restricted here to those individuals we formally call the patriarchs (Abraham, Isaac, Jacob, Moses, *etc.*), but has the more general sense of "ancestors." The phrase **long ago** is generic and sets up a contrast to the "recent" activity of God described in verse 2. It also suggests a long, drawn-out process in the past versus the relatively abrupt communication in verse 2. Immediately the author begins to draw a distinction between the old and the new (which has appeared in "these last days," v 2), which is foundational to the sermon. As he will make clear, the old becomes inferior when the new appears on the scene (8.13). For now, however, he is simply laying the groundwork. The author's concern is not with a particular episode of divine revelation, nor a particular situation a divine message was sent to address. Instead, he has the "big picture" in view. **God spoke** to the ancient Israelites, but our author wants to draw attention to the nature of that speaking, for that has everything to do with the purpose and nature of the message itself. However, also implicit in the statement is that God's speaking is meant to be heard by man. The fact that he speaks removes excuse for sin (see 2.1; 3.7, 16).

The author begins by pointing out three significant features of the old revelation. First, it was delivered **in many portions** (Greek *polumerōs*) or

[1] Daniel J. Ebert, "The Chiastic Structure of the Prologue to Hebrews," *TrinJ* 13 (1992): 163–79: A (vv 1-2a), B (v 2b), C (v 2c), D (v 3a-b), C′ (v 3c), B′ (v 3d), A′ (v 4).

in many separate parts. No single former revelatory episode contained a complete expression of the plan of God. To the ancients, this meant one thing: that the former revelation of God was imperfect (in the Greek sense of the word), it was incomplete, never finished.[2] It kept coming from God in parts, a piece at a time. There was always a sense of incompleteness in the method; the final word did not come (*cf.* 1 Pet 1.10–12).

Second, God spoke **in many ways** (Greek *polutropōs*). God used a variety of methods in his former speaking to the Israelite ancestors. Sometimes God communicated through visions and dreams (as in Gen 31.11; 37.5–10; 1 Kngs 22.19–23), sometimes verbally or audibly (as in Exod 20.1; 1 Sam 3.1–14; Jer 1.4), sometimes by signs (as in Dan 5.5–30), or by Urim and Thummim (*cf.* 1 Sam 28.6), *etc.* There was no single definitive method of communication in the prior period of God's revelation.

The picture from these two terms (**many portions** and **many ways**) taken together is that God's prior revelation was not delivered completely at one time to the ancient Israelites but was delivered in pieces and in different ways for hundreds of years over the span of their history. God kept speaking, another piece of the plan at a time. A message that was never finalized could not have been God's ultimate word to man. The old revelation was incomplete by design, because it pointed to its fulfillment in Jesus (*cf.* Rom 3.21; Gal 3.24).

Third, the old revelation was delivered through the **prophets**, the human mouthpieces, as it were, through whom God spoke. The author has in mind the *people* who were God's prophets and not just the writings of the literary prophets in the OT. The author was in no way suggesting that the prophets were low types or that they should be in any way discounted or despised (see Heb 11.32). His point lay instead in the fact that the word "prophets" is in the plural. God did not reveal himself fully to anyone of them, and no single prophet delivered all of God's word to Israel. Thus,

---

[2] *Cf.* Brooke Foss Westcott, *The Epistle to the Hebrews: The Greek Text with Notes and Essays*, 3rd ed., (London: Macmillan, 1903), 4. Repetition as an indicator of inefficiency and imperfection will also figure into the discussions of the priesthood in Heb 7.23–25 and the yearly Day of Atonement ritual in Heb 9.25–10.10. Generally, for Hebrews, the heavenly (the new) is characterized by singularity ("one"), whereas the earthly (the old) is characterized by repetition ("many"). See James Thompson, "*EPHAPAX*: The One and the Many in Hebrews," *NTS* 53 (2007): 566–81. Not all uses of plurality in Hebrews are necessarily negative, though. Multiple witnesses would be an example of positive multiplicity, as well as continual praise in 13.15. See Nicholas J. Moore, *Repetition in Hebrews*, WUNT 388 (Tübingen: Mohr Siebeck, 2015).

the old revelation came in a plurality of parts, on numerous occasions, and through a plurality of people and methods. Formerly there was no one time or person in which God delivered all of his message. Again, plurality was considered a mark of an ongoing process, and the point is that the old revelation, as great as it was, lacked finality. Although the author has pointed out a weakness of the old revelation, he still had a high view of it. It was nothing less than the word of God.

1.2 has spoken to us in these last days in a Son, whom he appointed heir of all things, and through whom he made the world,

Christianity is built, in a sense, on the fact that God has spoken again, but not just again in the sense of another piece of an ongoing process.[3] The same God who spoke to the Jewish ancestors has now **spoken**[4] his final word **to us**, that is, to Christians. Of course, God's word in Christ is meant for the entire world, but the focus in Hebrews is on the significance of that message for God's own people. God has spoken in one who is his **Son**, to whom God's former words pointed (*cf.* 1 Pet 1.10–11; Acts 3.18, 24; 7.52) and whose status is greater than that of the prophets (see below).

The term **son** is used to suggest several things in Scripture: 1) It can denote physical descent, but that is clearly not its meaning here. By extension, a descendant ("son") is also 2) an heir of his father's wealth (*cf.* Matt 21.38), and the sense of son as heir is certainly operative when used of Jesus in Hebrews. 3) It can be a term of endearment when used by the father (*cf.* Heb 12.5ff). 4) Since children bear the traits of their parents, "son" can mean "imitator" (as in Gal 3.7; Matt 5.45; John 5.19) or "partaker" in some quality or condition (Matt 8.12; Luke 16.8; John 12.36; 1 Thes 5.15). Jesus is the Son of God in that he shares in the nature and attributes of God (deity), as our author will point out below. 5) "Son" can also suggest the role of service to the father (Mal 3.17; Matt 21.28), but with a status greater than that of an ordinary servant (*cf.* Heb 3.5; Gal 4.1). 6) It is a title of honor that distinguishes one person in a household above others

[3] The Christian claim that God had revealed himself in Jesus ran counter to the beliefs of some Jews who believed that revelation had ceased after the time of Malachi. See 1 Macc 4.46 and 9.27. See also Josephus, *Against Apion* 1.41; and the rabbinic *Tosefta Sotah* 13.2. However, not all Jews believed that prophecy had ceased in their day. See David E. Aune, *Prophecy in Early Christianity and the Ancient Mediterranean World* (Grand Rapids: Eerdmans, 1983), 103–6.

[4] The aorist *elalēsen* has a perfective sense in this context.

in that same household (Heb 3.1–6) and is connected with the father's authority. As such it becomes a term denoting status. Sons, especially the firstborn (see v 6 below) are "viewed as the symbol of the father's might or strength,"[5] a point our author will emphasize in his statements below. While Jesus was, and is, always God's Son (Heb 5.8; Matt 3.17), the author of Hebrews here sees (based on the OT texts he quotes below) in this word a term that emphasizes the exaltation of Jesus. After Jesus' resurrection, the name "Son" declares his status as the exalted one.[6]

The word "Son" lacks the definite article in the Greek here, and possibly emphasizes the quality of sonship,[7] as opposed to "prophets" in the previous statement, without sacrificing the definiteness of the noun.[8] The contrast in status between the one who is God's Son and all others will be the object of the author's attention through the rest of chapter 1. Furthermore, the idea that God has spoken in a final (eschatological) way suggests that the long-awaited messianic order of things has now appeared, and this speaking is bound up with the fact that something has now *happened* in Jesus. Although it is legitimate to speak of Jesus as the Prophet by whom God spoke (*cf.* John 8.26; 12.49; 14.10), Jesus was more than just a messenger, and the Greek preposition *en* (which can be translated "in") may have a locative force here, although the instrumental sense of "by" works well also.[9] Due to the Son's unique nature and status, the revelation that comes through him is a qualitatively better revelation of God because the Son can speak for God in a way that no human prophet could (*cf.* John 8.38). Jesus was not simply another spokesman for God, but by

[5] "Son," *DBI* 805.

[6] Moises Silva, "Perfection and Eschatology in Hebrews," *WTJ* 39 (1976): 60–71, at 63.

[7] See Ronald D. Peters, *The Greek Article: A Functional Grammar of ho-items in the Greek New Testament with Special Emphasis on the Greek Article,* Linguistic Biblical Studies 9 (Leiden: Brill, 2014), 227.

[8] It is normal in Greek for nouns in prepositional phrases to lack the article, especially when the noun denotes a unique or divine person; BDF §255; A. T. Robertson, *A Grammar of the Greek New Testament in the Light of Historical Research,* 4th ed. (New York: Doran, 1923), 791–92. Furthermore, in Greek it is usual for the first mention of a person to be anarthrous, with subsequent mentions including the article. Stephen H. Levinsohn, "The definite article with proper names for referring to people in the Greek of Acts," *Work Papers of the Summer Institute of Linguistics, University of North Dakota Session 35* (1991): 91–102, at 93.

[9] Johnson, *Hebrews,* 65. However, the same preposition is used of the prophets in v 1, so Westcott (*Epistle to the Hebrews,* 6) saw the same locative force there, indicating that God was "the quickening power of their life."

virtue of his sonship all the qualities of the Father were *in* him so that he could speak for the Father in a unique way (Matt 11.27). He did not simply deliver God's truth; he was God's truth incarnate (John 1.17; 14.6).[10]

God's speaking also carries with it a sense of surety, since God is always true to his word (this will become a consideration in ch 6). Like the other NT writers, the author of Hebrews also understood that a new-creational order of things has come about as a result of God's speaking, although it has not yet reached its fullest realization. That fullness will be experienced in heaven (see ch 12), so the word of God both establishes a new order in the present, but it also brings a promise of an even greater measure to come. Endurance is therefore required on our part if we hope to share in it.

God's new revelation stands in contrast to the old one in at least three ways. First, instead of being delivered through a plurality of times, God has delivered his new revelation **in**[11] **these last days**. This phrase, when used in eschatological contexts, refers to the messianic age.[12] The same period is sometimes called "those days" by the prophets (see Jer 3.16; 31.33; Joel 2.29; *etc.*), and it is viewed in Scripture as a single time, as a whole, not as an indefinite period. The term **last** (Greek *eschatos*) can convey the sense of reaching a goal.[13] The word does not necessarily convey a chronological sense, so it need not imply that the author thought the end of the world was near. These days are the last days in the sense that they mark the attainment of that to which the previous order of things pointed, the age of the consummation and fulfillment of God's previous promises. The author also calls this time "the consummation of the ages" in 9.26 (*cf.* 1 Cor 10.11), and it is therefore paradoxically also the beginning of a new order of things in which the purpose and promises of God have begun to be realized. God's revelation has achieved its end, or its goal, in his Son. By the word **these** the author claims that the long-awaited "last days" are here; "those days" have now become "these days" by the work of Jesus. The Law and the Prophets pointed to him (Rom 3.21), and in him they find their "yes,"

---

[10] *Cf.* 2.3, where the author also says that the word we have heard was spoken *through* the Lord.

[11] The preposition here translated "in" (Greek *epi*) can denote what is contemporary, and thus enhances the sense of "now" in this statement. BDF §234.8.

[12] LXX Num 24.14; Jer 25.19 [49.39 MT]; Dan 10.14; Hos 3.5; Mic 4.1.

[13] Franco Montanari, *The Brill Dictionary of Ancient Greek* (Leiden: Brill, 2015), 831.

their fulfillment (2 Cor 1.20). The author will discuss other aspects of the final character of the new order of things in chapters 9 and 10.

We should also note here that from the very beginning, the author of Hebrews held a basic apocalyptic and eschatological viewpoint concerning Christianity, and this viewpoint colored his entire presentation. The viewpoint was that God had intervened in history, in a final and dramatic way, to deal with the problem of sin and to establish and confirm his righteous reign over the world. For Christians, *the* apocalyptic event was the coming of Jesus and his work which he accomplished on the earth, which included delivering God's final, consummative word to man. The result of this event was a new, heavenly, and spiritual order of things in which we participate now, but even more fully in the future.[14] This perspective informed how the author of Hebrews read (and quoted) the OT in this sermon.

Second, instead of being delivered through a plurality of methods and people, God has delivered his new revelation through one person. Third, the final word from God has not come through a prophet, but through one who is much greater than a prophet, God's own Son. The composite picture is that this one Son is sufficient to reveal the word of God in a final and complete way.

The fact that God has now spoken in one person (Jesus) reflects the finality of God's message through him. The new revelation was given once and for all (*cf.* Jude 3). Man needs no more revelation from God after this. The fact that the apostles received and delivered revelation after Jesus left the earth does not contradict this, because it was Jesus who was speaking through them (1 Cor 14.37; 1 Thes 4.2; 2 Pet 3.2). Nor does the fact that Jesus spoke through his apostles for a generation or so after he left the earth suggest that the word that came through Jesus

---

[14] This apocalyptic eschatological viewpoint should not be confused with the apocalyptic genre. Paul D. Hanson, *The Dawn of Apocalyptic: The Historical and Sociological Roots of Jewish Apocalyptic Eschatology*. Rev. ed. (Philadelphia: Fortress, 1979), 429–44; George H. Guthrie, "Hebrews' Eschatology in Hermeneutical Perspective" (paper read at the Annual Meeting of the Evangelical Theological Society, Danvers, MA, 1999); John J. Collins, "Introduction: Towards the Morphology of a Genre," *Semeia* 14 (2003): 1–29. For a study in how the apocalyptic viewpoint pervades the NT, see Ethelbert Stauffer, *New Testament Theology* (New York: Macmillan, 1955). There is a short summary in David McClister, *Relationships in the Messianic Time: A Commentary on Philemon* (Tampa: DeWard Publishing Company, Ltd., 2022), 69–95. This apocalyptic perspective should not be confused with speculative modern millennial theories.

was also ongoing, piecemeal, and thus incomplete. In the big picture, the relatively short period in which the faith was revealed is viewed by our author as evidence of the finality of the message. It is significant that nowhere does the author of Hebrews pretend to offer some recently- or newly received revelation as the answer to his readers' problems. He saw his task as explaining for his readers the deeper implications of the faith they had already received and bringing them back to what they had heard before. What was spoken in the Son is the fulfillment, end, completion, and climax of the progressive revelation that had been spoken before. God has now made a final revelation in Jesus, of whom God himself said "Hear him" (Matt 17.5). Hearing what God has said in his Son will be a major emphasis in the exhortations our author will present later. It is important to note that the author does not yet call him Jesus or the Christ. He calls him God's Son in order to prepare the reader for the argument in the following verses.

The author's statement in verses 1–2a asserts both continuity and discontinuity between the old and new revelations of God.[15] There is continuity, or unity, in that it is the same God who speaks in both. His former message led to the latter one, and his latter message is properly the completion of the former one. But there is discontinuity in that the latter message was delivered through a superior agent in a once-for-all way.

Verses 2b–4 list seven things[16] that describe the superior status and exalted greatness of the Son in whom God has spoken.

1) The first thing said about the Son is that God has appointed **him heir of all things** (*cf.* the parable in Matt 21.37f). **Appointed** (Greek *tithēmi*) here denotes the official conferring of a status, in this case the status of heir. To ask *when* God appointed him heir would be to miss the point. It is the *fact* of the appointment that is here asserted. In ancient times, just as the firstborn son was the primary **heir** and held a place of prominence in the family (see Gen 21.10; Matt 21.38), so God's Son, Jesus, is his heir and holds the first place with God the Father (Col 1.18). The term "heir" can emphasize the idea of having received or obtained

[15] Gene R. Smillie, "Contrast or Continuity in Hebrews 1.1–2?," *NTS* 51 (2005): 543–60. *Cf.* Westcott, *Epistle to the Hebrews*, 7.

[16] Allen argues for eight (Allen, *Hebrews*, 109). Victor Rhee ("Christology and the Concept of Faith in Hebrews 1:1–2:4," *BibSac* 157 (2000): 174–89, and again in "The Role of Chiasm for Understanding Christology in Hebrews 1:1–14," *JBL* 131 (2012): 341–62) argues (unconvincingly, in my opinion) that this list is arranged chiastically.

something, thus being possessor and ruler over what is received (*cf.* Gal 4.1). The Son has received all things from God (Matt 11.27; John 3.35; 13.3) and thus has the right to rule over them (Matt 28.18). In this way, "heir" suggests dominion.[17] It also suggests the closeness of the Son to the Father, since an heir receives his possession by virtue of the fact of his personal connection with the father.[18] The wording of this first statement echoes Psalm 2.8 (Psa 2.7 is quoted in v 5 below) in which God gives the nations to the exalted Son as an inheritance. In that context it means that the Son rules over them. Psalm 2 was a significant text for the early Christians. But the idea of being appointed over all things also echoes Psalm 8.5–6 (quoted in Heb 2), which is itself a summary of Genesis 1.26–28. Jesus fulfills the Adamic commission to reign over God's world.

2) By this appointed heir, God **made the world**. Jesus was the agent or instrument of the creation of the world. This is affirmed by other NT writers as well (1 Cor 8.6; Col 1.16; John 1.3). **World** translates the Greek word *aiōn*, which denotes the world and all its systems and activities. In the plural (as here) this word can denote what we call the universe,[19] but it likely includes more than just the physical creation. *Aiōnes* primarily means "ages," so the point here may include the idea that God made the history of salvation through the Son.[20] Since the Creator has authority over his creation, this second statement also describes the Son's reign over all things.

1.3 who, being the brightness of his glory and the image of his essence, holding up all things by the word of his power, once he had made cleansing for sins, sat down at the right hand of the majesty on high,

3) The Son is the brightness of God's glory. To ask if this is predicated of the Son as he existed before or after the incarnation is to inquire in a way that is foreign to our author's point here. The point instead is that the Son is equal to God himself. The word **brightness** translates the Greek word

---

[17] Westcott, *Epistle to the Hebrews*, 8.

[18] Westcott, *Epistle to the Hebrews*, 8.

[19] T. Holtz, "*aiōn*," *EDNT* 1:46; Louw-Nida, 1.

[20] See K. R. Harriman, "Through Whom He Made the Ages," *NovT* 61 (2019): 423–39: "It is through the Son that God's purpose for history was designed, made, and ultimately fulfilled" (439). Also Allen, *Hebrews*, 111.

apaugasma, which denotes either (active) shining or (passive) reflection,[21] and, to the Hebrew way of thinking, to speak of God's **glory** was a way of describing God's essence.[22] Thus Jesus shows forth the essence of God himself. Paul said that we see the glory of God in the face of Christ (2 Cor 4.6), and John said, "we beheld his glory, the glory as of the only begotten of the Father" (John 1.4).

4) The Son bears the image of God's essence. **Image** here renders the Greek word *charactēr,* from which we get our words "character" and "characteristic." This word was used in Greek to describe a portrait or authenticating mark on a coin[23] or the traits children acquire from their parents,[24] and denotes the visible expression of something, the traits by which a thing is recognized.[25] If God were pictured as a stamp, Jesus would be the impression made by the stamp. The word **essence** (Greek *hupostasis*) denotes the underlying, foundational reality of a thing, the basis of a thing,[26] its "actual being,"[27] and thus what it has permanently.[28] In this context it describes God's very being in which Jesus shares and parallels the term "glory" in the preceding line. The point in both statements is "the essential unity and exact resemblance between God and his Son,"[29] not any distinction between them. Jesus said, "he who has seen me has seen the Father" (John 14.9; *cf.* Col 1.15). The Son has the characteristics of the Father, and although he is distinguishable from God he is one with him in essence (*cf.* John 10.30; Col 2.9).

5) As deity, Jesus **upholds all things by the word of his power**. He is not only the creator of the universe (v 2), but also its sustainer (*cf.* Col 1.17). This also suggests that the Son is ruler of all things because as the sustainer of the universe he maintains its existence. Its continuance depends on him and in this sense, he controls it. The way he maintains all things is **by the word of his power**, a Hebraism meaning "his powerful

[21] O. Hofius, "*apaugasma,*" *EDNT* 1:118; Louw-Nida 175; the difference between the two is slight and often exaggerated.

[22] The Hebrew word was *kabōd;* John N. Oswalt, "*kābēd,*" *TWOT* 1:426–28; BDB 458–59.

[23] See Michael P. Theophilus, "The Numismatic Background of *charactēr* in Hebrews 1:3," *ABR* 64 (2016): 69–80.

[24] Ulrich Wilckens, "*charactēr,*" *TDNT* 9:418–20.

[25] Westcott, *Epistle to the Hebrews,* 12.

[26] H. W. Hollander, "*hupostasis,*" *EDNT* 3:407.

[27] BDAG 1040.

[28] G. Harder, "*hupostasis,*" *NIDNTT* 1:710–14.

[29] Ellingworth, *Epistle to the Hebrews,* 99.

word"[30] and a trait elsewhere ascribed to the Father (*cf.* Isa 55.11). God's word is different from man's word in that when God speaks, he does not simply make observations or declare a wish, but his word is living and active (4.12) and contains the power to create and cause conformity to what he says. The Son's word has the same power as the Father's word and he sustains the universe by it.

The Son who upholds the universe is also the one who came to earth and lived in the form of a man, and in that form accomplished[31] **cleansing for sins**. This is mentioned to set the proper context for the next thing that is attributed to the Son. The historical narrative about Jesus, as told in the gospels, is always the interpretive context for the truth of Christianity. The author will rely upon it to interpret Psalm 8 in Hebrews 2. Cleansing is an important theme in Hebrews (9.13f, 22f; 10.2). The reference to it here ("made purification" NASB) draws on OT sacrificial terminology and concepts (see Lev 16.30). The assertion implies that cleansing for sins had not been accomplished under any previous order of things, including the Mosaical system. Furthermore, the author does not, at this point, delve into how Jesus accomplished this cleansing, or what was required to achieve it; these ideas will receive more detailed treatment in chapters 2, 9, and 10. For now it is simply presented as part of the summary of the Son's claim to greatness. The work of the Son is presented for Jewish readers in terms of OT categories and procedures which, by design, pointed to him and which ultimately hinted at the idea that Jesus is our high priest. The preexistent Son humbled himself and purified us from our sins by the sacrificial shedding of his cleansing blood on the cross (Matt 26.28). The marvel of the gospel is that the creator and sustainer of the world is the one who died on the cross (Col 1.15–20).

6) Jesus' humiliation, in which he made a cleansing for sins, was the prelude to his exaltation to glory (*cf.* Phil 2.6–10). Therefore, the next thing predicated of the Son is that he has now taken his seat at the right hand of God the Father. God's **right hand** is a literary symbol of his

---

[30] See James Hope Moulton and Nigel Turner, *A Grammar of New Testament Greek: Syntax*. Vol. 3 (Edinburgh: T. & T. Clark, 1963), 214.

[31] The middle voice of the verb here (*poieō*) emphasizes the idea that this purification was not some external ritual but involved Jesus personally (again, explored more fully in chs 9–10). A textual variant (the phrase "by himself," excluded from the Nestle text but included in the Textus Receptus, and for which there is fair support) attempts to make this point more obvious.

power, strength, and authority (see in Exod 15.6; Isa 48.13; 62.8). The position at the king's right hand was a place of honor (*cf.* Matt 25.34), and to sit at a king's right hand was to share in his reign and wield his power. This statement about the Son echoes the words of Psalm 110.1, which will be an important text later in the sermon (and see v 13 below). The fact that Jesus has not continually been seated at God's right hand will be discussed more fully in 2.9–18. For now, however, the point is that Jesus occupies the highest seat in the universe, reigning with the power and authority of God (*cf.* Rom 8.34; Eph 1.10; Col 3.1; 1 Pet 3.22). God is here described in his greatness as **the majesty** in order to heighten the sense of the greatness of the Son's exaltation. This reverential way of referring to God also appears in 8.1 (*cf.* Jude 25) and shows the author's familiarity with the LXX.[32] God's right hand is a position **on high** (a term from the Psalms, LXX 98.2; 112.4; 137.6), far above any merely earthly honor (*cf.* Phil 2.9; Eph 1.21). The fact that Jesus **sat down** also suggests the finality of his work, which the author will later explore more fully; see comments on 10.12 and 12.2.

Our author has now previewed his presentation of Jesus as God's spokesman (v 2—God has spoken in him), priest (v 3—he made purification for sins), and king (v 3—he sits at God's exalted right hand). It is common in the NT documents that the opening lines contain a kind of summary of the major themes that will be explored. Hebrews is no exception.

1.4 by means of which, having become better than the angels, he has inherited a name superior to theirs.

7) The author wishes to direct us to the fact that the Son has a greater position or status than the angels, denoted by the word **better**. The idea that what God has done in the Son is better than what was available in Judaism is, in a sense, the driving argument of Hebrews.[33] Here is the first of thirteen times where Hebrews uses this term to describe Jesus and the order of things he inaugurated. The term (Greek *kreittōn*) has the specific idea of "more prominent," "higher in rank," or "greater."[34] In Hebrews it also takes on the sense of "eternal," as opposed to the earthly things

[32] *Cf.* Deut 32.3; 1 Chron 29.11; Psa 78.11 [79.11 MT]; 144.6 [145.6 MT]; *etc.*

[33] David Alan Black, "Hebrews 1:1–4: A Study in Discourse Analysis," *WTJ* 49 (1987): 175–94.

[34] "*kreissōn/kreittōn*," *EDNT* 2:316.

that characterized the old system (Judaism). Of course, the term "better" implies a comparison and thus implicitly evokes one of the rabbinic exegetical *middoth* (rules) known as *qal wahomer* (see Introduction).

The words **having become** do not mean that Jesus is a created (made) being, nor that he was not God's Son before the incarnation, but here denote the attainment of a status. Jesus became greater **than the angels** in the sense that he did not always (*i.e.*, while he was on earth) exist in a form that was demonstrably better than the angels, but afterward was exalted to greatness. The author will show in 2.9–18 that Jesus' time of humility on earth does not detract from his eternal greatness. The statement here in no way implies that Jesus was not greater than the angels until his exaltation. Jesus is now what he has always been. For now, however, the author's concern was to state the fact that after Jesus' earthly life God exalted him to a position far greater than that given to any angel.

Our author added that the Son has **inherited** a more excellent name than the angels. The perfect tense of the verb in the Greek indicates that it is already the Son's possession, and his lasting possession.[35] Inheriting, with its implication of *a goal to anticipate in the future*, will become important for the exhortations later in the book (6.12; 9.15; 11.8; 12.17). Here, however, "inherited" denotes *an obtaining*, as in 1.2, and with it the sense of dominion that an heir has over the father's estate. What is the superior **name** he has obtained? There are three ways to approach this statement:

1) It may be that the author was simply making a statement about the Son's exaltation, because to receive a great name from one in authority meant to be given great status and honor (*cf.* 2 Sam 7.9). That is, it may be that no specific name is meant, but that the phrase should be understood as an idiom meaning that Jesus has been exalted by the Father and recognized as a great person (we have a similar idiom in English).

2) Several have argued that the more excellent name of Jesus is his title, Son.[36] The significance of the name "Son" would be that a son bears the traits and characteristics of his father (1.3). Thus, to call Jesus God's

[35] Westcott, *Epistle to the Hebrews*, 17. The perfect tense in Koinē Greek can depict a state of being (as opposed to a process). Constantine R. Campbell, *Basics of Verbal Aspect in Biblical Greek* (Grand Rapids: Zondervan, 2008), 106.

[36] Ellingworth, *Epistle to the Hebrews*, 104; Lane, *Hebrews 1–8*, 7; Cockerill, *Epistle to the Hebrews*, 98; Koester, *Hebrews*, 182; Peterson, *Hebrews*, 68; *et al.* Thomas R. Schreiner (*Hebrews*, Evangelical Biblical Theology Commentary (Bellingham, WA: Lexham Press, 2021), 60–61) discusses this interpretation and the third one (below) and decides for "Son."

Son is a way of affirming his deity. This would contribute to the author's argument that Jesus is so much better than the angels, because angels are not deity.

3) The author had a specific name in mind, the name of God himself (*YHWH*).[37] In the ancient way of thinking a name was not just a tag, but represented the person who wore it. It was more like a description. For example, Jacob's name meant "deceiver," and Gideon was called Jerubbaal (which means "let Baal contend against him") after he tore down an altar of Baal (Jdg 6.32). And of course, there is the famous incident in Exodus 3.14, where the revelation of God's name at the burning bush said something about the kind of God he is. Bauckham has argued that the NT authors held what he calls a Christology of divine identity as their way of asserting the deity of Jesus and yet remaining within classic Jewish monotheism. "Early Christianity, very consciously using this Jewish theological framework, created a kind of Christological monotheism by understanding Jesus to be included in the unique identity of the one God of Israel."[38] According to him, one of the prime and unique identifiers of the God of the Old Testament is his name, *YHWH*, so here "The name that is so much more excellent than those of angels must be the Hebrew divine name, the Tetragrammaton."[39] Other identifiers are God's eschatological rule over all things, the fact that God alone is the creator of the universe, that he is eternal, that he is providentially sovereign over all things, and that He alone may be worshipped. According to Bauckham, the Old Testament quotations that follow establish these very points about Jesus. Since the Son, Jesus, shares in the identifiers of *YHWH*, he is therefore deity as well. A problem with this approach is that none of the texts quoted in Hebrews 1.5–14 originally used the

[37] Richard Bauckham, *Jesus and the God of Israel: God Crucified and Other Essays on the New Testament's Christology of Divine Identity* (Paternoster, 2008), 239. *Cf.* Phil 1.9, where Paul said that Jesus has been given the name that is above every other name, which can only be the name of God himself. In that context (v 10), Paul quotes Isa 43.23, in which God is *YHWH* from v 21. Paul often quoted OT passages in which the divine name *YHWH* was used and applied them to Jesus. See Gordon D. Fee, *Pauline Christology: An Exegetical-Theological Study* (Peabody, MA: Hendrickson, 2007), 631ff ("Appexndix B"); David B. Capes, "YHWH Texts and Monotheism in Paul's Christology," in *Early Jewish and Christian Monotheism*, ed. Loren T. Stuckenbruck and Wendy E. S. North (London; New York: T&T Clark, 2004), 120–37; and David B. Capes, *Old Testament Yahweh Texts in Paul's Christology* (Tübingen: Mohr Siebeck, 1992. Repr. Waco, TX: Baylor University Press, 2017).

[38] Bauckham, *Jesus and the God of Israel*, 234.

[39] Bauckham, *Jesus and the God of Israel*, 239.

name *YHWH*, so that particular point is not established by those quotations. However, given the clear interchange of "God" (*Elohim*; which does appear in the texts quoted in vv 5–13) and "Lord" (*YHWH*) in the OT, this objection is not strong.[40]

This third interpretation is preferable, since "Son" is not technically a name, but a title. Also, in the OT quotations that follow, the Son is also called God (v 8) and Lord (v 10). The point in the context is that Jesus has an exalted status greater than any angel (*cf.* 1 Pet 3.22), the crowning proof of which is that he wears the name of God Himself. The implications of such a statement cannot be explored in a commentary. We must content ourselves with noticing that for the Son to wear the name of God, and to sit with God on God's throne, and to be above even angelic beings—all of these are *strong* statements of the deity of Jesus. And if the original recipients of Hebrews were Jewish Christians, the phenomenon becomes even more impressive. It was once believed by most scholars that belief in the deity of Jesus evolved from lesser kinds of beliefs, and that this process came from Gentile Christian circles. The reason it must have come from Gentile circles, it was argued, is that Jewish Christians would never have created such an idea due to their strict monotheism. A growing number of scholars are becoming aware, however, that the NT indeed presents us with what is now called "early high Christology," that is, a belief in the full deity of Jesus at a very early time in the history of Christianity, even from the very beginning, including within Jewish Christianity.[41] Hebrews is witness to this very thing.

As noted in the comments on verse 2, the author of Hebrews saw in the word "Son" an expression of the authority Jesus wields in the father's name. In the verses below the author will quote several OT passages that speak of the Son's reign, leading to the observation in 3.6 that his status as Son gives Jesus a unique position of authority over God's house.

Why this comparison between Jesus and the angels, and the emphasis on Jesus' superiority over them? (See Excursus: Jesus and the Angels). Part of the answer is found in Hebrews 2.2, Acts 7.53 (see also Acts 7.30, 38), and Galatians 3.19. The Law of Moses was given from God to Moses *through angels*. This fact is not mentioned explicitly in the OT account of

---

[40] See Grindheim, *Letter to the Hebrews*, 102–103.

[41] See Crispin Fletcher-Louis, *Jesus Monotheism: Christological Origins: The Emerging Consensus and Beyond*, Vol. 1 (Eugene, OR: Whymanity Publishing, 2019).

the giving of the Law at Sinai, but hints appear in Psalm 68.17 and Deuteronomy 33.2 LXX. The ancient Jews believed that angels had a mediating role in the giving of the law.[42] The author's point is that since the Son is greater than the angels, the word God has spoken to us in his Son supersedes "the word spoken through angels" (2.2). Furthermore, in Jewish thought, angels were the administrators of God's will and the agents of his power throughout the universe (see Dan 10). In several OT stories angels provided protection for and deliverance of God's people. In some Jewish apocalyptic texts from the intertestamental period (especially 1 Enoch) angels were made to be important agents of God not only in his revelation at Sinai but in the salvation of God's people. It was claimed that the archangel Michael, among other things, stands at the right hand of God's throne and mediates and intercedes for God's people.[43] By the first century, the extant extra-Biblical literature paints a picture of Jewish belief that rescue from national enemies would involve God's use of angels to destroy the adversaries of his people. It is possible that Hebrews 1 is to be read in light of this confidence in angels.[44] It is probably safe to assume that in the thinking of some Jewish groups angels held extremely important positions which impinged on that of the Son and his uniqueness.[45] As great as the role of angels was, the Son is greater, and help (4.16) now comes from him, not angels.

1.5 For to which of the angels did he ever say, "You are my son, today I have begotten you"?, and again, "I will be a father to him, and he will be a son to me"?

The author was writing to people for whom the Jewish Scriptures provided the final, authoritative word in religious discussions. He will now therefore show that his assertions about the superiority and reign of the Son in verses 2b–4 come from Scripture itself by assembling a collection of texts that make the same basic point.[46] Such a collection is called a cat-

[42] Josephus, *Ant.* 15.136; *cf.* the rabbinic *Mekilta* on Exod 20.18; *Book of Jubilees* 1.27–29; 2.1,26f; *Damascus Document* 5.

[43] J. Daryl Charles, "The Angels, Sonship and Birthright in the Letter to the Hebrews," *JETS* 33 (1990): 171–78, at 172.

[44] Randall C. Gleason, "Angels and the Eschatology of Heb 1–2," *NTS* 49 (2003): 90–107.

[45] Charles, "The Angels, Sonship and Birthright."

[46] Herbert W. Bateman IV has proposed a chiastic structure for this section: A (1.5), B (1.6–7), C (1.8–9), B′ (1.10–12), A′ (1.13–14). "Psalm 45:6–7 and Its Christological

ena (the Latin word for "chain"). This method was common among the Jews,[47] including the NT authors.[48] It is tempting to think that the more OT citations that were adduced for a particular point, the more controversial or difficult to accept that point may have been, or that the point was not understood well. If that is correct, then the superiority of the Son to the angels, and the superiority of the word which came through the Son to that which came through angels, may have been either a contentious point or one that was not understood for its full implications, or both. It is possible that the recipients of Hebrews may not have grasped the full implications of the greatness of Jesus. See the Excursus: Jesus and the Angels. However, this is probably not all that was driving the quotations here. We must allow that the author was presenting what he saw to be the message presented by the OT, and especially by the psalms which described the coming Davidic king and his kingdom.[49]

While angels are collectively called sons of God in some OT passages (Gen 6.2; Job 1.6; Psa 29.1; 89.6), and all of God's people may be called his sons (Heb 2.10; Gal 3.26; Rom 8.14; *cf.* 2 Cor 6.18), Jesus is not just a son, he is *the* Son, and God calls him "*my* Son." This term is used in a special way of Jesus, just as Jesus claimed a special relationship with God by calling him "*my* Father" (Matt 7.21; Mark 14.36). Nowhere and at no time did God call any angel his Son in this special sense, and the author notes the Scriptural silence (**to which of the angels did he ever say ... ?**) in a rhetorical question to note that God has not bestowed such great status upon anyone other than *the* Son. What God *did* say was that the Messiah is his Son, and God gave him that name in a royal context as one who reigns over all others.

The quotations in verses 5–13 come from passages in which God is either describing the Son or speaking to the Son (with one passage about angels quoted for the sake of contrast). The list begins with quotations

Contributions to Hebrews," *TrinJ* 22 (2001): 3–21, at 20. More recently, also Heath, "Chiastic Structures in Hebrews."

[47] The list of quotations here shares many similarities with one of the Dead Sea Scrolls documents, *4QFlor*. See Herbert W. Bateman, "Two First-Century Messianic Uses of the OT: Heb 1:5–13 and *4QFlor* 1.1–19," *JETS* 38 (1995): 11–27. The procedure of creating a "chain" or "string" of Scriptural texts is still midrashic (Boyarin, "Midrash in Hebrews/ Hebrews as Midrash," 16–22).

[48] Some NT examples are Rom 3.10–18; 9.25–29; 15.9–12; 1 Pet 2.6–8.

[49] See Stephen Motyer, "The Psalm Quotations of Hebrews 1: A Hermeneutic-Free Zone?," *TynBul* 50 (1999): 3–22.

from Psalm 2.7 ("You are my son") and 2 Samuel 7.14 ("I will be a father to him," paralleled in 1 Chron 17.13), verses which Jews in antiquity already recognized as speaking of the Messiah's reign.[50] The verses from Psalm 2 and 2 Samuel 7 both refer to the reigning Messiah as God's **Son**. The combination of these two verses generally exhibits the rabbinic technique of *gezerah shawah*, where two verses were allowed to inform each other on the basis of verbal analogy (see Introduction).[51] In fact, the combination[52] of these two particular verses was already established in early Christian preaching (Acts 13.33; Rom 1.3).

Psalm 2 is a royal psalm that presents the authority of Israel's king (assuming an ideal, faithful king) as granted by the decree of God himself. It affirmed that the (ideal) king of Israel was a God-appointed man who reigned with God-given authority in a close, father-son kind of relationship. As the obedient servant of God, God declared the king to be a **son** to him. This ideal king was itself a messianic type, and thus the psalm spoke ultimately about the Christ. In fact, the messianic aspect of the scenario seems to outweigh those aspects that described any Israelite king. It is hard to overestimate the importance of Psalm 2 to the early Christians.

While the words **today I have begotten you** may at first seem to refer to the birth of Jesus, they are nowhere understood in Scripture in that way. In the psalm they refer to God's appointment of the king to reign, and that is how the words are to be understood of the Christ. Paul said that this statement from Psalm 2 is about Christ's *resurrection, his being begotten from the dead* (Acts 13.33), which was his triumph over death and the beginning of his triumphant reign. Psalm 2 was a key text for the early Christians, as was Psalm 110. The appearance of both together in this chapter is significant.[53] God appointed his **Son** to reign, but never any angel. Furthermore, a son is an heir, so when God calls Jesus his Son, this implies that Jesus stands to inherit all things that belong to the Father (v 3 above; see Matt 11.27; John 3.35). In fact, this is the very thing that the next verse of the psalm says: "Ask of me, and I will surely give the nations as your inheritance, and the very ends of the earth as your

---

[50] *4QFlor* also quotes these two verses in its messianic discussion.

[51] See Wenkel, "Gezerah Shawah as Analogy in the Epistle to the Hebrews."

[52] Together the verses form a chiasm. Ebert, "The Chiastic Structure of the Prologue to Hebrews," 166.

[53] See David Wallace, "The Use of Psalms in the Shaping of a Text: Psalm 2:7 and Psalm 110:1 in Hebrews 1," *ResQ* 45 (2003): 41–50, at 43.

possession" (NASB). We should also note that the psalm is not saying that Jesus became God's Son, or received that status, at his resurrection and exaltation. Jesus has always been the eternal Son of God. The resurrection and exaltation have simply made that clear to the world in way it had not been seen before.

The phrase from 2 Samuel 7.14 (**I will be a father to him** ...) is another text in which God made a solemn declaration concerning a regal figure whom he would call his **Son**. God's statement to David is part of the messianic promise that his descendant (the heir to his throne; v 12) would build a house for God and that this descendant would have a father-son relationship with God. The immediate historical object of that promise was Solomon, but Solomon was himself, in his great glory and kingdom, and as builder of God's temple, a type of Christ. Typologically, then, these are the words God speaks to the Christ, the ultimate occupant of David's throne.[54] It should be noted that not every detail or feature of a typological person, event, or institution contributes to the type itself. Solomon was a type of Jesus even though God warned that he would punish Solomon if he sinned (2 Sam 7.14b; note that the statement about punishing David's descendant is absent in the parallel account in 1 Chron 17, suggesting that it is not regarded as a central part of the promise).

1.6 And again, when he brings the firstborn into the world, he says, "And let all the angels of God worship him."

It seems better to understand **again** as signaling that another OT quotation is coming (as in the NIV, RSV, ESV, *etc.*) rather than to connect it with the verb **bring** (with the resulting sense of "he brings again," as in the NASB).[55] The exact source of the quotation in this verse has been debated. Deuteronomy 32.43 LXX is often suggested, but this is problematic. The quotation as it stands in Hebrews is not part of the traditional MT of that passage,[56] and manuscripts of the LXX vary on the exact word-

---

[54] According to Str-B (3:788), the rabbis did not read 2 Sam 7.12 messianically. This suggests that the messianic reading of this text was a Christian invention.

[55] Thus contra S. Lewis Johnson ("Some Important Mistranslations in Hebrews," *BibSac* 110 (1953): 25–31) who favors the NASB-type of translation and finds here a reference to the Lord's "second coming."

[56] However, one Hebrew text found among the Dead Sea Scrolls [4QDeut[q], also called 4QDeut32] contains the words "worship him all you gods," but with other variants.

ing of this verse.[57] The more likely source is Psalm 97.7 (96.7 LXX), which says "worship him, all you his angels."[58] The Hebrew text of Psalm 97.7 says "worship him all you gods," and the translators of the LXX took the word "gods" (*'elohim*) to mean heavenly beings, or angels, probably to avoid tacit recognition of other gods. More importantly, the LXX version of Psalm 97 used the Greek word *oikoumenē* (**world**, in v 4 of the psalm), which the author of Hebrews here used in introducing this quotation.[59]

It is possible that the subject of the verb ("**says**") is Scripture, and not God directly. However, since both the author and the original Jewish Christian recipients of Hebrews would have understood that it was God who was speaking in Scripture, this distinction would not have been significant. As noted before, it is the fact that God is *speaking* in Scripture that is important to the author of Hebrews. In midrashic fashion, he saw the words of the psalm as a fitting description of the conditions of the messianic age.

The term **firstborn** (Greek *prōtotokos*) does not refer to Jesus' birth in human history, much less does it imply that he is a created being. It is a term of status, not origin, and denotes preeminence and endearment. Therefore, it has a similar sense to "son" and "heir."[60] In ancient Jewish culture, the firstborn son had a status above all the other children in the family. He received a double portion of the inheritance and became the family leader when the family patriarch could no longer serve in that role. See comments on 12.23. The author deduced that the Messiah is the firstborn Son of God from Psalm 2.7 (quoted in v 5 above, the first quotation in the series), where God said to him "I have begotten you." As noted in the comments above, this refers to Jesus' resurrection. Jesus is the first of the new order of humanity, raised from the dead to be immortal. He is "the firstborn from the dead" (Col 1.18), the first man raised from the

[57] A complete discussion of the textual problem in the LXX text of Deut here is in Gareth Lee Cockerill, "Hebrews 1:6: Source and Significance," *BBR* 9 (1999): 51–64. See also Peter Katz, "The Quotations from Deuteronomy in Hebrews," *ZNW* 49 (1958): 213–23, at 217–19.

[58] Str-B 3:788: "Psalm 97:7 is the base text." While the LXX text of Deut 32.43 uses a third person plural imperative verb—the same as here in Heb 1.6—and Psa 97.7 uses a second person plural imperative verb, the difference is not significant enough to exclude Psa 97 as the source of the quotation here.

[59] This is a much simpler approach to the source of the quotation than one which requires reconstructing a now-lost Hebrew text behind the LXX reading (as in Cockerill, "Hebrews 1:6: Source and Significance," 53–55).

[60] Wilhelm Michaelis, "*prototokos*," *TDNT* 6:871–81.

dead never to die again (Rom 6.9). He came to create a new humanity that has overcome the blight of sin and death by the power of God, a new humanity who will join him in immortal resurrection (Rom 8.29), fully restored to the image and goodness of God (Eph 4.24). This is the sense in which Jesus is God's firstborn.

The phrase **when he brings the firstborn into the world** is a paraphrase of the preceding quotation, Psalm 2.7, and serves to introduce the next quotation. The idea of bringing God's Son into the world may at first seem to speak of Jesus' birth, but like the similar phrase in 1.5 ("I have begotten you") this is not its true referent for two reasons: first, the quotation from Psalm 97.7 calls for worship of the Son, and worship (in the author's way of thinking) has to do with the Son's exaltation, not his humiliation.[61] Verse 9 in the Psalm confirms that the Messiah's reign, and not his birth, is in view as it says "You are the Lord Most High over all the earth, you are exalted far above all gods" (NASB). Second, it must be understood that the **world** here is not the physical world, the *kosmos*, but translates the Greek word *oikoumenē* which has a political connotation and can mean "empire"[62] and thus is akin to "kingdom." The world of which the Psalm spoke is therefore the domain over which the exalted Son reigns. A look at verse 1 of the psalm confirms this, as it says, "The Lord reigns, let the earth rejoice" (NASB). To say that God brought the firstborn into the world is therefore a way of saying that God raised the Son from the dead and exalted him to reign over his domain.[63] Here is another verse, then, that speaks of the Son's reign over all things.

It may also be that the author of Hebrews read Psalm 97.4–6 as a reference to the resurrection of Jesus, or at least to his exaltation; verse 6 of the psalm says, "all the people have seen his glory" (NASB), and glory characterizes the risen Son (see comments on 2.7). The **worship** commanded in verse 7 of the psalm would then be worship to the Son who was exalted after his resurrection. When the Son was exalted to his glory and kingdom, he was pronounced worthy of worship from **all** other heavenly

---

[61] See Ardel B. Caneday, "The Eschatological World Already Subjected to the Son: The *oikoumenē* of Hebrews 1:6 and the Son's Enthronement," in *A Cloud of Witnesses: The Theology of Hebrews in Its Ancient Contexts*, ed. Richard Bauckham *et al*, LNTS 387 (London: T&T Clark, 2008), 28–39, at 31.

[62] H. Balz, *"oikoumenē,"* *EDNT* 2:503–4.

[63] See Kenneth L. Schenck, "A Celebration of the Enthroned Son: The Catena of Hebrews l," *JBL* 120 (2001): 469–85.

beings (**angels**), and this is what Psalm 97.7 foresaw. Implicit in the quotation is the idea that worship is always of a lesser being to a greater being. If the angels are commanded to worship the Messiah, then the Son is greater, or better in status, than the angels (1.4). Their worship of the Son also affirms his deity, since only the true God (deity) may be worshipped, as this is one of the unique identifiers of God.[64]

1.7 And with reference to the angels he says, "He is the one who makes his angels winds, and his servants a flame of fire."

The author now offers a quotation from Psalm 104.4 by way of contrast to the statements about the Son. The Psalm describes God as the controller and sustainer of all creation (reminding us of the assertion in 1.3 that the Son upholds all things, and thus exercises the power of God.) In that context, the psalm speaks of angels in a subservient role, and the quotation proves that God does not speak of angels with the same high language he uses to speak of the Son. The point the author draws from this verse lies in recognizing the parallelism of the words **angels** and **servants**. According to the parallelism, angels are only ministers, or servants, of God. This is far below the honor accorded to the Son, as seen in the next verse. In Hellenistic culture, families were organized with the father as the head, the firstborn son as the primary heir and co-ruler over the family estate and household, then other sons after him. At the bottom of the household ladder of status were the servants.[65] According to this imagery, Jesus (the Son) and angels (God's servants) are at opposite ends of the family status spectrum. The Son's status is far above the angels.

The LXX version of this statement, which our author has quoted, at first seems to have a different sense than the Hebrew original, which says "He makes the winds his messengers, flaming fire his ministers." The Hebrew text seems to have God using elements of nature as his servants, whereas the LXX rendering has spiritual beings subdued to God's glory—which is exactly the point the author wishes to make here. The reason this dual reading is possible is because of the double object construction (in both Hebrew and Greek). Switching which noun is treated as the object of the verb and which is treated as the product of the verbal action results in the different senses. Swinson has argued that this latter sense, preserved

[64] Bauckham, *Jesus and the God of Israel*, 11–13.

[65] Note this same imagery at work in Gal 4.1–7.

in the LXX rendering, may actually be more faithful to the point of Psalm 104 and the wider literary context within the Psalter.[66] Psalm 103.20f calls on heavenly beings in the same way as the LXX version of Psalm 104.4 depicts them, as servants of God. However, this approach is not necessary. The way the author of Hebrews understood the psalm is a perfectly legitimate reading of the text of Psalm 104.4, and in that reading he saw a declaration about the status of angels. According to this reading, God uses the angels as he would the winds and fire, as lesser agents of his reign. See further on verse 14 below.

1.8 But with reference to the Son he says, "Your throne, God, is forever and ever, and the scepter of your kingdom is the staff of righteousness.

This is a quotation from Psalm 45, which is often described as a royal wedding psalm. One of the difficulties of the psalm is determining who is speaking, and who is being addressed. The chief question here is exactly who is being referred to as **God**. Three interpretational possibilities are:

1) The psalm is strictly a messianic prophecy and none of it was about, nor addressed to, Israel's human king.[67] That is, it was not about an Israelite royal wedding, but only about the Messiah. This approach would not have been foreign to the original recipients of Hebrews. In Acts 2, Peter argued that Psalm 16 could not be about David, Philip seems to have argued that Isaiah 53 is directly about Jesus, and many have argued that Psalm 110 could not be anything other than a direct messianic prophecy. This same approach to Psalm 45 would claim that the psalm does not involve any typology and the name "God" refers directly to the Messiah. It is possible that the author of Hebrews read the psalm this way on the basis of the psalm's direct address, which it shares in common with Psalm 2.7 (quoted in Heb 1.5 above) and Psalm 102.25–27 (quoted in Heb 1.10–12 below). Since wedding imagery is a common Biblical image for the messianic age (*cf.* Isa 49.18; 61.10; 62.5; Jer 33.11; Hos 2.19f; Joel 2.16; John 2.1; 3.29; Luke 5.34; Rev 19.7), this also might have encouraged the author of Hebrews to read Psalm 45 as speaking about the Messiah. Fur-

---

[66] L. Timothy Swinson, "'Wind' and 'Fire' in Hebrews 1:7: A Reflection upon the Use of Psalm 104 (103)," *TrinJ* 28 (2007): 215–28.

[67] Seth D. Postell, "A Literary, Compositional, and Intertextual Analysis of Psalm 45," *BibSac* 176 (2019): 146–63.

thermore, the mention of a "throne," which is kingdom terminology, is easily read messianically (recalling Psalm 2).

2) An interpretation that attempts to see some historical context for the psalm in addition to its prophetic role is that the psalm's words "Your throne, O God" in v 6 were originally addressed to God as an acknowledgment of the true source of authority in Israel,[68] and perhaps the words of verse 7 ("You have loved righteousness ...") were addressed to the king of Israel. With this approach, the words "Your throne, O God" were not addressed to the king at all, but to God, whom the author of Hebrews understood to be the Son (probably based on v 7 in the psalm). There are many instances in both the psalms and the prophetic literature where there appears to be more than one speaker or addressee in the poetry, and determining who the various speakers are is difficult.

3) The most common modern interpretation suggests that the king of Israel was called "God" by metonymy, since he sat on the throne that rightly was God's (2 Chron 9.8; 1 Chron 29.23; *cf.* Psa 82.6) and he reigned with God-given authority (*cf.* Exod 7.1; John 10.34). Sometimes in OT typological texts, figurative language that historically concerned a human person is typologically addressed to the Messiah with literal connotations (note how Peter applies this same kind of hermeneutic in Acts 2.29–35; *cf.* also Heb 2.6–8). Typologically, then, God was here speaking about the Son. Psalm 45.7 mentions the God of the one who is himself called God in the previous verse, and the only one who could (literally) be called God other than the Father is his divine Son. The first interpretation seems the most likely to me, with the second also possible, but the first and second interpretations are, in my view, more likely than the third.

The author wished to establish, by this quotation, that nothing like this was ever said to any angel. As the author of Hebrews has read it, the psalm is yet another example of where God speaks to the Son[69] with regal language, in the same vein as Psalm 2 (quoted above). According to this reading, God clearly calls his Son "God,"[70] declaring him to be equal in deity

[68] Nancy deClaissé-Walford, Rolf A. Jacobson, and Beth LaNeel Tanner, *The Book of Psalms*, NICOT (Grand Rapids: Eerdmans, 2014), 419.

[69] Taking *ho theos* as vocative. See Murray J. Harris, "The Translation and Significance of '*ho theos*' in Hebrews 1:8–9," *TynBul* 36 (1985): 129–62; reprinted as chapter 9 in *Jesus as God: The New Testament Use of* Theos *in Reference to Jesus* (Grand Rapids: Baker Books, 1992).

[70] *Cf.* Raymond E. Brown, "Does the New Testament Call Jesus God?," *TS* 26 (1965): 545–73, at 561–66.

to the Father himself and fitting with the assertion in Hebrews 1.4 that the Son has inherited God's name. The divine Son sits upon a **throne**, which is the seat of a king. The picture of God's Son reigning complements both Psalm 2 (quoted above) and Psalm 110.1 (quoted below). God's throne is described in the Bible as being glorious (Jer 14.21; 17.12; see also Rev 4; Isa 6; Ezek 1), and Jesus described his post-resurrection throne as glorious (Matt 19.28; 25.31). In this way the Son also reflects God's own glory (v 3). Also, by taking this seat of authority (*cf.* 1 Kngs 16.11) the Son reigns in his **kingdom forever** (Isa 9.7). The eternal nature of the Son's work will be an important part of the exposition of his priesthood in chapters 7–10, and the statement in Psalm 45.6 provides a subtle link to Psalm 110.4 ("you are a priest forever"). "Kingdom" can denote a territory over which a king reigns, but the term more fundamentally refers to the authoritative power, or sovereignty, of a king.[71] The Messiah's kingdom is not a physical place, restricted by physical boundaries, but his conquest and reign over the power of sin and death, over the hearts and lives of men, over angels, and over all rival powers. See comments on 12.28. All who come into this kingdom share his victory over these evil forces. Angels might have been agents of God's kingdom (as Psa 104 demonstrated), but the Son reigns over it. He wields a kingly **scepter** of **righteousness**, which makes him the ideal king (see 1 Kngs 10.9). In a similar way, Psalm 2.9 portrays the Messiah's scepter as a "rod of iron" by which he destroys his enemies.

1.9 You have loved righteousness and you have hated lawlessness; for this reason God, your God, has anointed you with the oil of gladness above your companions."

The words "**You have loved righteousness, and you have hated lawlessness**" from Psalm 45.7 evoke divine attributes (Psa 11.5, 7; 33.5; 97.10; 99.1; Hos 9.15). Therefore, the Son has the same character as God and he embodies God's own righteous essence (v 3). The words also describe the obedience of the Son and hint at his perfection (see in 2.10). Because God was pleased with his Son's faithful obedience, he exalted the Son to reign over all, including angels.

---

[71] Schmidt, *TDNT* 1:579–90; Lampe, *EDNT* 1:201–5. See also George Eldon Ladd, *Jesus and the Kingdom* (Waco, TX: Word Books, 1964); Kevin Sulc, "The Gospel of the Kingdom: Jesus and the Kingdom of God," in *Jesus for a New Millennium: Florida College Annual Lectures 2001,* ed. Ferrell Jenkins (Temple Terrace: Florida College, 2001), 97–109.

It is obvious that the author of Hebrews saw this psalm as messianic, no doubt prompted by the presence of the term **anointed** (the Greek *chriō*, rendering the Hebrew *mashach,* is the word from which the title "Christ" derives). Anointing was a symbolic action in which oil was poured on the head of one who was thereby "marked" as belonging to God in some special way. Things could be anointed as well, thus making them holy objects. Here the oil is the figurative **oil of gladness**. The entire expression denotes that **God** has given a measure of joy to the Son that far surpasses what others possess, and that joy is the result of the greater status God has given him. This is further reflected in that God is "**your God**" to the Messiah, suggesting that he has a special relationship with the Father (see also on 1.5). The language of God as the God of one who is also God invites comparison with Psalm 110.1, where the Lord (God) speaks to David's Lord (the Messiah).The author of Hebrews understood the Son's **companions** to be other heavenly beings, specifically angels, over whom Christ reigns. Psalm 45.7 thus further "proves" (when read from the perspective that the OT is about Jesus) that the Son has a status that is much better (greater) than the angels (1.4). Whether as a direct messianic prophecy or through typological understanding of a royal wedding scene, the author of Hebrews heard a declaration about the Messiah in the words of the psalm, a declaration ultimately ascribed to God himself. That is, Psalm 45.7 is understood as a divine proclamation about the status of the Messiah just like Psalm 2.7 and 2 Samuel 7.14 (quoted in v 5 above).

1.10–12 And, "You, Lord, in the beginning laid the foundation of the earth, and the heavens are the works of your hands. They will perish; but you will continue, and they all will become old like a garment, and you will roll them up like a cloak, and like a garment they will be changed: but you are the same, and your years will not cease."

This lengthy quotation from Psalm 102.25–27 provides the foundation for three more of the assertions made about the Son's reign in 1.2–4. The overall key to reading the psalm, of course, is the author's Jesus-centered perspective on the OT. He is the **Lord**, and the creator, of whom the psalm speaks. First, verse 10 proves the assertion of 1.2 that the Son is the creator of the world who **laid the earth's foundation** at the very **beginning** of the world; and if he is creator, then he is also ruler over creation. God's role as unaided creator of the world is one of his unique identifiers.[72] Using the imagery of a potter or a craftsman (as in Gen 2.7), the psalm says that **the heavens are the works of** the Son's **hands,** the result of his skill and power, just as much as they are of God's (see Psa 136.5; and Psa 8.6, quoted in Heb 2). Again, this makes him equal to God (Job 38.4; Zech 12.1; *cf.* John 1.3; 1 Cor 8.6; Col 1.16) and greater than the angels.

Second, part of the greatness of God's nature is that he is eternal (*cf.* Rom 16.26) and unchanging (Mal 3.6). Likewise, the Son **continues** eternally in contrast to the created order that one day will **perish** (2 Pet 3.10). He is ever **the same** (unchanging) in contrast to the universe that grows **old like a garment** and eventually wears out, and his **years will not cease**. To say that God does not change sometimes emphasizes his faithfulness and trustworthiness, but in this context the parallelism suggests that the Son is unaffected by the passing of time and is, therefore, eternal (**your years will not cease**). Thus, the Son is the exact representation of God's eternal nature (1.3).

Third, the words **you will roll them up like a cloak** describe the Son's power over the universe, showing that its existence depends upon him and that he is therefore the sustainer of the world (1.3). The Psalm asserts that the universe **will be changed**, which stands in contrast to the unchangeable nature of the creator. The change envisioned in the psalm is arguably the same transformation that is mentioned in Hebrews 12.26–27 and the change that Paul had in mind in Romans 8.20–21. Isaiah 34.4 is also likely in the background here, with its larger context (Isa 35) of God's eschatological restoration.[73]

The author of Hebrews understood these words from Psalm 102 in the same way he understood the words from Psalm 45 (quoted in vv 8–9 above): as God speaking to his Son (indicated by the use of "**and**" to connect the quotations) and demonstrating that the Son has things ascribed to him that are never ascribed to any angel. The author quotes six passages about the Son in this chapter (Psa 2.7; 2 Sam 7.14; Psa 97.7; 45.6–7; 102.25–27; and 110.1), and four of them (Psa 2.7; 45.6–7; 102.25–27; and 110.1) are passages in which God is speaking directly to the Son.

---

[72] Bauckham, *Jesus and the God of Israel*, 233.

[73] The context in Psa 102 is the new-creational renewal of Zion and the end of Israel's exile. See Philip Church, "Hebrews 1:10–12 and the Renewal of the Cosmos," *TynBul* 67 (2016): 269–86.

The question arises, what in Psalm 102 suggests that this is how these words should be understood? This is a thorny question, because in the psalm it appears that the author of the psalm is talking to God, not God talking to the Son. There are, however, several hints in the psalm itself that it is supposed to be read messianically. The psalm mentions Zion (vv 13, 16, 21), which is a pointer to the messianic age, and speaks of the Lord appearing there in his glory (v 16; *cf.* Isa 24.23), which could easily be understood as a reference to the Messiah entering into his reign. The psalm also speaks of writing praise for the Lord for the generation to come (v 18), suggesting that the psalm was about a time beyond itself (*i.e.*, the messianic time), and hints at the preaching of the gospel (vv 21f). The language can be understood as the psalmist's praise of God, but those same words can also be understood as God's commendation of his Son. This latter understanding is a good example of the Jesus-centered perspective by which the early Christians read the OT (see the Introduction) combined with the Jewish hermeneutical technique of *midrash*.[74] Both are appropriate and "correct" readings of the psalm.

1.13 But to which of the angels has he ever said, "Sit at my right hand, until I make your enemies a footstool for your feet"?

The final and crowning quotation that establishes the reign of the Son and proves his superiority over the angels comes from Psalm 110.1, which, for the author of Hebrews, is arguably the most significant of the messianic psalms for his purposes in this sermon. It is introduced with another rhetorical question (the same one as from the first quotation, in verse 5, **to which of the angels** ...?) to highlight the unique content of God's declaration to the Son.

It has often been speculated that Psalm 110 was originally a coronation Psalm, but even then, the king of Israel (the office) was a type of Christ. The Jews of antiquity seem not to have known what to do with it,[75] and within ancient Judaism "there are no clear examples of its messianic interpretation."[76] It is from verse 4 of this psalm that the author of Hebrews will draw his presentation of the superiority of Jesus' high

[74] See Pickup, "New Testament Interpretation of the Old Testament."

[75] See David M. Hay, *Glory at the Right Hand*. SBLMS 18 (Atlanta: Society of Biblical Literature, 1989), 19–33.

[76] Grindheim, *Letter to the Hebrews*, 97.

priesthood (chs 5–10), for God's purpose in his Son is not exhausted in the revelation that came in him. The Son's introduction into the world of men and subsequent heavenly exaltation has also brought about a new way of access to God, *viz.*, the Son's high priesthood. The author of Hebrews routinely lays the groundwork for his discussions by introducing quotations or terms, reserving analysis until later.[77] For now the point is that God has exalted his Son to his presence at his own **right hand** (see 1.3), and from there he will reign and conquer (as in Psa 2). To sit at the right hand of a monarch means to share in his reign and authority. To say that Jesus occupies this position, then, is to assert the equality of Jesus with God (see Matt 26.64), and no angel was ever exalted to such a position. To make one's **enemies** a **footstool for** one's **feet** is a figurative way of describing conquest, defeat, and subjugation (*cf.* Josh 10.24f; 2 Sam 22.39; 1 Kngs 5.3; Psa 18.38; 47.3; Mal 4.3). This quotation then serves here a similar purpose as those in verse 5 above: it shows the Son to be the one who has received from the Father the right to reign as king over God's world, something no angel could ever claim. Nowhere did God promise to subdue enemies before the angels; this special treatment is reserved for the Son alone. Yet it is also the crowning, or climactic quotation of the catena, which brings the point home mostly clearly and powerfully. The author has placed this quotation in a rhetorical question, and last on the list, for emphasis.

The following chart[78] summarizes the possible relationship of verses 2b–4 with verses 5–13:

Trait of the Son:	*Demonstrated by:*
God appointed him heir of all things (v 2)	v 5: Psalm 2.7 and 2 Samuel 7.14 (son = heir)
God made the worlds through him (v 2)	v 10: Psalm 102.25

[77] The author also uses key terms from OT texts in his discussion, and then quotes the texts from which he borrowed those terms, in order to prepare his readers/hearers to receive the main point he wishes them to derive from the quotation. He also likes to link one section of his treatise with another by means of terms shared between the sections. See Longenecker, *Rhetoric at the Boundaries*.

[78] For other approaches to how the statements of 1.1–4 relate to the catena, see Bauckham, *Jesus and the God of Israel*, 238; Jason Maston, "The Son and Scripture in Hebrews 1–2," *JSNT* 44 (2022): 496–515.

He is the brightness of God's glory (v 3)	vv 8: Psalm 45.6 (his throne)
He is the image of God's essence (v 3)	v 9: Psalm 45.7 (God's righteousness) vv 11–12: Psalm 102.26f (his eternal nature)
He holds up all things by the word of his power (v 3)	v 12: Psalm 102.26 (he has power over the heavens)
He sat down at God's right hand (v 3)	v 13: Psalm 110.1
He has inherited a better name than the angels (v 4)	v 5: Psalm 2.7 and 2 Samuel 7.14 (Son) v 6: Psalm 97.7 (angels worship him) v 9: Psalm 45.7 (he is called God, and he is above his companions)

1.14 Are they not all ministering spirits, sent for service for the sake of those who are about to inherit salvation?

The final rhetorical question returns to the point of verse 7 and its quotation of Psalm 104.4. The antecedent of **they** is "angels" (from 1.13). Angels are not the objects of God's exaltation, nor do they (rightly) receive praise from others. Even though they are heavenly beings (they are called **spirits** from the quotation in 1.7), they are simply God's servants. They are beings who are in subjection, not beings to whom others are subject (*cf.* Rev 22.8–9), and their service is **for the sake of** the messianic people of God. By this remark about the angels' service the author brings his readers to the same kind of messianic perspective seen in 1 Peter 1.10–12. The prophets and the angels were servants who delivered a message that has found its fulfillment in the messianic people of God, the church. That is, the prophets were serving in something that went beyond themselves, to a time past their own time, and the work of the angels likewise concerns the last days. As the heirs of their work, then, we are in a privileged position that we ought not readily abandon. The idea of being **about to inherit** the Lord's promised **salvation**, with its implications of anticipation and waiting (or, endurance), will become prominent in the epistle's exhortation as the argument unfolds (6.12; 11.8).

It is probably a mistake to suppose that this verse teaches that angels presently provide personal assistance to the saints (such as "guardian angels"). The statement must be read in its context. The role of angels (**all** of them, see v 6) is always[79] only to serve for the benefit of the people over whom the Son reigns, for whom he died, and who are the heirs of the coming salvation. The service angels render is "for the sake of" these heirs, but not necessarily directly to them. The verb "inherit" combined with *mellousan* ("they are about to") reinforces the idea that these are people to whom something is promised but who have not yet received it. The verse also makes it clear that no angel was ever made a universal ruler by God. Only the Son, who is exactly like the Father in essence, sits reigning at God's right hand. He is superior to angels in both essence and rank. The overall point is that angels are always in a role of service. They serve, but the Son alone reigns. The author will return to his discussion of angels and subjection in 2.5, but only after he has paused for an exhortation (2.1–4) based on his main point of the Son's superiority.

The argument of chapter 1 is fundamental to the rest of the book. It establishes the superiority of Christ, which is fundamental to the discussion of Psalm 110 and the high priesthood of Jesus.[80] Hebrews' argument for, and recommendation of, that which is "better" begins with the better status of the Son and the word of God that has now come through him. This high view of the Son has also served as the initial point in understanding the true message of the OT and the true nature of Judaism. The Son is not the pinnacle of Judaism but stands in a position far above it. His work, therefore, is not the perfection of Judaism but the accomplishment of something new, to which Judaism, in many ways, pointed.

---

[79] Expressed here through the present participle *apostellomena*. The present tense communicates imperfective (ongoing) aspect contemporaneous with the main verb. Campbell, *Basics of Verbal Aspect in Biblical Greek*, 72.

[80] See Schenck, "A Celebration of the Enthroned Son"; also Wallace, "The Use of Psalms in the Shaping of a Text," 43: "The first chapter of Hebrews is an exceptional example of the literary and theological significance of both Psalms 2 and 110 for the entire document. As a prelude anticipating the message of exhortation that follows and that argues for the relative superiority of the work of Christ, Hebrews 1 encapsulates many of the themes emerging later in the book."

EXCURSUS: JESUS AND THE ANGELS

Why is there all this talk in Hebrews 1 about Jesus being greater than the angels? One reason is that the author will make the argument (in 2.1–3) that since Jesus is greater than the angels, then the word that has come through Jesus is greater than the word which came through angels (*i.e.*, the Law of Moses). A greater messenger brings a greater message. But is this all there is to it? Nowhere else does the author of Hebrews spend as much energy to prove a point than he does with this point about Jesus' superiority to the angels. From a rhetorical standpoint alone, the amassing of so much evidence and argumentation suggests that there might have been more than a point about the Law of Moses at stake here. This should be coupled with the fact that this effort to prove the superiority of Jesus over the angels comes at the beginning of the sermon. The placement of this discussion here at the head of the work suggests that, in the author's opinion at least, this matter had to be addressed before any other discussion about Jesus' role in relation to believers could proceed. There could be no exposition of how Jesus fulfilled the pattern of Melchizedek until the readers first had the correct estimation of Jesus.

Does this extended proof that Jesus is greater than the angels suggest that there may have been a serious flaw in the original readers' understanding of the exaltation of Jesus? In what way could beliefs about angels have conflicted with a correct view of the greatness of Jesus?[1]

Generally speaking, the Jews in the first century had a highly developed view of angels. Some of the Jewish extra-Biblical literature speaks extensively about this, especially 1 Enoch. There was no unanimity on the subject among the ancients themselves (which is nothing unusual), but from the data a general picture emerges of seven archangels whom God has placed in charge of various things like the supervision of spirits, the planets, God's retribution, *etc.* In the Bible, the archangel Michael is mentioned in Daniel

[1] See the brief review of scholarly opinions in Gert J. Steyn, "Hebrews' Angelology in the Light of early Jewish Apocalyptic Imagery," *Journal of Early Christian History* 1 (2011): 143–64.

(10.13, 21; 12.1), and Gabriel is mentioned in the gospels (Luke 1.26). Michael was the guardian of God's people, Israel according to Dan 12.1, and we are told that Gabriel stands in God's presence (Luke 1.19). The subject receives just enough Biblical attention to invite speculation, which indeed came. The fact that angels are heavenly beings, and that they are agents of God's activity, naturally led to the idea that it was appropriate to acknowledge and even venerate their heavenly status. The idea was common enough that it was addressed in the ancient Jewish literature, where worship directed at angels was clearly prohibited.[2] Stuckenbruck notes that although there is no hard evidence for the formal, or organized, Jewish worship of angels, "the polemical texts seem to suggest that attitudes and devotional practices relating to them were not only a hypothetical possibility but also posed a practical problem that was subject to internal debate."[3] There are also those interesting passages in John's Apocalypse (Rev 19.10 and 22.8–9) where John felt obliged to venerate the angel who had shown him the heavenly realities, only to be told "Do not do that."[4] The inclusion of these scenes in Revelation may reflect some sensibilities on the part of John's readers that such worship of angels was appropriate, and it is possible that Hebrews 1 was a contribution to such a discussion.

Along similar lines, the Jews of the first century believed that angels were the protectors of God's people.[5] If the original readers of Hebrews were mostly Jewish Christians, it is not hard to imagine that such beliefs may have persisted among them after their conversion to Christianity. If this were the case, it is possible that these beliefs could have compromised their thinking about Jesus to some extent. That is, if Jewish Christians were accustomed to turning to angels for help in times of difficulty (as the original audience of Hebrews was facing), Hebrews 1 (and passages such as Heb 4.16) could be read as a corrective to such reliance on the help of angels.[6] Or, as deSilva suggests, the

---

[2] The literature is covered in Loren T. Stuckenbruck, *Angel Veneration and Christology: A Study in Early Judaism and in the Christology of the Apocalypse of John*, WUNT 70 (Tübingen: Mohr Siebeck, 1995), 51–149.

[3] Loren T. Stuckenbruck, "'Angels' and 'God': Exploring the Limits of Early Jewish Monotheism," in *Early Jewish and Christian Monotheism*, ed. Loren T. Stuckenbruck and Wendy E. S. North (London; New York: T&T Clark, 2004), 45–70, at 51–52.

[4] For instances of this same kind of scene in Jewish apocalyptic literature, see David E. Aune, *Revelation 17–22*, WBC 52C (Dallas: Word, Incorporated, 1998), 1034–35.

[5] See Matthew L. Walsh, *Angels Associated with Israel in the Dead Sea Scrolls*, WUNT 509 (Tübingen: Mohr Siebeck, 2019).

[6] See Gleason, "Angels and the Eschatology of Hebrews 1–2."

Jewish belief in the role of angels as mediators for God's people may have been the issue, and Hebrews 1 served to correct Jewish views that angels served as priests in heaven on behalf of God's people.[7] Less likely, it seems to me, is the proposal that the talk of angels was actually code for talk about Moses, whom some Jews believed had been given angelic status.[8] It is true that Hebrews contrasts Jesus and Moses (Heb 3.1–6), but the more immediate context explicitly contrasts the *revelation* given through angels to that given through the Son (Heb 2.2–3). There is no suggestion in Hebrews that angels are a way of speaking about Moses.

Another part of the ancient context is the intriguing issue of how the earliest Christians came to understand the deity of Jesus within their Jewish framework of monotheism. That is, how did the earliest Christians come to believe that Jesus was deity but at the same time avoid saying that they now believed in two gods, and that the inclusion of Jesus within their conception of God did not violate classic Jewish monotheism? It would not be surprising if some Jewish Christians were still struggling with making sense of the exaltation of Jesus. Their monotheism might have given them some pause in recognizing the divine status of Jesus, and it might have been easier to think of Jesus as being some kind of exalted angel. Scholars have referred to this as "angel Christology."[9] It is possible that some of the original readers of Hebrews were thinking that Jesus came to earth as a heavenly, high angelic agent of God, and that after appearing as a human being (which angels can do), he returned to heaven, but not equal with God. Hebrews 1 could have been a direct answer to this thinking.[10] Although the earliest evidence for angel Christology comes from a time later than the writing of Hebrews,[11] it is possible that a strand of this thinking existed among some early Christians.

---

[7] deSilva, *Perseverance in Gratitude*, 94. Some Jews believed that the archangel Michael served a high priestly role for God's people. *b. Hag.* 12b. *Cf.* also Jubilees 31.13–15, which compared the Levitical priesthood to angelic worship. Walsh, *Angels Associated with Israel*, notes that angels were viewed as Israel's guardians, but also as priests on Israel's behalf.

[8] Sirach 45.2; the Dead Sea Scroll 4Q377 says of Moses that "God would speak through his mouth as though he were an angel." Michael O. Wise, Martin G. Abegg Jr., and Edward M. Cook, *The Dead Sea Scrolls: A New Translation* (New York: HarperOne, 2005), 428.

[9] See Charles A. Gieschen, *Angelomorphic Christology: Antecedents and Early Evidence*, AGJU 42 (Leiden: Brill, 1998).

[10] This is the approach of Gert Steyn, "Addressing an Angelomorphic Christological Myth in Hebrews?," *HTS* 59 (2003): 1107–28.

[11] The earliest such interpretation that is clear is in Justin Martyr, *Dialogue with Trypho*, dated *c.* 140–160 AD, where Justin thought that Jesus was the archangel.

Instead of thinking that Jesus was an angel, it is also possible that some of the original hearers of Hebrews either did not understand, or had not truly accepted, the deity of Jesus, and that Hebrews 1 confronted this. Allen has asserted that

> There was no need to argue for the superiority of Jesus over the angels as that was not in question among early Jewish Christians. What was an issue—indeed, it was the watershed issue between Jews and Christians—was the deity of Christ and the Jewish attempt to deny it by claiming to preserve monotheism. Early Jewish Christians faced accepting the deity of Jesus while preserving historical monotheism. This was the heart of the author's theological purpose in the first two chapters. ... Hebrews 1:5–14 was not intended to show the superiority of Jesus to angels; that was never in question. It is intended to show his deity to a monotheistic Jewish-Christian audience....[12]

Taking this one step further, Bauckham has proposed that, in Hebrews 1, angels serve as a kind of boundary marker in thinking about the status levels of beings. To be lower than an angel is to be human, but to be above the angels is to be deity. Therefore "... the angels in Hebrews add precision to the picture. They mark out the cosmic territory. They function, so to speak, as measures of ontological status."[13] The discussion of Hebrews 1, then, is part of the larger discussion which goes through Hebrews 2. Chapter 1 establishes that Jesus is now above the angels, whereas chapter 2 establishes the necessity that he become, temporarily, below the angels.

Of course, it is also possible that there was no crisis of understanding about the deity of Jesus among the first hearers of Hebrews, and that Hebrews 1 should not be read as a response to inadequate beliefs about it. It is possible that the author of Hebrews simply used angels as a point of comparison to describe the greatness of Jesus, which is foundational to the main discussion of the sermon. This would be consistent with the author's method throughout the sermon, where the old is used as a basis of comparison for the new. Cockerill suggests "Comparison with the angels was the most effective way of substantiating the supremacy of the Son .... There were none greater with

---

[12] Allen, *Hebrews*, 165.

[13] Richard Bauckham, "The Divinity of Jesus Christ in the Epistle to the Hebrews," in *The Epistle to the Hebrews and Christian Theology*, ed. Richard Bauckham *et al* (Grand Rapids: Eerdmans, 2009), 15–36. *Cf.* Andrew Ter Ern Loke, *The Origin of Divine Christology*, SNTSMS 169 (Cambridge: Cambridge University Press, 2017), 67: Christ is consistently portrayed as belonging "on the Creator side of the Creator-creature divide."

whom the Son could be compared. ... As ancient orators praised a ruler by comparing him with great rulers of the past, so the pastor magnifies the Son by comparison with the angels."[14]

We cannot know for certain if Hebrews 1–2 was partly a response to some misunderstanding about the deity of Jesus. We do not know exactly how the original readers thought of Jesus, what misperceptions they might have had, what ideas they had absorbed from Jewish circles, *etc.* But enough talk of angels has survived in connection with the Jews of ancient times, and it was widespread enough, to conclude that the original readers of Hebrews may have had some mistaken and inadequate understandings of Jesus, possibly understandings that placed him on the same level as the angels (if not identifying Jesus as an angel Himself). Of course, for the author of Hebrews, such inadequate views of Jesus would have ruined the Biblical picture of Jesus as the new and exalted high priest of God who now ministers at the right hand of God. But even if no misunderstanding was being addressed, the proper picture of still Jesus had to be established, even if by way of reminder, before the Biblical picture of Jesus' priesthood could be fully appreciated, and that appreciation was vital to the readers' motive for endurance.

Addendum

This is probably an expedient place to comment, briefly, on the view that Jesus was the angel of the Lord in the Old Testament. The view was common among the church fathers of the second century,[15] and still finds advocates today. Those who argue for identifying this angel with Christ himself would have to assert that this is an exception to what is asserted in Hebrews 1. However, it should be clear that Hebrews 1 has "closed the door" to any view that identifies Jesus with any angel.[16] In fact, if Jesus were the angel of the Lord, that is, if this is theological truth that explains Jesus in the Old Testament, Hebrews would have been the perfect vehicle to make that observation (as well as 1 Cor 10.1–5 and Phil 2.5–11). It would have fit well with the view, described above, that some Jews held, namely, that angels served as heavenly priests

---

[14] Cockerill, *Epistle to the Hebrews*, 100–101.

[15] Although they used it as a functional category, not an ontological one. Aloys Grillmeier, *Christ in Christian Tradition, Vol. 1: From the Apostolic Age to Chalcedon (451)*, 2nd rev. ed., trans. John Bowden (Atlanta: John Knox Press, 1975), 47–49.

[16] William Graham MacDonald, "Christology and 'The Angel of the Lord,'" in *Current Issues in Biblical and Patristic Interpretation: Studies in Honor of Merrill C. Tenney Presented by His Former Students*, ed. Gerald F. Hawthorne (Grand Rapids: Eerdmans, 1975), 324–35, at 325.

for God's people. Hebrews plainly asserts, however, that Jesus is greater than the angels (and that would include "the angel of the Lord"), and nowhere does he describe Jesus' current priesthood as angelic. Also, no NT author ever tried to fit Jesus into some hierarchy of angels, nor asserted that Jesus existed in the form of an angel before he came to the earth. The plain implication of John 17.5 and Philippians 2.6 is that, before his incarnation, Jesus existed in the glorious form of God, without any angelic form intervening or temporarily assumed. Nor did any New Testament author explicitly identify Jesus as the angel of the Lord from the Old Testament, nor even hint at such an identification. In fact, the argument of Hebrews 2.1–2 crumbles if Jesus is an angel. The contrast between revelation through angels and revelation through the Son disappears if the Son is, after all, an angel himself. But the author of Hebrews stated clearly that God never called any angel his Son (Heb 1.5). To suggest that Jesus could have occasionally taken the form of an angel without compromising his identity (so that he is still the Son even if at times he was an angel, as the view in question seems to demand) not only stands against the plain language of Hebrews 1 but is also pure speculation.

Other considerations argue against the identification as well. First, there is no title in the Old Testament "the angel of the Lord." None of the occurrences of this phrase have the definite article in Hebrew. The confusion is possibly caused for some by the rendering of the phrase in English Bibles, but in none of the occurrences does the phrase denote a special angelic being who stands in a kind of class by himself.[17] Second, the fact that "angel" and "God" seem to be interchangeable in some stories can be accounted for by the fact that God was speaking through an angel, and the angel represented God.[18] The words could be said to be God's, or the angel's, without contradiction and, more importantly, without any sense that the two were the same being. It may even be that the phrase "angel of the Lord" was meant as a way of speaking of God's presence.[19] Third, questionable assumptions are necessary to identify

[17] MacDonald, "Christology," 330.

[18] See René A. López, "Identifying 'The Angel of the Lord' in the Book of Judges: A Model for Reconsidering the Referent in Other Old Testament Loci," *BBR* 20 (2010): 1–18; Kristian A. Bendoraitis, *"Behold, the Angels Came and Served Him": A Compositional Analysis of Angels in Matthew*, LNTS 523 (London; New York; Oxford; New Delhi; Sydney: Bloomsbury T&T Clark; Bloomsbury, 2015), 22–35; also Susan R. Garrett, *No Ordinary Angel: Celestial Spirits and Christian Claims about Jesus* (New Haven; London: Yale University Press, 2008), 21–27.

[19] G. von Rad, "*malak* in the OT," *TDNT* 1:77: "when God enters the apperception of man, the *malak yhwh* is introduced." See also Garrett, *No Ordinary Angel*, 21–27; David

Jesus with the Old Testament "angel of the Lord." One must assume that, if this truly was a case of deity on earth, that it was the Son and not the Father who had come to earth in those episodes. But nothing in those Old Testament stories supports such an idea. If anything, they would more consistently be read as "appearances" of the Father, theophanies, not Christophanies.[20] It also requires us to assume that Jesus came to earth in angelic form several times before his birth as a man, and in that angelic form he spoke with Abraham, wrestled with Jacob, *etc.* (some would even have Jesus, as "the angel of the Lord," announcing his own birth to Mary), but that references to an "angel of the Lord" after Jesus' ascension (Acts 5.19; 12.7, 23) are not appearances of Jesus. However, these assumptions are neither warranted nor necessary to understand the Biblical stories in which angels appear. Of course, to say that Jesus is not "the angel of the Lord" is not to say that Jesus had no part in the events of the Old Testament. Passages such as 1 Corinthians 10.1–4; John 1.3; and 1 Peter 1.11 make it clear that he did. It is simply to say that an Old Testament encounter with a heavenly being known as an "angel of the Lord" was not an appearance of God's Son to men.

Francis Hinson (*Theology of the Old Testament* (London: SPCK, 2001), 60–61): "Probably the writers who used the distinctive phrase *the angel of the Lord* wanted to preserve the wonder and glory of the Lord. They recognized that God in his power and glory is separate from and greater than anything in the whole universe, and as such remains beyond our wisdom and understanding. ... They wanted to express the grandeur and detachment of God. To see God would tempt us to think that we understand him, and even that in some ways we can control him. Yet according to all these stories God really was aware of, and concerned about, his people. He was present in a mysterious way with people like Hagar, Abraham and Jacob. The writers used the term *the angel of the Lord* to talk about this."; *cf.* Stephen L. White ("Angel of the Lord: Messenger or Euphemism?" *TynBul* 50 (1999): 299–305): "The variation between the use of device of the 'angel of the LORD' and the name of Yahweh serves both to emphasize God's transcendence when it is applied and to remind us who is really acting when it is not." (305).

[20] Yet, as Simmers has shown, these episodes do not follow the normal ways of describing theophanies in the Bible. Gary Simmers, "Who is 'The Angel of the Lord'?," *Faith and Mission* 17 (2000): 3–16.

HEBREWS 2

Chapter 1 established, from Scripture, that Jesus in his exalted status is greater than the angels. However, the suffering and death of Jesus seemed to contradict any such ideas of superiority. Chapter 2, therefore, will demonstrate how the earthly lowliness of Jesus is compatible with the heavenly greatness predicated of him in chapter 1. The key lies in understanding the purpose for which Jesus came to this earth in the first place.

2.1 For this reason it is necessary for us to pay even more attention to the things that have been heard, lest we drift away.

The phrase **for this reason** draws the reader to a conclusion based on the facts presented in chapter 1. A greater messenger (Jesus) has delivered a greater message (the gospel), which should therefore receive greater attention than the word delivered through angels (the Law of Moses; see verse 2 below and comments on 1.4). Here is Hebrews' first "warning passage." If the readers had been zealously attentive to the old law, they ought to pay even more attention to the greater, new, and final revelation in Christ (*cf.* Matt 17.5). The time of which God spoke for hundreds of years (the "last days," 1.2) has now come; by the new word of God in Jesus the long-awaited kingdom of God has arrived, and while a taste of its blessings has been poured out, the greater portion of the inheritance (salvation) still lies ahead. Now is not the time to retreat from the kingdom but to enter it and hold onto it in order to obtain the full portion of the promised inheritance.

We/us recalls the fact that God has now spoken "to us" (1.2), the messianic people of God. The exhortation to **pay attention** to what we have **heard** lays the foundation for the upcoming discussion in Hebrews 3–4 ("... if you will hear," 3.7) and the rebuke in 5.11 ("dull of hearing"). Hearing God's word, and receiving it with faith, is an important part of the exhortation of Hebrews. The expression **things that have been heard** reminds us that in the first century the gospel was primarily communicated orally (even as it assumed written form). In the Biblical way of thinking, to hear is to receive, to accept; it is an act of the will (*cf.* Jam 1.21; Matt 13.13), and those who have heard become responsible to respond in faith. The fact that we have heard the gospel means that we are now liable to its demands. The original hearers of Hebrews had received the word of the gospel, but now they were retreating in their minds and hearts from its message. In light of the nature of what they had received (*i.e.*, God's final word that brings forgiveness, the new covenant, and salvation), they needed to maintain their commitment to it.

The reason constant and careful attention to the word of God delivered to us in his Son **is necessary** is that if we do not, we will **drift** away from it. The Greek word here (*pararreō*) is used of water that flows past in a river or stream, of ships that are not moored or anchored and therefore drift about, or of something that slips off its place[1] because it is not fixed and gets away from its proper position. Figuratively it can denote forgetting, to escape or slip from the mind,[2] and thus to leave the faith.[3] It is the opposite of the other word the author used here (*prosechō*, **pay attention**), which could be used in nautical contexts for keeping a ship on course.[4] We may drift away from our relationship with God by our inattention to his word, because inattention eventually turns into refusal (see Heb 6.3–6). The author will cite the historical example of Israel in chapters 3–4. The NT consistently teaches that it is possible for a believer, a child of God, to fall away from the faith and be lost. Several such admonitions appear in Hebrews (3.6, 12–14; 4.1; 6.4–6; 10.26–31, 35, 39; 12.25).[5] Constant attention to God's word, hearing it, reading it, and meditating upon it, is therefore necessary (*cf.* 1 Pet 2.2; 2 Pet 1.19; 1 Tim 4.13).

2.2 For if the word that was spoken through angels was firm and every transgression and disobedience received a just penalty,

---

[1] LSJ 1322; D. A. Carson, "Flow," *NIDNTT* 1:683.

[2] BDAG 770; Joseph Henry Thayer, *A Greek-English Lexicon of the New Testament* (New York: Harper & Brothers, 1889), 486.

[3] Louw-Nida 374.

[4] LSJ 1512.

[5] See Scot McKnight, "The Warning Passages of Hebrews: A Formal Analysis and Theological Conclusions," *TrinJ* 13 (1992): 21–59.

The word spoken by **angels** was the old Law, the Law of Moses. According to both the OT (Psa 68.17 and Deut 33.2 LXX) and the NT (Acts 7.30, 38, 53, and Gal 3.19), angels played a mediating role in delivering that law.[6] The author raised two points about the old Law here. First, it was **firm**, a word (Greek *bebaios*) that can mean "valid" (as the RSV and NRSV render it) or, more commonly, "sure" or "reliable" (ESV). *Cf.* Rom 4.16. The NASB renders it "unalterable" here. The point is that there was no question about the binding nature of the Law. Second, the old Law was **just**. It was a just Law because it came from a just God. The fact that it was only a pointer to something greater than itself did not in any way diminish its high concern for justice. No sin was ignored. Every violation of that law had some punishment (**penalty**) attached to it (*cf.* Rom 4.15). It should be noted that the author is here describing the Mosaic law itself, not necessarily the ancient practice of it. Even though the Law was not always enforced by those to whom it was given, the Law itself contained provisions for punishing every offense.

The reference here to the Law of Moses, and in particular its setting at Mt. Sinai, begins a string of allusions that gradually build a picture of a new exodus that is underway, explicitly comparing the journey of the ancient Israelites with the journey of the recipients of Hebrews. Israel came to Mt. Sinai after the exodus from Egypt, and from there God's intention was for that generation to enter the promised land and ultimately to Jerusalem, where God would live among them. The developing picture will set up the exhortations not only in Hebrews 3–4, but ultimately the exhortation in Hebrews 12 as well.

There are two terms for sin used here. **Transgression** translates the Greek word *parabasis* and is a general term for the failure to comply with the demand of a law.[7] **Disobedience** translates the Greek word *parakoē* and denotes an inward, intentional neglect to hear.[8] This term recalls the importance of hearing God's word mentioned in verse 1 above. However, the distinction between the two words should probably not be pressed very far, since the author of Hebrews liked to present things in parallelism for emphasis.

---

[6] The presence of angels at Sinai is also mentioned in extra-Biblical Jewish literature: Josephus, *Ant.* 15.136; the rabbinic *Mekilta* on Exod 20.18; *Book of Jubilees* 1.27–29; 2.1,26f; *Damascus Document* 5.

[7] BDAG 758.

[8] BDAG 484.

The author here made his point with a rhetorical conditional sentence, the protasis (the "if" clause) of which appears in this verse. He appealed to something his readers believed and understood well in order to make the apodosis (the "then" clause, in the next verse) all the more forceful.[9] The rhetorical question was one of his favorite persuasive tools.

2.3 how will we escape if we neglect so great a salvation, which, at first being spoken through the Lord, was confirmed to us by those who heard him,

The author here presents one of many arguments from the lesser to the greater (the rabbinic *qal wahomer*; see Introduction) in the sermon. If the facts of verse 2 are assured, then an even greater and more serious situation surely exists in the new order of things. The exhortation here, with its particular form of argument, previews the similar exhortation that will appear in 12.25–29. **We** is emphatic in the Greek here, contrasted with an implied "they"; if *they* did not escape punishment under a strict law that was inferior in so many ways, then how can *we* expect to escape divine wrath under a better law?

Escape, or **salvation** (Greek *sōtēria*; deliverance, rescue) from the guilt and consequence of sin—God's wrath—is available only in the gospel of Christ (*cf.* Rom 5.9; 1 Thes 1.10; Gal 3.13; Acts 4.12). It is here characterized as **so great** a salvation because of what it took to provide it, and because of the nature of that from which we are being rescued, *viz.* slavery to sin and death in this life (v 15 below) and the fierce wrath of God later (Heb 12.29; 1 Thes 1.10). **If we neglect** the gospel (that is, pay no attention to it; *cf.* Matt 22.5), which is the word which God spoke to us in his Son (1.2), we will have neglected the only avenue of salvation available and we will not escape God's wrath (John 3.36). We should note that "neglect" may be too mild a term for the translation here. In English, neglect can convey the sense of an accidental oversight, but the author of Hebrews had something much more deliberate and disastrous in mind here. As deSilva notes, this is the language of affront: "Inherent in the participle *amelēsantes* is the notion of showing contempt for the thing 'neglected.' … Neglect for God's gifts and revelation—thinking other concerns to be more weighty

[9] See Daniel B. Wallace, *Greek Grammar beyond the Basics: An Exegetical Syntax of the New Testament* (Grand Rapids: Zondervan, 1996), 694; Ellingworth, *Epistle to the Hebrews*, 137.

or deserving of attention—means dishonoring God."[10] To neglect is to commit the sin of ingratitude. Here, in a nutshell, lies the main exhortation of Hebrews. Stronger terminology will appear in the third warning passage (esp. 6.4–8, see comments there, and comments on 5.2). This first warning passage is relatively "mild" compared to the ones to come.

The message (the gospel) that saves us from the consequences of sin was first **spoken through the Lord**, the Son in whom God has spoken in a final way (1.1–2). Jesus presented himself in his preaching as the way of salvation from sin and its consequences (*cf.* John 5.34; 10.9; 11.25–26; 14.6; Matt 11.28–30). This escape is not given to anyone unconditionally. God offers it to all, but it may be accepted or neglected by one's own choice, and to neglect it is to abandon the only way of deliverance.[11]

The threat of punishment for unfaithfulness to God's word is a major theme in Hebrews (*cf.* 3.17–18; 4.1; 6.7–8; 10.26–31). There is no escaping accountability to the law of Christ. *Cf.* 4.12–13; 12.25. The original readers of Hebrews were contemplating abandoning Christianity under pressure of shame and social rejection (see Introduction). They therefore needed to hear this warning, as does anyone who would leave the Lord's church in times of hardship (*cf.* Gal 1.6–10). This same warning to hear lest they face the wrath of God will appear again in 3.7–19.

God's new revelation in Christ has also been confirmed and therefore stands as valid, if not more so, as the old Law ever was. When the apostles went out preaching the gospel, they were testifying about what they had seen and **heard** from Jesus (*cf.* Acts 4.20; 22.15; 1 John 1.1–3; 2 Pet 1.16–18). First-hand knowledge of the gospel was a prerequisite for being an apostle (Acts 1.21–22; Gal 1.11–12). As witnesses, the apostles **confirmed** (Greek *bebaioō*, the verbal form of the adjective used in v 2 above) what was first spoken by the Lord himself. The role of witnesses and testimony is important in the argument of Hebrews (see chs 3–4, 11–12). They offer encouragement but they also demand accountability. See the Introduction for the bearing of this verse on discussions of the authorship of Hebrews.

2.4 with God also testifying by signs and wonders and various miracles and by distributions of the Holy Spirit according to his will?

[10] deSilva, *Perseverance in Gratitude*, 106.

[11] See Brenda B. Colijn, "'Let Us Approach': Soteriology in the Epistle to the Hebrews," *JETS* 39 (1996): 571–86.

The veracity of the testimony of the apostles was further demonstrated by the various miracles they performed by the power of God. By these miracles **God** himself was also **testifying** along with them or adding his testimony to theirs in order to confirm it (*cf.* Acts 14.3). The significance of this would have been readily apparent to the original Jewish Christian audience, since according to the Law of Moses a fact was considered to be established (confirmed) if two or three witnesses testified to it consistently (Deut 19.15). There were three reliable witnesses to the gospel: Jesus (v 3), the eyewitness apostles (v 3), and God himself (v 4, through miracles).

Three terms are commonly used in the NT for miracles, and the author of Hebrews used all three of them here. To refer to a miracle as a **sign** (Greek *sēmeion*) is to emphasize its informational character. A sign is a pointer, that which gives information beyond itself. In this sense they too were witnesses (see Exod 4.8; Acts 14.3; John 5.36). The miracles performed by the apostles were information-giving signs that proclaimed God's confirmation of what they testified about Jesus. To refer to a miracle as a **wonder** (Greek *teras*) emphasizes its awesome nature. Miracles were also extraordinary and supernatural accomplishments that caused people to marvel when they saw them. This is not to say that any amazing thing is a miracle in the Biblical sense, but that genuine miracles had this effect on those who saw them (*cf.* Matt 8.27; 9.33; 12.23; Mark 7.37; *etc.*). The word **miracle** (Greek *dunamis*; from which we get our English word "dynamite") emphasizes the power behind, and exhibited in, these great deeds. They were not conjuring tricks or sleight of hand. They were the power of God at work (1 Cor 2.4–5; 1 Thes 1.5; Acts 8.9–13). The working of these miracles, either through Jesus or the apostles, was understood to be evidence of the presence and approval of God in and for the one who worked them, and for the preaching that always accompanied them. God's testimony was not explicitly verbal, but through demonstration of his power in his approved messengers (*cf.* 1 Cor 2.4). If the mention of the scene at Sinai in verse 2 hinted at a new exodus in which the recipients of Hebrews were involved, this verse would strengthen that hint, as Exodus 7.3 said that God worked signs and wonders as part of Israel's exodus experience.[12]

In addition to God's testimony through the miracles performed by the apostles was his testimony through miraculous gifts **of the Holy Spirit**

---

[12] David M. Moffitt, "Exodus in Hebrews," in *Exodus in the New Testament*, ed. Seth M. Ehorn, LNTS 663 (London: T&T Clark, 2022), 146–63, at 152.

which were exercised by some of the early Christians. Some of these gifts (such as prophesying) were designed to strengthen and edify the church, and others (such as speaking in tongues) were signs to unbelievers that the word spoken in the churches was the truth (1 Cor 14.22). These miraculous spiritual gifts served to confirm the gospel they accompanied, the same gospel from which the readers were falling away (*cf.* Gal 3.5). While every apostle was endowed with power to perform miracles, not every Christian in the early church received a miraculous spiritual gift. These gifts were **distributed** among his people as God saw fit (**according to his will**; 1 Cor 12.11). It is not clear whether the recipients of Hebrews had previously exercised spiritual gifts themselves, but if they were the Jerusalem church (see Introduction) they certainly would have at least known firsthand of miracles performed by the apostles.[13] At any rate, it is the confirmed nature of the word spoken through Jesus that is in view here. God himself confirmed the gospel the apostles preached; therefore it "stands" as valid, it is not to be ignored, and its message of faith in Jesus is the only way to escape the wrath of God.

2.5 For it is not to angels that he subjected the coming world, concerning which we are speaking.

The author returns from his brief exhortation to resume his demonstration (from 1.4–14) that the word which has come through the Son is greater than that which came through **angels**, with "angels" standing up front in the sentence for some emphasis. As noted in the comments on 1.4 and 2.2 (see also the Excursus: Jesus and the Angels), angels played a significant role in the thinking of some Jewish groups in antiquity to the extent that it was believed that they were the greatest of God's agents

---

[13] Wallace has argued that vv 3 and 4 present "some solid inferences that the sign gifts had for the most part ceased" near the end of the first century A.D. (Daniel B. Wallace, "Hebrews 2:3–4 and the Sign Gifts." < https://bible.org/article/hebrews-23-4-and-sign-gifts>). He argues that the author spoke of the performance of the miracles in the past tense, and "the aorist *ebebaiōthē* ["confirmed"] loses much of its punch if the author intends to mean that these gifts continue. He so links the confirmation to the eyewitnesses ... that to argue the continued use of such gifts seems to fly in the face of the whole context." Those who heard were simply "observers of such sign gifts; they were not performers of them. The eyewitnesses seem to be the only ones implied here who exercised such gifts." We might add that once the confirmation of the word had been given, the need for the things that provided confirmation (the miracles and spiritual gifts) were no longer needed. *Cf.* 1 Cor 13.8–12.

and that the word that came through them (the Law of Moses) was God's eternally authoritative message to man. Jews generally believed that angels not only had a role in the giving of the Law but that they also played a part in ruling the world. However, no Biblical text says that God placed any angel as ruler over God's new creation (the messianic age). The author thus intended that something new and different has started. Even though angels had extensive roles in the administration and governance of God's plan in former times (see Dan 10.13, 20; 12.1 and Deut 32.8 LXX), they do not hold the same roles in the messianic age (the quotations in ch 1 served to establish this point). And if angels do not rule over the messianic age, then the word that came through them (the old Law) is not the word that governs this age. The word of supreme authority in the present, messianic age comes from the one whom God has exalted to reign over all (*cf.* Matt 28.18), Jesus, his Son. A greater messenger has delivered a greater word.

The phrase **the coming world** might at first seem to denote the afterlife, the world that is to come after this one, but that is not its true referent here. It is rather the messianic age, the new life-situation made possible by the work of Jesus. The clue to this interpretation is that the word "world" is, in the Greek, the word *oikoumenē,* which denotes the world in a political sense, an empire. It is the same word the author used in 1.6 when he mentioned God bringing the firstborn (Jesus) into the world. In that context it clearly referred to Jesus' entrance into his reign, his exaltation to glory and his being placed over all things after his resurrection from the dead. The prophets spoke of the messianic age as a new world.[14] The world the author had in mind, therefore, is what is elsewhere in the NT called the kingdom of God, or the messianic time, the new order of things in which the Son has been made ruler over all, which is a new world, as it were, for mankind.

So why did the author speak of it as a *coming* world if it had already begun with Jesus' exaltation? It is likely that he said it is a "coming" world because he was speaking from the standpoint of the OT predictions (*cf.* Col 2.17). In support of this view, if "the powers of the world to come" in Hebrews 6.5 are the same things as the miracles mentioned in 2.4, then it follows that the "world to come" is the age in which those miracles were seen, the same age in which the readers lived and in which

[14] Isa 51.14–16; 65.17; 66.22. See also Psa 96.10. In the NT, see Rom 5.12ff; John 1.1ff.

the kingdom of Christ was established and opened for men to enter. In any case the author quickly added that this world to come is the very situation **concerning which we are speaking**, that is, the *present* reign of Christ far above the angels.

2.6 But one has testified somewhere, saying, "What is man, that you think of him? or the son of man, that you look after him?

To show that angels do not rule the present age, the author cited Scripture, which his readers would have considered the last word in any dispute. The **somewhere**[15] from which the author here (in vv 6-8a) quoted is Psalm 8.4–6, which meditates, with a rhetorical question, upon the role God has given to man within the created order. It expresses amazement that God would **think of** (Greek *mimnēskomai*, often meaning to "remember" and thus "to think of"; it can also have the sense of "be concerned about"), or **look after** (Greek *episkeptomai*, to look carefully at something, but also to visit in order to give help) a creature that is so comparatively weak and small. The author's selection of the psalm is apparent for two reasons: 1) it is another psalm (like Psalms 2 and 110) that speaks of someone's exaltation, and the author read it, with those other psalms, as speaking about Jesus[16]; and 2) Psalm 8 reveals an additional element to the Biblical picture of the exalted Messiah, one that is not explicitly mentioned in Psalms 2 or 110: that the Messiah's exaltation would be preceded by a time in which he was lower than the angels.

A key feature of this psalm is its use of the term **son of man**. While that expression may simply mean **man** (as the parallelism of Psa 8.4 suggests), this was, in fact, Jesus' most frequent self-designation.[17] The presence of

[15] That the author merely attributes it to "somewhere" in Scripture in no way suggests that he treated Scripture casually. This is actually a fairly common way of citing a quotation in Greek literature (see examples in BDAG 858) and places the emphasis on the content of Scripture's testimony rather than its location in the canonical arrangement of books. See also Heb 4.4.

[16] According to Kistemaker, the Jews did not read Psa 8 as a messianic psalm. Simon J. Kistemaker, *Exposition of the Epistle to the Hebrews*, NTC (Grand Rapids: Baker Books, 1984), 66; also, his *Psalm Citations*, 29.

[17] See Arthur J. Ferch, *The Son of Man in Daniel Seven*, Andrews University Seminary Doctoral Dissertation Series 6 (Berrien Springs: Andrews University Press, 1979). Jesus himself combined Dan 7.13 and Psa 110.1 in his statement before the Sanhedrin (Luke 22.69). The author of Hebrews possibly saw the same connection as he read Psa 8. Kistemaker, *Psalm Citations*, 81.

this phrase no doubt signaled to Christians that the psalm was about the Messiah. However, the psalm makes perfectly good sense as a meditation on the place of man in the universe as well. The question, therefore, is which of these two meanings did the psalm intend? Is the psalm about man or the Messiah? The answer is: it is both.[18] Man's lowly state and his disproportionately high relation to the world is a type of the Messiah's humiliation and supreme reign over all things. At the forefront in this context, however, is the messianic side of the psalm.[19] It is clear from the context that the author adduced this passage as yet another indicator that Jesus (and not just mankind in general) has been exalted overall and is another good example of the technique of *midrash* at work.

2.7 You made him a little lower than the angels, you crowned him with glory and honor,

The author is quoting from the LXX (but has omitted the first line of v 7 = v 6 in the English translations). There is one significant change between the MT and the LXX that requires attention. In Psalm 8.5 the MT reads "Yet you have made him a little lower than God" (NASB). The word translated "God" is the Hebrew *elohim*, a common name for God in the OT but which may also be translated as "gods" should the context warrant it (the word is, technically, a plural). The LXX, probably in a pious attempt to avoid direct comparison between God and man, has taken the latter route and interpreted "gods" to be heavenly beings (as does the NIV), or angels. A similar thing was noticed in the LXX of Psalm 97.7, which was quoted in Hebrews 1.6.

In Psalm 8 David considered the relative insignificance of man and wondered why God even pays attention to man at all (Psa 8.3). Man is, after all, a mortal being whose mode of existence is **a little lower than** that of **the angels**. The word *brachus* ("little") in Greek has a semantic range similar to that in English, and can refer to a small space, a short amount of time, something little in relative size, few in quantity, *etc.* Here the idea is that man is of a lower order **than the angels**. However, the

[18] deSilva proposes that the author of Hebrews might have been encouraging a "double reading" of the psalm in which both interpretations were in play. *Perseverance in Gratitude*, 110.

[19] See Jason Maston, " 'What is Man?' An Argument for the Christological Reading of Psalm 8 in Hebrews 2," *ZNW* 112 (2021): 89–104.

sense of "for a little while" is not out of the picture, as verse 9 will show. The thing that amazed David is that God had **crowned** (Greek *stephanoō*, here in a general sense of "honored") this lowly creature (man) with **glory, honor**, and dominion over all the earth. The reference is to Genesis 1.26–29; 9.2; but Psalm 2 is also part of the picture when the psalm is read messianically. With Adam, God took a weak and lowly creature and set him in a position disproportionate to his condition. Lowliness and greatness would ordinarily seem to be contradictory qualities, yet God's exaltation of the lowly (and his corresponding humbling of the great) is a common theme in the Bible (*cf.* 1 Sam 2.8; Psa 113; Isa 14.4–16; Ezek 21.26; 31.18; Jam 4.10; 1 Pet 5.6). God routinely exalts the lowly and brings down the proud so that God may receive the glory due him. This in turn became a pattern that God has followed with the Messiah (Phil 2.5ff; Eph 1.20ff). Jesus fulfills the Adamic commission to reign over God's creation, but only after he conquered the enemy of God's people through an experience of lowliness and death. But the psalm will also be fulfilled when God's people attain their glory.

2.8 and you subjected all things under his feet." Now in subjecting all things to him, he left nothing unsubjected. But we do not yet see the subjugation of all things to him.

The last line of the quotation, **you subjected all things under his feet**, not only summarizes Genesis 1.26–29, but also recalls a similar statement about the subjection of enemies in Psalm 110 (quoted in Heb 1.13) and a prominent theme in Psalm 2 (ruling over the nations). One of the ancient Jewish exegetical guidelines dictated that one text may be used to interpret another text where similar wording appears (*gezerah shawah*). By this method, if the subjection in Psalm 110 is messianic, then the subjection in Psalm 8 may be seen as messianic also,[20] so Psalm 8 can be used to interpret Psalm 110. This is exactly the procedure the author was here using. The resulting picture is that the Son's enthronement and exaltation (Psalm 110) was preceded by his lowly time in the flesh (Psalm 8) in which he made purification for sins (Heb 1.3) and became qualified to represent people as their high priest (Heb 5.7–10).

[20] Other rabbinic techniques are also at work in this passage. See George H. Guthrie and Russell D. Quinn, "A Discourse Analysis of the Use of Psalm 8:4–6 in Hebrews 2:5–9," *JETS* 49 (2006): 235–46, esp. 241–42.

In order to guide our understanding of the quotation from the eighth psalm, the author, in good midrashic fashion (see Introduction), added two important comments at the end of verse 8. The first one is: **Now in subjecting all things to him, he left nothing unsubjected.** The author emphasizes the absolute nature of the reign depicted in the psalm. Jesus' reign is not like the situation in which angels were put in charge of various facets of the plan of God (*cf.* 1.13). No angel was ever given—nor is presently given—the absolute kind of authority described in Psalm 8. Therefore, the Son of Man (Jesus) is shown, by Scripture itself, to hold a position far greater than that of the angels.

The second comment is: **But we do not yet see the subjugation of all things to him.** Who is the "him"? There are two possibilities:

1) It is possible to interpret "him" as "man" (mankind) from the psalm,[21] and thus understand the verse to say that we do not see man (probably understood as God's people) reigning over all things, but that this will be remedied because of the work of Christ. This understanding of Hebrews 2.8 could also work in connection with the next verse, which presents the contrasting situation of Jesus. It may be that reading the "him" as a reference to man was meant to include the original readers, considered as participants in the new creational work of Christ, in their present condition of being shamed and rejected by others. At the moment, those Christians did not seem to be reigning over the world, but the day is coming in which they will be glorified and victorious over it (*cf.* Heb 2.10).

2) Since the author's point is to establish from Scripture the high exaltation of God's Son, "him" must be Jesus. This is in keeping with how the psalm was understood among other early Christians and by Jesus himself. Paul quoted this same verse in 1 Corinthians 15.27 and also applied it to Jesus, and Jesus himself quoted verse 2 of the psalm in Matthew 21.16 and said it had reference to his ministry. The author's statement here simply notes that Jesus has not yet conquered all things completely, that the words of the psalm have yet to see their fullest realization. This is how Psalm 110.1 presented the picture: as a future reality ("... *until* I make your enemies of footstool"). There is no contradiction, however,

[21] So Westcott, *Epistle to the Hebrews*, 44; Franz Delitzsch (*Commentary on the Epistle to the Hebrews*, Clark's Foreign Theological Library (Edinburgh: T&T Clark, 1874)), 1:109; Kistemaker, *Hebrews*, 66.

between the assertion of a present reign of the Messiah by Psalm 8 and the assertion of a future reign by the Messiah in Psalm 110.[22] Both are correct and true; Jesus is presently reigning, but an even greater scope of his reign is still to come. The kingdom of God has appeared, but it has not yet attained its fullness. One enemy that is still active is death (1 Cor 15.26; although Jesus dealt a death blow to death in his resurrection). Eventually, Jesus will have conquered everything and everyone in the universe (Paul discussed this in more detail in 1 Cor 15.23–28). To him every knee will ultimately bow, including those in heaven (heavenly beings, or angels), those on earth, and those under the earth (Phil 2.10). For the author of Hebrews, the fact that all things have not been completely conquered at present in no way mitigates or diminishes the fact that Jesus has indeed begun to reign, even over death (see vv 14–15 below).[23]

In this context, the quotation from Psalm 8 confirms the statement from verse 5 that God did not subject the messianic age to angels, even if the fullness of that subjection has not yet appeared. God has rather subjected the world to the Son of Man, one who lived in a form lower than the angels. The irony and apparent difficulty that God would make one who was lower than the angels (the son of man) to be ruler (Son) over the new age will be explained by our author in verses 10ff below.

2.9 But we see Jesus, the one who was made a little lower than the angels on account of the suffering of death and who has been crowned with glory and honor, that by the grace of God he might taste death for everyone.

We do not see Jesus the Son of Man (or his people) yet completely fulfilling the words of Psalm 8 about absolute reign, but we do see[24] that

[22] Guthrie and Quinn, "A Discourse Analysis of the Use of Psalm 8:4–6 in Hebrews 2:5–9," 242.

[23] See Wilber B. Wallis, "The Use of Psalms 8 and 110 in I Corinthians 15:25–27 and in Hebrews 1 and 2," *JETS* 15 (1972): 25–29.

[24] There are two different Greek words for seeing in this context. The word in v 8 is *horaō*, and the word here is *blepō*. Just how much we should make of the difference is debatable. Sometimes *blepō* emphasized the physical act of seeing, or meant to notice something, and *horaō* emphasized mental perception, but the distinction was not always a sharp one. It may also be that the author simply chose different terms for the sake of variation. Wilhelm Michaelis, "*horaō ktl*," *TDNT* 5:316–17; K. Dahn, "*horaō ktl*," *NIDNTT* 3:511–12. However, Ellingworth (*Epistle to the Hebrews*, 154) notes that *blepō* occurs in contexts in Hebrews that involve faith, and that may be its distinction here.

Jesus has completely fulfilled the words about becoming lower than the angels and now existing in glory. This was accomplished in his incarnation and subsequent exaltation. This is the first place in this sermon where the author has referred to God's Son by the name he wore as a man: **Jesus**. Until now the emphasis has been on his exalted status as Son. In this context, however, the author wished to discuss the significance of his lowly existence for a while as a man. Using the Lord's earthly name emphasizes this.

For a while, Jesus was indeed **lower than the angels** (again picking up the wording from Psa 8.5, quoted in v 7 above). Jesus was made "a little" lower than the angels in two ways: first, he lived in this world, this lower realm (compared to the regular abode of the angels) in a flesh-and-blood body which is a lower mode of existence than what the angels enjoy in heaven, and second, he lived here for a little while. The ambiguity of the term *brachus* can cover both ideas, but in the present context, the temporal sense is the one our author saw most clearly. Jesus' existence in a fleshly body was only for a little while. It was not his original, true, or lasting mode or form of being. It was, in fact, a momentary kind of thing compared to his eternal existence. In his experience of lowlines Jesus **suffered** a horrible **death** (which angels do not have to experience; see v 16). After his brief existence in the form of a man, God then **crowned** Jesus **with glory and honor** (borrowing words from Psa 8, quoted in v 7 above; *cf.* Matt 28.18 and Phil 2.9; and Psa 2 is still in the background) to sit on an eternal throne (Heb 1.8).

The author therefore saw these successive lines in Psalm 8.5 ("a little while lower," "crowned with glory and honor," and "appointed him over the works of your hands") as depicting three successive stages in the experience of Jesus, namely 1) his humiliation for a little while in his incarnation, which was followed by 2) his heavenly exaltation, and 3) his absolute reign over everything (which, as the author noted, we do not yet see fully realized).[25] His entrance into the realm of man was the prelude to his exaltation in fulfillment of Psalm 8.

The original readers of Hebrews may not have understood all of this well. It certainly was a part of the gospel story that sounded like nonsense to some (l Cor 1.18ff). Lowliness and exaltation are usually opposites, not complements. If Jesus is the great exalted being the author claims he is,

[25] Maston, "'What is Man?,'" 98.

then why did he live such a lowly life? Why was he subject to inglorious and shameful suffering, and death? The answer is that not only did it fulfill prophecy (Psalm 8), but there was a gracious purpose behind it as well. He came to the world to die because of[26] (**by**) the **grace of God** toward us. All that God has done for our salvation is the gift of his kindness to us (*cf.* Rom 3.24; Eph 2.8). We in no way deserve or earn it. Jesus' humiliation, climaxed in his death, was God's gift (grace) to us. In the Hellenistic world, receiving a gift brought with it the obligation to reciprocate with a fitting response, whether it be another gift in return or, if that was not possible, expressions of gratitude and public praise for the giver.[27] The reception of a gift created a relationship between two people in which the recipient was expected to show loyalty to the giver. Refusal to reciprocate was considered shameful because it communicated an insulting scorn towards the giver and his generosity. The ancient dynamics of grace are a large part of the exhortation of Hebrews. As the original readers were in fact recipients of God's grace (in the lowly death of Jesus), responding to that grace with disloyalty to God would have been counted as an insult to God that rightly drew his anger (see Heb 10.29–31).[28]

The purpose of Jesus' incarnation was that he should **taste death**. The word "taste" is used figuratively here to mean "experience." Jesus experienced death even though death did not keep him (*cf.* Acts 2.24, 31). He died **for everyone**, bearing the sins of the world (*cf.* 9.28). The atoning death of Jesus was universal in its scope and in the forgiveness it offers (*cf.* Acts 10.43; John 3.16).

It may be that the original readers of Hebrews did not grasp all the greatness of Jesus. They knew that Jesus had lived as a man and had died, and they seemed to know quite well that Jesus had been raised from the dead. This much was not apparently in question. However, Jesus' existence as a man and his subjection to death possibly led some to think of Jesus as less than he is. They possibly did not fully appreciate what happened after Jesus was raised from the dead. They knew Jesus in his lowliness but perhaps did not fully know him in his exaltation, and

---

[26] "due to"; dative of cause with *hopōs* preceding, indicating purpose.

[27] See John M. G. Barclay, *Paul and the Gift* (Grand Rapids: Eerdmans, 2015); deSilva, *Honor, Patronage, Kinship, and Purity: Unlocking New Testament Culture,* 2nd ed., 96–124.

[28] deSilva, *Perseverance in Gratitude,* 111: the reminder of the death of Christ with the language of grace serves "to amplify the obligation that such a generous patron lays on the recipients of gifts that cost so dearly."

may well have thought that the former somehow diminished the latter. In God's way of doing things, however, humiliation is the way to exaltation (*cf.* Matt 18.1–4). The author of Hebrews has just shown, from Psalm 8, that in Jesus both lowliness and greatness are combined. He will now explain in more detail how the death of Jesus in no way makes him inferior, nor does it imply that he is less than the reigning king at God's right hand and God's equal as depicted in chapter 1. Jesus' lowly death was, in fact, absolutely necessary to the attainment of his present position as high priest. He will return to the subject of the superiority of the Son, and our need to hear him, in 3.1.

2.10 For it was fitting for him, for whom all things are, and through whom all things are, in leading many sons to glory to perfect the pioneer of their salvation through sufferings.

Why did God find it *necessary* (**fitting**) that Jesus should be humbled and die for every person? That question was, in fact, one of the things that made Christianity seem so strange to many people, since suffering is normally associated with rejection and degradation, not glory.[29] The short answer is that because of God's great love for us, Jesus was humbled so that he might be like us (thus qualifying to serve as our high priest, 4.15 and 5.2), and he died so that he could atone for our sins (9.14). God was working on a plan to bring his children to himself, and that plan required a perfect sacrifice to atone for their sins, and a perfect priest to offer it. In this way, then, it was entirely fitting, according to the demands of unconditional divine love, that God send the Son into the realm of men. That love knew no limits. In other words, God has not asked us to meet him "halfway"; Jesus came all the way to us and entered fully into our own world and our mode of existence in order to accomplish the divine plan. Therefore, rather than see the suffering of Jesus as implying weakness and inferiority, it demonstrates the Father's love for us (*cf.* Rom 5.8). It proves that God has spared nothing in his desire to bring his children home.

The one **for whom** and **through whom all things** exist is, in this context, God. The fact that the author has used this same language of Jesus in 1.2 shows that Jesus is equal to God in his deity. These words not only emphasize the sovereignty of God to do as he wills, but they

[29] Johnson, *Hebrews*, 95.

reveal that the paradox of the cross ("sufferings," below) was part of a larger plan **for** God himself (specifically, to bring his children to himself; see also Eph 1.11, 14). It was also accomplished **through** God in that he was in complete control of it at all times (Acts 4.28). The cross was no accident (Acts 2.23).

God is currently in the process of bringing his **many sons to glory** (through the gospel; *cf.* Rom 8.17; 2 Thes 2.14; 1 Pet 3.18). This suggests that they are on a journey to God from their present location. This adds to the picture of a new exodus that was first hinted at in 2.1–4. In the exodus, God sent Moses into Egypt and, through his leadership, brought Israel out of the enemy kingdom and to himself at Sinai. This becomes a major theme in Hebrews that will be explored by comparison with Israel's journey in chapters 3–4, and the arrival at the heavenly Jerusalem in chapter 12. The growing picture is that we are on a journey to God as well, paralleling in many ways the journey that ancient Israel undertook, and yet with much greater stakes. The word **glory** here echoes Psalm 8.5, quoted in verse 7 above, indicating that God's people, "man" in the psalm, are destined to join the Messiah in his glory (and see 13.20, where a compounded form of the verb here, *agō,* is used of Jesus' resurrection). It is also part of the ancient vocabulary of honor. Through the gospel God invites man to share in his own eternal glory (Rom 5.2). In order to accomplish this beneficent plan for us, God decided to send Jesus to be, for a while, lower than the angels (vv 7, 9; *i.e.,* to become a man) and in that form suffer and die (v 10) on our behalf, thus removing the obstacle (sin) that kept us from him. The picture is that God sent Jesus to get us and bring us to God. Since we live in a realm characterized by suffering and death, Jesus entered fully into it in order to take hold of us.

It is significant that God's people are here called his **sons**. Until now that term has been used in Hebrews in the singular and only of Jesus. But Jesus is not the only son God has (yet he is the only Son, the firstborn). Every person who comes to God in obedient faith in Christ is added to God's spiritual family and becomes a son, or child, of God (Eph 1.5; Gal 4.5). In this sense God has **many sons** and they are brethren to Jesus. The emphasis in this section (2.10–18) is on the solidarity of Christians with Jesus. Jesus came to earth to share our experience in mortality and then lead the way to God and glory. We come to God not only through Jesus, but *with* Jesus as well. Yet we must never think that this makes Christians equal to Jesus in terms of status in God's family. Of all of God's children, Jesus is preeminent and unique and deserves the praise, honor, and gratitude of his brethren.

The verb **perfect** (*teleioō*) here means to make something whole or complete so that it lacks nothing (it does not denote sinlessness). It may seem strange at first to think that the divine Son lacked anything, but this idea lays the groundwork for the upcoming discussion of his work as our high priest. As long as Jesus remained in the form of deity, he lacked the experience as a man that was essential to his work as our representative priest (as 5.2 will discuss). In this sense, then, Jesus needed to be "perfected," he needed to experience what we experience. It is also significant that the verb "perfect" is used in the LXX for the ordination of priests (Exod 29.33; Lev 21.10).[30] Jesus was ordained as high priest only after he lived and died as a man on earth (v 17). This thought will be further developed in chapters 9–10; see the same usage in 7.28. Silva points out[31] that for the author of Hebrews, the word "perfect" is associated with Jesus' exaltation and the fulfillment of God's promises in the messianic age. This parallels the statement in verse 9 ("crowned with glory and honor") and is a concept that echoes throughout the NT (*cf.* Luke 24.26; Rom 8.17; 1 Pet 1.11; 5.1, 10). It also resonates with Hebrews 12.2, where Jesus is called the "perfecter" of faith, having finished the "race" and entered heaven. With this understanding of the word "perfect" in Hebrews, this verse is then saying that Jesus was exalted and appointed to his high priesthood through his **sufferings**. Therefore, his sufferings are not to be viewed as a degrading of Jesus but as the means by which the new, messianic age has come to be. By implication, if Jesus was perfected through sufferings, so it will be for those who join themselves to him.[32] This anticipates the discussion of suffering and faith in chapters 11–12.

Jesus is here called **the pioneer of** our **salvation**. The Greek word (*archēgos*) denotes a leader or one who initiates something, one who is first, who goes before others and makes their passage possible. "Given its full range of meaning, the word designates an individual who opened the way into a new area for others to follow, founded the city in which they dwelt, gave his name to the community, fought its battles and se-

---

[30] Hübner, "*teleioō*," *EDNT* 3:345.

[31] Silva, "Perfection and Eschatology in Hebrews."

[32] Johnson, *Hebrews*, 97.

cured the victory, and then remained as the leader-ruler-hero of his people."[33] Hebrews uses the term again in 12.2, and Peter used the word in Acts 3.15 and again 5.31 along with "savior." A similar term, "forerunner," will appear in Hebrews 6.20. The idea of Jesus as a pioneer further reinforces the idea of God's people on a journey to a heavenly city, one which God has built for them (Heb 11.10, 16) and which is their true residence. On **salvation**, see comments on verse 3 above. Jesus leads us to a fellowship with God wherein we experience salvation (deliverance or rescue) from the guilt and terrible consequence of sin (which is God's wrath; see 10.26ff). Like a pioneer sent from God, he has trod the way ahead and cleared the path for us to follow in his footsteps. The concept is also similar to that of the work of the high priest, who annually took a "journey" from outside the tabernacle to its innermost place, the Holy of Holies, into the presence of God. In fact, one could argue that Israel's journey from Egypt culminated in the entrance of the high priest (who represented the entire nation) into the Most Holy Place in the Tabernacle.[34] Jesus has already reached the divine glory (Rom 8.17; Col 3.4), and we will join him in it if we remain faithful.

At this point we must return to Psalm 8 for a moment (quoted in vv 6–8 above). That the psalm finds its foremost fulfillment in the Messiah does not mean that it has no other aspect to its realization. Man reaches the fullest measure of the glory promised in the psalm in union with Jesus, whom God has exalted to glory ahead of his people (v 9). Those who join themselves to Christ share in his reign over sin and death. Those who have obeyed the gospel are raised up with Jesus and seated with him in the heavenly places (Eph 2.6). To use the terminology of Hebrews, we have become partakers of Christ (3.14) so that we might enter the Most Holy Place (10.19) with him. Jesus, by his sacrificial death, did more than merely open up the way (*cf.* 10.20) that leads us to fellowship with God (*cf.* John 14.2–6) and thus to salvation and eternal glory. In God's plan to bring his children to share in his glory, Jesus is the one who "brings" them there as they join themselves with him, and that required Jesus to take on a form lower than the angels, and to die.

---

[33] J. Julius Scott, Jr., "*Archegos* in the Salvation History of the Epistle to the Hebrews," *JETS* 29 (1986): 47–54, at 52; Gerhard Delling, "*archō ktl*," *TDNT* 1:487–88.

[34] See Michael L. Morales, *Who Shall Ascend the Mountain of the Lord?: A Biblical Theology of the Book of Leviticus*, NSBT 37 (Downers Grove, IL: InterVarsity Press, 2015), esp. 35–38.

2.11 For both the one who sanctifies and those who are sanctified are all from one, for which cause he is not ashamed to call them brothers.

To say that God's sons will enter into glory (v 10) is to say that they will come into the heavenly presence of God. No one, however, may be in the presence of God who has not been cleansed and **sanctified**. The sacrificial death of Jesus foreshadowed by Psalm 8 (above) provides that sanctification. The Jewish Christians who first read Hebrews would have been familiar with this OT concept. To sanctify (Greek *hagiazō*) is to consecrate, to designate something as holy or to make something holy by purifying it and putting it into exclusive service to God.[35] In the OT, things could be purified and consecrated by blood sacrifice (Exod 29.21; Lev 8.15, 30; 16.19; Zeph 1.7; *cf.* Heb 10.10).[36] Similarly, Jesus' sacrificial, atoning death on our behalf cleansed us from the defilement of sin and dedicated us to God (*cf.* 1 Cor 6.11; Heb 9.13; 10.29; 13.12). The sinner appropriates this cleansing and sanctification when he submits to the gospel (Acts 22.16; 1 Cor 6.11). Sanctification is important in Hebrews because of the typology of entering into the presence of God, into the Most Holy Place. Nothing, or no one, unsanctified, can be there (see 2.17).

The author says that **the one who sanctifies** (Jesus) **and those who are sanctified** (God's children, his sons) **are all from one**. Modern English translations have struggled with the precise meaning of this statement. Part of the problem is that the word **one**, Greek *henos,* could be either masculine or neuter. The NASB treats it as masculine and says, "are all from one Father," but a word corresponding to "Father" is not in the Greek text. The RSV treats it as neuter and says, "all have one origin." Neither of these translations should be taken to imply that Jesus is not eternal, as this is clearly not what Hebrews means to say (*cf.* 1.12). The key, it seems, lies in discerning the precise meaning of the word **from** (which translates the Greek preposition *ek*) and conveying it in translation. It can denote a "coming from" in the sense of origin (as when we say "automobiles come *from* factories"), but it can also denote belonging to a particular group or class (as in "he is *from* the Jews").[37] Since the context argues for the similarity between Jesus the sanctifier and those he sancti-

[35] Otto Procksch, "*hagios* in the NT," *TDNT* 1:111.

[36] See Jay Sklar, *Sin, Impurity, Sacrifice, Atonement: The Priestly Conceptions*, Hebrew Bible Monographs 2 (Sheffield: Sheffield Phoenix Press, 2015), esp. 105–59.

[37] BDAG 296.

fied, we may understand the author of Hebrews as saying that Jesus and God's children all belong to the same class or group.[38]

What is the class to which they both belong? There are three possibilities:

1) One interpretation is reflected in the NRSV when it translates "all have one Father" (again taking *henos* as masculine and adding the word "Father"). This interpretation suggests that what Jesus has in common with God's children is that they both have the same Father, God; they both belong to the class of God's sons (v 10).[39]

2) The second possibility is that what unites Jesus and God's children is mortality or existing in the form of humanity; they both belong to the class of humanity, including participation in suffering and death. Some scholars suggest that this interpretation basically means that both Christ and his people are descended from Adam (*i.e.*, Adam is the "one" (man)).[40] Whether Adam was in mind here or not, verses 9, 14 in the context could support this anthropological interpretation. What made Jesus our brother was the fact that he existed in the same fleshly form as us. The fact that Jesus did not *remain* in human form in no way alters the point. While he was here, Jesus shared fully in the same humanity that characterizes us as he fulfilled his mission to bring us to God. For this reason, he can call us his brothers.

3) If we view Jesus and his people as members of the new-creational reality inaugurated by Jesus' death and resurrection, with Jesus being the firstborn among many sons or brothers (Rom 8.29), then aspects of both the interpretations above could be in play. That is, Jesus and his people are all sons of one father, God, who begets them, as people of Abrahamic faithfulness,[41] from the death which they experienced as mortals subject to the ravages of sin. That is, the class or group to which both Jesus and his people belong is the class of those who, because of their faithfulness to God, have been brought out of the slavery of mor-

---

[38] Robert Doran, "The Persuasive Arguments at Play in Heb 2:11 and 7:12," *NovT* 60 (2018): 45–54, at 48–49: On the principle that "things to which the same predicate properly belongs are connected," the language here indicates that "The sanctifier and the sanctified belong to one group."

[39] Moffatt, *Epistle to the Hebrews*, 32; Peterson, *Hebrews*, 92–93.

[40] Grindheim, *Hebrews*, 175.

[41] *Cf.* James Swetnam, *"ex henos* in Hebrews 2,11," *Bib* 88 (2007): 517–25, at 521: "It is their faith-trust which links Jesus and the 'children'."

tality (v 15 below and 12.23) and raised to live in God's new-creational family. This would explain the sudden appearance of a reference to descendants of Abraham in verse 16 below.

Because Jesus existed as a man while he was on the earth, he is **not ashamed** to call those who come to God from among men his brethren. He in no way thinks less of them because of their lowly, mortal condition, because he shared fully in it himself. In a culture that dreaded dishonor among the worst of all possible social situations and in which acceptance by society at large was highly valued, this was a strong statement indeed.[42] Just as Jesus was not so high-minded that he refused to associate with the outcasts of society while he was on the earth (as numerous stories in the gospels show), even now the great and preeminent Son does not stand aloof from the rest of God's children even though they are shamed and marginalized by the world. Instead, he expresses his closeness to them by **calling them** his **brothers**. Family ties were important and strong in ancient Jewish culture, and the sense of having a place within God's spiritual family would have been a great encouragement to Jewish Christians who were possibly considered outcasts from Judaism and rejected from their families. They may have lost earthly families, but they gained a heavenly one (*cf.* Mark 3.33–34). Having Jesus as a brother is a benefit that was not available under the old Law, and it would have encouraged those who were thinking about abandoning Christianity to rethink their decision. Only in Christianity can one call a member of the Godhead "brother." If he is not ashamed to acknowledge his relationship with us, we should have that same boldness to acknowledge our relationship with him (Mark 8.38) and with each other (Heb 10.33–24; 13.3) despite the shame and rejection associated with him (see 12.2). The use of the word "brothers" prepares the reader/hearer for the quotation in the next verse.

2.12 Saying, "I will announce your name to my brothers, in the midst of the assembly I will sing praise to you."

The author of Hebrews returns to the OT to establish the claim he has just made in the preceding verse. He quotes from Psalm 22, a lament that prefigured the sufferings of the Messiah. The plight of the psalmist was a type of the sufferings of the Christ, and what was true figuratively for the

[42] *Cf.* deSilva, "Despising Shame: A Cultural-Anthropological Investigation of the Epistle to the Hebrews," 439–48.

psalmist became true literally for the Messiah (see especially vv 14–18 in the psalm). The part of the psalm that is quoted here was the psalmist's vow of praise that looked forward, by faith, to the time when God had delivered him from his troubles at the hands of his persecutors. Messianically, then, this part of the psalm is about the Messiah *after* his suffering, when God has rescued him from death and vindicated him above his enemies.

While the beginning parts of this psalm are quoted in the NT to show how it was fulfilled in the passion of Jesus (see Matt 27.35, 46), the author has here quoted this latter part of the psalm for a different purpose: to show that the exalted Christ refers to God's people as his **brothers**. The statements about **announcing** God's **name to** Jesus' **brethren** and **singing** God's **praise** in their **midst** use typical hymn language from the psalms to describe praise within the assembly of God's people, thus depicting the solidarity between them all (*cf.* Psalm 22:31; 78:3f), and reinforce the sense of the recipients relationship with the exalted Jesus.[43] It is significant that we see Jesus referring to his disciples as his brothers after he had died and was risen from the dead (John 20.17; Matt 28.10). After he had taken on human form (*cf.* Matt 12.48f) and especially after he had gone through the suffering of death (Heb 2.9) he fully ("perfectly") became a brother to us (Heb 2.11), and after he had been raised from the dead and was on his way to the Father (John 20.17) he became the pioneer who leads his brethren to God (Heb 2.10).

Psalm 22.22 was especially useful to the author here because it identifies, by its use of parallelism, exactly who the brethren of the Messiah are. His brethren are the group (Greek *ekklēsia*, **assembly**) of God's people. The KJV translates the word as "church," and that certainly is its ultimate referent, but translating it as "congregation" (as in most modern translations) or "assembly" preserves the typological background of the quotation. The original group to which the psalmist referred was Israel, and Israel as God's group of people was a type of the messianic Israel, the church. Thus, the psalmist and Israel were types of Christ and the church respectively. Furthermore, in Greek culture the term *ekklēsia* denoted the assembly of citizens who fully belonged to their city and enjoyed the special privileges of "insiders." This aspect of the "assembly" will surface later in the sermon (12.23).

[43] See Bryan R. Dyer, " 'In the Midst of the Assembly I Will Praise You': Hebrews 2.12 and Its Contribution to the Argument of the Epistle," *JSNT* 43 (2021): 523–38.

2.13 And again, "I will trust in him." And again, "Behold, I and the children whom God has given to me."

Another quotation, this one from Isaiah 8.17, also establishes the point that Jesus and God's new people are brethren to each other. Understanding the significance of this quotation requires that we remember the context in which it was spoken. As C. H. Dodd suggested, OT quotations were not isolated proof texts but instead served as pointers to the larger texts from which they were drawn.[44] The original speaker of these words was the prophet Isaiah. In that context God told the prophet not to be afraid of his opponents (vv 11–15). Isaiah's response was that he resolved to put his confidence in the Lord (vv 16–18) and said, "I will wait for the Lord." Our author, following neither the MT nor the LXX, has apparently paraphrased this as **I will trust in him**[45] to emphasize that it was an expression of the prophet's faith and trust that God would indeed do as he promised. The prophet in his faithfulness stands as a type, or model, of the final, greater messenger from God, Jesus (recall 1.1–2), who also put his trust in God (Heb 3.2).[46] While on the earth Jesus lived in perfect confidence that God would deliver, vindicate, and exalt him (*cf.* 1 Pet 2.3).[47] It is exactly at this point that Jesus proves himself to be like his brethren. Mortal men who come to God must do so in a posture of faith in God's word, and often that faith must face situations of opposition and persecution. The following quotation of Isaiah 8.18, **I and the children whom God has given to me**, reminds us that the prophet did not stand alone in his faith toward God. The prophet's family shared the same faith with him. The verb **given**, read messianically, might also suggest that

[44] C. H. Dodd, *According to the Scriptures: The Substructure of New Testament Theology* (London: Fontana Books 1965), 126, 132.

[45] Using a future perfect periphrastic, denoting an imperfective (continuing) condition of believing. The precise nuance of this construction is debated. Pragmatically, it likely communicates the notion of a permanent condition. BDF §352 suggested that "Periphrasis occasionally provides a rhetorically more forceful expression." For the verbal aspect of the perfect, see Campbell, *Verbal Aspect, the Indicative Mood, and Narrative*, 184–99; for the perfect periphrastic, see Stanley E. Porter, *Verbal Aspect in the Greek of the New Testament with Reference to Tense and Mood*, Studies in Biblical Greek 1 (New York: Peter Lang, 2010), 471–74.

[46] See Brian Pate, "Who is Speaking? The Use of Isaiah 8:17–18 in Hebrews 2:13 as a Case Study for Applying the Speech of Key OT Figures to Christ," *JETS* 59 (2016): 731–45.

[47] The early Christians turned to this part of Isaiah often to understand the life of Christ. See J. Cecil McCullough, "Isaiah in Hebrews," in *Isaiah in the New Testament*, ed. Steve Moyise and Maaten J. J. Menken (London: T&T Clark), 2005, 159–73, at 164.

God's people have presently been given over to the Messiah's care. In ancient times the older brother could serve as the guardian and tutor of his younger brothers until they came of age.[48] At any rate, Isaiah and his family prefigured the Messiah and his spiritual family, the church. The fact that the author separated this verse from the following one with a second introductory formula (**and again**) perhaps suggests that he wanted this verse to make its own emphatic point.

This double quotation served at least two important purposes for the author of Hebrews in this context. First, it showed that while he lived on earth, Jesus exhibited the same attitude toward God we must exhibit (faith). Jesus' life on earth by faith in God is another thing that makes him like us. That Jesus is the perfect example of living by faith will reappear in 12.1–3. Second, this quotation showed the relationship between Jesus and God's children. While Jesus is not ashamed to call God's children his brethren (v 11), they are not treated as full equals of Jesus. Instead, they are **children whom God has given** to his Son. While they are brethren to the Son, they are also subject to the Son and under his care.

2.14 Since the children, therefore, have shared in flesh and blood, he himself also shared the same things, that through death he might make powerless the one who has the power of death, that is, the devil,

For Jesus to be completely like us and be our sympathetic high priest, it was necessary (v 10; "it was fitting") for him to share fully in the form in which we exist. The **children shared** flesh and blood, that is, it is something they all held in common. The combination **flesh and blood** is a common Biblical designation for a human being (*cf.* Matt 16.17; Gal 1.16; Eph 6.12), a mortal. Jesus, however, did not have this in common with the people of God in his pre-incarnate state. He therefore **shared the same things** in the sense that he entered into a participation with them, taking on flesh and blood. In that form he died for us, shedding human blood to atone for human sin (see ch 9). There are two different words for sharing in the Greek text here. The children shared (*koinōneō*), and the Son participated (*metechō*). However, as with many other pairs of terms in Hebrews, the differences between the two words for "shared" may not be as sharp as they might first appear to us, and the variation in

[48] Patrick Gray, "Brotherly Love and the High Priest Christology of Hebrews," *JBL* 122 (2003): 335–51, at 340.

terminology may simply be for the purposes of parallelism or rhetorical effect. *Cf.* also on 2.9.

The death of Jesus for our sins involves tremendous ironies. In verse 10 the author noted that Jesus' exaltation (perfection) was possible only through his lowly suffering. Also, **through** his **death** he effectively invalidated the **devil** who wielded the **power of death** over man. The devil, otherwise known as Satan, has been working to turn man against God from the beginning. He oppresses man in many ways (*cf.* Acts 10.38), but ultimately by ensnaring him in sin, which brings death. It is one of the great ironies of the gospel that Jesus' subjection to death became the means by which he conquered both death and the one who wielded death as a weapon against us. That is, Jesus did not overcome our problem of sin and death from without, but by entering into it, as it were, and disabling it from within. What appeared to be Satan's defeat of Jesus turned out to be Jesus' victory over Satan. The reason for this seemingly strange method is that our salvation is not something that God or Jesus does apart from us, outside of us. God does not fix the problem of sin by "snapping his fingers" and making it go away. Instead, he fixed the problem by sending Jesus to disarm sin and death by the power of his own death and resurrection within our realm, and he bids us to follow him in the pattern of his own life (the pattern of the cross), which will lead us to God in glory. While we in no way earn our salvation, we are not passive in it either because we must, of our own will, follow the pioneer (v 10) who has gone before us.

2.15 and deliver those who through fear of death were held in slavery all their lives.

To sin is to enter into a bitter **slavery** under a hard taskmaster (Satan), a slavery from which there is no human remedy and that will result in the slave's death (John 8.34; Rom 6.16). As long as men were condemned as sinners, they had no hope, but only a **fear** of reaping the consequence of sin, which is **death** (Rom 5.12; 6.23; Jam 1.15). In his death, Jesus provided an atonement for our sins, and in his resurrection, Jesus defeated the taskmaster, thus making it possible for the slaves to be set free (**delivered**) into life. *Cf.* the larger, cosmic picture of this same thing in Romans 8.21. Those who respond in obedient faith to God's offer in Jesus no longer live in fear of death but in hope of eternal life (*cf.* Rom 5.12–21).

In the Roman world of the first century, the bitterness of **slavery** was a regular part of the social fabric, and the image of a liberated slave was perhaps more powerful to the original hearers than it is to us today. The use of the term "slavery" here strongly hints at the story of Israel's bondage in Egypt, since it is the same word (Greek *douleias*) used by the LXX to describe Israel's Egyptian bondage (Exod 6.6; 13.3, 14; *etc.*). Just as Moses came to his Israelite brethren in Egypt and led them out of bondage and into a covenant relationship with God at God's mountain, so Jesus took on existence as a man and leads his brethren in a new exodus out of the bondage of sin and into the liberty of a new covenant with God, ending at the heavenly mountain of God (Heb 12.22–24). This further contributes to the author's developing picture of a new exodus from 2.2, 10 (*cf.* Rom 8.29), and naturally suggests a comparison between Jesus and Moses. That Jesus is greater than Moses will be discussed in 3.1–6, and the idea of entering into the new relationship with God will occupy 3.7–4.11. Implicit in the context here is also the idea that the Law of Moses was not the way out of the slavery of death, but the author of Hebrews does not develop that idea explicitly.

2.16 For surely it does not take hold of angels; but it does take hold of the seed of Abraham.

This verse has been variously translated in the modern versions, partly because the subject of the main verb is unexpressed and must be derived from the context (but there is more than one possibility for it), partly due to disagreement about the meaning of the Greek word *epilambanomai* (**take hold**) here, and partly due to various understandings of the identity of "the seed of Abraham." *Epilambanomai* means to take hold of something,[49] but the idea of taking hold of something can itself be a figurative way of describing concern[50] and giving one's help, as when we say that someone took something to heart (this second understanding of the term is reflected in most English translations). We must determine 1) which meaning of the verb is intended here, 2) what the subject of this verb is, and 3) to whom the title "seed of Abraham" refers. Questions 1) and 2) are interrelated. We will begin with 3), since it seems easiest to answer.

[49] This meaning is reflected in the KJV rendering: "For verily he took not on him the nature of angels; but he took on him the seed of Abraham." See the usage in Heb 8.9, where it is said that God took (seized) Israel by the hand.

[50] BDAG 374.

Who is this **seed of Abraham**? It seems that the phrase does *not* mean humanity in general.[51] It is too Jewish and loaded with too much theological significance (Abraham was a man of faith and the recipient of the promise) for that. While one's interpretation of *epilambanomai* will have a bearing on this question, there are three basic options: 1) the seed of Abraham could be taken literally as a reference to the Jewish people, or 2) it could refer figuratively to God's people, a people of Abrahamic faith (*cf.* Gal 3.7; Heb 6.18, where "we" are the heirs of the promise made to Abraham). Even here we still need to decide if the people of faith are believers of all ages[52] or Jesus' brethren, the church (from v 12; this seems the better choice); or 3) it refers to the individual who completely fulfills the "seed" promise (Gen 22.18), Jesus. The second of these interpretations makes the best sense in this context, since the author is emphasizing the humanity of Jesus and his solidarity with God's people on earth. However, Israel (the first interpretation) could work if understood typologically, for it is this same people who became enslaved in Egypt and who needed to be rescued from an existence of living death, and thus they stood as a type of the people of Christ who also needed rescue from the slavery of death.

Concerning the first two problems, four approaches are feasible:

1) The subject of *epilambanomai* is Jesus, and the word means that Jesus did not take hold of (take on himself) the form (KJV "nature") of an angel, but instead took on (took hold of) the form of "the seed of Abraham." While this is the way the verse has often been understood,[53] there are two serious problems with it. First, if this truly is the meaning, it seems unusual that *epilambanomai* should be in the present tense here.[54] Second, there is no evidence that the verb means "to take on the nature of" something.

2) Attridge holds to a literal treatment of the verb here without referring it to Jesus' taking on a human nature. He takes this statement as de-

---

[51] Although Bauckham has defended this approach: "In his exaltation he is not one of the angels, but divine. In his incarnation he is not one of the angels, but human, as he had to be if he came to help humans, not, as 2:16 points out, angels." Richard Bauckham, "Monotheism and Christology in Hebrews 1," in *Early Jewish and Christian Monotheism*, ed. Loren T. Stuckenbruck and Wendy E. S. North (London; New York: T&T Clark, 2004), 167–85, at 170.

[52] Delitzsch, *Epistle to the Hebrews*, 1:138.

[53] See Westcott, *Epistle to the Hebrews*, 55.

[54] The KJV unjustifiably renders it in the English past tense.

noting Christ "taking hold of his followers on the way to glory"[55] in keeping with 2.10. In this way he also explains the present tense of the verb, since this is an action "in which he is yet engaged."[56] This solution is also in line with the fact that the author's words appear to be rooted in Isaiah 41.8–10. In that passage God encouraged Israel by reminding them that they were the descendants (seed) of God's friend, Abraham, and they should not fear because God will strengthen them. God says that he had taken them[57] from the ends of the earth. In support of this approach, the larger context in Isaiah (ch 40) evoked the idea of a new exodus, at which our author has hinted in verse 15 above.[58]

3) The subject of the verb is Jesus, and the word is being used figuratively. In this way the verse is saying that the object of Jesus' incarnation was to demonstrate his great concern for the descendants or "seed" of Abraham (*cf.* Gal 3.7, 29), a concern that was proven by his sacrificial death (v 9). This is how several modern versions have treated it. For example, the NASB renders it "For assuredly he does not give help to angels, but he gives help to the descendant of Abraham." In support of this interpretation is verse 18 where the author speaks of Jesus coming to the aid of others.

4) We may understand death (or fear of it, from the previous verse) as the subject of *epilambanomai* instead of Jesus. Understood this way, our author is saying that death (or fear of it) does not seize angels, but death certainly does take hold of the seed of Abraham.[59] This understanding of the verse has two advantages: it takes *epilambanomai* in its normal sense, and it explains the use of the present tense, for it is declaring what is usually true. When the verse is interpreted this way, it serves to give further explanation for why it was necessary for Christ to partake of flesh and blood to the point of death.[60] That is, Jesus took on flesh and blood (v 14) to deliver his brethren (**the seed of Abraham**) who were seized by the fear of death and enslaved by the devil. In order to free them he had to

---

[55] *Epistle to the Hebrews*, 94; similarly, Koester, *Hebrews*, 232; and Grindheim, *Letter to the Hebrews*, 187: "Jesus takes Abraham's descendants by the hand in order to lead them into this [v 5] future world."

[56] Attridge, *Epistle to the Hebrews*, 94.

[57] LXX *antilambanomai*.

[58] Lane, *Hebrews 1–8*, 63–4; Moffatt, *Epistle to the Hebrews*, 37.

[59] Michael E. Gudorf, "Through a Classical Lens: Hebrews 2:16," *JBL* 119 (2000): 105–108, at 106.

[60] Gudorf, "Through a Classical Lens," 107.

partake in a flesh-and-blood existence with them and die for them. Like Moses (see later in 11.25), he had to enter their situation in order to bring them out of it. This is something no angel could do, because death does not seize the immortal angels (Luke 20.36), so our deliverance from sin, which required a death, could not have been accomplished by them. In this way, then, by becoming lower than the angels (in fulfillment of Psalm 8.5) Jesus did something for us that was better than any angel could do, and it further argues to his superiority over the angels. I have reflected this interpretation in my translation (above), but only provisionally, since interpretation #2 is also attractive.

2.17 For this reason he was obligated to be like his brothers in everything, that he might become a merciful and faithful high priest in the things with reference to God, to atone for the sins of the people.

This verse both summarizes the preceding line of thought[61] and introduces another aspect to it, that of the high priesthood of Jesus (vaguely hinted in 1.13). In fact, it is about this new aspect that the author ultimately wants to say the most in this sermon.

Jesus **was like his brothers** (the ones mentioned in vv 12–13) **in everything**. The Greek phrase is *kata panta*, a common prepositional phrase meaning "in all respects." He became completely human (without loss of deity), including the experience of death. It was his full participation in humanity that enables him to call us his brethren. Since he is God's Son, and we are God's children, Jesus is like our older brother in the family of God (see below). See also comments on verses 11f above.

Jesus also had (**was obligated**) to become like us in order to be our **high priest**. This is the first time in Hebrews where Jesus is described in this way (although the previous quotation from Psa 110 in 1.13 suggested it), and our author is carefully dropping a hint about the main discussion to come in chapters 7–10. Another such hint will come in 3.1. The high priest in Israel was, of course, the chief religious figure in the nation, the man who represented the nation on the Day of Atonement when he offered sacrifices for the sins of the people. To the ancient Jews, priesthood meant at least two things: 1) the avenue of access to God: the high priest went ahead of the people (in this sense, like a pioneer) into God's presence, and

[61] Kistemaker (*Psalm Citations*, 131) notes that this verse neatly summarizes the sermon's uses of Psa 8, Psa 110, and Psa 40.

2) the security of the people he served by virtue of his accomplishing the rites that God demanded.[62] Both will become major topics in the author's discussion, and both are hinted at here. For now, the author explicitly calls attention to another feature of the high priest: the fact that he was one of the people he represented. God selected the high priest from among his people, and thus for Jesus to be our new high priest he had to have occupied a place among us. He had to take on human form (see 2.11) in order to be the mediator and representative of humans before God. The high priest could not represent a people of which he himself was not a member, because representation is possible only when the representative shares the qualities of those he symbolizes. It was proper, therefore, that Jesus become **like** us (**his brothers**) in taking on humanity fully (**in everything**), including its testing and death. We should not overlook the connection between the concepts of Jesus as our high priest and Jesus as our brother. The two roles are closely related and have in common a sense of care and sympathy. In the Hellenistic world, the ideal older brother within a family was expected to be the caretaker of his younger siblings, he was expected not to consider himself above helping the younger brothers, he was their defender and the one who made sure they got their rightful share of the inheritance.[63] Jesus' taking on the role of our high priest is therefore part of what he does out of brotherly love for us.

The author here notes two essential qualities of the high priest,[64] foreshadowing more developed discussions to come (3.1–4.14 and 4.15–5.10). First, he had to be **merciful**, that is, sympathetic or compassionate. The high priest's job was to intercede for his brethren before God. He had to know their problems intimately before he could stand as their advocate. Accordingly, it was necessary for Jesus to take on human form completely so that he might know intimately all that we experience. Second, the high priest had to be **faithful**. The Greek adjective *pistos* can be used in a passive sense to mean "trustworthy," "reliable," or "dependable" and in that sense "loyal," or it can be used in an active sense to mean "believing"

[62] Harold S. Songer, "A Superior Priesthood: Hebrews 4:14–7:28," *RevExp* 82 (1985): 345–59.

[63] Gray, "Brotherly Love and the High Priest Christology of Hebrews."

[64] W. Horbury ("The Aaronic Priesthood in the Epistle to the Hebrews," *JSNT* 19 (1983): 43–71) demonstrates that, along with an emphasis on the ethical character of priests, "the compassion of the high priest, and his solidarity with mankind, which come to expression with particular force in Hebrews, are Pentateuchal themes which received comparable development in other post-biblical sources" (65).

or trusting in God's word. Both could be said of Jesus; the two ideas are not exclusive.[65] In this context it has the sense of "accomplishing all that was required," which included his death, and which was due to trusting in God's will for him. That this sacrificial sense of Jesus' faithfulness is in view here is confirmed by the fact that the phrase "**the things with reference to** (or pertaining to) **God**" has a long history in the Greek language of referring to religious duties or rites of worship.[66] The fact that Jesus accomplished God's will and did not quit foreshadows an important element in the author's exhortation later. Jesus is also a reliable high priest in contrast to the mortal high priests of the old system, as 7.23–25 will discuss.

God's purpose in giving Israel a high priesthood was **to atone for** his **people's sins** on the annual Day of Atonement, and this is what Jesus has done in fulfillment of that paradigm. The term *hilaskomai* has been translated in some English versions as "make expiation," and in others as "propitiate." Expiation technically describes the cancellation of guilt, whereas propitiation describes the turning away of God's wrath. "To atone" captures both aspects.[67] The context here suggests a general sense of the term, not a specific one, as Jesus has been most recently described as "making purification for sins" (1.3) and sanctifying us (2.11). The author's discussion of the work of Christ emphasizes its cleansing effect (9.11–4; 10.19–22) because the goal of everything is to enter the Most Holy presence of God. The mention of atonement hints at the important discussion of the atoning death of Jesus in chapters 9–10, which was only possible if Jesus took on human form. His incarnation, far from being something that detracts from Jesus' greatness, is the very thing that makes our relationship with God viable.

2.18 For since he was tempted by what he suffered, he is able to come to the aid of those who are tempted.

This verse picks up on the idea of "merciful" in the preceding verse. Jesus' sharing in flesh and blood with those he came to save means that he can sympathize with them. The difficulty here is determining the proper

[65] See Todd D. Still, "*Christos* as *Pistos*: The Faith(fulness) of Jesus in the Epistle to the Hebrews," *CBQ* 69 (2007): 746–55.

[66] Andrie du Toit, "*ta pros ton theon* in Romans and Hebrews: Towards Understanding an Enigmatic Phrase," *ZNW* 101 (2010): 241–51.

[67] Peterson, *Hebrews*, 99.

sense of the Greek verb *peirazō*, which can mean "to test" or "to tempt." While the two ideas are related, they are not the same things. So, is the verse describing the testing of Jesus, or his temptation? The scales might tip toward "tempt" because the author was emphasizing the continuity between the experience of Jesus and that of the recipients of Hebrews. Since they were considering quitting because of ongoing hostility and shame (*cf.* 12.2–3), and Hebrews consistently identifies quitting as sin, the idea here is that the readers' temptation to quit under difficult circumstances was experienced by Jesus as well during his sufferings (see Heb 4.15). It is not a sin to be tempted, nor does it detract from the greatness of Jesus that he could be. It is sin to give in to a temptation to forsake the way of faith in God (something Jesus never did; see comments on 4.15). As Erickson puts it, in Jesus' case sin was possible but not actual.[68]

The word **suffered** is capable of two different meanings. It can mean to experience something (without necessarily suggesting that it is bad). If this meaning is operative here, then our author is simply saying that Jesus is able to represent us perfectly before God because he experienced the very same kinds of human difficulties as his brethren. Jesus was **tempted** while he was on this earth with the same kinds of temptations we face (Heb 4.15). However, **suffer** can also have a negative sense, meaning to experience pain and hardship. Since the context has mentioned Jesus' death and emphasizes the solidarity between Jesus and God's people who were subject to fear of death and slavery (v 16) and who, in this case, were experiencing social rejection, it seems that this second meaning is intended here. The point is that although Jesus was **tempted by** his sufferings with the thought of giving up, he did not allow the pain and rejection he suffered to drive him to quit. With such experience, Jesus is **able to come to the aid of** his brethren (vv 11–13) who face the same kind of temptation from the same kind of circumstances. The opposition Jesus faced tested his resolve and his trust in the Father's plan and promises. But he never quit. Instead, he blazed a trail of faith that leads to the Father and to glory, and he bids us to follow him in it. This serves as a fitting introduction to the second exhortation, or warning passage, of the epistle (3.1–4.13).

---

[68] Millard J. Erickson, *Christian Theology*, 3rd ed. (Grand Rapids: Baker Academic, 2013), 655–58.

HEBREWS 3

Chapter 1 emphasized that Jesus is the Son in whom God has spoken in a final way. Chapter 2 presented an exhortation to hear the word of the exalted Son and then discussed the incarnation, or lowliness, of the Son. As the second main section of the book opens, the author builds upon his most recent subject, the earthly life of Jesus. From this the author now wishes to emphasize a particular aspect of that life: Jesus' faithfulness (introduced in 2.17), which serves as an example and encouragement to the readers (3.1–6). This will lead to another exhortation to hear the word God has spoken in his Son (3.7–19).

3.1 Wherefore, holy brothers, sharers in a heavenly calling, consider the apostle and high priest of our confession, Jesus,

All Christians are **holy** people, or saints, by calling (*cf.* 1 Cor 6.2, 5). It behooves us to live accordingly. Referring to the readers as **brothers** reminded them of the fact that they were part of a brotherhood, a family, one that included Jesus himself (2.11ff). Christians are also **sharers** of **a heavenly calling**. Our calling, or invitation, from God is heavenly both in the sense that it originates from heaven (1 Pet 1.12) and in the sense that it calls us to heaven, to where God is bringing many sons to glory (2.10). God calls all people through the gospel (2 Thes 2.14) to come and enter his spiritual family with his Son. Those who respond positively, in obedient faith, become his spiritual sons (Rom 1.7; 1 Cor 1.2), and they comprise a heavenly, spiritual association. Eventually they will follow Jesus to the heavenly city and be in God's presence with him. See also 12.22f.

The author wanted his hearers to **consider** (which means to give careful notice, contemplation, and reflection; see also 12.3), their brother **Jesus**, who is here described with two significant terms. First, he is the **apostle** of our confession. Only Hebrews uses this term in reference to Jesus. An apostle is one who is sent out by one in authority to accomplish a commissioned task in the sender's name.[1] Jesus is an apostle in that he was sent from God (*cf.* John 4.34; 5.30; *etc.*) to execute the divine plan of salvation, a task at which he succeeded (John 17.4). As the author pointed out in 2.10, he was sent in order to retrieve us and bring us to God (if we will go). Second, he is the **high priest** of our confession, a description first mentioned in 2.17. The author continues to use this terminology to prepare his readers for the major discussion later, while he lays the groundwork for it in the present text. The job of the high priest was centered in offering atoning sacrifices for God's people on the Day of Atonement in order to make continued fellowship possible between them and God. Jesus came from God (as an apostle) to bring us to God (as a high priest). How he brought us to God will be discussed in chapters 7–10. Both roles, however, have in common the idea of representation. As apostle, Jesus represents God to us, and as high priest, he represents us to God.[2]

The word **confession** denotes more than a simple acknowledgment. The term (Greek *homologia*) denotes "a binding expression of obligation and commitment."[3] To confess, in the Biblical sense, is to acknowledge "in such a way that it is followed by definite resolve and action, by ready attachment to a cause."[4] To say that Jesus is the object of our confession means that we are committed to him who came from God and who brings us to God. Being a Christian involves confessing Jesus as Lord (Rom 10.9) in the sense of openly recognizing and accepting him and his authority (Matt 10.32). The original readers of Hebrews were, it appears, becoming reluctant to commit to him, or confess him, any longer. The author therefore reminded them that they had made a commitment which must be kept. He will make this appeal more plainly in 4.14 and 10.23.

3.2 who was faithful to the one who appointed him, as Moses also was faithful in all his house.

The chief characteristic of Jesus the author here wishes to emphasize is his faithfulness. Exactly what is meant by **faithful**? The word (Greek *pistos*)

---

[1] Karl Heinrich Rengstorf, "*apostellō ktl*," *TDNT* 1:398–400.

[2] Bruce, *Epistle to the Hebrews*, 55. James Swetnam ("*ho apostolos* in Hebrews 3.1," *Bib* 89 (2008): 252–62) has proposed that the author is here establishing the comparison with Moses that becomes explicit in the following verses, as Jesus is an apostle in the sense that he, like Moses, was sent to announce the name of God.

[3] Lane, *Hebrews 1–8*, 75.

[4] Otto Michel, "*homologeō ktl*," *TDNT* 5:200.

can be used in a passive sense to mean trustworthy, reliable, or dependable, or it can be used in an active sense to mean believing or trusting in God's word and following it explicitly. Which is meant here? The two are so closely intertwined that it may not be possible to separate them so neatly. The point is that Jesus never deviated from the commission God had given to him, even when it meant suffering. He accomplished this by his trust in God's plan, so the active and passive senses stand in a kind of cause-and-effect relationship. However, the active sense seems more in view here (as in 2.17). In Hebrews, Jesus is consistently presented, among other things, as the greatest example of faithfulness to God, along with the endurance that faithfulness generates (see 12.2f).[5] The author has already told us in 2.13 that the Messiah trusts in God, according to Isaiah 8.

The word **appointed** is the Greek verb *poieō*, which has a broad semantic range. Here it simply means that God put Jesus in the position he occupied, a fact also true of Moses (1 Sam 12.6). That Jesus was appointed high priest by God will be discussed again in 5.4–10. All Jesus did in executing the plan of salvation was done in perfect accord with the will of God who appointed and sent him. We must not think that Jesus was in any way reluctant to accept the position God willed for him, for his will and the Father's are ever one (John 4:34; 5:30; 6:38). It may be that 1 Samuel 2.35 is in the background here: "But I will raise up for Myself a faithful priest who will do according to what is in My heart and in My soul; and I will build him an enduring house, and he will walk before My anointed always" (NASB).[6]

The author here introduces a comparison between Jesus and **Moses**. The previous hints of God's people on an exodus-like journey that ends in the presence of God (2.2, 10, 15) naturally invited the comparison. Moses was the one who led Israel out of Egypt, went up to the presence of God on Sinai, the one to whom God gave the Law to give to the people, and a man with whom God spoke "face to face" (Exod 33.11). He too was an "apostle" of God, having been sent by God to Pharaoh and to Israel, and Moses also served as an intercessor for Israel (*cf.* Exod 32.11ff; Num 14.13ff).[7] To Jews he was one of the greatest figures in Judaism, rivaled only by the likes of Abraham and Elijah. The author has already shown

---

[5] See Still, "*Christos* as *Pistos*."

[6] Lane, *Hebrews 1–8*, 76.

[7] Bruce, *Epistle to the Hebrews*, 56.

that Jesus is greater than the angels through whom that old Law was delivered (1.1ff). Now he will show that Jesus is also greater than Moses.

Moses was **faithful in all his house**, a statement that alludes quite clearly to Numbers 12.7. The context for the statement was the rebellion of Miriam and Aaron, when they complained about the preeminence of Moses among the leaders of Israel. In response to this complaint God commended the faithfulness of Moses. The full statement was: "Hear now my words: If there is a prophet among you, I, the Lord, shall make myself known to him in a vision. I shall speak with him in a dream. Not so with my servant Moses. He is faithful in all my household; with him I speak mouth to mouth, even openly, and not in dark sayings, and he beholds the form of the Lord. Why then were you not afraid to speak against my servant, against Moses?" (Num 12.6–8 NASB). The **house** over which Moses was faithful was God's house, that is, God's family, Israel (who proved to be notoriously unfaithful, as our author will show below). The author of Hebrews did not depreciate the role and status of Moses in the old system (the fact that he compares Moses to Jesus actually exalts Moses[8]). Instead, he saw that Moses prefigured one who was even greater.

3.3 For he[9] has been considered worthy of more glory than Moses, to the degree that the builder has more honor than the house.

As great as **Moses** was, Jesus is greater. It would have been hard for many Jews to understand how Jesus, who died such an ignominious death, could be said to be greater than one of the founding figures of Judaism. The author thus argues for his case when he says that Jesus is **worthy of more glory** (honor) than Moses in the same way that the builder of a house is greater than the house itself. Our author does not say that Jesus is the builder, although passages such as Matthew 16.18 come to mind. It is instead an analogy based on the imagery of a "house"

---

[8] Attridge, *Hebrews*, 105.

[9] "He" translates the demonstrative pronoun *houtos*, which can be used as an emphatic personal pronoun (Herbert Weir Smyth, *Greek Grammar*, rev. ed. (Cambridge: Harvard University Press, 1956), 308). *Houtos* typically denotes what is thematic in the context. Here it identifies Jesus as the thematic subject in contrast to Moses. Stephen H. Levinsohn, "Towards a Unified Linguistic Description of *houtos* and *ekeinos*," in *The Linguist as Pedagogue: Trends in the Teaching and Linguistic Analysis of the Greek New Testament*, ed. Stanley E. Porter and Matthew Brook O'Donnell (Sheffield: Sheffield Phoenix Press, 2009), 204–16, at 211.

(from v 2). The author does not present Jesus and Moses as opposites, as some mistakenly thought Jesus to teach (*cf.* Matt 5.17), nor does he denigrate Moses in order to exalt Jesus. Instead, the focus is on a similarity between them. Both Moses and Jesus are associated with God's house, and both of them were faithful, yet one of them (Jesus) in a much greater role. The **builder** of a house **has more honor than the house** he builds, that is, the creator is greater than the thing he creates. The two are related, but one is definitely greater than the other. In this same way Jesus has more honor than Moses.[10] *Cf.* a similar comparison and contrast between Jesus and Aaron in 5.1ff.

3.4 For every house is built by someone, but the one who built all things is God.

The purpose of this remark is to sharpen the contrast begun in verse 3. The analogy associates Jesus with a builder (v 3), and a builder with **God** (v 4; *cf.* 1.2) and thus portrays Jesus as functioning at the divine level,[11] something that could not be said of Moses.[12] Jesus is a builder, or creator, in the same way that God is, therefore he is greater than Moses in the same way that God is greater than **all things**. Recall 1.3, 10. *Cf.* Matthew 16.18, Ephesians 2.22 and John 1.1ff. Jesus is the one who "built" (created) the new situation (*i.e.*, he has built God's new house, v 6) in which we have access to God. Furthermore, in the OT, God's creative nature also means that he delivers the creation from chaos.[13] This verse is not, then, simply parenthetical. Instead, it is the climax of the comparison. It further argues for the greater status of Jesus and also reminds us that the particular **house** of which the author here speaks is God's house.

3.5 And "Moses was faithful in all his house as a servant" as a testimony of the things that would be spoken later,

---

[10] See Brett R. Scott, "Jesus' Superiority Over Moses in Hebrews 3:1–6," *BibSac* 155 (1998): 201–10. He notes (202) that favorable comparison (Greek *sunkrisis*) was an ancient rhetorical device.

[11] The word "God" here lacks the definite article, so in the Greek the idea of deity is prominent.

[12] James Girdwood and Peter Verkruyse, *Hebrews,* College Press NIV Commentary (Joplin: College Press, 1997), 115.

[13] See Peter E. Enns, "Creation and Re-Creation: Psalm 95 and Its Interpretation in Hebrews 3:1–4:13," *WTJ* 55 (1993): 255–80. See also the Excursus: The Sabbath Rest in this commentary.

The verse begins with another strong allusion to Numbers 12.7 (*cf.* v 2 above), which specifies exactly how Moses is not as great as Christ. Again, our author in no way deprecated **Moses**, but at the same time he wished to correct the view common in some Jewish circles that there was no greater person than Moses.[14] While it is true that Moses was a **faithful** (see comments on v 2) member of God's **house** (spiritual family), the main point is that, for all his greatness, Moses was a servant in God's house. The Greek word for **servant** used here (*therapōn*) lacks the pejorative connotations usually associated with the idea of slavery in that it denotes one who serves willingly.[15] The word is often used of service in a religious (ritual) setting.[16] However, since the author already found the word in LXX of Numbers 12.7, perhaps not too much should be made of it. The more common word for servant (*doulos*) is applied to Moses in 2 Kings 18.12. While it could be argued that Moses was a good and faithful servant worthy of honor, the fact remains that he was never more than a servant.

Moses' faithful service, and God's explicit approval of it, was a testimony of the things that **would be spoken** later.[17] His part in the plan of salvation was to point ahead to Christ. The word **testimony** denotes a legal declaration presented as truth. It is true that Moses also testified by his words about one who was coming after himself (Deut 18.15). That, however, is not exactly the point here. Instead, the author is saying that Moses *himself* was a "testimony" about something that would be further explained later. That is, Moses, in his role in the house of God, was a type of Christ who would stand in a similar, yet even greater, role in the house of God. See also 11.24ff. In typological relationships, the antitype (the fulfillment) is always greater than the type. Of course, it is also true that Moses, in his role as prophet, was a type of Jesus who came and delivered God's final message to the new Israel. However, the author of Hebrews does not explore that aspect of the typology, possibly to avoid the implication that Jesus was simply a prophet on the same level as Moses.

The things that would be spoken later could refer to things that Moses himself spoke concerning Christ, but it is better to understand it as referring to the things God would later (*i.e.* after Moses' time) speak in,

[14] *Cf. m. Soṭah* 1:9: "We have none so great as Moses."

[15] Thayer, *Greek-English Lexicon,* 138.

[16] BDAG 453.

[17] Future passive participle, but the future inherently carries with it a sense of potential action. The speaking is understood as future from the perspective of Moses.

and about, his Son (Heb 1.1–2). What was future for Moses has now become "Today" (see 3.5ff below) for Christians.[18] Moses was therefore a servant whose position in God's family was itself a testimony, or type, of the things that would later be said about Jesus.

This statement about Moses' role in the larger scheme of things is a good example of the insight of the early Christians into the true nature of those things which were done in divine history before the coming of Christ. The patriarchs, Law, and prophets testified, in various ways, about things that would be fulfilled in Christ (*cf.* Rom 3.21). Their role as witnesses makes acceptance of Jesus all the more crucial (*cf.* John 5.46). The early Christians learned (from Jesus himself, Luke 24.27, 44) to see the things that came before Christ not simply as history, but as prophecy. This insight is one of the keys to understanding Hebrews' use of the OT.

3.6 but Christ was faithful as a son over his house, whose house we are, if we hold fast the boldness and the boasting of our hope.[19]

In order to sharpen the distinction between Moses and Jesus, our author refers to Jesus here as **Christ** for the first time in the epistle. Whereas the name Jesus tends to emphasize his humanity and humility, the title Christ often emphasizes his deity and exaltation.

There are two important distinctions made between Christ and Moses in this verse. The first is an important distinction in the prepositions the author uses to describe the relationship of Moses and Jesus to God's house. While both figures were **faithful** (see on v 2 above), Moses was *in* God's house (v 5), but Jesus is **over** God's house. That is, although Jesus is our brother (1.11ff), he is not just another member of God's family. He is the one who has been exalted to a position of authority over it (ch 1; see also 10.21).[20] This relates directly to the second distinction: Moses was a

[18] Ellingworth, *Epistle to the Hebrews*, 208.

[19] The words "firm until the end" are lacking in some of the oldest copies of Hebrews, but the editors of most modern English translations have felt enough confidence in their genuineness to include them in the text. The phrase is not absolutely crucial to the exhortation and simply emphasizes the idea of "holding fast." The words are attested in the text in 3.14. Their appearance here may have been due to the fact that the same verb ("hold fast") is used in both places, and a scribe familiar with 3.14, upon seeing the verb "hold fast," may have (unconsciously?) put these words in this place.

[20] The description of Jesus as over God's house maybe rooted in OT language of stewardship. See Scott C. Layton, "Christ Over His House (Hebrews 3.6) and Hebrew *asher ul-habaylt'*," *NTS* 37 (1991): 473–77.

servant; Jesus is God's **Son**—a title of preeminence emphasized in chapter 1 (see comments on 1.2). It was a common fact in ancient society that while the father was the unquestioned ruler of the house, among the subordinates in the household the father's firstborn son had a greater status than any servant (*cf.* John 8.35), even though the son was expected to serve the father. Upon maturity the son could become the ruler and heir of all that belonged to his father. Such is the imagery behind the argument here (*cf.* the same metaphor in Gal 3.23–4.7). God has placed his Son Jesus over his new house (family), the church. As great as he was, Moses never attained such a status in God's house. The point of this whole Moses-Christ comparison is, of course, to assert again the greater state of things in Jesus. It serves the same purpose as the Christ-angels contrast in chapter 1. Furthermore, it is to be understood that Jesus' faithfulness as the Son entailed his suffering and death (ch 2) according to the Father's great plan.

Here the author makes explicit the fact that Christians are God's house or family. **We** (Christians) **are** God's family (**house**), having been added by God through faith. *Cf.* 1 Timothy 3.15; 1 John 3.1–2. However, children may scorn their place in the father's house and leave it, as in the parable of the prodigal son (Luke 15.11–24). It is against such rebellion and renunciation on the part of the first readers that our author directed this exhortation. Christians have all the privileges associated with being part of God's family only **if** they remain at home, so to speak, in a right (faithful) relationship with the father. In order to receive all the benefits coming to God's children, we must be faithful children just as Christ proved himself to be faithful.

The exhortation to faithfulness is further specified as **holding fast the boldness and the boasting of our hope**. The term **hold fast** (Greek *katechō*) basically means, in its various usages, to hold onto something, to keep it in its place. It is used of keeping a secret, holding one's temper, holding a ship on course (recall 2.1), or staying true to God's word. Here the object is twofold. First, we must hold on to our **boldness**. The Greek word here, *parrēsia*, is difficult to render accurately in English translation. It denotes an openness, especially in speech, that is the product of courage. Although it is translated as "boldness," it should not be confused with a foolish kind of audacity or rudeness. In the LXX, with which our author was well acquainted, the word came to denote a confidence in God, and the author of Hebrews uses the term to denote the assurance Christians have of their access to God.[21] In a way, boldness is the opposite of being ashamed or timid (*cf.* 2 Tim 1.7–8). The bold Christian lives his life openly, not hiding his identity out of fear or shame. For the author of Hebrews, one of the marks of a Christian is that he is confident that he has fellowship with God, and this confidence translates into a way of living in the world. The bold Christian demonstrates his faith even in the face of being rejected for it. Second, we must hold on to **the boasting of our hope**. "Boasting" here is similar to "boldness." There is a worldly kind of boasting (in oneself) that is arrogant, but there is also a spiritual and godly kind of boasting, a justifiable pride (in the good sense) and rejoicing not in self, but in what God has done for us (*cf.* Rom 15.17; 1 Cor 1.31).[22] In the Bible, this boasting always involves the "paradox that man can truly boast only when he looks away from himself to God's acts."[23] This latter kind of boasting carries with it a sense of appreciation and gladness. The person who boasts in this way is happy (or as we would say in a similar English idiom, "proud") to be a member of God's family in the sense that he is not ashamed and, even more, he is positively joyous in it. God has given us the **hope** of eternal life (having taken away the fear of death, 2.14–15). Together, these two terms encouraged these Jewish Christians who were facing persecution not to hide who they were or feel as if they were lesser people for being Christians. Instead, they were to be proud of who they were and live like it, in a way that was open, public, and unashamed.

3.7 Therefore, just as the Holy Spirit says, "Today if you will hear his voice,

The comparison with Moses in the preceding section naturally suggests that Christ is leading God's people in a new exodus. If Christ is a greater figure than Moses, then he is leading a greater exodus to a greater destination, the ultimate promised land, the heavenly Jerusalem (12.22–24), as 2.2, 4, 10, and 15 suggested. The quotation here is from the LXX of Psalm 95.7–11[24] and begins the second "warning passage" in the sermon and

[21] H. Balz, "*parrēsia* and *parrēsiazomai*," *EDNT* 3:45–47.

[22] *Cf.* Heinrich Schlier, "*parrēsia, parrēsiazomai*," *TDNT* 5:881–84.

[23] Rudolf Bultmann, "*kauchaomai ktl*," *TDNT* 3:650.

[24] But the psalm is, itself, drawing upon the narrative in Num 14: "my voice" (Num 14.22) and "his voice" (Psa 95.7), "wilderness" (Num 14.22, 29 , 32, 33; Psa 95.8), "put me to the test" (Num 14.22) and "testing" (Psa 95.9), and the numbered generation (Num 14.29) and "this generation" (Psa 95.10).

establishes the point just mentioned in verse 6, that perseverance in faith is required for fellowship God. The verses quoted from the psalm are themselves a warning passage, a sermon as it were,[25] that surveys the attitude of the Israelites who came out of Egypt in the exodus. Those who followed Moses did not attain God's rest in the land because they did not hold fast, they did not persevere through the trials of the wilderness. Christians have an even greater leader, a pioneer (2.10) who is bringing us out of spiritual captivity to sin and death, and we must make sure that we do not repeat the mistake of the ancient Israelites.[26] We must endure in faith until the journey's end in the presence of God.

Here the passage is attributed to the **Holy Spirit**, emphasizing that it is the word of deity, but it is also attributed to David in 4.7. The Holy Spirit moved the human authors so that what they wrote was the word of God (*cf.* 2 Pet 1.21; 2 Tim 3.16). Even more, introducing the quotation as being the words of the Spirit is the author's way of emphasizing that this text speaks in a direct way to the people of the messianic age, the people who have received God's Spirit.[27] This is borne out also by the way the quotation begins. The word **today** is not a generic reference to a timeless "now," but specifically recalls the same word from Psalm 2.7 (quoted in Heb 1.5). The "today" of Psalm 2 is the time when God raised his Son and made him ruler over the nations. That is, "today" is the time that began with Jesus' resurrection, the time of the Messiah's reign, the messianic age, or "these last days" (1:2). Our author then used that same understanding of "today" to read Psalm 95. This results in a reading of Psalm 95.7–11 that understands it to be speaking to the people of the messianic time. This is an example of the Jewish exegetical method of *gezerah shawah,* in which two verses are read together because they share common terminology (see Introduction). Further support for this messianic reading is found in the fact that the text obviously addresses a later generation whose fathers (ancestors; see 1.1) did not trust in God.

---

[25] Boyarin, "Midrash in Hebrews / Hebrews as Midrash," 25.

[26] Moffitt, *Exodus in Hebrews*, 153: "the larger narrative arc of the exodus tradition provides much of the underlying plotline the author uses to shape and inform the imagination of his readers, whom he exhorts not to waver in their confession about Jesus."

[27] Martin Emmrich, "*Pneuma* in Hebrews: Prophet and Interpreter," *WTJ* 63 (2002): 55–71; Pierce, *Divine Discourse in the Epistle to the Hebrews*, 2: In Hebrews, "The Father and Son speak primarily to each other. The Spirit speaks to the community."

Psalm 95 is famous for its drastic change in tone starting in the last line of verse 7 (the point at which our author begins his quotation). The first part of the psalm celebrates the greatness of God as savior of his people and enjoins the hearer to give God the worship due him. The psalm then radically shifts to a warning not to repeat the characteristic mistake of the generation of Israelites that came out of Egypt (faithlessness), following themes from Deuteronomy.[28] God's power will either save or destroy, depending upon one's response to him (*cf.* Matt 3.11–12; Rom 11.22). Two things unite the two parts of the psalm and connect the wilderness generation of Israelites to another, later generation: 1) both parts of the psalm refer to creation. There is the original cosmic creation in the first part, and the creation of Israel climaxed in the exodus in the second part.[29] It is addressed, however, ultimately to the eschatological Israel, the church, the new house of God ("whose house we are" v 6) built by Jesus the Messiah (v 4). This creation motif, and its realization in the work of Jesus, also contributes to the interpretation that it speaks ultimately about the Messiah's people (2.13), the church. 2) In both scenarios, a rest with God was available, but rejected.[30]

The psalm's exhortation is based on the condition that one **will hear** what God has to say (**his voice**).[31] The opening message of Hebrews—that God has spoken his greatest message through his Son (1.1–2), and it is important that we hear it (2.1) and hold on to it—is thus seen to be grounded in the words of Psalm 95. In the Bible, true hearing consists of receptivity and acceptance, and thus is nearly synonymous with faith. It is characteristic of the stubborn sinner that he will not hear God's word (Isa 65.12; Jer 5.21; 7.13; Ezek 12.2; Zech 7.12). The exodus generation of Israel "heard" in a superficial sense, but did not trust what they heard. "Today" in the psalm, then, is not just the time of the Messiah, it is also supposed to be the time of hearing, the time of obedience.[32] The rabbis

---

[28] See David Allen, "More Than Just Numbers: Deuteronomic Influence in Hebrews 3:7–4:11," *TynBul* 58 (2007): 129–49. The idea of two ways or two options in life is Deuteronomic; "as I swore" in Psa 95.11 echoes Deut 2.14 "as the Lord had sworn to them"; 'voice" in Psa 95.7 echoes Deut 4.33, 5.24, 26.17, *et al*; "forty years" in Psa 95.10 echoes Deut 8.2.

[29] See Enns, "Creation and Re-Creation."

[30] See the Excursus: The Sabbath Rest.

[31] Pierce notes that "Throughout the text of Hebrews, the author never portrays scripture as written, but instead as heard or spoken." (Pierce, *Divine Discourse in the Epistle to the Hebrews*, 33). For the author of Hebrews, Scripture is a living voice.

[32] Boyarin, "Midrash in Hebrews / Hebrews as Midrash," 24.

connected "Today" with repentance as well.[33] A response of faith brings the experience of God's power to save, but a response of faithlessness brings an experience of God's power in destruction. The original readers of Hebrews were contemplating abandoning Christianity. Our author used this text to warn them that such a move would be the same kind of faithlessness that characterized the exodus generation of Israelites and would just as surely bring the destructive wrath of God upon them.

3.8 do not harden your hearts, as in the rebellion, as in the day of trial in the wilderness

The problem with that generation was that they **hardened** their **hearts**. In the Bible, the heart is regularly credited with thinking[34] and therefore is often set in parallel with one's mind.[35] It is also the source of feeling,[36] or can refer to one's inner being.[37] It is the part of a person that determines one's morality and conduct.[38] Because of the fluidity of the concept, the heart could be understood as involved in hearing as well (Deut 29.4; Isa 6.10; Matt 13.15), as Psalm 95.7–8 attests. The hard heart is a mind or attitude that is unreceptive to the word of God, a heart that will not listen (Pharaoh is the classic example, Exod 8.15). It is **hard** in the sense of impervious. God's word cannot get inside it because the hearer refuses to accept it (Deut 29.4; Zech 7.11f). It is a Biblical way of speaking of a stubborn refusal to trust in what God says. Our author will return to this problem in 6.1–8.

The LXX text of this psalm (which our author has quoted) differs from the MT in one basic way. Where the MT refers to Meribah and Massah, the LXX has interpreted these names as **rebellion** (Greek *parapikrasmos*) and **trial** (Greek *peirasmos*) respectively.[39] Meribah (which means "strife")

[33] David Flusser, "Today If You Will Listen to His Voice: Creative Jewish Exegesis in Hebrews 3–4," in *Creative Biblical Exegesis: Christian and Jewish Hermeneutics through the Centuries*, ed. Benjamin Uffenheimer and Henning Graf Reventlow, JSOTSup 59 (Sheffield: JSOT Press, 1988), 55–61, at 59.

[34] Gen 6.5; Deut 15.9; Psa 64.6; 139.23; Matt 15.19; *etc.*

[35] 1 Chron 28.9; Psa 26.2; Jer 17.10; 20.12; Matt 22.37; *etc.*

[36] Exod 4.14; Lev 19.17; Psa 27.3; *etc.*

[37] 1 Sam 16.7; Zech 7.10; 2 Cor 5.12; 1 Pet 3.4. The Biblical authors did not make sharp distinctions between the "heart," the mind, feelings, thoughts, desires, intentions, *etc.* as we tend to do today. See "Heart," *DBI* 368–69.

[38] See Friedrich Baumgärtel, *"leb, lebab," TDNT* 3:606.

[39] The LXX at Exod 17.7 rendered Meribah as *peirasmos*, and Massah as *loidorēsis* ("railing" or "abuse").

and Massah (which means "test") were two names for the same place to which God led the Israelites on their way to Sinai, also called Rephidim (Exod 17.1, 7). Meribah also became the name given to a place in the wilderness of Zin at Kadesh (Num 20.1–13), where both Israel and Moses sinned. These were remembered as places where Israel demonstrated their refusal to trust in God. Psalm 95 recalls the Biblical account of Exodus 17.7, which says "He named the place Massah and Meribah because of the quarrel of the sons of Israel, and because they tested the Lord, saying, 'Is the Lord among us, or not?' " (NASB). God had led Israel to this place, but there was no water there. The Israelites had seen God defeat the Egyptians, they had been eating his manna, and he had turned bitter water sweet for them at Marah (Exod 15.23–25). By this time, they should have learned to trust that he would use his power to bring them water, but instead they acted as if God could do nothing for them. In a stubborn refusal to trust, they complained and demanded that God prove himself, which provoked God's anger.

The term **day** (v 8) in the phrase "day of temptation" is used generically to refer to a period of time. This is a normal Hebraic use of the term. That is, it was not a particular date on the calendar to which the psalm looked back. Instead, the parallelism here indicates that it refers to the entire wilderness wandering period (forty years, v 9), and the events at Meribah and Massah were cited because they were typical of Israel's attitude throughout their sojourn in the **wilderness** of Sinai. The time Israel spent there was a time of training (this theme will reappear in ch 12). It was supposed to be a time when they learned to trust in God (Deut 8.16). Instead, however, it became notorious as the time when Israel became hardened and refused to trust God any longer.

3.9 where your fathers tried me by testing and saw my works for forty years.

The Israelite ancestors (the **fathers**) developed hard hearts in reaction to the training (Deut 8.16) God put them through. The exodus and the wilderness period is one of the heaviest concentrations of miraculous activity and revelation in all of Biblical history. When confronted with a challenge, what the Israelites should have done was turn in faith to God to provide their needs, based on their past experience with him and his covenant word to them. God had sufficiently demonstrated his faithfulness to them. Instead, however, they complained, they acted in a faithless way, and on several occasions, they actually longed for Egypt (Exod 14.11–12; 16.3; 17.3; Num 11.5; 14.2–4; 20.5).[40] God interpreted this as their **testing** him, demanding that God prove himself to them after he had already proven himself in the past. It was, simply, a lack of trust. Instead of seeing the hardships of the wilderness as an opportunity to demonstrate their trust in God, they became bitter and increasingly refused to follow God's leading. They acted as if God would do nothing for them.

At Numbers 14, God had had enough, and, upon his own person, swore (v 11 below) that the Israelites who refused to trust him and his word (and thereby put God to the test) would not enter the land of rest but would die in the wilderness (Num 14.28ff). Even after that, they still had not learned their lesson. Throughout that period (**forty years**) they **saw** God's mighty **works** of provision and deliverance, and they heard his voice from Mt. Sinai (see comments on 12.18ff). God generally characterized the entire wilderness wandering period of forty years as one of faithlessness (and thus also of divine anger, v 17). Since forty years was also roughly the span of a generation (v 10), the phrase "forty years" takes on the sense of "all their (adult) lives."

The author intended that the behavior of the original hearers of Hebrews was becoming dangerously parallel to that of the ancient Israelites.[41] He emphasized the typological continuity of Christianity and Judaism and portrayed his readers as walking, as it were, in the footsteps of a former generation of God's people, yet at the same time in a better and greater situation. Like the Israelites, the hearers of Hebrews had also heard God's word and saw signs (2.3f), but this time it was God's greater word delivered not through angels but through his Son (ch 1). The Son came to lead them to God, but the hardship of the way (opposition and reproach) was causing some to want to quit following Jesus, which would also be a wandering away from God in their hearts (v 10). Our author emphasized the faithlessness of such behavior and its terrible

[40] Some strands of Jewish tradition downplayed or ignored the failures of the exodus generation in the wilderness, and emphasized the positive aspects of the period. See Johnson, *Hebrews*, 120. Hebrews, however, stands in the Biblical tradition that criticized the wilderness generation. See Psa 77.5ff; Ezek 20.1–31.

[41] See Matthew Thiessen, "Hebrews and the End of the Exodus," *NovT* 49 (2007): 353–69. See also the Introduction to this commentary, and Jacob Neusner, "Paradigmatic Thinking Versus Historical Thinking: The Case of Rabbinic Judaism," in *Approaches to Ancient Judaism Vol 11*, ed. Jacob Neusner (Atlanta: Scholars Press 1997), 163–92.

consequences. He warned them that they were about to make the same mistake as the generation of old, but this time the consequences would be far worse (*cf.* 2.2ff).

3.10 Therefore I was angry with this generation, and I said, 'They always wander in their heart, and they have not known my ways.'

The phrase **this generation** (v 10) is a justifiable expansion of the MT (which simply says "generation"). The addition of "this" is sometimes used in a negative way in the OT to indicate God's disgust of a godless people. See Genesis 7.1 and especially Deuteronomy 1.35 ("this evil generation"); Psalm 12.7; *cf.* Matthew 12.41. That the author of Hebrews should quote a text speaking about "this (wicked) generation" and apply it to his readers certainly must have been a surprising rebuke to them. Perhaps they did not see themselves in this way because they had not fully appreciated Christ or the new order of things they enjoyed in him. Our author, however, shows them the full force of their error by applying a "this generation" text to his readers.

God's specific complaint was that the **heart** (see on 3.8 above) of his people was not what it should have been. They were not truly committed to God; they had not entered into a close relationship with him in order to **know** his **ways** (see Exod 33.13; Psa 25.4; Jer 5.4; *etc.*). If they had, they would have seen God as a beneficent being who gives many good things to those who show faith in him, and they would have walked boldly and confidently in the way he laid out before them. Instead, however, they lacked trust in God's promise and were willing to sacrifice a future good for the sake of their immediate physical comfort. For this they reaped the **anger** of God from which they could not escape (see Heb 4.1; 10.26–31; 12.29). The Israelites' propensity to **wander** from God in their hearts echoes the warning of Hebrews 2.1, not to drift away from what we have heard.

3.11 So I swore in my wrath, 'They shall not enter into my rest.' "

For wandering in their hearts, God sentenced that generation to wander in the wilderness and not enter the promised land. As our author will point out in chapter 6, it is always a serious thing when God takes an oath. God's word is always reliable and sure. What he says, he will do. When God **swears** on top of his sure word, it is God's way of emphasizing the surety of his intentions in the matter (see 6.13f). There was no way these faithless people (here, the Israelites) were going to enjoy the promised land, because these Israelites who came out of Egypt had provoked God to anger (**wrath**) by their repeated refusal to trust in him. Trust would have put them into the good land of Canaan, but their faithlessness enraged God and he swore an oath[42] that there was no way[43] they would **enter into** the rest he had prepared for them to share with himself. God's oath made the matter final and their fate irreversible. See comments on 4.1. The author will address again the prospect of facing the wrath of God as a result of a lack of faith in 10.26f. For now, the point was simple and forceful: a lack of faith brought the wrath of God, and it will be no different for anyone who repeats the conduct of that generation of Israelites.

Often in Hebrews the emphasis of an OT quotation comes at the end of the quotation (although sometimes at the beginning).[44] In the verses that follow, our author calls special attention to the first and last words of the quotation ("today" and "rest"), but the climax of the exhortation comes with the more extended treatment (in 4.1–11) of the last word in the text, **rest**. See the Excursus: The Sabbath Rest. While it may seem distant here, the connection between this exhortation and the discussion of Jesus' high priesthood are always coupled. As noted in the Excursus, Israel's journey out of Egypt was always designed to end in the presence of God, initially at Sinai, but ultimately in the temple that would be built once Israel entered the promised land. That is, entering into God's rest would be achieved by the high priest's entering into the presence

[42] The statement "as I live" in Num 14.21 and 28 was oath language; *cf.* Deut 2.14; similar language in Jer 4.2. Psa 95.11 "as I swore in my wrath" is from Deut 1.34 "he was angry and took an oath."

[43] Psa 95 stated the oath of Num 14.28 as *ei eiseleusontai eis tēn katapausin mou*. The word *ei*, in this construction means "if" only in an elliptical sense, either using ancient oath language (BDF §372), or by positing an illogical assertion: "The 'then' clause is so obviously false that it turns the 'if' clause into a strong negative assertion." (Richard A. Young, *Intermediate New Testament Greek: A Linguistic and Exegetical Approach* (Nashville, TN: Broadman & Holman, 1994), 229). It therefore matches the similar Hebrew idiom that expresses an emphatic negative using *im* (BDB §50; Moulton and Turner, *A Grammar of New Testament Greek: Syntax*, Vol. 3, 333). There is no evidence the original recipients of Hebrews knew Hebrew or had read this phrase in the original Hebrew, but the Greek language (with which Hebrews was written) had the same kind of construction (Robertson, *Grammar*, 94, 1024). When used with a future verb, it expressed certainty.

[44] Ellingworth, *Epistle to the Hebrews*, 40.

of God in the temple, because the temple (and specifically the ark in the Most Holy Place) was God's resting-place. "Arise, O Lord, to Your resting place, You and the ark of Your strength" (Psa 132.8). The Aramaic paraphrases (the Targummim) of the Hebrew Bible reflected this thinking. In the Targum for Psalm 95, verse 11 reads "concerning whom I swore in the strength of my anger that they should not come into the rest of the house of my sanctuary."[45] Israel's refusal to enter God's rest is also reflected in the Targum for Isaiah 28.12: "to whom the prophets were saying, 'This is the sanctuary, serve in it; and this is the heritage of the house of rest;' yet they would not listen to teaching."[46]

3.12 Watch out, brothers, lest there be in any of you an evil heart of unbelief that withdraws from the living God.

3.12–4.11 consists of the author's midrashic exposition of Psalm 95.7–11,[47] one in which he draws out key terms to show their application to his readers in their situation. He advances methodically through his text, commenting on key words and making their significance explicit.

Again, it is entirely possible for children of God, members of God's house (v 6), to be and act in such a way that they will forfeit their salvation. If a child of God can never be lost, then there is no reason the author should tell his readers to **watch out** (NIV more literally "see to it"). The plural imperative puts the responsibility on the entire group (see 12.15ff). *Cf.* 2.1, but the exhortation here is worded more strongly (the warnings in Hebrews get progressively stronger). The words here recall Joshua's rebuke to the Israelites: "do not rebel against the Lord" (Num 14.9),[48] as the author draws a parallel between his readers and the ancient Israel-

---

[45] Kevin Cathcart, Michael Maher, and Martin McNamara, eds., *The Aramaic Bible: The Targum of Psalms*, Vol. 16, trans. David M. Stec (Collegeville, MN: Liturgical Press, 2004), 179.

[46] Kevin Cathcart, Michael Maher, and Martin McNamara, eds., *The Aramaic Bible: The Isaiah Targum*, Vol. 11, trans. Bruce D. Chilton (Collegeville, MN: The Liturgical Press, 1990), 55.

[47] A detailed discussion of how this passage uses Jewish methods of interpretation is in Pasquale Basta, "Only the One Who Works Enters into Rest: The Homiletic Logic of Heb 3,7–4,11," *Biblica* 99 (2018): 567–91. Also, since Psalm 95 (LXX) referred to Num 14, the author of Hebrews used several of the details from Num 14 in his exposition. See Bryan J. Whitfield, *Joshua Traditions and the Argument of Hebrews 3 and 4*, BZNW 194 (Berlin: De-Gruyter, 2013), 43–44.

[48] Whitfield, *Joshua Traditions and the Argument of Hebrews 3 and 4*, 43.

ites: "It happened to them; be careful that it does not happen to you." We should not overlook the word **you**. The author wants his readers, his beloved **brothers** in Christ, to know that the warning of Psalm 95 finds its ultimate audience in them, the people of the messianic time (the time called "Today"), God's house (v 6), the church.

The first term for consideration is the hard, straying **heart** mentioned in verses 8 and 10 of the psalm. See on verse 8 above. Disobedience in actions stems from a heart that harbors wickedness, or **evil** (v 10 above; see also Matt 9.4; 15.18–20), but if the heart is right, good and righteous deeds will follow. Christianity is designed not just to reform a person's deeds but to create a new heart (Ezek 36.26; *cf.* 2 Cor 5.17; Eph 4.24). Jesus' sermon on the mount (Matt 5–7) was aimed at this very thing. The author of Hebrews thus began with the real root of the problem among his readers, an internal problem of the heart, which was the specific problem God identified in the Israelites in Psalm 95.8, 10. A **heart of unbelief** (a Hebraic way of saying "unbelieving heart") is a heart that is not faithful, one that does not take in God's word and refuses to know God's ways (v 10 above), one that remains unconvinced in spite of signs from God (Num 14.11; Heb 2.3–4), and most of all, a heart that does not trust that God will provide and protect, especially in times of hardship (as in the wilderness of Sinai). The picture is not necessarily that of a complete absence of belief, but of a refusal or failure to trust in God's promise to sustain further.[49] The author called this refusal to trust **evil**. The one with such a heart typically departs or **withdraws from God** and seeks to follow his own way. He turns his back on God's instruction and stubbornly refuses to hear or follow what God says (*cf.* 2.2), like Israel wanted to return to Egypt, because he does not believe it will result in his happiness or safety, but instead believes it will result in his harm. Thus, he decisively rejects the divine promise.[50] Such was the attitude of the Israelites as recounted in Psalm 95, and for that attitude they suffered God's wrath. The translation "fall away" (NASB, RSV, ESV) may not communicate fully the true nature of the problem. Faithlessness is not something one passively "falls" into, but is an active, deliberate and willful turning away from God. The term (Greek *aphistēmi*) means "to distance

[49] Randall C. Gleason, "The Old Testament Background of Rest in Hebrews 3:7–4:11," *BibSac* 157 (2000): 281–303, at 291.

[50] Lane, *Hebrews 1–8*, 142; J. C. McCullough, "The Impossibility of a Second Repentance in Hebrews," *BTB* 24 (1974) 1–7, at 3.

oneself from some person or thing," and can be translated "go away" or "withdraw."[51] The exhortation in Hebrews is to do the opposite, to draw near. To depart from Christ is to depart from God, for it is only through Christ the high priest that anyone has access to God.

God is here called **the living God**. This phrase sometimes has the sense of "true God" when it is used to describe God in contrast to idols (Hos 1.10; Acts 14.15), and it is also used in the Bible to emphasize that he is the source of life (*cf.* Psa 84.2; Acts 14.15; 1 Tim 4.10) or to emphasize the spiritual nature of God (2 Cor 3.3; in contrast to ink and tablets of stone; Heb 9.14). To depart from God is to depart from the one who gives life (*cf.* John 5.26) and is thus to face only death (like the disobedient Israelites in the wilderness). Even more, God is sometimes called the "living God" in OT contexts where his ability to destroy is being asserted (*cf.* Josh 3.10; Jer 10.10; 23.36). The phrase recalls God's oath language, especially in contexts of punishment. In Numbers 14, where God pronounced the punishment for the unfaithful Israelites, he prefaced the sentence with "As I live, says the Lord" (v 28), the same oath referenced in Psalm 95.11 (and here in Hebrews 3–4). Similarly, in Hebrews this designation of God also appears in 10.31 in a context of warning which emphasizes that God acts in punishment against the faithless. Both 3.12 and 10.31 have in common that they refer to texts where God took an oath. In 10.31, the author quotes Deuteronomy 32.35f, and in that context God promised to punish saying "'Indeed, I lift up My hand to heaven, and say, 'As I live forever''' (v 40; NASB). It is possible, therefore, that the phrase **living God** echoes this oath language by which punishment of the unfaithful is made sure.

3.13 But encourage one another day by day, while it is called "Today," lest anyone of you might be hardened by the deceitfulness of sin.

In order to remain faithful, Christians are commanded to **encourage** (Greek *parakaleō*) **one another**, to exhort each other in the moral sense, to appeal to each other in a way that is uplifting. See Hebrews 10.24f; 12.15; Romans 15.1ff; 1 Thessalonians 5.11, 14. The Lord in his wisdom put Christians together in local churches that they might help each other to remain faithful (*cf.* 10.24–25). This encouragement should be offered not just weekly at worship gatherings, but on a continual basis, "daily" as it were (**day by day**, drawing on the word "today" from the psalm),

[51] BDAG 157.

because we routinely face some form of temptation to unfaithfulness. We are to do this **while,** or as long as, **it is called "Today."** As a skilled orator, the author used the vocabulary of the Biblical text ("today ... hardened") as the foundation of his midrashic exhortation. The opening word of the quotation from Psalm 95, **Today**, can have the rhetorical sense of "now" or "while the opportunity exists." To this extent, it encourages the hearer to obey today rather than put it off until later. But, as noted in the comments on 3.7, we also hear the echo of the same word from Psalm 2.7 (which was quoted in Heb 1.5). In that context "today" refers to the messianic age, the time when God has exalted his Son to a position far above the angels (*cf.* Acts 13.33). It should also be noted that the author still read the psalm as having historical referents (as is clear in vv 16–18 below). However, the Psalm's warning was not written to the wilderness generation of Israelites. It was *about* them, but it was directed *to* a later generation, and that later generation is the people of the messianic age. It is, instead, a reminder that we are now living in "the last days" (Heb 1.2), the time of the consummation of God's plan, the time when it is most crucial to turn to God and be faithful. The time is coming in which the "window" of opportunity to listen to God and obey his voice in this final time will be closed, and once it is closed it will not be opened again. Part of the warning of Hebrews is that people can (and have) put themselves into situations from which they cannot escape, with the result that they lose their opportunity for future blessing. See comments on 12.17.

Unfaithfulness is here described as being **hardened by the deceitfulness of sin**. The term **hardened** echoes the exhortation from Psalm 95.8 ("do not harden your hearts"), and is the same condition called "an evil heart of unbelief" in Hebrews 3.12. It seems likely that the **deceitfulness** in view here is the idea the readers of Hebrews had, that if they renounced Christ their lives would be easier. While such a move would eliminate the social pressure, ostracism, and persecution, it would also reap the wrath of God. Sin's appeal is deceiving. It appears to offer something enjoyable or easy when in fact it is an invitation to destruction. As Solomon wrote, "There is a way which seems right to a man, but its end is the way of death" (Prov 14.12). Furthermore, sin has a hardening effect upon the sinner's heart. This is a crucial part of the author's exhortation. He is convinced that harboring doubt and a failure to trust in God is not a condition that *may* cause a person to become hardened against God; it *will,* if left unchecked, result in a recalcitrant hardness of the worst kind (as he will describe in 6.4–6). The more one concentrates on his fleshly well-being, the more hardened he becomes against God's message to value spiritual well-being above physical comfort. Each foray into sin's deceitful pleasures makes it easier the next time until we reach the point that we will no longer listen to what God says. The conscience can become seared and insensitive if it is violated enough (1 Tim 4.2), and one may be deceived to the point that he calls evil good and good evil (*cf.* Isa 5.20) and rejects God's word because he is convinced it is untrue. Right now, the author saw that the hearers of Hebrews were starting down the path to unfaithfulness through weakness, and path that would only lead to them becoming hardened in their hearts. He knew where that path would take them, but the hearers did not yet see this. They therefore needed to encourage each other to endure the hardships associated with faithfulness lest their condition turn into something much worse. Moses himself will later be introduced as an example of one who chose "rather to endure ill-treatment with the people of God than to enjoy the passing pleasures of sin" (11.25). See also comments on chapter 5.

3.14 For we have become sharers of Christ, if we hold onto the beginning of our resolve firmly unto the end.

The word **sharers** recalls 3.1, where it was said that Christians are sharers of a heavenly calling, and 2.14 where it was said that Jesus shared with us in flesh and blood. Christians are also sharers in **Christ**[52] and brethren to him (2.11ff) in God's house, as well as partakers in the Holy Spirit (6.4). In our relationship with him we have come to participate in the heavenly blessings and realities of the messianic age which he has inaugurated. See 12.22ff. As partakers of Christ, we stand to be glorified with him (Heb 2.10; Rom 8.17; Col 3.4). But we are also called to share in his faithfulness, his endurance in faith (3.2, 6; 12.2). Hence the conditional statement here, **if we hold onto the beginning of our resolve firmly unto the end**, a phrase similar to the one in 3.6 (using the same

[52] The Greek phrase here can denote companionship ("partners with Christ") or participation ("sharers in Christ"). While the two ideas are not mutually exclusive, and may both be in view here, a case can be made that the sense of participation is in the forefront in this context. Enrique Nardoni, "Partakers in Christ (Hebrews 3.14)," *NTS* 37 (1991): 456–72. See also Benjamin J. Ribbens, "Partakers of Christ: Union with Christ in Hebrews," *Pro Ecclesia* 31 (2022): 282–301.

verb, "hold on") and that concisely encapsulates the exhortation of Hebrews. Endurance in faithfulness is always a part of being a partaker with Christ and a member of God's household. Here, a different Greek word for confidence is used than was used in verse 6. The word here is *hupostasis*, which at its most basic meaning denotes "something that underlies visible conditions,"[53] a foundation, as it were,[54] and which was used in 1.3 of the "essence" or "true reality" of the divine nature. Gelardini has suggested the notion of "substrate."[55] The word can also denote a situation or condition, or an undertaking,[56] but with the special sense of an undertaking pursued with resolve, which could also fit the context here.[57] The recipients of Hebrews had begun an undertaking of following Christ, but now they were shrinking back from it (*cf.* 2.1). They needed to regain a firm grip on the resolve they had when they first became Christians and see it through to its **end** (its completion or goal), which is to be glorified in heaven (2.10; *cf.* Rom 8.17), and that meant not quitting in their faith. That the apostle John said a similar thing to the churches in Ephesus (Rev 2.4f) and Smyrna (Rev 2.10 "be faithful unto death") reminds us that this is an exhortation all Christians need to heed. The word **end** recalls a form of the same word ("perfect") used in 2.10 to describe Jesus, who reached the goal (or "end") of glory through suffering. Jesus was faithful and reached the goal set before Him (*cf.* 12.2–3). The author of Hebrews encouraged his readers to consider this same Jesus (3.1; 12.2) as their example to follow.

3.15 While it is said, "Today if you will hear his voice, do not harden your hearts, as in the rebellion."

The introductory phrase **while it is said**[58] reminded the readers that a limited opportunity was open to them (see "as long as" in v 13 above). For now, there was a moment to correct their thinking and resolve to be faithful. If they did not give careful attention to the present condition of

---

[53] MM 660.

[54] Teresa Morgan, *Roman Faith and Christian Faith:* Pistis *and* Fides *in the Early Roman Empire and Early Churches* (Oxford: Oxford University Press, 2015), 339.

[55] Gelardini, "Faith in Hebrews and Its Relationship to Soteriology," 255.

[56] MM 659.

[57] H. W. Hollander, "*hupostasis*," *EDNT* 3:407.

[58] The phrase is an articular infinitive with the preposition *en*, which normally communicates a temporal situation (either "when" or "as").

their hearts, however, they would eventually come into a spiritual condition from which there was no rescue (*cf.* 2.3 "how will we escape?"; see on 4.1 and 12.17).

Here the author re-quoted Psalm 95.7b–8a for rhetorical effect, to let the words of Scripture ring in the ears and minds of his audience (this technique is fairly common in Hebrews). Yet there is more than repetition for the sake of emphasis going on here. The line from the Psalm said negatively ("do not harden ...") what the author said positively (v 14, "hold fast ..."). Moreover, the emphasis is on the last line of the quotation and its reference to Israel's **rebellion**. The original hearers of Hebrews were headed toward making the very same mistake the Israelites in the wilderness had made, yet the stakes were higher this time. He used these words to speak to the hearers directly and say, "don't do it!"

3.16 For who was it who provoked God after they had heard? Was it not all those who came out of Egypt through Moses?

A series of rhetorical questions are now adduced to explain just exactly who it was that rebelled in wilderness, that is, who Psalm 95 was describing. But the description is not simply an historical identification, but one that highlights the similarities between Israel and the recipients of Hebrews. Just as the exhortation to hear in 2.1 was followed by a warning about punishment in 2.2–3, so here the author followed the exhortation to hear in the previous verse (from Psa 95:7–8) with a warning about what happens to those who do not remain faithful to what they have heard. His warning is based upon what Psalm 95 said about the ancient Israelites, who were a type of the messianic Israel, the church. We may paraphrase the point of this verse as: "So who was it that **provoked God** (an echo of Psa 95.9) to the point that he unleashed his wrath against them and destroyed them? Was it not with all those who came out of Egypt, God's own people, those who were in covenant relationship with him?" By stating his case in a set of rhetorical questions the author made his point seem all the more obvious and his conclusion inescapable. The guilt of the Israelites was further established by the fact that they provoked God **after they had heard**. They could not claim that their lack of faith was due to ignorance of what God would do, for he had been speaking repeatedly of how he was going to give them the land (see Exod 6.8; 12.25; 13.5, 11; 20.12; 33.1). They heard the "good news" (see 4.2), but they refused to trust it. The original readers of Hebrews were, typologically, in the same situation. Therefore, "we must pay close attention to what we have heard" (2.1) and continue to accept it in full trust.

Our author has used the word **all** in a general, rather than an absolute, sense for the sake of emphasis (a form of hyperbole, in which something is overstated in order to make it emphatic). Of the multitude that **came out of Egypt through**[59] **Moses**, Joshua and Caleb did not provoke God, but they were the only ones (Num 14.24, 30, 38). The rest, or the majority, acted in disbelief. *Cf.* 1 Corinthians 10.1–5. It was not just the vilest Israelites who died in the wilderness, the murderers, *etc.*; *every* faithless Israelite died under the sentence of God. The sin that brought the death sentence upon them was a simple failure to trust what God had told them and that he would keep his word. See Hebrews 6.4.

It is safe to say that there is no NT mention or allusion to the exodus from Egypt without significance.[60] The exodus is the most-remembered event from Israelite history in the Bible and served as a foundational pattern for what God does for his people. Through the death of a lamb God's people were spared from death, and God led them through water, out of slavery, and into a covenant relationship with himself. The NT draws upon exodus typology heavily. Christians have their own exodus experience in Christ. His death spares us from death and he, like **Moses**, leads us through the water of baptism out of the slavery of sin and into the new covenant relationship with God (*cf.* 1 Cor 10.lff). The mention of Moses here is hardly casual. It recalls the point from verses 1–6 that Christ is greater than Moses and implicitly argues that if unfaithfulness under Moses' leadership was condemned, so much more will unfaithfulness under Christ's leadership be (*cf.* 2.2–3).

3.17 And with whom was he angry for forty years? Was it not with those who had sinned, whose corpses fell in the desert?

---

[59] Greek *dia*, here in the sense of "under the leadership of."

[60] See Seth M. Ehorn, *Exodus in the New Testament*, LNTS 663 (New York: T&T Clark, 2022); Michael L. Morales, *Exodus Old and New: A Biblical Theology of Redemption*, Essential Studies in Biblical Theology (Downers Grove, IL: IVP Academic, 2020); Bryan D. Estelle, *Echoes of Exodus: Tracing a Biblical Motif* (Downers Grove, IL: IVP Academic, 2018); Alastair Roberts and Andrew Wilson, *Echoes of Exodus: Tracing Themes of Redemption through Scripture* (Wheaton, IL: Crossway, 2018); Michael R. Fox, ed. *Reverberations of the Exodus in Scripture* (Eugene, OR: Pickwick Publications, 2014).

Another pointed rhetorical question drives the readers to consider an additional fact. It was not just that the exodus generation had provoked God to the point of making him **angry** (Psa 95.10). Throughout the Bible, God is angry with those who refuse to trust him after he has demonstrated his trustworthiness to them. The entire **forty years** of Israel's wandering in the wilderness was viewed by God as one rebellion after another. In Numbers 14.22 God spoke of the Israelites as "all the men who have seen my glory and my signs which I performed in Egypt and in the wilderness, yet have put me to the test these ten times and have not listened to my voice" (NASB). There the number ten is symbolic, meaning that God had had enough of their constant complaining and faithlessness. The incident at Kadesh-barnea, when the multitude followed the ten faithless spies who told them they could not take the land of Canaan, was the "last straw" with God. By that time, the Israelites should have developed a healthy trust in God because they had seen his mighty works. Their faithlessness was nothing else but rebellion, and for it God sentenced the unbelievers to die in the wilderness. That is exactly what they experienced over the next 38 years.[61] The specific circumstances of that incident were relevant to the original readers of Hebrews. The Israelites "feared the hostility and strength of the Canaanites more than they trusted God,"[62] which was the same attitude towards unbelievers that had begun to take root in the recipients of Hebrews. If they did not check this unhealthy attitude, it would lead them to the same end as the exodus generation of the Israelites.

In Hebrews, the word **sinned** primarily refers to the refusal to trust in God's promise of care, the refusal to trust in his power to sustain and protect his people, and thus putting God to the test (*i.e.*, putting him in a position where man demands that God prove himself), and turning one's back on him. It should be clear from this context that sin is not just a wrong deed, but we may sin in our hearts when we do not trust God. Sin often manifests itself in some action, but the sinful heart, the attitude of faithlessness, is just as sinful as the sinful deed it produces.

In order to emphasize the terrible consequence of the Israelites' sin, the author added an echo from Numbers 14.29, where God said to that faithless generation: "your carcasses shall fall in this wilderness," and

---

[61] The sentence of wandering for forty years included the two years they had already spent in the wilderness. Deut 2.14.

[62] deSilva, *Perseverance in Gratitude*, 145.

Numbers 14.32 "your corpses will fall in this wilderness" (NASB). The author's choice of the specific Greek word for dead bodies (**corpses**) vividly puts the scene before us. The **desert** (wilderness) littered with the corpses of unfaithful Israelites is a stark warning to all who would wish to turn back from following the way of God in faith. While the wilderness is sometimes remembered in Scripture as a symbol of God's care for his people, the author of Hebrews concentrates exclusively on another Biblical aspect of its symbolism, that of testing. The implication of the rhetorical question here is that those who commit the same sin as Israel will reap the same result. They will not enter into God's rest (see the Excursus: The Sabbath Rest), they will not live in God's land.

3.18 And to whom did he swear that they would not enter into his rest, except to those who were disobedient?

A third rhetorical question makes the final, climactic point. It echoes Psalm 95.11 (he **swore** that **they** would **not enter into** his **rest**) to keep the words of Scripture fresh in the hearers' ears. The exodus generation had *provoked* God by the sin of **disobedience** (parallel to "sinned" in the previous verse). The root of the Greek word here (*apeitheō*) is the word from which we get our English word "apathetic" and emphasizes disobedience that came from being unconvinced or unpersuaded about what God said. The sin of the Israelites lay in not trusting in God and his promise to give them the land of Canaan, and this lack of trust manifested itself in a refusal to enter the land into which God intended to lead them and which he had repeatedly promised to them. It is ironic that the author can use this same exodus generation as an illustration of faith later in the epistle (11.29). This is no contradiction, but instead points up the sad irony that the group who had, by faith, walked across the bed of the Red Sea did not continue in that faith to enter the land of Canaan. The original recipients of Hebrews were repeating this pattern of faith followed by faithlessness, typologically speaking.

3.19 So we see that they were unable to enter because of unbelief.

Here the failure of the Israelites, who are the subject of Psalm 95.7–11, is stated most succinctly as the author summarized his warning. God refused the Israelites entry into the promised land of rest because they did not trust in God enough to follow him into it. *Cf.* Deuteronomy 32.20.

Even though they had experienced so much of God's good care of them in the wilderness and had witnessed firsthand God's reliability (*cf.* 10.23) in his saving displays of power against their enemies, they still did not trust that he would be with them in the hardships that lay before them. Similarly, the original readers of Hebrews, in thinking of quitting the faith, were showing that they lacked the same kind of basic trust in God. That failure of faith could cost them their inheritance as God's sons if it was left uncorrected (see Heb 6.1ff). The risk of not finishing what we have started because of a lack of faith will be raised again in the exhortation of chapters 11 and 12. The word **unbelief** (Greek *apistia*) was repeated from verse 12 above to remind the readers of the main point of the warning from Psalm 95. Note also that unbelief is parallel to the disobedience mentioned in the previous verse. *Cf.* 1 Pet 2.7–8; Tit 1.15–16; John 3.36. Failure to trust in God is *the* sin that concerned the author of Hebrews about his readers. Generally speaking, whenever Hebrews mentions sin, this is the sin that is meant.

Excursus: The Sabbath Rest[1]

The story of the Biblical Sabbath begins with the opening scene of the Bible, the creation of the universe by God. After the description of God's creative activity, we read "By the seventh day God completed His work which he had done, and He rested on the seventh day from all His work which he had done. Then God blessed the seventh day and sanctified it, because in it he rested from all his work which God had created and made" (Gen 2.2–3). Here begins the concept of the seventh day as a day of rest, yet immediately we are forced to come to grips more precisely with the Biblical idea of rest. God did not rest because he was exhausted, for as Isaiah said, "the Everlasting God, the Lord, the Creator of the ends of the earth does not become weary or tired" (40.28). Nor was God's rest a cessation from all activity, for Jesus plainly said that God has been working since the creation, including on the Sabbath day (John 5.16–17). Even the Mosaic Sabbath was not a complete cessation of all activity (more on this below). Rest, then, is something else.

Before we come to that, however, we should notice that God's rest on the seventh day of the creation week is no incidental part of that narrative. The links within Genesis 2.1–3, and with the account in Genesis 1, are too strong to allow us to read Genesis 2.2–3 in a casual way. We have "completed" in 2.1, followed by "completed" in 2.2. "His work" in 2.2 is repeated in 2.3. "Seventh day" (which appears twice in 2.2) is followed by the same phrase in 2.3, and "rested" in 2.2 is likewise picked up again in 2.3. "Created" in 2.3 relates the passage to 1.1, as does the phrase "the heavens and the earth" in 2.1. Even more, the completion of creation in 2.1 leads naturally to God's rest in 2.2, which in turn naturally leads to the sanctification of the seventh day in 2.3. "The tight sequence of argument" in this passage "cannot be broken so lightly."[2] It is clear,

[1] This essay originally appeared in Daniel W. Petty, ed., *The Gospel in the Old Testament: Florida College Annual Lectures 2003* (Temple Terrace: Florida College, 2003), 213–32. It has been slightly modified for this commentary. All Scripture quotations in this excursus are from the NASB unless noted otherwise.

[2] Howard N. Wallace, "Genesis 2:1–3—Creation and Sabbath," *Pacifica* 1 (1980): 235–50, at 237.

then, that Moses intended to show that the origin of the Sabbath lay in God's rest at the end of the creation week. The idea of a Sabbath rest was an integral part of the original order of things.

It must not escape our notice that God rested at the end of his creative work. This was not just because God simply finished all he had set out to do. The last thing God did before he rested was he "created man in His own image" (1.27). Of all the earthly creatures God made, only man was made in God's image, which means that only man was endowed with a spirit capable of fellowship with God, who himself is spirit. Note also that immediately after the statement about God resting on the seventh day (Gen 2.3) comes the more detailed account of the formation of man, the goodness of the garden, and God's terms that would sustain Adam's life (2.4ff). God's rest must be understood in light of this sequence, for this is the first Biblical clue concerning the meaning of the Sabbath. When God entered into his rest after creating the world, it was with the intention of enjoying fellowship with the man he had made with the capability of that fellowship. God had placed Adam and Eve in a place that was ready-made for them, a place that would sustain them comfortably. All they needed to live was provided for them so they would not be burdened with hard labor for their survival. In such an environment God had made it possible for man to live without giving all his time, energy, and thought simply to staying alive. With their survival provided by God, Adam and Eve were supposed to direct their attention to God. Given their circumstances, it should have been relatively easy. Adam and Eve had no reason to distrust God, and God's provision of all their needs in a productive, beautiful garden was proof that they could, and should, trust him.

This brings us to another clue concerning the significance of the Sabbath. After the creation account comes the story of the sin of Adam and Eve. The fellowship God wished to have with man did not materialize. Adam and Eve were deceived into a distrust of God, sinned, and were expelled from Eden. One then searches in vain through the rest of Genesis and the first half of Exodus before encountering the next mention of the Sabbath.[3] The introduction and rise of sin in the world meant that God was unable to enter into a fellowship with man. Only when God brought Israel out of Egypt to make them his own people do we again begin to hear of a Sabbath. After Israel

---

[3] The closest the text comes to this is with Noah, whose name is a form of the Hebrew word for "rest" and of whom it was said in Gen 5.29 "This one will give us rest from our work." However, Noah has his downfall in Gen 9.20f, and no Sabbath ordinance comes from the story of Noah.

crossed the Red Sea and entered into the wilderness of Sin, God began to lead them to Sinai where he would enter into a covenant with them, a covenant that created (and had provisions to maintain) a fellowship between them and God. On the way to Sinai God began to feed them with manna, and with the coming of the manna came the first mention of a Sabbath rest since the creation. The command to do no work at all did not come at this time, but it certainly is foreshadowed here. God said that on the seventh day no manna would come (Exod 16.25), thus making the work of gathering manna impossible. On the sixth day the Israelites were to gather twice as much as they normally needed. Only on the sixth day would the manna not rot on the next day (Exod 16.5, 19f, 24). So the Israelites gathered no manna on the seventh day (for there was none to gather), and Moses records "so the people rested on the seventh day" (Exod 16.30).

There are two important things to notice from this account. First, there is the idea that the Sabbath was a time when the Israelites were relatively free from the concerns of their physical existence. It was a day in which they lived not because they had worked on that day, but because God blessed them. It was the day they lived by God's hand and not their own. This echoes the story of Genesis 1–2, where God provided everything Adam and Eve needed in the garden of Eden. God was doing for Israel with the manna what he had done for Adam and Eve with the garden. This brings us to the second point. God provided Israel with an abundance of manna on the sixth day for the same purpose he had provided Adam and Eve with the garden: that the Israelites might not be distracted with their survival and instead turn their attention to God. The Sabbath was a day in which they were called upon to demonstrate their faith and trust in God. Before the manna first came, God said "I will rain bread from heaven for you; and the people shall go out and gather a day's portion every day, that I may test them, whether or not they will walk in My instruction. On the sixth day, when they prepare what they bring in, it will be twice as much as they gather daily" (Exod 16.4–5). It required trust on Israel's part to remain in the tent on the seventh day and believe that the previous day's supply of manna would get them through that day (when every other day the manna would not). They were to trust that God would provide for them, and God proved himself trustworthy by sending the extra manna on the sixth day and preventing it from rotting on the Sabbath. This was an opportunity for Israel to live by faith in God, which was the very thing that God had desired from man since the creation.

The Law revealed at Sinai made the connection between Sabbath and fellowship with God more explicit. While there is much about the Mosaic Sabbath regulations to notice, we will have to content ourselves with a few key considerations. First, while the Sabbath day was commanded in the Decalogue and thus formed a pillar of Israelite law, more instructions for the Sabbath came in Exodus 31. This was not a case of poorly organized laws. The ten commandments were a kind of index to the more detailed laws that followed.[4] Furthermore, again the sequence of the material is instructive. It is not without significance that the Sabbath regulations in Exodus 31 came immediately after the instructions for building the tabernacle in chapters 25–30. The juxtaposition of the tabernacle and the Sabbath was another important clue as to the character of the Biblical Sabbath. The Sabbath was about worship, just as the tabernacle was about worship. Thus, the regulations for the *time* when Israel was to worship God (the Sabbath) came in the same context as the instructions for the *place* where God was to be worshiped (the tabernacle). This same juxtaposition of tabernacle and Sabbath laws appears in Leviticus 26.2–9, where God plainly tied the two together when he said "You shall keep My Sabbaths and reverence My sanctuary" (v 2).[5] The worship character of the Sabbath was further underscored by the fact that on the Sabbath day the priests not only continued to do their service of worship in the tabernacle, but the Law required additional sacrifices for the Sabbath day (Num 28.9–10). In other words, there was "more" worship on the Sabbath day than on the other six days, and this highlighted the fact that the Sabbath was a special day for man and God to enjoy each other's fellowship.

We may also remind ourselves that the fourth commandment explicitly recalled God's rest on the seventh day of the creation week (Exod 20.8–11 and 31.12–17). The verbal links between Exodus 20.8–11 and the creation story reinforce the connection. The terms seventh day, bless, sanctify, make, and work appear in both texts.[6] As noted above, the Sabbath was an integral part of the original order of things. This should not be mistaken to mean that the observance of the Sabbath day is for all time. Instead, it means that part of God's original design in creating the world was to enter into fellowship with man.

---

[4] Walter C. Kaiser, *Toward Old Testament Ethics* (Grand Rapids: Academie Books, 1983), 129, following the earlier work of Stephen Kaufman ("The Structure of the Deuteronomic Law," *MAARAV* 1/2 (1978–79): 105–58).

[5] See Jared C. Calaway, *The Sabbath and the Sanctuary: Access to God in the Letter to the Hebrews and Its Priestly Context*, WUNT 349 (Tübingen: Mohr Siebeck, 2013).

[6] Gerhard F. Hasel "Sabbath," in *AYBD* 5:851.

When God connected the Mosaic Sabbath with the creation account, this was to make clear that God was offering to Israel what he had originally offered to Adam: a relationship with himself. It was God's intention to have a people and to enjoy his relationship with that people. Adam refused to enter into that relationship, so God's Sabbath rest had gone unrealized since that time. The opportunity to enjoy what Adam rejected was now being given to Israel. God was still seeking to enter into his rest, his fellowship with man. When God gave Israel the instructions for the tabernacle, God was providing the means by which Israel could enter into God's rest.

It is sometimes noted that there are actually two reasons for the Sabbath given in the Law of Moses. As noted above, the first reason is that the Israelite Sabbath imitated (or more properly, was designed to realize) God's rest on the seventh day of creation (Exod 20.8–11 and 31.12–17). The second reason is given in Deuteronomy 5.15. It says, "You shall remember that you were a slave in the land of Egypt, and the Lord your God brought you out of there by a mighty hand and by an outstretched arm; therefore the Lord your God commanded you to observe the Sabbath day." Here the reason for the Sabbath is to commemorate the freedom of the exodus. Upon closer inspection, however, it becomes apparent that these are not two different reasons, but two ways the Bible has of speaking of the same thing. The exodus itself is described in terms of the creation. For example, in Isaiah 43.15–17 God referred to himself as the creator of Israel, and then proceeded to describe the exodus from Egypt. In Psalm 74.12ff the psalmist spoke of God's "deeds of deliverance" (which certainly included the exodus) in words that could equally describe the creation of the world. In both the creation and exodus accounts God separated the waters and made dry land appear for the benefit of his people. In both, God "conquered" the waters and gathered them into one place. Exodus 15 says that the flowing waters of the Red Sea "stood up like a heap" when God parted it, and that same term ("heap") is used in Psalm 33.7 of God's gathering of the waters in the creation. In both accounts God provided objects of reference in the sky for both day and night (in the creation: sun and moon; in the exodus: the pillars of cloud and fire), and in both accounts there is the idea of God bringing a new thing into existence (creation: the world; exodus: Israel as God's people). Time on earth began with the creation, and the Israelite calendar was reset to zero the month of the very first Passover (Exod 12.2; *cf.* 1 Sam 8.8; 1 Kings 6.1). Most of all, in both accounts there is the idea of God acting or doing something so that, when God was finished, man could have a relationship with God. In the beginning a good world was made for man, and man was placed in that good environment (Gen 2.15) where all his needs were provided so that he might have every reason to trust in God and enjoy his relationship with his creator. Similarly, in the exodus (and the plagues against Egypt that preceded it), that generation of Israelites saw God's power at work, and their witnessing of his power against Egypt on their behalf was supposed to instill in them a sense that they could trust God to care for them (*cf.* Exod 19.4; Deut 11.2–7). God then brought them to Sinai for the purpose of entering into a covenant relationship with them (called a "rest" in Exod 15.13). The exodus, then, was patterned after the creation of the world. In both events God made a new situation, and when he was finished there existed a circumstance where man and God could live in fellowship together. Therefore, Deuteronomy 5.15 was not a second reason for the Sabbath but is actually another way of relating the Sabbath to the creation.

The Sabbath regulations reached their OT climax, as it were, in the instructions for the Sabbath year (Lev 25.3–7) and the Year of Jubilee (Lev 25.8–28). The Sabbath year was every seventh year, and the Jubilee came after every seventh Sabbath year (or, every fifty years). In the Sabbath year Israel was not to plant crops. In an agricultural society, this surely was a tremendous challenge! God's promise was that the land would produce enough on its own to sustain them, and Israel was called upon to trust God and his promise (and live like it). That is, Israel was to practice for an entire year what they normally practiced for one day each week (especially as seen in the Sabbath regulation given when the manna came). The highlight of the Sabbath concept, however, came in the Jubilee. The Jubilee year was specifically called a year of release (Lev 25.10). Land that had been forfeited through debt was returned to the original clan that owned it, and people who had become slaves because of debt were freed from service. Also, like the Sabbath year, there was to be no planting or sowing. This meant that every fifty years the Israelites faced a period of about three years in which they did not have an ordinary harvest. They could not sow in the (seventh) Sabbath year, and then they could not sow the next year either (for it was the Jubilee year). They could sow the year after the Jubilee year, but then they had to wait for the harvest. So God said, "But if you say, 'What are we going to eat on the seventh year if we do not sow or gather in our crops?' then I will so order My blessing for you in the sixth year that it will bring forth the crop for three years. When you are sowing the eighth year, you can still eat old things from the crop, eating the old until the ninth year when its crop comes in" (Lev 25.20–22). Just as Eden provided Adam and Eve with all they needed, and just as God provided an abundance of manna on the sixth day to cover Israel's needs on the Sabbath, so would it be on a larger scale in the Jubilee cycle. We should also note that the Jubilee cycle was observed on a smaller scale in the Feast of Weeks. The fiftieth day (that is, the day after seven Sabbath days) after the harvest of the first fruits was a special day of worship on which no work was allowed and special sacrifices were offered (Lev 23.10–21).

While we are thinking about these things we should return to the Biblical concept of rest, which is at the heart of the meaning of the Sabbath. Perhaps the first thing that comes to our minds when we think of rest is a cessation of activity, even in the sense of inactivity. This, however, does not do justice to what the Biblical writers meant by this term. In fact, Genesis 49.15 shows that one could have "rest" even though one was working hard. Also, as Jesus pointed out in Matthew 12.5, "Or have you not read in the Law, that on the Sabbath the priests in the temple break the Sabbath and are innocent?" As noted above, the priests actually had more to do on the Sabbath than on regular weekdays. The Sabbath certainly was not a day of inactivity for them. Consider also that the rest the Israelites were promised in Canaan (Deut 3.20) certainly did not mean they would not have to work. They would have to sow, harvest, cut wood, and draw water to survive. Even when God rested on the seventh day of the creation week, this does not mean that God stopped doing everything, for Jesus, responding to a complaint of his healing on the Sabbath, said "My Father is working until now" (John 5.17).

Rest in the Biblical sense does not mean a cessation of activity, but instead refers to "the ideal living condition in the promised land"[7] where one's activity is not burdensome but is blessed by God and productive. This brings us to an important fact at which our observations above on the Sabbath and Jubilee years has hinted: there is a strong connection in the OT between *rest* and the *land*. One form of the Hebrew word for rest (*nahala*) "is used almost as a synonym to ... the promised land of Israel."[8] Deuteronomy 12.9f; 25.19; Josh 1.13; 22.4 are some examples. What made the land a place of rest was the fact that there the Israelites would enjoy a freedom from the oppressive slave labor they knew in Egypt, and their work in the land would be repaid with an abun-

---

[7] Gnana Robinson, "The Idea of Rest in the Old Testament and the Search for the Basic Character of Sabbath," *ZAW* 92 (1980): 32–42, at 42.

[8] Robinson, "The Idea of Rest in the Old Testament," 35.

dance of goods. They would still have to work, but their labors would bring bountiful harvests (see Deut 28.2–13). The character of the land itself as fertile and productive, "flowing with milk and honey," provided a measure of this rest to Israel, and God's provision for his people in the Sabbath and Jubilee years were extraordinary demonstrations of this very idea. Again, this was rooted in the scene of the bountiful garden of Eden, and later echoed in God's provision of abundant manna for Israel on every sixth day in the wilderness.

To rest in the Biblical sense, then, was to live in a situation where one's work was pleasurable and productive, and it also involved enjoying a situation of safety and peace, where one could settle down. Again, Genesis 49.15 is instructive. It says, "When he saw that a resting place was good and that the land was pleasant, he bowed his shoulder to bear burdens, and became a slave at forced labor" (NASB). What Issachar saw as good was the opportunity to settle down in the land, and for that he was willing to take up forced labor.[9] The Hebrew verb *nuach* (often translated "rest" in our English Bibles) has exactly this connotation of "settling down" in several places, as in Exodus 10.14 and Isaiah 7.19. In the case of the Israelites, the rootless and vulnerable existence they knew in Egypt would, in the promised land of rest, be turned into a condition of settlement and tranquility.[10] Thus in Deuteronomy 12.10 and 25.19, rest refers to peace, the cessation of war. Generally, the word refers to a condition of remaining in a situation (see Jdg 2.23). Rest, then, also involves the idea of continuance, and when used of the Sabbath it suggests a continuing relationship between man and God. Again, the Sabbath and Jubilee years especially highlighted the long-term nature of rest when Israelites were to spend an entire year (not just one day a week) of their lives living off of God's gracious provision, not working in the fields but instead devoting their time that whole year to God.

A further significance of the connection between rest and the land is seen in the fact that this same word (*nuach*) was used when God spoke in Psalm 132.8, 13–14 of Zion as his resting-place. That is, Zion was the place where God settled among his people. This passage is especially instructive, because Zion was not just the place where God himself rested but was preeminently the place where God and Israel met in fellowship, and the erection of a permanent structure there for God's dwelling-place (the temple) indicated that God was settling down in the midst of Israel for a long-term relationship. That

---

[9] Robinson, "The Idea of Rest in the Old Testament," 35.

[10] John N. Oswalt, *"nuach,"* *NIDOTTE* 4:1133.

is, God's rest was institutionalized in the tabernacle/temple. There was already a hint of this concept in Numbers 10.33. When Israel left Sinai "the ark of the covenant of the Lord went before them a three days' journey to provide rest for them." Already the presence of God (which was centered around the ark of the covenant) was being associated with Israel's rest. The building of the temple turned this into a more permanent reality.

Living in a land where one could enjoy a continuing situation of freedom from oppressive labor specifically meant that time would be available for the worship of God. This is especially apparent from Deuteronomy 12.9–11, where Israel's entering into rest meant going to the land where God would be worshiped. The text says "for you have not as yet come to the resting place and the inheritance which the Lord your God is giving you. When you cross the Jordan and live in the land which the Lord your God is giving you to inherit, and he gives you rest from all your enemies around you so that you live in security, then it shall come about that the place in which the Lord your God will choose for his name to dwell, there you shall bring all that I command you: your burnt offerings and your sacrifices, your tithes and the contribution of your hand, and all your choice votive offerings which you will vow to the Lord." At a particular place in that land God would cause his name to dwell, and there Israel would present offerings to the Lord (v 11). This would be the essence of Israel's rest in God. Yet it is important to note that while the land and God's rest are closely connected in the OT, we must not make the mistake of thinking the connection amounts to an equation of those terms. The land would be the place where the rest would be achieved, but one could live in the land without necessarily entering into God's rest. As Oswalt says, "The land was a metaphor, God was the reality."[11] The land, then, was the place where God would be worshiped among his people, and resting in that land always primarily meant devoting time to fellowship with God through worship.

The connections between the entrance into the land and the establishment of the temple are important for Hebrews. As noted above, God explicitly linked living in the land, having rest, worship, and being at the place where God's name would dwell (Deut 12.9–11). Another way to see this is that the exodus was intended to be a journey not only into the land of Canaan, but into the presence of God, initially at Sinai, but ultimately in the temple. That is where the journey properly ended. This is previewed in the latter chapters of Exodus, where the instructions for the tabernacle were given. The book of

[11] Oswalt, *"nuach," NIDOTTE* 4:1135.

Exodus ends with a problem, though. When the tabernacle was assembled, the cloud of glory settled upon it and no one was able to enter. The question of how to enter, and who could enter, is left unanswered at the end of the at narrative. The answer comes in the next book of the Pentateuch, Leviticus, which describes who may enter, and when, and under what conditions (purity and holiness).[12] The center of Leviticus is the instructions for the Day of Atonement, the highest holy day in the Israelite calendar. The big picture is that rest was accomplished not just by living in the land, but by being in the presence of God in the land in the designated place of worship, the temple,[13] and through the role of the high priest who entered God's presence for the nation on the Day of Atonement.

Rest, then, involves the ideas of God's provision of one's needs, a resulting freedom from constant attention to one's physical needs which produces both a condition of peace and time for fellowship with God expressed especially in worship, and enjoyment of these conditions over one's lifetime. All of these aspects of rest were to be found ultimately in God. Oswalt has said it well: "What is the Biblical understanding of rest? It is the rest of faith, a life of trust, belief, and obedience in God. In him who is eternal there is permanence; in him who has no rival there is security; in him who has made us in his own image there is freedom; in him who combines complete power, complete holiness, and complete love there is tranquility."[14]

The concept of fellowship with God that was at the core of the Sabbath was no minor or marginal part of the relationship between God and Israel. The Sabbath observance on Israel's part was explicitly said in the Mosaic law to be inextricably tied to the covenant with God. Exodus 31.16 said "So the sons of Israel shall observe the Sabbath, to celebrate the Sabbath throughout their generations as a perpetual covenant." This makes perfect sense in light of what we have already discerned about the character of the Sabbath rest. In the Sabbath Israel participated in the goal for which God had created them. The Sabbath was to be a time of fellowship with God. That fellowship was now to be effected through the covenant of Sinai. The Israelite who despised the Sabbath and used it for himself was by that disobedience indicating his disdain for Israel's re-

---

[12] Morales, *Who Shall Ascend the Mountain of the Lord?*

[13] See Daniel E. Kim, "Jewish and Christian Theology from the Hebrew Bible: The Concept of Rest and Temple in the Targummim, Hebrews, and the Old Testament," in *Hebrews in Contexts*, Gabriella Gelardini and Harold W. Attridge, eds., Ancient Judaism and Early Christianity 91 (Leiden: Brill, 2016), 31–46.

[14] Kim, "Jewish and Christian Theology from the Hebrew Bible."

lationship with God. The one violated the Sabbath paid for his disregard of fellowship with God with his life (Exod 31.15; Num 15.35). Similarly, it was a refusal to observe the Sabbath years (which indicated a refusal to live by faith in God) that the Bible itself gives as the reason for the exile (Lev 26.31–35, 43; 2 Chron 36.21). This is why Amos complained that even though Israel was outwardly observing the Sabbath, they were using the day to plan their dishonesty for the coming week (8.4–6). It was supposed to be a time for God's people to demonstrate the one thing God wanted to see from them most: their faith in him. The Sabbath was designed to be the time when man and God enjoyed each other's fellowship, the time when man put off physical concerns and came to God in faith, and God enjoyed the heartfelt expression of thanks and adoration from man. It was, in a sense, the time when man and God came together.

Like everything else in the old law, the design of the Mosaic Sabbath belied its character as merely the shadow or type of something greater. That is to say, it was eschatological, it pointed to a fuller version of itself in the future, in the "last days," the Messianic time.[15] The Sabbaths of the Mosaic code were observed only periodically (once every seven days, or every seven years). Its periodic character indicated that it was not the ongoing, ultimate, or perfect rest itself. A fuller and permanent expression and enjoyment of the God-man relationship was in the works. The Mosaic Sabbath simply bore witness to it. Isaiah spoke of the Messianic time as a time of God resting with his people: Isaiah 11.10; 14.3; 32.18; 56.4, 6; 66.23. Because the Sabbath rest was associated with the worship of God in the temple, prophecies of a coming new temple were also, in their way, predictions of a coming Sabbath rest for God's people (Isa 2.3; 44.28; Jer 7.26f; Hag 2.7, 9; Zech 6.12f).

God had offered to Israel what Adam had refused: rest, or an ongoing fellowship, with God. The sad story, however, is that Israel refused that rest as well. In general, Israel preferred fellowship with the false gods of her pagan neighbors over the fellowship of the one true and living God who made her and formed her. Ironically, the worship of those false gods (especially Baal) involved a concentration on Israel's physical existence, whereas God had offered to guarantee Israel's physical existence if she would draw near to him through the Sabbath.

There were a few moments in Israel's history where it seemed that Israel might realize the rest God had offered. Israel had rest from war after the ini-

---

[15] See Jon Laansma, *'I Will Give You Rest.' The Rest Motif in the New Testament with Special Reference to Mt 11 and Heb 3–4*, WUNT 98 (Tübingen: Mohr Siebeck, 1997), 58–61.

tial conquest of Canaan under Joshua (Josh 21.44), and thus the conditions for achieving a lasting, settled relationship with God were in place, but Israel did not go on to obey the stipulations of God's covenant. The history of the Judges was a cyclic repetition of unfaithfulness and punishment from God. Israel would learn the consequences for unfaithfulness and for a while would be faithful, but later generations failed to learn from the experiences of their ancestors and as Nehemiah later confessed, "but as soon as they had rest, they did evil again before You" (Neh 9.28). When the monarchy came along, it appeared that perhaps Israel was now on a course to realize true rest with God. David was a righteous man, and with his legacy came the potential for the nation to achieve a lasting fellowship between Israel and God. Although David was not allowed to build the temple, God said to him "Behold, a son will be born to you, who shall be a man of rest; and I will give him rest from all his enemies on every side; for his name shall be Solomon, and I will give peace and quiet to Israel in his days. He shall build a house for My name, and he shall be My son and I will be his father; and I will establish the throne of his kingdom over Israel forever" (1 Chron 22.9–10). Note the ideas of being settled and enjoying one's situation in that passage. The idea was that with Solomon a time of lasting fellowship with God would be possible. Solomon acknowledged "But now the Lord my God has given me rest on every side; there is neither adversary nor misfortune" and expressed his initial desire for the nation to enter into its ideal relationship with God when he said "Behold, I intend to build a house for the name of the Lord my God" (1 Kings 5:4–5). With this assessment and plan David himself concurred (1 Chron 22.18–19). Note again the connection between having rest and building the temple, the place where God was worshiped, the place where fellowship between man and God was achieved. When Solomon dedicated the temple he said, "Blessed be the Lord, who has given rest to his people Israel" (1 Kngs 8.56), and David's view of the situation was "The Lord God of Israel has given rest to his people, and he dwells in Jerusalem forever" (1 Chron 23.25). Solomon had turned his attention to solidifying the nation's relationship with God by building the temple, but alas, Solomon's own unfaithfulness ruined the plan.

The next we hear of Israel approaching entrance to God's rest is under king Asa. He said "'The land is still ours because we have sought the Lord our God; we have sought him, and he has given us rest on every side.' So they built and prospered" (2 Chron 14.7). Here Israel had turned to God, which was the principle behind the Sabbath rest, and God had responded by blessing them.

Asa's reforms prompted the Chronicler to note that "the Lord gave them rest on every side" (2 Chron 15.15). But Asa also became unfaithful, and so again a continuing fellowship between God and Israel did not materialize. He was succeeded by his son Jehoshaphat who was also a good man, yet the inspired account says that during his reign "The high places, however, were not removed; the people had not yet directed their hearts to the God of their fathers" (2 Chron 20.33). The next king, Jehoram, led Judah back into idolatry. When Jeremiah appeared at the end of the southern kingdom's existence, he asserted that Sabbath-keeping was the key to understanding both Judah's destruction and its hope (17.19–27). Similarly, from captivity Ezekiel also explained Judah's woes as a failure to observe the Sabbaths (20.12) and spoke of a time when God's priests would sanctify the Sabbath (44.24), and Isaiah spoke of the restoration of Israel as dependent upon its sincere observance of the Sabbath when he said "If because of the Sabbath, you turn your foot from doing your own pleasure on my holy day, and call the Sabbath a delight, the holy day of the Lord honorable, and honor it, desisting from your own ways, from seeking your own pleasure and speaking your own word, then you will take delight in the Lord, and I will make you ride on the heights of the earth, and I will feed you with the heritage of Jacob your father, for the mouth of the Lord has spoken" (Isa 58.13–14; see also 56.2–7).

The OT closes with the rebuilding of the temple after the exile, but it is hardly a picture of faithfulness and fellowship with God. When Nehemiah discovered that the returned Jews were not observing the Sabbath, he reprimanded them severely and said "What is this evil thing you are doing, by profaning the Sabbath day? Did not your fathers do the same, so that our God brought on us and on this city all this trouble? Yet you are adding to the wrath on Israel by profaning the Sabbath" (13.17f). Nehemiah's use of the word "Sabbath" eleven times in that short scene underscores the centrality of the Sabbath concept to Israel's well-being.[16] Nehemiah understood the failure of faith that neglect of the Sabbath reflected. Even as the Jews labored to rebuild the temple, God said through Isaiah, "Heaven is My throne and the earth is My footstool. Where then is a house you could build for Me? And where is a place that I may rest?" (66.1), indicating that the true rest would not be tied to some physical location like Jerusalem. Like the Sabbath itself, the temple was a symbol of something greater, a symbol of a more perfect

[16] Stanley L. Jaki, "The Sabbath-Rest of the Maker of All," *Asbury Theological Journal* 50 (1995): 37–49, at 45.

fellowship that was to come. God's rest would not be achieved in the temple the returned exiles were building (and thinking that it would seems to have been a crucial mistake of the Jews of Jesus' day). That rest would instead be realized in that to which the temple pointed.

The author of Hebrews understood that the OT was not a story of a rest achieved, but of a rest unrealized.[17] He made his case from Psalm 95, which ends with a warning based on Israel's failure to enter into God's rest. King David (according to Heb 4.7) had urged God's people to succeed where former generations of God's people had failed. The place of David's warning in the chronology of OT discussions of rest implies that in David's day God's rest was yet unrealized. Neither Genesis 2.2 nor Joshua 21.44 meant that God had achieved his fellowship with his people, "for if Joshua had given them rest, He would not have spoken of another day after that" (Heb 4.8). Thus the author can say "So there remains a Sabbath rest for the people of God" (Heb 4.9). That is, since the seventh day of the creation week God had not entered into the lasting fellowship with man he has desired, but God's longing for an ongoing relationship with man is now being fulfilled in the new system of things in Jesus. The goal of creation is achieved through Jesus who brings us into God's rest through his blood.

The long-awaited Sabbath rest between God and man was inaugurated in the ministry of Jesus. To the attentive reader, many things in the gospel narratives proclaim this fact. For example, when Jesus began his public ministry in Galilee, he read from Isaiah 61 in the synagogue of his hometown, Nazareth. The text he read said "The Spirit of the Lord God is upon me, because the Lord has anointed me to bring good news to the afflicted; he has sent me to bind up the brokenhearted, to proclaim liberty to captives and freedom to prisoners; to proclaim the favorable year of the Lord" (vv 1–2). While the words "Sabbath" or "rest" do not appear in that text, it is plain that the language ("proclaim liberty") is that of the announcement of the Jubilee from Leviticus 25.10 ("proclaim a release").[18] When Jesus said "Today this Scripture has been fulfilled in your hearing" (Luke 4.21), he meant that the fellowship (rest) between God and man that was symbolized in the Jubilee was now being fulfilled in

[17] Herold Weiss, "*Sabbatismos* in the Epistle to the Hebrews," *CBQ* 58 (1996): 674–89; Walter C. Kaiser, "The Promise Theme and the Theology of Rest," *BibSac* 130 (1973): 135–50; see also his *Toward an Old Testament Theology* (Grand Rapids: Zondervan, 1978), 127–30.

[18] Andrew. T. Lincoln, "Sabbath, Rest, and Eschatology in the New Testament," in *From Sabbath to Lord's Day*, ed. Donald A. Carson (Grand Rapids: Zondervan, 1982), 197–217, at 201.

himself and his work. Some have argued that Jesus' ministry actually began in a Jubilee year according to the Jewish calendar.[19] If correct, that is surely significant. From a broader point of view, we may note that Luke's presentation of the beginning of the public ministry does not begin with an announcement of the kingdom, but with Jesus preaching in the synagogues of Galilee (which would have been done primarily on Sabbath days) and reading Isaiah 61 in his hometown synagogue. In his own subtle way, then, Luke is trying to present the ministry of Jesus first in terms of the fulfillment of the Sabbath.[20]

Other indicators of the Sabbath nature of Jesus' work appear in his sayings. "Seek first His kingdom and His righteousness, and all these things [physical provisions—from the context] will be added to you" (Matt 6.33). In those familiar words Jesus was describing the kingdom of God as a relationship with God like the Sabbath of old. Remember that the first mention of Israel's Sabbath appeared in connection with God sending the manna to feed Israel. God provided them with food for that day so they could turn their attention to God, having been given assurance that they could trust in God. That is the same idea Jesus set forth in Matthew 6.33. Then there is the clear reference to rest in Matthew 11.28f, where Jesus invites all saying "Come to me, all who are weary and heavy-laden, and I will give you rest. Take my yoke upon you and learn from me, for I am gentle and humble in heart, and you will find rest for your souls" (echoing the same call issued by God through Jer 6:16, but spurned by Israel). Even when Jesus says "I am the good shepherd," he was evoking imagery that partakes of the ideas inherent in the Sabbath rest. Recall that "rest" involves the idea of living in safety and security. Jesus' claim to be the good shepherd surely evoked Ezekiel's prophecy of the Davidic shepherd who would come and of the corresponding time when Israel would live securely on the land and enjoy its blessings (Ezek 34), which are Sabbath concepts.

One of the most obvious things about Jesus to his contemporaries was that he often worked his miracles specifically on Sabbath days. This was not coincidence but was deliberately intended by Jesus (*cf.* Mark 3.2ff). These healings appeared to the Pharisees to violate the Sabbath day, and they were so perturbed by this that they did not see that Jesus was in fact demonstrating that in himself the Sabbath—a freedom from physical concerns to enjoy lasting fellowship with God—was being fulfilled. Perhaps this is best illustrat-

[19] Jack Finegan, *Handbook of Biblical Chronology*, rev. ed. (Peabody, MA: Hendrickson, 1998), 342.

[20] Eduard Lohse, "*sabbaton, sabbatismos, paraskeuē*," *TDNT* 7:26.

ed in the story Luke preserved about the healing of the woman who was bent over with illness. When the Pharisees objected to this cure being worked on the Sabbath, Jesus responded "this woman, a daughter of Abraham as she is, whom Satan has bound for eighteen long years, should she not have been released from this bond on the Sabbath day?" (13.16). What more appropriate day was there to set someone free from physical hardship than the Sabbath? This takes us back to the exodus from Egypt and the reason given for the Sabbath commandment in Deuteronomy 5.15. But we must not fail to understand that the miracles Jesus worked were illustrations of what he came to accomplish spiritually. Setting the woman free from physical ailment was an illustration of Jesus' power to free people from slavery to sin and the flesh and make their fellowship with God possible. Just as the Sabbath remembered the new situation God made when he liberated his people so they could enter into covenant fellowship with himself, so Jesus, when he healed on the Sabbath day, was proclaiming that in him a new time of fellowship with God was dawning and the old Sabbath was fulfilled.

This brings us to an important consideration. Sometimes it is suggested that the Lord's day (Sunday) has replaced the Sabbath day now that Christianity has come. This, however, fails to see the true significance of both the old Sabbath and Christianity. Remember that the Sabbath came at the end of the week. The days of labor led up to the Sabbath, making the Sabbath a day of completion or, in the Biblical sense, "perfection."[21] Therefore, that old institution by its nature pointed forward. Also, by having only an occasional (even if regular) day that was devoted to the Lord, the old Mosaic system was showing its imperfection. God's rest is achieved not when man gives God one day each week, but when man spends his entire life living in faithful, trusting fellowship with God. When Jesus said "seek first his kingdom and his righteousness, and all these things will be added to you," he certainly indicated what is to be the way of life every day for those in the kingdom of God. Thus *the Messianic age is God's Sabbath rest realized.* In the Messianic age every day is a Sabbath day, every year is a Sabbath year, and the Messianic age is a spiritual Jubilee to God. Jesus rose from the dead (and we worship) on the first day of the week proclaiming that the time of looking forward to completion had, in one sense, ended. The time when God enters into a lasting fellowship with man has arrived, and those who enter into that fellowship begin each week in the very thing that old Sabbath emphasized: worship. But it would

[21] Robinson, "The Idea of Rest in the Old Testament," 39.

surely be a mistake to think that the formal worship of God on the first day of the week fulfills the old Sabbath. All of life in the Messianic age is to be devoted first to the worship and fellowship of God with the promise that God will take care of the other aspects of our existence.

We noted above that the Jubilee cycle was observed on a smaller scale in connection with the harvest of the first fruits. The day following the next seven Sabbaths after the harvest of the first fruits was a holy day dedicated to God. In NT times this was called the feast of Pentecost, and was the day on which the Spirit Jesus had promised to his disciples came upon them and they first proclaimed the forgiveness of sins in the name of the crucified and resurrected Jesus. It hardly seems coincidental that the age of freedom from sin and of fellowship with God began on the day that was itself part of the larger Sabbath pattern of the OT.

The OT's perspective on rest was summed up by God when he said through the prophet Jeremiah "I will come to give rest to Israel" (31.2 NIV). The psalmist anticipated the outcome of the story when he testified "My soul finds rest in God alone" (61.2 NIV). The OT presented a picture of God who desired to rest with man, but whose offer of rest was repeatedly rejected. In Jesus, however, that rest has begun. In Jesus God has made a new Israel with whom his rest is realized. But the story is not yet over, for although the rest has begun, it remains to find its perfect fulfillment in heaven.

HEBREWS 4

4.1 Therefore let us fear, lest, while a promise of entering into his rest remains, any of you might seem to have failed to attain it.

The faithless behavior of the Israelites (3.19), along with its consequence (they were denied entrance into the land of promised rest), stands as a warning to God's new Israel, the church. **Fear**, therefore, is the appropriate response. We should not diminish this to mean "respect" here (although the word can bear that meaning depending on the context). Genuine fear of facing the wrath of God is a legitimate, Biblical motive for obedience.

The last words in Psalm 95 are "my **rest**," and the author of Hebrews will now focus on it. See the Excursus: The Sabbath Rest. The warning to the church from Israel's history is appropriate not only because of the typological correspondence between Israel and the church, but because, as our author will show in the following verses, the rest of which the Psalm speaks is a messianic, eschatological rest. He has already treated the word "today" as a reference to the messianic age (3.13), and his treatment of the "rest" as messianic is consistent with this. In Psalm 95 God announced the time when the kind of relationship he had always wanted with man would be achieved, *viz.* the messianic age (v 7 below). Thus, our author says that a **promise of entering into** God's **rest remains**, *i.e.* Today, in the now-present messianic age, "these last days" (1.2). God is offering to the church what was offered to, and refused by, Israel. That this is indeed the case will be argued in verses 2–9. This is the first explicit mention of God's **promise** in Hebrews, and the concept lies at the core of the epistle's exhortation to faithfulness and endurance. There is no OT text where God promised, in so many words, "I will bring the Messiah's people into my rest." A messianic reading of Numbers 14.31 might be in the background here, but more likely is the idea that the author was able to refer to a promise because he read Scripture as constituting a holistic narrative[1] in which we all are still participants. God has always determined to rest with his people. That goal was not reached with Adam, nor with Israel, but God *will* achieve his purpose and fulfill his promise to the true descendants of Abraham. It is in this sense, then, of God's eternal intention, that the author could speak of entering God's rest as a promise.

The original readers of Hebrews were thinking about forsaking Christ, or had already begun to forsake him, to avoid the shame and rejection that was coming from unbelievers, and the point here is that to forsake Christ is an act of unfaithfulness which would prevent them from entering into the rest—the ongoing, continual fellowship with God—that God has prepared for them in the heavenly Jerusalem. The ongoing nature of Biblical rest seems to be the key idea here. It is not enough to become a Christian; rest is achieved only by those who persevere. From the author's position of observing this group who had become Christians but were now contemplating quitting, it **seemed**, therefore, as if they had failed to truly attain it. Although they had become Christians, the hearts (see 3.12) of the recipients were not set on continuing in it because the shame heaped upon them as Christians had created a crisis of faith. But their reluctance to continue in it jeopardized their place in God's rest. Entering into God's rest is not an event that one accomplishes once and then it is over. It is more like a process, something that we begin now but must also continually maintain until the full measure of rest is granted in the presence of God. Past faithfulness does not guarantee anyone a place in the heavenly Jerusalem, and quitting (*i.e.*, failing to persevere) will cause one to fail to attain to God's rest. At the moment, the matter was not settled because the original recipients were only contemplating quitting (and perhaps showing its first signs). They were on the edge, as it were. Their decision to stay or to quit would determine it. The verb translated "**failed to attain**" (Greek *hustereō*) brings to mind the end of Moses, who got close to the land of promised rest but was denied entrance for his unfaithfulness (Num 20.12; Deut 34.4), but it in this context it refers primarily to the wilderness generation of the Israelites, who are the subject of Psalm 95.7–11. To abandon Christ is to repeat the mistake of Israel, to

[1] Boyarin describes the author's exposition of Psalm 95 as "the interpretation of the Bible by the Bible, the reading of the Bible as one giant literary context." That is, the method is midrashic. Boyarin, "Midrash in Hebrews / Hebrews as Midrash," 26.

miss out on a lasting fellowship with God, because it is Christ who brings us all the way into the presence of God as our high priest.

There is another aspect to the story of the Israelites which, if it is not explicitly mentioned here, is latent in the words **failed to attain**. The verb is used again in 12.15 and means to miss out on something. When Israel heard the punishment for their unbelief—that they would die in the wilderness—they changed their minds and attempted to enter the land. At that point God intervened with a judgment, a final decision concerning their future, and no more progress was possible. Although they attempted to enter the land, they were repulsed (Num 14.39–45). They had made a choice that brought them into judgment from which there was no escape. The message here is that the same thing can happen to Christians who have experienced the same good treatment from God as the ancient Israelites. If they make their choice not to continue on, they may put themselves into a situation from which they cannot escape (*cf.* 2.3; 12.25). They will face God's wrath on judgment day and wish to change their minds then, but it will be too late. Our author will discuss another similar case, that of Esau, in 12.16–17.

4.2 For we have been the recipients of good news, just like them. However, the word they heard did not benefit them, because they were not united in faith with those who accepted it.[2]

In what sense was **good news** preached to the Israelites? Our author is here using the term (the same word used in the NT for "gospel") in a broad sense to mean "good news about entering God's rest" or "good news about the possibility of fellowship with God." The Israelites had experienced the saving power of God in the exodus and were exhorted to enter the land of Canaan that awaited them where they would worship God and enjoy the blessings of his presence among them (Num 14.7

[2] There are two ways the latter part of this verse might be translated depending on a textual variant here: 1) the heard word did not benefit them who were (or, because they were) not joined in faith with those who heard (ESV, HCSB, NET, NIV, NRSV) or 2) the heard word did not benefit them because it was not joined with faith among those who heard (NASB, RSV). The first reading is the one in the Nestle[28] text, and defended in Bruce Manning Metzger, *A Textual Commentary on the Greek New Testament, Second Edition a Companion Volume to the United Bible Societies' Greek New Testament*, 4th rev. ed. (London, New York: United Bible Societies, 1994), 595.

"they spoke to all the congregation"). It is in this sense that they **heard** the same kind of good news that is contained in the gospel of Jesus (see the Excursus: The Sabbath Rest).

Just hearing the good news about the possibility of fellowship with God does not **benefit** anyone unless they respond to it **in faith**, trusting God's promise and living like it (*cf.* Jam 1.22). The fate of the Israelites is proof enough of that. The problem lay not with the message, but with the hearers (*cf.* the parable of the sower, Matt 13). God's promise of fellowship with him is not unconditional. Israel of old made the (common) mistake of thinking that God would bless them regardless of their behavior because they were the chosen people. They learned, however, that God's fellowship is enjoyed on the condition that those who are invited to share in it accept the offer in faith. Those who do not respond in humble, obedient faith suffer the destructive wrath of God. Their punishment is our warning.

Of course, not every Israelite from the exodus generation died under the wrath of God. There were a few who heard the good news about entering into God's rest and accepted it. **Accepted** here literally means "heard," but in the Biblical way of thinking, there is more to hearing than simply being exposed to, or listening to, a message. To hear in the Biblical sense is to receive, to accept, and to internalize so that the word affects both the mind and the behavior. In the Biblical sense, to hear is to believe (*cf.* Jesus' often-repeated call, "He who has ears to hear, let him hear"; *cf.* Jam 2.21). The problem with the majority of people in the exodus generation is that they did not join themselves (they **were not united**), **in faith**, to those few who did "hear" God's word. The importance of joining in faith with other believers is a constant theme in Hebrews; see especially 10.24f; 12.1, 22–24.

4.3 For we who have believed enter into rest, just as he has said, "As I swore in my wrath,[3] they will not enter my rest," even though his works were finished from the foundation of the world.

In verse 1 the author said that there remains a promise for us to enter into God's rest. He will now demonstrate that this is a fact, as the use of the word **for** (Greek *gar*) indicates, since it may not have been such an

[3] The KJV here translates the Greek particle *ei* with the word "if," which makes the reader expect a conditional sentence. However, when *ei* is used in an oath (as here, where God swore in his wrath) it does not mean "if" but instead denotes a strong negation (a Hebraism, BDF §372). The newer translations correctly render it "They shall not enter" or "They shall never enter...."

obvious thing to his readers. Perhaps some thought that God's rest was something God already gave to the Jews. Our author has already rejected such a view in 3.19, and here he argues that God's rest was still open.

The emphasis here, however, is not just on the possibility of entering into God's rest, but also on the faithfulness required for it. God's rest is for **we who have believed**, who respond to God's offer in persevering faith. The Israelites were invited to share in God's rest in the promised land, but they refused the invitation by their unwillingness to trust what God told them. The case of the Israelites shows, then, that the faithless cannot enter into God's rest (3.19; 4.2). Believers (*i.e.*, those who endure in their trust), however, do indeed **enter** that **rest**. The readers of Hebrews, therefore, needed to prove themselves true believers in the gospel that had been preached to them (*cf.* 2.1) and continue in their faith, lest they meet the same end as the ancient Israelites. The present tense of **enter** should not here be explained away as a use of the present tense to denote the surety of a future event. People of faith enter into God's rest now, although the fullest experience of that rest will be realized in the heavenly Jerusalem (see Excursus: The Sabbath Rest; also see comments on 12.22–24).

The author again quotes Psalm 95.11 (**As I swore ...**) to prove the assertion from verse 1 that the possibility of entering into God's rest still exists. As a careful exegete, the author is working his way through the text of Psalm 95.7–11, having covered verses 7–10 from the psalm in his discussion in Hebrews 3.12–19. The fact that the exodus generation of Israelites did not enter into God's rest means that it was still open for someone to enjoy. The last phrase of this verse (**even though his works were finished ...**) highlights this yet-available nature of God's rest. God had done his part to make a blissful relationship with man possible. He has been waiting, as it were, since the time his works of creation were finished, for man to accept the invitation. The invitation to fellowship with God "was something long present and lying in readiness,"[4] and Israel had an opportunity to enter into it but failed because of their unbelief. Moffatt put it well when he said "When God excluded that unbelieving generation from his Rest, he was already himself in his Rest. The *katapausis* [rest] was already in existence; the reason why these men did not gain entrance was their own unbelief, not any failure on God's part to have the Rest ready."[5]

---

[4] Lünemann, *Epistle to the Hebrews*, 171.

[5] Moffatt, *Epistle to the Hebrews*, 51.

4.4 For he has spoken somewhere concerning the seventh day in this way: "And God rested on the seventh day from all his works."

The "**somewhere**" from which the author now quotes is Genesis 2.2, which simply notes that after God created the world in six days, on the seventh day he rested. The function of this quotation in the author's argument is to prove what was said at the end of verse 3, that God entered his **rest** after he finished creating the world and has been waiting for his people to join him in it. The author is following a regular rabbinic exegetical method where one verse is used to interpret another (see Introduction); Jewish readers would have recognized this as a valid argument. The most natural way to understand the phrase "my rest" from Psalm 95.11 is that there is a rest that God himself owns and enjoys. The quotation from Genesis 2.2 establishes quite clearly that God has a rest, that he entered into it after his work of creating the universe, and that he was then ready for man to come and join him in an enduring fellowship.

Even though God rested **from all his works** on the seventh day of the creation week, the Bible distinguishes between God's work in creating the world and his work in sustaining the world. God has done many things since the creation (*cf.* John 5.17). That is, God's rest is not God's cessation from all activity. Instead, it denotes God's readiness and desire for a permanent fellowship with man. Since he finished the creation of the world God had been waiting for the time when man would join him in his rest, and that time began when the messianic age commenced. This was the time Psalm 95 predicted ("today").

Another important function of this quotation is that it connects God's rest mentioned in Psalm 95 with the Sabbath. The word "Sabbath" in Hebrew means "seventh," and Genesis 2.2 explicitly says that God's rest was on the **seventh**, or Sabbath, day. In this sense, one can say that God has already entered into his Sabbath. The rest which God entered on the seventh day after creating the world was, of course, the primary model for the Sabbath day of the Jews (Exod 20.8–11). It is interesting that the Sabbath is also specifically linked to the exodus from Egypt (Deut 5.12–15). This is no contradiction but instead underscores the correspondence between rest and a situation of enduring fellowship with God which was possible only after the exodus. See the Excursus: The Sabbath Rest. The Sabbath itself was a type of the relationship with God that would be available in the Messiah, a relationship in which man would be free from the hard slavery of sin to devote his energies to worshiping God and to enjoy his blessings. Those who come to God through Jesus our high priest leave the bondage of sin and enter into God's own rest, which he has been waiting to enjoy with man since the creation of the world was finished.

4.5 And in this place again, "They will not enter my rest."

This place is Psalm 95, which has been the main object of our author's comments since 3.12.[6] By means of a technique which the rabbis called *gezerah shawa* (see Introduction), the author coupled Psalm 95 with the preceding quotation from Genesis 2.2 (both contain the word "rest"). By quoting this line from Psalm 95 **again** (for the third time now; *cf.* 3.11 and 4.3) the author wanted to focus on the fact that God, *after* the creation and *after* he entered his rest, was still speaking about the possibility of people entering into his rest with him. The gist of the argument lies in the chronological sequence of the statements and the implications of that sequence. The fact that God told the Israelites that they would be denied entrance into his rest implies that such entrance was possible. God did not say "no one can enter my rest" or "there is no rest to enter," but "*they* (the unfaithful Israelites) will not enter my rest." *They* could not enter, but the faithful may (4.3).

4.6 Since, therefore, it remains for some to enter it, and those who formerly received the good news did not enter because of disobedience,

Verses 3–5 established, by careful use of Scripture, the conclusion stated here that **it remains** for **some** to **enter** God's rest. The "rest" of which Psalm 95 speaks was not something accomplished by Israel and finished. Instead, it is an enduring relationship between the creator and his creature (man) that was still vacant for the faithful to enter, because Israel had not entered it. As Weiss put it, "God's rest on the seventh day did not take place in a past buried in a chronological time. It is a permanent reality in the life of God. It is on account of the permanent nature of God's rest that the author sees the possibility of entering it open to successive generations."[7] Someone can still enter it since Israel, the people to whom **the good news** about the possibility of entering God's rest was first an-

---

[6] See comments on 3.3: "this" refers to what is thematic in its context.

[7] Weiss, "*Sabbatimos* in the Epistle to the Hebrews," 682.

nounced, did not enter into God's rest with him **because of** their **disobedience** (same term as in 3.18), which is the same thing as their failure to believe (3.19) or to "hear" (4.2). They **received** the good news about entering into God's rest only in the sense that God announced it to them. He did this when he sent Moses to bring them out of Egypt and into Canaan (Exod 3.8ff; 6.8). However, from the very beginning those Israelites did not believe that God was going to bring them into the land (see Exod 6.9). They grew weary of the hardships of the wilderness, and finally they became frightened when they saw its inhabitants and concluded that there was no way they could possess it. It was a failure to trust God's promise (Exod 23.23), which was a failure to trust God himself. The author of Hebrews calls their refusal to go forward in faith **disobedience**.

We should be careful to note that the author of Hebrews does *not* say that a promise remains for us to enter God's rest *because of* the failure of the Israelites. Paul shows in Romans 9–11 that this would be a misreading of Israel's history. Our author will later show (in ch 11) that even those who lived faithfully under the old covenant did not receive what was promised because the ultimate reward, the messianic rest, was always designed to include us as well (11.40).

4.7 he again appoints a certain day, "Today," speaking through David after so long a time, just as it has been proclaimed beforehand, "Today, if you will hear his voice, do not harden your hearts."

The author has shown from Scripture that God has a rest, and it is still open for some to enter it. This means that the promise of entering his rest remains (v 1), which is expressed in the call of Psalm 95.7, **Today if you will hear his voice ....** The word **appoint** (Greek *horizō*) means to determine or to set something,[8] here indicating that it was the plan and purpose of God. God did not have the kind of relationship he wanted with man in times past, but he purposed, planned for, and appointed a time (**a certain**[9] **day**) in which he would enjoy that relationship in a new order of things he would bring about. God spoke of that appointed time in Psalm 95 a **long time** after the time of Joshua (roughly four hundred years). The

[8] BDAG 723.

[9] "Certain" not in the sense of "particular" or "sure," but in the sense of "non-specific" or "some" (BDAG 1008). Greek does not have an indefinite article, but the use of *tis* can sometimes be similar to the English indefinite article.

argument here is the same as in verse 5: the chronological sequence of the Biblical statements implies that God's rest was not filled by the ancient Israelites, for if they had filled God's desire for rest with man, God would not have been talking about the need for people in the messianic age ("today") to have the proper hearts in order to enter it.

The Hebrew Psalter does not explicitly ascribe Psalm 95 to **David**, but the LXX does. However, ascription to David does not necessarily mean that David was literally the author.[10] "David" could here be a reference to the book of Psalms that is so closely associated with David and his kingdom. Whether "David" here means "the Psalter" or that David wrote Psalm 95, either way the *speaker* in Psalm 95 is clearly God. Hagner is correct as he notes "David is referred to here in order to stress the chronological distance between the time of the wilderness wandering and the repetition of the promise with the word 'today'."[11]

The time when God's purpose for an enduring relationship characterized by worship on man's part and blessing on God's part would be fulfilled is **Today**, the key word in Psalm 95, which our author understood from Psalm 2 to be the messianic time, the time inaugurated by the exaltation of the Son (see comments on 3.13). In the present order of things under the exalted Christ, God finally realizes his goal of having continual fellowship with a people of faith who worship him and whom he blesses. Those who enter God's rest are those who humbly **hear** the **voice** of God in his Son (1.2) and who do not faithlessly **harden** their **hearts** (see 3.12) but instead respond in enduring faith.

4.8 For if Joshua had given them rest, he would not have been speaking about another day after these days.

The author now draws out the implication of Psalm 95.7, 11. The use of "Jesus" in the KJV translation conveys to the modern reader an idea almost exactly opposite of what the author of Hebrews meant. The author was arguing on the basis of the chronological sequence of the Biblical events (see vv 5 and 7 above). Therefore, our author was not here speaking of Jesus Christ but of **Joshua** the son of Nun, the leader of the Israelites after the death of Moses. How did this confusion arise? Josh-

[10] Peter C. Craigie, *Psalms 1–50*, 2nd ed., WBC 19 (Nashville: Nelson, 2004), 33–35.

[11] Donald A. Hagner, *Hebrews*. Understanding the Bible Commentary Series (Grand Rapids: Baker Books, 2011), 76.

ua's name, in Hebrew, is Yehoshua. This was later shortened to Yeshua (as in Neh 8.17). When the Hebrew Bible was translated into Greek (the LXX), this shortened form of Joshua's name became *Iēsous*, and English has transliterated this Greek version of the name roughly as Jesus. There can be little doubt that our Lord's name was the Hebrew name Yeshua, the same as that of Joshua, and people familiar only with the LXX version of the Scriptures would have known Joshua as *Iēsous*, or "Jesus." Technically the KJV has not erred since Joshua and Jesus had the same name. Furthermore, we must be open to the possibility, if not likelihood, that the author of Hebrews wished to evoke a subtle contrast and comparison of the two great "Joshuas." Both share the status of great leaders of God's people, and Joshua was an "apostle" in the sense that he was sent into the held by the enemy, but the son of Nun and his conquests was only a type of the Son of God who leads (*cf.* 2.10) God's people into the true rest. However most modern readers, unaware that Jesus' and Joshua's names were actually the same, know our Lord only by the Greek name Jesus and the son of Nun only by the Hebrew name Joshua, and in the interests of clarity the modern English versions are careful to observe the distinction.

The fact that God ("**he**") was still speaking about the possibility of people entering his **rest** such a long time **after** Joshua (v 7) clearly implies that the true rest God offered to Israel was not realized in Joshua's days (**these**[12] **days**). Joshua did not bring the Israelites into God's rest. If he had succeeded in this, if Israel had attained it and God's desire for an enduring fellowship with man was fulfilled and further opportunity closed, then God would not have spoken later (in Psa 95, in the time of David) about his rest in such a way to imply that participation in it was still possible. Israel did not enter God's rest, and so it remained "vacant" in the sense that although God was already there, man had not joined God yet.

Immediately, however, we think of Joshua 21.4: "And the Lord gave them rest on every side, according to all that he had sworn to their fathers, and no one of all their enemies stood before them; the Lord gave all their enemies into their hand" (NASB). Does Hebrews' claim that Joshua did not give Israel rest contradict this? Not at all. Simply occupying the land was not the essence of the promised rest. As Bruce noted, "The people addressed in the ninety-fifth psalm were already living in the

---

[12] See comments on 3.3.

land of Canaan, as their ancestors had been for generations now."[13] And yet God was still speaking about entering into his rest. God's rest was to be Israel's enduring fellowship with God, but she refused it. The history recorded in the book of Judges further shows that even after the Israelites entered the land of Canaan, they generally failed to accept God's invitation of fellowship and to worship him. They may have entered the land, but they did not enter the true rest God desired them to enter. Their entrance into the land got them closer to realizing this spiritual rest, but the occupation of the land was not itself the rest. What the Israelites experienced under Joshua, therefore, was rest only in a limited sense, and it was not the true spiritual rest God had designed for them. That is why God later, after the time of Joshua, was still speaking about his rest being open and unrealized.

4.9 Consequently, a Sabbath rest for the people of God remains.

Our author has now used a different word for "rest" than he has been using in verses 1–8. Until this point the author has used the Greek word *katapausis* (in both the noun and verb forms) because it is the word used in Psalm 95.11 LXX. Here, however, he substitutes the theologically loaded word **Sabbath**.[14] The Greek noun (*sabbatismos*) is rare,[15] although other words built on the *sabbat-* stem are frequent enough in Jewish Greek writing. The suffix *-ismos* is normally added to a verb stem to make a noun that denotes an action.[16] *Sabbatismos*, then, would mean "a Sabbath-keeping"[17] or Sabbath observance. It conjures up the idea of the festivity and joy of the Sabbath celebration.[18] The author could make this switch in terminology because he has already shown from Genesis 2.2 (quoted in v 4 above) that God's rest was on the seventh, or Sabbath, day. God's rest, therefore, is a Sabbath rest. God entered his Sabbath, or his rest, on the seventh day after the creation of the world, but Israel failed to join God in it because of her faithlessness. It is still possible (it

[13] Bruce, *Epistle to the Hebrews*, 108.

[14] The substitution of synonyms was a common practice in Jewish expositions of Scripture. Kistemaker, *Psalm Citations*, 74.

[15] Only here in the NT, and in secular Greek only in Plutarch, *On Superstition* 3 (Johnson, *Hebrews*, 129).

[16] Robertson, *Grammar*, 151; BDF §109.

[17] LSJ 1579.

[18] Lane, *Hebrews 1–8*, 101–102.

remains), therefore, for **the people of God** in the present ("Today")—believers, the church—to join God in his Sabbath rest.

We should also remember that, in Judaism, Sabbath-keeping was considered one of the most important duties of any Jew, so much so that it was considered one of the fundamental marks of Jewish identity.[19] Our author presents them with the true Sabbath of God, a messianic eschatological rest, of which the Jewish Sabbath ordinance was a symbol.[20]

4.10 For the one who has entered his rest has himself also rested from his works, just as God did from his.

Here the author focuses on a particular characteristic of the Sabbath, *viz.* that entering into it involves a cessation from one's works. This is in imitation of God's own resting after his work of creation (v 4 above; Gen 2.2; Exod 20.8–11).

One question here concerns the identity of **the one who has entered**. Does this phrase denote anyone who enters into rest?[21] Or does it refer specifically to Christ?[22] That is, is this verse saying that when anyone enters into God's rest, that person, like God, ceases from his works? Or is it saying that a particular and special "he" (singular in the Greek), Christ, has entered into God's Sabbath rest having "ceased" from his ordeal in the flesh (*cf.* 2.9–18)? Since the exhortation in this passage is built on an analogy between Israel and the church, it would seem best not to see here a reference to Christ. In verse 9 the author was speaking about the people of God, and it is best to understand "the one who has entered" as a generic statement, referring to anyone from among God's people.[23]

---

[19] Pagans often noted that the Jews did not work on the seventh day; Horace, *Satires* 1.9; Tacitus *Hist.* 5.4; Juvenal 14.105–106; Petronius, *Satyr.* frag. 37; Seneca, as reported in Augustine, *City of God* 6.11; Dio Cassius 37.17. Older Greek writers such as Agatharchides of Cnidus were also familiar with this custom (quoted to this effect by Josephus in *Against Apion* 1.209–12).

[20] The idea that this passage teaches Christians to continue observance of the seventh day fails to follow the author's argument and tends to make the identification of "rest" with a physical condition, which the author was trying to refute (in v 8). The rest that the faithful presently enter is not the observance of a Sabbath kind of day *a la* the OT Law. The Sabbath day was only a type of the true, spiritual rest that the faithful enter through Christ.

[21] Ellingworth, *Epistle to the Hebrews*, 255–57; Cockerill, *Epistle to the Hebrews*, 211.

[22] So Henry Alford, *Alford's Greek Testament: An Exegetical and Critical Commentary* (Grand Rapids: Guardian Press, 1976), 4:81.

[23] Ellingworth, *Epistle to the Hebrews*, 257: "The whole argument is designed to encourage the readers to take their own place in God's [rest]."

A similar question involves the phrase **his rest**. Who is the antecedent of **his**? God, or a generic "person"? That is, does it refer to someone entering into one's own rest, or does it refer to someone entering into God's rest? Does the statement mean to rest *like* God, or does it mean to rest *with* God? Since the "rest" of which the author has been speaking at length has up to this point exclusively been God's own rest, a good case can be made that this is what it means here too.[24] The verse would then be saying that the believer who enters into God's rest with him there finds rest for himself in that relationship, and therefore states the reason the promised rest of God into which believers are invited to enter is called a Sabbath rest (v 9): because the one who enters into it **has rested from his** own **works,** which is exactly what **God did** when he entered his Sabbath after the creation of the world. This means, then, that the believer's rest is a Sabbath-type of rest because it is an entrance into God's own Sabbath rest, and this would confirm the assertion of verse 9.

A third and even more difficult question concerns what the author of Hebrews meant by the term **works** (Greek *ergon*) here. What are the works that a believer ceases when he enters into God's Sabbath rest with him? At least four interpretations have been offered:

1) They are the works of the old Law. It is possible that our author here meant that once one has entered into God's rest through Christ, one finds relief (rest) from the obligations (works) of the Law of Moses, which certainly were difficult (*cf.* Acts 15.10). However, the author of Hebrews nowhere depicts Judaism as a religion that could be summed up by the word "works." See comments on 6.1 and 9.14.

2) The author was using "works" as a synonym for "hardships."[25] Understood in this way, the statement would need to refer to a future rest (*cf.* Rev 14.13), because nowhere else does the author of Hebrews suggest that by remaining faithful to Christ his readers' earthly trials would end in the present. Similarly, "works" here could be the works of faithful endurance, on analogy with Hebrews 6.10f. "Works" does need not have a negative sense. Again, this would require that the rest spoken of here is future.

---

[24] Grindheim, *Letter to the Hebrews*, 255: "To rest from one's works is to enjoy fellowship with God in his blissful state of rest."

[25] Lünemann, 176; Attridge, *Hebrews*, 131: "Christians can expect rest after the 'toils' of this life."

3) Guthrie has suggested that these are "the hard-hearted works that see the works of God mentioned in the psalm and yet provoke him."[26] It is not clear, however, how this could stand in parallel with God resting from his works.

4) Maybe the best approach is to realize the obvious, that "The author does not specify what are the believer's 'works' which correspond to God's works of creation."[27] Similarly Hagner: "The most plausible interpretation, however, is that the author has in mind the ideal qualities of the sabbath-rest, namely, peace, well-being, and security—that is, a frame of mind that by virtue of its confidence and trust in God possesses these qualities in contradiction to the surrounding circumstances,"[28] and "In exegeting the meaning of 'works,' it is a mistake to put too much stress on the analogy of God's having rested from his works. The analogy centers on the reality of the rest, not what one rests from."[29] In this case, the phrase is simply a generic, negative way of reinforcing the idea of rest: "when you rest, you cease from your works." This view has the most to commend it.

4.11 Let us be diligent, therefore, to enter that rest, lest anyone fall by the same pattern of disobedience.

With these words the author summarizes and repeats the main point of his exhortation (*cf.* 3.19–4.1). While believers have already entered into God's rest (v 3), entering is conditioned on perseverance. With the original recipients wavering in their commitment, it seemed as if they had not truly entered yet (v 1). Hence the exhortation **to enter** it. The hortatory **be diligent** reminds us that entrance into the full measure of God's rest is granted only to those who endure in faith in God's promise concerning it. Here, in this context, it carries the sense of making sure that one is not deceived (see v 12; recall 3.13). In saying that we must be eager or earnest to enter God's rest, however, we must not think that what we do (even our faith) earns us a place within it. Nothing man can do can possibly earn him a right relationship with God (Eph 2.8–9; 2 Tim 1.9). The exhortation to be earnest to enter God's rest is an

---

[26] Guthrie, "Hebrews' Eschatology in Hermeneutical Perspective, 18.

[27] Ellingworth, *Epistle to the Hebrews*, 257.

[28] Hagner, *Hebrews*, 72.

[29] Hagner, *Hebrews*, 76.

exhortation not to "refuse him who is speaking" (12.25), not to reject God's invitation to join him in his Sabbath rest but instead to continue faithfully on, even if that means hardship.

Once again, the plain sense of the statements in Hebrews is that it is entirely possible for a child of God to **fall** and be lost (*cf.* 2.1; 3.6, 12, 14; 4.1; 6.6). The word "fall" here recalls the statement in 3.17 that the corpses of those who did not trust in God fell in the wilderness (from Num 14.29, 32). The analogy here is clear. If Christians follow **the same pattern** (example) **of disobedience** as exhibited in the case of the Israelites (as Psa 95 so clearly points out), they will suffer the same consequence, *viz.* permanent exclusion from God's rest. The word "pattern" (or example; Greek *hupodeigma*) is often used in Greek literature for a positive model, but Hebrews uses it negatively;[30] the word can denote that which is the basis for instruction.[31]

4.12 For the word of God is living and active, and sharper than any two-edged sword, and pierces to the separation of soul and spirit, and of the joints and marrow, and is able to judge the reflections and thoughts of the heart.

The conjunction **for** establishes a connection with the exhortation of verse 11. The reason we must be diligent to enter God's rest, and not follow the same pattern of faithlessness as the ancient Israelites, is because we can deceive ourselves into a false sense of security (recall 3.13). In contrast to our self-deception, God's word reveals our true disposition towards God.

There is no indication in this context that the term **word** is being used in this verse as a designation for Jesus (as in John 1.1ff),[32] although our author has noted that God has spoken through his Son in the messianic age (1.2). Instead, our author has in mind the message that has come from God, the "good news" (v 2), the message consisting of an invitation to join God in his rest. The author's statement here is presented as a general truth that is true of any of God's communication to man.

---

[30] Johnson, *Hebrews*, 131.

[31] E. Kenneth Lee, "Words Denoting 'Pattern' in the New Testament," *NTS* 8 (1962): 166–73, at 168.

[32] Although there is a long interpretive tradition that sees Jesus as the word here. See James Swetnam, "Jesus as *Logos* in Hebrews 4,12–13," *Bib* 62 (1981): 214–24; Angela Costly, "A New Look at Hebrews 4:12–13," *PIBA* 40 (2017): 23–42.

The word that has come to us is **living**, because it comes from the living God (see on 3.12). It is not a static word on a page. Instead it speaks, it has a living voice (recall Psa 95.7); all the Biblical quotations in Hebrews are introduced with verbs of "saying." "Living" sometimes emphasizes the divine ability to judge (condemn), and no doubt that is prominently in view here (see the comments on "living God" in 3.12 and 10.31). The word of God is also **active** (Greek *energēs*, from which we get our English word "energy"), a description that emphasizes its effectiveness. The power of God's word is a familiar theme in the Bible (*cf.* Isa 55.11; Psa 33.9; 1 Cor 1.18; Rom 1.15; Heb 1.3). The word of God is active, here, in the sense that it actively confronts every person in a way from which we cannot escape. The comparison of the word of God to a **sharp sword** is found elsewhere in the Bible (Eph 6.17; Isa 49.2; *cf.* Rev 2.16; 19.15, 21). To the ancients a **two-edged** sword was especially lethal. Just as a sharp sword could cut through muscle and bone and expose one's internal parts, so God's word has the ability to penetrate (**pierce**) into our deepest, innermost parts (**soul and spirit, joints and marrow**) and judge the **heart**, the seat of our faculties, personality, and character.

The connection of this warning with the context goes back to the quotation from Psalm 95.7–11, in which the word "heart" appeared twice (and this was re-quoted in 3.15 and 4.7). The term was also repeated, by the author, in 3.12. The word "heart" has been ringing constantly in this exhortation, making a strong rhetorical appeal. The problem with the Israelites was with their hearts. Their disobedience, and their subsequent failure to enter God's rest, started when they went astray *in their hearts*. The warning, therefore, was that not only must the readers not turn back from following Christ in its outward expressions, but also that they must not turn back in their hearts. Apostasy, falling away, starts on the inside. Quitting the "external" practices of a Christian is the sign of having already quit in one's heart. This raises the important question of how one might know the condition of one's heart without self-deception. The answer here is: the condition of your heart will be made plain by its reaction to God's word. The hard heart will not take it in, it will not trust God's word, and it will go another way (like the Israelites did). The "soft" heart (*cf.* Ezek 11.19; 36.26, a "heart of flesh") will respond correctly to God's word by trusting it. In this way, then, the word of God judges not only our actions, but our hearts as well. Our reaction to God's word reveals even our heart's most secret **reflections** and **thoughts**. When confronted with God's word our innermost contemplations and motives are judged and made obvious for what they are. We may hide our thoughts from others, but we cannot hide them from the scrutiny of God's word which exposes their true nature. This is true for our response to God's word now, and will be true of the day "when, according to my gospel, God will judge the secrets of men through Christ Jesus" (Rom 2.16; *cf.* also 1 Cor 4.5; John 12.48 "the word which I spoke, this will judge him in the last day").

4.13 And no creature is hidden from his presence, but all things are naked and open to his eyes, to whom we have to account.

The penetrating power of God's word derives from God's own nature, who is fully cognizant of all that is in his people. David confessed that God knew him so completely that he could not hide anything about himself from God:

> O Lord, you have searched me and known me, you know when I sit down and when I rise up; you understand my thought from afar. You scrutinize my path and my lying down, and are intimately acquainted with all my ways. Even before there is a word on my tongue, Behold, O Lord, you know it all. You have enclosed me behind and before, and laid your hand upon me. Such knowledge is too wonderful for me; it is too high, I cannot attain to it. Where can I go from your Spirit? Or where can I flee from your presence? (Psa 139.1–7 NASB).

The antithetic parallelism of this verse emphasizes God's omniscience, especially concerning the hearts of his people. The first line of this verse (**no creature is hidden from his presence**) is a circuitous way of saying "God knows all." If God's people go astray in their hearts like the Israelites did (3.10), God will know it. God sees everything about us, "for God sees not as man sees, for man looks at the outward appearance, but the Lord looks at the heart" (1 Sam 16.7) and "the Lord searches all hearts, and understands every intent of the thoughts" (1 Chron 28.9). To speak of God's **eyes** is, of course, a common Biblical anthropomorphism, a figure of speech whereby God is ascribed human qualities. To say that God is all-seeing or omnipresent (as in Psalm 139) simply means that he is omniscient. We may present ourselves a certain way before others, and we may even fool ourselves, but God sees (knows) us as we really are. The expression also implies that we ought to have a sense of shame when we act or think unfaithfully before God's scrutiny. Aristotle said, "They are also more ashamed of things that are done before their eyes and in broad daylight; whence the proverb 'The eyes are the abode of shame.' That is why they feel more ashamed before those who are likely to be always with them or who keep watch upon them, because in both cases they are under the eyes of others."[33] The phrase **naked and open** portrays us as stripped of all pretension and all false appearance. That is how God sees us, and it is him, not our peers nor even our own self-scrutiny, that we must please (*cf.* 1 Cor 4.3–4). It is possible that the original readers of Hebrews were relying on their Jewishness for a sense of rightness with God. If that were the case, the author here dismantles it. It is the right heart, not the right ethnicity, that makes one right with God.

God is the one ultimately **to whom we have to account.** The word **account** translates the Greek word *logos*, the same term translated "word" in verse 12, and the two appearances of this term therefore neatly brackets the exhortation. God has given a word to us, and we will have to give a "word" (account) back to him.[34] The stance of NT moral exhortation is forward-looking (*i.e.*, eschatological). We must learn to look past the present circumstances and consider standing before the judgment seat of the Lord one day to account for our lives in light of his word (2 Cor 5.10; *cf.* Luke 16.2). We are accountable to him and his word for all we are, think, and do. Every thought, plan, decision, word, action, feeling, or trait is subject to his judgment. The force of this statement is that God is not one with whom we may trifle, and his perfect knowledge of what we truly are means that we must not harbor any unfaithfulness in our hearts, for God will see it and judge us for it. This is because God's invitation to join him in his rest is offered at great cost to himself. He does not take rejection lightly (*cf.* 10.29f). We must, therefore, give diligence (v 11) to accept his offer of rest.

4.14 Therefore, since we have a great high priest who has passed through the heavens, Jesus the Son of God, let us hold to our confession.

---

[33] Aristotle, *Rhetoric* 2.6.18 (Freese, LCL).

[34] Gene R. Smillie, "'The Other *logos*' at the End of Heb 4:13," *NovT* 47 (2005): 19–25; see Johnson, *Hebrews*, 136.

With this verse our author returns to the high priesthood of Jesus, a discussion he left in 2.17–18 to deliver his exhortation to be faithful in order to enter into God's rest. The discussion in 3.1–4.13 has not been a digression, however. This is now the third time in the sermon (previously in 2.17 and 3.1) that our author has referred to Jesus as our **high priest** and indicates that this greater theme still dominates the discussion. Only through the high priest of our confession, Jesus (3.1), is it possible to enter into God's rest. He is here called our **great** high priest, hinting that his priesthood is better than that of the old Law. The proof of the greatness of his priesthood will come later in the sermon. The author mentions it now to motivate the readers to remain faithful.

A chief aspect of the greatness of Jesus' high priesthood is that he has **passed through the heavens. Heavens** was a Jewish way of denoting the realms above the earth. A good case can be made that "passed through the heavens" here refers not to Jesus ascension, but to his incarnation. That is, he passed through the heavens "downwardly" to come to earth, and his subsequent experience in this flesh is what makes him sympathetic to the sufferings of God's people.[35] In this connection our author calls him **Jesus the Son of God** (*cf.* Luke 1.35). The combination of his earthly name and his exalted title is significant. Because he shared in flesh and blood (2.14), is he perfectly able to sympathize with his followers, and because he is God's exalted Son, he is able to approach God for us in a way no former priest ever could. The title **Son** recalls, of course, the discussion of chapter 1, where it was demonstrated that he is greater than the angels, and thus the word that has come through him (the same word described in v 12 above) is greater than the word that came through angels. But there is more to come: the Son's priestly service is also greater than the ministry that was exercised under the old Law.

The words "**let us**" render a hortatory subjunctive in the Greek and is one of the author's favorite ways of delivering encouragement (he uses it about a dozen times; 4.1, 11, 14, 16; 6.1; 10.22–24; 12.1, 28; 13.13, 15). It is a way of expressing a command by way of urging rather than with an outright demand,[36] although the author also knows how to be stern. Furthermore, his gentle urging is always based on some fact he has care-

[35] So Mark A. Jennings, "The Veil and the High Priestly Robes of the Incarnation: Understanding the Context of Heb 10:20," *PRSt* 37 (2010): 85–97, at 95. See the comments on 10.20.

[36] Wallace, *Greek Grammar*, 464.

fully established from Scripture. Here the fact is that we have a great high priest by whom we can enter God's rest. The encouragement, then, is that we must **hold to our confession**, the same idea as "the obedience of our confession" in 2 Corinthians 9.13. As noted in the comments on 3.1, confession denotes not just an acknowledging of something, but a pledging of oneself as a commitment. The exhortation is for the recipients to continue in the commitment they made to Jesus, to continue in their identification with him who calls them his "brethren" (2.11–13),[37] regardless of the social cost. Only by imitating Jesus' faithfulness will God's people be able to follow him as he leads them to glory (2.10) and rest. However, the content of that commitment or confession is in view as well, as the full title of Jesus as the Son of God here suggests. Commitment to Jesus because we believe that he is the Son of God is the foundation of all else (see John 6.69). To acknowledge Jesus as the Son of God, and to live in a way that reflects that acknowledgement, is to make "the good confession" (*cf.* 1 Tim 6.12f).

4.15 For we do not have a high priest who is unable to sympathize with our weaknesses, but one who has been tested in every way just like us, yet without sin.

Cf. 2.18. From the negative tones of verses 12–13 the author now shifts to a more positive, encouraging tone. Both the wrath and the grace of God are legitimate incentives to seek a right relationship with him. Verses 12–13 emphasized the former, verses 15–16 emphasize the latter.

As our sympathetic **high priest**, Jesus knows just how difficult it is to live faithfully in a world in which God's people are surrounded by unbelievers. He also lived here in the flesh and "endured such hostility by sinners against Himself" (12.3). Faithful endurance is often difficult, and Jesus knows this from his own experience on this earth. He was subject to cruel treatment at the hands of his own fellow-countrymen, the same situation in which the readers of Hebrews now found themselves. The double negative (**we do not have. . . who is unable**) means "we have a high priest who can be touched … ." This choice of phrasing suggests that some of the readers may have thought "how can Jesus help me when he is not even here anymore?" But far from this being a

[37] See Scott D. Mackie, "Confession of the Son of God in Hebrews," *NTS* 53 (2007): 114–29.

flaw in Christianity, just the opposite is the case. The reason we cannot see Jesus now is that he is at God's right hand interceding for us as our high priest. His absence from us physically does not mean that he is unconcerned or unable to help us. It means, in fact, that he is at the very place where he can help us the most.

The exhortation here thus comes from a different perspective than the preceding one. Verses 12–13 were a warning based on our inescapable accountability to God and his word, but verses 15–16 offer encouragement based on the Lord's sympathy with our trials. The Lord certainly sees what is in our hearts (vv 12–13), but he also sees our difficulties and knows first-hand what his people must endure. This is the sense of **sympathize** (this one of the things that qualifies him to be our high priest, as 5.2 will discuss); it is a sharing in an experience, and not just thinking about someone else's problems.[38] The picture here is that we should not think of our Lord as some cold, uncaring tyrant who gives orders from heaven without caring how difficult they may be for his disciples to follow. Instead, the exhortation to faithful endurance comes from one who has faced the same experiences of opposition from hostile unbelievers as his own followers (12.3; *cf.* John 15.18). The **weaknesses** of the flesh, associated with a fear of pain, can tempt us to be unfaithful.

The comparison between our experience with opposition the Lord's is qualified in one important way. He was **tested in every way just like us, yet without sin**. The word *peirazō* can mean either to test, or it can have a more negative sense, to entice (tempt). Often, however, situations that test our faith also tempt us to quit, so the two senses of the word are closely connected. Jesus' commitment to God was put to the test while he was on this earth. He had a physical body that had all the same limitations and weaknesses as ours, which made the accomplishment of his mission difficult. It is not a sin to be tested or to be testable. Jesus was both, as Matthew 4 plainly shows. See also the comments on 2.18. The crucial difference between us and Jesus, however, is that not once did Jesus allow testing, or temptation, to turn into sin. In case it might be argued that this could only make Jesus *less* sympathetic to others ("how could he be sympathetic to the plight of sinners if he never sinned?"), it should be noted that enduring is always harder than surrendering. Jesus, by his sinlessness, actually endured more than those who give up the

[38] Lane, *Hebrews 1–8*, 108. It is synonymous with a need for help, v 16.

fight and give in to temptation. It is not just that Jesus knows how hard it is to struggle against sin, but that he knows it perfectly.

4.16 Therefore, let us approach the throne of grace with boldness, that we might receive mercy and find grace for timely help.

Since Jesus is sympathetic to his followers who must resist hardship to be faithful, they should go to him for encouragement. The word **approach** (Greek *proserchomai*) is regularly used in the LXX for approaching God in worship and parallels the exhortation to "hold fast our confession" (v 14). The **throne of grace** is the throne Jesus now shares with God as his exalted Son (*cf.* Heb 1.13, fulfilling Psa 110.1; Heb 2.7–8). It should be remembered that Jesus was presented in verse 14 as our great high priest, but he is a high priest on a throne, he is both priest and king (the author will expound upon this later). Who else is so perfectly suited to give aid to those who are being tested? Where else could they find the comfort they needed? This is partly the point of the phrase **with boldness** here, which uses the same word rendered "confidence" in 3.6. The idea of approaching a king on his throne with boldness would have seemed unusual to the ancients. Kings were powerful figures and were to be approached with fear (*cf.* Esth 4.11, 16). While we must maintain a healthy fear of our Lord's power (*cf.* 4.1, 12–13), the reigning Jesus is not a king who feels annoyed by the personal petitions of his people. We may approach him freely with our concerns.

While we may think of **mercy** as something only for the guilty, the word here (Greek *eleos*) can more broadly denote compassion, pity, or concern.[39] Furthermore, mercy is not just a thought of sympathy, but something *done* for someone in a difficult situation that relieves their distress (illustrated in the parable of the good Samaritan, Luke 10.37). To **receive mercy**, therefore, is to get help for one's plight. Similarly, **grace** denotes God's favorable disposition towards man, but we should also realize that his grace is often accompanied by his power that actually accomplishes the good that he wills (*cf.* Acts 4.33; Eph 3.7). To draw near for grace, therefore, is to rely on the Lord to act so as to help us in our time of need. The language of "grace" here depicts Jesus (or God) as a beneficent patron-king who loves his people and is eager to help them. Because he is kindly disposed towards them, his subjects should be "bold" in approaching him when

---

[39] BDAG 316.

they need help. He is our sympathetic high priest who wants to see us endure successfully and is ever ready to give **timely help** and support to those who find it difficult to do so. Since this is the case, we should not be reluctant to go to him for help when we need it. We should, instead, draw near to him with all assurance that he can and will help.

Here the author has made a forceful appeal for his readers to remain faithful to Jesus. They were thinking about abandoning Jesus in order to avoid the persecution that accompanied their faithfulness to Christ. This, our author says, was the wrong solution to the problem. Rather than abandon Christ, his persecuted followers needed to draw closer to him. The way to deal with hardship is not to forsake one's commitment to the Lord, but to increase it. Only by drawing closer to the enthroned and reigning Christ could such persecuted Christians find help.

HEBREWS 5

5.1 For every high priest selected from men is appointed on behalf of men in the things pertaining to God, that he might offer both gifts and sacrifices for sins.

The discussion from chapter 4 continues (the chapter breaks were not original to the text), as the word **for** suggests. 4.14–16 emphasized the sympathetic nature of our great high priest, Jesus. This was actually a trait necessary for any high priest of God, and the author now wishes to show that Jesus fits the fundamental requirements **every high priest** had to meet. Of course, the most fundamental requirement was that the high priest was selected **from men**, to represent humans before God (2.17). Jesus once lived in human form (2.5ff; Phil 2.5ff) and therefore he too is a high priest taken from the ranks of men. Jesus was more than just a man, but he was not any less than a man.

So important was this choice that God did not leave it up to Israel to choose their own high priest. The high priest was also **selected** and **appointed** by God (see v 4). The word the author of Hebrews used here for "appointed" (Greek *kathistēmi*) is the same word used of the appointment of Aaron in the LXX (Num 3.10).[1] God appointed the high priest **on behalf of men**, for his role was primarily that of service to others. The sphere of his service was **in the things pertaining to God**, that is, in helping them attain a right relationship with God (see the same phrase in 2.17). He was the mediator between God and man. This specifically involved that he **offer** the designated sacrifices. Our author has here used the normal word for offering a sacrifice in the LXX (Greek *prospherō*). In Hebrews it always means "to accomplish the sacrifice."[2]

[1] The same verb could be used of the appointment of a king, as in Psa 8:6 (8:7 LXX; in the line which the author of Hebrews omitted in his quotation of the Psalm; see comments on 2.8) and in Psa 2.6. Since the exaltation of Jesus as messianic king was apparently not an issue among his readers, the author did not need to establish that point.

[2] Konrad Weiss, *"pherō, ktl,"* *TDNT* 9:67.

Our author here broadly describes the various offerings in the Mosaic system as **gifts** and **sacrifices for sins**. This could refer to two kinds of offerings, *viz.* voluntary and required sacrifices. Not all sacrifices under the old Law were obligatory. Anyone could bring a sacrifice to the Lord at any time as a free-will offering, and such offerings could be described as **gifts**. Other sacrifices were mandatory in the case of sins and offences and could be classified together as **sacrifices**. We probably should not make too much of this distinction, however, since there is considerable overlapping in the usage of these terms in the LXX and in the NT. For example, both terms are used of Abel's offering in Heb 11.4. Either way, **sins** (transgressions of God's commands) were the problem, and under the Law of Moses a worshiper could not approach God for himself for forgiveness. A priest was required, and the efficacy of everything centered around the high priest and the annual Day of Atonement.

5.2 He is able to deal gently with those who are ignorant and who go astray, since he himself is also encumbered with weakness.

The high priest was able to serve not as a mere workman but as one who was sensitive to the problems of those he represented. Because he was a fellow-human being, this produced in him a natural sympathy for the people's difficulties as he took their sacrifices before God. For this reason, the high priest of Israel could **deal gently** with his fellow-Israelites. The verb means to moderate one's feelings toward another[3] or to bear reasonably with someone,[4] and thus is close to (but not identical to) the idea of sympathy (see 4.16).[5] The high priest's ability to deal gently with others came from the fact that he was a human being just like those he represented. He experienced the same kinds of weaknesses as his brethren, he was vulnerable to the same limitations and temptations as any other. Our author has already discussed this trait in Jesus in 4.14–16.

Notice that the high priest approached God for **those who are ignorant** and **who go astray**. This latter expression literally denotes those who have wandered, and comes to mean, figuratively, being misled, deluded, mistaken, or deceived.[6] The two terms probably describe the same peo-

---

[3] BDAG 643.

[4] LSJ 1122.

[5] Ellingworth, *Epistle to the Hebrews*, 275; Lane, *Hebrews 1–8*, 108.

[6] *cf.* NASB "misguided"; same word used in 3.10 of the Israelites.

ple, because only those who sinned due to weakness or who went astray without intending in their hearts to forsake God had remedy available in the sacrificial system under the Law of Moses. Under that Law, sin was broadly classified into two categories: unintentional sins, and defiant sins (presumptuous sins, done with a "high hand" (ASV, ESV)). *Note carefully Leviticus 4–5; Numbers 15:22–31; and Deuteronomy 17:12–13.*[7] For example, the law of Moses distinguished between unintentional homicide and (intentional) murder. The one who killed someone unintentionally was not liable to capital punishment by the nation (Deut 19.4), but the murderer was (*cf.* Exod 21.12–14; Num 35.15–25). This did not mean that ignorance, weakness, confusion, or being deceived was excusable, or that the sin that resulted from it was not serious in God's sight. It was still sin (*cf.* Psa 25.7 and Num 12.11). However, God considered the sinner's heart as well as his action. Those whose actions failed to meet God's standards but whose hearts were fundamentally directed toward God and who wanted to return to fellowship with him were offered forgiveness through the sacrifices. An entirely different matter was a sin that was deliberate, willful, and fully intent on disobeying God, and the sinner whose heart had become hardened, who was not sorry for his sin and had no intention to repent. For such a one no sacrifice, and therefore no forgiveness, was available.

This same distinction between unintentional and deliberate sins is valid in the new covenant through Jesus as well. It is implicit in the discussion of Hebrews and the sacrifice of Jesus (see 10.26) and had a direct bearing on the sermon's exhortation. The original readers were faced with renewed persecution and some of them, through simple weakness, had begun to shrink back. Their situation was critical and they needed to resolve to hold fast to their commitment to the Lord (4.14; 10.23), but they had not yet reached the point of no return. The exhortation of Hebrews was that they needed to renew their commitment and remain faithful lest their hearts become hardened and they commit the willful sin of refusing to trust in God, for which there is no remedy. See 6.4–6 and 10.26ff. While the distinction between unintentional and presumptuous sin might be hard for us to make (the two might outwardly

[7] The fact that the author used Numbers 14 in the preceding exhortation in Hebrews lends weight to the idea that he still had Numbers in mind, and particularly the distinctions of Numbers 15, here in this discussion. Matthew McAfee, "Covenant and the Warnings of Hebrews: The Blessing and the Curse," *JETS* 57 (2014): 537–53, at 546–47.

appear the same to us), we must remember that ultimately it is God with whom we have to do, and he, with his word, sees and judges the thoughts and intents of the heart (4.12–13).

It was not a nuisance for the high priest to intercede on behalf of his fellow Israelites before God, as if he were a superior being who had to put up with the failings of inferiors. The fact is that he was such an "inferior" himself; **he himself** was **also encumbered with weakness** (*cf.* 7.28). The word **weakness** (Greek *astheneia*) denotes a lack of strength and thus comes to mean frail, lacking or limited in power.[8] It is not, however, a synonym for sin (*cf.* 2 Cor 13.4), nor does it refer here to moral weakness. Instead, it refers to the human condition in general, the weakness that is inherent in having a fleshly body and that leads us to sin.

There is a subtle encouragement in the author's emphasis on the high priest's sympathy with his brethren. So far, the original readers of Hebrews had started down the path of unfaithfulness because of weakness in the face of persecution. The point here is that Jesus, our high priest, would deal gently with them and accept them back upon their repentance and renewal of faithfulness. Having lived in the flesh and having been tempted in all things like we are (yet without sin; 4.15), Jesus understood why they were reluctant to continue in their commitment. They stood at a crossroads, and a critical decision was before them. They could repent of the measure of unfaithfulness they had already committed and return to a right relationship with God through Jesus the high priest who was fully sympathetic with their plight because he too suffered persecution during his time in the flesh (2.10–18); or they could decide to continue in their unfaithfulness after having heard the warnings against it, they could allow their hearts to become hard (3.8), and "go on sinning willfully" (10.26). Our author appeals to them to maintain the right disposition of heart, for that is the crucial thing. Right now, the door back to God was still open and Jesus stood ready to forgive them, sympathetic toward their situation. If they persisted in further unfaithfulness, however, they would, like ancient Israel, go astray in their hearts (3.10), become hardened (3.13), and fall away from God (3.12) with only his wrath to face (10.26ff). The readers had to decide, therefore, whether they would continue to hear God's voice or refuse it.

---

[8] J. Zmijewski, *"asthenēs, ktl," EDNT* 1:170–71.

5.3 And on account of this he is obligated, just as he is for the people, so also for himself, to make offerings for sins.

Because (**on account of**) the high priest of Israel was a human being like everyone else within the congregation of God's people, and therefore just as prone to sin as the rest, it was necessary for him (**he is obligated**[9]**) to** offer sacrifices **(make offerings) for** his own **sins** (**for himself**) as well as **for** those of **the people** whom he represented. In speaking of the need for the high priest to offer sacrifice for his own sins, the author probably has in mind primarily the high priest's duties on the Day of Atonement (see Lev 16.5f). In fact, most of the references to priests and sacrifices in Hebrews have the Day of Atonement in mind. However, the high priest had to offer sacrifices for his own sins whenever he sinned (Lev 4.3–12), not just on that day. The point of this verse is to confirm the assertion of verse 2, that the high priest really was beset with weaknesses. It shows the extent to which he was just like those whom he represented. Israel's high priest needed God's forgiveness just like those he represented, and so he had no reluctance to perform his duty for them because he himself needed it too, and he understood intimately their need for it.

The high priest's sharing in weakness also highlights one of the problems inherent in the Mosaical system, specifically that the high priest was also a sinner. This stands in sharp contrast to Jesus, our new and great high priest, who lived without sin (4.15) and thus is able to approach God in a better way. The limitations of the old Levitical priesthood will be an important part of the author's presentation in chapters 7 and 9. For now, the emphasis here is not so much on the sin of the high priest but on his completely sympathetic nature (due to his sin). Since the high priest shared in the weakness of those he represented, he was able to represent them with true understanding and sensitivity.

5.4 And no one takes the honor for himself, but the one who is called by God receives it,[10] **just like Aaron.**

---

[9] The present tense need not imply that the rituals of Judaism were still going on at the time of writing. See Introduction. The present tense in Greek can also denote what is customary in a situation (even a past one). We have a similar usage of the present tense in English.

[10] The words "receives it" are supplied here to make a smoother rendering of the ellipsis in the Greek.

This verse picks up from verse 1 the fact that the high priest was appointed by God. The high priest stood at the apex of Israel's religious system, and serving his fellow-Israelites in this way certainly was a great **honor**. It was not, however, an honor one could assume (**take**) or achieve **for himself**. It was bestowed only by the will of God upon the one he **called** (another way to say "appointed"; *cf.* "designated" in v 10 below). **Aaron** became Israel's high priest in exactly this way (Exod 28.1). We must understand that our author was viewing the OT high priesthood in an ideal way. He was thinking about the pattern presented in the OT regulations for high priests, not the actual practice in the first centuries BC or AD in which the high priesthood was occupied by men who attained it through their own ambition and self-promotion. Under Roman rule, the office of high priest had basically become a vassal political post filled by the appointment of Rome.

In verses 1–4 our author is simply listing requirements for the high priesthood *in general*. That is, these are qualities required in any high priest. He mentions **Aaron**'s appointment as one example of the larger point he is making (that high priests are appointed by God).

5.5 Thus also Christ did not glorify himself in order to become high priest, but the one who said to him, "You are my Son, today have I begotten you" glorified him.[11]

Having established in verses 1–4 the basic requirements for any high priest (especially that he is able to sympathize with those he represents), our author will now show that **Christ** (his title that reminds us that he was chosen, or anointed, by God) meets those requirements (vv 5–10). This demonstration accomplishes two things: 1) it lays the groundwork for the author's exposition of Jesus as the high priest of the new covenant, and 2) it is meant as an encouragement for the readers to draw near to him. The argument proceeds in inverse parallelism (see below).[12]

Jesus Christ has become our great high priest in the new covenant because God appointed him to that position, and thus he fulfills the requirement for high priests noted in verse 4. Jesus did not **glorify himself**, that is, he did not take the honor of the high priesthood for himself (v

---

[11] The last two words, "glorified him," are added here to make a smoother rendering of the ellipsis in the Greek.

[12] *Cf.* Lane, *Hebrews 1–8*, 111; Ellingworth, *Epistle to the Hebrews*, 271.

4). However, to acknowledge that God appointed Jesus as high priest is not to say that Jesus is a high priest according to the Mosaic regulations. Verse 6 will show clearly that this is not the case. Instead, the point is that God's general pattern involved God choosing the man for the office, not a man choosing the office for himself.

In this connection the author quotes Psalm 2.7 again: **You are my Son, today I have begotten you**. This same passage was previously cited in 1.5 to establish Jesus' position as **Son**, greater than Moses or the angels. It is cited in this context, however, for a different reason, namely because it is an example of God addressing the Messiah directly. This, in turn, prepares us to hear another direct proclamation by God to the Messiah in the next verse. As we noted at 1.5, this statement from Psalm 2 is not about the birth of Jesus, much less does it imply that he had an origin. It is instead a declaration of God concerning his exalted post-resurrection status. Jesus took that position **Today**, which as we have already seen, designates the messianic age (see comments on 3.7, 13).

- **A** The high priest offered gifts and sacrifices for sins (5.1)
  - **B** The high priest was sympathetic with those he represented (5.2–3)
    - **C** The high priest was appointed by God (5.4)
    - **C′** Jesus was appointed priest by God (5.5–6)
  - **B′** Jesus' incarnation made him sympathetic with us (5.7–8)
- **A′** Jesus is the reason we can be saved (5.9–10)

5.6 Just as he also says in another passage, "You are a priest forever according to the order of Melchizedek."

Another quotation is now drawn from **another passage**—Psalm 110.4—(*cf.* comments on 2.6) to show that Jesus is indeed our high priest by God's appointment. This quotation shares in common with the one in 5.5 that both are statements in which God makes a direct declaration to the Messiah about his status. This juxtaposing of two verses that contain the same words (**You are**[13]) is a good example of the rabbinic exegetical method known as *gezerah shawah* (see Introduction) and would have been a convincing argument to those accustomed to Jewish interpreta-

[13] Psa 2.7 *ei su*, Psa 110.4 *su ei*.

tions of Scripture. The quotation proves, from Scripture, that God himself appointed Jesus, his Son, to hold his office of high priest over God's people. For this reason, then, the high priesthood of Jesus is perfectly legitimate. The verse from the psalm shows that Jesus meets one of the basic qualifications any high priest must have (vv 1, 4), and the God who declares Jesus to be his Son (Psa 2.7) is the same God who declares him, in Psalm 110.4, to be a **priest**.

This brings the author, for the first time in this sermon, to Psalm 110.4, which could arguably be called the most important Biblical verse for the purposes of Hebrews. There is a sense is which every point and every exhortation is grounded in this one verse.[14] The author has already quoted from the first verse of this psalm in 1.13 to show that the Son sits at God's right hand as king, an honor never accorded to any angel. Here he quotes another verse from the same psalm to establish another point about Jesus, *viz.* that God has appointed him high priest. If the exalted, regal sonship of Jesus is valid (according to God's direct statement in Psa 2.7), so is his priesthood, for the same God decreed both things (**he also says**) about him. That Jesus is high priest in the new covenant is not just an assertion the author of Hebrews makes about him. It is instead something that *God* said about him. In this way the author establishes this important fact from Scripture itself, and also makes a transition from his discussion of Jesus the Son to Jesus the high priest.[15]

Many scholars have read Psalm 110 as a royal psalm, that is, a psalm about Israel's king. The kingship, like the high priesthood, was a model or pattern that would ultimately be fulfilled in Christ, and this, it is claimed, allowed the early Christians to apply this psalm to Jesus. However, what is unique about Psalm 110 is that it combines the offices of king (v 1) and high priest (v 4). This was in stark contrast to the requirement of the Mosaic law which always sharply distinguished between the two. In pagan religions it was quite common for the two offices to be combined, but in Judaism they were kept separate. In fact, when Israel's kings took it upon themselves to do what only the high priest was allowed to do, God punished those kings severely (see Saul's action in 1 Sam 13.8–14 and Uzziah's action in 2 Chron 26.16–21). In fact, so anom-

[14] "Hebrews' exposition—its theo*logical* argument—turns, in large part, on successive inferences drawn from Ps. 110:1 and 4." Compton, *Psalm 110 and the Logic of Hebrews*, 12 (emphasis his).

[15] Ellingworth, *Epistle to the Hebrews*, 281.

alous (within the OT[16]) is Psalm 110's picture of a combined king-priest that some scholars[17] have concluded that, unlike the majority of psalms, it was not rooted in any historical situation but was a direct messianic prophecy. With this view we concur.

The combination of king and priest caused the ancient Jews to wonder about this psalm. The solution among the sectarians at Qumran near the Dead Sea was to expect not one, but *two* Messiahs, a king from David and a priest from Aaron.[18] The roots of this approach appear to go back to the Maccabean period.[19] The idea of a single person who embodied both offices concurrently was apparently not entertained in antiquity (*cf.* similar confusion in John 1.19–21). The author of Hebrews, however, understood that these offices were combined in a single person, Jesus. Of course, **Melchizedek** was the king Abraham encountered after his rescue of Lot (Gen 14) and will also be the object of more detailed discussion in chapter 7.

The sole exception to the separation of the offices of king and priest was David, who offered a sacrifice to stay the plague that came upon the land in consequence of his numbering of Israel (2 Sam 24 and 1 Chron 21). The singularity of this event has led some scholars to propose that David was being presented (or he thought of himself) in Psalm 110 in terms of Melchizedek, as exercising a royal priesthood.[20] This makes good sense when we see David's kingship in light of the larger Biblical story. As we have seen in Hebrews 2, Psalm 8 reflected upon Adam's role of being God's vice-regent over God's created domain (referring to Gen 1.26–28). However, Adam was also the world's first priest, as Eden is described

---

[16] Zech 6.13 refers to the one called "Branch" as a priest on his throne. However, the text can also be translated "there will be a priest by his throne" (RSV; see also NET, ESV).

[17] Such as: M. J. Paul, "The Order of Melchizedek (Ps 110:4 and Heb 7:3)," *WTJ* 49 (1987): 195–211, at 200–202, and Barry C. Davis, "Is Psalm 110 a Messianic Psalm?," *BibSac* 157 (2000): 160–73. An attempt to retain a Christological reading and also see an historical context in ancient Israel for the psalm is Herbert W. Bateman IV, "Psalm 110:1 and the New Testament," *BibSac* 149 (1992): 438–53.

[18] Adam Simon van der Woude, *"chriō ktl,"* *TDNT* 9:517–20.

[19] John J. Collins, "Messianism in the Maccabean Period," in *Judaisms and their Messiahs at the Turn of the Christian Era*, Jacob Neusner, Williams S. Green, and Ernest Frerichs, (Cambridge: Cambridge University Press, 1987), 97–109, at 105.

[20] See Eugene H. Merrill, "Royal Priesthood: An Old Testament Messianic Motif," *BibSac* 150 (1993): 50–61; Matthew H. Emadi, *The Royal Priest: Psalm 110 in Biblical Theology*, NSBT 60 (Downers Grove, IL: IVP Academic, 2022), 116–28.

as the world's first temple.[21] In Eden, Adam exercised "a type of *priestly* rule by fulfilling his commission from the garden-temple."[22] That is, Adam was himself a king-priest of God. Of course, Adam failed in his responsibilities, but one intriguing person comes along later in the Biblical narrative to suggest that God's ideal of a king-priest accomplishing his will had not been abandoned. That person is Melchizedek, who, interestingly, appears in the story of Abraham, another man who represents the Adamic ideal. The appearance of Melchizedek in the Biblical narrative right before the episode of God's reaffirmation of his covenant promises to Abraham in Genesis 15 (and Abraham's famous reaction in v 6 of that text) is significant. Moses intended for readers to connect the covenant promises to Abraham with Melchizedek.[23] In general, David's reign (its good side) is presented in the Bible as recapturing the Adam-Melchizedek ideal, at least typologically.[24] In fact, in David (and especially in his psalm, 110) the threads of Adam, Melchizedek, and Abraham all come together.[25] The author of Hebrews also combined these threads in his sermon. When viewed in this way, David's action in 2 Samuel 24, while unusual under the Law, fit with the larger picture of God's plan to rule over the earth through a faithful king-priest, and all of it—Adam, Abraham, Melchizedek, and David—pointed to Christ and his people as the ultimate fulfillments of God's eternal intentions for the world.

It must be remembered that the point the author is making is that Jesus meets the general requirements of a high priest of God. This is *not* to say, however, that Jesus is a *Levitical* priest. The Levitical priesthood may have contributed some typology to the messianic picture of the Bible, but because of Psalm 110 there are some fundamental differences between Jesus' priesthood and the Levitical priesthood. Instead, Jesus is a priest **according to the order of Melchizedek**, which is different in significant

---

[21] See G. K. Beale and Mitchell Kim, *God Dwells among Us: A Biblical Theology of the Temple*, Essential Studies in Biblical Theology (Downers Grove, IL: IVP Academic, 2021); Emadi, *Royal Priest*, 32–36; Andrew S. Malone, *God's Mediators: A Biblical Theology of Priesthood*, NSBT 43 (Downers Grove, IL: InterVarsity Press, 2017), 52–57.

[22] Emadi, *Royal Priest*, 32.

[23] Emadi, *Royal Priest*, 48.

[24] See G. K. Beale, *A New Testament Biblical Theology: The Unfolding of the Old Testament in the New* (Grand Rapids: Baker Academic, 2011), 65–66.

[25] On David and Abraham see G. K. Beale, *The Temple and the Church's Mission: A Biblical Theology of the Dwelling Place of God*, NSBT 17 (Downers Grove, IL: InterVarsity Press, 2004), 107–109.

ways from the Levitical priesthood under the law of Moses (as our author will show in ch 7). Yet this idea was so difficult that some in the post-apostolic church apparently believed Jesus was also from the tribe of Levi![26] However, there is no Biblical evidence for such an idea, and the express statement of Hebrews 7.14 rules it out. How the priesthood changed from that under the law of Moses will be demonstrated in chapter 7.

Similarly, the phrase **the order of** should *not* be taken to denote a succession of priests. This is the last thing it can mean in the argument of Hebrews. The word **order** (Greek *taxis*) denotes nature, kind, or type.[27] That is, Jesus' priesthood is the same kind or type as Melchizedek's. Furthermore, in Hebrews, to say that Jesus' priesthood is the same kind as Melchizedek's does *not* specifically refer to the combination of king and priest within the same person (although that feature of Melchizedek is likely always assumed). Instead, the emphasis is on the fact that Melchizedek became priest by God's direct appointment (*cf.* v 10 below), not by descent, and that he was the sole officeholder of that priesthood.[28]

The interaction between verses 1 and 4 of Psalm 110 is important to notice, for it is the basis of the author's contention that Jesus is now the high priest (2.17; 3.1; 4.14f; 6.20; *etc.*) of God's people. Melchizedek is not specifically called a *high* priest in the OT. So how does the author of Hebrews conclude that Jesus is a high priest? The logic derives from the situation described in Psalm 110 itself. The words **You are a priest** were spoken by God to the Messiah whom he had (in v 1) exalted to his right hand. Since the Messiah is at God's right hand, he is therefore in heaven, in the very presence of God, which also means that he is in the actual (true) "Most Holy Place" in heaven itself (see 9.11f). Since the kingly Messiah was in heaven when God appointed him to his priesthood, then the Messiah is not just an ordinary priest but a *high* priest, because the defining characteristics of a high priest are that he was directly appointed by God and that he alone was able to be in the presence of God in the Most Holy Place. The prominence in the comparison with Melchizedek lies in the term **forever.** The significance of this term will receive our author's fuller attention later (ch 7). For now, the point is that Jesus is high

---

[26] *Testament of Simeon* 7.2.

[27] *Cf.* Ellingworth, *Epistle to the Hebrews*, 283–84; in 7.15 our author used the word "likeness," which is perhaps the best explanation of the term in Hebrews.

[28] M. J. Paul, "The Order of Melchizedek," 203–204.

priest by the appointment of God himself, and thus he fits the general requirement for all high priests. But he is also so much greater than the Levitical high priests, as indicated by his appointment to the priesthood that is like Melchizedek's. *Cf.* a similar comparison and contrast between Jesus and Moses in 3.1ff.

5.7 Who, in the days of his flesh, offered prayers and supplications with strong crying and tears to the one who was able to save him from death, and he was heard because of his piety.

As the author discussed earlier (2.9ff), Jesus spent time in the **flesh** and lived on earth in the form of a man (*cf.* Phil 2.7–8). This did not detract from his greatness but instead qualified him to be our high priest, for he could not be sympathetic to us if he had never experienced the difficulties we face (2.17; 4.15). During Jesus' time in the flesh, he felt the brunt of the difficulties and weakness associated with mortal life on earth, which caused him to turn to God with **prayers and supplications with strong crying and tears**. Prayer characterized by boldness, piety, and emotion was the way Jews thought of the prayers of righteous men like Abraham and Moses.[29] Although Jesus' agony and fervent prayers in the garden of Gethsemane may immediately come to mind, that should not be thought of as the only time he felt the need to rely on God (*cf.* Luke 6.12). It is interesting that **offered** translates the Greek word used of priestly service in the LXX (*prospherō*, the same word used in 5.1), in keeping with the context's emphasis on the priestly role of Jesus. It is also used of the prayers of Christians in 13.15.

At this point two important questions arise. For what was Jesus asking? And what was the answer God gave to him? Consider two interpretations. One way of understanding our author's statement here is that Jesus was praying that God would rescue him *out of* death (the Greek preposition *ek* here can bear this meaning), that is, after he had died.[30] This is based on the fact that our author specifically said that Jesus prayed to God who **was able to save him from death**. According to this first interpretation, the author mentioned this fact about God precisely because it was this attribute of God that was in view in Jesus'

---

[29] Harold Attridge, "'Heard Because of His Reverence' (Heb 5:7)," *JBL* 98 (1979): 90–93, citing Philo, *Who is the Heir of Divine Things* 7.

[30] Attridge, *Hebrews*, 150.

request. God then **heard**[31] this prayer by raising Jesus from the dead. Although Jesus asked that his life be spared, if possible (Matt 26.39), it is equally clear that Jesus understood the necessity of his death and was perfectly willing to accept it as necessary (Matt 16.21; John 12.27; *etc.*). The answer to Jesus' prayer, then (according to this interpretation) was that God did not allow death to have *lasting* dominion over him. Yet this explanation is problematic, for Jesus' prayers in Gethsemane (if indeed that is the referent here[32]) do not seem to be prayers for resurrection after death,[33] and a prayer to be saved from death naturally seems to be a prayer to avoid death.[34]

A second interpretation focuses on the Greek word translated **piety** (*eulabeia*), which denotes godly fear or respect, reverence, and devotion to God.[35] Jesus always placed doing the Father's will and pleasing him first, even to the point of death. Jesus was singly and whole-heartedly devoted to God and his will, and Jesus prayed that God's will would be accomplished (Matt 26.39, 42) even though he was speaking to the one who had the power to save him from that death. That is, Jesus did not ask for deliverance from the death of the cross, even though he was praying to the one who had such power. Instead, he prayed for God's will to be done, and this request, even though it meant Jesus' death, constituted Jesus' piety.[36] God answered the Son's prayer made out of reverence and devotion to God's will, and fulfilled Jesus' request that God's will be done. The difference between these two views might prove to be slight. Both display Jesus' willingness to endure even death, and it is that experience of suffering to the point of, and including, death that makes Jesus fully sympathetic to our difficulties.

---

[31] *eisakouō* in the passive, with reference to a prayer, means that God responded. BDAG 293.

[32] Christopher Richardson has argued that Jesus' sufferings on the cross are the referent here. Christopher Richardson, "The Passion: Reconsidering Hebrews 5:7–8," in *A Cloud of Witnesses: The Theology of Hebrews in Its Ancient Contexts*, ed. Richard Bauckham *et al*, LNTS 387 (London: T&T Clark, 2008), 51–67. This line of interpretation may receive some support from the author of Hebrews' own discussion in Hebrews 10, where the Messianic speaker of Psa 40 had the cross in view.

[33] Attridge, *Hebrews*, 150.

[34] Delitzsch, *Epistle to the Hebrews*, 1:242.

[35] H. Balz, "*eulabeia*," *EDNT* 2.79.

[36] Neil R. Lightfoot, "The Saving of the Savior," *ResQ* 16 (1973): 166–73, at 172. So also Spicq (cited in Peterson, *Hebrews*, 141).

The picture presented of Jesus here is like that of the righteous innocent sufferer so often portrayed in the psalms of lament and depicted in graphic detail in the messianic Psalm 22, which was, among the early Christians, "*the* psalm and *the* OT text in general for interpreting the death of Jesus on the cross."[37] Compare Hebrews 5.7 with Psalm 22.24.[38] It is this allusion to the righteous sufferer of the psalms that probably best explains the statements about Jesus' loud crying, tears, and piety rather than the scene in Gethsemane. In the laments of the Psalter one of God's children is typically facing or enduring some severe hardship at the hands of adversaries (who are often wicked fellow-Israelites), a hardship that he fears will end in his death, and he cries out in his distress to God to rescue him, defeat his adversaries, or both. He trusts that God will hear him because he has been righteous and zealous for good, or at least penitent when he has done wrong. It is not unusual for such psalms to end in a note of joy, expressing thanks for deliverance received from God. The righteous Israelite suffering at the hands of wicked fellow-Israelites or foreign enemies and crying out to God in distress was a type of Jesus in the days of his flesh. His righteousness was perfect, for he was without sin (4.15), and when he cried to God, God responded.

The author of Hebrews had a special interest in the thanksgiving section of Psalm 22.[39] Another verse from this same section of the psalm has already been quoted in Hebrews 2.12. One should also note that Psalm 22.28 mentions the Lord's kingdom. When read from a messianic perspective, the order of statements in this section of the psalm, and indeed the movement of the psalm from lament to praise, is instructive. God allowed the Messiah to suffer because that suffering would bring about the establishment of the Lord's kingdom. It is obvious that Jesus saw himself as fulfilling Psalm 22 (*cf.* Matt 27.46).

This picture of Jesus as the consummate example of the righteous sufferer[40] whose prayers God heard is important for two related reasons. First, it contributes to the author's point that even though Jesus is the

---

[37] James Swetnam, "The Crux at Hebrews 5,7–8," *Bib* 81 (2000): 347–61, at 355, emphasis his.

[38] The LXX of Psa 22.24 has three words that also appear here in Heb 5.7 ("supplication," "cry," and "heard"), suggesting that the author of Hebrews may have had this text in mind.

[39] Swetnam, "The Crux at Hebrews 5,7–8" 357.

[40] *Cf.* Timothy Bertolet, "Hebrews 5:7 as the Cry of the Davidic Sufferer," *IDS* 51 (2017), https://doi.org/10.4102/ids.v51i1.2286.

exalted Son, his exalted status does not mean that he is so far separated from us that he cannot appreciate our hardships. Second, Jesus' suffering in the flesh parallels the circumstance in which the original readers of Hebrews found themselves. If our theory about the destination of Hebrews is correct (see Introduction), then these converted Jews were suffering ongoing shame and social pressure at the hands of unbelievers, and this caused them to cry out to God in their distress. Jesus' crying out to God in time of distress parallels the situation of the readers, and that demonstrates that he certainly is sympathetic towards them as he serves them in the capacity of high priest. Therefore, Jesus meets this criterion for a high priest and the original readers were thereby encouraged to draw near to him.

5.8 Even though he was Son,[41] he learned obedience from the things which he suffered.

The word **Son** recalls the discussion in chapter 1 and denotes Jesus in his exalted greatness and uniqueness (see comments on 1.2). Recent English translations uniformly render "was a Son," which is not the English past tense but the subjunctive mode. It in no way suggests Jesus' Sonship was only a thing of the past. The Greek is a present (concessive) participle, the significance of which is possibly to emphasize the eternal, ongoing nature of Jesus' Sonship.[42] The great and exalted Son, however, was humbled, as our author has discussed previously (2.5ff). Jesus left heaven and came to earth to live in the likeness of a man (Phil 2.6ff). His status as Son did not exempt him from any of the difficulties of obedience to the Father's will during his life in the flesh.

By pointing out the fact of the savior's suffering the author has established that Jesus is able to serve as a sympathetic high priest for us (v 2). However, there is a subtle yet important difference in how the high priest under the old system became sympathetic to those he served, and how Jesus became sympathetic to us. The high priest under the Mosaical sys-

[41] The entire phrase **even though he was** (a) **Son** modifies what comes after it. Normally the word **though** (Greek *kaiper*) introduces a clause related to a preceding main verb (*cf.* Phil 3.4; Heb 7.5), but there is nothing to forbid placing the *kaiper* clause before the verb to which it relates for the sake of emphasis (*cf.* Prov 6.8 LXX). That is, the statement here does not mean that Jesus was heard (v 7) even though he was a Son, but that Jesus learned obedience even though he is God's Son.

[42] Ellingworth, *Epistle to the Hebrews*, 293.

tem was able to deal compassionately with those he represented because he too shared in the problem of sin, which is part of the human situation. Thus, he had to offer sacrifice for his own sins as well as those of the people (v 3). Jesus, however, was sinless (4.15), but he certainly did share fully in every other way in the human situation, including suffering. It is this participation in life in the flesh that enables Jesus to be sympathetic toward us as he serves as our high priest today.

Although the word **suffered** in Greek (*paschō*) can mean "experience" without denoting grief or agony, it seems that in this context the word denotes the negative experiences Jesus had as a mortal, his experiences in hardship, temptation, distress, and death. In these things Jesus **learned obedience**. It may sound strange to us that Jesus learned obedience, because we normally do not think of the divine Son as having to learn anything. However, the word **learned** (Greek *manthanō*) can denote appropriation through experience.[43] The ancients generally acknowledged that the experience of suffering can teach us some important things.[44] The Greek expression was *mathein pathein*, which means "to suffer is to learn," as well as "to learn is to suffer."[45] It was part of the larger experience which the Greeks called "training" (Greek *paideia*; see comments on 12.5). Jesus found out, or experienced for himself, what it is like to live in obedience to God as a man, especially in a hostile environment (see 12.3),[46] as he submitted reverently to God's will that entailed his own death. The Greek word translated **obedience** is *hupakouō*, which is a form of the Greek word that denotes hearing. We have a similar usage in English for the word "listen." It means to submit to what one is told, and it stands in contrast to the disobedience of the wilderness generation of Israelites in 3.7ff. It was God's will that his Son leave heaven, come to earth, and here suffer and die for the sins of the world. Jesus' response to his father's will was that he "listened," he humbled himself (Phil 2.5ff) and did what his father wanted (*cf.* John 4.34; 5.30; 6.38; Rom 5.19; Phil 2.8; Isa 50.5). In He-

---

[43] Grindheim, *Hebrews*, 289: "His learning consisted of experiencing obedience in practice."

[44] *E.g.*, Herodotus has Croesus saying "disaster has been my teacher" (1.207). See the references in Johnson, *Hebrews*, 147; see also Bryan R. Dyer, "The Wordplay *mathein-pathein* in Hebrews 5:8," *NovT* 63 (2021): 489–504.

[45] Johnson, *Hebrews*, 147.

[46] Cockerill, *Epistle to the Hebrews*, 247–48: "he learned or experienced what it was like to be perfectly obedient though that obedience elicited unrelenting antagonism from the unbelieving world."

brews 11.8 we are told "by faith Abraham, when he was called, obeyed" (NASB). That is how people on this earth must live in order to be right with God, and that is also how Jesus lived when he was on this earth. Therefore, Jesus is shown to be a sympathetic high priest, for he lived under the same circumstances, and with the same dependence upon God, as those he was appointed to represent. *Cf.* Hebrews 2.10, 17.

5.9 And having been perfected, he became the source of eternal salvation for all those who obey him.

How are we to understand the word **perfect** here? The Greek word (*teleioō*) basically denotes making something complete, and can also mean "bringing something to, or having something arrive at, its appointed end."[47] When used of Jesus in this sermon (see 2.10 and 7.28), it seems to take on the sense of "exalted," thus inaugurating the messianic age.[48] However, the normal sense of "complete" is not out of the picture. If Jesus had never come to this earth and lived in human form, subject to hardship, suffering, and death, he would have lacked an important experience crucial to his high priesthood. He could not truly sympathize with us until he had experienced for himself what we must go through as we live on earth. His incarnation, then, perfected him in this sense. These two senses of the word "perfect" are not, however, at odds with each other. Jesus' suffering both made him sympathetic with us and was followed by his exaltation and appointment to his high priesthood (Jesus' suffering and glory are often presented in the NT as two aspects of a single event; *cf.* Acts 3.13; Rom 6.4; Heb 2.9; *etc.*).[49] We should also remember that in the LXX the word is used of the ordination of priests (see comments on 2.10). Jesus' complete obedience was also preliminary to his appointment as high priest.

Once he had fully experienced life in the flesh, including death, Jesus was raised to glory and **became the source** of our **salvation**. The word translated **source** is the Greek word *aitios*, which denotes the cause, reason, or source of something. In this context Jesus **became** (past tense, in

[47] deSilva, *Perseverance in Gratitude*, 196.

[48] Silva, "Perfection and Eschatology in Hebrews," 64–68.

[49] For the role of Jesus' resurrection in his high priesthood, see David M. Mofitt, *Atonement and the Logic of Resurrection in the Epistle to the Hebrews*, NovTSup 141 (Leiden: Brill, 2011).

contrast to the present participle in v 8) the source or cause of salvation because of the redeeming quality of his death, the eternal nature of his resurrected life, and because he has been appointed high priest (see v 10 below). Only after he had suffered and thus entered into complete sympathy with us was Jesus appointed high priest. God's rescue (**salvation**) from the consequence of sin became fully available through him when Jesus began his high priesthood on our behalf.

What God offers man through Jesus is **eternal salvation** (*cf.* Isa 45.17) from the consequences of sin. Sin reaps the wrath of God. Because of the work of Jesus, however, sin can be forgiven and the wrath of God can be abated (Rom 5.9). This rescue from the guilt and consequence of sin has, in Jesus, an eternal quality about it. This does not mean that once a sinner is forgiven he may never again incur guilt and the wrath of God. The book of Hebrews, with its many warnings against apostasy (2.1–3; 3.12; 4.1, 11; 6.4–8; 10.26–31, 39; 12.15, 25; 13.9), argues clearly and strongly against such an idea. Participation in salvation is conditioned upon faithfulness. That is, to say that salvation is eternal is not to say that it is unconditional. So, what is eternal salvation? The author of Hebrews uses the word **eternal** as a key term associated with the new covenant, and it is closely associated with his claims that the new order in Jesus is "better." In this same way he speaks of eternal redemption (9.12), the eternal Spirit (9.14), the eternal inheritance (9.15), and the eternal covenant (13.20). Thus, eternal salvation is the salvation available in Jesus in the new covenant. The salvation offered in Christ is not a temporary fix for the problem of sin. That was the weakness of the old Law. In Jesus, however, a "permanently valid,"[50] once-and-for-all solution to the problem of sin has been offered to sinners (*cf.* 7.25; 9.26), corresponding to the fact that he is high priest forever (5.6).

Eternal salvation is offered to **all those who obey** the Son. Salvation is granted to those who obey, who submit to God's demands through the Son and who do what he says. Such obedience must be the fruit of one's faith (Jam 2.14–26; Heb 3.18–19; 11.4ff) and does not earn anyone the right to be saved from sin's terrible consequences, for salvation springs always first from the love and grace of God (Eph 2.4–9; Heb 2.9). Obedience out of faith in the reigning Son is simply the condition God has placed upon receiving the salvation he gives in Jesus. Faithful obedience is, after all,

[50] Bruce, *Epistle to the Hebrews*, 105.

what Jesus himself rendered to God (he "learned obedience," v 8), and this becomes the paradigm for his followers.

5.10 Having been designated by God as high priest according to the order of Melchizedek.

This verse completes the thought of the previous verse and also completes the transition from the discussion of Jesus the Son to Jesus the high priest. Jesus has become the source of salvation to all those who obey him because he now occupies the high priesthood **according to the order of Melchizedek** (according to **God**'s own decree, or **designation**, in Psa 110.4, quoted in v 6 above). God's salvation (v 9), God's rest, is attained through our great high priest. It is only through Jesus' role as high priest that anyone today can have fellowship with God, for in that role Jesus atones for our sins and brings us into God's presence. Discussion of the full significance of the Melchizedekian high priesthood of Jesus must wait, however, until our author has first paused in the discussion to deliver a rebuke to his readers.

5.11 Concerning whom we have much to say, and hard to explain, since you have become lazy in hearing.

Beginning with this verse and going through the end of chapter 6, the author temporarily leaves the discussion of the Melchizedek, the one **concerning whom** he had **much to say** (as he will, in ch 7), and its significance for the high priesthood of Jesus to deliver a rebuke, and then an encouragement, to his readers. This is the sermon's third "warning passage." The discussion and the rebuke-encouragement are not, however, unrelated.[51] The perfection of Jesus (see comments on v 9 above) calls for the followers of Jesus to strive for a similar completeness, which the original readers of Hebrews were failing to do.

Some things in the Bible are **hard to explain** (*cf.* 2 Pet 3.16), especially for Christians who have not grown in their knowledge of God's word as they should. Yet the difficult things of God's word are not optional reading. They are given to us for the purpose of increasing our faith, but they require a certain amount of spiritual maturity and previous understanding of the simpler things in God's word in order to understand them. God

[51] See Ron Guzmán and Michael W. Martin, "Is Hebrews 5:11–6:20 Really a Digression?," *NovT* 57 (2015): 295–310.

wants us to take in *all* of his word, the simple and the difficult. *All* of it is helpful to our faith. Preachers and teachers of God's word today must take a cue from the author of Hebrews not only to delve into the deeper things of the word for themselves but also to bring their hearers into the profound depths of the word with them. A teacher or preacher who only feeds his hearers with the fundamentals (spiritual milk, v 12 below) does them a great disservice, for by doing so he keeps them at a level of spiritual weakness that proves dangerous when they must rely upon their faith in times of trouble. It is by *increasing our knowledge of the word* that we gain strength to fight off the temptations to unfaithfulness.

The recipients' flirtation with the idea of abandoning Christianity was, partly, the product of their ignorance of what the Bible has to say about Jesus. Had they grown more in knowledge and faith they would have seen just how superior the priesthood of Jesus is, and this would motivate them to persevere. As it was, however, they had become **lazy in hearing**, which means to be "hard of hearing," and thus unreceptive.[52] *Cf.* the earlier exhortations to hear (2.1; 3.16). The word **lazy** (dull; Greek *nōthros*) appears also in 6.12 and thus frames this exhortation.[53] Because of this spiritual slowness they had not increased in knowledge as they should, and this left them spiritually weak and vulnerable in the face of opposition. There is a tremendous lesson here for Christians today. The more we learn of God's word, the stronger we will be. *God's word* builds us up (Acts 20.32). What God tells us *in his word* motivates us to remain faithful and equips us to resist every attack against our faith (2 Tim 3.16–17). There is no substitute. However, if we go along simply content with whatever knowledge we have, too lazy to increase it, we put ourselves in peril for the day of testing, since a better knowledge of our relationship with Jesus has the effect of drawing us closer to him. Our perseverance is directly related to our ability to hear and grow in knowledge.

5.12 For although you ought to be teachers by this time, you have need for someone to teach you the elementary principles of the oracles of God again, and you have become those who need milk and not solid food.

---

[52] Herbert Preisker, "*nōthros*," *TDNT* 4.1126.

[53] Also, Johnson (*Hebrews*, 152) sees an inverse parallelism extending from 5.11 to 6.3: *a* they are lazy and need to learn the basics, *b* they must mature, *b'* the author will move them on to maturity, *a'* they must progress past the basics.

The author told his readers **you ought to be teachers**. This does not contradict James 3.1, which says "Let not many of you become teachers, my brethren" (NASB). James was discouraging the egoistic desire to be a teacher for the prestige it brought. The author of Hebrews meant that his readers should have by now attained the level of knowledge sufficient to be teachers, and that rather than being in need of encouragement, by now they should have become teachers who could have been an encouragement to others who were facing doubt. The phrase **by this time** is literally "on account of the time," *i.e.*, a sufficient time had passed since their conversion to learn much more than they had. It takes time to grow in knowledge of the word, although how much time it takes to reach a particular level of maturity in the word may differ from person to person. The author of Hebrews apparently knew his readers well enough to say that they had been Christians a sufficiently long time to have grown in spiritual knowledge, but they had not taken advantage of the opportunity. Now instead of being spiritually mature they needed to rehearse things they had learned before. Knowledge that is not being constantly supplemented and used is quickly lost, but it has moral consequences as well. Truths that are ignored are not practiced, and unfaithfulness results. Failure to progress results in regress.

Instead of being able to teach and encourage because of their accumulated knowledge, however, these Christians had become unfamiliar with certain truths and now needed to become students **again** of the things they had once learned. Not only this, it was not as if they had forgotten the difficult things of the word of God. No, they had forgotten **the elementary principles**, the basics (Greek *stoicheia*). The first principles here are not just foundational OT concepts but include basic teachings of Christianity, as 6.1ff shows. The word **oracle** in Greek thought denoted a message from deity, especially one that was heard (in keeping with the author's emphasis on hearing God's word, 2.1, 3; 3.7, 16; 4.2). The phrase **oracles of God** is a synonym here for the "word of righteousness" in the next verse. Both phrases refer to God's word recorded in the canonical Scriptures.

In order to drive his rebuke home, the author takes up an analogy concerning growth and food. When people are young and small their diet consists of **milk** (milk was a common image of elementary teaching in ancient pedagogy[54]). As they grow, however, children gradually develop

---

[54] *E.g.*, Quintilian (Roman rhetorician, 1st century): "I would urge teachers too like nurses to be careful to provide softer food for still undeveloped minds and to suffer them

the ability to eat **solid food**. Weaning from milk to the ability to eat solid food is a recognized mark of physical maturity, and a good diet was especially required for athletes (this imagery will come up later, in Heb 12).[55] This is analogous to spiritual growth. When one first becomes a Christian he must take in the milk of the word, the simple and fundamental truths from the Bible. As time passes, however, he should grow in knowledge so that he can progressively learn more and take in the more difficult or profound truths from God's word. Clearly, the author intended to shame his readers for their failure to have grown in the faith. There may be an echo here of Isaiah 28.9: "To whom would he teach knowledge, and to whom would he interpret the message? Those just weaned from milk? Those just taken from the breast?" 1 Peter 2.2 is not parallel to this passage, but it is not unrelated either. There Peter used the "milk" metaphor in a different way, encouraging his readers to desire God's word like a baby desires milk. Peter's point is about one's eagerness to take in God's word (which will result in growth unto salvation), while the point here is about the need to advance from one level of knowledge to another. A closer parallel to the present passage is 1 Corinthians 3.2.

5.13 For everyone who lives on milk is unacquainted with the word of righteousness, for he is an infant.

The phrase **word of righteousness** appears only here in the NT, and the context indicates that the Biblical message is its referent. Its precise nuance is less clear. It may denote the word about righteousness (objective genitive), or the word which is God's righteousness (epexegetical genitive; similar to Paul's idea in Rom 1.16), or (best, I think) the righteous word (genitive of quality). At any rate, a spiritual **infant** is one who has learned only the basic truths (first principles, v 12) from God's word. This in itself is not shameful *if* one has not been a Christian for long. The problem

to take their fill of the milk of the more attractive studies" (*Inst. Or.* 2.4.5; *Quintilian, With an English Translation*, ed. Harold Edgeworth Butler (Cambridge: Harvard University Press, 1920), 227); Epictetus: "Are you not willing, at this late date, like children, to be weaned and to partake of more solid food?" (*Discourses* 2.16.39, from Johnson, *Hebrews*, 156). Compare Philo, *On Agriculture* 9: "But since milk is the food of infants, but cakes made of wheat are the food of fullgrown men, so also the soul must have a milk-like nourishment in its age of childhood" (Charles Duke Yonge, *The Works of Philo: Complete and Unabridged* (Peabody, MA: Hendrickson, 1995), 174).

[55] Moore, *Repetition in Hebrews*, 143–44.

with the original readers of Hebrews was that they had been Christians for some time (v 12), enough to have matured in the word, and yet they were still like spiritual babies. Failure to grow in knowledge keeps us **unacquainted** with the word and thus prevents us from receiving the encouragement that a fuller knowledge brings. Conversely, to be acquainted with the word is to have skill in it, to understand it correctly and handle it accurately (*cf.* 2 Tim 2.15) and, as a result, to be more confident in our faith.

5.14 But solid food is for those who are mature, who because of their state have their senses exercised to discern good and evil.

In contrast to a spiritual baby who knows only the basic truths from God's word is the one who is spiritually **mature**, which translates the Greek term *teleios*, rendered "perfect" elsewhere. For the author of Hebrews, perfection (completeness) is a trait of the messianic age. See comments on 2.10; 5.9; *etc*. Those who are complete, therefore, are those who have come to participate in the things of the messianic age. To continue the metaphor from verse 13, such a one is like a grown person who can eat **solid food**. The need for spiritual maturity is a recurring NT idea (Eph 4.13f; Col 1.28; 4.12; Jam 1.4; *etc.*; *cf.* Num 14.23).

The middle part of this verse has been variously translated. Some English versions translate "because of practice" or "by constant use." Many lexicons claim that the Greek word *hexis* denotes practice in the sense of repetition or drilling.[56] It is probably better, however, to understand the word as denoting "a physical and/or mental state" or condition.[57] In the present context it refers to the state of maturity. Thus the author is saying that solid food is for adults, who **because of their** mature **state** have their senses trained **to discern** (distinguish, differentiate) between **good and evil.**[58] This ability was crucial to the original readers, who seem not to have understood fully that their reluctance to press on in faith was the first step toward acquiring evil, unbelieving hearts (3.12) that would sin and rebel against the Lord's leading (3.17). The word **exercised** translates the Greek verb *gumnazō*, from which we get our word "gymnastics." It

[56] *Cf.* Louw-Nida, 1:512.

[57] John A. L. Lee, "Hebrews 5:14 and *hexis*: A History of Misunderstanding," *NovT* 39 (1997): 151–76, at 155; *cf.* LSJ 595.

[58] Lee, "Hebrews 5:14 and *hexis*," 166; Mark Kiley, "A Note on Hebrews 5:14," *CBQ* 42 (1980): 501–503.

probably originally denoted athletic training and conditioning but came to be used figuratively as well. It is used in the NT metaphorically (*cf.* 1 Tim 4.7; 2 Pet 2.14). Here it refers to moral training of the **senses**, by which our author means one's spiritual discernment, the ability to make moral judgments[59] (*cf.* Phil 1.9; Luke 9.45). Proper training of one's spiritual and moral senses comes from the word of God (*cf.* 2 Tim 3.17). When we constantly use God's word to guide our lives, our sense of moral judgment becomes trained in what is right and wrong and we develop, as a result, a mature godly character. The author will have more to say about God's training for us in chapter 12.

Why this emphasis on spiritual maturity? It is because those who neglect to study and grow in knowledge of God's word thereby neglect the spiritual training (exercise) that will make them stronger Christians. By their failure to grow, such Christians keep themselves weak and ill-prepared to face trials and are prone to go astray in their hearts (*cf.* 3.10). Spiritual growth is not an academic exercise but is protection against unfaithfulness. The original readers of Hebrews were struggling under the pressure of social rejection and shame, and some of them wanted to quit Christianity. This exhibited a weakness of character which was directly attributable to their failure to grow in God's word. Had they grown in their knowledge of the word they would have understood better the high priesthood of Jesus, which itself is a great motive for faithfulness. It is therefore not just that these readers had failed to progress intellectually in God's word, or that they had forgotten some important basic truths. Their real problem was that their inattention to Christian doctrine was making them weak in their faith and they were not persevering.

---

[59] Gerhard Delling, *"aisthanomai, aisthēsis, aisthētērion,"* *TDNT* 1:188.

HEBREWS 6

6.1 Therefore leaving the matter of the first principles about Christ, let us move on to maturity, not laying a foundation again of repentance from dead works and of faith in God.

While a failure to grow in understanding and the ability to handle God's word is a serious problem indeed (5.11–14), the real problem is what such a defect may produce: a hardness of heart (recall Psa 95.7) that falls away from God and has no avenue of forgiveness. It is this danger that our author will discuss in 6.1–8.

First principles translates the Greek word *archē*, which simply means "first" and here denotes primary, elemental truths. It recalls the similar term (*stoicheia*) in 5.12. One may review the basics from time to time to make sure he is thoroughly grounded in them (*cf.* 2 Pet 1.12), and there is a sense in which every Christian always needs them. To use Hughes' illustration, one does not dispense with the alphabet once he learns to read.[1] But there comes a time when every Christian must advance beyond (**leave**) the basics, the "milk" (from 5.13), and progress in his knowledge of God's truths. However, it is not intellectual knowledge for its own sake that is in view here. The "meat" gives greater hope, which brings about faithfulness. In the context of chapters 1–5, the **first principles about Christ** are not elementary truths about the OT picture of the Messiah in general but are likely the truths the author has most recently rehearsed for his readers, *viz.* that Jesus is the Son of God who lived among us in order to qualify to represent us sympathetically before God in heaven, where he now reigns in fulfillment of Psalm 110.[2]

---

[1] Hughes, *Epistle to the Hebrews*, 194.

[2] Since the author regularly uses "Christ" as a specific reference to Jesus (3.6,14; 5.5; 9.11; *etc.*), it seems best to take the title in that sense here as well and not as a generic reference to "the Messiah." However, "Christ" was not Jesus "last name," but his title, "Messiah."

The recipients' reluctance to continue in faithfulness was becoming manifest in their spiritual slothfulness (6.12) and inattention to God's word (5.11). The author knew where such lethargy would lead them, as he will point out below. They needed instead to decide to **move on**. The word here (*pherō*) has a broad semantic range. From its basic idea of "bring" it also came to mean "endure" (press on or bear onwards) as well as "produce" (as in produce fruit; see vv 7–8 below), and "aim at."[3] Although it means "move on" in this particular context, in keeping with the pilgrimage theme of Hebrews,[4] these other ideas are not far behind. The readers needed to aim at and produce spiritual maturity, which included advancing in their knowledge. His exhortation, therefore, is that they not follow the course they have contemplated but understand why they should not abandon Christianity, and determine anew that they will continue faithfully as Christians.

The author's exhortation is to **move on to maturity**. The word here translated **maturity** employs the same root (in the Greek) used in 5.14 (there translated "of full age"). It is, in fact, a form of the word "perfect" which appears so often in the sermon. For the author of Hebrews, maturity, or completeness, is possible only in the new order of things inaugurated by Jesus (*cf.* Paul's argument in Gal 3.23–4.6); the old system, or covenant, was characterized by imperfection and could make nothing perfect (7.19). *Cf.* also 5.9; 12.1–2. The exhortation to press on thus specifically refers to coming to understand the significance of Christ's Melchizedekian high priesthood, and participate fully in it, which will be the subject in the chapters that follow.[5] If the readers could grow to appreciate the importance of Christ's role to them, they would have every incentive to persevere in the faith.

An important question about this passage concerns the nature and precise understanding of the things mentioned in verses 1–2. Are these basic religious principles found in Judaism which served as types of Mes-

---

[3] LSJ 1923–24; BDAG 1051–52.

[4] William G. Johnsson, "The Pilgrimage Motif in the Book of Hebrews," *JBL* 97 (1978): 239–51.

[5] *Cf.* Craig Allen Hill, "The Use of Perfection Language in Hebrews 5:14 and 6:1 and the Contextual Interpretation of 5:11–6:3," *JETS* 57 (2014): 727–42, although I think he presses the idea too far in suggesting that the present passage is not about increasing in Christian knowledge and maturity but about abandoning "the messianic and covenantal imperfection of the previous covenant" (742).

sianic realities? Or are the things on this list to be understood as fundamental teachings of Christianity?[6] Or a mixture of both?[7] If we take the first view, then presumably the exhortation was to leave behind the limited and imperfect teachings of Judaism and press on to the fullness of things that exists only in Christianity. If we take the second approach, and we understand verses 1–6 as referring to specifically Christian doctrines, then the text becomes an encouragement for Christians to understand deeper truths. However, an either-or approach is not necessary. Nothing says the list could not be a combination of elementary teachings that were both fundamental Christian doctrines and Jewish issues that needed to be understood properly or clarified.[8]

The author proceeds to give a short list of some of the things that comprise the basics of the teaching about Christ and past which he expected his readers to advance. However, this list also has connections with the discussion in the following chapters of Hebrews.[9] Dead works are mentioned in 9.14; faith will be the theme of chapter 11; washings are mentioned again in 9.10, and the laying on of hands was part of the sacrificial procedure under the old Law, which pointed to Christ. The things on this list are thus also basic to the discussion of the high priesthood of Christ, which is the "solid food" the author wants to feed his readers. The futility of remaining in the basics is indicated by the phrase **laying a foundation again**, which is somewhat of a contradiction in terms because a foundation, by its nature, is something laid only once.

The list consists of six items, probably meant to be read as three pairs. First on the list is **repentance from dead works**. **Repentance** is not simply feeling sorry for something; note Paul's contrast between sorrow and repentance in 2 Corinthians 7:8–10. It is instead a change of mind (with sorrow involved) that leads to a change in one's actions. Note Jesus' illustration in Matthew 21.28–31, and the prodigal in Luke 15.18–20. It

[6] Cockerill, *Epistle to the Hebrews*, 264–65. Beasley-Murray suggested that the six things mentioned in vv 1–2 were elements of the "confession" of the early Christians. George R. Beasley-Murray, *Baptism in the New Testament* (Grand Rapids: Eerdmans, 1962), 242.

[7] Grindheim, *Letter to the Hebrews*, 305; Peterson, *Hebrews*, 150.

[8] F. F. Bruce cut through the question by suggesting that "Each of them, indeed, acquires a new significance in a Christian context; but the impression we get is that existing Jewish beliefs and practices were used as a foundation on which to build Christian truth." *Epistle to the Hebrews*, 139.

[9] Lane, *Hebrews 1–8*, 140.

is otherwise called "turning" in the NT.[10] The phrase **dead works** can cover any work (deed, conduct, behavior) that is not pleasing to God. They are, generally, the things that unbelievers do (*cf.* Eph 2.1, 5).[11] Such works are dead in the sense that they do nothing positive spiritually, they are things done with no benefit (*cf.* Col 2.23) or, perhaps better, they are works that produce the spiritual death of the one who does them (Rom 6.21).[12] Some[13] have suggested that the phrase refers to works of the old Law (9.10, 14; Rom 7.10), in which case the teaching here refers to turning from Judaism to Christ (about which the readers were apparently doubtful). However, this does not seem likely because nowhere did the author of Hebrews present the old covenant as something sinful and from which people needed to repent. Besides, there is no suggestion in Hebrews that the recipients were turning "back to Judaism" (see Introduction). A better interpretation is that the author viewed the life of an unbeliever as a life of dead works, a life of not trusting in God that results in spiritual death. This fits well with the overall exhortation of Hebrews to Christians who were thinking about quitting and becoming unbelievers again.

Faith in God is the complement to repentance (*cf.* Mark 1.15; Acts 20.21); both repentance and faith pertain to the Christian's mind,[14] the former as a decision to turn from sin and the latter as a decision to give oneself to God. Faith has always been the basic requirement for all who would come to God (Heb 11.6; *cf.* Rom 4). In fact, in the ancient Roman cultural world in which Hebrews was originally written, faith involved a reciprocal relationship between a patron and a client (or more generally, between the giver and the recipient of a gift).[15] Faith is not merely mental assent to an idea, but denotes a comprehensive, positive response to God that not only believes what he says but is also manifested in one's life in many ways.[16] It involves believing in the heart and mind what God says, but true, Biblical faith also includes a corresponding way of living. To

---

[10] Luke 1.17; 22.32; Acts 3.26; 9.35; 11.21; 14.15, 19; 26.18; esp. 26.20; 1 Thes 1.9.

[11] So also Grindheim, *Letter to the Hebrews*, 306.

[12] Cockerill, *Epistle to the Hebrews*, 265: they are "works of unbelief," like those of the Israelites who came out of Egypt but never made it to Canaan.

[13] *Cf.* Westcott, *Epistle to the Hebrews*, 146.

[14] Westcott, *Epistle to the Hebrews*, 144; Lane, *Hebrews 1–8*, 140.

[15] Gelardini, "Faith in Hebrews," 253.

[16] Morgan, *Roman Faith and Christian Faith*, 335: "the author's understanding of *pistis* is complex, making use of a wide range of meanings, including trust, faithfulness, belief, confidence, obedience, and hope."

believe means to trust and accept what God says, even when what God says seems highly unusual, and to live upon that basis. True faith in God will be illustrated richly in our author's discussion in chapter 11.

6.2 Of instruction about baptisms, and laying on of hands, and resurrection of the dead, and eternal judgment.

The reference to **baptisms** is problematic for two reasons. First, this is a different word than is normally used for baptism in the NT. The usual word is *baptisma*,[17] but the word here is *baptismos*.[18] The difference may seem slight,[19] but it prompts us to wonder if the author truly had baptism into Christ in mind, or if his choice of a different word means that he was referring to some other kind of immersion. It is possible that he was referring to the various purification rituals of the Jews that involved submersion in water (the NASB seems to have this in view as it renders "instructions about washings"), since the word *baptismos* is used in the plural in exactly this sense in Mark 7.4 and Hebrews 9.10.[20] The Jewish background of the recipients of Hebrews would make such an interpretation possible. If the author was indeed referring to these Jewish ritual washings, then "the teaching about washings" would be about how such Jewish ceremonies were no longer necessary in Christ,[21] or about their typological significance. It is possible, however, that the two words were basically synonymous. We probably do not know enough about how the wider Christian community used such terms to make a definitive judgment. If *baptismos* here refers to the same baptism elsewhere called in

[17] It appears that this became the "Christian" term, since this word does not appear in literature outside of the NT (or literature related to it). Neither term occurs in the LXX. Albrecht Oepke, "*baptismos, baptisma*," *TDNT* 1:545.

[18] Josephus referred to the baptism of John the Baptist as a *baptismos*, but the NT consistently refers to it as a *baptisma*, suggesting either two different perspectives on what John administered, or that the terms were basically synonymous.

[19] In koine Greek, nouns that derived from verbs and that end in *-mos* denote an action, and those that end in *-ma* denote the result of an action (Robertson, *Grammar*, 151–53; BDF §109), but it is not clear that these nuances were always operative in the way the language was actually used (Richard Chenevix Trench, *Synonyms of the New Testament* (London: Macmillan and Co., 1880), 370).

[20] Col 2.12 may be the exception; manuscripts vary between *baptisma* and *baptismos* for that verse.

[21] *Cf.* W. Bieder, "*baptismos*," *EDNT* 1:195: "instruction in which the baptismal candidate is taught the difference between Christian baptism and ritual washings in Judaism and paganism."

the NT *baptisma*[22] (baptism into Christ), then we encounter the second problem, namely, that the word is in the plural. This could most easily be understood as a reference to the baptism of John and baptism into Christ. While there is only one baptism in water that is valid for Christians (Eph 4.5), it was anticipated by the baptism of John the Baptist. Some early Christians had heard of John's baptism but were unacquainted with baptism into Christ (Acts 18.24–26; 19.1–5), so it is not unreasonable to suppose that teaching about the differences between the two may have been a regular part of instruction for new converts from among Jews. Delitzsch may have been correct to combine all the options when he proposed that the phrase referred to the practice of teaching Jewish converts the differences between Jewish purification baths, the baptism of John, and baptism into Christ.[23] That is, perhaps the word (in the plural) here means "washings of all kinds, Jewish, Christian, *etc.*"

The **laying on of hands** probably refers to the miraculous impartation of spiritual gifts, a phenomenon extant in the first century church. There was a non-miraculous function of this same symbol,[24] but it is hard to imagine why the non-miraculous use of this gesture would have required explanation as one of Christianity's "first principles." In the early church, laying hands on a person was known as the means by which divine power was conferred by the apostles[25] or by which miracles were performed (Acts 28.8). There seems to have been confusion in some early churches over the reception and use of such spiritual gifts (*cf.* 1 Cor 12–14; Acts 8.17ff), and it could have become common practice in the churches to instruct new Christians about this phenomenon.

The teaching about the **resurrection of the dead** was part of the preaching of the early Christians from the very beginning (Acts 2, 3, 4, *etc.*), and proved to be a doctrine that some people found hard to accept.[26] The doctrine of the resurrection of Jesus in particular is the cornerstone of Christianity. Everything else in Christianity revolves around that histor-

---

[22] *NIDNTTE*, 2nd ed., "*baptō ktl*," 1:462: "both terms refer to Christian baptism."

[23] Delitzsch, *Epistle to the Hebrews*, 1.274f; Beasley-Murray takes a similar approach, suggesting that our author here refers to teaching about the "contrast between Christian baptism and other religious 'washings'." Beasley-Murray, *Baptism in the New Testament*, 243; so also Trench, *Synonyms*, 371–72; so also Grindheim, *Letter to the Hebrews*, 307.

[24] See 1 Tim 5.22, Acts 6.6, 13.3, where no miraculous result is suggested.

[25] Acts 8.17f; 19.6; 1 Tim 4.14; 2 Tim 1.6.

[26] See 1 Cor 15.12–19; Acts 4.2; 17.18, 32; 26.24.

ical fact. His resurrection gives hope of the general resurrection to those who follow him (1 Thes 4.14) as well as supplies the chief reason for living according to the Lord's demands. It also gives significance to Christian baptism, for in baptism one joins Christ in his death and resurrection (Rom 6.3–11). Most importantly for Hebrews, Jesus' resurrection was the inauguration of his exalted reign (see comments on 1.5, 6) wherein he also serves as the new high priest of God's people. **Eternal judgment** could refer to the doctrine that when the dead are raised, they will be gathered to the judgment seat of Christ.[27] However, a good case can be made that, in this context, it refers specifically to the **judgment** (which in the NT sometimes has the sense of "condemnation") of God against those who reject the reign of his exalted Son (Heb 10.27). Such judgment is **eternal** in that it is "final" (*cf.* "eternal salvation" in 5.9), but also in that it has no end (Matt 18.8; 25.46; *etc.*). It is worth noting that the list ends with a mention of judgment (condemnation), because the original readers of Hebrews, by their contemplated unfaithfulness, were making themselves liable to God's wrath (see 10.26ff). Therefore, the placement of the word here at the end of the list was undoubtedly for rhetorical impact.

6.3 And this will we do, if God allows it.

Do what? It seems best to understand this statement as meaning "we will move on to maturity" (v 1), rather than "we will lay again a foundation." It is a note of encouragement to the readers. The phrase **if God allows it** should not be taken to imply that God has predetermined the course of every life in a fixed or detailed way. The phrase simply acknowledges that there are opportunities in life (including opportunities to mature as Christians) because God makes them possible. It also imparts the sense that the opportunities for the readers to achieve spiritual maturity may not be endless, and the time to be busy growing in the faith is now.

6.4–6 For it is impossible for those who were once enlightened, and tasted the heavenly gift, and became sharers of the Holy Spirit, and tasted the good word of God, and the powers of coming age, and who fell away, to renew them again to repentance, since they crucify to themselves the Son of God anew, and publicly disgrace him.

---

[27] 2 Cor 5.10; Matt 25.31ff; John 5.28; Heb 9.27.

In these verses the author paints a picture of Christians who had fallen away. It is not a hypothetical picture. The language (**those who were once enlightened...**) recalls real cases of real people. If it happened to them, it could happen to the readers of Hebrews (and it can happen today just as well). In fact, our author inserted this discussion here precisely because he was convinced that his readers had already started down the path of apostasy and hardness of heart (recall Psa 95.7). He wrote to warn them of what would happen if they continued on that path.

The author began with a list of things these lapsed Christians experienced prior to their falling away. The list spells out some of the many blessings that come with being a child of God in Christ. Other such lists of blessings occur in the NT (see Eph 1.3–14; Rom 5.1ff).[28] The purpose and effect of the list needs to be appreciated. As the list piles up the blessings received from God, it creates a sense of debt which ancient readers would have understood well. As deSilva has shown, the dynamics of the patron-client relationship were powerfully active in the ancient Hellenistic world. Patrons granted gifts for petitioners who then became their clients. As recipients of such great blessings from God, the readers of Hebrews stood as clients to God, their patron, and they were obligated to reciprocate with loyalty.[29] Failure to act appropriately toward God in light of these blessings would only constitute an insult to the giver (*cf.* Heb 10.29). Aristotle said "The experiencing of good from another person, and experiencing it often, and then throwing the good things he did in his teeth, these are all signs of smallness and baseness of soul."[30] To receive a gift and then to refuse to show loyalty in return not only insulted the giver, it also all but ensured that no more opportunities for asking and

---

[28] Some have argued for seeing parallels between the items on this list and the experiences of the Israelites who fell in the wilderness, so that the image of Israel's failure at Kadesh-barnea stands implicitly in the background of this passage. See Dave Mathewson, "Reading Heb 6:4–6 in Light of the Old Testament," *WTJ* 61 (1999): 209–25; Randall C. Gleason, "The Old Testament Background of the Warning in Hebrews 6:4–8," *BibSac* 155 (1998): 62–91; Martin Emmrich, "Hebrews 6:4–6—Again!," *WTJ* 65 (2003): 83–95. Cockerill (*Epistle to the Hebrews*, 272, esp. fn21; and *idem*, "A Wesleyan Arminian Response to a Moderate Reformed View," *Four Views on the Warning Passages in Hebrews*, ed. Herbert W. Bateman IV (Grand Rapids: Kregel, 2007), 415–29) and deSilva (*Perseverance in Gratitude*, 222, esp. n. 28; *idem*, "Hebrews 6:4–8: A Socio-Rhetorical Investigation (Part 1)," *TynBul* 50 (1999): 33–57, at 44, fn24) disagree. To the extent that there are legitimate typological correspondences between Israel and the church, some of the parallels seem valid, but perhaps not all.

[29] See deSilva, "Hebrews 6:4–8: A Socio-Rhetorical Investigation (Part 1)," 33–57.

[30] *Rhetoric* 2.6.10 (my translation).

receiving would be available in the future.[31] No self-respecting person in the ancient world would have thought of treating a human patron in such a way, and so all the more they must give the same consideration to their divine patron, God (*cf.* Mal 1.6–8). Our indebtedness to God our great benefactor is what makes the offense of the one who falls away so heinous in God's sight, and this list is intended to highlight the sense of shame that ought to go with refusing to trust, honor, and obey the God who has blessed us so greatly. See also on 12.22.

First, they had been **enlightened**, which means they had either learned or obeyed the truth. This word was a metaphor for baptism in post-apostolic times,[32] but no such usage appears in the NT. To learn the truth of the gospel is to come out of the darkness of ignorance (John 8.12; 12.46; Eph 4.18) and into the new-creational light of the knowledge of God (2 Cor 4.6). *Cf.* John 1.9; Eph 1.18. The same term appears in Hebrews 10.32, where apparently it is the same thing as receiving the knowledge of the truth in 10.26. Darkness is also a Biblical metaphor for sin, and to come out of the darkness and into the light also denotes repentance and regeneration.[33]

These Christians had also **tasted the heavenly gift**. The author's mention of "tasting" does not mean this is a reference to the Lord's Supper, nor does it mean to sample something partially.[34] "Tasting" is a common Biblical metaphor and means to experience something (2.9; see also 1 Pet 2.3; Matt 16.28), sometimes with an emphasis on its delightfulness (Psa 34.8). The **heavenly gift** may be the forgiveness of sins, for salvation is God's gift (Rom 3.24; 6.23; Eph 2.8). Alternately, it could be some miraculous spiritual gift (*cf.* the mention of laying on of hands in v 2 above, and 2 Tim 1.6). In Acts 8.20 and 10.45 the miraculous manifestation of Holy Spirit is called a gift and could thus easily also be called a heavenly gift. Either way, to accept a gift and then repudiate the giver would have been considered an insult and affront of the severest kind.[35] It is

---

[31] See deSilva, *The Hope of Glory*, 1–33, 144–77, and his *Honor, Patronage, Kinship, and Purity*, 2nd ed., 96–124.

[32] Philip Edgcumbe Hughes, "Hebrews 6:4–6 and the Peril of Apostasy," *WTJ* 35 (1973): 137–55, at 139; *idem*, *Epistle to the Hebrews*, 208.

[33] Acts 26.18; Rom 13.12; Eph 5.8, 11; Col 1.13.

[34] Thus arguing that these apostates were not truly Christians in the first place; see McKnight "The Warning Passages of Hebrews," 46, 50–51; Cockerill, *Epistle to the Hebrews*, 270.

[35] deSilva, *Perseverance in Gratitude*, 223–24.

significant that the author does not argue here on the basis of a coming benefit, but on the basis that the first hearers were already experiencing some of the goodness of the messianic time, and participating in the eschatology of the larger Biblical narrative.[36] This has the rhetorical effect of making their thoughts about quitting seem even more unreasonable. Furthermore, Christians have tasted goodness from God just as ancient Israel had tasted the manna in the wilderness.[37]

They also had become **sharers of the Holy Spirit**. Whether the author meant a miraculous mode of the Spirit's presence with these early Christians (such as in Acts 10.44–46 or 19.6), or whether he meant the "ordinary" (*i.e.*, non-miraculous) union of all believers with the Spirit (Rom 8.9–11), is not possible to determine. This is the only place in Hebrews where this phrase appears. Either way, a real relationship with God through the Spirit was part of the experience of these people.

These Christians had also **tasted the good word of God**, which perhaps means that they had experienced (see comments on "tasted" above) for themselves the fact that God's promises in his word were reliable. "Good word" echoes Joshua 23.14–15 (*cf.* also 1 Kngs 8.56), where the covenant with God, specifically the covenant blessings, is called God's "good words."[38] Here it undoubtedly refers to the gospel, but the choice of terminology casts the gospel as God's new-covenant word and implicitly recalls the story of the Israelites from Hebrews 3–4. They too had heard God's good word (at Sinai; Neh 9.13).[39] *Cf.* 1 Peter 2.2–3 for a similar metaphor of tasting God's word and its benefits (although the point of the metaphor here is different). Finally, these Christians had experienced **the powers of the coming age. The powers** may be a reference to signs, wonders, and miracles (2.4) that confirmed the word. The presence of miraculous activity in the ministry of Christ and of his apostles was a sign that the age predicted by the prophets had come, the new age had begun. "Power" in the NT often describes the miraculous.[40] However, the word "power" is

[36] Scott D. Mackie, "Early Christian Eschatological Experience in the Warnings and Exhortations of the Epistle to the Hebrews," *TynBul* 63 (2012): 93–114.

[37] Mathewson, "Reading Heb 6:4–6 in Light of the Old Testament," 216; Gleason, "The Old Testament Background of the Warning in Hebrews 6:4–8," 77; Emmrich, "Hebrews 6:4–6—Again!," 84.

[38] McAfee, "Covenant and the Warnings of Hebrews," 541.

[39] Mathewson, "Reading Heb 6:4–6 in Light of the Old Testament," 218.

[40] Acts 6.8; 10.38; Rom 15.19; 1 Cor 2.4.

also used in the NT to describe the gospel's ability to forgive sins,[41] and so this phrase may be yet another way of speaking about salvation, but living by divine power is also possible here.[42] We should not overlook that "signs and wonders" characterized God's formation of Israel into his own nation (Exod 4.30; 7.3; Deut 7.10, *etc.*),[43] and the generation that died in the wilderness was the same generation that witnessed God's devastation of Egypt in the plagues, the parting of the Red Sea, the manna, and water from rocks in the desert. Their experience of God's power should have led them to trust in God's care for them as they came to the land of promise, but they did not. Accordingly, the phrase **the coming age** should be understood as in 2.5, as an age that was coming from the perspective of the OT but has now arrived in Christ. The word of God, and the signs accompanying it, was proof that the divine had broken into the world of men.[44]

Whether the things on this list of Christian experiences were primarily miraculous in nature or non-miraculous is not critical, because it is the genuine experience in the benefits of Christianity that is the point, as well as the greatness of these gifts from God's hand. The miraculous, external manifestations of the Lord's power were outward expressions of the spiritual power of the gospel for every Christian. What makes Christianity so blessed is not that some Christians once could work miracles, but that through the gospel *every* Christian experiences divine love, grace, kindness, mercy, and forgiveness from the Father.

Even though these Christians had experienced the wonderful things in this list, they **fell away**. The verb here recalls the same term from 3.17 ("... corpses fell in the wilderness") and 4.11 ("so that no one will fall, through the same example of disobedience"). The KJV (also NKJB, NIV, and RSV) unnecessarily weakens the force of the warning by translating "if they shall fall away," but there is nothing in the Greek text nor the grammar[45] of verse 6 to warrant treating the participle "fall away" as condi-

---

[41] Rom 1.16; 1 Cor 1.18; 2 Cor 6.7; Eph 1.19.

[42] *Cf.* 2 Cor 4.7; 12.9; Eph 1.19; 3.16, 20; Col 1.11; 2 Tim 1.8.

[43] Mathewson, "Reading Heb 6:4–6 in Light of the Old Testament," 219; Gleason, "The Old Testament Background of the Warning in Hebrews 6:4–8," 78.

[44] *Cf.* Emmrich, "Hebrews 6:4–6—Again!," 86. B. Nongbri notes the apocalyptic nature of the scenario here (Brent Nongbri, "A Touch of Condemnation in a Word of Exhortation: Apocalyptic Language and Graeco-Roman Rhetoric in Hebrews 6:4–12," *NovT* 45 (2003): 265–79).

[45] Wallace, *Greek Grammar*, 633.

tional. Like the other aorist[46] participles in the series, *parapesontas* here is a (substantival) adjectival participle, not a (circumstantial) adverbial participle.[47] It simply states the fact just as surely as the previous aorist participles ("were enlightened," "tasted," *etc.*), so the falling away was as much a reality as their being enlightened, having tasted God's word, *etc.*[48] A rendering such as the NRSV ("and then have fallen away") is correct. Comparison with the experience of the Israelites makes the case even stronger. The Israelites really were God's people, but they perished because of their disobedience, and the same thing could happen to the readers of Hebrews (as the exposition of Psa 95 in chs 3 and 4 has already exhorted). *Cf.* Paul's similar warning in 1 Corinthians 10.1–12. Attempts to show that these people were not truly Christians in the first place fall in light of the plain language here. "The author believes them to be, and presents them as, believers in the fullest possible sense."[49] Others have tried to soften the full force of this passage by suggesting that the falling away does not mean these people became lost but that a lesser problem is indicated, such as a failure to bear fruit,[50] but this does not hold up to the language our author uses either.

What does it mean to "fall away"? It is the response to God that was demonstrated by the exodus generation of the Israelites (Heb 3.12; 4.11), which the author later calls a refusal and a repudiation of God (12.25). This is not an act that a person commits once and then is forever lost

---

[46] The significance of the aorist here is not the "pastness" of the things described, but simply the fact that they have happened. The aorist is often the "unmarked" tense in terms of discursive prominence. Steven E. Runge, *Discourse Grammar of the Greek New Testament: A Practical Introduction for Teaching and Exegesis* (Bellingham, WA: Lexham Press, 2010), 129.

[47] See John A. Sproule, "*Parapesontas* in Hebrews 6:6," *GTJ* 2 (1981): 327–32; Allen, *Hebrews*, 346–47

[48] If Christians cannot fall away and be lost, "Why, then, all this earnest warning about a matter which never did occur…?" Robert Milligan, *A Commentary on the Epistle to the Hebrews* (Nashville: Gospel Advocate Company, 1973), 179–80.

[49] McKnight, "The Warning Passages of Hebrews," 44. Also I. Howard Marshall, *Kept by the Power of God* (Minneapolis: Bethany Fellowship, 1969), 144: "the conclusion is irresistible that real Christians are meant"; Allen, *Hebrews*, 350: "The obvious implication is that these four phrases describe someone who is a believer," and "There is a growing consensus crossing the Calvinist/Arminian divide that the language of Heb 6:4–6 describes genuine believers" (353).

[50] J. B. Rowell, "Exposition of Hebrews Six: "An Age-Long Battleground," *BibSac* 94 (1937): 321–42, at 323. Similarly, Gleason ("The Old Testament Background of the Warning in Hebrews 6:4–8," 79) suggests that "they faced the danger of falling into a permanent state of immaturity."

but is the result of a process. It begins with spiritual laziness (v 12; see also 5.11) and gets progressively worse to the point that the believer develops "a total attitude reflecting deliberate and calculated renunciation of God."[51] Our author is not speaking of the case of the occasional sin committed by one who sincerely wants to do right, and it is more than drifting (2.1) or being sluggish (v 12). He is speaking of the Christian who has known for himself what a wonderful thing it is to live in fellowship with God (vv 4f) and then eventually, through a process of continuing weakness and disinterest, deliberately and willfully (see Heb 10.26) turns his back completely upon God and his goodness. He is like the Israelites who saw God's goodness and power on their behalf and yet still refused to trust in God and to follow his leading. "A total renunciation of Christianity is meant."[52] "…the sin the author has in mind is a willful rejection of God and his Son, Jesus the Messiah, and open denunciation of God and his ethical standards."[53] It is a picture of one who has deliberately chosen to step off the path and to go in another direction because he just does not trust God.[54] It is what Paul called disowning the Lord (2 Tim 2.12 NIV) and becoming faithless (2 Tim 2.13). Such a Christian deliberately sins, he knows that he is sinning, he deliberately abandons walking by faith in God's word, and he has no intention of ceasing his sin. He has developed an evil, unbelieving heart (3.12).

On the one hand, the specific things (such as circumstances, problems, fears, *etc.*) that caused these Christians to fall away is not stated. This in itself is instructive, for the precise cause of the failure is not ultimately the chief concern. Many things may tempt or challenge us as we journey toward heaven, and what distracts one may not affect another. In truth, there is no one cause of falling away, no one thing in life that negatively affects every Christian uniformly. For some, the cares of the world or the deceitfulness of riches may be the chief problem (Mark 4.19), while others may be turned from the path by the lusts of the flesh or by pride (*cf.* 1 John 2.16), and others may be deluded by false teaching. The situation for the readers of Hebrews was no doubt equally complicated and not

---

[51] Lane, *Hebrews 1–8*, 142.

[52] Marshall, *Kept by the Power of God*, 144.

[53] McKnight, "The Warning Passages of Hebrews," 39.

[54] See Wayne R. Kempson, "Hebrews 6:1–8," *RevExp* 91 (1994): 567–73; Johnsson, "The Pilgrimage Motif in the Book of Hebrews," 239–41, 246; Emmrich, "Hebrews 6:4–6—Again!," 87–89.

reducible to a single thing, and included in the matrix of factors affecting them was, no doubt, social pressure from unbelieving family and friends to give up Christianity. However a person arrives at this point, the nature of the result is the same. On the other hand, it is equally correct to say that the basic cause of falling away is a hard heart that refuses to trust in God and his promises any longer (3.12, like the wilderness generation of the Israelites), regardless of how that hard heart developed.

Those who fell away reached such a point that the author says **it is impossible to renew them again to repentance.**[55] The verb **renew** (Greek *anakainizō*) here has the sense of "restore."[56] The author is actually describing two scenarios here. One is the person who sins, but then repents. This is being "renewed again," and it is possible as long as a sinner is open to hearing God's word. It is entirely possible for a Christian, by his or her own choice, to return to the "old" ways of sin and become just as morally and spiritually corrupted as before, if not more so (2 Pet 2.20–22). Such people need to be **renewed again**, that is, they need to return to the truth that sanctifies them and to the Lord who cleanses them from sin. There is no hint in the NT that a Christian who has sinned needs to be re-baptized in order to be renewed again. Instead, the erring Christian must be renewed in his mind (Rom 12.2) and heart and decide to be faithful again (*i.e.* repent), acknowledge his sin to God (1 John 1.9), and go forward in faithful service. The parable of the prodigal in Luke 15 illustrates this scenario. The prodigal could not be restored as long as he determined to be away from his father's house. Only when he determined *for himself* to get up and go home was his restoration possible.

The second scenario, which is the point of the present text, is the one who goes beyond this point, into a situation even worse than that of the prodigal: a person can become so hard-hearted and hateful of Jesus that they will never want to repent. This person sins and then allows this rebellion to develop into a repudiation of Jesus that grows stronger and stronger. They eventually become permanently set in their opposition to

---

[55] This is *not* a reference to the specific sin of blasphemy against the Holy Spirit, for which Jesus said there is no forgiveness (Matt 12:31f). Nothing in this context suggests that. Furthermore, there is a difference between saying that a sinner will not repent (Hebrews) and that there is a sin which God will not forgive (Matt 12); these are clearly two different problems. Nor does our author here say that God would not forgive those who repent. Repentance, with God's forgiveness following, is always possible for the one who *wants* to return to God (*cf.* Acts 8:22; 1 John 1:9; 2 Pet 3:9).

[56] J. Baumgarten, "*kainos ktl*," *EDNT* 2:232.

Jesus, and nothing anyone says to them will change their mind or heart, because they have allowed their hardness to become complete. The result is that he or she becomes so hardened in their rejection of Jesus that it becomes **impossible** for someone to renew them again. The verb **renew** is transitive, which means that it requires an object to complete its sense. The object is the people (**them**) who are described as "those who were once enlightened, who tasted … and then fell away." Also, the verb is in the active voice, which means that it conveys the idea of a subject acting upon an object, not a subject being acted upon (*i.e.*, passive voice) nor a subject acting for itself (*i.e.*, middle voice). The verb here is therefore describing what one person cannot do to or for people who have fallen away.[57] In the strictest sense, another Christian cannot renew such a one. Renewal requires the personal decision and determination of the one who needs it, but in this case that decision will never come. One can urge others to repent, (2 Tim 2.25; Eph 4.23f), but each one decides it for himself.

As noted above (v 1), **repentance** is a decision or determination to quit sinning that is put into action. It is in this vein that our author speaks of the repentance of these apostate Christians as **impossible**:[58] they cannot be renewed because they will not. They have allowed their hearts to reach the point that they care nothing for God or Christ any longer; they have acquired the "evil heart of unbelief that withdraws from the living God" (3.12). The scenario is described in Jeremiah 8.4–6. If one will not be renewed by his own volition, by his own humble acceptance of the gospel of Jesus Christ, then that person cannot be restored to a right relationship with God. If a person refuses to repent, then he has made repentance impossible by his own decision.

Our author here describes the sin of apostasy as **crucifying the Son of God anew, and publicly disgracing him.** The words "crucify anew" and "publicly disgrace" here are present participles, indicating an ongoing activity by the one who has fallen away. The postverbal position of the participles indicates that they are offered as descriptions of, or the reasons for, the action of the main verbal clause of the sentence ("it is im-

---

[57] Westcott, *Epistle to the Hebrews*, 150; Peterson, *Hebrews*, 153: the text is about "those who cannot be brought back to their initial repentance."

[58] Hughes ("Hebrews 6:4–6 and the Peril of Apostasy") argues that the impossibility here is the impossibility of being baptized again. However, there is no indication whatsoever in the NT that, in apostolic Christianity, Christians who sinned were required to be re-baptized.

possible to renew …").[59] If we read the participles as expressing cause,[60] then the reason this apostate Christian will not repent is because he has become hardened in his opposition to Christ, and even hateful of Christ. Jesus was crucified because his own people blatantly rejected him (Mark 8.31; 12.10; 1 Pet 2.4, 7). They hated Jesus so much that they wanted him dead; no other outcome was acceptable to them. Those who have followed Jesus and then fall away eventually become so hard-hearted that they duplicate that same evil, unbelieving rejection in their own hearts, and it is in this sense, then, that they **crucify the Son of God anew**[61] with respect to themselves. While the Lord certainly agonizes over those disciples who abandon him, that is not the point of our author's statement here. The point instead concerns the attitude of disciples who decide to reject Jesus. Their attitude is not just that they will have nothing to do with him, but that they want him out of their lives altogether. Persecution and hardship have made them frustrated and angry with Jesus, and they come to reject the Lord in the strongest possible way. They do not simply refuse the Son's word, but they will not tolerate him at all, they want Jesus to be dead **to themselves**. By their repudiation they also **publicly disgrace** Jesus, since crucifixion did not simply involve pain but it especially denoted a shameful death reserved only for the worst criminals.[62] It was a public statement of rejection and degradation (*cf.* Heb 12.2 "the shame of the cross"). Just as the mob hated Jesus to the extent

---

[59] Adverbial participles that follow the main verb "elaborate the action of the main verb, often providing more specific explanation of what is meant by the main action." Runge, *Discourse Grammar,* 262.

[60] So Gareth Lee Cockerill, "A Wesleyan Arminian View," in *Four Views on the Warning Passages in Hebrews,* ed. Herbert W. Bateman IV (Grand Rapids: Kregel, 2007), 257–92, at 276; Bruce, *The Epistle to the Hebrews,* 124; Marcus Dods, *The Epistle to the Hebrews,* vol. 4 of *The Expositor's Greek Testament,* ed. W. Robertson Nicoll (repr., Grand Rapids: Eerdmans, 1979), 4:298; Koester, *Hebrews,* 315; Lane, *Hebrews 1–8,* 133.

[61] "Anew" comes from the prefix *ana-* on the verb here. Some suggest that the prefix only denotes the vertical, "up" position of a crucifixion. The word is certainly used this way in Greek literature (see references in Koester, *Hebrews,* 315 ; Attridge, *Hebrews,* 171; Ellingworth, *Epistle to the Hebrews,* 324). However, the word "again" in this context (v 6) argues for understanding that the author was describing a new demonstration of the hatred that led to the crucifixion of Jesus. Cockerill, "A Wesleyan Arminian View," 276 fn44; Ellingworth, *Epistle to the Hebrews,* 324; Johannes Schneider, *"stauros, stauroō, anastauroō,"* *TDNT* 7:583–84.

[62] See David W. Chapman, *Ancient Jewish and Christian Perceptions of Crucifixion,* WUNT 244 (Tübingen: Mohr Siebeck, 2008), 217–18 and 252–53; Jerome H. Neyrey, *Honor and Shame in the Gospel of Matthew* (Louisville: Westminster John Knox Press, 1998), 139–40.

that they purposefully handed him over to the disgraceful, humiliating treatment he received from the Romans, these apostate Christians despise Jesus to that same extent. Those who once professed love for the Lord now hate him as apostates. They come to hate Jesus so much that they *want* him to be harmed and shamed. Note that Jesus is here called **the Son of God**, his exalted title from chapter 1, which underscores the greatness of the apostate's offence.[63] For such a contempt-driven, willful, wholesale, and remorseless rejection, no provision for forgiveness exists. *Cf.* 1 John 5.16f.

6.7–8 For the ground which has drunk the rain that often comes upon it, and has produced vegetation useful for those for whom it is cultivated, partakes in a blessing from God; but the ground that bears thorns and thistles is rejected and is near to being cursed, and its end is burning.

These verses are a short parable that brings the discussion to a warning. Like all Biblical parables, its purpose is to illustrate, not to prove. The main point of the parable is about reciprocity. Judgment parables drawn from agriculture and especially the harvest are plentiful in the Bible. Examples are Jesus' own parables of the soils (Matt 13.1–9), the wheat and tares (Matt 13.24–30), and the wicked vine-growers (Matt 21.33–43), as well as a similar metaphor in John the Baptist's preaching (Matt 3.10–12). The parable of the vine from Isaiah 5 (which is also echoed in Matt 21.33ff, John 15.1–6 and Rom 11.17–24) may also be in the background here, and possibly the destruction of the cities of the plain (Sodom and Gomorrah). That area was well-watered (Gen 13.10) but was burned for its wickedness (Gen 19.24–25), and it was held up as a model of God's judgment (Gen 29.22ff).[64] However, well-watered ground is also an image of the promised land (Deut 11.11), which itself reflected the well-watered garden in Eden (*cf.* Gen 13.10, Canaan was "like the garden of the Lord"). The idea of cultivating, or working, the land also echoes Eden (Gen 2.15), as well as the mention of fruit (Gen 1.29; 2.9). However, the parable here is not about Eden, but about two kinds of people and their responses to God.

There are two basic situations considered in this parable, but the point is the same for each: they are about how one "repays" the goodness of

[63] Westcott, *Epistle to the Hebrews*, 151.

[64] Lane, *Hebrews 1–8*, 143.

God. There are some Christians who accept God's offer of salvation, with its accompanying gifts, and respond with faithfulness and its fruits; and there are some who accept God's salvation and favors but then never repay God's goodness with good things in return, but instead with scorn. The former are **blessed** by God (explained in greater detail in vv 13ff below), but the latter are **rejected**. Like the **ground** that receives **rain**,[65] so is a Christian who has been enlightened, who has tasted the heavenly gift, *etc.* (vv 4–5). The farmer's hope is that in season the ground will produce good, mature (Heb 6.1) fruit for his benefit. In our case, God is the one who has planted and cared for this "garden," which is his people (here, Christians), and they in turn are expected to bear good fruit for God (Rom 7.4). They exist by his grace and for his good pleasure. Note the order here. Our author does not say that the ground will be productive if God blesses it. He says if the ground is productive, then God blesses it; the blessing is God's response to the ground's fruitfulness. A future reward is what is ultimately in view here, but our author will also specify the nature of this blessing in verses 12ff.

But what if the plot of ground produces only **thorns and thistles**? In the present passage the thorns and briars represent Christians who have fallen away (v 6), who have turned against God and his Son. Instead of maturing and producing something good, such ground has produced something useless and even harmful. Likewise, these apostate Christians become rebels against God who begat them by the seed which is his word (1 Pet 1.23–25). We should also remember Isaiah's parable (see Isa 5.6) and consider the influence of passages such as Isaiah 7.23–25 and 32.13 on the point here. The word **rejected** translates the Greek word *adokimos* and refers to that which fails to pass the test and hence is disqualified, unfit, unworthy, or useless.[66] It is entirely possible for one to be a Christian and yet so think and live as to fail to meet God's approval (1 Cor 9.27; 2 Cor 13.5). These Christians are **near to** being **cursed**, that is, they stand on the verge of receiving the wrath of God for their disobedience. Just as harmful and unwanted weeds in a field are gathered up and **burned** (*cf.* Matt 13.30), so these apostate Christians face, in that state, only the fiery

---

[65] Early and latter rains in the Palestinian agricultural cycle are often, in the OT, a way of speaking of God's provision for his people; *cf.* Deut 11.11, 14; Psa 84.6; Lev 26.4. Joel 2.23 uses it as a figure of the blessings of the Messianic age.

[66] *"adokimos," EDNT* 1:33; BDAG 21.

wrath of God.[67] See also Isaiah 10.16f. There is no avenue of reconciliation available in their rebellious, hardened condition, only the judgment of God against them. The fact that they are only *near* being cursed points to the fact that their situation has not become permanent yet.

6.9 But we are convinced of better things concerning you, beloved, even those things that belong to salvation, even though we are speaking in this way.

If a Christian who once turned from God could never decide to come back to God under any circumstance, then the author of Hebrews would not have turned from warning to encouragement. Christians who have stumbled (in this case, contemplating quitting) always have the choice to return to God. The key is that they must not allow their sin to breed the hardness of heart that eventually makes this impossible (vv 1–8). It is possible to snatch them from the fire (Jude 23) in the sense that it is possible to encourage them to return to faithfulness before that level of hardness sets in. This our author will now attempt to do.

The warning in verses 1–8 is stern and frightful. The author did not apologize for that. The horrible consequences of disobedience are a legitimate incentive to righteous living, as are the rewards of obedience. While the author was **convinced** ("persuaded," and in that sense, "sure"; it is a rhetorical statement and does not indicate an absolute state on the part of his readers) that his readers had not yet reached the point described in verses 4–6, it was necessary to depict the consequences they faced if they continued in their spiritual regression. But while the author has not been reluctant to warn them with talk about what happens to the reprobate (**though we are speaking in this way**), neither does he dismiss his readers nor treat them as enemies (*cf.* 2 Thes 3.15). They were still **beloved** to him (and to the Lord), and the goal of his correspondence was to avert their further progress toward destruction. He was optimistic that **better things** would be true of them, that is, that they would be renewed like the good, fruitful ground of the parable in verses 7–8, and not like the land that produces only thorns and briars.

[67] Matt 13.49f; 25.41; Heb 10.27; 12.29; 2 Pet 3.7. While the reference to burning here could refer to hell, the focus in Hebrews is on God's wrath, not the place where unbelievers exist for eternity. "Fire" is a frequent symbol in the Bible for God's consuming, destroying anger against sinners. Deut 9.3; 32.22; Psa 21.9; 68.2; 79.5; 89.46; Isa 30.27; *etc.*

The expression **things that belong to salvation** refers to the alternative to ending up under God's punishment. Broadly speaking, there are two kinds of "things" in which one may be involved: the things that belong to the scenario of destruction, and the things that belong to the scenario of salvation. In Hebrews, however, one particular "thing" is in view, and that is perseverance (see below). Thus, the author was optimistic that his readers would return to faithfulness and exhibit perseverance in their faith.

6.10 For God is not so unjust so as to forget your work and the love which you showed for his name, in your having served, and still serving, the saints.

In the previous verse, the author referred to things that appear in the lives of saved people and that belong to salvation, which things are evidence of their perseverance. Here he reminded his readers that they had manifested such good works before. Their spiritual regression had not yet become a dissociation from other Christians. **God** would **not** be so **unjust** or unfair so as **to forget** such loving service, implying that the reward for faithful service was still theirs to have. To turn back from Christianity after already having done such good works was to throw away their hope of reward (10.35). Exactly what they had done for other Christians (**the saints**) is not stated. To **serve** (Greek *diakoneō*) someone can mean to provide financial aid (as in Acts 20.24; Phil 2.25; 4.16), but it could refer to any kind of assistance. Whatever it was, it had been done by the original readers of Hebrews as **a work**. This in no way implies that their efforts of service to others merited or earned them anything before God, much less that the author here thought so. The word (Greek *ergon*) can have the sense of "demonstration" or a practical proof of something, but it can also have the ordinary sense of "deed" ("what you did").[68] Their service to others did not consist in mere thought or sentiment, but in deeds that demonstrated their concern for others (see Jam 2.15f). What they had done was also an expression of **love** toward their brethren. Love is the mark of a genuine Christian (John 13.34f), especially when it involves giving to others (1 John 3.17f), and the author here reminded his readers that they had indeed been living the kind of life that God would reward. Their Christianity had been genuine, not superficial, and it would be a

[68] BDAG 390.

tragic shame to turn back from it. To do something of love toward a disciple is to do it for the Lord (Matt 25.40), and thus the author of Hebrews added that their loving care of other Christians was ultimately **shown for his name**. The readers of Hebrews had already shown that they were capable of sacrificial, faithful service to God, for their loving care of other Christians was exactly that (see comments on 10.33f). In fact, they were **still** doing it. In a sense, the solution to their current problem was a simple one: they needed to keep doing what they had been, and were still, doing. They had already proven that they could persevere. They just needed to continue in it. Having shown love, they now needed to show their faith (v 12) and hope (vv 18f).[69]

6.11 And we desire for each of you to show the same diligence to the full assurance of hope until the end.

The readers had already proved, by their sacrificial assistance to the saints, that they could be sincere, faithful Christians. We should note the little phrase **each one of you**. Entrance into heaven is not granted simply because one associated himself with other Christians in the group, the church. Each person within the group of God's people will be judged for his own deeds (2 Cor 5:10), and each person who has persevered in faith will be saved (Luke 8.15; Matt 10.22).

Their expressions of love to others demonstrated that they had within themselves the attitude necessary for endurance and a willingness to be associated fully with Christians, even sacrificially. The author simply encouraged them to continue in that same vein. The key was perseverance, or **diligence** (Greek *spoudē*, which can also denote zeal, willingness, or enthusiasm, reflecting "earnest commitment in discharge of an obligation or experience of a relationship"[70]). They already attained a measure of hope for the good things they had done before, but no Christian may ever be content to rest on any imagined merits of past good works. **The full assurance of hope** comes not when one has done good things only in the past, but by serving faithfully **until the end**. The word **until** (Greek *achri*) may refer to time, but it can also refer to place ("as far as") or extent ("up to the point of").[71] The **end** here may be the end of one's

---

[69] Attridge, *Hebrews*, 174.

[70] BDAG 939.

[71] BDAG 160–61.

life, or better, the end or goal of Christian service, which is a glorious, heavenly life with God (see comments on 3.14).

6.12 So that you might not become lazy, but imitators of those who, through faith and patience, inherit the promises.

The problem with the original readers of Hebrews is precisely that they had become **lazy** or sluggish (NASB) in their faith, which had produced inactivity for the Lord and a failure to maintain their faithfulness. The word **lazy** is the same word (Greek *nōthros*) used in 5.11 where the current discussion of the readers' problem began, and thus neatly brackets the conversation. They had become tired from the hardships of suffering and were unwilling to persevere any longer. What they needed to do was come out of their lethargy, rekindle the hope that would motivate them to endure, and follow the example of so many others who either had been faithful in past generations or who were continuing in the faith as their contemporaries. The word **imitators** translates the Greek word *mimētēs*, a form of the word from which we get our English word "mimic" (*cf.* 1 Cor 4.16). *Mimesis*, or imitation, was a standard rhetorical and pedagogical tool in antiquity.[72] The author will therefore come back to this encouragement with a long list of examples of faithfulness to be imitated (in ch 11). For now, however, he notes two qualities of those they should follow: their faith and their patience. **Faith**, or trust, is the essential element in any right relationship with God (see 11.6). Its importance has already been mentioned in 4.2. For Hebrews, however, the emphasis is usually on the perseverance that true faith exhibits. **Patience** translates the Greek word *makrothumia*. Although this word can sometimes refer to holding one's temper, and in this sense mean "longsuffering," it can also be used in a broader sense (as here) to denote endurance under difficulty and is virtually synonymous with the Greek word *hupomonē* ("patience," which is not used in Hebrews, but appears in similar contexts, *cf.* Jam 1.4, or appears together with *makrothumeō*, as in Col 1.11, *etc.*).[73] Those who endure do so because they trust in God (see ch 11), and therefore, in Hebrews, faith and patience are basically two aspects of the same thing.

Those who patiently maintain faith in God **inherit the promises** God has made to them. The word **inherit** here is in the Greek present tense, in-

[72] See Rubén R. Dupertuis, "Mimesis," *NIDB* 4:89.

[73] BDAG 612.

dicating in a proverbial kind of way what is usual for these circumstances. In a Jewish context, "the promises" first refers to the promises God made to Abraham. Like Paul in Galatians 3, the author of Hebrews understood that people of faith are the true children of Abraham, and therefore they are the heirs of what God promised to the patriarch (who was himself a man of faith). The significance of the plural **promises** should not be emphasized too much, since all the things that comprise salvation are also sometimes lumped together under the term "the promise" (as in Gal 3.22; Eph 3.6). However, the plural communicates that God has many good things in store for those who demonstrate their loyalty to him.

6.13–14 For when God was promising to Abraham, since he had no greater by which he could swear, he swore by himself, saying, "Surely I will bless you, and I will multiply you."

For now, one example of faithfulness is presented as an encouragement before the author returns to his discussion of the high priesthood of Jesus (which holds the greatest encouragement for his readers). The example would have been especially powerful to Jewish Christians, for it is the example of **Abraham**, the man all Jews claimed as their "father." In the NT Abraham is consistently remembered as a man of exemplary faith in God (Rom 4; Jam 2; *etc.*). The true descendants of Abraham are those who imitate (v 12) his faith.

God made several promises to Abraham, no less than nine different ones in all.[74] The promise God made in Genesis 22.16–17 was, in fact, a repetition of a promise made in Genesis 12.2: "I will bless you." However, God did not simply repeat the promise. On this occasion God **swore** to it, or took an oath. Normally God's promise word needs no oath to secure it. God keeps his word, and when he says he will do something, men may count on the fulfillment of that word as if it were already done. "He who promised is faithful" (Heb 10.23). But God wanted Abraham to be doubly

[74] They are: 1) God would make him a great nation (Gen 12.2; 13.16; *etc.*); 2) God would bless Abraham (Gen 12.2; 15.19; *etc.*), which means that God would give him life; 3) Abraham's name would be great (Gen 12.2); 4) Abraham himself would be a blessing (Gen 12.2); 5) God would bless those who blessed Abraham, and curse those who cursed him (Gen 12.3; 15.1); 6) through Abraham divine blessing would come to the Gentiles (Gen 12.3; 18.18; 22.18); 7) Abraham's descendants would occupy the land of Canaan (Gen 12.7; 13.14f; *etc.*); 8) kings would be descended from Abraham (Gen 17.6); and 9) the Lord would be the God of Abraham's offspring (Gen 17.7f).

certain, as it were, of the surety of his promise. Thus God, for Abraham's sake, took an oath. Oaths are normally sworn by a **greater** authority (see v 16 below), but in God's case there is no one greater. So, God **swore by himself** (Gen 22.16 "By Myself I have sworn" NASB). The significance of this can scarcely be overemphasized. When God swore by himself, he was affirming his word against his own being. God could not have been God and failed to keep his word to Abraham. The English translations struggle to do justice to the oath language of God on this occasion. In the Hebrew text of Genesis 22.17, these words are spoken in a construction known as an infinitive absolute, which is one of the strongest ways the Hebrew language had of making an affirmation.[75] The KJV (*cf.* also the ASV) renders it somewhat woodenly as "blessing I will bless thee, and multiplying I will multiply thee," but that captures the repetition of the verbal idea in the Hebrew. The term **surely**[76] was an ancient and regular part of oath language.[77] The emphatic construction, along with God's self-adjuring, made God's promise as guaranteed as it could be.

The specific context here, and the order of events in it, is important to note. The quotation (**"Surely I will bless ..."**) is from the last occasion on which God spoke this promise personally to Abraham, after he had demonstrated his loyalty to God in offering Isaac (Gen 22.17). The Jews called that story the *Aqedah* (the "binding" of Isaac). It was a unique moment in Abraham's experience with God and one of the most significant moments in the Abraham story. After God saw that Abraham would hold nothing back, that he was willing to sacrifice all for the sake of following and obeying God, and that he trusted God's word fully, God then made a solemn promise to Abraham, to which our author now directs our attention. The word **bless** here recalls the word "blessing" from the parable in verse 7 above, but more importantly, it refers back to Genesis 12.2, where God first promised to Abraham "I will bless you." The two statements from Genesis 22.17 are basically two ways of saying the same thing. God's promise to bless Abraham was a promise to give him life (*cf.* 2 Tim 1.1; by God's Spirit, Gal 3.14), and that life would be seen in the

---

[75] GKC 342.

[76] *ē mēn* in the LXX, rendered *ei mēn* in Hebrews; *cf.* MM 182.

[77] Gustav Adolf Deissmann, *Bible Studies: Contributions Chiefly from Papyri and Inscriptions to the History of the Language, the Literature and the Religion of Hellenistic Judaism and Primitive Christianity*, trans. Alexander Grieve (1901; repr., Winona Lake, IN: Alpha Publications, 1979), 205–208.

multitude of living people who came from him. Just as the land that is fruitful receives God's blessing in response, so Abraham's faith bore the fruit of endurance, and God's response was to promise life (blessing) to him and his descendants. The order is: bear fruit (*i.e.*, show faith), then receive life from God (see next verse).

God's response to Abraham's great demonstration of faithfulness was to reaffirm the promise that Abraham would have countless descendants and they would possess the gate (*i.e.*, the fortified land) of their enemies.[78] The promise of living in God's land is always connected with the promise of blessing (life). The land is the place where the life is enabled and enjoyed, it is where rest with God is achieved (Heb 3–4). The Hebrew and LXX record the promise as "I will multiply your seed," but our author has here shortened to "**I will multiply you**" to keep the emphasis on Abraham.[79]

6.15 And in this way, after he had endured, he obtained the promise.

The verb **endured** recalls the noun form of the word in verse 12, and Abraham's endurance (patience) is a model for Christians, specifically for those first readers of Hebrews who were tempted to quit in the midst of pressure and hardships brought upon them by their own fellow-countrymen. The specific endurance of Abraham in this case was the demonstration of his perseverance, by faith, through his testing in the matter of the offering of Isaac. After that trial, God affirmed his promise with an oath (vv 13f above).

In what sense did Abraham **obtain the promise**? The phrase cannot mean that Abraham obtained everything God had promised to him, because Abraham did not live to see his descendants become a great nation of people in their own land (*cf.* 11.13), or kings come from them, *etc.* He died with only one son and two grandchildren (*i.e.*, children of promise, Isaac and his sons Jacob and Esau), both still living in a land controlled by Canaanites. Some have suggested that Abraham received in his lifetime some, but not all, of the things promised to him, with the partial fulfillment sufficing as proof that the whole would come.[80] Others suggest that

[78] The picture is one of ultimately sharing in the conquest of the Messiah, as depicted in Psa 2 and 110.

[79] Lane, *Hebrews 1–8*, 151; Ellingworth, *Epistle to the Hebrews*, 337.

[80] *E.g.*, Cockerill, *Epistle to the Hebrews*, 286.

it means that Abraham received Isaac back after the attempted sacrifice in Genesis 22 (*cf.* Heb 11:19),[81] and this, I think, gets closer to the meaning here. The rescue of Isaac from certain death proved that God would provide life (through his descendants) to Abraham, and God used that occasion to reiterate, with an oath, that this would be God's provision for Abraham always. In this context, receiving life seems to be more than living on the earth (Abraham did, after all, die). It points to an eternal life in the future, in God's land and city (Heb 11.10, 13–16), something that God guaranteed to the faithful patriarch. Additionally, the author's remark demonstrates the faithfulness of God.[82]

6.16 For people swear by the greater, and the oath is the end for confirmation of their every dispute.

This verse explains what happens in an oath. Oaths are sworn upon a **greater** power or authority than oneself. In an **oath** one makes himself liable to the destructive power of one who is greater if his words should prove false.[83] The oath-taker willingly places himself in such risk to affirm the truth of what he says. When someone places themselves under such risk in making a statement, the presumption is that no one would do such a thing and then lie (and thus bring down the destructive power of the greater one upon himself). So, when someone swears an oath, it is normally considered evidence enough (or **confirmation**) that the words spoken are true. If anyone's words are in doubt, an oath normally settles the matter; the oath is understood to be the **end** of the matter as far as confirmation is concerned. Because an oath is such a high and solemn pledge of truthfulness, the making of false oaths is forbidden by God.[84]

6.17 In which God, wishing even more to show to the heirs of the promise the unalterable nature of his will, guaranteed it with an oath.

God's promise of life, confirmed by his oath, concerned not only Abraham but his descendants as well. The true descendants (or "sons") of Abraham are those who imitate his faith in God (*cf.* Gal 3.7, 9; Heb 2.16). The promise of life is just as valid to Abraham's true, spiritual descendants as

[81] *E.g.*, Rhee, "Christology and the Concept of Faith"; Koester, *Hebrews*, 326.

[82] Cockerill, *Epistle to the Hebrews*, 285.

[83] *Cf.* the ancient oath formula in Ruth 1.17; 1 Sam 14.44; 2 Sam 19.13.

[84] Matt 5.33–37; 23.16–22; Jam 5.12; *cf.* Lev 19.12; Num 30.2.

it was to Abraham. This is the significance of the phrase **in which**. The NASB and NRSV renders as "in the same way," NKJB "thus," RSV "so."

This verse shows that what is true in human oath-taking (v 16) is also true of God's oath-taking. The **heirs of the promise** are ultimately Abraham's spiritual descendants, Christians. God wanted to impress upon them (us!) the **unalterable** or unchangeable nature[85] of his **will** (Greek *boulē*), which is his resolution, decision, or purpose.[86] The word "unalterable" (Greek *ametathetos*) is also "the standard term in inheritance discussions for a will being 'unchanged' at the testator's death,"[87] which fits well with the discussion of the "heirs" in this verse. God's will was specifically his decision to grant an abiding eschatological rest to Abraham and his true descendants.

As noted in the comments on verse 13 above, God's determination ordinarily is reliable enough. But God wanted to show **even more to the heirs of** the **promise** (those who will receive what is promised) that his will was absolutely reliable, and so he **guaranteed it** (see v 16) with his **oath**. The word translated **guaranteed** is not the same word used in verse 16 above, but renders the Greek word *mesiteuō*, which means to act as surety or to guarantee.[88] The point is that there is no way God, by virtue of his own being, will fail to give eternal life to his faithful people. This discussion of God's oath prepares also the way for the discussion in chapters 7 and 8 of the relationship between Christ's priesthood, God's oath, and the new covenant (testament) that expresses God's will.

6.18 So that through two unchangeable things, in which it is impossible for God to lie, we who have fled to take hold of the hope lying before us might have a strong encouragement.

The **two unchangeable things** are 1) God's promise and 2) God's oath. Worley, based on a study of litigant oaths in antiquity, suggests that the two immutable things are 1) God's dependability and 2) God witnessing his own oath,[89] which interpretation should not be discounted. Sup-

[85] BDAG 53, the neuter form of the adjective being used as a substantive ("unchangeableness").

[86] BDAG 181–82; H. J. Ritz, "*boulē*," *EDNT* 1:224.

[87] David R. Worley, "Fleeing to Two Immutable Things, God's Oath-Taking and Oath-Witnessing: The Use of Litigant Oath in Hebrews 6:12–20," *ResQ* 36 (1994): 223–36.

[88] BDAG 634.

[89] Worley, "Fleeing to Two Immutable Things," 227.

porting this is Westcott's observation that the word **God** here lacks the definite article, emphasizing God's quality as deity.[90] That is, the statement can have the force of "in these things deity cannot lie." However, the mention of "promise" and "oath" in the preceding verse makes them seem the most obvious referents. The word **unchangeable** is the same word from verse 17 above. By repeating it so quickly the author intended to emphasize it. Once promised, and once confirmed by God's oath, what God said could not be changed, and there is no possibility that God was lying. It is **impossible for God to lie** in this matter because such would be a violation of God's fundamental, absolutely righteous nature. He could not have promised or sworn falsely and still be God, for he swore by himself (v 13 above).[91] God is not capable of any kind of sin, and hence his oath is true. We must remember that God's oath is for our sake, not his. God did not need to guard his own words with an oath, as if sometimes God did not keep his word. Instead, God's oath is his attempt to assure *us* that there is no way his promise will fail.

The transition to the word **we** is significant. Believers in Christ are the true, spiritual descendants of Abraham (*cf.* Gal 3.7, 9). Abraham believed in a God who could bring life out of a situation of death (see Rom 4.19–24; Heb 11.17–19) and thus is the prototype of those who believe that God raised Jesus from the dead. The church is ultimately the great nation God had in view that would come from Abraham (*cf.* Rom 4.13–17). What God promised to Abraham he also promises to Abraham's spiritual descendants (Gen 17.8), Abraham's "seed." The same promise was for both (see 11.39f), and that promise was guaranteed by God's own oath. God's promise-oath to Christians is every bit as sure and reliable as it was to Abraham, but the promise is theirs to obtain only if they, like Abraham, prove their faith through endurance.

Christians have **a strong encouragement** in God's promise, just as Abraham did (because it is the same oath-guaranteed promise). Although the Greek word *paraklēsis* can mean consolation (KJV), here it has the sense of encouragement.[92] Christians are also described as those **who have fled** to God for refuge in his power to protect, which is part of God's covenant obligations to his people. The picture is one of God's people finding safety

---

[90] Westcott, *Epistle to the Hebrews*, 162.

[91] *Cf.* Num 23.19; 1 Sam 15.29; 2 Tim 2:13; Titus 1:2.

[92] BDAG 766.

from the hardships and difficulties of living in a hostile world of sinners, similar to the picture often depicted in the OT psalms, and this picture will be evoked again in 11.8ff. It also generally recalls the exodus from Egypt.[93] Although they were maligned and even persecuted, the original readers of Hebrews could take refuge in the surety of God's promise. The author thus took their social situation, which was causing them to rethink their commitment to Christ, and used it as an encouragement for them to draw even closer to God through Christ. By his oath-confirmed promise God has **laid hope before** his people, a hope of rest, a better life in a better place (more on this in ch 11). In Hebrews "hope" is never merely an attitude but includes the content of hope, what is hoped for.[94] The author's encouragement was no doubt very powerful in its original context. Jewish Christians certainly considered themselves children of Abraham, but even more, as Christians they were spiritual sons of Abraham the believer. To them belongs God's promise-oath which gives hope of life and rest with God. The encouragement was for them to be true sons of Abraham and continue in faith like Abraham did. If they maintained their faith, then God's immutable promise would give them hope which, in turn, would help them to persevere. To **take hold of the hope**, then, means to be faithful so as to be a true, spiritual descendant of Abraham and thus also a recipient of God's promise. The Christians to whom Hebrews was addressed needed to continue in the faithfulness they had already shown themselves capable of exhibiting (v 10), so they might have "the full assurance of hope until the end" (v 11).

We should note that the author of Hebrews understood that those who had gone before in faith "did not receive what was promised" (11.39). The picture is that the faithful of old have not yet entered into their ultimate rest because God's plan "provided something better for us, so that apart from us they would not be perfected" (see comments on 11:40). We do not join them, they join us. Until the end, God's people of all ages wait in hope, based on God's promise, to enter the heavenly country together and enjoy eternal life there (yet see v 20 below).

6.19 Which we have as an anchor of the soul, firm and sure, and which enters into that which is inside the veil.

---

[93] Attridge, *Hebrews*, 182.

[94] Lane, *Hebrews 1–8*, 153.

Hope is the product of God's oath-guaranteed promise. The importance of hope in the Christian life can hardly be overemphasized. The hope of glory motivates Christians to persevere in faithfulness. Hope in this sense is **as** (like; Greek *hōs*) **an anchor of the soul**. The word **soul** (Greek *psuchē*) is used in the Hebrew sense of "person."[95] Hope gives the Christian spiritual stability, like the anchor of a ship. The storms of life may rage (especially things such as hardship and persecution for being a Christian), but hope keeps a Christian "in place." A ship without an anchor will be driven by the waves of the storm and will eventually drift away and wreck (see the imagery in Jam 1.6; 1 Tim 1.19; *cf.* Heb 2.1), but a ship that is securely anchored will not move. An unfaithful Christian, who has lost sight of the hope before him, is like a ship without an anchor. The waves of hardship will drive him about and he will eventually flounder in his doubt.

Of course, an anchored ship is safe only if the anchor is **firm** (Greek *asphalēs,* meaning "certain" or "secure")[96] **and sure** (Greek *bebaios,* meaning "reliable, dependable"),[97] that is, if it has caught hold of something immovable. It is useless to quibble over whether "firm and sure" modifies "anchor" or "hope" (either is grammatically possible), for the anchor is a symbol of the Christian's hope in this discussion. The hope in a Christian's soul is grounded in God himself who cannot lie about what he has promised.[98]

The imagery now transitions to that of the tabernacle/temple, the most sacred part of which was the Most Holy Place (the Holy of Holies). The Most Holy Place was partitioned off by a **veil**,[99] or curtain (Exod 26.33), past which no one could go except the high priest alone. The significance of the tabernacle typology will be explored in chapter 9 (see also comments on 8.2). It was understood that the Most Holy Place was where God dwelt, for in there was God's footstool, the ark of the covenant (1 Chron 28.2). Therefore, **that which is inside the veil** is a circumlocution

---

[95] BDAG 1099; like the Hebrew word *nephesh*.

[96] BDAG 147.

[97] BDAG 172.

[98] So strong was this image in Christian tradition that the anchor became the predominant funerary symbol for Christian burials in the catacombs of Rome in the second and third centuries. See Jason A. Whitlark, "Funerary Anchors of Hope and Hebrews: A Reappraisal of the Origins of the Anchor Iconography in the Catacombs of Rome," *PRSt* 48 (2021): 219–41.

[99] See Daniel M. Gurtner, "LXX Syntax and the Identity of the NT Veil," *NovT* 47 (2005): 344–53.

for God himself, God's presence. There is nothing surer in the universe to which the soul could be anchored. It may be noted in passing that our author says nothing of "cables" connecting the Christian to his anchor, or of "taking up the slack" of such imagined cables. Instead, entering inside the veil, or entering into God's very presence, is always the goal Hebrews has in mind.

6.20 Where a forerunner has entered on our behalf, Jesus, having become a high priest forever according to the order of Melchizedek.

The mention of the tabernacle imagery in verse 19 brings the author neatly back to Jesus, the Christian's high priest who has entered into the true Holy of Holies, heaven itself (9.11), to intercede with his own blood in the presence of God (9.12). But this statement is not merely some piece of rhetorical skill by which the author resumes a previous topic. Like the high priest of the OT, Jesus has entered into the Most Holy Place **on our behalf**. But unlike the arrangement of the OT, *our new high priest brings us into the presence of God with him*. Jesus, and faith in him, is essential and crucial to the Christian's relationship with God, which relationship is the anchor of the soul's hope and is based on God's immutable promise secured by his own oath. Hope draws one near to God (7.19), and drawing near to God is mediated through the high priesthood of Jesus (7.25). In this way, the author has skillfully combined the Biblical threads of Abraham and the promise, rest, and the high priesthood of Jesus. As noted in the remarks on 2.10, Israel's journey out of Egypt culminated in the high priest entering into the Most Holy Place. Entering into rest—an ongoing, worshipful fellowship with God—was to be achieved by faithful endurance on the part of Abraham's descendants until they entered into the land and, finally, the high priest (who represented them all) entered the presence of the living God. This is the large-scale paradigm driving Hebrews.[100]

Jesus has entered into the presence of God as a **forerunner on our behalf**. *Cf.* the comments on 2.10 where Jesus is called the "pioneer of our salvation." The author is not saying that Jesus is the anchor within the veil. He is saying instead that Jesus is the way to God (who is inside the veil) in whom the Christian's hope is anchored (*cf.* 7.19). Jesus' ascension to God's right hand was not solely for his glorification (although that is certainly a significant part of it; Heb 1.13; 2.17f), but also that he

[100] See Thiessen, "Hebrews and the End of Exodus."

might open up the way and make it possible for others to follow him there, into perfect (*i.e.* fully realized) and eternal fellowship ("rest," ch 4) with God. Jesus has already entered where the faithful hope to be. That is, God has not simply invited us to join him in heaven, but he sent his Son who trod the way ahead of us to make the path clear and to bring us to him (2.10). See also John 14.6.

Jesus is again described as a **high priest after the order of Melchizedek** (see comments on 5.6), a subject which our author approached back in 5.1–10. The author paused in that discussion to both rebuke (5.11–6.8) and encourage (6.9–19) his readers, and has now brought the discussion back to where he left it.

The last phrase in the Greek text of this verse is rendered **forever** in English, picking up the term from Psalm 110.4. In Greek composition the end of a sentence is one of the places to put something for prominence. Our author has put this phrase last at this point because the eternal nature of the Melchizedekian high priesthood is his next topic (ch 7). In fact, the order of words in the Biblical quotation "(1) priest (2) forever (3) according to the order of Melchizedek" is the agenda for the discussion. The author has already established (1) that Jesus is qualified to be high priest (3.17; 4.14–5.6). After having paused to deliver his rebuke and encouragement, he will now proceed to discuss the significance of the phrase (2) "forever" in Psalm 110's description of the Melchizedekian priesthood (7.1–10), and then discuss how the priesthood changed from that of Aaron to (3) the order (type or kind) of Melchizedek (7.11–28).

HEBREWS 7

The author has wished to bring his readers to a discussion of the high priesthood of Jesus, which is like that of Melchizedek, because this teaching held a tremendous encouragement to faithfulness. The author had begun the discussion earlier (4.14–5.10) but paused in his presentation to deliver a rebuke and encouragement (5.11–6.19). Here, at last, the author now begins to lay out his picture of the priesthood of Jesus in contrast to the priesthood of the old law in an extended midrash (see Introduction).[1] Our author has already quoted Psalm 110.4 ("you are a priest forever according to the order of Melchizedek") in Hebrews 5.6, 10 and most recently in 6.20. The fuller meaning of those words will now be demonstrated by a return to the only other place in Scripture where Melchizedek is mentioned, Genesis 14. While the subject of the priesthood of Jesus establishes his superiority over the Levitical system, it should also be noted that in the Judaism of antiquity, the Levitical priesthood with its sacrifices was viewed as the backbone of the religion. Thus the author's comparison between the priesthoods of Aaron and Jesus also served as a thorough critique of the former in order to magnify the latter.

7.1 For this Melchizedek, king of Salem, priest of the most high God, who met Abraham as he returned from the slaughter of the kings and blessed him.

For the meaning of the name **Melchizedek** and the significance of the place where he reigned, see comments on verse 2. The point of this verse is to introduce formally the historical character of Melchizedek and mention the key facts about him. Jewish Christians would have been already familiar with the Genesis story of Melchizedek (Gen 14.18–20), so the pur-

[1] For a demonstration of how Heb 7 fits the character of midrash, see Jospeh A. Fitzmyer, "'Now This Melchizedek…' (Heb 7,1)," *CBQ* 25 (1963) 305–21, reprinted in his *Essays on the Semitic Background of the New Testament* (Grand Rapids: Eerdmans, 1997), 221–43.

pose of our author's words was not to inform them about the episode, but to remind them of the details, which were particularly relevant to the discussion he now enters. It is worth noting the method of the author of Hebrews here. Like a good Bible student, he went back to the original story and collected the data to lay the foundation for his exposition of the topic.

As far as we can tell, **Melchizedek** was a Canaanite king. There is no suggestion in the Bible that he was related to Abraham in any way. His kingdom was the city-state of **Salem** (probably along with its satellite villages), which was probably the same place later called Jerusalem. The parallelism of Salem and Zion in Psalm 76.2 suggests this, although Shechem and a place near Scythopolis have (unconvincingly) been suggested as well.[2] The Genesis narrative seems to suggest that Salem was an important city in Abraham's day. This is similar to cities such as Hazor, which was a kingdom-city with other satellite cities and villages around it (Josh 11.10). It is interesting, given the messianic significance of Jerusalem, that the author of Hebrews did not explore its typological potential (see below). This was perhaps due to the fact that the author may have seen the Jerusalem of his day as the symbol of an approach to God that has now been replaced through the work of Jesus (*cf.* 12.18ff). The focus of Hebrews is not on the fact that Melchizedek was a **king** (as significant as that was), but on his priestly role (and its typological value for the nature of Jesus' priesthood). M. J. Paul has convincingly argued that the significance of Melchizedek in Psalm 110 is not the combination of king and priest in one person (because the expression "according to the order of Melchizedek" is connected only with Melchizedek's priesthood), but the single, abiding nature of his priesthood.[3]

In addition to being king of Salem, Melchizedek was also a **priest of the most high God**. The phrase **most high** describes **God**, as is common enough in the Bible (Num 24.16; Deut 32.8; *etc.*); the phrase does not describe the priesthood of Melchizedek (see on 5.6). It is not a high priestly status of Melchizedek that is the real significance of this character, but the abiding nature of his priesthood.

The priesthood of Melchizedek is that aspect of him our author will now discuss in great detail. We do not know the circumstances in which he came to be a priest of the true God, nor do we have any indication of

---

[2] See Michael C. Astour, "Salem," *AYBD* 5.905.

[3] Paul, "The Order of Melchizedek," 203–4.

what his priestly duties were, or how he carried them out. One thing is certain, however, for the author of Hebrews: Melchizedek did not become a priest by receiving that office from a predecessor. The sudden interjection into the Genesis narrative of the fact that this man was a priest of God therefore reflects the very nature of that priesthood. The Bible gives scant mention of the priesthood that served God before the Aaronic priesthood described in the Law of Moses. Jethro was priest of Midian (Exod 2.16ff; 3.1), and we read of priests at Mt Sinai before the giving of the law (Exod 19.22, 24). But we simply do not know how these people came to be priests, what they did in their service, or the nature of any communication they had with God. Nevertheless, we must understand that behind the author's remarks was the understanding that in the thinking of many Jews the Levitical (Aaronic) priesthood stood at the apex of Judaism. Without the Levitical priesthood the Jews had no access to God. The priesthood was not, therefore, an incidental part of Judaism. Instead it lay at the very center of the God-man relationship.

The only historical narrative in the Bible about Melchizedek appears in Genesis 14.18–20, where he met **Abraham**[4] who had just rescued his nephew Lot, after Lot had been taken captive by a coalition of kings from the east. After defeating those kings, Abraham returned to southern Palestine and there was met by Melchizedek, who **blessed him**. The Genesis account states: "He blessed him and said, 'Blessed be Abram of God Most High'" (14.19 NASB). To bless someone can mean to praise someone (as when man blesses God), but it can also mean much more. Often, to bless someone means "to provide with benefits" or to call down God's beneficent power upon another.[5] Consider, for example, the scene where Jacob blessed his children (Gen 49), or the familiar story of Jacob stealing Isaac's blessing from Esau (Gen 27). To receive blessing was to be granted a measure of success (note the usages in Gen 30.30; Deut 1.11; Job 1.10), and thus it was deemed a valuable thing. When this kind of blessing is under consideration, it comes from one who has the status and authority to impart benefit from God upon one who lacks such status. In typical fashion, our author simply introduces this idea for now, but will return to comment on its significance below (vv 6–7).

---

[4] Technically, at this point in the Genesis narrative his name was still Abram, but the NT authors consistently refer to him by the name that reflected his status as father of Israel: Abraham (see Gen 17.5).

[5] BDAG 408; Hermann Wolfgang Beyer, *"eulogeō ktl," TDNT* 2.755.

7.2 To whom Abraham also parted out a tenth of everything, is first interpreted as King of Righteousness, but then also King of Salem, which is, King of Peace.

Abraham's reaction to being blessed by Melchizedek was that he **parted out**, or divided, to the king **a tenth of everything** he had with him. Genesis simply says "He gave him a tenth of all," but the author of Hebrews has inferred, from the context, that it was Abraham who gave a tenth to Melchizedek and not vice versa. A gift consisting of one-tenth of one's goods was called a tithe. Giving a tithe was a gesture that honored the recipient, and thus it implied that the recipient was of a higher status or position in some sense. This surely signaled that Abraham believed he was in the presence of a greater person who deserved to be honored with treasures. Although Abraham had just defeated a great enemy and was worthy of the gratitude of the kings of Canaan, Abraham's reaction to Melchizedek shows that Abraham considered the king to be worthy of greater honor than himself. How Abraham knew about Melchizedek is not stated in Genesis. It is not unlikely that Abraham had at least heard of this king before, since Abraham had lived not far from there in Bethel and in Hebron.

We may also note that the practice of giving a tenth of one's possessions (tithing) as a sign of honor to one who is greater did not originate with the Law of Moses, as this story shows. It is also seen as an expression of honor and gratitude in the story concerning Jacob in Genesis 28.22. Our author will discuss the significance of Abraham's action in verses 4–10 below.

The greatness of Melchizedek, and hence his worthiness of the honor Abraham showed to him, is indicated by his name and his title. The point of the author's etymological observations is to show that Scripture itself pointed to Melchizedek as a messianic type.[6] The name Melchizedek means, in Hebrew, **King of Righteousness**; *melek* is the Hebrew word for king, and *zedakah* is the Hebrew word for righteousness. Righteousness was one of the ideals toward which all Israel's kings were to strive (2 Sam 8.15; 2 Kngs 10.9), and became a type for the Messiah's reign.[7] Also, Melchizedek was **king of** the city named **Salem** (see com-

---

[6] Johnson, *Hebrews*, 177.

[7] *Cf.* the messianic prophecies in Isa 11.5; 32.1, Jer 23.5f; 33.15, and Psa 45.6 (quoted in Heb 1.8), which mention the messianic king reigning in righteousness, or according to God's measure of rightness.

ments on v 1). **Salem** is a variant of the Hebrew word *shalom* (note the consonants *s-l-m*), which means peace. Therefore, Melchizedek was also **King of Peace**. The Messiah is called the Prince of Peace in Isaiah 9.6, and peace is another hallmark of the messianic age (Mic 5.5; Isa 9.7; 52.7; 54.10; Jer 33.6; *etc.*). Righteousness and peace are often paired together in OT messianic texts.[8] As messianically suggestive as Melchizedek's name and title were for the kingly aspect of Jesus, our author does not dwell on them because his main concern is with Melchizedek's priesthood.[9] It is enough to point out the messianic significance of his name and title to establish him as a messianic figure.

7.3 Without father, without mother, without genealogy, having neither beginning of days nor end of life, but similar to the Son of God, he remains a priest continually.

This verse has proved to be the most difficult part of the author's comparison between Jesus and Melchizedek, and has generated many different interpretations over the years.[10] Our author's treatment of the Melchizedek story is often compared with Philo's allegorical treatment of the same subject,[11] but there is no reason to suppose that the author of Hebrews was presenting an allegorical treatment of Melchizedek. We should begin by noting that it is surely incorrect to think that our author understood these observations about Melchizedek literally. There is no indication that Melchizedek was more than a human being, nor is there any hint the author of Hebrews actually thought that Melchizedek literally had no earthly parents, that he never died, *etc.* As a matter of fact, there are several good reasons why we should not interpret Hebrews' statements about him in this way:

1) Such an understanding of Melchizedek ignores the context of Hebrews 7 and of Psalm 110, which is that Melchizedek is an illustration of the kind of *priesthood* that Jesus now holds.[12] It is the uninherited and uniheritable nature of Melchizedek's *priesthood* that is in view, not the man himself.

---

[8] See Psa 72.3; 85.10; Isa 9.7; 32.17; 60.17; *cf.* Rom 14.17; Jam 3.18.

[9] Lane, *Hebrews 1–8*, 164.

[10] For a survey of approaches to this text, see Bruce A. Demarest, "Hebrews 7:3: A *Crux Interpretum* Historically Considered," *EvQ* 49 (1977): 141–62.

[11] In his treatise *On the Allegorical Interpretation of the Laws* 3.79ff.

[12] *Cf.* Lane, *Hebrews 1–8*, 165.

2) Messianic figures or types in the Bible (of which Melchizedek is one), by their nature, are not equal to the things to which they point. Messianic figures regularly had features that prefigured messianic realities, but they lacked the essential qualities of the Messiah himself. To make Melchizedek an eternal being is to make the figure and the reality equal to each other in this regard. This leads to:

3) If Melchizedek was an eternal being, then he was already nearly the perfect high priest, at least as far as the argument of Hebrews 7 goes. The concern of the author of Hebrews is to show that Jesus is our perfect high priest by virtue of his indestructible life (vv 16, 24). Since he will never die, his priesthood will never fail nor be interrupted by death. But if Melchizedek was already an eternally-living priest, this emphasis on Jesus' eternal life is moot. Furthermore, if Melchizedek is literally an eternal being, he would stand as a competitor to Jesus in his priesthood, but that is certainly not what the author of Hebrews intended to show.[13]

4) There are other people, including kings, in the Bible for whom we are not given the names of their parents or their descendants (*e.g.*, Cyrus, the kings of the east in Gen 14.8–9, Abimelech, a later king of Jerusalem named Adoni-zedek, Hoham, Piram, Japhia, *etc.*; *cf.* also people like Abraham's unnamed servant, Elisha's servant Gehazi, *etc.*). We do not, however, on that basis, assume that these people are eternal beings.

5) This literal approach completely fails to understand how the terms "without father, ..." were used in the ancient world (see below).

What is interesting about the features our author notes here in verse 3 about Melchizedek from the Genesis narrative is that they are all things that are *not* said about him. It should not surprise us that the author would note the failure of the Biblical text of Genesis to mention anything about Melchizedek's lineage. To Jewish minds steeped in the Mosaic Law (to whom we suppose this epistle was originally addressed), priesthood and lineage went hand in hand. According to the Law, only men of the lineage of Aaron could be priests, and they had to have genealogical proof to serve in that capacity (*cf.* Neh 7.64). For Scripture to mention a priest and say nothing about his lineage was thus an unusual thing,[14] and this unusual feature becomes the point of departure for our author's treatment of Melchizedek's significance. Whatever kind of priest Melchizedek

[13] Cockerill, *Epistle to the Hebrews*, 302–06.

[14] Bruce, *Epistle to the Hebrews*, 137.

was, he was not a Levitical priest (which depended upon descent from Aaron), which is to say his priesthood was of a different kind or order. The author finds the lack of a mention of a lineage for Melchizedek, and the implication that Melchizedek's priesthood was of a different kind than the Levitical priesthood known in the Law of Moses, to be **similar to** Jesus, **the Son of God**, in his priesthood.

In Genesis 14, Melchizedek is introduced as a priest, yet his parents are not mentioned, and thus nothing is said about his **genealogy**. It is unclear if this genealogy refers to Melchizedek's ancestors or to his descendants. A case could be made for the latter view, since **without father** and **without mother** describes his ancestry, but it is also possible that the qualification "without genealogy" is a summary of the other terms. The terms "without father" and "without mother" (Greek *apatōr* and *amētōr*) were used to describe children who were orphaned, abandoned, estranged, or otherwise disconnected from their parents.[15] The point is not that Melchizedek was an orphan, or abandoned, *etc.*, but that no father was recorded for *legal* purposes.[16] He did not inherit his priesthood from his father, therefore his parentage is "unrecorded" in the Bible.[17] If we had a form documenting Melchizedek's priesthood, in the box that asked for "Father:" it would say "unknown," or "no father's name given." That is what "without father" meant. As noted above, the parentage of a priest was important to Jews who were familiar with the Levitical system. A priest's father had to come from the line of Aaron (Exod 28.1), and his mother had to be a pure Israelite woman (Lev 21.7). Melchizedek had an ancestry, as verse 6 clearly says, but it was not one that would have enabled him to be a Levitical priest. To say that he was without parents thus meant that his genealogy played no consideration in his priestly status.[18] That Melchizedek was a priest and yet no mention is

---

[15] BDAG 54, 99.

[16] Paul, "The Order of Melchizedek," 207.

[17] LSJ 181; MM 54–55: the term *apatōr* means "father unknown" in the Greek papyri. Also Gottlob Schrenk, *"apatōr,"* *TDNT* 5:1019–20: the term meant "of unknown (parental) origin," which could make a person ineligible for certain rights. A gentile who converted to Judaism was considered "without father" as far as Jewish law was concerned.

[18] This approach is to be preferred to that which reads the terms "fatherless" and "motherless" as Hellenistic descriptions of divine beings (as advocated by Jerome H. Neyrey, "'Without Beginning of Days or End of Life' (Hebrews 7:3): Topos for a True Deity," *CBQ* 53 (1991): 439–55). Such an interpretation goes against the argument of Hebrews concerning the uniqueness of Jesus and against the plain sense of the Genesis account.

made of his lineage implies that Melchizedek's priesthood was not based on genealogy, hence it was a different kind of priesthood than the Levitical office. Likewise, Jesus' priesthood is the same kind (or "order") as Melchizedek's in the sense that it is not a Levitical priesthood, and thus it is not received by being of a particular physical descent, but is the kind of priesthood that is held by a single person at God's appointment.[19] Melchizedek's priesthood was of such a nature that he did not succeed a previous priest, nor did he leave that office for another to take after him. His was *a one-person priesthood*. Similarly, Jesus did not become priest as a successor to someone who went before him,[20] nor will another priest take his place after him. Jesus was appointed directly by God (3.2; 5.4–6) and serves as priest eternally, as Psalm 110.4 ("You are a priest forever according to the order of Melchizedek") indicates. In this way, the priesthood of Jesus and the Biblical portrait of Melchizedek are similar: they are priesthoods held by only one person.[21]

In the same way, nothing is said in the historical record about Melchizedek's birth (**beginning of days**) or death (**end of life**). This should not be taken to mean that Melchizedek was an immortal being, because the point here concerns the *kind* of priesthood Melchizedek occupied. The lack of information about the birth and death of this priest implies that this information was unnecessary for his appointment, since he did not receive his priesthood as part of a hereditary series. It is worth noting, with Westcott,[22] that the Bible describes the death of Aaron in detail (Num 20.24–28). The Bible also specifically mentions his birth, with the names of his father and mother (Exod 6.20). Therefore, the priesthoods occupied by Aaron and Melchizedek stand in stark contrast, the former held by a succession of men connected by genealogy, the latter by one man alone. Most commentators view the statement about Melchizedek having neither beginning of days or end of years to be the author's way of suggesting that the timeless quality of the literary portrait of Melchizedek in Genesis 14 echoes the eternity of Jesus. While the author of Hebrews later mentions the eternal nature of Jesus

---

[19] Paul, "The Order of Melchizedek," 203.

[20] See Westcott, *Epistle to the Hebrews*, 174.

[21] See Martin Pickup, "'According to the Order of Melchizedek': The Use of Psalm 110 in Hebrews 7," in *A Tribute to Melvin D. Curry, Jr.*, ed. Ferrell Jenkins (Temple Terrace: Florida College, 1997), 112–135; Paul, "The Order of Melchizedek," 208–209.

[22] Westcott, *Epistle to the Hebrews*, 173.

(in contrast to the mortal nature of the Levitical priests, vv 23–25 below), that does not seem to be the point in this verse.

It is interesting to note that the author does not say that Jesus is like Melchizedek, but that Melchizedek was like (**similar to**) Jesus **the Son of God**. This is a good example of how the early Christians read the OT with the truths about Jesus as their interpretive guide. Yet the author was not reluctant to say that Jesus is a high priest according to the order of Melchizedek (as in 5.10), and thus in that sense Jesus' priesthood is similar to something that preceded it. Yet he did not call Melchizedek a type,[23] for that could conceivably suggest that Jesus was in some way a successor to Melchizedek. Instead, the similarity of the two is all he wished to note (see comments on v 15 below). Specifically, the similarity consisted of the personally abiding quality of their priesthoods. Therein lay our author's main point. The kind of priesthood Jesus occupies continues with a singular priest, in contrast to the Levitical priesthood that was characterized by a succession of multiple priests (explored in vv 11ff below). Nothing is said in the Genesis narrative about Melchizedek being a successor to someone else in his service as priest of God, nor of someone assuming his priestly office after him. Melchizedek is presented in the Genesis narrative as the sole holder of his office, and as such his priestly office was like Jesus'. It is in this sense that the author could say that Melchizedek **remains**[24] **a priest continually** in the narrative of Genesis. The particular expression used here (Greek *eis to diēnekes*) "marks his priesthood as continued to the end in his person without break."[25] As Demarest stated, "The fact that Melchizedek neither took up the priesthood from a predecessor nor handed it on to a successor points to the corresponding reality that Christ is the eternal, absolute and undying high priest of the New Covenant."[26]

---

[23] Lane, *Hebrews 1–8*, 171.

[24] The present tense is used often in Hebrews for things or people who no longer exist (see 9.7; 13.10 *etc.*). It does not mean here that Melchizedek is an eternal being, that he somehow is still a priest today, *etc.* It means that within the story in Genesis, Melchizedek never gives up his priesthood. "Melchizedek remains a priest continually for the duration of his appearance in the biblical narrative" (Bruce, *Epistle to the Hebrews*, 138). "He therefore abides a priest 'perpetually,' 'for ever,' not literally but in the Scriptural portraiture" (Westcott, *Epistle to the Hebrews*, 174).

[25] Westcott, *Epistle to the Hebrews*, 174. He goes on to note that "The phrase does not describe absolute perpetuity, duration without end, but duration continued under the conditions implied or expressed in the particular case."

[26] Demarest, "Hebrews 7:3: A *Crux Interpretum* Historically Considered," 162.

The strange nature of the Melchizedek story in Genesis prompted all kinds of speculation about him among some quarters in Judaism. In the writings from Qumran (in a manuscript known as 11QMelch, dated to the first century AD) and in some of the Pseudepigrapha (2 Enoch), Melchizedek appears to be treated as a character of cosmic, apocalyptic proportions who functions for the benefit of God's people, even as the agent of divine judgment.[27] He certainly is a mysterious character, but the author of Hebrews has neither bought into, nor borrowed from, Jewish speculations about him.[28]

7.4 Consider how great this man was, to whom even Abraham, the patriarch, gave a tenth of the spoils of war.

Abraham was the **patriarch** (founding father) of the nation of Israel (*cf.* Matt 3.9; John 8.39). In this sense one could argue that there was none greater than him. He was even called God's friend (2 Chron 20.7 and Isa 41.8; *cf.* Jam 2.23), and it must not escape our notice that Abraham offered sacrifices to God (Gen 22.13) and in this sense was a priestly figure himself. Yet one greater than him appears in the narrative of Genesis 14, and **even Abraham** himself acknowledged the greater status of Melchizedek when he honored him with the gift of a **tenth** (see comments on v 2) of all he had from the spoils of his recent victory over the kings of the east. If Melchizedek was greater than Abraham—and Abraham's actions confirm this—then Melchizedek must be a **great** figure indeed. Furthermore,

---

[27] For a translation and analysis of the Qumran document, see Joseph A. Fitzmyer, "Further Light on Melchizedek from Qumran Cave 11," *JBL* 86 (1967): 25–41. For a survey of how Melchizedek was interpreted, see Fred L. Horton Jr., *The Melchizedek Tradition: A Critical examination of the Sources to the Fifth Century A.D. and in the Epistle to the Hebrews* (Cambridge: Cambridge University press, 1976).

[28] James W. Thompson, "The Conceptual Background and Purpose of the Midrash in Hebrews vii," *NovT* 19 (1977): 209–23 correctly argues that Hebrews' treatment of Melchizedek is not like that of 11QMelch, but then argues that it is like Philo's treatment. Philo, however, uses Melchizedek to expound allegorically upon the difference between the spiritual and the world of sense perception, which the author of Hebrews does not do. It is not unthinkable, however, that the author of Hebrews was taking advantage of a well-known, if not varied, Jewish tradition that understood Melchizedek to be an exceptional OT character whose significance was more than historical. See Anders Aschim, "Melchizedek and Jesus: 11QMelchizedek and the Epistle to the Hebrews," in *The Jewish Roots of Christological Monotheism*, ed. Carey C. Newman, James R. Davila, and Gladys S. Lewis, JSJSup 63 (Leiden: Brill, 1999), 131–47; Gard Granerød, "Melchizedek in Hebrews 7," *Biblica* 90 (2009): 188–202.

if this cannot be denied, then surely one must acknowledge the greatness of Jesus, who "fulfills" the pattern of Melchizedek.[29]

The goods of which Abraham gave a tenth to Melchizedek are here called **spoils**, because Abraham had just profited from his defeat of the kings from the east. Genesis 14.16 reports that Abraham "brought back all the goods." In ancient times plundering the enemy was an accepted practice and part of warfare. The winner profited financially from the victory. Thus Abraham gave Melchizedek a tenth of the plunder he had just gotten from the kings he defeated. But in the Greek text of Hebrews, the matter is even more emphatic. The usual Greek word for the spoils of war is *skula*, but the author has here used the word *akrothinia*, which denotes the choicest spoils.[30]

There is evidence that suggests that the Melchizedek story in Genesis was troublesome if not embarrassing to some Jews in ancient times, precisely because it presents Melchizedek as greater than Abraham. In the Targumim (Aramaic paraphrase-commentaries), different things were done to soften this implication of the story, including making Melchizedek a relative of Abraham (many Jewish rabbis identified Melchizedek as Shem, Noah's son) or reading the story in such a way that God takes the priesthood away from Melchizedek and gives it to Abraham.[31] If this story was indeed a sore spot in Jewish exegesis, then our author's straightforward handling of it and dwelling on such an "embarrassing" implication from it is an indicator of his boldness.

7.5 And on the one hand, those who receive the priestly office from among the sons of Levi have, according to the Law, a commandment to collect tithes from the people, that is, from their brethren, even though they had come out of the loins of Abraham.

The purpose of reciting the facts about Melchizedek (vv 1–4) was to enable a comparison between the Melchizedekian and the Levitical priesthoods. The comparison will show the superior nature of the former.

One point of comparison is tithing, which is part of both the Melchizedek story and the regulations for the Levitical priesthood. Outwardly it

[29] Allen, *Hebrews*, 413: for all his greatness, Melchizedek "only resembles someone greater."

[30] BDAG 40.

[31] Martin McNamara, "Melchizedek: Gen 14,17–20 in the Targums, in Rabbinic and Early Christian Literature," *Bib* 81 (2000): 1–31, at 15–16.

would appear that all tithing is equal, but our author will now argue that the circumstances in which a tithe is given can make one example of tithing more significant than another. Accordingly, our author now compares the story of Abraham giving a **tithe** (tenth) of his goods to another tithe with which Jewish Christians were certainly familiar, the tithe prescribed in the Law of Moses, in order to set up a contrast (explored in v 6). Priests under the Law of Moses came exclusively from the family of Aaron within the tribe of **Levi**, and were devoted to the service (worship) of God (Exod 28.41). Non-Aaronic Levites were designated as helpers to the priests (Num 3.6–9). The tithe supported both groups, and the Levites comprised the larger of the two. Technically, the tithe went to the tribe of the Levites, and the Levites then gave a tenth of that to the priests (Num 18.21–28), but since part of the tithe went to the priests, our author's statement here is not incorrect. Hebrews instead seems to reflect the actual practice, which was that the priests collected the tithe.[32]

The giving of the tithe to the Levitical priests was not just for the provision of their needs (although it served that purpose), but also to recognize their higher status on the principle that the one who receives tithes is greater than the one who gives them. The Mosaical tithe was therefore a way of honoring the Levitical priests for the special role they had in the nation's relationship with God, and it is likely that the status of the Levitical priesthood was bolstered by exactly such an argument in the thinking of many Jews. Yet the genuineness of the honor involved in the tithe for the Aaronic priests was relativized by two considerations. First, even though the Israelites gave tithes to the priests, the fact remained that they were all—both givers and recipients—**brethren**, all descendants of **Abraham**. The force of this observation is that while the special role of the Levites and priests was recognized by the institution of the tithe, it was still, in another sense, something done between relatives. Second, the tithe of the Mosaic system was **collected** by a **commandment** in their **Law**. It was not voluntary, but was something that the Levites *took* from their brethren, which also relativized the honor the tithe represented. By pointing this out, the author begins his critique of the priesthood (and its service) of the law of Moses, which continues into chapter 10.

At this point it is appropriate to note that the author of Hebrews saw both continuity and discontinuity between the Levitical system and the

[32] See Horbury, "The Aaronic Priesthood in the Epistle to the Hebrews," 50–51.

new priesthood of Jesus, a perspective shared by the rest of the NT. In the following verses the author of Hebrews will point out several dissimilarities between the Levitical priesthood and that of Jesus, but in chapters 9 and 10 he will also touch upon the similarity of those systems. This is not contradictory. The old system had features that served as models and patterns of the system that would come in Jesus, and thus many similarities can be seen. However, the old was at the same time only a pointer to the new. As a pointer only, the old lacked the fullness and effectiveness of the new, and thus many dissimilarities between the two systems may be seen also. In general, it could be said that the major features of both systems bear superficial resemblance to each other (in both the old and new systems there is a sanctuary, a high priest, a sacrifice for sins, *etc.*), but the essential characters of those two systems were quite different.

7.6 But on the other hand, one whose genealogy is not reckoned from them received tithes from Abraham, and blessed the one who had the promises.

This verse summarizes the fact that there are two indicators that Melchizedek was greater than Abraham: 1) Abraham gave a tithe to Melchizedek (the significance of which was discussed above), and 2) Melchizedek blessed Abraham. As for the first indicator, the tithe Abraham gave to Melchizedek was different in two significant ways when compared to the situation described in verse 5. First, in Genesis 14 **one** (Melchizedek) **whose genealogy is not reckoned from** the Israelites, that is, who stood outside the family tree of Abraham, received the honor of a tithe from Abraham. Abraham and Melchizedek were not relatives, and therefore Abraham's giving a tithe to Melchizedek is a more significant example of the honor involved in tithing than was the tithe under the Law of Moses. Second, Abraham's tithe to Melchizedek appears to have been freely prompted by pure respect for the priest-king and not because some law required it. Therefore, the tithe Abraham gave to Melchizedek is a more significant honor even though outwardly it would appear to be the same thing.

As for the second indictor, see comments on verse 1 above for a discussion of **blessed**. Melchizedek blessed Abraham in Genesis 14.19 as he said "Blessed be Abram of God Most High, Possessor of heaven and earth." In order to underscore the greatness of Melchizedek, our author particularly notes that Abraham was the one **who had the promises.** This is mentioned as an indicator of the high status of Abraham. God had spoken his promises to Abraham exclusively, and this made Abraham a special person among all other people in the world at that time. It would be hard to imagine someone of greater status than Abraham, whom God chose to receive the promises and be the progenitor of God's own people. Yet there was one person who was greater: Melchizedek, as the facts noted above show.

7.7 And without any dispute the lesser is blessed by the greater.

The phrase "without any dispute" (Greek *chōris pasēs antilogias*) expresses certainty.[33] The last word in the English translation of this verse is, again, the Greek word *kreittōn,* which normally means "better," but in this context has the sense of "**greater** person" or "person superior in rank." This verse makes a simple yet powerful observation that establishes the greater status of Melchizedek over Abraham, and draws out the significance of the observation our author first made, in verse 1, that Melchizedek blessed Abraham. Certainly, the one giving the blessing (who calls down God's favor upon another) is in a higher position than the one who receives the blessing. For Melchizedek to bless Abraham means that Melchizedek was of such a status that he could call down God's favor upon Abraham (something Abraham could not do for himself), and Abraham's acceptance of the blessing implies that he acknowledged the greater status of Melchizedek.[34] Thus of these two characters, Melchizedek was of a higher (greater, superior) status.

7.8 And in the former case, men who die receive tithes; but in the latter case one receives them of whom it is testified that he lives.

The words translated **in the former case** and **in the latter case** render the Greek words *hōde* ("here") and *ekei* ("there") respectively, used in combination with a *men … de* construction (which denotes "on the one hand … on the other hand") to mark the contrast between the Levitical priests and Melchizedek. **The former case** is the one described in verse 5, that of the Levitical priests receiving tithes from their fellow-Israelites.

[33] MM 48.

[34] Bruce, *Epistle to the Hebrews*, 141.

Correspondingly, **the latter case** refers to Melchizedek. Even though both Melchizedek and the Levitical priests received tithes (which would outwardly make them appear to be "equal"), there was an important difference in the natures of those two priesthoods.

The words **receives them** are regularly rendered in italics in the English versions, indicating that there is nothing in the Greek text that particularly corresponds to it. The additional words simply attempt to supply a verb that is lacking in the sentence in the Greek text. That verb is understood to be the same one used in the first part of the sentence ("receive"), and in Greek usage it is not necessary to repeat the verb in another clause when the verb is the same as the previous one.[35] We must make sure, however, that we do not let these added words distract us from the main point of our author here. His point is not about receiving, but about the contrast in the natures of the priesthoods that comes to light when the tithe given to Melchizedek and the tithe given to the Levites are compared. Both priesthoods received tithes, but the Levitical priesthood consisted of a succession of **men who die**. The priesthood of Melchizedek, however, consisted of one man who **lives**. That is, the point here is not that the Levites died but Melchizedek never died (for surely he did). The author will call attention to the contrast between the mortality of the Levitical priests and the immortality of Jesus in verses 23–25, but this is not the point here. Instead our author is saying that the difference between the Levitical and Melchizedekian priesthoods is the difference between one that is occupied by a succession of priests, and one that is occupied by a sole office-holder respectively. It is the difference between a priesthood that continued because priests were continually replaced (due to death), versus a priesthood that continued because the priest lived.

7.9–10 And, so to speak, through Abraham even Levi, who receives tithes, paid tithes, because he was still in the loins of his father when Melchizedek met him.

A further consideration serves to establish the superior status of Melchizedek over the Levitical priesthood. There is a sense (thus our author says **so to speak**) in the Bible in which it is possible to speak of a person as the embodiment of all his descendants. For example, in the prophets God sometimes referred to the nation of Israel as "Jacob," from whom they de-

[35] This is called ellipsis; BDF §§ 479–81.

scended (as in Isa 40.27 and 41.8). Similarly, God referred to the Edomites as "Esau" in Jeremiah 49.10.[36] See also Genesis 25.23 and Malachi 2.1–3.[37] Here our author saw **Levi** as embodied in his great-grandfather **Abraham**, and the Levitical priests embodied **in** their **father** Levi. The Levites were so closely connected with the priesthood that there was no problem for the author to make an argument about priests by simply citing what was true about Levites.[38] When considered in this way, it is possible to say that when Abraham acknowledged the superior status of Melchizedek with his tithe, Abraham's descendants did also, including the Levitical priests. In this sense, the Levitical priests themselves recognized that Melchizedek and his priesthood was greater than their own, even before they and their priesthood were ever established by the Law.[39] Given the special role and status of the Levitical priests within Judaism, this might have been a shocking argument to first-century Jewish readers.

The basic idea here is the same as that presented in earlier chapters. In Hebrews 1–2, the author discussed the Mosaic law that was delivered through angels. There it was argued that another word from God has come through one who is greater than the angels, a fact acknowledged by Scripture itself. In chapter 3 the author showed that Jesus is a greater figure than Moses. So here, there is a kind of priesthood that is greater than the Levitical priesthood, and Jesus belongs to this other, greater order. It is this greater priesthood that the readers of Hebrews were to consider more carefully, because this greater priesthood is now man's only access to God.

The author of Hebrews shared the perspective of other NT writers, that the old system in Judaism acknowledged its own inferiority. It

---

[36] This is not the same idea as what some have commonly called "corporate personality" in the OT, a psychological concept that has largely been abandoned by modern OT scholars. See J. W. Rogerson, "The Hebrew Conception of Corporate Personality: A Re-examination," *JTS* 21 (1970): 1–16. Porter prefers to speak of "corporate representation," a concept common to many ancient cultures (Stanley E. Porter, "Two Myths: Corporate Personality and Language/Mentality Determinism," *SJT* 43 (1990): 289–307). It is true, however, that "The biblical writers were aware that our individuality can only be understood in relation to the various collectivities in which we participate," (Joel S. Kaminsky, "Corporate Personality," in *Eerdmans Dictionary of the Bible*, ed. David Noel Freedman, (Grand Rapids: Eerdmans, 2000), 285–87, at 287), and that is more in line with the point of this passage, which views the Levites as a group and sharing in their forefather's deference to Melchizedek.

[37] Peterson, *Hebrews*, 174.

[38] Horbury, "The Aaronic Priesthood in the Epistle to the Hebrews," 53–54.

[39] Peterson, *Hebrews*, 174.

is possible that some Jews thought that since the Levitical priesthood came after that of Melchizedek, then the Levitical priesthood was a replacement for the imperfect priesthood of Melchizedek.[40] In a surprising turn, then, our author will now make the same argument concerning the priesthood of Jesus.

7.11 Now if there was perfection through the Levitical priesthood (for on its basis the people received the law), what further need was there for another priest to arise according to the order of Melchizedek, and who is not said to be according to the order of Aaron?

Our author likes to use rhetorical questions for emphasis, and here is a good example of it. The word **perfection** (Greek *teleiōsis*) lies at the heart of the author's critique of the old, Mosaical system, since the underlying assumption is that the purpose of religion is to "perfect" the worshipper in his conscience and his relationship with God.[41] "Perfect" does not refer to absolute sinlessness, but to that which does not lack anything. The old, Mosaical system was an imperfect and inadequate answer to the problem of sin, as our author will discuss at length in chapter 10. That old system lacked the elements that are necessary to provide the kind of answer to the problem of sin that was truly needed, so a complete, final solution to the problem of sin was not available under it. The elements that existed under that system to address the problem of sin were weak and unable to deliver a forensically adequate forgiveness (see vv 18–19 below).

The author's critique is not limited to **the Levitical priesthood** alone. **On** the **basis** of that priesthood **the people** of Israel also **received the law** of Moses. The law and the priesthood were integrally joined, and came together as parts of one "package."[42] The priesthood functioned in the context of the covenantal law, it was the foundation or basis of the Law which the people (the Jews in general) received. The author thus intends to show the inadequacy (imperfection) not just of the Levitical priesthood, but of the entire Mosaic system.

The argument here is the same kind as was presented in Hebrews 4, which took careful note of the sequence of Biblical statements and

---

[40] Leon Morris, *Hebrews*, The Expositor's Bible Commentary (Grand Rapids: Zondervan, 1996), 66.

[41] Johnson, *Hebrews*, 185.

[42] Horbury, "The Aaronic Priesthood in the Epistle to the Hebrews," 56–59.

events. In chapter 4, the author said that the promise of rest in Psalm 95 implies that Joshua, who lived earlier than the time of the psalm, must not have delivered the anticipated divine rest to Israel. Similarly, the argument here is that if the answer to the problem of sin lay in the law of Moses, then why, after that law was given, did God still speak of **another** priest (of a different kind, Greek *heteros*, as the priesthood of Melchizedek was a different kind of priesthood than the Levitical order) who was to come later (*cf.* Gal 2.21; 3.21)? If the law remedied the problem of sin perfectly, then we should expect to hear nothing about any other system after that. But such was not the case. Psalm 110.4 spoke of a coming priest who would occupy a priesthood like that of Melchizedek, and this implied that the priesthood that was **according to the order** (likeness) **of Aaron** was inadequate and not meant to be God's final address to the problem of sin. See verse 28.

Although the word "new" is not used in Hebrews until 8.8, it is clear that the foundation for the idea of newness is being laid in the present discussion. For the author of Hebrews, "new" (akin in meaning to the term **another**) means "better." This would have been contrary to the widespread way of thinking in the ancient world that "old" was better, because it had proven its worth through the test of time.[43] That which is new is the latest, which serves as a replacement for the old which was inferior (or else it would not have been replaced). The conceptual groundwork for this idea was first laid in chapter 4 with the discussion of the divine rest which is available even after the time of Joshua. Here, however, in the discussion of Melchizedek, the concept of a "new" and better (7.19) order replacing an old inferior order becomes important for the exhortation.

The author's careful method here may reflect that some of his original readers may not have contemplated these matters at this level before. It would be difficult for some Jewish Christians to see how a system that came from God through angels to Moses could be flawed, and we even get a glimpse here of just what the gospel sounded like to unbelieving Jews. Against the Jewish reluctance to entertain any criticism of God's old Law we can appreciate the careful, Scriptural argument of the book of Hebrews.

[43] See James W. Thompson, *Strangers on the Earth: Philosophy and Rhetoric in Hebrews* (Eugene, OR: Cascade Books, 2020), 28–38. "In both philosophical discourse and daily life, ancient people shared the opinion that the old is better and that the new is dangerous. … Indeed, one of the major challenges faced by the apologists was to respond to the ancient charge that Christianity was new." (30).

7.12 For since there has been a change of the priesthood, there has necessarily been also a change of the law.

The implication of Psalm 110.4 is not only that the Levitical priesthood was inadequate (as argued in v 11), but that it would eventually be replaced. God promised to make the Messiah a priest like Melchizedek, so with that change would necessarily also come a change in the law because, as noted in verse 11, the old priesthood only functioned in connection with the old Law. The two were bound together; a change in one meant a change in the other also.[44] When the promise of Psalm 110.4 was fulfilled at the ascension of Jesus, **the priesthood** was thus **changed,** a new law with a new priesthood was inaugurated, and the old priesthood was nullified. What is changed is removed (same word in 12.27, *metathesis,* "removal"). The author will demonstrate in chapter 8 that this change in the law reflects a change in covenant as well.

Again, we ought to be sensitive to just how difficult it must have been for Jewish ears to hear statements about the Levitical priesthood being inadequate and being changed or removed. This is why the author was diligent to ground his message in a careful handling of Psalm 110.4. Only by showing that these things were grounded in Scripture, whose authority they accepted without question, could the author hope to make his case sure before his readers. By simply unfolding the implications of Psalm 110.4 and by presenting the argument in the form of a logically compelling rhetorical question, the author was making an irrefutable case.

7.13 For the one of whom these things are spoken shares in another tribe, from which no one officiated at the altar.

This verse serves to bring the discussion of the superior nature of Melchizedek's kind of priesthood to its application. The greater nature of the Melchizedekian priesthood is not just an academic observation. There now exists a priest whose priesthood has these superior qualities, namely Jesus. The argument in verse 12 about a change of both priesthood and law was not just a theoretical proposal, but has indeed taken place with Jesus, for he is **the one of whom** the **things** in Psalm 110 **are spoken**. As we have noted earlier, the author of Hebrews read the OT in the light of

[44] The concept goes back at least to Aristotle, who argued that changing the institutions that defined a city meant that the city was no longer the *same* city. See Doran, "Persuasive Arguments at Play in Heb 2:11 and 7:12," 50–54.

Jesus. The promise of a new priest (from Psa 110.4) has been fulfilled in Jesus, and Jesus was from **another tribe**, that is, he was not of the tribe of Levi (or even the family of Aaron in that tribe) from which the old Law required that all Levitical priests come. Under the old Law, no one outside of the tribe of Levi was allowed to **officiate**[45] **at** God's **altar** as priest.[46] If the legitimacy of Jesus in his priesthood is beyond question (which is predicated on the fact that the same person who is proclaimed king in Psa 110.1 is also proclaimed high priest in v 4 of that same psalm; if Jesus fulfills v 1, he must also fulfill v 4), then the only way to explain how Jesus can presently be a priest is to acknowledge that the old Law, which required that priests come from the tribe of Levi, must no longer be in force.

7.14 For it is clear that our Lord descended from Judah, for which tribe Moses spoke nothing about priests.

This verse makes the same point as verse 13, but more explicitly. Apparently the author did not want simply to assume that his readers would catch the full significance of what he had said in verse 13, so he here spelled it out for them to make sure they got it. Jesus came from (**descended from**) the tribe of **Judah**, as the genealogies in Matthew 1 and Luke 3 show (see also Rev 5.5). This was apparently common knowledge among Christians by the time Hebrews was written, because the author here can say that this fact was **clear** (Greek *prodēlos,* meaning "known to all," describing something that is quite obvious[47]). In asserting that the Lord came from the tribe of Judah, our author also affirmed the real humanity of Jesus.[48]

It is instructive to note how the author here treated the silence of the OT concerning anyone other than Aaronites serving as priests. His thought is that since the Law that came through **Moses spoke nothing about** someone outside of the tribe of Levi serving in that capacity, this

---

[45] The word here (Greek *prosechō*) has a range of meanings. Its basic meaning is to occupy oneself with something, to pay attention to something (BDAG 880; *EDNT* 3.169–70) and hence to apply oneself to something or to look after something. To occupy oneself at the altar clearly means to present an offering, or to "officiate."

[46] The sacrifice of David in 2 Sam 24 is a special case, ordered by God, nor does Scripture ever suggest that it invalidated the requirement that priests be from the tribe of Levi. See comments on 5.6. The sacrifices of Saul in 1 Sam 13 and of Uzziah in 2 Chron 26, as well as the incident of Korah's rebellion (Num 16), show that the Mosaic requirement was to be respected.

[47] BDAG 867.

[48] Westcott, *Epistle to the Hebrews,* 182.

meant that no one outside of that tribe was allowed (authorized) to serve in that capacity. That is, God's silence was interpreted as a lack of authority, and effectively constituted a prohibition. Only those who had been authorized by God could serve in the priesthood, and God only authorized the sons of Aaron for that service (this was stated in Exod 28.41, but the incident of Korah's rebellion in Num 16 removed all doubt). This understanding of God's silence was reinforced by the story of Jeroboam's religion in 1 Kings 12.31. See the same principle in Acts 15.24; Jeremiah 19.5; 29.23. Jesus was not authorized to be a priest under the law of Moses (see 8.4). Under that system, only Levites from the family of Aaron could serve God as priests, and Jesus was from the tribe of Judah. Therefore he could not be a priest under the old Law. But Jesus *is* a priest in fulfillment of Psalm 110.4, and this necessarily implies that the old Law that restricted priests to the tribe of Levi must no longer be in effect.

7.15–16 And it is even more clear, if another priest rises up in the likeness of Melchizedek, who has become a priest not according to a physical requirement, but according to the power of an indestructible life.

Our author has said that the Levitical system was inferior (v 11) and that it has been annulled (vv 12–14). So when he here says **it is even more clear**, to which of these observations does **it** refer? This is not a trivial question, because it has to do with following our author's argument correctly. We agree with Westcott[49] that the consideration is the inferiority of the old system, because that inferiority is the cause for its annulment, as verse 19 makes clear. Furthermore, the point he now raises is about the superior nature of Jesus compared to the Levitical priests, which is to say he here further speaks about the matter of the inferiority of the Levitical system and not its demise.

Likeness renders the Greek term *homoiotēs*, which denotes a "state of being similar to something."[50] This is what the author understood the phrase "according to the order of Melchizedek" (from Psa 110.4) to mean. That phrase from the psalm (especially the word "order"[51]) should *not* be

[49] Westcott, *Epistle to the Hebrews*, 183.

[50] BDAG 707.

[51] That is, the word "order" here does not denote sequence (as the English word commonly denotes), but a class of something, as in the group of people who have been knighted in England and belong to "the Order of the Garter."

understood as denoting a succession of priests. Instead that phrase means "like the kind of priest Melchizedek was," specifically referring to a priest who is the sole holder of that office by direct appointment from God. In other words, there are only two ways one could conceivably become a priest of God: one could inherit that position from one's forefathers in a system in which the privilege of the priesthood is passed on through physical descent, or apart from such a system God could declare an individual to be his priest. Since Melchizedek's genealogy does not come into the Biblical picture (v 3), his priesthood is not the former type but the latter. So also it is with Christ, who became high priest not because he was related to someone who could pass that office on to him (he was not, as v 13 above plainly says) but because God appointed him (5.5f)—and him alone—to hold that office, just as in the case of Melchizedek.

The word **another** translates the Greek word *heteros*, which can denote another of a different kind.[52] Indeed another kind priest (that is, different from the Levitical kind of priesthood) has arisen[53] whose priesthood is like Melchizedek's, namely Jesus. Verse 16 further explains what is different and makes explicit the point of the discussion in verses 3, 8, 13–14. The Levitical priests served on the basis of their genealogy, that is, on the basis of a **physical requirement**. More specifically, as noted in verses 13–14, only Levites from the family of Aaron were authorized to serve under the old system. But the priesthood of Jesus is different in that Jesus has no predecessor and no successor, and thus has come to serve (**has become a priest**) by direct appointment of God as the sole holder of his office. In that way he is similar to Melchizedek. Again, the unquestioned assumption here is that Jesus has fulfilled Psalm 110.4. If that is accepted as true, then it is quite obvious that the Levitical priesthood has been superseded, for Jesus does not meet the "physical requirement" for Aaronic priests (and yet he is a priest nonetheless—a priest of a different kind).

But Jesus fills up the paradigm of Melchizedek in an even greater way in that Jesus lives forever (see v 24 below). Melchizedek held his priestly appointment from the day he was appointed until the day he died. His

[52] BDAG 399; same word used in vv 11, 13.

[53] The term "rise up" or "arise" (Greek *anistēmi*) can refer to resurrection from the dead, but there is nothing in this context to suggest that sense of the word. Instead the word here has its ordinary sense of "come into existence" or "appear on the scene." The word is used in this sense of several people in the Bible who appeared on the scene at God's appointment.

priesthood was a one-person priesthood, but it eventually ended at his death. But Jesus' one-person priesthood will never end, because he lives forever. This is how he is truly able to be the sole holder of that office, and is one of the reasons his priesthood is perpetually efficacious. When Jesus was raised from the dead he entered into **an indestructible**, and hence endless, **life**. As Paul says, "Christ, having been raised from the dead, is never to die again; death no longer is master over Him" (Rom 6.9). Jesus' priesthood functions by **the power** of that eternal life which he now lives. That is, it is not that Jesus has met some physical requirement external to himself, but the fact that Jesus lives forever that enables him to be priest forever. This is the ultimate fulfillment of Psalm 110.4, which spoke of the priest like Melchizedek serving in that position forever. This is a tremendous improvement over the Levitical system where priests had to be constantly replaced because they succumbed to death (see vv 23–25 below).

The true significance of the word "forever" from Psalm 110.4 may not have been immediately apparent to the original readers of Hebrews, since the Aaronic priesthood was described with this same term in Exodus 29.9, 40.15, and other passages. Yet there are two important differences between the "forever" of the Aaronic office and that of Jesus in his priesthood. First, the Aaronic priesthood continued through means of a succession of priests, but Jesus' priesthood continues through Jesus alone. That is, the ways by which these priesthoods endured are fundamentally different. Second, the "forever" of the Aaronic priesthood did not mean "for all eternity," as the argument in verse 11 has shown. "Forever" in the OT, specifically the Hebrew word *'olam*, can mean "for a long time." The Aaronic priesthood lasted for a long time, but Psalm 110.4 implied that the Levitical priesthood would not last (literally) eternally. Jesus, however, literally serves as priest forever since he now lives an eternal life. The eternal nature of Jesus in his priesthood makes it abundantly clear that the old Aaronic system was inferior.

There is no indication that the post-resurrection ascension and exaltation of Jesus was a new idea to the original recipients of Hebrews. They knew it and believed it. They may not, however, have appreciated the significance of that doctrine. If Jesus is the object of Psalm 110 (and it is assumed that he is), then these readers must not quit following him, for the exaltation of Jesus fulfilled Psalm 110, which means that a new priestly system is now in place as verses 11–14 have carefully demonstrated.

7.17 For it is testified, "You art a priest forever according to the order of Melchizedek."

For the word **order**, see on verse 15 above and on 5.6. A note concerning the prepositional phrase **according to** is appropriate in this discussion also. This renders the Greek preposition *kata*, which can mean "according to" or "in conformity with."[54] It does *not* mean "later" (nor should the KJV translation "after" be taken in that sense). We must avoid thinking that this means that Jesus is in some way the successor to Melchizedek. The argument in verse 3 above rules this out (see also comments on the word "likeness" in v 15 above). Jesus does not occupy Melchizedek's priesthood. The idea is that Jesus' priesthood conforms to the *kind* of priest Melchizedek was, that Melchizedek's priesthood is a particular *kind* of priesthood (specifically, a one-person priesthood), and Christ's is the same kind (and yet even greater in some respects).

This verse quotes again the OT passage that is the key to this discussion (Psalm 110.4). The author wanted these words of Scripture to ring in his readers' ears (especially the term "**forever**") as they pondered his exposition of it so they would see how the exposition made perfect sense of the text. The last time he had quoted this verse to his readers was in 5.6, so as a good teacher he again reminded them of the words of the Scriptural text. Quoting the verse again served to reinforce for his readers that his assertions about the superior priesthood of Jesus were not baseless or philosophical, but came from the words of Scripture itself.

7.18 For on the one hand there is an annulment of a previous commandment on account of its being weak and useless.

Having presented his arguments in verses 1–17, the author now makes some straightforward conclusions. The **previous commandment** is the old Law of Moses. That Law has now been annulled by reason of the considerations laid out in verses 11–13 above, specifically because it was of an inferior nature. The ascension of Jesus fulfilled Psalm 110.1 and 4, which means the priesthood has now changed from the Levitical system, which in turn means the Law has changed.

Now the author makes his strongest critique yet concerning the old Law. He says that it was **annulled** (Greek *athetēsis*), a legal technical term

[54] BDAG 512.

which means it was set aside or done away with.[55] The same term is used of sin in 9.26. But here he gives a stronger reason for the setting aside of the old system than he has argued previously. Here he says that the old Mosaic system was canceled because it was **weak** and **useless**. Both of these words must be understood relatively. No NT author argues that the old law was absolutely powerless or completely useless (see, for example, Rom 3.20; 7.12). The criticism is, instead, that the old system of things was but a pale and limited imitation of the true answer to the problem of sin. As such it lacked the power of the ultimate reality to which it pointed. The word **weak** renders the Greek term *asthenēs*. To be weak does not mean to have no power at all, but to have insufficient power or relative ineffectiveness,[56] so this word can have the sense of "limited." Paul used this same term of the old law in Romans when he spoke of "what the Law could not do, weak as it was through the flesh" (8.3). The old system provided an approach to God, but that approach to God (all of it, not just the part that pertained to priests[57]) was limited by the nature of the elements of that system (discussed in chs 9 and 10). That system provided a remedy, but it was not the kind of remedy that was truly needed, for by its design that system was inherently unable to provide it. The word **useless** renders the Greek word *anōphelēs*, which refers to that which is not of any advantage[58] or has no special benefit.[59] Again, this must be understood in a relative sense. The old Law offered the Jews an approach to God, but that approach was only a model of the true and greater approach that would come in Jesus.

7.19 (for the Law perfected nothing), but on the other hand there is the bringing in of a better hope through which we draw near to God.

See the discussion of the term "perfection" in verse 11 (*cf.* also 5.14; 6.1; *etc.*). **The Law** of Moses was not able to provide all that was necessary for

---

[55] BDAG 24; MM 12.

[56] BDAG 143.

[57] Contra Donald A. Hagner, *Hebrews*, NIBCNT (Peabody, MA: Hendrickson, 1990), 109. The view he represents is fairly common. But according to Hebrews, if the priesthood has changed, so has the law (7.12), and if the law has changed, the covenant has changed as well (Jer 31; Heb 8). This is an important consideration for those who advocate that we are somehow still under the old Law (or parts of it), or those who argue that the Mosaical covenant was never annulled.

[58] BDAG 92.

[59] Louw-Nida 2:626.

the forgiveness of sins. What it provided was not the full and final answer to the problem of sin. That law instead provided things that were themselves pointers to the perfect remedy for sin that would appear in Jesus (discussed in chs 9 and 10). Inasmuch as those things were only pointers or models, they lacked the power to deal with sin in a truly effective way. The author was not saying that any or all law is unable to provide a way to God, for two reasons: 1) in a Jewish context (as here), "law" only means the Law of Moses, and 2) the new order of things in Jesus (which provides our way to God) certainly contains law (Rom 8.2; Gal 6.2; Jam 2.12; 1 Cor 9.21; John 13.34; 15.12). Law (as a way of spelling out God's demands) is not inherently incompatible with the grace that characterizes the new covenant. Our author was simply stating what the rest of the NT affirms, that (specifically) *the* Law of Moses **perfected nothing**. To perfect something is to bring it to full measure or completion, or to bring something to its intended goal.[60] If the goal of religion is to bring man into a close and right relationship with God, the NT authors taught that Judaism (as a religion) did not accomplish this. Of course, the Jews had *a* relationship with God, but the Christian gospel basically said that the relationship with God afforded in Judaism was not the fullest relationship possible. It was, in fact, a mistake for the Jews to think otherwise (see, *e.g.*, Rom 2–3, 9). The author of Hebrews asserted that Judaism was itself unable to bring man into a close, full, and open fellowship with God, but instead pointed to that which could (this is explained further in chs 9–10).

The assertion that the Law of Moses was unable truly to achieve reconciliation between God and man was a radical idea for the Jewish culture of first century Palestine. It was so radical that the gospel was considered blasphemous by devout Jews (*cf.* Acts 6.11), because to them, to say that the Law did not perfectly succeed in bringing man into a relationship with God was to say that Judaism was a failure, but even more so, since that Law came from God, it laid the blame for that failure at God's feet! Again, we can understand why the gospel sounded so blasphemous to some. The early Christian teaching was that God Himself designed the Mosaic system to be limited and inefficacious because that system was intended from its beginning simply to point beyond itself to the real solution in Jesus.

The good news is that the better system of things whereby we may finally **draw near to God** has come in the new covenant that includes the

[60] BDAG 996; H. Hübner, "*teleioō*," *EDNT* 3:345.

priesthood of Jesus. The author refers to this new system of things as **a better hope**. The word **hope** recalls the exhortation in 6.9–20. In Jesus we have a hope of eternal glory based upon nothing less than God's own immutable promise word, a word which establishes access to himself perpetually and continually in the high priesthood of Jesus. It is called hope, however, because salvation is not unconditional for anyone, and because the full measure of salvation is yet in the future (*cf.* Rom 8.24). God will bring to himself (2.10) those who demonstrate their faith by persevering (an exhortation our author will take up in greater detail in ch 11). It is exactly here where the original readers of Hebrews had begun to slip. The point the author wished them to see was that the *only way* man can **draw near to God** is through the hope made possible in the new priesthood of Jesus, a hope that enters within the veil to the presence of God (6.19). If they were to quit Christianity (in order to get relief from opposition), they would be turning their backs on the only access to God that is available.

Of course, **better** is one of the key terms in Hebrews. To say that the new order of things in Jesus is a better hope implies that some hope was offered through the previous (Mosaical) system. The Levitical priesthood provided a relationship with God, but it was imperfect because the system that created it was imperfect. What we have in Jesus is therefore a much **better hope** because in the new covenant we are "brought near" through the perfect priesthood of Jesus. The Melchizedek-like priesthood of Jesus accomplishes what the Levitical priesthood could not (this will be demonstrated in chs 9 and 10 especially). In this light, then, **better** has a final (eschatological) sense to it. The word "better" here in Hebrews denotes not only what is superior in quality to what went before it, but also what is perfect and therefore last, or final.

7.20–21 And to the degree that it was not without an oath—for they on the one hand became priests without an oath, but he has become priest with an oath through that which was said to him: "The Lord swore and he will not change his mind; You are priest forever"

There is another consideration that shows the superiority of the priesthood of Jesus: his priesthood was ordained by an **oath** from God, which our author cites in verse 21. Recall from the discussion in chapter 6 that God's oath has the effect of making God's word even more sure and reliable to *us*. Lest someone should suggest that the author's treatment of

Psalm 110.4 up to this point has drawn conclusions that are not wholly warranted, the fact that Jesus' priesthood was established with a divine oath proves that it certainly was God's plan to do away with the Levitical system and bring in another, better one.

The pronoun **they** refers to the priests under the Mosaic system, and stands in contrast to **he**,[61] which refers to Jesus. The Levitical priests were indeed appointed by God (Exod 28.41), and our author was in no way calling that into doubt. But there is an element in the priesthood of Jesus that makes his office even more established, and that is the divine oath. Therefore, it is not a contrast of an illegitimate priesthood versus a legitimate one, but rather of a priesthood authorized by God's command versus a priesthood authorized by God's command accompanied by an oath. The priesthood of the old law stood **without an oath** from God, which to our author meant that the old system was never guaranteed by God to last permanently. The lack of a divine oath was another indicator of the inferior, and thus transitory, nature of that system and the better nature of the new system in Jesus.

The **oath** that guaranteed the permanence of the priesthood of Jesus is reported in the opening words of Psalm 110.4, where we are told that **the Lord swore**. The parallel statement that the Lord **will not change his mind** adds yet more emphasis to the unchangeable intention of God in this matter. Note the emphasis on the surety of God behind Jesus' priesthood: God declared it, he swore to it, and he said he would not change his mind. A more certain foundation cannot be imagined. The Messiah's priesthood will never be replaced or superseded.

7.22 To this same degree Jesus has become the guarantee of a better covenant.

The added surety of God's oath to establish the priesthood of Jesus has the effect of placing Jesus in his priestly office forever. Because Jesus' priesthood is established forever on the basis of God's own oath (vv 20–21), and because Jesus lives forever as that priest (vv 16–17), the relationship with God available through him is of a surpassingly better quality than was available through the Mosaic system. To the degree that the

[61] The contrast in the Greek is simply between two definite articles used demonstratively: *oi men … ho de*. In such constructions, the definite article has the force of a personal pronoun. BDF §250.

oath makes Jesus' priesthood better, **to** that **same degree** Jesus **has become the guarantee of a better covenant**. A **guarantee** is an expression of assurance. It means that something will work, or perform, as promised. Since the priesthood and the covenant were linked, a better priesthood naturally means a better covenant situation. The assurance of a covenant relationship with God exists in the person of Jesus who holds his high priestly position forever and who, because of the oath of God, will never leave that position (see vv 22 and 23 below).

This is the first time the author of Hebrews has mentioned the **covenant** (Greek *diathēkē*). The KJV rendered it as "testament." We must here be careful because the English word "testament" has acquired legal connotations in modern usage that are not always reflected in the Biblical usage of the Greek word, and we must not take modern English usage as the basis for discerning the author's meaning (this is a consideration in any Biblical text, not just here). *Diathēkē* was the word consistently used in the LXX to translate the normal Hebrew word for covenant (*berith*). The Hebrew word *berith* emphasized a binding relationship[62] that was described through legal statutes. It is more than a "contract." A contract is a legal agreement between strangers, but a covenant is based on the knowledge and trust of both parties (see on 8.9). The Greek word *diathēkē* still retains some of the sense of "relationship," but the emphasis is on the expression of God's will,[63] and the word denotes a declaration of initiative or purpose.[64] In the Bible it specifically refers to God's revealed plan by which man can enter into fellowship with him. In typical fashion, the author only introduces this topic for now, reserving fuller discussion of the new covenant for later (8.6–13).

In verse 19 our author mentioned a better hope. Here he mentions a **better** covenant (also in 8.6). The Israelites had a covenant with God, but it was imperfect by design. God had expressed and revealed a means whereby Israel could have a relationship with him, but that old system was simply a pointer to another system that was to come later. Hence the relationship with God through Jesus constitutes a better covenant, a better expression of God's will and intention toward us. Here again "better" has the sense of "perfect" and "final" (see comments on v 19).

---

[62] Gottfried Quell, "*diathēkē*," *TDNT* 2:112–14.

[63] Johannes Behm, "*diathēkē*," *TDNT* 2:126–7.

[64] BDAG 228.

7.23 And they had become a greater number of priests because they were hindered, on account of death, from continuing.

Here is yet another defect of the old system. The Levitical priesthood was staffed with mortals who were prevented from serving forever because of their deaths. The context suggests that high priests are particularly in view here. No one high priest under the Mosaic system was able to effect a continuing, lasting mediation for the people. Thus **a greater number of priests**[65] were required over the years to sustain the nation's relationship with God. But Jesus now lives forever, never to die again (*cf.* Rom 6.9). By virtue of his eternal life (see v 24), Jesus himself is a guarantee (v 22) of an access to God that will never be interrupted. His mediation will never fail. Recall the same kind of argument in chapter 1, where it was noted that, in the ancient way of thinking, that which was ongoing (in the sense that more parts and pieces were always being added) was considered incomplete or imperfect. Like the former revelation, so the former Levitical priesthood was characterized by a series of "pieces" (here, persons), none of which was the full or final manifestation of God's will.

7.24 But he, because he lives forever, holds a permanent priestly office.

The pronoun **he** renders the same kind of Greek construction as noted in verse 21 above. The author is thus setting forth another set of contrasts between the priesthoods of the Law and Jesus. The advantage of Jesus' priesthood is that since he lives forever (*cf.* v 16) and has been appointed to an eternal priesthood (as Psa 110.4 declares), he is able to provide continuing, uninterrupted, and unending access to God for all those who come to him. Instead of the many high priests (in succession) required under the old temporary system, the new system has a single high priest who serves forever in a priesthood that is established forever. The **priestly office** of Jesus is thus **permanent** in that Jesus holds it absolutely.[66]

7.25 Therefore he is able to save completely those who come to God through him, since he always lives in order to intercede for them.

---

[65] Or, "they had become more numerous priests." There is no word in the Greek that precisely corresponds to the word "number" in our translation, but it is the sense of the comparative form of the adjective *polus* ("much") as it modifies the word "priests."

[66] Westcott, *Epistle to the Hebrews*, 190.

The eternal life and priesthood of Jesus means (**therefore**) that he is constantly and perpetually **able to save** those who draw near **to God through him**. Our author has spoken before of the salvation available through Jesus in 2.3, 10, and 5.9. Salvation is rescue from the bondage of sin and the terrible wrath of God, which is the consequence of sin. That salvation is effected by Jesus, because of his death in which his blood was shed for our forgiveness (see in chs 9 and 10). Other NT passages speak of God saving us because the initiative and the plan that saves us came from God, who sacrificed his Son Jesus for us (Rom 5.8–10; 2 Tim 1.8–9; Tit 3.5); yet man must respond to that initiative by accepting the salvation God offers, as the words **come to God** indicate. However, our author here emphasizes Jesus as savior because his readers were apparently contemplating, if not already, abandoning their relationship with Jesus. To do so would be to abandon the only way of salvation now available.

Our author emphatically says that Jesus **is able to save completely** (other versions: "to the uttermost"). This phrase translates the Greek phrase *eis to panteles*, an idiom that means "completely."[67] Bruce explains it as meaning that Jesus' "saving power is available without end."[68] Since there is no defect in either the person or priesthood of Jesus, that priesthood accomplishes the goal of bringing man to God perfectly. The salvation Jesus gives is perfect, in contrast to the imperfect rescue from sin available in the old law (see v 19 above). *Cf.* the "eternal salvation" mentioned in 5.9. Only in Jesus—that is to say, not in the old Law—is full and complete forgiveness, and hence salvation, available. If the original readers of this epistle were to abandon Christianity, they would be abandoning the only thing that provided them with complete salvation.

Because Jesus now lives forever, he can intercede continually for us before God. This was the goal of all Jesus has done. The word **intercede** highlights Jesus' work as our high priest who brings us to a relationship with God (*cf.* Rom 8.33–34; Isa 53.12). As the Jews knew well, there is no direct, unmediated access to God for man. A mediator is required who will represent us before God and intervene for us to repair the fellowship with God that was broken by our sin. Since Jesus will never die and since God's oath has established Jesus in his priesthood never to be changed, then Jesus truly is our perfect, uninterrupted, and eternal access to God.

---

[67] *Cf.* Luke 13.11; BDAG 754.

[68] Bruce, *Epistle to the Hebrews*, 153.

The picture here is not necessarily that Jesus is continually busy in heaven making pleas on our behalf to God, but that "his very presence in heaven in his character as the one who died for mankind and rose again is itself an intercession."[69]

7.26 For such a high priest was fitting for us, one who is holy, innocent, undefiled, separated from sinners, and who has become higher than the heavens.

To say that **such an** eternally efficacious **high priest was fitting for us** means that it was appropriate, proper, or right for our situation that such a high priest should be appointed on our behalf. As the NIV renders it, "Such a high priest meets our need." What we need is a way to God that is not constantly being interrupted by the death of the one who mediates for us, one who is not burdened by that which prevents his own access to God, and one who is ever close to God. Such a priest we have perfectly in Jesus. The old system did not provide such a mediation and was thus imperfect and short of being truly adequate. That is, the old Levitical system, as revered by the Jews as it was, truly did not meet man's need to provide a lasting, continuing relationship ("rest") with God. With Jesus, however, the kind of high priest we have always needed is available.

The author lists five attributes that define the perfection and superiority of Jesus' high priesthood. First, he is **holy**. The word most often used to denote the concept of "holy" is the Greek word *hagios*. A less-frequently used word is *hosios*, and this is the term the author of Hebrews uses here. *Hosios* appears to have more of a moral connotation than *hagios*[70] and describes one who is distinct from others by virtue of his obedience to God.[71] *Cf.* 5.8. It is thus a way of speaking of the sinlessness of Jesus. Second, he is **innocent**. This translates the Greek word *akakos* and literally means "without evil." The quality of innocence makes Jesus the perfect sacrifice for sin (see v 27 below). Third, he is **undefiled**, which renders the Greek word *amiantos*. While it was not necessarily sinful to be ceremonially defiled (unclean) under the old Law, no *priest* who had become defiled could serve until he was made clean again. However, the word "defiled" can be used figuratively to

[69] Morris, *Hebrews*, 71.

[70] Friedrich Hauck, "*hosios ktl*," *TDNT* 5:489–90.

[71] "*hosios ktl*," *NIDNTTE* 2:237.

describe the guilt of sin (*cf.* 2 Cor 7.1; Tit 1.15; 2 Pet 2.20), and that is probably how the author of Hebrews was using the term here. Because Jesus is undefiled, there is no hindrance that would prevent him from interceding for us as high priest. It is yet another way of describing the moral purity of Jesus and his fitness for this role. Fourth, he is **separated from sinners**. The word **separated** is the Greek term *chorizō*, which is also used in the Bible of divorce and other kinds of division between people. The priests of the Mosaical system were separated from their brethren by virtue of the fact that they held a special office and did special work. For this reason, the nation could be referred to as "the priests and the people" (Exod 19.24; Lev 16.33; *cf.* 2 Kngs 23.2; Jer 1.18). Jesus is separated from sinners in the sense in that he holds a position none of them hold, but it can also mean that with reference to sin Jesus is unlike all others, who have sinned. Of course, while Jesus was on earth he was known as the friend of sinners and ate with them (Matt 11.19), but he was not a sinner like they were although he shared fully otherwise in their humanity (Heb 4.15). Alternately, the phrase could be synonymous with the next and fifth description, that he **has become higher than the heavens**. As is typical, our author has here introduced an idea that he is about to discuss in more detail (chs 8 and 9). Jesus has ascended to the right hand of God (Psa 110.1; Heb 1.13) to a position of exalted status (Eph 1.20–21; Phil 2.9; Heb 1.4). While this marked the beginning of his reign as king, it also put him in the presence of God where is he now mediates for us as high priest.

7.27 Who does not need daily, like those high priests, to offer up sacrifices first for his own sins and then for the people's; for he did this once and for all when he offered up himself.

The high priests under the old system were not sinless people. Before they could approach God on behalf of the nation of Israel, they had to offer a sacrifice to atone for their own sins (*cf.* Heb 5.3), because no sinner or defiled person can stand before God. Then, and only then, could the high priest offer sacrifice to God for the sins of others. This was clearly spelled out in the procedure for the Day of Atonement (Lev 16.6, 11; Heb 9.7).

However, the author of Hebrews says this was done **daily**. Since there is no law in the Mosaical code that required a high priest to offer such sacrifices every day, how are we to understand our author's statement here? A few Greek manuscripts here read "priests" instead of "high priests." Adopting this reading would eliminate the difficulty, and the context could conceivably support such a reading, since "priests" appears in verse 23. However, the reading "high priests" is well-attested and is no doubt the correct one. Furthermore, verse 26 clearly mentions Jesus as a high priest, and that establishes the contrast with the Levitical high priests mentioned in this verse.

Some possible solutions are:

1) It is possible that the author is thinking of the whole priestly system as being centered around the high priest. Thus, in a kind of metonymy, the author used the term "high priests" to refer to the whole system of which they were the head, so the daily work of the priests was attributed to the high priests collectively.[72] *Cf.* 10.11.

2) Bruce alternately suggested that sin on the high priest's part could well have been a daily problem.[73]

3) The best solution is that which Westcott[74] and others have proposed, that this statement means that Jesus' daily intercession does not require a daily sacrifice, in contrast to the Levitical high priests who had to offer a sacrifice every time they approached God (even if it was only yearly). That is, "daily" does not describe the duties of the high priests in the Levitical system, but simply refers to Jesus' high priesthood. As Guthrie explains, "He has no need in his daily ministry to offer sacrifices for himself as those priests did."[75]

It seems that the real significance, however, is that for the author of Hebrews, **daily** denotes a repetitive action. The phrase *kath' hēmeran* could conceivably have the sense of "regularly" or "constantly" without necessarily literally denoting something done every single day (*cf.* Matt 26.55). The phrase is used synonymously with *pollakis*, which means "often" or "frequently" or "repeatedly" in 10.11, and it is also used in the LXX to translate the Hebrew word *tamid*, which means "continually" (as in Num 4.16 LXX). Repetition was a weakness of the old system, for repetition indicates incompleteness (*cf.* on 1.1). The sacrifices needed to be offered repeatedly because no sacrifice in that system was able to

---

[72] So Milligan, *Epistle to the Hebrews*, 215.

[73] Bruce, *Epistle to the Hebrews*, 157.

[74] Westcott, *Epistle to the Hebrews*, 196.

[75] Guthrie, *The Letter to the Hebrews*, 69.

secure a lasting atonement and fellowship with God (see Heb 10.2). For the relationship with God to continue, the sacrifices needed to be offered over and over again. The need for the sacrifices to be offered repetitively showed their weakness (v 18). This observation complements the author's observation in verse 23 about the need for high priests under the old system to be replaced continually. Just as no one high priest could achieve a lasting mediation between God and his people, so also no one sacrifice had lasting effects. Thus by the limited nature of both the priests and the sacrifices, the old system was unable to effect a truly ongoing relationship with God.

The fact that the high priest under the Levitical system was himself prone to sin was another weakness in that system. How much better to have a high priest who himself does not struggle under the burden of sin (4.15) but who, by virtue of his own sinlessness, can boldly approach God with no other burden than the sins of the people he represents. The fact that Jesus did not need to **offer up** a **sacrifice for his own sins** is an important consideration in appreciating the better quality of the new system of things in Jesus. If Jesus had sinned, he would have been required to die for his own sins, his death would have been the punishment for his own transgression, and thus his death would not have had any power to help anyone else. However, since Jesus committed no sin (4.15; 1 Pet 2.22), his death was not for himself but wholly for others (1 Pet 2.24; 2 Cor 5.21). His sinlessness is the quality that makes it possible for his death to be a substitution for ours.

The better nature of the new system in Jesus is that the sacrifice Jesus has offered for our sins is eternally effective. It was offered **once and for all**, indicating its final and permanent quality (10.10; Rom 6.10; 1 Pet 3.18), and hence it does not need to be offered repeatedly. As noted, in the ancient way of thinking, something that was done repeatedly was by definition incomplete. The fact that Jesus' sacrifice was offered only once means that it is completely efficacious and lacks nothing, so no further sacrifice is needed. Furthermore, Jesus did not offer an animal sacrifice for our sins, but he **offered up himself** for us (9.14; *cf.* Gal 2.20). Jesus is not only our high priest who presents a sacrifice to God on our behalf, but he is also the sacrifice. The blood he takes before God to make atonement for us is his own blood (9.12).

7.28 For the law appoints as high priests men who have weakness, but the word of the oath which came after the law appoints a Son who is perfected forever.

This verse summarizes the argument made in verses 20–25, but adds a significant detail as well. The priests of the old Mosaical system had **weakness** (see 5.2). Specifically, they were mortals (v 23), so the access to God they provided was not permanent; their mediation for the people ceased when they died. Thus, again, the old law had a built-in inadequacy. It was designed to function imperfectly because it was not the final answer to the problem of restoring sinful man's fellowship with God.

The **oath** was mentioned in verses 20–22. God's oath in Psalm 110.4 appointed his **Son** as a high priest like Melchizedek. The mention of God's **Son** is the detail our author has added to this summary. It is significant because it reminds the readers that Jesus is both the exalted Son who lives and reigns forever by God's appointment (as shown in ch 1, especially vv 8–13) and the great high priest who mediates forever by God's appointment as well. The verbal link between Psalm 2 and Psalm 110 led our author to conclude that both are fulfilled in the same person (recall 5.5–6). It would not be wholly inaccurate to say that Hebrews 1–7 is an exposition of the fulfillment and implications of Psalm 110. The eternal life of the exalted Son who is eternally appointed as our high priest by God's own oath stands in stark contrast to the **weakness** and mortality of the Aaronic priests under the Mosaical system.

Again (as he did in v 11) the author notes the historical sequence in which God's pronouncements occurred, for that sequence has important implications. God's **oath** to appoint his **Son** as a high priest like Melchizedek came chronologically **after** the institution of the Levitical priesthood in the Law of Moses. This implies, therefore, that the Levitical system was not intended by God to be a permanent institution (see v 11). It would be replaced by another (different, v 15) priesthood that was superior in nature, one occupied by a single priest who is perfected forever. Jesus was **perfected** in the sense that he was appointed (see comments on 2.10) to his position as high priest. This same word is used of the appointment of priests in the LXX,[76] but in Hebrews it has a messianic, eschatological connotation.[77] God's oath in Psalm 110.4

[76] H. Hübner, "*teleioō*," *EDNT* 3:345.

[77] Silva, "Perfection and Eschatology in Hebrews," 64–65.

placed Jesus in his high priesthood **forever** without any possibility of that priesthood changing. Jesus' priesthood is thus the last and final priesthood, the full and perfect way to God and the fulfillment of the Levitical priesthood that preceded it.

HEBREWS 8

8.1 Now the point of the things that are being said this is: We have such a high priest, who is seated at the right hand of the throne of the majesty in the heavens.

As is quite typical of his style, our author now focuses (v 1) on his preceding point (from chapter 7) and introduces themes he is about to explore in more detail (vv 2–3). Lest his readers get lost in the details of the argument in chapter 7, the author makes clear the main **point**[1] (Greek *kephalaion*, "head") of his discussion. **The things that are being said** refers to the discussion in chapter 7, specifically the qualities of the Melchizedekian priesthood mentioned in Psalm 110.4, and how it is better in many ways than the Levitical priesthood. Psalm 110 foretold that such a priest would appear for God's people, and the good news of the gospel is that the figure who fulfills Psalm 110 has appeared, and he is Jesus. Jesus became our **high priest** after having lived and suffered as a man (*cf.* 2.14–18; 4.15; further explanation comes in ch 9). He ascended to the **right hand of** God, the place of supreme honor, to reign over all (thus fulfilling Psalm 110.1), at which time God also appointed him high priest over the new Israel after the likeness of Melchizedek (thus fulfilling Psa 110.4; Heb 7.2–ff). Psalm 110 does not mention the **throne** of God, but the OT regularly portrays God as the great king who occupies a heavenly throne (the ark of the covenant was the "footstool" of his throne, 1 Chron 28.2).[2] It is a natural inference that if the Messiah sits at God's right hand according to Psalm 110, then the divine throne is where he sits. The heavenly coronation of the Messiah in Psalm 2 is surely in the picture here as well. The effect of the language here should be noted. The terms "high priest," "seated at (God's) right hand," "throne," and "majesty" all combine in a picture of exaltation. The fact that Jesus exercises his priesthood in this

[1] See Johnson, "Some Important Mistranslations in Hebrews," 28–29.

[2] See 2 Chron 18.18; Psa 11.4; 45.6 (quoted in Heb 1), 47.8; Isa 66.1; Matt 5.34.

exalted state, in heaven, is the **main point** of the discussion of the significance of Psalm 110.4 (in ch 7).[3]

This verse possibly reflects Zechariah 6.13[4] as well, since that passage says that the Messiah "will sit and he will rule upon his throne" (Psalm 110 does not explicitly mention a throne). The inclusion of the word **throne** emphasizes Jesus' regal status. The throne is the symbol of the authority and power the king possesses and wields and stands for the king's right to rule. As noted in 7.1, while the kingly role of Jesus is not the object of detailed discussion in Hebrews, this does not mean that our author regarded that aspect of Jesus' nature as insignificant. Its frequent mention indicates that it is not to be ignored. The mention of God's throne also serves to direct our attention to the heavenly sphere. God is here referred to as "**the majesty**" (*cf.* the same word in 1.3). The phrase enhances the idea that Jesus **is seated**[5] at the highest possible position, also using a word (Greek *kathizō*) that was used in the LXX of the appointment of priests. On God's **right hand**, see comments on 1.3. This picture of a messianic priest-king is also found in Jeremiah 30.21: "Their leader shall be one of them, and their ruler shall come forth from their midst; and I will bring him near and he shall approach me [*i.e.*, as a priest]" (NASB).

Because he is seated at God's right hand, Jesus exercises his regal and priestly functions **in the heavens**, which is to say, not on earth. The heavenly realm is the abode of God (Psa 115.3; Eccl 5.2), and Jesus performs his duties as high priest not in some crude model of what exists in heaven (as the tabernacle was; see 9.9), but in the very presence of God himself (discussed further in 9.11–12). The plural **heavens** reflects the Jewish way of thinking about the realm beyond this world, which was conceptualized as having several parts (*cf.* 2 Cor 12.2). Not too much should be made of this, however, because the NT writers also speak of the same realm in the singular as "heaven" (*cf.* Matt 6.10; Col 4.1).

---

[3] As Kistemaker notes, "If Christ had merely fulfilled the Aaronic priesthood—thereby effecting the atonement for his people—there would not have been a new covenant, and there would not have been a heavenly high priest" (*Psalm Citations*, 125).

[4] The Zech passage also associates the Messiah's reign with a priesthood. The NASB says "he will be a priest on his throne," but the text can also be translated "there shall be a priest [*i.e.*, with him] on his throne" (ESV, NET) or "by his throne" (NRS).

[5] The Greek word here (*kathizō*) is aorist, but it has a perfective sense in this context ("has been seated, is seated"). A similar Greek word (*kathistēmi*) is used in 5.1 and 8.3 of the appointment of priests.

8.2 A minister of the sanctuary, and of the true tabernacle, which the Lord pitched, and not man.

The author now undertakes to explain more fully the function of Jesus as our high priest, and he will do so by way of both comparison and contrast with the Levitical priesthood (as he did in ch 7). He will proceed by taking his readers to Scripture. Instead, he will show them that *Scripture itself* testifies to the better nature of the relationship with God offered through Jesus.

The word **minister** here should not be confused with an evangelist of the gospel. Those who preach the gospel are indeed called ministers (*cf.* Eph 3.7), but the Greek terms involved are different. It would be a mistake to think of Jesus as an evangelist in this context, and it would also be a mistake to think of an evangelist as some kind of special priest. An evangelist is called a *diakonos* in Greek, but the word here is *leitourgos,* which (with its cognate forms) has a rich history in the LXX of denoting the kind of service done by a priest (yet not exclusively so[6]). In this context, however, the public religious sense is intended, and means that Jesus is now the one who performs priestly service in the **sanctuary**.[7] This sanctuary of which the author speaks here is not the physical structure that stood in Jerusalem, the temple,[8] or its predecessor, the earthly tabernacle. Instead, our author has in mind the actual presence of God in heaven itself, which he also calls the **true tabernacle**. Our author's use of the word **true** does not imply that the tabernacle on earth was a false one. **True** in this context is the antonym of "copy" or "shadow" (v 5).[9] To say that God has **pitched** (set up) a tent in heaven means that there is a heavenly reality behind the earthly tabernacle, which was merely a model of

[6] The word could also denote servants of the state (empire), public servants (*cf.* the same word in Rom 13.6), or servants of the king, but "always with sacred connotations." BDAG 591–92. Paul used the word of his service as an apostle in Acts 27.23, Rom 1.9, and 2 Tim 1.3, giving his apostleship a priestly character.

[7] In the Greek the sanctuary is *ta hagia,* a plural either because the term includes both parts of the tabernacle (the ESV has "a minister in the holy places"), or as a Hebraism meaning "holiest." It is a normal shortened expression in Biblical Greek for the "most holy place" within the tabernacle.

[8] The author of Hebrews avoids the normal Greek terms for the temple, *naos* and *hieron,* perhaps influenced by the LXX which completely avoids the use of *hieron* and does not use *naos* in the Pentateuch.

[9] *Cf.* BDAG 43.

what exists in heaven, a model of heaven itself.[10] See further comments on 9.2–7. By its very nature, what is heavenly is better than what is earthly, but the heavenly sanctuary is also better because it was built by one who is greater than any human being (*cf.* 11.10). Jesus does not serve as our high priest in a model of heaven (as the priests of the old system did), but in heaven itself. There is no contextual warrant for the idea that the true sanctuary of which our author speaks is the church.

This is the first explicit mention in Hebrews of the **tabernacle** (the veil was mentioned briefly in 6.19; the features of the old tabernacle are discussed in 9.2–7). Nowhere does the author of Hebrews discuss the temple in Jerusalem, which was the more permanent replacement for the tabernacle and which, perhaps more than anything else, was the symbol of Judaism in the first century. The question naturally poses itself, why did our author avoid mentioning the temple? Some have taken this as an indirect indicator of the book's date (see Introduction), but that is probably not the answer. There are other reasons the tabernacle would have appealed to the author instead of the apparently more obvious temple:

1) Some have suggested that the author of Hebrews likes to appeal to the original of a thing as being the true representation of its kind. Just as the concept of God's rest is a feature of the first story in the Bible, and Melchizedek was the first priest encountered in the Bible, likewise the tabernacle was the original house of God's presence. This suggestion is seriously weakened, however, by the fact that here our author argues that the second covenant is better than the first.

2) A better explanation is that the tabernacle was a tent, by its very design something transitory, temporal, and provisional. The tabernacle was provided for Israel during its time of wandering, until they would achieve rest in God's land (which they also ultimately failed to do). The author has already asserted that God's rest is now attainable in Christ (ch 4). The author thus found in the tabernacle the perfect vehicle to represent the old system that was temporary by design and that has been rendered obsolete now that God's rest has come in Christ.

---

[10] See Phil Roberts, "The Story of the Tabernacle," in *Hebrews for Every Man: Florida College Annual Lectures 1988*, ed. Melvin D. Curry (Temple Terrace: Florida College, 1988), 65–83.

3) Similarly, the tabernacle corresponds to the abundant imagery in Hebrews of wandering and sojourning and with the messianic warning, from Psalm 95, based on Israel's experience in the wilderness (Heb 3–4).[11]

The addition of the phrase **and not man** is significant. The author did not wish simply to say that Jesus serves as high priest in heaven itself, but to say that the old tabernacle was inferior to the true one in heaven because that old tabernacle was the product of human labor. Perhaps our author is drawing on the language of passages such as Exodus 33.7 or Numbers 1.51, which describe the tabernacle as a tent which men set up. Even though it was appointed and designed by God himself, there was always this human, earthly element to it.

Can we detect here an echo of the kind of criticism of Judaism raised by Stephen in Acts 7.44–50? It seems that we can. Stephen accused the Jews of turning the religion of God (via the temple) into something that conformed to their own image, their own ideas and wishes, their own designs, and did not accurately express the kind of relationship God willed between himself and his people. Stephen said that God does not dwell in something made by human hands (Acts 7.48, used of idols in v 41), implying that God cannot be controlled. In the true worship of God, it is God, **and not man**, that designs the relationship. Such is the nature of Christianity. The relationship we have with God through our high priest Jesus is not something created by men nor given into the hands of men to maintain but is accomplished by Jesus himself in heaven where it is truly effectual. This serves as another reason the readers should draw even closer to Jesus. But what Stephen said more directly, our author here says in a less confrontational way.

8.3 For every high priest is appointed to offer gifts and sacrifices, for which reason it is also necessary that he have something to offer.

The phrase **every high priest** does not denote only earthly high priests, but any high priest of God whether in the old system or the new (thus including Jesus; *cf.* the discussion in 4.1ff). It is inherent to the office of

[11] It is possible that the author avoided reference to the temple because he understood that the tabernacle was built at God's insistence, whereas the temple was David's idea. In fact, when David first suggests building a temple, God says, in effect, that he never asked for one (2 Sam 7.5ff). Therefore, it may be that the author of Hebrews concentrated on the tabernacle because it, and not the temple, was part of the Law of Moses, but there is nothing in Hebrews that would explicitly support this explanation.

high priest that the holder of that office offers **gifts and sacrifices** (on that phrase see comments on 5.1) to God on behalf of the nation he represents. It stands to reason, therefore, that if the high priest's job is to offer things to God, he must have **something to offer**. In the exercise of his high priesthood for the new Israel, Jesus likewise offers something to God for us: himself (7.27). A more detailed discussion of this will wait until 9.12ff and 10.1–18 because some other things must be discussed first to set Jesus' high priesthood in its proper context.

Every (true or legitimate) high priest is **appointed** by God himself. That Jesus was appointed to his position as high priest by God was discussed in 5.1–6, and his likeness to those he represents was discussed in 2.17f. The discussion now turns toward the function of the high priest (chs 9–10), but it is crucial that Jesus' high priesthood be understood as the truest of all high priesthoods (for it is exercised in heaven itself) that is exercised within the context of the new covenant of which Jeremiah spoke. The present priesthood of Jesus means that the law has changed (7.12), which means that the covenant that embodied that law has also changed. It is the establishment of this change of covenant as the proper frame of reference that occupies our author in verses 4–13.

8.4 Now if he were on earth, he would not be a priest, since that there are those who offer gifts according to the Law.

Jesus is not a priest after the earthly, Levitical system established in the Law of Moses. In fact, **if he were on earth**[12] **he** could **not** serve as **a** high **priest** at all, because he is of the wrong lineage. As noted in 7.14, Jesus is from the tribe of Judah, but the Law specified that priests of the Levitical system had to come from the family of Aaron in the tribe of Levi. Furthermore, Jesus' ascension (which seems to be unquestioned among the readers) necessarily means that he has fulfilled Psalm 110.1 and 4, and therefore he is a *heavenly* priest. Jesus could not be a priest like Melchizedek and be an earthly priest at the same time, for Psalm 110 clearly puts the Melchizedek-like priest of Psalm 110.4 in heaven, at God's right hand (Psa 110.1; Heb 8.1).

---

[12] This is an example of what Greek grammarians call a present unreal condition (present contrary-to-fact). It is unreal in the view of the speaker. See also v 7 below, 4.8, 7.11, and 11.15. BDF §360. The inclusion of the particle *an* in the apodosis (which was not necessary) makes it somewhat emphatic (Robertson, *Grammar*, 1013).

The phrase **those who offer gifts according to the Law** of Moses recalls the similar phrase in 5.1 and refers to the men who served as high priests of Judaism. The present tense in the statement,[13] along with the present tense verb **serve** in the next verse, should not necessarily be taken to suggest that at the time Hebrews was written the temple and its services in Jerusalem still existed. The Greek present tense can describe what is generally true[14] under contextual circumstances (we have a similar use of the present tense in English). Hagner[15] suggests that the present tense here describes an ongoing action, and thus highlights the imperfect or incomplete nature of the old system under Moses.

The author of Hebrews connects the Levitical priesthood (with the high priest foremost in mind) and the relationship with God that attained under the Mosaical covenant with the **earth**. Certainly, all would agree that, when compared to that which is heavenly, that which is earthly is inferior. As the author will state in verse 5, the earthly is but an imitation of the heavenly. By placing Jesus' high priesthood unequivocally in the sphere of the heavenly, our author underscores its better nature. The high priesthood of Jesus functions on an entirely different (and better) plane, and this is meant to serve as an encouragement to us not to abandon our relationship with him.

The idea of a Jerusalem and sanctuary of heavenly origin was part of Jewish theology and eschatological hope and is grounded in the OT itself (*cf.* Ezek 40–48 and Isa 65.17ff). Paul spoke of "the Jerusalem above" (Gal 4.26) and John portrayed a new Jerusalem coming down out of heaven (Rev 21.2, 10). Some Hellenistic Jews, possibly influenced by Platonic philosophy, believed that the heavenly sanctuary existed in parallel with the earthly one, but was of greater significance.[16] Other strands of this theology envisioned the day when God would bring a new Jerusalem down from heaven and place it on earth, where it would be the center of the messianic kingdom of glory and dominion (2 Baruch 4, 4 Ezra 10). These

---

[13] A "genitive absolute" in Greek, giving background information. Lois K. Fuller, "The 'Genitive Absolute' in New Testament/Hellenistic Greek: A Proposal for Clearer Understanding," *JGRChJ* 3 (2006): 142–67, at 151.

[14] The present participle is perhaps best interpreted here as "gnomic" and not having a present-time (to the author) temporal reference.

[15] Hagner, *Hebrews*, 120.

[16] Leonhard Goppelt, "*tupos ktl*," *TDNT* 8:257; *cf. Wisdom of Solomon* 9:8; *Testament of Levi* 3:4–10.

Jews believed the new Jerusalem would be a heightened (in what sense, was debated) version of the old (with Judaism still firmly in place as the religion of God's people). Christians believed in a coming new Jerusalem that truly was the perfection and consummation to which Judaism's realities pointed, and that this new city of God is already prepared (see Heb 11.16) for the benefit of God's true people, the true sons of Abraham. Consistent with the NT perspective, our author here envisions that we already partake of the benefits of the new Jerusalem in that our high priest, Jesus, is already there ministering on our behalf. God's people will experience their fullest enjoyment of that place, however, when they are gathered to God. We must also remember that the idea that the priest of this heavenly sanctuary is the crucified Jesus was certainly radical in its day, as well as the idea that his assumption of his priestly office entailed the annulment of Judaism.

8.5 Who serve as an example and shadow of the heavenly things, just as Moses was directed by God when he was about to erect the tabernacle: for, "See to it," he said, "that you make everything according to the pattern which was shown to you on the mountain."

Priests **who**[17] served in the temple exercised their functions in something that was only **an example and shadow** of a true reality that stood behind that system, a reality that was **heavenly** in nature. The word **example** translates the Greek word *hupodeigma*, which denotes "an indication of something that appears at a subsequent time" and hence conveys the idea of an outline, a sketch, or a symbol of something else.[18] The word **shadow** renders the Greek term *skia*, which is here used figuratively to mean the representation of a thing. A shadow cannot exist by itself; it requires something else to provide its form and shape. The shadow is not the reality of the thing it represents but is instead simply something that looks like the substance it portrays. Those familiar with Plato's *Republic* would have known this kind of illustration from Plato's famous allegory of the cave,[19]

[17] The Greek simply has a plural indefinite relative pronoun. Whereas a regular relative pronoun would have sufficed, sometimes the Greek indefinite relative pronoun seems to have an inclusive sense to it, and that perhaps explains its use here.

[18] BDAG 1037. LSJ 1878: "illustration, picture showing how something is to be done" or "pattern." Grindheim, *Letter to the Hebrews*, 386: "It is used not for a copy but for something that is copied, or, rather, for a plan that needs to materialize."

[19] *Republic* 7.514f–520a.

but we do not need to insist that either the readers or the author of Hebrews needed to, or must have been, familiar with that famous piece of literature to employ the point here, let alone that the author of Hebrews was using that imagery in a Platonic way.[20] The image of a shadow representing some reality is obvious enough. Together the two terms **example** and **shadow** suggest that Judaism itself was not the true, final religion by which man could reach God, but was instead only a resemblance of that true way to God that was to come in Christ (see Col 2.17). Judaism's features were not ends in themselves, but illustrations or examples of the features of the approach to God that would be available through the work of Jesus.

We should remember that the purpose of pointing out Judaism's limitations in Hebrews was not to criticize Judaism, but to show the better nature of what we have in Jesus. Therefore, in order to prevent this statement from coming across as a mere criticism of Judaism, the author shows that he has taken his point from Scripture itself, specifically Exodus 25.40. In that context Moses was receiving the instructions for how to build the tabernacle and its furnishings. He was told "**See to it that you make**[21] **everything according to the pattern which was shown to you on the mountain**" of Sinai. Our author has added the word **everything** (literally "all things"; Greek neuter plural *panta*) to the LXX text which he here quotes,[22] not only to supply an explicit direct object for the main verb, but also as an interpretive (midrashic) amplification that takes its clue from the context of Exodus 25.9.[23] The addition allows the writer

---

[20] "Platonism" is probably not the best way to describe the worldview in Hebrews. The sermon simply reflects the worldview of the OT, which posited that God lives in heaven, and man lives on earth. A two-story universe was a common idea in the ancient world, including in the Bible. Furthermore, the author of Hebrews was making a very different point with this imagery than Plato was. See Lane, *Hebrews 1–8*, 207; Peterson, *Hebrews*, 192: "The distinction between the earthly and the heavenly in Hebrews is Christologically driven, rather than philosophically inspired." Also Grindheim, *Letter to the Hebrews*, 378: "The author's understanding differs from the idealism of Philo. To Philo, the biblical account provided illustrations of the world of ideas. He understood "the holy tabernacle and its contents to be a representation [*apeikonisma*] and copy [*mimēma*] of wisdom" (*Who Is the Heir?* 112). To the author of Hebrews, the earthly tabernacle does not correspond to an ultimate reality consisting of timeless ideas but to God's historical intervention in the person of Jesus."

[21] Translating the combination of the imperative *hora* plus the future indicative of *poieō*. Future indicatives are sometimes used as imperatives in Biblical Greek ("thou shalt").

[22] Although codex F (5th cent.) of the LXX has this reading. See Ellingworth, *Epistle to the Hebrews*, 407.

[23] In the MT of this text, the word for "pattern" has a 3rd person personal plural suffix ("their pattern" or "the pattern for them"). "Them" implies the command in v 40 is for "all."

to treat not only the tabernacle in his discussion, but the entire ministry centered in the tabernacle.[24] Some have taken the phrase **shown to you on the mountain** to imply that God showed Moses a model or heavenly vision of what the tabernacle was supposed to look like while he was on Mt. Sinai, but it is better to understand that the "pattern" refers to the instructions received on the mountain. God wanted to be worshipped according to the pattern he dictated. The Israelites were not free to make the tabernacle as they wished.

The quotation from Exodus 25 is presented here because it says that what the Israelites received from God at Sinai was a type, a pattern, an example, or a shadow of something else. God himself called what he gave Moses on the mountain (*i.e.*, the Law) a "type." The text in the LXX contains the word *tupos* (here translated **pattern**), from which we get our English word "type" and which our author obviously understood as a synonym of the words "example" and "shadow." This is the only place where our author used this word. Technically, he did not use the word himself, but approvingly quoted a verse that used it. This apparent reluctance to use the word "type" when describing the relationship between the old and new systems might seem surprising, but it may be due to the fact that our author wanted to avoid the idea of succession that could be implied in saying that the old was a type of the new. Alternately, it could be that he wanted to avoid the idea that this was something that could be repeated over and over again,[25] thus violating the idea of the finality of the new system of things in Christ. Our author instead wanted to say that the new is better, and in many ways, different from, the old (even though the old and new are certainly related). In typical fashion, our author has detected a fuller sense in the words of Exodus 25.40 when they are read with the messianic time in view. In ancient thought, gods were associated with mountains (see Heb 12.18–24). They lived above the world of men, and mountains were understood to be the places where heaven and earth intersect. "Mountain," then, suggests heavenly. The words of Exodus 25.40, therefore, suggest that there is a heavenly reality to which the tabernacle corresponded in a more limited, earthly way.

---

[24] Lane, *Hebrews 1–8*, 207.

[25] Goppelt, *"tupos ktl,"* *TDNT* 8:252.

8.6 But now he has attained a superior ministry, by as much as he is also the mediator of a better covenant which was enacted on better promises.

Jesus does not serve in something that is only a pattern or model of the true worship and fellowship of God. He serves in that higher, true order in heaven itself. For this reason, he has **attained a superior ministry** than that which approached God under the old covenant. The word **ministry** is from the same root as the word "minister" in verse 1, which was used extensively in the LXX for the priestly service. This new service, after the order of Melchizedek, is **superior** (literally "more excellent"; it is the same word used in 1.4 of Jesus' name) than the priestly system under the Law not only because of its heavenly nature (which was discussed in vv 1–5), but also for another important consideration (**by as much as**, rendering the Greek correlative adjective *hosos* which means "to the degree that" or "to the extent that")[26]: Jesus is the mediator of the better covenant that rests on better promises (which will be discussed in vv 7–13). That is, to the extent that Jesus serves in the context of a better covenant that has been enacted on better promises, to that same extent he has a ministry (priesthood) that is superior to the Levitical system.

A high priest is a **mediator** by virtue of the office itself. A mediator (Greek *misitēs*) is one who arbitrates or interposes between two parties in order to achieve a reconciliation.[27] The primary role of the high priest of Israel was to represent the nation before God as he offered special expiatory and consecratory sacrifices for their sins on the Day of Atonement. A central fact of the old system was that no ordinary person could approach God with a sacrifice directly for himself. Sacrifice was brought to God only through his appointed intermediaries (the priests), whose function culminated in the office of the high priest. In the new covenant we approach God sacrificially through the mediation of the exalted Jesus who occupies his place at the right hand of God in heaven. But a finer nuance is discernible in Hebrews. Our author always uses the word **mediator** in connection with the word **covenant**, and comparison with 7.22 suggests that a mediator, for the author of Hebrews, was more than just a "go-between." A mediator is also a guarantor, and the word was used this way in Hellenistic Greek.[28] This turns out to be important

---

[26] BDAG 729.

[27] BDAG 634.

[28] Albrecht Oepke, "*mesitēs, mesiteuō,*" *TDNT* 4.598–624, at 599–601.

for the thought of the book of Hebrews. The author's understanding is that God had promised (4.1) with an oath (6.17–18) a relationship between himself and the new people (the new Israel) he would create (Jer 31.31–34). Jesus is the one who guarantees that this relationship becomes reality. Jesus is thus not merely the one who stands between God and man, neither is he merely a detached guarantor of God's promise. Jesus actually accomplishes what God had promised, and he does this with his death that ratifies the new covenant, delivers that covenant's forgiveness of sins, and provides the only truly efficacious way to fellowship with God. Jesus thus becomes the guarantor of God's promise by acting so as to fulfill God's promise to his people.[29] Portraying Jesus as the mediator, including the notion of a guarantor, of the new covenant thus prepares the way for understanding the necessity of his death (discussed in ch 9). This understanding of the death of Jesus came from Jesus himself, as he explicitly connected his blood (death) with the establishment of the new covenant of which Jeremiah had spoken (Matt 26.28; Mark 14.24; Luke 22.20; 1 Cor 11.25).

The point our author here wished to emphasize is the new and better nature of the covenant in which Jesus serves as our mediator. The author hinted at this in 7.12, where he noted that the fact that Jesus is a priest implies there must now be a law other than the Mosaical Law (which would have prevented Jesus from serving as a priest at all; *cf.* also v 4 above). Until this point he has not said what that new law must be, but now he will launch into a discussion of that subject, again firmly basing his argument on an explicit OT text (Jer 31). Note that the passage he will quote is about a new covenant. Law and covenant go together.

The new covenant has been **enacted upon better promises** from God. In terms of their surety, one promise from God is not better than another, for God's promises are all equally reliable. By **better promises** he refers to the *content* of those promises. God promised better things, a better situation, in the new covenant (see 12.22–24). Covenants are, by their nature, based on promises or pledges which the parties involved make to each other.[30] What this better situation entails we will hear from Jeremiah, which our author quotes in verses 8–13 below.

---

[29] Oepke, "*mesitēs, mesiteuō,*" 620.

[30] Koester, *Hebrews*, 364.

8.7 For if that first one was faultless, an occasion for a second one would not have been sought.

Before quoting Jeremiah, our author prepared his readers for a proper hearing of the text. He wanted his readers to see the logic implied by the fact Jeremiah spoke of a *new* covenant. Just as Psalm 95's warning, given *after* the time of Joshua, about entering God's rest implied that Joshua had not led Israel into God's rest (Heb 4.8), and just as the promise of a priest according to the order of Melchizedek, which promise was given *after* the institution of the Levitical priesthood, implied that the Levitical priesthood was inadequate (Heb 7.11), so here also Jeremiah's mention of a new covenant, *after* God already had a covenant with his people, certainly implies that the Mosical covenant was inferior and bound to be replaced. If the Mosaical covenant (with its law) had been the perfect way to God, then why would God speak through Jeremiah about another one to come?

Note the terms **first** and **second**, which correspond respectively to the similar terms "old" (*cf.* v 13) and "new" (in Jer 31.31). By the phrase **first covenant** our author meant the covenant God entered with Israel at Sinai through Moses. That was not the first covenant in history, but it was the first covenant God made with Israel as a nation, with Israel as God's own people. The Israel of old failed to become the kind of people God wanted to have for himself, so God spoke of the day when he would make for himself a "new" Israel, and enter into a new, or second covenant with that new people.[31] This new Israel would be all that the old Israel was

---

[31] The concept of "group" operates heavily in Hebrews, as it does in all the NT. An "important aspect of ancient Mediterranean culture was its sense of group identity. Whereas contemporary Westerners tend to define themselves and their identity first of all as individuals, ancient Mediterranean cultures tended to define the self primarily in terms of group membership. … The importance of group identity did not, however, mean that the individual as individual was insignificant. Rather, it meant that the creation of individual identity was impossible apart from the dynamics of solidarity with others in one's group(s)." (Michael Gorman, *Apostle of the Crucified Lord: A Theological Introduction to Paul and His Letters, 2nd ed.* (Grand Rapids: Eerdmans, 2017), 12–13). See also Jerome H. Neyrey, "Group Orientation," in *Biblical Social Values: A Handbook, 3rd ed* , ed. John J. Pilch and Bruce J. Malina, Matrix: The Bible in Mediterranean Context 10 (Eugene, OR: Cascade Books, 2016), 88–91. The NT documents served, among other purposes, to give the early Christians a new sense of identity, defined with different parameters than the identities they formerly held. See Johnson, *Going Outside the Camp*; Seth Kissi and Ernest van Eck, "An Appeal to Personality in Hebrews; A Social-Scientific Study," *Neot* 51 (2017): 315–35: "Hebrews portrays its readers as typical collectivists persons with a group orientation, who are concerned primarily with the pursuit of goals and interests related to the group"

not. This second Israel would enter into God's rest in contrast to the first Israel who had failed to attain that rest (see 3.12–4.13). Jeremiah specifically described this new Israel as a people who would be close to their God, and a people to whom God would draw close. It is this loyal, spiritual quality of the new Israel that is emphasized in Jeremiah's vision of the new people of God.

The discussion that has begun here (in v 1) goes to 10.18. Its point is a simple one: the old law with its Levitical sacrificial system was merely a model of the true and better order that exists in the new covenant which has been established by the work of Jesus. With the new covenant established, the old covenant has been done away. Everything the author will say through 10.18 will contribute to establishing that point.

8.8 For, finding fault with them, he says, " 'Behold, days are coming,' says the Lord, 'and I will effect a new covenant with the house of Israel and with the house of Judah.'

Verses 8–12 are a quotation from Jeremiah 31.31–34, the core of a passage some scholars have come to call the "Book of Consolation." Here, at the literary center of his book,[32] Jeremiah looked past the impending destruction of Jerusalem in his day, and the sins of Judah that prompted it, to the time when a reconstituted Israel would enjoy a new relationship with God that would rest on a basis quite different from that of the old Mosaic covenant. The assumption and assertion behind our author's citation of this text is that Jeremiah's prophecy has been fulfilled in Jesus and his work and is therefore another example of how the author of Hebrews (like the rest of the early church) read the OT on the basis of the life and work of Jesus of Nazareth. This quotation is a key piece of the author's larger argument. He has reasoned that if Jesus fulfills Psalm 110, and he is

(315). Grindheim has noted "The author's hermeneutic has been compared to that of the Qumran community. In both cases, the original passage is reapplied to the community's own situation. The eschatological interpretation of Scripture specifically concerns the community in contradistinction to Israel as a whole. For such an interpretive approach to be possible, it is necessary that the community being addressed has developed a distinct group identity. The eschatological fulfillment of Israel's Scriptures now concerns them, not Israel." (Grindheim, *Letter to the Hebrews*, 219). See also Matthew Marohl, "Letter Writing and Social Identity," in *T&T Clark Handbook to Social Identity in the New Testament*, ed. J. Brian Tucker and Coleman A. Baker (London: Bloomsbury T&T Clark, 2014), 93–104.

[32] See Joel Rosenberg, "Jeremiah and Ezekiel," in *The Literary Guide to the Bible*, ed. Robert Alter and Frank Kermode (Cambridge: Harvard University Press, 1987), 184–206, at 190–94.

currently the new high priest of God's people, then there must have been a change in the law (7.12; since Jesus could not be an earthly, Levitical priest). If there has been a change in the law, there must also have been a change in the covenant that contained the law (7.22), and this is exactly what Jeremiah 31 predicted.

The prophecy of Jeremiah 31 is part of a larger theme in the OT, the theme of a coming day when Israel's exile from God would be completely reversed. The prophets spoke of the time when Israel would not only be restored to her land, but most importantly, to her covenant faithfulness with God.[33] Before Jesus came to this earth, Israel's exile was not fully over, even though some Jews had returned to Palestine.[34] That is, several of the things God promised would happen when Israel returned had not yet happened. The temple was incomplete (there was no ark of the covenant), and so the Day of Atonement ritual was incomplete, the Romans appointed the high priest, and there was no messianic kingdom (among other problems). The day was promised, however, when God himself would set everything right and accomplish all of these things, and more, for his people. This is what Jeremiah 31 was about. It does not describe every facet of the return, but instead focused on a new covenant. Our author's logic has already shown (7.12–16) that this is part of a larger, or wider, messianic renewal that also involved a new (and better) high priest. The arrival (or "rising up," Heb 7.11, 15) of a new high priest of a new covenant were parts of a larger experience (in the work of Jesus) which signaled that the exile of Israel had now been remedied.

The quotation from Jeremiah 31.31–34 mainly follows the LXX translation (it is 38.31–34 in the LXX). See notes below for significant differences. The promise basically held out two things: a new kind of people for God (Jer 31-34a = Heb 8.8–11), and the forgiveness of sins (Jer 31.34b = Heb 8.12). It is the latter of these features upon which our author will con-

---

[33] Passages include but are not limited to: Deut 30.3; Isa 1.26; 49.6, 8; Jer 29.13f; 30.18–22; 31.23–26; Mal 4.6.

[34] On this topic, see N. T. Wright in *The New Testament and the People of God* (London: SPCK, 1992), 268–72, 299–301; James M. Scott, ed., *Exile: Old Testament, Jewish, and Christian Conceptions*, JSJSupp 56 (Leiden: Brill, 1997); Nicholas G. Piotrowski, "The Concept of Exile in Late Second Temple Judaism: A Review of Recent Scholarship," *CurBR* 15 (2017): 214–47; Craig A. Evans, "Jesus and the Continuing Exile of Israel," in *Jesus and the Restoration of Israel: A Critical Assessment of N. T. Wright's Jesus and the Victory of God*, ed. Carey C. Newman (Downers Grove, IL: IVP Academic, 1999), 77–100; James M. Scott, ed., *Exile: A Conversation with N. T. Wright* (Downers Grove, IL: IVP Academic, 2017).

centrate. He will show, in chapters 9–10, that this forgiveness has been realized by the death of Jesus.

The phrase "**days are coming**," anarthrous in the Greek, is present tense from the standpoint of the original context, and also suggests God's plan for (and control over) history. Although our author did not explicitly comment to this effect, he undoubtedly understood the **days** of which Jeremiah spoke to be the same as "the last days" (in Heb 1.2), the messianic age. His exegesis of the OT, in which those texts are viewed as finding their true fulfillment in Jesus and what he accomplished, certainly supports such a conclusion.

The phrase **says the Lord** employs a different Greek verb in the LXX (*phēmi*) than it does in the quotation here (*legō*). The same is true whenever the LXX has *phēmi* in this text (vv 9, 10). There is often no discernible difference between these two words in their meaning. It may be that the author of Hebrews simply preferred the verb *legō*, because the author otherwise used the verb *phēmi* only once (in 8.5). Furthermore, the author preferred to introduce quotations with a form of the verb *legō*. The Greek word for **make** is also different in the LXX (*diatithēmi*; Hebrews uses *sunteleō*). The former (or some compound of *tithēmi*) is the more usual term for the establishment of a covenant in the LXX and appears in verse 10 below, whereas the latter term has the sense in Greek of bringing something to its end, conclusion, or fulfillment, or to accomplish.[35] *Sunteleō* is used of making a covenant in the LXX of Jeremiah 34.8 and 34.15, so the words appear to be fairly interchangeable. Perhaps our author preferred this term for the sense of finality it suggested (it is a compound word built on the Greek word for "perfect," "end," or "last").

On the word **covenant**, see on 7.22. Jeremiah was the only OT prophet to speak of God's future relationship with (the second) Israel as a **new** covenant. The word translated "new" is *kainos*, which can mean new in kind or quality (as opposed to *neos*, which can mean new in time, "young"[36]). The Jews of antiquity thought of Jeremiah's new covenant as a renewal of the Mosaic covenant (along the lines of Josh 24.22–26; 2 Kngs 11.17; *etc.*).[37] The author of Hebrews, however, understood the new

[35] BDAG 975.

[36] BDAG 496–97 and 669, although the words sometimes seem to be synonymous (see Roy Harrisville, "The Concept of Newness in the New Testament," *JBL* 74 (1955): 69–79).

[37] See Peter Gräbe, "The New Covenant and Christian Identity in Hebrews," in *A Cloud of Witnesses: The Theology of Hebrews in Its Ancient Contexts*, ed. Richard Bauckham *et al*,

covenant in a much more radical way: the new covenant would *replace* the Mosaical covenant and make it obsolete. **New**, in both the Jeremiah passage and in Christian texts, comes to mean "messianic." In the larger context of Hebrews, "new" is akin to other antithetical terms like "better," "heavenly," "eternal," and "true" (see on 7.11). The full meaning of this OT prophecy (like many others) was unclear until it was understood in the light of Jesus and his work.

It is significant that the Lord says his new covenant would be completed **with the house of Israel and with the house of Judah**. The name of the original kingdom of Abraham's descendants was Israel (as in 1 Sam 14.47). After the death of Solomon that kingdom split into two parts and was thereafter known as the kingdoms of Israel in the north and Judah in the south (*cf.* 1 Kngs 12.20). The kingdom of Israel had been gone for over a hundred years when Jeremiah spoke his prophecy, so the prophecy also implied a regathering of God's people (see Jer 31.10; also Psa 147.2; Isa 11.12; 27.12f; *etc.*), that is, an end of their exile (see above) and a reconstituted Israel. The NT perspective is that this regathering of Israel is fulfilled in God's call to men through the gospel of Jesus (2 Thes 2.14). Through the gospel God would call men to himself, and those who believed in the message and responded to the call would constitute the "new" Israel of God (*cf.* 9.15; 11.8; Rom 9.24, especially Jewish Christians). God mentioned both Israel and Judah in the prophecy to indicate that in the new situation he would create, the covenant relationship would be available to all, and his new people would not be divided. The new people would once again simply be known collectively as Israel (as in v 10 below, Jer 31.33). In addition to being part of the larger messianic picture that the author saw in the OT, the emphasis on the new covenant in Hebrews also served to create a sense of "distance" between the recipients' past, and their social ties with the "old" Israel, and their new lives as Christians. "The author of Hebrews has chosen the term 'New Covenant' in order to confirm the self-understanding of the church he addresses. This identity has roots in the cultic heritage of Israel. Hebrews, however, gives primacy to the fact that the church participates in a new, qualitatively *superior*, worship and identity rooted in a heavenly reality."[38]

LNTS 387 (London: T&T Clark, 2008), 118–27, at 120.

[38] Gräbe, "The New Covenant and Christian Identity in Hebrews," 126.

8.9 'Not according to the covenant which I made with their fathers in the day when I took their hand to lead them out of the land of Egypt; because they did not continue in my covenant, and I disregarded them,' says the Lord.

The word **made** is different here (*poieō*) than in the received LXX text (*diatithēmi*). The word in the LXX has the sense of "enact," but the word our author has used here is a more general term that can also denote doing the things specified in a covenant agreement so as to fulfill the covenantal obligations.[39] The word **continue** in this verse suggests that God performed his required duties in the covenant, but Israel did not.

To understand this verse, it is important to remember that a **covenant** is a *relationship*. That relationship is governed and maintained by laws (commandments that express God's will), but it is first and foremost a relationship. More importantly, a covenant is a relationship based on trust, on faith (see on 7.22). When God said that the new covenant with the new Israel would **not** be like the one he **made with their fathers**, he meant that that he would create a different kind of relationship with the new Israel, different in its quality from the kind of relationship he had with the Jewish forefathers. What kind of relationship did God have with old Israel? Through Jeremiah's words the author of Hebrews again takes his readers back to consider the generation of Israelites who wandered and died in the wilderness because of their unbelief (recall Psa 95 in Heb 3.12–19). God **took** that generation by their **hand** as it were, an expression that conjures up the image of a father holding the hand of his child as they walk together. It is a picture of tenderness and gentleness. The sad story, however, is that the Israel of old was ungrateful for what God did for them, and their history was one of rebellion (*cf.* Deut 1.26, 43; 9.23; 2 Chron 36.15f). They did not keep God's laws, and thereby exhibited a refusal to have a relationship with God. See the Scriptural summary in 2 Kings 17.13–18. Through Jeremiah, God was saying, in effect, "I am not going to have a relationship like that again," and the way God would avoid another such disastrous relationship would be by entering into a relationship with a different kind of people. This, according to this passage, is one of the things that is new about the new covenant. The old Israel became a disobedient, unfaithful people with whom God had to plead, strive, and fight. In the new situation which God would create, his people would be characterized by faithful-

[39] LXX Lev 26.15; 2 Kngs 18.12; Psa 103.18; Jer 41.18.

ness. God would have for himself a people who would not rebel, but who love God and who want to abide in their relationship with him.

This point was appropriate to the original readers of Hebrews. To turn away from God through Christ would be to act just as the Israel of old had acted: unfaithfully, rebelliously (see Heb 10.29), turning to vanity, and refusing what God had offered them. If they acted just like the old Israel, they could not be the people of God's new covenant.

8.10 'For this is the covenant that I will make with the house of Israel after those days,' says the Lord; 'I will put my laws into their mind, and I will inscribe them on their hearts, and I will be God for them, and they will be a people for me.'

After those days refers, in the context of Jeremiah, to the time when God had satisfied his wrath against old Israel. The phrase is another way of referring to the messianic age (along with "last days"; see comments on 1.2). God looked forward to the time when he would ordain a relationship (**make** a **covenant**; using the Greek word *diatithēmi*, the term commonly used in the LXX for this) of a different nature with the new Israel. The Israel of old never truly adopted God's ways for themselves. God had given them his instructions for how they were to live, but they did not appropriate them, they did not allow those commandments to mold them into the image God wanted them to have. The Law was therefore always something that was external to them. In the new relationship with the new Israel, however, things would be different. The new Israel would internalize God's demands. This is what God meant when he said **I will put my laws into their mind, and inscribe them on their hearts**. They would be truly obedient to God, but we certainly must not make the mistake of reducing the relationship of the new covenant to obedience (because obedience can be rote and insincere, Isa 29.13). Acceptable obedience is the outward demonstration of an inward spirit, heart, and mind that is loyal and dedicated to God. It is this inward commitment, which makes obedience meaningful, that would be the basis of the new covenant with God. The word **inscribe** here is *epigraphō*, which can mean to mark or to engrave (in the sense of making a deep impression), as opposed to the more generic word *graphō* (which means simply to write). The Law of Moses was carved on tablets of stone, reflecting the hard-heartedness of Israel, but the new covenant is carved on the soft hearts of a new people (*cf.* 2 Cor 3.3).

In the new covenant God would inscribe his laws (his covenant demands) for his people on their **hearts** and **mind**. On the heart, see on 3.8. The combination of heart and mind appears several times in the Bible as a kind of summary expression for a person's inward self or his character.[40] The mention of "heart" here recalls the extended discussion of Psalm 95 in Hebrews 3–4, where the condition of the hearts of the Israelites was a central issue. The important point is that God's new people would be characterized by a dedication and faithfulness to God that consisted not simply in their actions but resided in the core of their being. It is the same thing that God envisioned when he spoke through Ezekiel: "Moreover, I will give you a new heart and put a new spirit within you; and I will remove the heart of stone from your flesh and give you a heart of flesh. I will put my Spirit within you and cause you to walk in my statutes, and you will be careful to observe my ordinances" (Ezek 36.26f NASB). The possession of the new heart, mind, and spirit of dedication and faithfulness would motivate and produce obedience to God's commands. It would be inaccurate to say that the old covenant only addressed Israel's actions and that the new covenant addresses the new Israel's inner being. God certainly wanted the old Israel to internalize his laws. "Oh that they had such a heart in them, that they would fear me and keep all my commandments always" (Deut 5.29, NASB). *Cf.* also Proverbs 7.3. God exhorted Solomon "know the God of your father, and serve him with a whole heart and a willing mind" (1 Chron 28.9 NASB). According to Jesus, the foremost commandment of the old Law was to love God with all the mind, heart, soul, and strength (Matt 22.36–38). The difference instead is that whereas the old Israel failed to internalize God's demands because of the hardness of their hearts (Heb 3.8), the new Israel would succeed because they would possess "soft" hearts that were penetrable and receptive to God's word. The new Israel would only be comprised of people such as are described here.

The phrase **I will be God for them, and they shall be a people for me**[41] is somewhat of a refrain in prophecies of the messianic age. Examination of the contexts in which it appears reveals that it denotes an exclusive relationship (*cf.* Ezek 14.1; 37.23, 26f). The phrase means, in essence,

---

[40] *Cf.* 1 Chron 28.9; Psa 7.9; 26.2; Jer 17.10; 20.12; Matt 22.37; Phil 4.7; Rev 2.23.

[41] The datives could also be understood as possessive, hence "their God" and "my people." *Cf.* Paul's paraphrase in 2 Cor 6.18.

that God will be Israel's only God (*cf.* Lev 19.4), and Israel will be God's only people (*cf.* Deut 14.2; 27.9). It denotes a relationship characterized by loyalty and faithfulness. This was indeed the kind of relationship God wanted to have with the old Israel (Exod 6.7; Lev 26.12; Deut 29.13; *etc.*) but which he did not get from them. Instead, he got quite the opposite in the unfaithfulness (the OT prophets called it "harlotry") of old Israel as they worshipped idols. The new Israel would be faithful to God in contrast to the wanton unfaithfulness of old Israel.

8.11 'And each one will not teach his fellow-citizen, nor each one his brother, saying, "Know the Lord," because all will know me, from the least of them to the greatest.'

To **know the Lord** is not to know about him, but to enter into a personal relationship with him, to know him intimately, to know his ways, his mind, his likes and dislikes, his intentions, and his character. We often use the word "know" in this same sense in our language. Knowing the Lord was a theme in Jeremiah's preaching.[42] The old Israel did not know God, but God's plan was to create a new Israel that knew him well. In Jeremiah 24.7, God spoke of the new Israel with these words: "I will give them a heart to know me, for I am the Lord; and they will be my people, and I will be their God, for they will return to me with their whole heart" (NASB). The fact that God's new people would know God complements the condition described in the previous verse where it was stated that God's new people would have God's law written in their hearts and mind. Not only would God's people be inwardly dedicated to God, but they would also have such dedication for the best of all reasons: because they are close to their God, because they know their father.

The importance of knowing God as a characteristic of the new Israel can hardly be overstated. Here God said **each one will not teach his fellow-citizen, nor each one his brother, saying, "Know the Lord."** That is, the new covenant would not be a situation where God had a people who had to be encouraged, exhorted, and admonished to draw close to the Lord and to be the kind of people they were supposed to be. Such was the character of the old Israel. They were God's people, but often only in name. They never really drew close to God as he wanted them to do, and God said of them through Jeremiah "they do not know me" (9.3).

[42] Jer 2.8; 4.22; 8.7; 9.3, 6; 10.25; 16.21; 22.16.

But God's new relationship with the new Israel would be vastly different in this regard. "**All will know me**" was God's design for the new Israel. Rather than call a people and then try to get them to know the Lord, the new situation would be one where all those who belonged to the Lord would belong to him on the basis that they know him. Knowing the Lord intimately would be the basis, the identifying mark, of the new Israel. It would be unnecessary for God's new people to exhort each other to draw close to God, for that would be the fundamental basis on which they were God's people in the first place. **Fellow-citizen** here translates the Greek word *politēs*[43] and implies that these people would be united in a city-kingdom, which lends itself naturally to understanding that this passage speaks of the messianic kingdom in which we are not only fellow-citizens under the reign of Christ (see the terms in 12.22–24), but also God's family and thus brethren (see 2.11ff).

We see here (and in many other similar passages in the OT) God's picture of the new Israel, the church of Jesus Christ. It is not nearly enough to imitate the early Christians outwardly. Having a Scriptural name, worship, organization, *etc.* is surely part of the pattern, but it is by no means all of the pattern. The pattern for the new Israel includes every Christian being a person who is close to the Lord and who does his will because of an inward dedication and conformity to God's design for his people's heart, mind, and character. To conform to the outward parts of the pattern only, and to leave undone the inward part, is to fail to attain to the "new Israel."

8.12 'For I will be merciful to their wrongs, and their sins will I remember no more.' "

The final, and crowning, part of the description of the new covenant is the feature of the forgiveness of sins and is the essence of the "better promises" it contains (v 6). It is typical in Hebrews that the author ends a quotation with the part he wishes to emphasize, and this is a good example of this practice. The two expressions **I will be merciful** and **I will remember no more** stand in parallel to each other, which our author interprets in 10.18 to mean forgiveness. The expressions **their wrongs** and **their sins** also stand in parallelism. How this promise of forgiveness is fulfilled in the new covenant is discussed at length in chapter 10. There was a for-

[43] The KJV follows a textual variant that reads *plēsion*, "neighbor."

giveness available under the old system, but it was an imperfect, forensically inadequate forgiveness that God in his grace provided and accepted until the coming of the perfect solution it reflected, *viz*. the death of Jesus. The author of Hebrews saw in the promise that came through Jeremiah the true and permanent fix to the problem of sin.

There is, however, a connection we must not fail to see. We noted briefly above that the promise concerning the new covenant holds out two things: a new kind of people for God, and the forgiveness of sins. There are two things that are important about the juxtaposition of these two things in the promise:

1) The promised forgiveness would be available to the new kind of people. Consequently, to refuse to abide in the new covenant is to forfeit the true forgiveness available in it. This recalls the warning in chapter 6 and is an important consideration for those who were thinking in their hearts (see Heb 3.10, 12; 10.22) of abandoning Christianity (see Introduction).

When we speak of a "new people," however, we should not take this to mean a rejection of the Jews (and replacing them with the church). Instead, it refers to a change in the character of God's people. That is, there is every reason to believe that the new people of which Jeremiah spoke was Jewish Christians (*cf.* Paul's discussion in Rom 9). That the new people would eventually be comprised of more than ethnic Jews—as true as that is—is not the point in Jeremiah. The point is that "Israel" herself would be fundamentally different in the new covenant (compared to the Israel of the prophet's own day), and what ultimately makes them different is their faith in God's Son (with the corresponding transformation of self that comes with it) who brings them to God and provides the forgiveness of which God spoke. In this sense, Jeremiah 31 spoke quite directly to the original (Jewish Christian) readers of Hebrews. What was "new" in the new covenant was not that God had an entirely different group of people as his own, but that the Jews who entered into this relationship (through Jesus) were what God had always wanted them to be: a people of faith—which is another way of saying that God finds his true "rest" with this new Israel (Heb 3 and 4).

2) Jesus himself perfectly embodied and demonstrated the kind of dedication God described for those in the new covenant, and it was in that mode of true dedication, commitment, and knowledge of God that he died to provide the very forgiveness God promised to give. This re-

minds us that Jesus is the guarantor (see comments on 7.22) and mediator (see comments on 8.6) of the new covenant in a most significant way. Jesus fulfills the promise made by God through Jeremiah by becoming the perfect example of the kind of people envisioned for the new Israel. Jesus' preeminence in this way will be mentioned again in 11.1ff.

The argument in Hebrews is partly driven by the force not only of explicit OT statements, but by their implications as well. The implications of Jeremiah 31.34 are significant. If God is going to enact a new covenant (Jer 31.31), and if that covenant will feature true forgiveness of sins (Jer 31.34), then a blood sacrifice will be needed for both. The fulfillment of these implications will be explored in Hebrews 9–10.

8.13 When he says 'new,' he has declared the first one to be obsolete. And that which has been declared obsolete, and is growing old, is near disappearing.

The quotation is bracketed by another observation (see vv 7–8a) by the author that the whole gist of the promise is that God was speaking of replacing the Mosaical covenant with something else.[44] Thus he quotes

[44] This is not to say that God has rejected the Jewish people. We must let the author of Hebrews say exactly what he said: God has made the former covenant old by inaugurating a new covenant. That is, God has brought a new and better way of relating to him, and with the coming of that new and better way, the old one ceases to be operational. As Skarsaune put it, "It has to do with the Christological exclusivism that is so integral to all known varieties of early Christianity." (Oskar Skarsaune, "Does the Letter to the Hebrews Articulate a Supersessionist Theology? A Response to Richard Hays," in *The Epistle to the Hebrews and Christian Theology*, ed. Richard Bauckham *et al* (Grand Rapids: Eerdmans, 2009), 174–82, at 181). Also Allen, *Hebrews*, 83: "one will not find in Hebrews any notion that the Jewish people have been replaced by any other group, including the church. However, and this is crucial, it is clear there is a form of supersessionism in Hebrews. It is vital that this notion be defined properly. In Heb 8:13 the old covenant is superseded by the new. But this point is made by the author in his appeal to the Old Testament Scriptures themselves, namely Jer 31:31–33, which predicts this very thing." It is worth noting, too, that what God replaced the old covenant with was itself thoroughly Jewish in its origins and designs. As Hays put it, "On the one hand, Israel's story is continued, reaching a climax in the figure of Jesus.... Yet, on the other hand, Jesus, as the climactic figure of the story, also introduces a major plot twist: he becomes the mediator of a new covenant that not only sustains but also *transforms* Israel's identity." (Richard B. Hays, "'Here We Have No Lasting City': New Covenantalism in Hebrews," in *The Epistle to the Hebrews and Christian Theology*, ed. Richard Bauckham *et al* (Grand Rapids: Eerdmans, 2009), 151–73, at 155). Emphasis his. Wright holds basically the same view (N. T. Wright, *Paul and the Faithfulness of God*, vol. 4 of *Christian Origins and the Question of God* (Minneapolis: Fortress, 2013), 809–810; see his survey of different supersessionist views on pp. 805ff). The talk of new vs. old in Hebrews is not anti-Semitic (as some brands of supersessionism are).

again the crucial word **new** (most modern English versions except the NIV supply the word "covenant" here, but the focus in the Greek is solely on the word "new"), and specifically states that the promise of a new covenant implies that the **first** (or former) covenant would, from the point of the new covenant's enactment onwards, be considered old. There is no single English word that captures the sense of the Greek verb *palaioō,* which we have translated as **declared obsolete**. In the active voice (as here) it can mean either to make something old, or to treat something as old, or to declare something to be obsolete.[45] The latter idea fits best with this context, since our author is here making a point about the implication of God's prophetic statement through Jeremiah.

The words **near disappearing** (*engus aphanismou*) can also mean "near destruction."[46] Some, following this meaning, have taken this as evidence that the Jerusalem temple was still in existence at the time of writing. While this sense is possible, that is not the point in this context. The author was here speaking about the covenant, not the temple. The point is not that God would destroy the outward symbol of Judaism (*i.e.,* the temple; although he did), nor even that the old Law of Moses would be decisively cancelled (as true as that was; Col 2.14). With this in mind, the statement can be understood generically, in the sense of "when something gets old, it eventually disappears." And the fact that Judaism, as a religion, still exists does not nullify the author's statement here. His concern was not with the existence of Judaism, but with its operational status. Instead, the point is that the language of Jeremiah 31 clearly implies that the old, Mosaical covenant (which included the Law and the Levitical priesthood) was, by God's own word, not meant to be the final solution to the problem of sin nor the consummation of his plan to have a "rest" with man. As soon as God referred to the coming covenant as a "new" one, by that statement God pronounced the eventual demise of the first one, which then became the "old" one. Of course, the author of Hebrews understood that this promise had been fulfilled by the death of Jesus, which (as he will show in ch 9) ratified the new covenant.

---

[45] BDAG 751.

[46] BDAG 155; it literally means "not appearing," but by extension, what is destroyed no longer appears.

HEBREWS 9

Hebrews 9.1–10.18 is arguably the heart of the sermon, where the author describes how the major elements of the old system (especially those connected to the Day of Atonement ritual) served as shadows of the reality that has now come in the work of Jesus.

9.1 The first covenant also had regulations of service, and an earthly sanctuary.

The author will now take his readers through a review of the **earthly sanctuary**, the tabernacle, to point out two things: 1) its role as a shadow, model, or copy of what was to come, and thus to show its inadequacy, and 2) to remind the readers of its earthly and temporary nature, and thus of the earthly and temporary nature of the entire Mosaical system. The discussion will prepare the reader for an explanation of how the promise of the new covenant (Jer 31; quoted in Heb 8) is fulfilled.

The tabernacle was part of the **first** covenant. The words "first" and "second," introduced in 8.7, will become important for the contrast our author is about to discuss (*cf.* 9.3, 7, 28; 10.9), and correspond to the terms "old" and "new" respectively. Although the word **covenant** is not in the Greek text here, it certainly is the object of the discussion as the context from 8.8ff shows. This was the covenant God made with Israel at Sinai. In that agreement God specified the **service** (Greek *latreia;* the word commonly used in the LXX of the worship offered through the priests) Israel was to give to him, and that service centered in a physical (**earthly**; *cf.* the word "fleshly" in v 10) **sanctuary** known as the tabernacle. As noted in the comments on chapter 8, the fact that the tabernacle was physical or earthly in nature is important, for this speaks to its inferior nature when compared to the heavenly reality to which it attested.

9.2 For a tabernacle was prepared, the first one, in which was the lampstand and the table and the presentation of the loaves, which is called the Holy Place.

The word **tabernacle** renders the Greek word *skēnē,* which denotes a tent. As a tent, the tabernacle was a temporary structure and thus reflected the nature of the covenant that ordained it. However, the term can also mean "a covered place," and in this sense the author of Hebrews uses the term here of each part of the larger structure. He therefore speaks of a first tabernacle (v 2) and a second one (v 3), which are otherwise called the Holy Place and the Most Holy Place respectively. While this way of referring to the internal parts of the tabernacle might seem strange to us, there is evidence that this is how the Jews spoke of such things. Josephus referred to a "second temple," by which he meant what we call the inner courtyard of the Jerusalem temple.[1] The Jewish tabernacle was basically destroyed in the time of Samuel, in the Philistine victory at Aphek (although the Bible does not specifically record the event; see 1 Sam 4.11 and Jer 7.14). What was left of the tabernacle was later stored in Solomon's temple (1 Kngs 8.4), and that is essentially the last we hear of it in the Old Testament.

The tabernacle proper (*i.e.*, not counting the courtyard) had two parts. There was only one entrance and exit, through the front, which faced the east. The **first** room, immediately inside the entrance, was called the **Holy Place.**[2] In the holy place, on the south side, was a **lampstand**. This special lamp had seven branches, each terminating in an oil-burning lamp (Exod 25.31–37). The lamps were apparently extinguished each morning and lit each night, and burned all night whenever the tabernacle was assembled.[3] The lamp was in the form of a tree whose branches ended in a

[1] *Jewish War* 5.193.

[2] The adjective *hagia* here could be either feminine singular or neuter plural. Normally the neuter plural form in Hebrews denotes the Most Holy Place (8.2; 9.8, *etc.*), not the Holy Place. It therefore seems likely that the form should be read as feminine singular, modifying the word *skēnē* ("tent"). Alternately, if we read the indefinite relative pronoun *ētis* as inclusive, the verse could be saying that everything (the tent, the lamp, the table, *etc.*) is collectively called "the holy things" (*cf.* Exod 20.30 LXX). Unlikely (it seems to me) is the suggestion of Swetnam, who sees the adjective as describing the loaves (following the Vulgate) and makes a connection with the Eucharist. James Swetnam, "Hebrews 9,2 and The Uses of Consistency," *CBQ* 32 (1970): 205–21.

[3] Exod 30.8; Lev 24.3; *cf.* 1 Sam 3.3; 2 Chron 13.11.

lamp (light),[4] and it symbolized the Spirit of God (*cf.* Rev 4.5; see also the vision in Zech 4.1–6). There was also a **table** that is sometimes called in English translations the table of showbread (Exod 25.27–30) and which stood opposite the lampstand, on the north side of the room (Exod 26.35). On this table was spread a blue cloth (Num 4.7), and on it was placed twelve loaves of bread in two rows of six loaves each (Lev 24.5f; and some other items), and this bread was sometimes called the bread of the Presence (Exod 25.30; Num 4.7; *etc.*). Our author here calls it **the presentation of the loaves**, a description that seems to be taken from 2 Chronicles 13.11 (LXX). In Exodus 39.17 LXX the table is called the "table of the setting forth" (of the loaves), and the bread is regularly called "the bread of the presentation" (Exod 40.23 LXX). It symbolized God's provision of food (and generally, his care and sustenance) for his people.

9.3 And beyond the second veil there was the place which is called the Most Holy Place,

A **veil**, or curtain, separated the two rooms of the tabernacle (Exod 26.33). This is here called the **second veil**, because another veil served as the front door of the tabernacle (mentioned in Exod 26.36; 39.38). The innermost room of the tabernacle was called "the Holy of Holies" (which renders the Hebrew quite strictly) or the **Most Holy Place.**[5] Again, the author of Hebrews refers to it as a *skēnē,* not in the sense of a separate tent, but simply as a covered **place**. By speaking of them as separate places, the author emphasized the sense of separation that characterized the Most Holy Place, which was no incidental feature. Inside the Holy of Holies was the ark of the covenant (see v 4 below) before which the high priest alone stood in God's presence only on the Day of Atonement (Lev 16). Otherwise, the Holy of Holies was strictly off limits to everyone (Lev 18.7). The tabernacle, in a sense, kept people away from God (even though God was near his people insomuch as his tent was in the midst of theirs). See verse 8 below.

---

[4] For a discussion of the symbolism of the tabernacle's features, see Phil Roberts, "The Story of the Tabernacle"; also Vern Poythress, *The Shadow of Christ in the Law of Moses* (Brentwood, TN: Wolgemuth & Hyatt, 1991), 9–40.

[5] But called "the holy place inside the veil" in Lev 16.2f, and "the holy place" in Lev 16.16f, 27 where the context (v 15) makes it clear that it is "inside the veil" where atonement was made.

9.4 which had the golden altar and the ark of the covenant covered all over with gold, in which was the gold pot that had manna, and Aaron's rod that budded, and the tablets of the covenant,

The word here translated **altar** is the Greek word *thumiatērion*. In secular Greek the word normally denoted a censer (so the KJV), but Jewish authors used this same word for the incense altar, and there are other examples in Hellenistic Greek of this word being used in this sense. It was a small altar made of wood overlaid with **gold** (Exod 30.1ff). The author here places this incense altar inside the veil, but the OT says it was in the Holy Place (Exod 40.26). Is this a mistake? Not at all. The picture we get from the OT description of the tabernacle is that this altar stood at the very entrance to the Most Holy Place, perhaps partially inside it (as it apparently did in Solomon's temple, 1 Kngs 6.22; 2 Baruch 6.7 also depicts this altar in the Most Holy Place with the ark of the covenant). Exodus 40.5 says it was to be placed "before the ark of the testimony." It stood in the approach to the Most Holy Place and it was treated with blood on the Day of Atonement in a way similar to the ark of covenant.[6] Its location was especially designed to fill the Most Holy Place with smoke for the ritual of the Day of Atonement. When that room was full of smoke from the burning incense, the glory of God dwelt in the cloud of smoke (Lev 16.2, 13) over the ark. It is clear that one of the most significant uses of this altar was in relation to the ark of the covenant, and this accounts for its location and description in connection with the Most Holy Place. That is, this item in the tabernacle is being described more in terms of its function than its precise location.[7] Otherwise, incense was burned twice a day on this altar (Exod 30.7f), and the smoke from this incense symbolized the prayers of God's people going up to God (*cf.* Rev 5.8; *cf.* Psa 141.2; Luke 1.10).

The only thing in the Most Holy Place was **the ark of the covenant**, a wooden chest also overlaid with **gold** (Exod 25.10f). The ark was the footstool of God,[8] and ancient kings had footstools of approximately this size in their throne rooms. What was strikingly different about Israel's sanctuary was that it had a footstool in it, but no throne and no visible

[6] Westcott, *Epistle to the Hebrews*, 247f.

[7] Harold S. Camacho, "The Altar of Incense in Hebrews 9:3–4," *AUSS* 24 (1986): 5–12.

[8] 1 Chron 28.2, corresponding to the idea that the earth was God's footstool and his throne was in heaven (Isa 66.1; Matt 5.35; *cf.* Psa 99.5; 132.7). The ark was, in a sense, the place where God's "feet" touched the earth.

image (*i.e.*, idol) of their God. Pagan temples normally had an image of the god inside, but Israel's God was unseen. The ark symbolized God's presence, but again, it was in the Most Holy Place, which was inaccessible to all but the high priest, and even his access to that place was limited to one day each year, the Day of Atonement (Yom Kippur).

While it might seem superfluous to us to rehearse the contents of the ark (since the author does not expound on them at length), these items are mentioned because they actually have a bearing on the author's point (that a new and better covenant has been ratified in the work of Jesus). The three things inside the ark all came from Israel's time in the wilderness, which recalls Hebrews 3–4 (and Psalm 95). Inside the ark of the covenant was:

1) A **gold pot** of **manna** which reminded Israel of their time in the wilderness and God's care for them there, and hence was a reminder of God's faithfulness to his part of the covenant. This connection in itself recalls the exhortation in Hebrews 3–4, based on Psalm 95, which warns Christians in the messianic age not to repeat the sin of the wilderness generation, the generation that ate God's manna. The fact that it was a **gold** pot is recorded in the LXX but not in the MT, but this is not necessarily a reason to doubt the veracity of this detail since the LXX may have been based on a Hebrew text that described the pot as gold, and many holy vessels were made of gold. Commentators quibble over the fact that the OT says this pot was "before" (in front of) the ark (Exod 16.33f; Num 17.10), and the author of Hebrews says it was *in* the ark, but the language of Exodus 16 can also describe something that was placed in the ark next to the tablets of the covenant. Moreover, the fact that a pot, made of an earthly material containing earthly food, was inside the ark of the covenant subtly reinforced the fact that the former covenant (and how it dealt with the problem of sin) was earthly (9.1) by nature, and dealt with things like food (9.10). Such things are inferior to what is heavenly (8.1f, 5) and inadequate for what is inward (9.9).

2) **Aaron's rod that budded**, which affirmed God's choice of Aaron as priest (Num 17). Its inclusion in the ark alongside the tablets of the Law reinforced the idea that the covenant and the priesthood went together. This is significant for the author of Hebrews, as he has noted this connection in 7.11. The fact that this rod was part of something that was but a temporary model of an eternal spiritual reality possibly hints at

the fact that the priesthood of Aaron, which the rod legitimized, would be replaced.[9]

3) The **tablets** (or "tables," translating the Greek term *plakes*, flat stone tablets) of the Law which Israel received at Mt. Sinai. These tablets contained the Decalogue (Exod 34.28; Deut 4.13), which was itself a summary of the entire Law.[10] Since the Law was the stipulations of the covenant between God and Israel, the tablets containing the ten commandments were rightly called the tablets **of the covenant** (*cf.* Exod 34.28; Deut 4.13; 9.9, 11, 15). The original tablets were destroyed by Moses (Exod 32.19), but replaced by God (Exod 34.1ff), which actions represented the breaking and restoration of the covenant relationship respectively.[11] It is not without significance that the tablets were stone, which reflected the hard, unbending character of that Law (see Heb 10.28) and of the people to whom it was given (*cf.* Ezek 11.19; 36.26; 2 Cor 3.3). Note also that the Law which God gave to Israel was kept in the ark, which was in turn kept in the Most Holy Place away from everyone but the high priest. In this sense, the Law was "remote" to the people. But as God said through Jeremiah, in the new covenant God would put his law *in* his people and write his laws on their hearts (Jer 31.33, quoted in Heb 8.10 above). Also, the same kind of connection that existed between the covenant and the priesthood existed between the Law and the covenant, for the Law spelled out the covenant obligations. If God has enacted a new covenant in fulfillment of Jeremiah 31, then the Law has also changed, as is evident also by the fact that Jesus is now our high priest (see Heb 7.12).

The last we hear of the ark of the covenant in the Bible is in Josiah's reform, 2 Chronicles 35.3, sometime in the 620s BC. Presumably the Babylonians took it (2 Chron 36.18). In the first century, Josephus said of the Most Holy Place of the Jerusalem temple: "There is nothing at all in it."[12] The Mishnah describes what was done in the temple on the Day of Atonement without the ark: "Once the ark was taken away, there remained a stone from the days of the earlier prophets, called Shetiyyah. It was three fingerbreadths high. And on it did he put [the fire pan]. He took the blood from the one who had been stirring it [M. 4:3B]. He [again] went into the

---

[9] Hagner, *Hebrews*, 132.

[10] Kaiser, *Toward Old Testament Ethics*, 127–31 (following the analysis of Stephen A. Kaufman, "The Structure of the Deuteronomic Law," *Maarav* 1, 2 (1978–79): 105–58).

[11] Meredith Kline, *Treaty of the Great King* (Grand Rapids: Eerdmans, 1963), 74.

[12] *Jewish War* 5.219.

place into which he had entered and again stood on the place on which he had stood. Then he sprinkled some [of the blood], one time upwards and seven times downwards. ... He went out and he set down [the bowl of blood] on the golden stand in the Sanctuary."[13] Jeremiah said that there would be no ark of the covenant in the messianic order of things: "It shall be in those days when you are multiplied and increased in the land, declares the Lord, they will no longer say, 'The ark of the covenant of the Lord.' And it will not come to mind, nor will they remember it, nor will they miss it, nor will it be made again" (3.16 NASB).

9.5 and over it the cherubs of glory overshadowing the mercy seat. It is not possible to speak piece-by-piece about these things now.

The lid of the ark was called the **mercy seat**. The Greek term is *hilastērion*, which, in the OT, means the place where expiation is achieved.[14] The mercy seat had two images of **cherubs**[15] on top of it, facing each other with their wings spread toward each other (Exod 25.17ff), and thus they **overshadowed** the mercy seat. Between these two cherubs God's presence was manifested in the cloud of incense on the Day of Atonement (Lev 16.2; *cf.* Psa 80.1). This presence is called God's **glory**, or what the rabbis called the *shekinah*. Here is where the high priest sprinkled the blood in the ritual of the Day of Atonement (Lev 16.15), at the feet of God, as it were.

At this point the author of Hebrews breaks off from the description of the details of the tabernacle. The overall purpose of the description is to set up the coming discussion of the significance of the fact that the tabernacle had two rooms (vv 6ff below).[16] There is also a broader point to be made from the overall function of the tabernacle and the Day of Atonement ritual that was its most important use, so our author now turns from the physical details to the ritual that employed them. His goal now (chs 9–10) is to show that a better sacrifice has taken place, offered by a better priest, and better blood has been provided in the heavenly sanctuary, with better results, and the new covenant has been ratified. Our

[13] *m. Yoma* 5.2A-3G (Jacob Neusner, *The Mishnah: A New Translation* (New Haven: Yale University Press, 1988), 272–73).

[14] BDAG 474.

[15] The KJV "cherubims" is technically incorrect. The singular is "cherub," and the plural in Hebrew is "cherubim."

[16] Allen, *Hebrews*, 467–68.

author had no interest in the fanciful, allegorical treatments of these items such as appeared in the writings of Philo of Alexandria.[17]

9.6 Now when these things were thus prepared, the priests[18] always entered into the first place, performing their services.

While the old covenant was in effect, the worship of God was ordinarily performed by **the priests** who, on a daily basis, went (**always,** continually, or regularly[19] **entered**[20]) into the Holy Place (**the first place** within the tabernacle). The repeated entrances and exits by the priests remind us of the author's insistence that repetition is a sign of imperfection (see 1.1f and 7.23, 27). The **services** they had to perform on a daily basis were: in the morning the lamps of the seven-branched lampstand were extinguished, and they were lit again in the evening; the lamps were also trimmed (*i.e.,* they trimmed the wicks, to keep them the proper length; Exod 30.7f) twice each day, and the lamps had to be kept filled with oil; incense was burned on the small altar twice each day, once in the morning and once in the evening (Exod 30.7f), which corresponded to daily prayers (*cf.* Luke 1.10). Once each week, on the Sabbath, the loaves of showbread were replaced and the priests ate the old loaves (Lev 24.5–9). All of these duties were given to the ordinary priests, but in these duties they were not in the presence of God, for God did not dwell in the Holy Place. The main point here is that God's presence was inaccessible to ordinary Israelites, because only priests could enter the Holy Place.

9.7 But only the high priest entered into the second place, once a year, and not without blood which he offered for himself and for the people's sins which were committed in ignorance.

---

[17] For example, see his *On Drunkenness* 1.85ff.

[18] Since there were hundreds of priests within the population of the nation, and not all of them lived in Jerusalem, nor could all of them have served in the daily rituals at once, David, in order to give as many priests as possible the opportunity to serve in these capacities in the temple, divided the priesthood into twenty four groups, who took turns performing the services in Jerusalem (1 Chron 24).

[19] See Dennis Hamm, "Praying 'Regularly' (not 'Constantly'): A Note on the Cultic Background of *dia pantos* at Luke 24:53, Acts 10:2, and Hebrews 9:6, 13:15," *ExpTim* 116 (2004): 50–52.

[20] The Greek has the present tense here, to convey the usual and ongoing nature of this activity under the old system. The verse therefore implies nothing about the existence or non-existence of the Jerusalem temple in the author's day.

Not only was God's presence inaccessible to ordinary Israelites, but it was also off limits even to the regular priests, because none of them could enter the Most Holy Place. Only **the high priest** could go **into the second** room of the tabernacle, the Most Holy Place, where God's presence dwelt, and then only for a few minutes **once a year** on the Day of Atonement (the tenth day of the seventh month of the year, Lev 16.29). These restrictions emphasized the relative inaccessibility of God in the old system.[21]

Even more significant for the author's discussion is the fact that when the high priest entered the Most Holy Place, he had to take with him the **blood** of a bull and the blood of a goat (Lev 16.14f); he could not enter God's presence without it. The procedure in Leviticus 16 was that the high priest would offer a bull as a sin offering **for himself**, (*i.e.*, for his own sins, since he had to be purified before he could go into the presence of God), and a goat as a sin offering for the people. He would first slaughter the bull and sprinkle its blood on and in front of the mercy seat to atone for his own sins, and then, once he himself was thus purified, he would go back outside, slaughter the goat, and then go back into the Most Holy Place and sprinkle that blood on and in front of the mercy seat **for the people's sins.**[22] These sins were "things done **in ignorance**" (Greek *agnoēmata*), inadvertent sins, which were the only kind of sin dealt with in the Law (Lev 4.2, 13, 22, *etc.*; *cf.* Num 15.30; see comments on 5.3; 7.27.). Yet as Moffatt rightly noted, "There is no hint that people were not responsible for them, or that they were not serious."[23]

---

[21] Steve Stanley ("Hebrews 9:6–10: The 'Parable' of the Tabernacle," *NovT* 37 (1995): 385–99, at 386) has suggested that the contrast between "first" and "second" still seems to be operative here, yet on a smaller scale. In 8.7 the author contrasted the first covenant with the second, or new, covenant. The second is better because it is obviously replacing a "first" one that was deemed insufficient in some way. Here also, there were two parts to the tabernacle, a "first" accessible to the priests, and a "second" part in which only the high priest went, once. In its own way, therefore, the tabernacle itself, with its two parts, suggested something of the inferior nature of the "first" compared to the "second."

[22] The author of Hebrews did not assign typological significance to every part of the Day of Atonement procedure. He never mentions the burning of incense, the casting of lots, and other such items. He purposefully concentrated on those parts of the ritual that lay at the core of the atonement "process" and which were essentially messianic. See Gabriella Gelardini, "The Inauguration of Yom Kippur according to the LXX and Its Cessation or Perpetuation according to the Book of Hebrews: A Systematic Comparison," in The Day of Atonement: Its Interpretations in Early Jewish and Christian Traditions, ed. Thomas Hieke and Tobias Nicklas (Leiden: Brill, 2012), 225–54, at 242–45.

[23] Moffatt, *Epistle to the Hebrews*, 117.

Three things stand out here: 1) The high priest could do nothing for God's people as long as he himself was considered a sinner. Only one who was himself right with God could act on behalf of others, so he had to make atonement for himself before he could intercede for the nation. 2) The high priest took blood before God to atone for the sins of the people. Animal blood, which symbolized its life (Lev 17.11), was required for atonement under the old system. 3) The high priest entered into God's presence once each year. While the yearly repetition of this ritual points to its defective nature (*cf.* Heb 10.1), that it was done only once in a year's time is also significant. There was a sense of culmination to it. These features of the Day of Atonement ritual were also shadows, copies, or models of the true, spiritual procedure that was required to obtain that perfect forgiveness which Jesus has now accomplished. Jesus was without sin (Heb 4.15; 7.27) and is thus qualified to approach God for us. He has entered God's presence for us through and "with" his own blood, as verses 11ff below will show, and he has performed this service only once because it is wholly efficacious and thus does not need to be repeated.

9.8 The Holy Spirit is making this clear, that the way into the Most Holy Place had not yet been shown while the first tabernacle was standing,

The author of Hebrews understood that the directions for the ritual of the Day of Atonement came through **the Holy Spirit**, who often in Scripture is presented as the means by which God revealed his will (*cf.* 1 Cor 2.12). In Hebrews, when the Spirit is said to be speaking from Scripture, the church is the intended addressee.[24] Furthermore, the Spirit is envisioned as "speaking" concerning the eschatological, messianic *significance* of what Scripture recorded. The Scriptural record of the layout of the tabernacle and its annual ritual of national atonement is, therefore, a communication from the Spirit of God in which the Spirit is **making this** important point **clear**: the design and regulation of the tabernacle offered only the most limited kind of access to God. Although the tabernacle was near to Israel (in the middle of their camp), the place where God dwelt was always off limits to the average Israelite. Specifically, the tabernacle had a built-in barrier to God. God's presence was **in the Most Holy Place**, but between God and everyone else was the Holy Place. As long as (**while**) there was a Holy Place ("**the first tabernacle**") in front of the

[24] Pierce, *Divine Discourse*, 2; see on 3.7.

Most Holy Place (mandated by the Law of Moses), access to God's presence by God's people themselves was **not yet** possible. God's presence was inaccessible under the old covenant, and the tabernacle was itself a statement of this inaccessibility. God's people were barred from coming to him, and even the one who was allowed to come before him could do so only once each year. Otherwise, there was no access to God, and the place where God dwelt was kept inaccessible by the veil that separated the Most Holy Place from everything, and everyone, else.

Two finer points of exegesis need to be addressed. First, there is a minor question whether the phrase **Most Holy Place**, which translates the Greek plural *tōn hagiōn*, refers to the most holy place or the entire tabernacle. The author's normal way of referring to the holy place is *hagia* (v 2, neuter plural), so a good case can be made that the plural here is to be understood in the same way.[25] Alternately, the genitive case here may be understood as a genitive of comparison, which is also how the most holy place is described (Greek *hagia hagiōn*, v 3). The ESV opts to make the phrase refer to the whole tabernacle ("the holy places"). The answer one gives to this question is related to the second point: there is also some question about the referents of the terms **Most Holy Place** and **the first tabernacle**. Two basic possibilities emerge for this second problem: 1) the author refers in both cases to the earthly tabernacle. In this case he is saying that the holy place in the tabernacle served as a barrier to the most holy place in that same tabernacle. Or 2) the **Most Holy Place** refers to the heavenly, true tabernacle (8.2; 9.11), and **the first tabernacle** refers to the earthly one. In this case he is saying that no one had access to the true presence of God in heaven as long as the earthly, inferior tabernacle was in place. Either way the point is that full and open access to God was not possible as long as the old tabernacle and its system was in place.

9.9 which is a parable for the present time, according to which both gifts and sacrifices are offered that are not able to perfect the worshipper in conscience,

To what does **which** refer? To 1) the entire tabernacle (the focus of vv 6–8), 2) only the Holy Place (most recently mentioned in v 8), or 3) the entire preceding statement? The second option seems most likely, in

[25] Norman H. Young, "The Gospel According to Hebrews 9," *NTS* 27 (1981): 198–210, at 198–99.

which case the author was saying that the Holy Place, with its multitude of priests and constant offerings (v 6 above) was an illustration, or **parable**, of the "**present time**."[26] But what was, or is, this "present time"? Is it 1) "now,"[27] *i.e.*, the messianic time? If so, then the parable would need to work in a strange kind of "opposite" way, illustrating that what was not possible "then" is possible "now."[28] Or 2) is it the present time from the standpoint of the operation of the tabernacle, the then-present time?[29] With this approach, the verse is saying much the same thing as verse 8 said: the tabernacle's layout indicated that access to the presence of God was not available, the access-blocking nature of the Holy Place was itself a parable (illustration) of the whole Levitical system. Since whatever the "parable" is seems to be the same situation described immediately next ("... gifts and sacrifices are offered which cannot make the worshiper perfect in conscience"), this interpretation seems better.

In this context, the developing picture includes: 1) a contrast between multiple priests (in the Holy Place, v 6) and one high priest (in the Most Holy Place, v 7), 2) a continual, daily entering into the Holy Place (v 6) versus one entrance (per year) into the Most Holy Place (v 7), 3) an unrestricted entrance into the Holy Place (v 6) versus access only by blood into the Most Holy Place (v 7), and 4) a cleansing of the flesh (vv 9,13) vs. the cleansing of the conscience (v 14).[30] All of these serve as pointers or illustrations of greater and better realities in the messianic approach to God.

For **gifts and sacrifices**, see comments on 5.1. These offerings, which were prescribed under that old covenant, did not perfect the ones who brought them. The word **perfect** translates the Greek verb *teleioō*, which

---

[26] So Lane, *Hebrews 9–13*, WBC 47B (Dallas: Word, 1991), 224. Stanley ("Hebrews 9:6–10: The 'Parable' of the Tabernacle," 395–96) argues that the "parable" lies in the comparison between the two parts of the tabernacle on the one hand, and the tabernacle vs. heaven on the other hand. The fact was that the Holy Place prevented entrance into the Most Holy Place, so the tabernacle was a system that did not allow for open and full access to God, which is available only in the work of Jesus.

[27] Such would be the naturally sense of the Greek phrase. See the references in Attridge, *Hebrews*, 241 fn 133.

[28] Attridge, *Hebrews*, 241.

[29] KJV. Perfect participles, of which we have one here, encode the spatial value of narrative proximity. This would suggest that the "present time" is the time being discussed in the context, the time when the tabernacle was operational.

[30] Felix H. Cortez, "From the Holy to the Most Holy Place: The Period of Hebrews 9:6–10 and the Day of Atonement as a Metaphor of Transition," *JBL* 125 (2006): 527–47, at 543–46.

denotes bringing something to completion so that it does not lack any parts. Our author has already noted in 7.19 that the old Law made nothing perfect; "perfect" is a characteristic of the things in the new messianic order. The old covenant's procedure for forgiveness of sins was simply unable, by its design, to do everything that was necessary for true atonement. The forgiveness it provided was incomplete, lacking in something.

What was incomplete about the forgiveness offered under the old system? In a word, it provided *a* cleansing, but not *the* cleansing. Our author frames this in terms of a contrast between rituals that were aimed at the flesh (v 10) but failed to fix the deeper aspect of the problem. The failure of the forgiveness offered under the old system was that it could not cleanse the **conscience**. The conscience is that part of our minds that retains moral instruction, and thus it is only as good, and only as reliable, as its training (*cf.* Tit 1.15). When we act against what we have been taught, our conscience accuses us and produces a sense of guilt. One does not have a complete sense of forgiveness until the conscience ceases to accuse. One of the chief problems with the sacrificial system of the old covenant was that it failed to soothe the guilty conscience (see 10.1f). Even when the offeror complied with God's requirements that promised forgiveness (Lev 4.20, 26, 31, 35; 5.10, 13, 16, 18; 6.7; 19.22), the worshiper was still left with a sense of inadequacy because what was offered for sin did not match the guilt of that sin. How could the blood of a dumb animal forgive the sin of a rational human being? Technically, it could not (see Heb 10.1). The prophet Micah wrestled with this very inadequacy as he said "With what shall I come to the Lord and bow myself before the God on high? Shall I come to Him with burnt offerings, with yearling calves? Does the Lord take delight in thousands of rams, in ten thousand rivers of oil? Shall I present my firstborn for my rebellious acts, the fruit of my body for the sin of my soul?" (Mic 6.6f NASB; *cf.* also Psa 51.16). This lingering sense of incompleteness (imperfection) is what is meant when the author says the old system was **not able to perfect the conscience**. By his grace God temporarily accepted those technically inadequate offerings with a view to the perfect remedy to which they pointed.[31] However, in the new covenant perfect forgiveness is available,

[31] Hobart E. Freeman, "The Problem of the Efficacy of the Old Testament Sacrifices," *Bulletin of the Evangelical Theological Society* 5 (1962): 73–79. He rightly notes that nowhere does the OT make the claim that the Levitical sacrifices only remedied "ceremonial" sins.

according to the promise he made through Jeremiah (Jer 31.34, quoted in Heb 8.12), on the basis of the perfect death of Jesus on our behalf. The forgiveness offered in the new covenant is not only forensically perfect in that human blood (*i.e.*, death) has been offered for human sin, but it is also perfect in that this totally adequate sacrifice of Jesus is able to cleanse the conscience (*cf.* 1 Pet 3.21).[32] The incomplete solution of the old system highlights, in relief, the perfect solution to the problem of sin offered in a relationship with Jesus, and is presented as an incentive for the readers not to forsake their commitment to him.

9.10 dealing only with food and drink and various washings, fleshly regulations imposed on them until a time of reformation.

The features and focus of the old system were primarily physical in nature, and its sacrifices left a guilty conscience behind. This is not to deny that God also wanted the inward affections of his people. "You shall love the Lord your God with all your heart and with all your soul and with all your might" (Deut 6.5 NASB). Our author's point is instead about the overall thrust and focus of the old Law. Cleanliness was spelled out in terms of **food and drink** (a general reference to the kosher laws), **washings** or purifications with water, and other such **regulations** that addressed the matter of cleansing in an outward, fleshly way. But rites and regulations centered around physical things could not touch the real problem, which was the guilty conscience, and no one with a guilty conscience is in a position to approach God. Keeping the flesh free from defilement, as significant as it is, was not enough, because man is more than flesh, and sin involves more than just the body. The fleshly cleanliness demanded by the Law was itself an illustration of a deeper, inward cleanness. Jesus himself spoke about the need for this inner cleanliness (Matt 23.25f; *cf.* Mark 7.18f) as part of the new order of things he came to establish.

The external items of the old system were only shadows and models of the true system that came to light in Jesus. Specifically, the cleansing of the flesh served as an illustration for the messianic cleansing of the conscience.[33] The rituals and procedures of the Levitical system were to stand as temporary measures **until** the time when God would execute his

---

[32] See Gary S. Selby, "The Meaning and Function of *suneidēsis* in Hebrews 9 and 10," *ResQ* 28 (1985–6): 145–54.

[33] Cortez, "From the Holy to the Most Holy Place," 537.

plan and enact a new covenant (Jer 31; quoted in Heb 8). The word **reformation** (Greek *diorthōsis*) can be used in a legal context to mean revision or correction (of a law),[34] but the verbal form is used in the LXX of Isaiah 16.5 to mean "establish." Either idea fits here.

9.11 But Christ having appeared as high priest of the good things that have come, entered[35] through the greater and more perfect tabernacle, not made with hands, that is, not of this creation.

The contrast between the high priesthood of Christ (established in chs 4–7) and that of the old system can now be laid out in full, with the result that what we have in Christ can be most fully appreciated. The "parable" continues. Whereas the tabernacle of the first covenant was earthly (v 1), in the new covenant Jesus exercises his high-priestly role in **the greater and more perfect tabernacle**, heaven itself. We respectfully disagree with the idea that the greater tabernacle is the church[36] or Christ's physical body.[37] There is no contextual warrant for either interpretation. The greater and more perfect tabernacle is heaven itself, the reality of which the tabernacle was a copy. Verse 24 below confirms this.

The Israelite tabernacle was a model (8.5) of the true presence of God in heaven.[38] Like everything else in the old covenant, physical things were the illustration and model of the **good** spiritual **things that have come** (through the work of Jesus in the messianic order). Just as the daily offerings of the many priests in the Holy Place paled in their significance compared to the single ritual on the Day of Atonement administered by the high priest, so the benefit available under the Levitical system pales in comparison to what Jesus has accomplished for us.[39] The earthly tab-

---

[34] Westcott, *Epistle to the Hebrews*, 254, Attridge, *Hebrews*, 243.

[35] I have supplied the main verb, which does not appear in the Greek until v 12, at this place for the sake of English translation, and I have repeated it in the next verse for the same reason. In the Greek, however, it only appears once, with v 11 serving as a long string of verbal modifiers.

[36] Bruce, *Epistle to the Hebrews*, 200; see Philip Edgcumbe Hughes, "The Blood of Jesus and His Heavenly Priesthood in Hebrews. Part III, The Meaning of 'the true tent' and 'the greater and more perfect tent'," *BibSac* 130 (1973): 305–14; at 309ff.

[37] See Hughes, "The Blood of Jesus and His Heavenly Priesthood in Hebrews. Part III," 305–309; James Swetnam, "'The Greater and More Perfect Tent': A Contribution to the Discussion of Hebrews 9,11," *Bib* 47 (1966): 91–106.

[38] See Roberts, "The Story of the Tabernacle."

[39] Stanley, "Hebrews 9:6–10: The 'Parable' of the Tabernacle," 397–98.

ernacle was prepared by men (9.2), but the true tabernacle in which Jesus serves is **not made with** human **hands** (*cf.* Acts 7.48), it is not fashioned out of earthly materials from the physical, created world. The phrase "not made with hands" is used in Scripture to denote what is made by God, and hence what is spiritual, perfect, and lasting (see 2 Cor 5.1; Acts 7.48).[40] While there was a manifestation of God's presence in the earthly tabernacle, God's true abode is in heaven (1 Kngs 8.27; Acts 17.24; Psa 11.4), and Jesus has gone there to enter into the true presence of God for us. Judaism dealt with physical copies, but Christianity deals with the true, spiritual realities. This, again, is meant to be an incentive for the readers not to abandon Christianity.

9.12 Nor was it via the blood of goats and calves, but by his own blood he entered once into the sanctuary, having obtained eternal redemption.

Just as the Aaronic high priest was required to approach God in the Most Holy Place with atoning blood (v 7), so the new high priest, Jesus, has **entered** into **the** true **sanctuary** of God, the very presence of God in heaven, through blood. But there is a crucial difference not only in the place into which our high priest has entered (heavenly vs. earthly, v 11), but in the source for the blood by which he enters God's presence. Jesus entered into the presence of God not through the blood of an animal, but with human blood, **his own blood**. The Son of God became a man, having a body of flesh and blood, when he humbled himself and "was made a little lower than the angels on account of the suffering of death" (2.9, 14; *cf.* Phil. 2.7f). Bruce rightly notes that the author of Hebrews avoids saying that Jesus took his blood into heaven.[41] In the sacrifices, blood was not considered to be some magical element that, by its own constitution, made atonement. The blood of the sacrificial victim represented the complete dedication of a life to God, and this is probably

---

[40] "Made with hands" had a consistently negative connotation in Jewish literature. Stephen used it of idols in Acts 7.41, and in secular Greek the phrase meant "inferior." James W. Thompson, "Hebrews 9 and Hellenistic Concepts of Sacrifice," *JBL* 98 (1979): 567–78, at 570 fn21. We are skeptical, however, of Thompson's suggestion that the author has appropriated in this chapter a religious critique that was current in Hellenistic forms of Platonism (such as in Philo of Alexandria). The author's perspective is eschatological, not Platonic. See David J. MacLeod, "The Cleansing of the True Tabernacle," *BibSac* 152 (1995): 60–71. at 61–62.

[41] Bruce, *Epistle to the Hebrews*, 200.

how we should understand Jesus entering into heaven with his own blood. It describes Jesus entering into heaven having given his life perfectly and fully, in its entirety, to God for the sins of others.[42] As noted in the comments on verse 9, the old rite was a figure of the reality in Jesus, but we must not think that the figure dictates every detail of the thing it describes. Similarly, debates over the precise moment in history when our redemption (which is itself a figure) was accomplished (was it on the cross? was it when Jesus reached heaven?) are misguided.[43] The NT speaks of how our forgiveness was accomplished using figures that illustrate what has happened in a greater, spiritual way. It is in this vein that we should understand the messianic significance of the sacrificial procedures of the old covenant.

It is crucial to know that what Jesus did, he did only **once**. This points to the abiding and perfect quality of what Jesus did. Whereas the priests under the old covenant repeatedly came before God with sacrifices (9.6), thus indicating the weakness (*cf.* 7.18) of those offerings, Jesus enters the presence of God one final time, thus indicating the full potency of his action forever. The sacrificial death of Jesus suffices once for all and does not need to be repeated. See verses 25f below.

By this blood Jesus has **obtained eternal redemption** (*cf.* Eph 1.7) for all those who join themselves to him and approach God through him. **Redemption** is a transaction in which something that had been forfeited is bought back or otherwise reacquired. It is used in the New Testament figuratively to describe the effects of the death of Christ for us and is a way of speaking about forgiveness (Col 1.14). Through Jesus' death God brings man back to himself. God's just decree was that "the soul who sins will die" (Ezek 18.4; *cf.* Gen 2.17; Rom 6.23a). Yet God did not create man to lose him to sin and death, nor to kill every person when they sinned, so God, in his great love, mercy, and grace, executed his plan whereby he would forgive man of the guilt of sin and restore him to fellowship with God. That plan involved offering his own sinless

[42] See Brandon D. Crowe, "Son and Priest, Then and Now: Christology and Redemptive History in Hebrews in Light of the History of Interpretation," *WTJ* 84 (2022): 19–39, esp. 28–30; R. B. Jamieson, "When and Where Did Jesus Offer Himself? A Taxonomy of Recent Scholarship on Hebrews," *CBR* 15 (2017): 338–68; Moffitt, *Atonement and the Logic of Resurrection in the Epistle to the Hebrews.*

[43] See Philip Edgcumbe Hughes, "The Blood of Jesus and His Heavenly Priesthood in Hebrews. Part I, The Significance of the Blood of Jesus," *BibSac* 130 (1973): 99–109, and "Part II, The High-Priestly Sacrifice of Christ," 195–212.

Son as a substitute for those who had sinned (everyone, Rom 3.23), thus redeeming, or reclaiming, man.

This is not called **eternal** redemption because the redeemed may never be guilty of sin again. There are too many warnings about falling away not only in Hebrews but throughout the Bible for any such notion to be correct (see Heb 6.1ff). Instead, it is eternal in that it is sufficient for all time. Jesus does not have to offer his blood (that is, die) repeatedly, for his one offering is sufficient to cover the sins of all (7.27; 9.12; 10.10; 1 Pet 3.18). *Cf.* 5.9 and 9.27.

9.13 For if the blood of bulls and of goats and the ashes of a heifer sprinkling those who were defiled sanctifies for the purity of the flesh,

Our author already pointed out in verses 9f that the old covenant provided only for a kind of ritual cleanliness **of the flesh** but did not completely cleanse the worshiper because the conscience was left guilty. He is now using that established fact to lay down the first part of an argument from the lesser to the greater, a common type of argument in Jewish exegetical practice (the rabbis called it *kal wahomer*, and the modern term for it is *a fortiori*; see Introduction). This verse contains the lesser premise of the argument, and the next verse contains the greater premise.

Verse 12 mentioned the blood of goats and calves, and this verse mentions **bulls and goats**. Both phrases are probably meant to be summary, not precise, and thus refer to animal sacrifices in general. However, it is likely significant that a bull and a goat were the prescribed sacrificial victims for the ritual of the Day of Atonement, and the author undoubtedly had that particular ritual in mind as *the* figure for understanding the redemptive work of Christ.

A little more problematic is the mention of the **ashes of a heifer**, which refers to the rite described in Numbers 19.1–10 that provided ritual purification for those who had become defiled. That rite was not technically part of the ritual of the Day of Atonement. So why did he mention it here? At least two explanations are possible: 1) our author here cited it simply as a prime example of the external nature of the cleansing the old covenant afforded,[44] or 2) the actual practice in Hellenistic times was that the high priest was purified with this procedure. Josephus said that the killing of a heifer was regularly used to cleanse

[44] Cockerill, *Epistle to the Hebrews*, 397.

from impurity (*Ant.* 4.79), and *m. Parah* 3.1 (attributed to the first century) says that the heifer rite was used to purify the high priest seven days before the Day of Atonement.[45]

9.14 how much more will the blood of Christ, who through the eternal Spirit offered himself unblemished to God, cleanse your conscience from dead works to serve the living God?

If sacrificial animal blood was effective to cleanse the flesh from defilement under the old covenant (v 13), **the blood of Christ**, the Son of God, in the new covenant is surely effective for **much more**, namely purification of the **conscience** (on which see v 9). If inferior blood provided a measure of cleansing, then better, perfect blood must provide better and perfect purification. The problem of the guilty conscience, which the old Law could not fix (v 9), is fixed in what Jesus has done (and nowhere else), and with this problem fixed we have full access to, and fellowship ("rest") with, God.

We should remember two things here: 1) The reason animal blood was efficacious to remove defilement and make atonement under the old covenant was because God said it was. There is no logical, inherent connection between killing an animal and becoming ceremonially clean; it worked only because God accepted it when the worshiper acted by faith in God's instruction. Offering an animal sacrifice to become ritually pure was an act of faith in God's decree that the sacrifice would indeed obtain the desired purification for the worshiper. What is greater about the death of Christ is that his was a human life (in contrast to the animal sacrifices of the old covenant) offered for human sin, thus the sacrifice matches the nature of the offense. It is because a *person* died in our place that forgiveness can be obtained and the guilty conscience can finally feel true relief. 2) The blood is the seat of life when it comes to sacrificial theology, and the shedding or pouring out of a victim's blood meant the victim's death. Note how the phrase **the blood of Christ** becomes "death" in the next verse.[46] More properly, perhaps, it meant *giving a life, wholly,* to

---

[45] See Horbury, "The Aaronic Priesthood in the Epistle to the Hebrews," 51–52; and below on 10.4. Also William Loader, "Revisiting High Priesthood Christology in Hebrews," *ZNW* 109 (1018): 235–83, at 243–48.

[46] So we reject hard distinctions between Jesus' "blood" and his "death" in such contexts (see Hughes, "Part II," 200ff).

God. The point of giving a life to God in the sacrificial reconciliation ritual was to demonstrate the sinner's dedication to God (that is, his faith, his loyalty) and pledge of his good faith going forward in the relationship. Dedication, or faith, has always been what God has wanted to see from those who would have a relationship with him. By becoming partakers with Christ (Heb 3.14), we share and participate in the dedication and loyalty to God that he himself showed in his life and death on this earth, and that participation in the complete self-giving of Jesus brings us into close fellowship with God, "within the veil."

Jesus **offered himself** in his sacrificial death on the cross (*cf.* John 10.17f). As the perfect sacrifice he was **unblemished**, he had no defect that would render him unfit for presentation to God (*cf.* Exod 29.1; 12.46 and John 19.36; Lev 1.3; 3.1; *etc.*; 1 Pet 1.19). Jesus was without any moral spot (4.15), which enabled him to give his life for the sins of others (see comments on 7.27). Like every other sacrifice, his death was offered **to God** as a substitute for the life of another (in this case, the world; *cf.* John 6.33), for all sin is against God and he is the one who must be satisfied. Furthermore, he offered himself to God **through the eternal Spirit**. All that Jesus did, he did by the Spirit of God (*cf.* Luke 4.1; Acts 10.38) and it was that same divine Spirit within him, which he followed perfectly and that empowered him, that led him to the cross. It seems pointless to debate whether the "spirit" here is the Holy Spirit or Jesus' own spirit,[47] for the two are the same thing (*cf.* Isa 42.1; Rom 8.9). The fact that the **Spirit** is here noted to be **eternal** suggests again the perfection of all things within the messianic order (see 5.9; 9.12, 15; 13.20),[48] but may also suggest that it had always been God's plan to offer his Son for the sins of the world (1 Pet 1.20). Although Hebrews does not make it explicit, the Biblical picture reflected here is that the atonement was a "trinitarian" effort.[49]

What are the **dead works** from which the conscience is cleansed? The same phrase was used in 6.1, and it refers to the same thing here. It is a

---

[47] So Westcott, Delitzsch, Johnson ("Some Important Mistranslations in Hebrews," 29–31), *et al.*

[48] *Cf.* Attridge's suggestion that the phrase refers to the spiritual quality of Jesus' sacrifice (*Hebrews*, 251).

[49] Peterson, *Hebrews*, 210. See Colin E. Gunton, *The Actuality of Atonement: A Study of Metaphor, Rationality, and the Christian Tradition* (London; New York: T&T Clark, 2003), 142–71; Joel Scandrett and William G. Witt, *Mapping Atonement: The Doctrine of Reconciliation in Christian History and Theology* (Grand Rapids: Baker Academic, 2022), 176–200.

way of referring to the life of an unbeliever in general. All the works of sin are dead works because they have no value (*cf.* 1 John 3.8) and because they produced the sinner's death.

The purpose of the cleansing available by means of the blood of Christ is that we might **serve the living God** in the ultimate fulfillment of the scenario described in Jeremiah 31.33f. The word **serve** again renders the same word used of priestly worship in earlier verses, but here it does not refer to the sacrificial rituals of the OT priesthood but to a life dedicated to the glorification of God in all things (*cf.* Luke 1.74; Acts 27.23). The language implies that God's new people are a priesthood (*cf.* Exod 19.6; 1 Peter 1.9). The new priesthood in the new covenant offers spiritual sacrifices to God, including what we do in public worship but in no way limited to this (see 1 Pet 2.5; Heb 13.15f). Christians (all of them) are priests in this sense, and our lives are a continuous spiritual, priestly service and sacrifice (Rom 12.1). See also Heb 12.28; Eph 2.20–22. The phrase **living God** can denote God in his judgment (3.12 and 10.31), but here it probably suggests God as the giver of life, or God generally associated with life, in contrast to the deadness of the life of an unbeliever.

9.15 And for this reason he is the mediator of a new covenant, so that (since a death has taken place for the redemption of the transgressions that were under the first covenant) those who have been called might receive the promise of the eternal inheritance.

In 8.6 our author has already said that Jesus **is the mediator of** the **new covenant** predicted through Jeremiah. It is important to remember that the crowning element of that new covenant was the forgiveness of sins (Jer 31.34). The prophecy of Jeremiah implied that something less was being done for sins in the old covenant (see Heb 10.3), but the promise of a new covenant also implied that a death would be required to enact it. A **covenant**, by its nature, is an agreement that consists of acknowledgements and promises. Each party promises to act on behalf of the other party in ways that are spelled out in the covenant. Loyalty and dedication are the ideas that drive a covenant relationship. In the new covenant with God, God promises to bless those who enter the relationship with him with life and save them from the eternal consequences of their sins. They in turn promise to trust him in all things. The word **mediator** denotes a guarantor, one who not only arbitrates but who actually enacts or accomplishes the reconciliation. That same sense of the word is operative in this context. The new covenant is a reality because of what Jesus did; it is in place because he enacted it by his death. 8.7–9.14 has established that a new covenant was indeed coming (as Jeremiah predicted), the old covenant was imperfect, and that what the animal sacrifices under the old covenant could not do (cleanse the conscience) is finally accomplished by the blood of Jesus in the new covenant. Now, therefore, we are in a position to see the full significance of the new covenant and Jesus' role in it. Jesus' blood not only cleanses the conscience but also has inaugurated the **new** covenant of which Jeremiah spoke, and thus he fulfills that promise. With that covenant thus enacted, the promised blessings of that covenant are now available. The easy shift from blood (vv 11–14) to **death** (vv 15–17) shows the intimate, inseparable connection between the two.

On the word **redemption**, see comments on verse 12 above. The words **for the redemption of the transgressions that were under the first covenant** require careful attention. They are not the main point of the sentence, and it would be easy to direct too much significance to them. In Greek they form a grammatical construction known as a genitive absolute, which is used to inject additional or background information into a sentence, but which does not supply the main thought. The author's argument so far has demonstrated that the Levitical sacrificial system was flawed. It was so by design, because it was always meant to be a pointer to something else, but not itself the definitive solution to the problem of sin. The clear implication, then, is that those who lived under that system did not receive the kind of forgiveness that was truly needed. So what is their fate? The answer is: the blood of Jesus provides the full forgiveness for their sins. The author's statement should not be taken to mean that there was no forgiveness of any kind before Christ died, that no one was forgiven of anything before Christ's sacrifice (see comments on v 9 above). Hebrews does *not* offer a contrast of no forgiveness in the old covenant versus forgiveness in the new covenant. Instead, he offers a contrast between an incomplete forgiveness versus a better, new, and perfect forgiveness. The death of Jesus is not like the animal sacrifices in that his blood is forensically sufficient to make atonement and meet God's demand for justice (see Rom 3.25f). It is in this sense that we must understand the author's reference to **the trans-**

gressions[50] **under the first covenant**. It took the death of Jesus, and the ratification of the new covenant, to deal fully and perfectly with those sins.[51] Moffatt brought out the sense as he rendered it "He mediates a new covenant for this reason, that those who have been called may obtain the eternal inheritances they have been promised, now that a death has occurred which redeems them from the transgressions involved in the first covenant."[52]

With the new covenant ratified, and forgiveness of sins fully possible, those who have been called (*cf.* 3.1) can now receive the promise of the eternal inheritance (recalling the discussion in 6.13–19). This is the main point of the verse. **Those who have been called** are first, in this context, those who heard God's voice and lived by faith under the old covenant. The author is previewing the statement he will make later in 11.40. He envisioned the faithful of both covenants joined together in the presence of God by the blood of Jesus (see 12.23). The saints of the OT lived in hope of the fulfillment of **the promise** God made to Abraham, *as do Christians*. Therefore, the group of "those who have been called" is not just those who lived by faith under the old covenant, nor is it just those who have been called by the gospel (2 Thes 2.14), but ultimately consists of *both*. This promise, as we have noted, is ultimately a promise of eternal life, and in this sense it is the **eternal inheritance** of the true children of Abraham (recall 6.13–19). Ultimately, it is eternal life in the presence of God. However, the realization of that promise depended on some means of forgiveness when God's people sinned (for people defiled by sin cannot stand in God's presence). The death of Jesus, and the new covenant it has enacted, provides that forgiveness, so now the heirs of the promise can inherit that for which those under the old covenant could only hope, and to which the elements of the old system pointed like a parable. It has now become reality in the new covenant that was ratified by the death (blood) of Jesus on the cross. The Abrahamic

---

[50] *Cf.* Paul's statement that even though the Jews had the sacrifices of the Law of Moses, that entire period was characterized as one in which God "passed over" their sins. That is, those sacrifices did not provide the full efficacy that was needed.

[51] Peterson and Grindheim go too far, in my opinion, in asserting that "transgressions" covers all sins of any kind under the old covenant. As noted in the comments on Heb 5.2, "defiant" sins had no remedy available, and it is not clear why people who stubbornly and defiantly rebelled against God would now be forgiven by Christ although they were impenitent.

[52] Moffatt, *Epistle to the Hebrews*, 125.

blessings of the messianic age are now available to be enjoyed by all the faithful because of the new-covenant-enacting death of Jesus.[53]

9.16 For where there is a will, there must necessarily be the death of the one who made the will.

The word here translated **will** is, in the Greek, the same word translated as "covenant" in the previous verse (*diathēkē*). The normal word for **covenant** (Hebrew *berith*) in the LXX is *diathēkē,* but the more usual word in secular Greek usage was *sunthēkē*. Technically, a *sunthēkē* was the word for a covenant between parties who were considered equals, but a *diathēkē* was one between two parties, one of whom was acknowledged as greater than the other (an overlord) and who imposed his will on the lesser party (the vassal).[54] The LXX possibly preferred *diathēkē* because it suggested the inequality of status that operated in God's covenants with people (where God and the people are not seen as equal parties in the relationship). Whatever the rationale of the translators was, the fact is that the Greek word *diathēkē* came to mean "covenant" in Biblical Greek and acquired, within that corpus, the theological significance of the original Hebrew term. However, in the secular *koine* Greek of the first century, *diathēkē* was the normal word for a testament or (last) will.[55] The author of Hebrews drew on this dual usage of the word to make a point here.[56,57] Just as a person's last will and

---

[53] In its bare outlines, the argument here is similar to Paul's in Gal 3.15–18, where Paul argued that salvation is through the promise, not the old Law. The author of Hebrews has added the detail that the new covenant promised through Jeremiah is the covenant vehicle through which the Abrahamic promises would be realized.

[54] H. Hegermann. *"diathēkē," EDNT* 1:299. *diathēkē* has a sense of the imposition of control on another that *sunthēkē* lacks. However, caution must be exercised here; the terms could be used interchangeably (as in Isa 28.15 LXX).

[55] Westcott, *Epistle to the Hebrews,* 299; Hegermann, *"diathēkē," EDNT* 1:299.

[56] John J. Hughes, "Hebrews IX 15ff and Galatians III 15ff: A Study in Covenant Practice and Procedure," *NovT* 21 (1979): 27–96, argued that *diathēkē* can only mean "covenant" here, but surely this is at the expense of the context.

[57] Scott W. Hahn ("A Broken Covenant and the Curse of Death: A Study of Hebrews 9:15–22," *CBQ* 66 (2004): 416–36) argues that vv 16f mean that a death (sacrifice) was necessary since the old covenant had been broken. The death of Jesus thus atones for Israel's breaking of the old covenant and establishes the new one at the same time. This interpretation is endorsed by Cockerill, *Epistle to the Hebrews,* 405–406. The problem with this approach, however, is that Hebrews nowhere argues that the old covenant had been broken (even though the argument can successfully be made that Israel had broken it). The author's consistent argument was, instead, that the old covenant was weak and ineffective for what was needed because it was a shadow of what was to come. Besides, certain threads

testament goes into effect upon their death, so the new relationship with God of which Jeremiah spoke went into effect at the death of Jesus. Paul used the word *diathēkē* in this same sense of "testament" in Galatians 3.15. Technically, a covenant is not the same thing as a testament. The author of Hebrews was not asserting that they are, and it would be incorrect to impose the idea of a testament (either modern or ancient) on every context in Hebrews where the word *diathēkē* appears. The necessity of a death for enactment makes the new covenant like a will and is the reason the author now uses that metaphor. In the Biblical world, a covenant was effected by the death of an *animal* (as the author will note below), but in the case of the new covenant which Jeremiah predicted, it is effected by the death of a *person,* and *in this way* it is like testament. But covenants and human testaments have in common that they contain promises that are realized by a death. Our author is simply drawing upon these shared features, upon the fact that the word *diathēkē* had two connotations in the secular and religious spheres, and upon the fact that a human death is involved in the new covenant, to illustrate an aspect of God's new covenant that could be seen as implicit in the promise made through Jeremiah, namely, that a death would be required for it to go into effect.[58]

The author points out the common process by which a last will and testament works: when **the one who made the will** dies, his "last will and testament" goes into effect, and the things promised in the will are distributed to the heirs. This corresponds to the mention of "the inheritance" in the previous verse. The point is to show how the death of Jesus has enacted the new covenant which God had promised through Jeremiah, and that the enactment of that covenant by a death has now brought great promises to those who enter into that covenant relationship. Remember also that in Biblical usage **death** and blood are often synonymous, for this fact sets up the point in verses 18–20 below.

9.17 For a will goes into effect at death, since it never has force while the one who made the will is alive.[59]

in the OT argue that the exile was the punishment, or atonement, for Israel's breaking the covenant (*cf.* Lev 26.43; Isa 27.8f).

[58] Ellingworth, *Epistle to the Hebrews,* 462. It is not at all unusual for a Biblical author to see several facets of a single event. For example, the author of Hebrews presents Jesus as both the sacrifice and the offeror of the sacrifice in the new covenant.

[59] Stevens has argued that the latter part of this verse can be rendered as a rhetorical

This verse simply states in a negative way what was said positively in verse 16 concerning the way a will works. A **will** (again, the same word can be translated "covenant" or "testament" according to context) goes into effect only **at** the **death** of the one who made it.[60] As long as he lives, his will is not executed. Since Jesus has died, we may then fairly infer that a testament has been put into effect, namely the new covenant of which God spoke through Jeremiah.

9.18 Therefore the first covenant was not put into effect without blood.

The comparison between God's covenant and human testaments continues, as well as the interchangeability between "blood" and "death." In the ancient world, covenants were inaugurated by a death (the shedding of **blood**), including the **first** (old) **covenant** of Sinai. This is nothing new in God's dealings with man, and is another way in which the old covenant prefigured the new covenant of which Jeremiah spoke and which was enacted by the death of Jesus.

9.19 For after every commandment had been spoken to all the people by Moses according to the Law, he took the blood of calves[61] along with water and scarlet wool and hyssop and sprinkled both the book and all the people,

When God entered into the covenant with Israel at Sinai (that included the Levitical priesthood), that covenant became effective upon the death **of calves** (specifically, young bulls) whose **blood** (which was proof of

---

question: "After all, is a testament ever valid while the one who made it lives?" Daniel Stevens, "Is It Valid? A Case for the Repunctuation of Hebrews 9:17," *JBL* 137 (2018): 1019–1025.

[60] J. Hughes ("Hebrews IX 15ff and Galatians III 15ff: A Study in Covenant Practice and Procedure") argues that this cannot be the sense of this verse, since this was not true of wills in Hellenistic times. Instead, he argues, wills were considered valid when they were witnessed and deposited with a notary (60), and distribution of an inheritance did not always have to wait until the death of the testator. However, the author's point here is not about the validity of a will, but its execution, and occasional and unusual exceptions do not invalidate the general fact that the instructions of a will were, usually, not carried out until the testator died.

[61] A textual variant inserts the words "and goats." Exod 24 does not mention them, and the oldest copy of Hebrews (P^{46}) lacks the words. Accepting the variant as genuine, Westcott supposed that goats were offered by others on this occasion (267). The phrase "goats and calves" was used in v 12 synonymously with the designation "goats and bulls" in v 13, and it seems more likely that our author simply used these animals somewhat interchangeably as the source of the blood used in the rituals of the old system.

their death) was **sprinkled** on the things that represented the essence of the agreement (Exod 24.6ff), including **the book** (the written document containing God's requirements, Exod 24.4, which represented the validity of the relationship, like a signed contract in modern times[62]) and **the people** themselves. The point is the covenant of Sinai was enacted upon a death (in this case, the death of an animal), and it is also another way in which the old prefigured the new.

There are, however, several details that our author has added to the picture. Exodus 24 does not say that Moses sprinkled the blood on **the book** of the covenant in which he had recorded God's words. It only mentions sprinkling blood on the people. Furthermore, the Exodus account does not record anything about **water, scarlet wool,** or **hyssop**. Similarly, Exodus 24 mentions an altar that Moses had built, and which he also sprinkled with the blood, but the author of Hebrews omits this feature of that scene. How may we account for these differences? The point in this section is not about a particular sacrifice and its specific requirements, but about the old system in general. Therefore, the author included various features together as all belonging to the same order, and omitted details that were not directly pertinent to his point. This accounts for the mention of the **water, scarlet wool, and hyssop**, which were used on some occasions that required blood or water to be sprinkled (*cf.* Lev 14.1–9, 49ff; Num 19.1–10, 18; Psa 51.7) as well as his omission of the altar. What Moses did on this one occasion was typical of what was done on other occasions and with other objects (see v 21 below), and our author saw the incident in Exodus 24 as representing the old Law's use of blood generally. We may understand the otherwise-unknown reference to Moses sprinkling the book in the same way. In addition, there is no reason why these additional details cannot be factual if we accept the inspiration of Scripture. Inspired NT writers sometimes reveal things about OT stories that are not in the OT records.[63]

9.20 saying, "This is the blood of the covenant which God ordained for you."

---

[62] Kline, *Treaty of the Great King*, 43.

[63] A few examples: God's communication with Abraham in Mesopotamia (Acts 7.2f), the Law of Moses given through angels (Acts 7.38), and Saul's reign of forty years (Acts 13.21).

The author quotes the words of Moses from Exodus 24.8, which explicitly connect the **blood** and **the covenant**. The covenant was **ordained** (Greek *entellō*, commanded, ordered, here in the sense of "became binding") on the basis of blood that had been shed for it. The quotation grounds the author's point in Scripture itself.

9.21 And he similarly sprinkled with blood both the tabernacle and all the vessels of the ministry.

Exodus 40.9ff describes how the tabernacle and its furnishings were anointed with oil, and Leviticus 8.15ff describes a blood ritual in which the altar of sacrifice and the priests were consecrated. While there is no specific mention in the OT of the tabernacle and its vessels being sprinkled with blood, there is every reason to believe this would have been done to consecrate the sacred tent in the same way as the altar, the priests, and the people had been consecrated. Again, the inspiration of Scripture allows us to accept these details just as confidently as if they were stated explicitly in the OT itself. These things are here cited as additional examples of how things under the old covenant—especially those things that had to do with drawing near to God—were inaugurated and dedicated **with blood**. The point the author is developing is that a covenant, and the things that are provided in the covenant, does not "go active," or is not put into effect, until blood has been shed. Blood puts things into service, blood makes things "work," blood makes things operational with respect to God.

9.22 And according to the Law, almost all things are cleansed with blood; and without the shedding of blood there is no forgiveness.

There were a few things specified in the **Law** of Moses that were cleansed by water (see Lev 11.32; 15.1ff; 17.15; Num 31.23f), and some with fire (Num 21.21ff; *cf.* other minor variations in Lev 5.11; Num 16.46; 31.50). However, in the case of God's sanctuary (which is the focus in this context), the tabernacle could not be used if it was defiled, and since the tabernacle was connected most closely with God's presence, the only way to make the tabernacle clean, and therefore to make it holy (usable for God), was by blood sacrifice.[64] Here therefore, as in verse 23 below, "**cleanse**" has the sense of "inaugurate" or "enact." Once the tabernacle

[64] See Sklar, *Sin, Impurity, Sacrifice, Atonement*, 127–36.

was cleansed of its impurity by a blood sacrifice, it was then "put into service" or made usable. The sprinkling of the blood in Exodus 24 ratified or enabled all it touched as now belonging under the covenant agreement with God. He says **almost all things** under the old covenant were cleansed, or put into use for the service of God, **with blood**, that is, in a procedure that required the shedding of blood (the sacrifice of a life). It is a statement of a general principle found in the Law of Moses.

The author then takes his argument one step further and connects the two major elements of Jeremiah 31.31–34 (quoted in Heb 8). Those two elements are 1) a covenant ("I will make a new covenant," v 31), and 2) forgiveness "I will forgive their iniquity," v 34). He has established that blood is required for a covenant and its provisions to go into effect (vv 16–21 above). However, the crowning provision of the covenant God promised through Jeremiah was the complete forgiveness of sins ("I will forgive their iniquity, and their sin I will remember no more," Jer 31.34). This too requires the shedding of blood. The prophecy of Jeremiah 31 therefore implied that death would be required for both of these things, and the sacrificial death of Jesus has provided the "blood" for both of them. **Without the shedding of blood there is no forgiveness** is also a general statement that finds validation in the new covenant as well. Note the connection between blood and **forgiveness** in the various procedures spelled out in Leviticus 4–5. In the same way in the new covenant, the forgiveness God promised in the new covenant (Jer 31.34) is obtained through a new covenant enacted by blood. Jesus himself connected his blood with the new covenant and forgiveness in Matthew 26.28 (*cf.* Eph 1.7). The blood of Jesus has enacted the new covenant (vv 16f), and this put the heavenly sanctuary in use, but also with the result that the forgiveness of sins promised in the covenant (Jer 31.24) is now available because the death of Jesus serves as the offering for sins.

The word **forgiveness** renders the Greek word *aphesis*, which can denote release (Luke 4.18), and when used of sin it refers to release from the guilt and consequences of sin. Generally speaking, the Law laid down as a principle that serious defilement and estrangement from the covenant relationship was corrected by **the shedding of blood** offered in the place of the one who had violated the terms of the covenant.[65] Restoration to fellowship with God required the giving of a life, symbolized by its

[65] Sklar, *Sin, Impurity, Sacrifice, Atonement*, 165–82.

blood. The statement here is true whether the inferior, limited kind of forgiveness under the Law is in view, or the full and complete forgiveness available with Jesus is in view. With God, blood is always the prerequisite for forgiveness because, as noted above, God demands loyalty as the condition of a relationship with him, and the greatest expression of loyalty is the giving of life.

9.23 It was necessary therefore that the patterns of things in the heavens were to be cleansed with these things, but the heavenly things themselves were to be cleansed with better sacrifices than these.

It was fitting, in fact **necessary**, that an earthly system use earthly, physical sacrifices. But it would be incongruent for the heavenly, spiritual system to use those same earthly sacrifices. The tabernacle and the rites and institutions of the Law of Moses generally were **patterns** of **heavenly things**, examples of spiritual realities that would operate in the messianic age (see 9.9). The plane on which Jesus enacted the new covenant and on which he provides perfect forgiveness is the heavenly plane, not the earthly plane. As our author has already noted, Jesus would not be a priest in the earthly system enjoined under the Law of Moses, for Jesus was not of the proper lineage to serve under that system (7.13f). His service is rendered in the heavens, where he has gone to sit at God's right hand in fulfillment of Psalm 110.1.

The word **pattern** is the same word (*hupodeigma*) that was translated "example" in 4.11 and 8.5. Every pattern, example, or model is a demonstration or suggestion[66] of something else. By its nature a pattern or example speaks of something beyond itself. So it was with the features of the sacrificial system of the OT. These external, physical things in the old covenant were but earthly demonstrations of heavenly realities. As patterns they lacked the power of the realities to which they pointed, but they imparted a basic understanding of the working of those heavenly realities. It is only in those heavenly realities that perfect forgiveness, extending to the conscience, could be obtained.

The earthly tabernacle and its accoutrements had to **be cleansed** (purified) through a blood ritual before it could be used (v 21; see Lev 16.16). But in what possible sense could the same be said of the heavenly sanctuary, of which the tabernacle was just a copy? Was there defilement in

[66] Lee, "Words Denoting 'Pattern' in the New Testament," 167–69.

God's presence that had to be removed by the blood of Christ? Of course not. Two interpretations are worth considering here:

1) The contrast between the earthly (9.1) and the heavenly (9.11ff) corresponds to the contrast between the flesh (9.10) and the conscience (9.9). Thus, the term **heavenly things** refers to the spiritual realities addressed and fixed (cleansed) in the work of Jesus, and in particular the conscience, which the Levitical sacrifices could not cleanse (9.9; 10.1). "... if the conscience is that part of man which belongs to a higher world, the perfection and cleansing of the conscience can occur only when the way is opened into the heavenly world."[67] Thus the cleansing of the conscience (v 14) is here called the cleansing of the heavenly things.

2) As noted in the previous verse, once a thing was cleansed it was available for use in the service of God (*cf.* Exod 29.36; Lev 8.15; 1 Chron 23.28), and it is this *result* of purification that is in view here. That is, the point in this particular part of the author's presentation is that blood (because it cleanses) consecrates or inaugurates (vv 16ff), and this, then, is the sense conveyed in this verse.[68] It is not that the heavenly sanctuary was defiled and need to be cleansed that is the point, but that that the new system of things that involved the use of the heavenly sanctuary had to be put into service or enacted, and blood is what enacts or puts something into the service of God. The old covenant was ratified or put into service with animal blood, but the new covenant was enacted by the blood of Christ. This interpretation fits the context best.

The heavenly things themselves were cleansed (enacted, put into service) **with better sacrifices.**[69] In Hebrews, "heavenly" is akin to what is messianic and eschatological. Understood in this way, the "heavenly things" refers to the process by which true forgiveness of sins is accomplished in the new covenant. As Jesus serves as our high priest in heaven, it is not on account of the death of an animal that he provides forgiveness and intercedes for us. It is rather through a better sacrifice, namely his own death, given through the eternal Spirit (v 14), that the priestly work of Jesus on our behalf is performed. Recall that **better** is akin to "new" and "perfect," and is a characteristics of the messianic order inaugurated

[67] Thompson, "Hebrews 9 and Hellenistic Concepts of Sacrifice," 572.

[68] Ellingworth, *Epistle to the Hebrews*, 477.

[69] The plural "sacrifices" may be understood as an instance of grammatical attraction, agreeing with the plural "these" (Lane, *Hebrews 9–13*, 247), or as a plural denoting a category, "a better kind of sacrifice" (Moffatt, *Epistle to the Hebrews*, 132).

by the work of Jesus. The new covenant is better (7.22; 8.6) because it operates on a greater (heavenly) level (9.11), has a better priest (because he lives forever, 7.24), provides a better hope (7.19), is enacted on better promises (8.6), and involves a better sacrifice (9.23), in a better sanctuary, with better blood (12.24), and with better results (9.14).

9.24 For Christ did not enter into a sanctuary made with hands, which is an antitype of the true one, but into heaven itself, now to appear in the presence of God for us.

The **sanctuary** (Greek plural *hagia*) is our author's regular way of referring to the Most Holy Place. In this context it refers to the actual heavenly presence of God, the true Most Holy Place. It is the same place as "the greater and more perfect tabernacle" in verse 11, which is a symbolic way of referring to heaven (God's right hand, Psa 110.1). Christ's work for God's new Israel was not accomplished in some earthly model **made with** human **hands** (see comments on 9.11), but in a better place that can truly bear the designation "the Most Holy Place," **heaven itself**. There is nothing in this context to suggest that the word **heaven** is being used to refer to anything other than the abode of God beyond this world. Jesus went to heaven at his ascension, at which point he became both king and priest in fulfillment of Psalm 110.1 and 4.

The earthly tabernacle (described in vv 2ff) was an **antitype,** a "copy" or something that corresponds to,[70] or visibly resembles or represents,[71] something else. The type is the real thing (here, the true, heavenly sanctuary), and the tabernacle was the inferior copy, the antitype. The author of Hebrews was not explicitly laying out a fully developed typological presentation here. He simply meant that the earthly tabernacle prescribed in the Law of Moses was a visible representation of heavenly realities. Moreover, the point is not that there is a literal tabernacle in heaven corresponding to the earthly one. In verses 1–5 our author mentioned the details of the tabernacle briefly to turn to the significance of the procedure that was carried out in it. The greater point throughout the discussion is that there is a heavenly *process* by which God has forgiven our sins, and the rites performed in the old, earthly tabernacle prefigured that heavenly, spiritual work of Christ that would be accomplished in the new covenant.

[70] BDAG 90.

[71] Lee, "Words Denoting 'Pattern' in the New Testament," 171.

In heaven itself Jesus now appears **in the presence of God**, ministering as high priest on our behalf (**for us**). Our author has explained the death of Jesus in terms of its OT antecedent the tabernacle in the effort to encourage his readers not to abandon Christ. If Christ is presently at God's right hand as our advocate, then it is clear that he wants us to succeed and to overcome, that he is willing and eager to help us (4.16) until we join him in the end. The NT does not depict God or Christ as detached and unconcerned in connection with our salvation. God has always wanted us to be with him, and so has Jesus, and even now our Lord stands in heaven interceding on our behalf. These truths were meant to encourage the readers to hold fast to their commitment (4.14), and they serve the same purpose for us today.

9.25 Nor is it necessary that he should offer himself many times, like the high priest enters into the sanctuary every year with foreign blood.

As we have noted before (see comments on 1.1), in the ancient way of thinking a thing that was done repeatedly was considered imperfect because it was never finished. The fact that the sacrifices of the old covenant had to be offered repeatedly (**many times**) should have been an obvious indicator that those sacrifices lacked the efficacy to deal effectively with the problem of sin. The present tense **enters** emphasizes the ongoing nature of those old sacrifices in their time and does not necessarily imply that those sacrifices were still being offered when the author wrote this letter.[72] **Every year**, that is, year after year, the high priest had to perform the ritual of the Day of Atonement. A similar point was made in 7.23, where it was noted that the high priests themselves had to be replaced often because they died. The old system required a repetition of both personnel and procedure, indicating the weakness and ineffectiveness of both. The fact that the high priest took **foreign blood** (that is, the blood of animals) into the tabernacle on the Day of Atonement has already been noted in verse 12. It is mentioned here again to emphasize the inferior nature of that blood, which further highlights the inferior nature of the ritual that used it. The point of the verse, however, is that none of this describes Jesus and his sacrificial death. His death suffices once and for all.

---

[72] Ellingworth, *Epistle to the Hebrews*, 482.

9.26 Otherwise it would have been necessary for him to suffer many times since the foundation of the world; but now once, at the completion of the ages, he has appeared to remove sin by the sacrifice of himself.

Although the earthly tabernacle and its pinnacle procedure on the Day of Atonement was a model, figure, or representation of the work of Christ, the latter far excels the former in its nature and quality. As a figure (v 9) the tabernacle and its ritual of atonement conveyed some, but not all, aspects of the work of Christ, and it surely would be incorrect to think that the old and new systems are alike in every regard. The following table points out the similarities and differences:

Common Features	**Old**	**New**
high priests	replaced because of death (7.23)	one high priest who lives eternally (7.24)
the holy place	earthly tabernacle (9.1)	heaven itself (9.24)
blood (sacrificial death)	of animals, not human (9.25)	of Christ, human (9.12)
sacrifices	offered repeatedly, yearly (9.25)	offered once (9.26), eternal (9.12)
effect	outward cleansing (9.9, 13)	cleanses the conscience (9.14)

The old sacrifices had to be offered repeatedly, but Jesus' death suffices once and for all. If Jesus' **sacrifice of himself** was like the sacrifices of the old covenant, then Jesus would have to offer himself repeatedly, over and over again, **since the foundation of the world**. Clearly, however, this is not the case, and the one-time nature of Jesus' death indicates its superior, final quality. It achieves what the old sacrifices could not. It is fully efficacious (and in this sense, eternal) and thus does not need to be repeated.

The phrase **the completion of the ages** does not refer to the end of the world's existence at the day of judgment but refers instead to the time at which Jesus **appeared** on earth (implying his pre-existence) and fully consummated and executed God's plan in his death and resurrection.

It is another way of saying "the last days," which, as we have noted, is not a reference to time but means that these are the days in which God's plan has reached its goal and has been executed. We now live in the time when God's plan and goal (namely, for man to join him in his rest), which was prophesied for long ages, is realizing its completion. Christ **appeared** in the fullness of times (Gal 4.4) to bring the old system to a close and to establish the promised new and better system. In many ways the old system itself pointed to the new one and thus implicitly testified to its own replacement (*cf.* Rom 3.21). Jesus both fulfilled (Matt 5.17) and removed (Col 2.14) the old Mosaical system in his death and resurrection. His death was the ultimate **sacrifice** for human sins, and it fully suffices **to remove** the guilt of **sin** that plagues the conscience (9.14), something the old sacrifices could never do (9.9). Removing sin is what Jeremiah 31.34 said would happen in the new covenant (see on 10.3 below), and the covenant-enacting death of Jesus has also supplied the "blood" that makes the promised forgiveness possible and real. The word translated **remove** (Greek *athetēsis*) is the same word used in 7.18 to describe how the old Law was set aside. In Jesus' **sacrifice of himself** (v 12 "through his own blood") sin is effectively removed, thus fulfilling the promise of Jeremiah 31.34. This is not to say that no one sins again, much less that those who have been forgiven and redeemed by Christ's blood may never be guilty of sin again. Instead, it means that sin will never be the same kind of problem it was before Christ appeared and offered himself. Since Christ has died, a way of perfect forgiveness is now available and sin's power over man has been defeated.

9.27 And to the extent that it is reserved for men to die once and after this comes the judgment,

The statement has a proverbial quality to it.[73] This verse does two things: 1) It shows why the hypothetical suggestion of Jesus' suffering and dying many times (v 26) does not happen, and 2) it introduces the fact that the death of Christ, as important as it is, is not the end of God's plan. As for 1), the normal human experience is that a person dies only once. That is, normally, one death is enough. The sacrifice of Jesus fits this normal expectation. The multiple, repeated sacrificial deaths of the OT turn out to be the oddball when viewed in this way. As for 2), the sequence of things

[73] Grindheim, *Letter to the Hebrews*, 464.

revealed in the Bible is that the death of our fleshly body is followed by **judgment** at the last day (John 12.48) in which all will give account before the Lord (2 Cor. 5.10; Rom 2.16; Matt. 25.31ff). This is not to say that the judgment *immediately* follows death, for other passages reveal that the judgment for all will take place on an appointed day (*cf.* Acts 17.31; Matt 10.15; Rom 2.5; 2 Tim 4.8). It simply means that judgment is the next significant thing that happens after death.

9.28 so Christ, having been offered once in order to bear the sins of many, will appear a second time, apart from sin, for the salvation of those who eagerly await him.

The activity of Christ follows the same basic sequence of one experience of death followed by a judgment as laid out in verse 27.[74] In accordance with the usual pattern, he has died **once** (see v 26; that is, once and for all), not as the consequence of his own sin (for he himself was sinless, 4.15) but that he might **bear the sins of many** others (the sins of the world). The language is drawn from Isaiah 53.12, which is also echoed in 1 Peter 2.24 and Romans 5.15, where we also see that **the many** in fact refers to everyone (*cf.* Heb 2.9). In his death Jesus was taking upon himself the punishment that was due to others. He is both the sacrificial victim from which atoning blood came, and the high priest who enters into God's presence in the Most Holy Place to offer it to God as an atonement for us.

After his death, the next major thing Jesus will accomplish will be his return to judge the world. He will not return to die for sins again, for his death is fully sufficient and does not need to be repeated (v 26). Thus, our author says that his return will be **apart from sin**, that is, not for the purpose of dying to provide forgiveness for sin (RSV "not to deal with sin"). Instead, he will come **for** the purpose of **salvation**, to raise the dead and bring the faithful to glory in heaven (1 Thes 4.13–18; Heb 12.22–24) where the fullest measure of salvation will be experienced.

We may detect here a continued dependence on the OT imagery of the tabernacle. The high priest went into the presence of God with blood and, after presenting the blood for atonement, came back out of the tabernacle to be seen by the people (*cf.* Lev 16.17). In the same way Jesus has gone to heaven itself, into the actual presence of God, to offer his own blood for

[74] Grindheim, *Letter to the Hebrews*, 464.

our sins, and we now await his return, where he will be seen by all, and at which the fullest benefits of his heavenly work will be enjoyed.[75]

To those who have joined themselves to Christ and have faithfully followed him, the coming of the Lord in judgment is not something to be feared but something for which we **eagerly await** (Rom 8.23, 25; 1 Cor 1.7; Phil 3.20). The term denotes an enthusiastic anticipation. At this point our author wished to encourage his readers with the positive prospects which are before the faithful. He will discuss the negative prospects for the unfaithful in 10.26–39.

[75] Lane, *Hebrews 9–13*, 250; Hagner, *Hebrews*, 149–50; Bruce, *Epistle to the Hebrews*, 223–24.

HEBREWS 10

10.1 For the Law (having a shadow of the coming good things and not the image itself of those things) can never, by means of the same yearly sacrifices which they offered continually, perfect those who draw near.

Using a familiar Platonic metaphor,[1] the author describes the old Levitical system of the law of Moses as the **shadow**, but the new system in Christ is the reality (**the image itself**) behind it. Some have suggested that **the image** is Christ himself, based on 2 Corinthians 4.4 and Colossians 1.15, but the author of Hebrews, in this context, was thinking of the sacrifice of Christ and its effect. A shadow represents the form of the object that casts it but lacks the substance. Likewise, the approach to God through the ritual of the tabernacle expressed the form of the true approach to God (an approach that involved a mediator who went into the presence of God with atoning blood), but it remained for the heavenly order of things to accomplish perfect forgiveness. The forgiveness that was obtained under the old system was itself a shadow of the forgiveness to be offered in Christ. While the idea that the Law was just a shadow of something else that is better sounds perfectly correct to Christians today, we must try to be sensitive to how radical that idea must have sounded to Jews of the first century. Goppelt put it well when he said "It would scarcely have been possible for Judaism in the time of the NT to consider the biblical history of the past as the inferior pattern of something great in the present. On the contrary, they considered the present to be wretched in every respect and looked to the past as having been much brighter."[2] This was especially true when it was claimed that the better thing was the religion centered around the shamefully crucified Jesus.

---

[1] See on 8.5.

[2] Leonhard Goppelt, *Typos: The Typological Interpretation of the Old Testament in the New*, trans. Donald H. Madvig (Grand Rapids: Eerdmans, 1982), 57.

While the old Levitical system was still in place, the **good things** of the messianic age were still **coming**. Accordingly, those who **drew near** to God through those **sacrifices** were not made **perfect** (complete), because the sacrifices of that system did not cleanse the conscience (9.9f). The author had the sacrifices of the Day of Atonement specifically in mind here. An obvious indicator of the incomplete and weak nature of those sacrifices was the fact that they had to be repeated **yearly** and **continually** (see 9.25), and this particular feature of the old system will be in view through verse 10. Recall, for the author of Hebrews, repetition is an indicator of ineffectiveness and imperfection. The word **never** is emphatic. Not even when they were done correctly and sincerely could those old sacrifices provide the kind of cleansing that was truly needed.

10.2 For then would they not have ceased to be offered, because the worshippers would no longer have a consciousness of sins once they had been cleansed?

Our author now poses a rhetorical question[3] in the attempt to persuade his readers of the validity of the assertion of verse 1. The construction in the Greek poses a question which expects a positive answer. The question shows that the contrary position (*i.e.*, that the Levitical system indeed perfected those who worshiped under it) cannot possibly be correct. If the sacrifices under the old covenant were truly effective to deal conclusively with the problem of human sin, then why did they have to be offered over and over again? If they were the solution to the guilt of sin, **would they not have** been offered only once and then have **ceased**? Yet the law itself demanded that those sacrifices be offered year by year, and so the law itself was proclaiming that its own sacrifices were imperfect. Their repetitive character indicated their weakness. Furthermore, if those sacrifices were truly the answer to the problem of sin, then the consciences of those **worshippers** would have been cleared of guilt **once** and for all. Yet, as noted in 9.9f and 7.19, such was not the case.

10.3 But in those sacrifices there was a yearly remembrance of sins.

---

[3] There were no punctuation marks in written ancient Greek, so the difference between a statement and a question is one of context (and sometimes word order). This verse is best read as a rhetorical question. See Philip Church, "The Punctuation of Hebrews 10:2 and Its Significance for the Date of Hebrews," *TynBul* 71 (2020): 281–92.

The old system of sacrifices did not clear the conscience. In fact, it had just the opposite effect: it kept an awareness of sins ever before the people.[4] How did the author come to this conclusion? The answer is that it is the clear implication of Jeremiah 31.34 ("their sin I will remember no more"), and in particular the words "no more." If someone says, "I do not ride a motorcycle anymore," the clear implication is that they used to do so. Therefore, when God said, "I will remember their sins no more," it clearly implied that he had been remembering them, that the Day of Atonement **sacrifices** had not "erased" them. Every year, especially in the ritual of the Day of Atonement, the people of Israel were caused to remember that they needed to be made truly right with God. That day was a day characterized by the trappings of mourning for sin (fasting and confession, Lev 23.26ff; 16.2ff), not the joy of forgiveness. This stands in stark contrast to the promise of God concerning the new covenant, in which he said, "I will remember their sins no more" (Jer 31.34; see Heb 10.15–18).

We must be careful not to make the author of Hebrews say more than he actually says. He does not say that no one was ever forgiven of anything under the Law, nor does he say that the old Law only dealt with "ceremonial" infractions, or that "sin" was somehow accumulating over the years like a yearly credit advance that was never being paid. His point instead is that the Law's mechanism for dealing with sin was inadequate. Forgiveness was given by the grace of God according to his promises in the Law itself (see comments on v 4 below), but there was a real sense in which the debt was never truly paid, so the sense of guilt remained. Moreover, the fact that the national ritual was done every year served to remind everyone that the issue of their sin was still very much a problem.

10.4 For it is impossible for the blood of bulls and of goats to take away sins.

In this context, to **take away sins** (*cf.* 9.26) is to deal properly, adequately, and finally with them, and thus to cleanse the conscience (9.13f) and make the worshipper whole. Why could animal **blood** not take away sins? The first answer is: because the animals had not done the sinning. How could the death of a dumb animal (**bulls and goats**[5]) suffice to atone

[4] *Cf.* Paul's statement of the same fact in Gal 3.10; Rom 3.20: the Law engendered an ongoing awareness of sin's curse.

[5] An allusion to Isa 1.11, expressing the abuses of the temple and its sacrifices in Isa-

for the guilt of a rational human being? Technically, it could not. There was no intrinsic connection between the sinner and the sacrifice. God's penalty for sin is death, and the sinner, not some animal put in his place, must die to pay for his sins (Ezek 18.4). Human blood was required to atone for human sin. This verse further explains why the assertion made in verse 1 is true. However, it is also **impossible** for animal blood to take away sins because sin is a matter of the human heart. The problem with sin is that it is not external to us, but it is something that comes from a defiled heart (Matt 15.18f) and a perverted will. That is, it is a moral issue and not a matter of ritual.[6] No animal sacrifice can fix such a problem.

We should note that although there is no inherent connection between the death of an animal and any forgiveness from God, God through his grace did indeed grant forgiveness through the animal sacrifices of the old Law.[7] But, as our author has pointed out in 9.9f, this forgiveness did not console the conscience because what was offered in those animal sacrifices was only a figure or shadow of the true, perfect means of forgiveness that would come in the new covenant. What was needed was a sacrifice that met the nature of the offense, and this the Law of Moses did not provide. The remedy came in the death of Jesus (9.15). Perhaps this illustration may help: suppose someone owed you $10,000, but they were unable to pay it. Then out of pure kindness you say to them "I will accept $10,000 in Monopoly[8] money for the payment of your debt." They give you the "money," with both of you knowing fully that it is not what was really needed to pay the debt. In a real sense, the debt did not get paid; you only accepted an inferior repayment out of kindness. The repayment had some of the characteristics of what was required (made of paper, had value printed on it, *etc.*), but everyone knows it was nowhere near sufficient. Although the debtor no longer owes you anything (because of your gracious offer), he still feels badly because you actually suffered loss in the deal, but there is nothing he can do about it. Then, one day, someone else comes along and pays you $10,000 in real money for that other person's debt. The debt is then really ("perfectly") paid and the debtor can

---

iah's day, but also possibly summarizing the Day of Atonement ritual as well. See Justin Harrison Duff, "The Blood of Goats and Calves … and Bulls? An Allusion to Isaiah 1:11 LXX in Hebrews 10:4," *JBL* 137 (2018): 765–83.

[6] Johnson, *Hebrews*, 250.

[7] See Lev 4.20, 26, 31, 35; 5.10, 13, 16, 18; 6.7; 19.22; Num 15.25f, 28; Deut 21.8.

[8] *I.e.*, the "play" money used in the famous Parker Brothers board game.

rest assured that you no longer suffer loss. In this illustration the debtor is the sinner, the Monopoly money is the animal sacrifices of the old covenant, and the payment of the real $10,000 is the death of Jesus. Just as Monopoly money cannot pay a debt (even if forgiveness was graciously granted), so the blood of animals cannot atone for sin.

10.5 Therefore when he comes into the world he says, "You did not want sacrifice and offering, but you prepared a body for me."

As he has done before, the author takes his readers to the words of the Scriptures to show that his remarks about the insufficiency of the old covenant sacrifices are rooted in the divine writ itself, but also to show that Scripture pointed to a sacrifice that would be effective for sins (in contrast to the animal sacrifices, v 4). He goes to the messianic Psalm 40 to show how the death of Jesus provides what the Law of Moses lacked. When Jesus came **into the world**, that is, when he took on human form and lived on this earth, he fulfilled a pattern that had been noted in Psalm 40.6–8. The author of Hebrews saw the ultimate speaker of these words as the Messiah, Jesus. *Cf.* the passages quoted in chapter 1, where the author also detected the Messiah speaking in the OT. Our author here produces yet another example of the eschatological word of God which has come through the Son and that speaks to a greater and better reality than the Law.[9] We need not go looking through the gospels for a record of Jesus literally having said these words (no such story is to be found; yet Jesus spoke often about the fact that he had come, Matt 5.17; 9.13; 10.34; John 8.42; 10.10), but instead we should understand our author to mean that these words of the psalm express the attitude Jesus had in his heart and mind as he lived on earth. His incarnation was itself a living expression of the sentiment of the words from the psalm.

Psalm 40 is a type of psalm known in modern classification schemes as a lament, although the feature of trust and praise is prominent. In the laments of the OT Psalter, we meet a typical picture of the innocent righteous sufferer who called upon God for rescue from his distresses, usually his godless enemies. That picture is itself a type of Christ, who is himself the ultimate personification of the innocent, righteous sufferer. The fact that it is a psalm of David may have initially suggested its messi-

[9] Karen H. Jobes, "The Function of Paranomasia in Hebrews 10:5–7," *TrinJ* 13 (1997): 181–91, at 186.

anic application.[10] The author of Hebrews quotes verses 6–8 of the psalm, in which the psalmist declared his commitment to God in the midst of his distress. It becomes a revealing portrait of Jesus' commitment during his time on earth and encapsulates much of the argument the author of Hebrews has been advancing in this part of his letter. Johnson notes that there are at least four other elements in the psalm (besides the one the author of Hebrews quotes here) that resonate with the argument of Hebrews: 1) Psalm 40.10, where the psalmist speaks of God to the congregation of God's people (recall Heb 2.12a), 2) Psalm 40.3, where the psalmist sings a hymn to God (recall Heb 2.12b), 3) Psalm 40.2, where the psalmist has been delivered from destruction and established in safety (the exaltation of Jesus is a constant theme in Hebrews), and 4) Psalm 40.1 speaks of the psalmist's cry to God in his distress, which recalls Hebrews 5.7.[11] Furthermore, there is a connection between this psalm and the passage about the new covenant in Jeremiah 31. The Jeremiah passage spoke of God's people having his law written in their hearts in the messianic age (Jer 31.33, quoted in Heb 8.10). Foremost of all, then, the Messiah himself would be such a person, and that is exactly what the last line of Psalm 40.8 says of the Messiah: "your law is within my heart." The author of Hebrews stopped his quotation of Psalm 40 just short of these words, so he did not make the explicit connection between them and the verse in Jeremiah 31. However, the presence of those words in Psalm 40 may further explain why the author chose to cite the psalm.

You did not want sacrifice and offering, from Psalm 40.6, is not to be taken as an absolute statement, as if God never wanted them at all. The fact is that God was the one who ordered them. Nor was it meant to criticize the sacrifices. The statement is a kind of hyperbole to emphasize what God wanted even more, or most of all. If the animal sacrifices were not what God primarily "wanted," it implies their insufficiency to deal with the problem of sin, that more was needed. *Cf.* Psalm 51.16f. Psalm 40.6 thus supports the contention of 10.1 that animal sacrifices were inadequate. God graciously accepted inferior sacrifices for the sins of his people in the first covenant, but they were not what was truly needed or wanted in order for God to be absolutely just (see Rom 3.26). The shed-

[10] Peterson, *Hebrews*, 225. Paul alluded to it in Eph 5.2, using the language of the psalm to describe the death of Christ (Grindheim, *Letter to the Hebrews*, 477–78).

[11] Johnson, *Hebrews*, 251.

ding of human blood (which represented absolute dedication and commitment to God in one's body) was what was really needed. We must remember that a sacrifice in the OT was the giving of a life to God, partly as payment for the penalty of sin, and partly as a token expression of the dedication, faith, and loyalty of the offeror, and was meant as a pledge of continued commitment to God. The problem with them, however, is that the life of an animal was insufficient to pay the penalty and to express the dedication of a person. A human sacrifice with which the offeror could truly identify was needed for those things. On the various kinds of sacrifices mentioned here, see comments on verse 8 below.

The MT of Psalm 40.6 says rather strangely "you dug (or opened) ears for me" (the exact phrase appears nowhere else in the Bible). As the author of Hebrews quotes it, however, it reads **you prepared a body for me.** What did the original text mean, and how did "ears" become "body"?

One suggestion that can be dismissed quite readily is that there was some confusion between the words for ears and body, and that one was written for the other as the LXX was copied and transmitted. In Greek ears is *ōtia,*[12] and body is *sōma.* There is not enough similarity in the Greek letters to make a believable case that a scribe copying this passage wrote one word for the other, although this possibility is defended by some.[13] Besides, scribes in ancient times often produced manuscripts by writing down what someone was reading aloud, and the two words were not pronounced similarly enough to be confused. Briggs suggested that the Hebrew text read *'etsem* (another Hebrew word that can mean "body"), but the evidence for this is slim.[14] Several good LXX manuscripts read *sōma* (body) at this place in the psalms.[15] This complicates the matter, for it raises the question of whether the Hebrew text behind the LXX here had the Hebrew word for "body" and if that better attests to the original. However, the reading "ears" is the only one known in the manuscript traditions in the Hebrew.

---

[12] The normal Greek word for ear was *ous.* The word used in the LXX of Psa 40.6 is a diminutive form, *ōtion.* The diminutive came to be equivalent to *ous* in late Greek (BDAG 1107).

[13] Ellingworth, *Epistle to the Hebrews,* 500.

[14] Charles Augustus Briggs, *Messianic Prophecy* (New York: Charles Scribner's Sons, 1886), 328–29, fn 6.

[15] The uncial manuscripts Sinaiticus, Vaticanus, and Alexandrinus; the Göttingen LXX (Psa 39) reads *ōtia,* but the apparatus shows that scribes were challenged by this reading.

Upon the assumption that the original Hebrew said "ears," most scholars suggest that "you prepared a body for me" is the LXX translator's interpretive paraphrase[16] of "ears you have dug for me," based on the principle of the part (ears) standing for the whole (body).[17] Isaiah 50.4f can be adduced to show how such an interpretation can be defended. It says "...He awakens me morning by morning, he awakens my ear to listen as a disciple. The Lord God has opened my ear; and I was not disobedient nor did I turn back" (NASB). Similarly, Jeremiah 6.10 says "To whom shall I speak and give warning that they may hear? Behold, their ears are closed and they cannot listen. Behold, the word of the Lord has become a reproach to them; they have no delight in it." To have an open ear can be understood as a figurative way of denoting willingness, readiness, receptivity, and obedience. Thus, the RSV translates the Hebrew of Psalm 40.6 as "thou hast given me an open ear." This approach also fits well with the exhortation of Hebrews 3–4, based on Psalm 95's warning to hear, which means to obey and to faithfully follow God's leading.[18]

Those who hold to this explanation believe that the LXX paraphrase represents no substantial change in the meaning and that the text is highly reminiscent of Samuel's famous statement: "Has the Lord as much delight in burnt offerings and sacrifices as in obeying the voice of the Lord? Behold, to obey is better than sacrifice, to heed than the fat of rams" (1 Sam 15.22 NASB). In fact, there is a long tradition in the OT of prophetic criticism of the sacrifices.[19] "God desires not sacrifices but hearing ears, and consequently the submission of the person himself in willing obedience."[20] The prophets did not object to the sacrificial system *per se*, rather they objected to an attitude toward it that viewed sacrifice as some kind of "magic wand," an impenitent attitude that effectively disregarded the covenant obligations because, it was thought, all they had to do to be

---

[16] In defense of the LXX translator, all translation requires interpretation. The debate emerges not over the fact of interpretation in translation, but over the balance between literalness and understanding in translation.

[17] So also Cockerill. *Epistle to the Hebrews*, 436; S. Lewis Johnson, *The Old Testament in the New: An Argument for Biblical Inspiration* (Grand Rapids: Zondervan, 1980), 62.

[18] Also Duff, "The Blood of Goats and Calves," 782: "The appearance of Ps 39 LXX thus seems to resonate with Isaiah's critique of disobedient worship."

[19] See Psa 50.8–10; 51.16f; Isa 1.11–17; 66.2f; Jer 7.21–24; Hos 6.6; 14.2; Mic 6.6–8; Amos 5.22–24. *Cf.* also the allusion to Isa 11.1 in Heb 10.4 (above).

[20] K&D 5:302.

right with God was offer a sacrifice.[21] Psalm 40, however, is not just another such text, for the author of Hebrews notes that this text spoke of how the *Messiah* would supply what the Levitical sacrifices lacked.[22] The LXX, therefore, has apparently paraphrased this difficult text in order to communicate its sense, and the author of Hebrews saw in that sense a clear reference to Jesus. The point of the passage, from our author's Jesus-centered perspective on the OT, is that Jesus accomplishes (once and for all) the will of God in a way that the animal sacrifices of the old Law never could. Not even when the old sacrifices were performed with sincerity could they cleanse the conscience, because they were not what was needed (see comments on v 4).

Other explanations have been put forth for the change from "ears" to "body" in this text, but none seem to work as well. Among them we may mention Hagner's suggestion that the LXX translator understood here an allusion to the creation of Adam, and rendered the text accordingly.[23] Also unlikely is the suggestion that relates the pierced ears to the ritual for slaves in Exodus 21.5f. Jobes has put forward the idea that the author of Hebrews has carefully reworded the passage into order to achieve a phonetic assonance in the Greek which would have served as a verbal underlining of the passage for emphasis.[24] While we would not deny such talents to the author of Hebrews, his point is still about the *meaning* of Psalm 40.6–8.

If such rewording of a passage (changing "ears" to "body") bothers us, we should take four things into account. 1) The ancients were not as concerned about verbatim quotation as we might be today. In fact, in ancient times verbatim quotations of a source were the exception, not the rule. Instead, 2) the preferred literary practice was to reproduce the sense of what was said, which was done in this case.[25] 3) The Jew-

---

[21] See Artur Weiser, *The Psalms*, OTL (Philadelphia: Fortress, 1962), 338.

[22] Westcott, *Epistle to the Hebrews*, 309.

[23] Hagner, *Hebrews*, 154.

[24] Karen H. Jobes, "Rhetorical Achievement in the Hebrews 10 'Misquote' of Psalm 40," *Bib* 72 (1991): 387–96; *idem*, "The Function of Paranomasia in Hebrews 10:5–7." Her thesis involves the idea that the author of Hebrews is the source for the word "body" here, and that this then accounts for mss. of the LXX that contain this reading. But this seems to run counter to the evidence. See Jared Compton, "The Origin of soma in Heb 10:5, Another Look at a Recent Proposal," *TrinJ* 32 (2011): 19–29.

[25] And in many other NT examples (see Nicole, "New Testament Use of the Old Testament," 145). NT authors often "quoted" passages according to their sense, in a kind

ish method of exposition, called *midrash,* combined quotation and commentary to produce a kind of expanded citation that aimed to clarify the meaning and application of the Scriptural text to the hearers. The original recipients of Hebrews would have been very familiar with this technique and would not have thought the author of Hebrews was taking careless liberties with the text of the psalm (see Introduction). 4) The kind of alteration we see in going from the Hebrew to the Greek in this particular case is no worse than what is done in hundreds of similar cases in modern English translations. In this case the LXX and the author of Hebrews were simply practicing a well-known procedure in translation and interpretation.

When Jesus entered the world, he inhabited a human **body** (1 John 4.2; 2 John 7) which had been given to him by God for use in his service as a sacrifice (*cf.* Rom 12.1). In his obedience to God Jesus offered his own body on the cross as an offering for the sins of others (see Rom 8.3; 1 Pet 2.24; 3.18; 4.1; *cf.* John 6.51).[26] In so doing he was accomplishing what the animal sacrifices of the old Law never could, for now a human death was being offered for human sin. Jesus' death is the better sacrifice.

10.6 You were not pleased with burnt offerings and sacrifices for sin.

This continues the quotation from Psalm 40, verse 6c. It stands in simple parallelism with Psalm 40.6a ("you did not want sacrifice and offering"). The alternating lines from this part of the psalm stand in antithetical parallelism, and may be illustrated as:

A Sacrifice and meal offering you have not desired (Psa 40.6a),

  B My ears you have opened. (Psa 40.6b)

A' Burnt offering and sin offering you have not required. (Psa 40.6c)

  B' Then I said, "Behold, I come; In the scroll of the book it is written of me. (Psa 40.7)

---

of quotation-paraphrase, rather than reproduce a strict verbatim quotation (we do the same thing today in sermons). As long as the sense of the passage has not been changed, no violence has been done to the text. This method was common not only among Jewish exegetes (see Introduction) but was quite common in secular Hellenistic literature as well.

[26] The emphasis is on the sacrifice. The obedience makes the sacrifice. See Benjamin J. Ribbens, "The Sacrifice God Desired: Psalm 40:6–8 in Hebrews 10," *NTS* 67 (2021): 284–304.

The lines thus alternate between what is not, and what is, acceptable to God, as the *A* lines describe what is not desired and what is ineffective, the *B* lines present what is effective.

There is a slight alteration in the quotation from the Hebrew (and LXX). The following table lays out the differences:

text	wording
Hebrew (MT) text of Psa 40.6c	"You have not required" (NASB) "you did not ask for" (NET)
LXX	"you did not ask for"
Hebrews	"you were not pleased with"

The psalm says, "you have not asked," which is an acceptable translation of the Hebrew term (*ša'al*), which primarily means "request" or "beg," but can also mean "demand."[27] The Greek word used in the LXX here (*aiteō*) has a similar semantic range.[28] However, the author of Hebrews has substituted a different verb (*eudokeō*), **you were not pleased**. This is another example of how NT authors employed the technique of *midrash,* in which they interpreted as they quoted in order to draw out the point they wished to make from the quoted passage. Some modern scholars call this kind of interpretive alteration "implicit midrash."[29] This is quite common for the NT writers in general (other examples include 1 Pet 2.4–10 and Acts 4.11). The author has just made the point in 9.19–23 that the Law of Moses required sacrifices. However, even though God demanded those sacrifices, they were insufficient for the problem at hand. By changing the wording to **you were not pleased** our author brings out the true sense of the statement in the psalm and also harmonizes it with the fact that the sacrifices were indeed required by God. On the various kinds of sacrifices mentioned here, see comments on verse 8 below.

10.7 Then I said, "Behold, I have come (in the roll of the book it is written concerning me) to do your will, O God."

[27] KBL 4.1371–73.

[28] BDAG 30; LSJ 44.

[29] Ellis, "Biblical Interpretation in the New Testament Church," 703–706.

The psalmist here declares his commitment to do the will of God. He pictures himself as the very embodiment of the Law of God, so much that he can say (in a kind of hyperbole) that the obedience demanded in the Law is a description of himself, thus **in the roll** (scroll) **of the book it is written** about **me**. Our author saw that this statement ultimately reflected the attitude of the Messiah, Jesus.

The psalmist's assertion **I have come**[30] recalls the statement in verse 5 about Jesus as he came into the world. As with other passages he has already quoted, the author of Hebrews reads the OT Scriptures with Jesus in mind, for he is the key to understanding them (2 Cor 3.14; Luke 24.27). Jesus ultimately fulfills the psalm's picture of dedication to the accomplishment of God's will. In other words, the means to perfect forgiveness appeared when Jesus arrived in this world as a man, to offer his body as a sacrifice for sin according to the will of God.

It is not clear what "**scroll**" the original author of Psalm 40 was referring to. It could refer to the Law concerning kings, that the king had to have a heart directed toward God and the doing of his will (Deut 17.19f).[31] If this is correct, the psalm noted that the king (in this case, David) needed to do more than offer sacrifice to be right with God. Full, heartfelt obedience was required. In typical midrashic fashion, however, the words take on a messianic sense when read in light of Jesus. With Jesus in view, the statement **in the roll of the book it is written of me** takes on new meaning, that the words of Psalm 40 are to be regarded as referring to Jesus who would fulfill the **written**, recorded prophecies of the OT, specifically those such as Isaiah 53 and Jeremiah 31.

The chief purpose of the Messiah's coming into the world was **to do** the father's **will**, which was to offer himself as a sacrifice for the sins of the world.[32] As James Denny put it, the atonement explains the incarnation.[33] Jesus did not offer an animal sacrifice to God, but in complete submission and obedience, stemming from a heart and spirit that was completely devoted to God, he gave his own body on the cross (7.27; 914;

---

[30] Technically a present tense in the Greek, but this particular word (*hēkō*) is unusual in that it uses perfect tense endings. Its sense is perfective, "I have come and I am now here." BDAG 435; BDF §101.

[31] Peter C. Craigie, *Psalms 1–50*, 2nd ed., 315.

[32] Matt 20.28; John 6.51; 10.10; 12.27; 1 Tim 1.15; although this was not the only thing the incarnation accomplished.

[33] Cited in Bruce, *Epistle to the Hebrews*, 243.

cf. 1 Pet 2.24). This was the perfect demonstration of obedience to the will of God, the perfect expression of commitment and dedication that lay imperfectly behind the animal sacrifices of the OT.

10.8 When he says above, "You did not want sacrifices and offerings and burnt offerings and offerings for sin" (which are offered according to the Law),

Like a good bible student, the author of Hebrews now quotes again the specific part of the psalm he wants to emphasize (recall this same technique in the author's exposition of Psa 95 in Heb 4). This time, however, he rearranges the lines in order to combine the parallel lines of Psalm 40.6–7 and place them immediately next to each other (see the arrangement in comments on v 6). The immediate repetition achieved by placing the parallel lines together accomplishes two things: 1) It lumps the various kinds of sacrifices together as part of a single system, and therefore 2) the multiplicity of offerings makes the inadequacy of the sacrificial system of the old covenant all the more obvious.

By combining the parallel lines from Psalm 40.6 and 7, the author has produced a kind of catalog of OT sacrifices, although it certainly does not attempt to be systematic or comprehensive. **Sacrifices** renders the Greek word *thusia,* which is the generic word for sacrifice. It is the word normally used in the LXX for the corresponding generic word for sacrifice in Hebrew, *zebach.* **Offerings** translates the Greek word *prosphora,* which in turn renders the Hebrew term *minchah* in the psalm. *Minchah* in the Levitical texts usually denotes the grain offering. **Burnt offerings** were, in one sense, the "highest" kind of offering under the law, because of a unique feature. In most sacrificial procedures, only part (the most inward parts) of the animal was offered to God on the altar. The remaining parts were eaten by the priests or the family that brought the offering, depending upon the circumstance and the Levitical regulations. In the burnt offerings, however, no part of the animal was kept back; all of it was consumed on the altar and thus it was given wholly to God. When we remember that part of the ordinary procedure for offering an animal involved the worshiper laying his hands on the animal in order to identify the animal with himself (Lev 1.4; 3.2, 8, 13; 4.4; *etc.*), then the significance of the burnt offering becomes even clearer. A burnt offering symbolized the worshiper's complete dedication to God. The animal represented, or stood in the place of, the worshiper, and it was given wholly to God on the altar. **Offerings for sin** refers to the sacrifice known as the sin offering (Hebrew *hatta't*; see Lev 5), which was designated for inadvertent sins. This is the kind of offering that was presented on the Day of Atonement.

The words **which are offered according to the Law** are an explanatory comment, again to emphasize that the Hebrew Scriptures themselves spoke of the inadequacy of the Levitical sacrificial system. He wanted to make sure his readers saw that the sacrifices mentioned in the psalm, which the psalm says God did not desire, were the very sacrifices that were prescribed in the Law of Moses. By bringing the various sacrifices listed in Psalm 40 together in this way the author was allowing Scripture to make his point that the Levitical sacrifices were insufficient for the problem of sin. If his readers wanted to think otherwise, they would have to argue with Psalm 40, and hence with God.

10.9 and then he said, "Behold, I have come to do your will, O God," he takes away the first, in order to establish the second.

The last line of the passage quoted in verses 5–7 above is now presented again, for rhetorical emphasis. The author of Hebrews often ends his quotation of an OT passage at the point he thinks is the most important. Accordingly, the last line quoted is the most significant part of the quotation for the author's purposes here. However, the next line in the psalm, "Your law is within my heart," could quite easily be understood of Jesus as well, for he was the perfect embodiment of the spirit that God desired to dwell in all those in the new covenant ("I will put my law within them, and on their heart I will write it," Jer 31.33).

The author added an explanatory comment to the line from the psalm in order to draw out what was implicit in the words he quoted. The alternating lines in the psalm, describing what God did not want and what truly sufficed, are now interpreted as describing the old and new covenants respectively. In other words, the psalm was the perfect companion text to Jeremiah 31 as it spelled out exactly what was inadequate with the old covenant, and why the new covenant would be so much better. The combination of the terms **first** and **second** brings us back to the same words which introduced the quotation from Jeremiah concerning the new covenant (Heb 8.7ff), where they refer to "first covenant" and "second covenant." The terms are akin to "old" and "earthly" on the one hand, and "new" and "heavenly" or "messianic" on the other hand. When Jesus entered the world in human form (v 5) **to do** the **will** of **God**, which he accomplished on the cross, he provided that perfect sacrifice which definitively atoned for sins and thus fulfilled the pattern of Psalm 40.6–8. The **second**, or new, covenant about which Jeremiah spoke (see 8.7) was thus established "in these last days" (the messianic time, 1.2) with Jesus' death (9.16f), having been enacted with a better sacrifice (9.23). With the accomplishment of the perfect sacrifice for sin, the **first** covenant and its Levitical animal sacrifices became "old" (8.13), it was no longer needed and was thus taken away. To put that differently, once the image itself had arrived, we did not need to look at the shadow (8.5; 10.1). This becomes a central consideration in the rest of this section of the sermon (through v 18).

10.10 By which will we are sanctified through the offering of the body of Jesus Christ once and for all.

This is a compact statement that summarizes the point the author has drawn from Psalm 40.6–8, and indeed summarizes the gospel message. It was God's **will**, plan (Acts 2.23), or purpose (John 12.27; Acts 4.28; Eph 3.11; 2 Tim 1.9; 1 Pet 4.1) that fellowship with himself ("rest") should be made available for all who wanted it. Since entering the presence of God is the goal envisioned in Hebrews, sanctification is absolutely necessary for anyone who would wish to stand there (see 12.14). The **offering** of the human **body of Jesus**, in fulfillment of Psalm 40, was a sacrifice that **sanctifies** his followers and therefore enables them to stand in God's presence—if they endure in faith.[34] His death was sufficient to cleanse the defilement of human sins **once** and **for all** (7.27; 9.12, 26, 28) and thus is infinitely greater in its power than the animal sacrifices of the old covenant, which were only pale illustrations of the sacrifice of Christ that was

[34] Debates over whether Jesus' high priestly work is done exclusively in heaven, or whether it included his earthly life, seem (in my opinion) to propose a dichotomy that does not exist in Hebrews. All of Christ's work was priestly. According to the Day of Atonement paradigm operative in Hebrews, the earthly death of Jesus was necessary for him to "have something to offer" (8.3) as he entered the heavenly sanctuary. "It is ... artificial to bracket off the resurrection or ascension from the death of Christ (or, for that matter, from his lifelong obedience). The work of Christ is a unified whole." Crowe, "Son and Priest, Then and Now," 31. Similarly, "... the author understood already Jesus' taking human flesh as a high priestly act, taking on the body prepared for him (10, 5–6)." William Loader, "Revisiting High Priesthood Christology in Hebrews," 237.

to come. The result is that, because of what Jesus has done, man who was once defiled by sin can now be cleansed and forgiven, and enjoy a **sanctified**, or holy, status before God. Sanctification is the act by which something is made clean and holy to God, and thus dedicated for his use exclusively. The gospel does both concurrently (Acts 26.18; 1 Cor 6.11; Eph 5.26; 2 Thes 2.13). However, sanctification is also something in which we may grow, and we are ever to perfect our sanctification by making ourselves more holy each day (1 Thes 4.3–7; 5.23).

10.11 And, on the one hand, every priest stands daily ministering and offering the same sacrifices many times, which are never able to take away sins.

Verses 11–18 are a summary, and tie together the main points raised in the foregoing discussion. This chart shows the elements of the summary:

Hebrews 10:	Summarizes:
11 repeated sacrifices, ineffective	Heb 9.6, 25; 10.1
12 one sacrifice, effective, "sat down"	Heb 9.26; 10.1, 4; Psa 110.1 (Heb 1.3, 13)
13 waiting for his reign to be complete	Psa 110.1; Heb 2.8
14 one offering has perfected God's people	Heb 9.9, 13–14; 10.1
15–17 quotation	Heb 8.8–12 (quoting Jer 31.31–34)
18 true forgiveness means no more sacrifices need to be offered	Heb 7.27; 9.12, 25–28; 10.2, 10

The finality of Jesus' sacrifice is what did away with the need for the sacrifices of the old Law (and thus also first covenant, v 9). It was therefore important to the author's point to establish beyond question this vital characteristic of Jesus' death. He has already drawn from Psalm 40 the fact that the old sacrifices were insufficient. There is, however, another text that speaks to the greater sacrificial activity of Jesus, and that is Psalm 110.1, which was fulfilled by Jesus after he died on the cross as an offering for sin, when God exalted him to heaven. The fact that Jesus died and then was exalted to heaven, in fulfillment of the messianic Psalm 110.1, implies something very important about the nature of Jesus' death. Our author will now draw out that implication in verses 11–14. In order to do this, he must first set the work of Jesus in contrast to the work of the Aaronic priests, which he does in this present verse.

The word **stands** is a term used in the OT of the priestly service (Deut 10.8; 17.12; 18.7; 1 Kngs 8.11) and in this context, together with the present participles **ministering** and **offering**, emphasizes the continuous, repetitive nature of their work. The idea is that their standing means that they are occupied with their work. Furthermore, the one-time nature of Jesus' sacrificial death creates a stark contrast to the sacrificial deaths of thousands of animals under the old covenant, which deaths did nothing to cleanse the conscience and hence could not truly **take away sins** because they were forensically inadequate. See verses 1–4 above, and 7.27. Because those old sacrifices could not take away the guilt of sin from the conscience, the priests who offered them spent their lives presenting those **same sacrifices** over and over again (**many times**; over the course of their ministries). The repetition of the old sacrifices was a clear indicator of their inability to provide the definitive solution to the problem of human sin.

10.12 But on the other hand he,[35] after having offered one sacrifice for sins for all time, sat down at the right hand of God,

The antecedent of the pronoun **he** is clearly Jesus (v 10), whose single sacrificial act stands in stark contrast to the repetitive offerings of the Levitical priests. Jesus, out of complete dedication and obedience to the will of God (v 9), **offered** his human body on the cross as the definitive, sufficient **sacrifice for sins**, effective **for all time** (forever). The aorist participle **offered** is in contrast to the present participle of the same word in v 11; what the priests *were doing* (continuously) Jesus *did* (once).[36] This is

[35] Literally "this one," a Greek demonstrative pronoun being used as a personal pronoun. This usage marks what is thematic in the context. See comments on 3.3.

[36] The aorist tense does not itself denote a "once for all action," although it can communicate this sense according to context. More accurately, the aorist participle

further emphasized by the singular **sacrifice** of Jesus, in contrast to the many sacrifices of the old system (v 11). Since his sacrifice suffices eternally,[37] he does not need to offer himself ever again (7.27).

The words **sat down on the right hand of God** are drawn from Psalm 110.1, which were first cited in Hebrews 1.3 where the author previewed the message of the sermon as he described Jesus, the Son, who, "once he had made cleansing for sins, sat down at the right hand of the majesty on high," a position never afforded to any angel (1.13). This psalm was also quoted in 8.1 to summarize the discussion about the Melchizedekian priesthood of Jesus, as the author said, "Now the main point in what has been said is this: we have such a high priest, who has taken his seat at the right hand of the throne of the majesty in the heavens." The words from the psalm not only proclaim the greater status of Jesus, but there is an emphasis here on "sat down" in contrast to the priests who "stand." The fact that Jesus has **sat down** means that his sacrificial work is done;[38] he does not need to "stand" in order to offer further sacrifice for sin because his one sacrifice suffices for all time (*cf.* 12.2). Also, in contrast to the Levitical priests who were constantly occupied on earth with the repetition of the animal sacrifices of the Law, Jesus has ascended to heaven to reign and to serve in the greatest position of honor possible, **the right hand of God**. Jesus is thus a greater kind of priest than the Levitical ones, for in addition to the superior nature of his offering there is his additional status as divine monarch. The significance of Jesus' position at God's right hand was discussed in chapter 1, and the fact that he is a regal priest like Melchizedek was discussed in chapter 7. However, the author of Hebrews has now quoted Psalm 110.1 in this context not to show the greater nature of Jesus' priesthood, but to show the all-sufficient nature of Jesus' sacrificial death (in the contrast between "stands" and "sat down"). Psalm 110.1 shows that after Jesus made his offering to God, he did not return to offer himself again (*cf.* 9.25). Because his offering sufficed once for all, he went instead to sit at God's right hand.

---

denotes perfective verbal aspect (Constantine R. Campbell, *Verbal Aspect and Non-Indicative Verbs: Further Soundings in the Greek New Testament*, Studies in Biblical Greek 15 (New York: Peter Lang 2008), 17).

[37] The phrase "forever" (a prepositional phrase in the Greek text) could modify either "offered" or "sat." Either would make a true statement. The major modern English versions uniformly connect it with "offered."

[38] Leon Morris, *The Cross in the New Testament* (Grand Rapids: Eerdmans, 1965) 282: "The posture of sitting is that of rest. It indicates that one's work is complete."

10.13 waiting from now on until his enemies are placed as a footstool for his feet.

This line also paraphrases from Psalm 110.1 and our author asserts that Jesus is fulfilling this part of the psalm as well. **Waiting** can denote "expecting," with a sense of eagerness (*cf.* the same word in 11.10). Since his exaltation to heaven, Jesus has been waiting until the time when all **his enemies** will become **a footstool for his feet**, which is an ancient image of conquest (*cf.* Josh 10.24f). That Jesus is waiting for this means that this particular element of the prophecy has not yet been completely fulfilled (see Heb 2.8); it will be fulfilled when Jesus comes again (9.28; see 1 Cor 15.24ff). Furthermore, to say that Jesus is waiting does not mean that Jesus is wholly passive in his reign, for he is also depicted as active in history, judging and defeating his enemies (as we see in the book of Revelation), particularly through the gospel (2 Cor 10.3–5; Rom 1.5), and protecting his people. Jesus is ever expanding his reign and will continue to do so until no enemies are left. *Cf.* Phil 2.9f; 1 Cor 15.25f. Nothing like this could be said of any Levitical priest, and this further serves to highlight the greater priesthood of Jesus.

10.14 For with one offering he has perfected forever those who are sanctified.

The author now plainly brings out for his readers the implication of Psalm 110.1 in connection with the death of Jesus, to make sure it does not escape them. What the Law could never do with its many animal sacrifices (9.9; 10.1), Jesus did with his **one** sacrifice (**offering**) of himself: namely, he has perfected God's sanctified worshippers in their consciences. When Psalm 110.1 said that the Messiah would sit in divine reign over all things, it thereby implied that he would *not* be occupied with repeated sacrifices. In other words, the psalm effectively says that after Jesus died he ceased (*cf.* v 2) to make any further sacrifice for sin, for none was necessary. Psalm 110.1, then, is further indication of the fact that Jesus' sacrifice was sufficient **to perfect forever those who are sanctified** by it. Of course, appropriation of the benefits of that sacrifice does not automatically extend to all men but comes by faithful obedience to his gospel (Acts 26.18). On **sanctified**, see comments on verse 10 above. If the death of Jesus suffices forever (as Psa 110.1 indicates), then the old Levitical system of animal sacrifices is no longer needed and has been done away (v 9).

Again, the word **perfect** in Hebrews does not denote sinlessness, but a wholeness, a condition in which no necessary thing is lacking. The old system was imperfect because it allowed only a limited access to God, and it lacked an adequate way to atone for sin and thus lacked the ability to cleanse the sinner's conscience. What Jesus has done, however, is able to perfect us in the sense that it provides true atonement and complete cleansing, and it brings us into the very presence of God in a kind of fellowship that was simply unknown in the OT.

10.15–17 And the Holy Spirit also testifies to us, for after having said "This is the covenant that I will make with them after those days, says the Lord, I will put my laws on their hearts, and I will inscribe them on their mind," he then says, "and I will not remember their sins and lawless deeds anymore."

As he brings his summary to a close, our author now quotes Jeremiah 31.33f again, in a condensed version, for the benefit of his audience (he had quoted it before at length in 8.8–12). Here, however, the quotation is prefaced by noting that the Holy Spirit is testifying in it. In what sense does **the Holy Spirit** testify to us? However we answer this question, it should be clear from the text that this testimony is delivered by means of the words of Scripture. There is no hint of any kind of miraculous testifying through personal visions, personal insight, *etc.* The Scripture came through the Holy Spirit who moved Jeremiah to speak these words (2 Pet 1.21). When the Spirit spoke, it was to communicate what **the Lord says**. However, a closer look at the introduction to the OT quotations in Hebrews suggests that this particular way of introducing a quotation is the author's way of emphasizing that the quoted text speaks directly to the people of the messianic age.[39] Thus the emphasis lies in the fact that in this text the Holy Spirit testifies **to us**, the people of the Messiah. This coincides exactly with the author's understanding that the OT is ultimately about Jesus and the situation created as a result of his work. With this perspective, the text is not just a prophecy, but a living word that continues to speak to God's people today; what was formerly understood as a promise can now be read as a description of the present situation in Jesus. The author of Hebrews clearly believed that the Holy Spirit communicated the truths concerning the new cov-

[39] Emmrich, "*Pneuma* in Hebrews: Prophet and Interpreter." See comments on 3.7.

enant (*cf.* 3.7; 9.8). This is an important consideration in the exhortation that follows in vv 19ff below (see v 29).

A quick glance at the quotation from Jeremiah 31 in Hebrews 8 shows that the quotation of that same text here does not follow the earlier one word for word. It is yet another example of how the NT authors quoted Scripture with a view to its meaning first, and to verbatim reproduction second. The following table summarizes the differences (in italics):

Jer 31.33f MT (NASB)	Heb 8.10, 12	Heb 10.16–17
But this is the covenant which I will make with the house of Israel	This is the covenant which I will make with *the house of Israel*	This is the covenant which I will make with *them*
I will put my law within them	I will put my laws *into their mind*	I will put my laws *on their hearts*
and on their heart I will write it	and I will inscribe them on their *hearts*	and I will inscribe them on their *mind*
and their sin	and their sins	and their sins and their lawless deeds
I will remember no more	I will remember no more	I will remember no more

Replacing "house of Israel" with "them," switching the places of the words "mind" and "hearts," inserting the term "lawless deeds," and replacing one kind of strong negative statement with another does nothing to change the sense or meaning of the passage.

The author divided the quotation into two parts, separated by **and then he says**, to show two things about which the Spirit testifies. He laid two parts of the larger text in juxtaposition to each other so his hearers / readers could see the connection. In the first part of the quotation the Spirit speaks of the internal nature of the relationship with God that will avail in the new covenant. This internalization of God's law envisioned in the prophecy corresponds to the cleansing of the conscience that has been accomplished through the sacrificial blood of Christ (9.14). With the conscience thus cleansed, God's law can take its place in the **minds** and **hearts** of God's people. Second, the Spirit testifies that in the new covenant God would **not remember**[40] the **sins and lawless deeds** of his people **anymore**. Our author has already established in verse 3 that in the Levitical sacrifices there was a remembrance of sins every year. Even though God graciously forgave his people's sins, the inadequate nature of that entire system for dealing with those sins meant that, in a real sense, the debt still existed. That fact was brought to mind every year on the Day of Atonement. So, when God said through Jeremiah that he would remember his people's sins no more (Jer 31.34), he therefore meant that sin would be dealt with perfectly in the new covenant, which was accomplished in the sacrificial death of Jesus (9.16ff). In the new covenant, a perfect sacrifice for sins has been offered. Since our sins have been dealt with in a truly satisfying way, they are not counted against us anymore. The debt is completely erased, divine justice has been met, and now full "rest" with God is possible. Consequently, the old system in which sins were remembered would serve no purpose anymore and would be done away.

10.18 And where there is forgiveness of these things, there is no longer any offering for sin.

Where a final, sufficient solution has been achieved with reference to the problem of sin, then there is no more need for further atoning sacrifice. Forgiveness has been secured, in a perfect way, by the one sacrifice of Jesus' own body, and this eliminates the need for any subsequent sacrifice.[41]

10.19 Having therefore, brethren, boldness for access into the most holy place by the blood of Jesus,

---

[40] The difference in these last phrases does not come across in English translation, but the statement in 8.12 uses an aorist passive subjunctive form of *mimnēskomai* in an idiomatic negation, whereas 10.17 uses a (somewhat unusual) future passive indicative form. Some manuscripts have the more usual aorist form in this place.

[41] This ought to weigh heavily against any ideas that the sacrifice of Jesus is repeated over and over again, either in heaven or in the Lord's Supper.

The rest of this chapter is devoted to another exhortation to faithfulness. The exhortation is based on the truths that have been presented in 6.20–10.18. In the Bible, moral exhortation is always grounded in the truth and is never presented for merely utilitarian concerns. *Cf.* 2 Pet 3.10–12 for another clear example. There are also several verbal parallels in verses 19–23 with the warning in 4.14–16: "having therefore a great high priest" (4.14), "let us hold fast the confession" (4.14), "boldness" (4.16), and "let us draw near" (4.16).[42] In fact, it is possible to understand that the appeal made in chapters 3–4 is now being presented again, this time with the presentation of 6.20–10.18 behind it.[43]

The paragraph made up of verses 19–25 neatly lays out two premises and three conclusions or imperatives that follow from them:

Premises:

1. We have confidence to enter the holy place by the blood of Jesus (vv 19f)
2. We have a great high priest over the house of God (v 21)

Conclusions/imperatives[44]:

1. Let us draw near (v 22)
2. Let us hold fast the confession of our hope (v 23)
3. Let us consider how to stimulate one another to love and good deeds (vv 24f)

The exhortation aims to encourage the readers to continued faithfulness in the face of persecution. Already their situation of ongoing opposition by unbelievers was causing some of these Christians to retreat from the faith. The appeal continues to draw upon both the tabernacle imagery and comparison with the old Law that have been the basis for presenting the better way available in Jesus. In 9.11 the author showed that the priestly work of **Jesus** is carried out in the true sanctuary, heaven itself, where he entered with his own **blood** to make perfect atonement for us.

---

[42] deSilva, *Perseverance in Gratitude*, 334.

[43] Moffatt, *Hebrews*, 141.

[44] In the Greek: aorist hortatory subjunctives. Campbell suggests that the aorist subjunctive typically refers to events that are particular, as opposed to those that are generic. *Verbal Aspect and Non-Indicative Verbs*, 56. Fanning suggests that an aorist subjunctive presents an occurrence in summary, viewed as a whole (*Verbal Aspect in New Testament Greek*, 361).

There is no warrant for the idea that the most holy place is the church; 9.24 makes this clear. Through Jesus we have a kind of **access**[45] to God that was not possible under the old system (9.8). The word **boldness** is the same word in 3.6 (see comments there). *Cf.* Eph 3.12. The author of Hebrews will further develop this concept of boldness in contrast to the fearful approach through God under the Mosaical system in 12.18–24. It should also be noted that the author does not encourage his audience to become bold, but instead says that we have boldness. That is, the situation resulting from the work of Jesus is one that bestows an unprecedented ability to approach God. This situation is to our advantage, and it behooves us to avail ourselves of it. This boldness is specifically a confidence **to enter into the most holy place**, that is, into the very presence of God. The author has in mind here not an approach through prayer or a worship service, but a spiritual approach through Jesus our forerunner (6.19f) who has opened the way for us and who brings us to the heavenly realm (9.11f) with him, into fellowship with God and ultimately into the very presence of God in the end. *Cf.* Ephesians 2.6. In Jesus we are empowered and emboldened to live on the heavenly plane and to attain a closeness with God that previously was impossible. That we may enter into the heavenly most holy place would seem to imply the priesthood of all believers, but the author of Hebrews, in order to keep the focus on Jesus, does not specifically explore that dimension in the exhortation. We would have no access to God without him.

10.20 which[46] he inaugurated for us as a new and living way through the veil, that is, his flesh,

Our author is keen to remind us that the tabernacle was a physical, earthly model of a spiritual reality. Even more, it was the ritual performed within that tent that served as an illustration of the Messiah's work. By offering his body as a sanctifying sacrifice for us (v 5), Jesus opened up (**inaugurated**; the same Greek word was used in 9.18 to say the covenant was *ratified*) the true **way** to God's presence. While we now enjoy a mea-

[45] The word (Greek *eisodos*) can refer to the place of entrance or to the act of entering (BDAG 294). The context suggests that the latter meaning fits best.

[46] The antecedent of the pronoun could be either "access" (*eisodon*) or "boldness" (*parrēsian*), but the context (stating *hodon*, "way") makes it clear that it refers to our access from the previous verse.

sure of the benefits of having this way open for us, its fullest measure will be enjoyed in heaven along with the rest of the faithful (11.39f) and thus the writer can also say that we enter into the veil through hope (6.19f). Because of what Jesus did for us, nothing now hinders us from a close relationship with God. Under the old system there were physical barriers—the Holy Place itself (9.8), and the veil—which were symbols of the fact that under that system people were unable to approach God. The author specifically had in mind here the inner veil (the "second veil," 9.3) that separated the holy place from the most holy place.[47]

There are two ways to understand what is said next:

1) Jesus' passing through the veil of his flesh refers to his death on the cross and his subsequent ascension to God's right hand.[48] Interpreted this way, the inauguration is the "event" of Jesus reaching heaven, and thereby opening up the way for us to come after him (thus fitting with descriptions of Jesus as "pioneer" (2.10 and 12.2) or "forerunner," (6.20)). In the tabernacle, the veil kept everyone out of the presence of God, and no one but the high priest could pass beyond it. Now, however, the barrier has been breached by the work of Christ (*cf.* the symbolic phenomenon in Matt 27.51), the way in has been opened up (inaugurated). The exclusion symbolized by the tabernacle's veil has been done away by the work of Jesus. Thus, he proclaimed, "I am the way, and the truth, and the life; no one comes to the father but through me" (John 14.6).

2) Jesus' passing through the veil of his flesh refers to his incarnation, his taking on human form. Thus the statement recalls the discussion in Hebrews 2. When interpreted this way, the term "inauguration" summarizes the earthly work of Jesus. Using the imagery of the Day of Atonement, this interpretation says that it was not Jesus entering into the Most Holy Place that constitutes the inauguration here, but Jesus' leaving heaven, his passing through the veil to come outside the presence of God into the world of men, that is meant here. While on the earth he shed his blood, and, as Hebrews 9.19–22 has shown, that blood inaugurated the new system of things, the new covenant. Therefore, the blood mentioned in the previous verse has the function of chapter 9 in view, blood that put something into service and made it operational.[49] The difference between

47 Gurtner, "LXX Syntax and the Identity of the NT Veil."

48 This is the interpretation defended by most modern commentators.

49 Jennings, "The Veil and the High Priestly Robes of the Incarnation," 85–97.

the two interpretations has almost no effect on the thrust of the exhortation here. The balance may be slightly in favor of the first view, because it is the believer's access to God, which was not previously open, that is under discussion here. Whether it was Jesus coming from heaven, or returning to heaven, a new and better way to God has been opened up for us.[50]

The way that Jesus opened as our pioneer is **new and living**. It is **new** in that it is a way that did not exist before and has only recently been established,[51] and it is **living** in that Jesus did not pass through a physical object (like the veil of the tabernacle) or even by means of the sacrificed body of a dead animal, but through his own experience in the flesh. Just as men may build a new highway to take people to places they could not go before, so Jesus has opened a fresh, newly established way to God.

10.21 and having a great priest over the house of God,

That Jesus is the new high **priest over God's house** (which is the church, 3.6) was established in chapter 7, where it was shown that Jesus fulfills Psalm 110.4, which spoke of the Messiah as a priest after the order of Melchizedek. Since we still live on earth, we now enjoy in earnest our delight in the very presence of God in heaven through our connection with Jesus ("partakers of Christ," 3.14). Without him, or apart from him, no fellowship with God would be possible. The point is, however, that we do indeed have a marvelous high priest who makes possible for us unprecedented access to our God.

10.22 let us approach with a true heart in full assurance of faith, having our hearts sprinkled from an evil conscience and our bodies washed with pure water,

Since we now have in the new covenant an unparalleled access to God through Jesus our new high priest, we should take advantage of the way that has been opened up for us and **approach** our God (*cf.* 4.16). The term here (Greek *proserchomai*) is used of entry into the presence of deity.[52] This

---

[50] The Greek phrase *tēs sarkos autou* ("his flesh") can be understood as appositional to "blood" in v 19, to "way," or to "veil." For a discussion of the grammatical possibilities, see Norman H. Young, "*tout' estin tēs sarkos autou* (Heb, x.20): Apposition, Dependent or Explicative?," *NTS* 20 (1973): 100–104.

[51] BDAG 886.

[52] BDAG 878; MM 547.

fits what we know about the original recipients of Hebrews, who were on the verge of falling away (3.12; 6.6), who had begun to shrink back (10.39). God wants us close to him, and he sent his Son to make that possible. While entering the presence of God would otherwise be unthinkable, and even frightful for man, through the work of Jesus we are invited to come close. With all of heaven's encouragement, then, we should draw near to the God who loves us and has redeemed us.

However, only the pure may approach God, so one must come **with a true heart**. That is, we must approach God with sincerity and genuine trust. *Cf.* Isaiah 38.3. The **heart** that is insincere, or untrue, or lacking in authentic faith is defiled. Recall also that it was a hard heart that caused the Israelites to fail to enter Canaan (Psa 95.8, 10, quoted in Heb 3.8–10). Jeremiah 31.33 (quoted in 8.10) stipulated that a changed or "new" heart is supposed to characterize those who live in the new covenant, and that is the **true heart** of which our author here speaks. *Cf.* Ezekiel 18.31: "Cast away from you all your transgressions which you have committed and make yourselves a new heart and a new spirit!" (NASB; also, Psa 51.10). Those in the new covenant must therefore adopt this new heart if they wish to keep fellowship with God. Furthermore, there is no need for us to fear the prospect of drawing near to God. What Jesus has done for us makes it possible for us to approach God with surety, certainty, confidence, or **assurance**. This in no way suggests that we may come into a relationship with God in a flippant or casual way; the utmost respect for God is always necessary. However, it means that in the new covenant access to God is fully available. Whereas the Israelites under the Mosaical system were basically told to keep away from God (lest they die!), now we may come close to him without any fear of reprisal. The ground of this new confidence is not in ourselves. No one should think that he is in any way personally sufficient to approach God on his own. No, we approach God in a way that requires **faith**, specifically through our relationship with Jesus; and in Hebrews, faith always includes endurance. While "faith" and "assurance" might seem like contradictory ideas to some, our author will illustrate in chapter 11 that it is entirely possible to have a confident faith (he has already mentioned a "full assurance of hope" in 6.11, which is a very closely related idea). This meant, for the original readers, that they must hold on to their relationship with Jesus, trusting that he alone is the way to fellowship with God. Persecution and ongoing opposition had caused these disciples to rethink their commitment to Christianity, but the one who truly pleases God is the one who follows God's way, trusting that it is right, even when it brings hardship.

Antecedent to the true heart and sure faith is a cleansing of all the heart's impurities. The author thus describes, with two perfect participles,[53] this cleansing with terms that employ figurative language based on the Levitical system. He uses the features of that old system in this way because he viewed them eschatologically as illustrations of the new system in Christ (9.9, 23), yet he stops short of explicitly identifying Christians as a new priesthood to God, probably so as not to detract from the priesthood of Jesus. **Our hearts** must be **sprinkled from an evil conscience**. Sprinkling was a method used in the Law of Moses, often in connection with a sacrifice, to purify and sanctify certain things,[54] so it here becomes a figurative way of saying "cleansed." We have seen in 9.19 that Moses sprinkled the people and the book of the covenant with blood in order to purify them and bring them into the covenant relationship with God. Such is the idea here as well. No one who is guilty of sin can hope to approach God. Ezekiel 36.25–26 is likely in mind here: "Then I will sprinkle clean water on you, and you will be clean; I will cleanse you from all your filthiness and from all your idols. Moreover, I will give you a new heart and put a new spirit within you; and I will remove the heart of stone from your flesh and give you a heart of flesh" (NASB).[55] The word **evil** here recalls the same term from 3.12, where the heart like the Israelites was called "an evil, unbelieving heart," that "falls away." This is undoubtedly the idea here as well. The evil from which we must be cleansed in order to approach God includes the sin of unfaithfulness within one's heart. The mention of the conscience here reinforces the idea, as the conscience, like the heart, is an internal part of a person. An **evil conscience** is probably parallel to the evil heart of 3.12 and is one that is defiled by unfaithfulness. The conscience must be cleansed first (which is the same

---

[53] The perfect participle can denote an action that is contemporary with the action of the main verb (Campbell, *Verbal Aspect and Non-Indicative Verbs*, 26), describing the current state of affairs. The idea here would be something like: "with our hearts sprinkled … and our bodies washed, we must approach …."

[54] Exod 29.16–21; Lev 1.5, 11; 3.2, 8, 13; *etc.*

[55] Jason P. Kees, "Having Our Hearts Sprinkled Clean: The Influence of Ezekiel 36:25–26 on Hebrews 10:22," *WTJ* 83 (2021): 237–50. The allusion suggests that the "new exodus" envisioned in Hebrews is the ultimate fulfillment of Israel's coming out of her exile.

thing as saying that the heart must be purified, *cf.* Acts 15.9; Jam 4.8) having been sprinkled, as it were, with the blood of Christ (9.14). Without a good (clear) conscience, one cannot serve God acceptably (1 Tim 1.19; 1 Pet 3.16). A similar combination of a pure heart, a good conscience, and sincere faith appears in 1 Tim 1.5.

Also, **our bodies** must be **washed with pure water**. There are two general ways this may be understood. First, this can be read as a reference to Christian baptism, which is the view of most commentators. If this is the referent, it is a figurative one, for Peter says that baptism is not to be understood as a washing of the body but is a cleansing of the conscience from the guilt of sin (1 Pet 3.21; Acts 22.16). The imagery here comes from various OT regulations in which the priests of the Mosaical system had to wash themselves with water before they could approach God (Exod 30.20; 40.12), or unclean persons had to wash in order to resume fellowship in the covenant community.[56] Here it is a figurative way of describing one who is pure. It is possible that the original recipients, from their Jewish background, would have seen this as a reference to their baptism. A second way to understand this washing is in connection with the sprinkling, so that the two participles combine to present a single picture. Together, sprinkling the heart and washing the body would denote one who is clean in every way, "inside and out."[57] The combination of heart and body can be a way of describing the whole person (Eccl 11.10), and priests under the old covenant were consecrated with sprinkled blood and washing their bodies with water (Exod 29.4, 21; Lev 8.6, 30). In this interpretation, the author was saying that we have been purified to enter the presence of God through the shed blood of Jesus (v 19; Matt 26.28; Eph 1.7; Heb 9.22). Either way, the overall point is that this cleansing (sprinkling and washing), whether it refers specifically to Christian baptism or not, purifies the heart or conscience, which enables us to draw near to God through Jesus.

10.23 let us hold to the acknowledgement of our hope without wavering, for the one who promised is faithful,

---

[56] Lev 14.8f; 15.5ff; 16.26ff; 17.15; Num 19.8; *etc.* The priesthood of believers is implied here.

[57] Like "clean hands and pure heart" in Psa 24.3–4, which discusses access to God's presence; *cf.* Jam 4.8; Matt 23.26; Ezek 36.25f; 2 Cor 7.1; Tit 3.5.

A second imperative for those who now have access to God through Christ is to adhere firmly to what we confess, namely that for which we hope (objective genitive in the Greek). The word **acknowledgement** here translates the Greek word that is elsewhere translated "confession;" a confession is an open acknowledgement of what one believes. However, confession also carries with it the idea of commitment; see comments on 3.1 and 4.14. Under difficult circumstances (like social shame), early Christians were no doubt tempted to suppress expressions of their loyalty to Jesus in order to protect themselves from hardship. The author here bid them to exactly the opposite. He wanted them to keep on acknowledging their relationship to Jesus in every way even though it was difficult to do so, because this is a demonstration of faithfulness, of trust. Furthermore, we must hold on to our hope **without wavering**, for vacillation is the fruit of unbelief (*cf.* Jam 1.6–8; Psa 26.1; Jer 4.1; Rom 4.20). The grounds for this courage lie in the fact that there is no way that the promise of eternal salvation will fail, because it is made by the God who is **faithful** and reliable when he speaks, and thus he can be counted on to do what he has promised. Christian faith, and faithfulness, is not the "leap" that it is sometimes made out to be. Although faith always involves an element of risk, with God we are called to trust in him not blindly, but because he has proven himself to be worthy of trust. He has shown himself, through repeated demonstrations in the Biblical narrative, to be faithful to his word.[58] God cannot lie (6.18a), and so he will be absolutely loyal to his promise (1 Cor 1.9; 10.13; 2 Cor 1.18) and will indeed reward those who persevere. Those who persevere in their faith will join God in his rest in heaven. Therefore, as those who have fled for refuge to the sure promises of God (6.18b), we must not stray from that hope which sustains and motivates us to persevere. To abandon what we have openly confessed to hope is to abandon the only thing that is truly sure and reliable. Since the promised reward is based on the surety of God himself, the only thing that may cause a person not to attain it is his own unfaithfulness. If God is faithful to us, we ought to be faithful to him (v 22).

---

[58] This aspect of faith is what is commonly in view in the LXX use of the term. See Dennis R. Lindsay, "Pistis and 'Emunah: The Nature of Faith in the Epistle to the Hebrews," in *A Cloud of Witnesses: The Theology of Hebrews in Its Ancient Contexts,* ed. Richard Bauckham et al, LNTS 387 (London: T&T Clark, 2008), 158–69.

10.24 and let us be mindful of each other, for stirring up love and good works,

The third imperative is to **be mindful of** one's brethren in the faith and encourage them. In situations of difficulty, it is quite easy to become self-absorbed and inactive. Yet the instruction here is not that we should find someone to encourage us but that we should contemplate others in order to encourage them. It is not without significance that the author has already told us to consider Jesus (3.1). Christ and others are the two basic objects of the thoughts of every Christian, and to consider the former leads us to consider the latter. The example of Christ is that we must always think of others first (Rom 15.2f), be devoted to them first (Rom 12.10), and spend ourselves for them (Gal 5.13). This is especially important in times of testing. The Lord's wisdom is revealed in his instructions for how his church is to be encouraged: by each member looking for the good they may do for the others (Rom 14.19; 1 Cor 10.24; Phil 2.4). Specifically, we are **to stir** one another **up**, to rouse and incite each other in a positive sense. The specific goal is two things. First, **love**. This is the same kind of selfless, sacrificial love Jesus showed to us. We in turn are to show that same love to each other (John 13.34f; 15.12; 1 John 4.11), especially when trials come along. In times of hardship, such as these Christians faced, brotherly love is especially needed (*cf.* 13.1). Biblical love must not be reduced to an action, but neither is it only an internal disposition. Love resides sincerely in the heart (Rom 12.9f; 1 Pet 1.21) and always manifests itself in sacrificial deeds (1 Thes 1.3; Gal 2.20; Eph 5.2, 25). A true and sincere love for others encompasses both emotions and actions. Second, we are to stir each other up to do **good works**. These are public expressions of our faith (*cf.* Jam 2.14ff) and of our brotherly love (*cf.* 6.11) and are the opposite of the dead works mentioned in 9.14. Here it may be read as a way of summarizing the Christian life. The exhortation is "keep on living your Christian lives in public, doing what Christians do and not stopping it or hiding it," even though this is the very thing that was bringing opposition to the group. In times of hardship, when faith is tested, it is typical for some Christians that their faith wanes and they become inactive. They cease to do the good things that are characteristic of Christians. However, we must not cease to do good to all and especially to each other.[59] The picture here is like that in Ephesians 4.16, of a church made up of intercon-

[59] Matt 5.16; Gal 6.10; Eph 2.10; Col 1.10; 1 Tim 2.10; 6.18; 2 Tim 2.21; 3.16.

nected members who support each other and in so doing build each other up in love. *Cf.* also 1 Thessalonians 5.11; Colossians 3.14. When some become weak in faith and cease to contribute to the well-being of the group, the entire group suffers. It therefore behooves every member to show love to the rest, and to encourage others to continue in the good works that reflect our faith. With each one contributing to the support of the others, the Lord's church can remain strong even in times of persecution.

10.25 not abandoning the assembling of ourselves, as is the habit of some, but exhorting one another, and so much more as you see the day approaching.

One of the ways we may encourage each other to continued faithfulness is in our **assembling** together. The Greek word is *episunagōgē*, and the preposition *epi* at the beginning of the word imparts a local sense, so the word means "the local gathering" or the gathering at a particular location.[60] It would seem that the gathering together for worship on the Lord's day is the assembly in view here (Acts 20.7; 1 Cor 16.2; 5.4; 14.23, 26; Jam 2.2), as this would more likely be simply designated "the assembling of ourselves together" without further qualification rather than an assembly of the church for some other purpose. The implication is that the normal desire and practice of Christians is to attend the public worship assembly which edifies the church through the word that is taught, and sung, in that gathering (*cf.* 1 Cor 14.3–5, 12, 26; Eph 5.19; Col 3.16);[61] it is likely that this sermon was intended to be read precisely in such a gathering. Apparently, the opposition these Christians were facing, and the fear it generated, had caused some to dissociate themselves from other Christians, at least to the point of willfully absenting themselves from the worship gathering (contrast 11.25; 12.3). Although it was undoubtedly done in an attempt to distance oneself from the group that was the object of continual social reproach, the author described it in terms of weakness in their faith in Jesus. Rather than isolating themselves from the faith and from others who identified with it, these Christians needed

---

[60] *Cf.* Mark 1:33; Koester, Hebrews, 446; BDAG 382.

[61] See Jason N. Yuh, "Abandonment and Absenteeism in the Letter to the Hebrews and Greco-Roman Associations," *JBL* 138 (2019): 863–82, at 864: "Documentary texts reveal that attendance and absenteeism were fundamental concerns for most associations" in the ancient world. However, the way those were handled was different between churches (with exhortation and moral warning) and civic associations (with monetary fines).

to maintain their public confession of Jesus and exhort each other, both of which were accomplished in their worship assembly. It should be noted that withdrawal from the public assemblies was not the problem per se, but was a sign or symptom of another, deeper problem. It is important to keep that in mind, because it is possible to place an improper emphasis on attendance at the worship assemblies for its own sake.

Not only was the presence of every member normally essential to the encouragement of the group, but this was especially important (**so much more**) in light of **the day** which was **approaching**. What is this day? The understanding one has of "the day" in this particular context will determine whether the author's words are an encouragement or a warning, and will also determine the specific referent of verses 26–31.

There are at least four possibilities as to the meaning of "the day":

1) "The day" is the day of judgment at the end of the world.[62] That day will be a day of both salvation for the righteous and condemnation for the wicked. Given the fact that the early Christians so often used this phrase "the day" (of judgment, or of the Lord) with this meaning, this would appear to be the most natural meaning here as well. The author mentioned the return of the Lord in 9.28, and mentions God's judgment in verse 27 below, so the idea belongs to this context. A possible weakness of interpreting "the day" as referring to the day of judgment at the world's end is that the author of Hebrews says, "you see the day approaching." When taken in its plain sense, that statement says the readers of Hebrews could tell that "the day" was getting near. However, the day of the Lord at the end of the world will come without prior signals (*cf.* 1 Thes 5.2; 2 Pet 3.10). One would have to interpret the words "you see the day approaching" as figurative language for hope (*cf.* Rom 13.11) in order to maintain this position. It would remain to be established whether the author intended his readers to think of "the day" in this particular exhortation as something positive or negative, since the day of judgment holds out either prospect depending upon one's stance toward the Lord (*cf.* Rom 2.5–8). In this context, verses 26–31 might be understood to support the latter, but verses 36–38 might be understood to support the former. Nothing would prohibit both aspects being operative here.

2) "The day" refers to the destruction of Jerusalem. This would be in accord with OT judgment language, where "the day" refers to God's vis-

[62] Matt 10.15; 12.36; 25.13; Acts 17.31; Rom 2.5, 16; 1 Cor 1.8; 5.5; Eph 4.30; Phil 1.6; *etc.*

itation in condemnation on a nation and especially upon its chief city.[63] The author of Hebrews has been speaking at length of the demise of the old Levitical system (8.7–10.18). Furthermore, Jesus taught his followers to look for certain signs that would mean the destruction of Jerusalem was near (Matt 24), and this would make sense of the author's words here "you see the day drawing near." However, this interpretation suffers from several weaknesses, two of which stand out: first, such an interpretation must be established on other grounds, and we have suggested (in the Introduction) that it is not easy to make a solid case for a pre-70 date for Hebrews. Without supporting evidence, this reading of the text is weak, and reading this passage as a reference to the coming destruction of the city only creates a circular argument. Second, this interpretation is connected to the questionable thesis that the readers had abandoned the practices of Judaism and were contemplating a return to it. As we have shown in the Introduction, this is not a plausible approach.

3) "The day" refers to coming persecution, as Biblical authors sometimes referred to "the day of my trouble" or "the day of my distress."[64] On this reading, we would need to imagine a persecution that was facing the readers, and the exhortation thus becomes "encourage one another to be faithful in Christ, and especially as you see that persecution is about to begin again." This interpretation is possible, but it cannot be confirmed from the available evidence either. We simply do not know enough about the actual situation of the original audience to speak with certainty.

4) "The day" refers to growth in the faith and the attainment of maturity. 2 Pet 1.19; *cf.* Eph 5.14. Understood in this way, growth in the faith is pictured as a coming out of darkness into the light of day. This would understand the author's exhortation to mean "as you see yourselves growing in the faith, then especially be about the business of encouraging each other." Against this view it could be objected that the author has already rebuked his audience for failure to grow as much as they should (5.11ff), but this is no real objection since the author obviously cycles his warnings, and repetition of such an important point could be expected. The author was still confident that his readers would mature (6.1, 9; 10.39).

Which of these views is the correct one? The author has left us few definite clues but on the whole the first interpretation described above

[63] *Cf.* Exod 32.34; Deut 32.35; Isa 10.3; 13.6, 9, 13; Jer 47.4; Joel 1.15; *etc.*

[64] *Cf.* Psa 18.18; 20.1; 27.5; 50.15; 59.16; 77.2; Jer 16.19; 17.17; *etc.*

seems preferable, or is the least problematic. The first view fits well with the normal NT practice of basing ethical instruction on the fact of the coming day of reckoning before the Lord. A strong case can be made for the fourth interpretation as well.

10.26 For if we sin willfully after receiving the knowledge of the truth,[65] a sacrifice for sins is no longer available,

The alternative to drawing near to God (vv 19ff) is now laid out to show its horrible end. The **sin** the author here envisions is not a refusal to attend the public worship gatherings, but is the same sin he has been discussing throughout the sermon: the sin of apostasy, falling away from God (6.6), "deconfessing Jesus Christ,"[66] **willfully** withdrawing from Christ and quitting one's relationship with him,[67] the sin of unfaithfulness to Christ, the sin of refusing to follow in faith (like the Israelites of old, Heb 3–4), of which withdrawal from the group gatherings was a symptom. This is important in order to understand the warning here correctly. As in 6.4ff (see comments there), the author is not speaking of those sins which sincere Christians occasionally commit out of ignorance or temporary weakness, nor is the author speaking of the sin Jesus described in Matt 12.31. Instead, he speaks of the one who deliberately severs his relationship with Christ and renounces him. The author has warned the readers that they may have already begun to walk down the path that would lead them to reject Jesus, and they now had to decide whether they would continue in their faith even though it meant hardship, or quit. The author of Hebrews was here warning them (and us) that the latter choice would bring the worst of all consequences.

What would make apostasy so terrible is that they had **received the knowledge of the truth**. In the NT the phrase "the truth" often denotes the teaching about Christ (John 5.33; 8.32, 40; 14.6; 18.37) delivered through the apostles (John 16.13; Tit 1.1), and is synonymous with the gospel (Gal 2.5, 14; Eph 1.13; Col 1.5). Those who have a knowledge of the

---

[65] Although it is translated as a conditional statement here, the first part of this verse is a construction in the Greek known as a "genitive absolute," which provides background information. The force of the entire statement is not so much "if…then" but "with this state of affairs (sinning after receiving the knowledge of the truth), here is the situation that now exists (no more sacrifice for sins)."

[66] McKnight, "The Warning Passages of Hebrews," 42, 54.

[67] McKnight, "The Warning Passages of Hebrews," 42.

truth are in a position to have fellowship with God (1 Tim 2.4; 2 Tim 2.25; Tit 1.1). The fact that they had received (accepted) the saving truth that came through Jesus means that they could not plead ignorance before the judgment seat of God if they were to turn away from Jesus. *Cf.* 2 Pet 2.20f. They knew the truth, so any rejection of it could only be viewed as defiant rejection of Jesus. Ultimately, their refusal to follow Jesus was a refusal to trust in God (John 12.44; 14.24).

The author of Hebrews has shown that a new and better way to God has become available through the death of Christ. In Christ we finally have that at which the sacrifices of the OT only hinted. If one knows that only in Christ we have perfect cleansing and access to God, and yet refuses him, then he has cut himself off from the only avenue whereby fellowship with God is possible for, as Jesus said, "no one comes to the father except through me" (John 14.6). Also, in Hellenistic culture, receipt of a gift by a patron obligated the recipient to honor the giver in such a way that displayed gratitude. Those who did the unthinkable and insulted the giver were cut off from receiving favor in the future. See comments on 12.22. In the same way, to receive God's great gift of forgiveness and then to go on sinning, acting contrary to his will, would be considered a terrible insult to God (see v 29 below) and would result in the loss of all positive relationship with him. Hence **a sacrifice for sins is no longer available** for such a one. See comments on 5.2 and 6.6. For what the Bible called the "high-handed" or defiant sin (Num 15.30), no forgiveness was available under the Law, and similarly, in the new covenant there is no other way to obtain forgiveness if one consciously and purposefully cuts himself off from Jesus who provides it. God's forgiveness now comes through our relationship with Jesus, or it does not come at all.

10.27 but a frightful expectation of judgment and of intense fire that is coming to consume the adversaries.

Where no atonement for sin is available, only punishment remains. One is either a friend of God or his enemy, and no middle ground is possible (see Matt 12.30; *cf.* Jam 4.4). Those who willfully choose apostasy thus make themselves enemies, or adversaries, of God, and the only thing they have to anticipate is **judgment**, or condemnation from God. The latter part of the verse echoes Isaiah 26.11. In that context God's **adversaries** were his own people who had turned from him. The author of Hebrews found in those words a fitting indicator (now read messianically) of the fact that God will indeed punish his own people under the new covenant if they prove faithless. The things that operated under the old covenant were shadows or models of the greater realities that would be possible in the new covenant, and this holds true for judgment as well. God's judgment of his people in the past confirms that he will not exempt his own people from punishment in the future, for God's people have had an unfortunate history of thinking that either his judgment will not come (*cf.* 2 Pet 3.3ff) or that it will always be upon someone else (*cf.* 1 Pet 4.17; Jer 7.4, 12–14). The judgment that God brought upon his own people through the Babylonians was but a model of an even greater condemnation and punishment for those who reject the fullness of God's blessings in the new covenant. Recall Hebrews 2.1–4: a greater offer brings a greater punishment for rejection. The final judgment of God upon the unfaithful will be one of **intense fire**,[68] indicating the intensity of God's wrath. The word **consume** here should not be taken literally in the sense that it will annihilate them. The word literally means "eat," and it is used figuratively here in the sense that God's anger will completely engulf those who have rejected him and his Son.

10.28 The one who set aside the Law of Moses died without mercy on the basis of two or three witnesses.

The author here presents another of his many arguments from the lesser to the greater (see Introduction), which is designed to prove the assertion of verses 26f. As in chapter 9, the author does not have a particular legal scenario from the OT in mind here but is thinking about the Law as a whole. His statement thus combines the regulations in Deuteronomy 19.10ff and 17.6–7. The former text describes the cities of refuge and their purpose. In that context God said that the cities of refuge were not to be a haven for murderers, who **set aside**, or willfully ignored, God's law against premeditated murder (Exod 20.13; Deut 5.17). For their disobedience they were to be executed **without** pity (**mercy**; Deut 19.16). The latter text says that no one was to be convicted of a capital crime and executed unless it was upon the testimony of **two or three witnesses**. The general principle was that the consistent testimony of at least two witnesses was considered enough evidence to establish the truth. If two or

[68] 1 Cor 3.13; 2 Thes 1.7; 2 Pet 3.7ff; *cf.* Rev 20.12–15; Gen 19.24.

three witnesses consistently testified to a person's guilt, that person was considered to have been proven guilty and he faced execution without any other recourse. There was a procedure to guard against false witnesses (Deut 19.16–19), but the author of Hebrews is simply thinking about normal cases where the sinner's guilt was beyond doubt. The point in this verse is that when one committed willful sin and was duly convicted under the law of Moses, the offender was executed and the law had no provisions for leniency or pity. This was designed to instill fear (12.21) as well as administer justice.

10.29 How much worse punishment do you think he will deserve who has trampled the Son of God under foot and has regarded the blood of the covenant, by which he was sanctified, as common, and has insulted the Spirit of grace?

Here is the latter part of the argument from the lesser to the greater, again in the form of a rhetorical question to make the point forcefully. The old Law was a shadow or figure of the realities in Christ (10.1). Now if the shadow had no provisions for pity for those who blatantly violated it, will we find the reality of the new covenant to be any less demanding? If no mercy was granted to the one who deliberately refused to abide by God's word in an inferior system, could any mercy be expected for such a one in the better system? If punishment under the old system was harsh, will not **punishment** under the new system be even **worse**? Indeed, the things of the new covenant are of a greater nature, and to spurn a greater gift will certainly bring a greater punishment.

But there is more to it than this. The author describes the sin of apostasy from the new covenant in three ways, to impress upon his readers just why it is such a terrible offense. First, to forsake Christ is to **trample the Son of God under foot**. The title "Son" recalls the discussion from chapter 1 where it was demonstrated that Jesus, as the Son, has received the greatest possible status and honor from God. Those who despise the Son will reap the father's wrath (*cf.* the parable in Matt 21.33ff), just as Jesus said, "he who rejects me rejects the one who sent me" (Luke 10.16) and "He who rejects me and does not receive my sayings has one who judges him" (John 12.48). To "trample under foot" is an idiom meaning to treat something in a despicable way, to consider it as garbage (see the similar illustration in Matt 5.13; *cf.* 2 Kngs 9.33; Luke 21.24). To refuse to follow Jesus is to treat him as if he has no significance, like garbage that is not worthy of our attention and to which we give no respect or consideration. It is the same kind of treatment as described in 6.6, of treating Jesus contemptuously and putting him to open shame. Second, to quit following Christ is **to regard** (consider) the **sanctifying blood of the covenant** (10.10) as if it were **common**. The blood that sanctifies us and puts us into close fellowship with God is not the blood of an animal but the blood of Jesus (13.12), God's own Son whom he sent in loving sacrifice for the sins of the world. God paid the most precious commodity in the universe in order to redeem us from our sins (Eph 1.7; Heb 9.12; 1 Pet 1.18f). The payment of such a cost on our behalf should prompt us to gratitude, thanksgiving, and devotion. The one who turns from Christ demonstrates no such responses, but instead shows that the precious blood of Christ means absolutely nothing to him. He is without appreciation for what the Lord has done for him. To such a one, the blood of Jesus has no special value and thus is considered **common**, that is, of no special importance (Greek *koinon;* common or profane). To think of the blood of Jesus as anything less than precious and holy is to treat it with great disrespect. Third, to quit is to **insult the Spirit of grace**. To turn one's back on God's offer of fellowship in Christ, after having accepted it, is an *outrage* to deity. There is no polite refusal of God's offer of fellowship and salvation as far as God is concerned. The one who willfully abandons Christ insults deity! While this is equally insulting to the Son and to God the father, it is also an insult to the **Spirit** through whom we have received and experienced the **grace** of God. To return insult for grace is the strongest kind of rejection. deSilva notes that this particular consideration would have been significant in the ancient world with its well-rooted system of patronage and honor.[69] To insult the one who provided a gift was considered the worst kind of shameful behavior because it violated the sense of grateful indebtedness that bound the recipient to the giver. The designation **Spirit of grace** appears in Zechariah 12.10, a messianic text that references the crucifixion of Jesus ("they shall look upon me whom they have pierced"). Recall also that Christ offered himself on the cross through the eternal Spirit (9.14), so to abandon Christ is to insult the Spirit by which Jesus was offered for our sins. The Holy Spirit is typically presented in the Bi-

[69] David A. deSilva, "Exchanging Favor for Wrath: Apostasy in Hebrews and Patron-Client Relationships," *JBL* 115 (1996): 91–116.

ble as the divine agent through whom God blesses and communicates to his people. To spurn the gift of God also involves spurning and insulting the divine Spirit who graciously brought it to us.

10.30 For we know him who said, "Vengeance is mine, I will repay," and again, "The Lord will judge his people."

Two OT quotations confirm that God will indeed take vengeance upon his own people when they become unfaithful. The phrase that introduces the OT quotations is significant. One of the characteristics of those in the new covenant is that they know the Lord (Jer 31.34; quoted in Heb 8.11), in contrast to the Israelites who did not know him (Jer 2.8; 9.3; Hos 4.6; 5.4). Through the Scriptures we know the character of the God we serve. If **we know him** at all, we must know that he is a just God who will not tolerate affronts to what he has so graciously provided. If we know this about our God, we should act accordingly and remain faithful.

Both quotations are from Deuteronomy 32, the "Song of Moses" in which the patriarch reminded the Israelites of the failure of the former generation that had perished in the wilderness. That generation had died as punishment from God for their unfaithfulness, and Moses called upon the new generation to remember what had happened, to learn a lesson about the character of their God, and to avoid the mistakes of their predecessors. This scenario fits perfectly into the thought of Hebrews, where the author has made the same kind of appeal (with an eschatological dimension) in chapters 3 and 4. The new Israel must not act faithlessly as the old Israel did. If they do, they will not enter into God's rest and they will face the wrath of God just as surely as old Israel did, yet even more so (v 29).

The first quotation is from Deuteronomy 32.35,[70] and the second is from 32.36 (which is also echoed in Psa 135.14). Although **vengeance** is sometimes a judicial act that God executes on others on behalf of his people, it

[70] The quotation of Deut 32.35 does not come from the LXX (which says "I will pay back in the day of vengeance") but reflects the reading of the MT ("vengeance and recompense are mine"). There may have been a Greek textual tradition that rendered the verse in this way (following a variant in the original Hebrew text; see Katz, "The Quotations from Deuteronomy in Hebrews"), or these words may simply represent the way the verse was commonly paraphrased among the Jews, since this same kind of rendering appears in the Aramaic Targumim, which were interpretive paraphrases of the Hebrew text (in Tg. Onqelos and Tg. Pal (texts quoted in Attridge, *Hebrews,* 295 fn60)).

can also be something he does for himself when his honor has been violated, which is the point here.[71] When God's own people refuse to honor him for who he is and what he has done for them, their ingratitude reaps God's wrath. In the first quotation there is an emphasis on God's exclusive right to judge his people. We could translate them "*To me* belongs vengeance," and "*I* will repay." Their failure to remain faithful would put them in jeopardy with God himself (*cf.* v 31). The second quotation emphasizes the surety of the fact that God will judge. The word **judge**, in Greek, has a broad semantic range. It can mean "decide," "condemn," or, as it sometimes means in the LXX, "vindicate," according to the context in which it appears. Since the word could mean either "condemn" or "vindicate" here, the reader must decide which meaning best suits this context. If we adopt the sense of "condemn," the verse from Deuteronomy is then being quoted as a warning not to fall under God's condemnation of the faithless. If we adopt the meaning "vindicate,"[72] then the verse is not a warning but an encouragement that God will vindicate his faithful ones in the end if they persevere. The negative context in Hebrews 10.26–31 argues for the meaning of "condemn."

10.31 It is a fearful thing to fall into the hands of the living God.

This verse summarizes the exhortation of verses 26–30 by condensing the point to a single maxim and thus bringing the warning to a climactic crescendo. *Cf.* 12.29. The context from which the quotations in the previous verse were drawn goes on to say "See now that I, I am he, and there is no god besides me; it is I who put to death and give life. I have wounded and it is I who heal, and there is no one who can deliver from *my hand*. Indeed, I lift up *my hand* to heaven, and say, *'As I live forever,* if I sharpen my flashing sword, and *my hand* takes hold on justice, I will render *vengeance* on my *adversaries*, and I will repay those who hate me" (Deut 32.39–41 NASB; emphasis added). This verse therefore summarizes the point of Moses' speech and applies it to those in the new covenant, through the *a fortiori* argument in verses 28f above. **To fall into** someone's **hands** means to come under their power (*cf.* Jdg 15.18; Luke 10.36).[73] God is here called

---

[71] deSilva, *Perseverance in Gratitude*, 350.

[72] As argued by John Proctor, "Judgement or Vindication? Deuteronomy 32 in Hebrews 10:30," *TynBul* 55 (2004): 65–80.

[73] Koester, *Hebrews*, 453.

the living God, echoing Moses' words to Israel (Deut 32.40), especially God's oath language in guaranteeing punishment against his enemies, to emphasize God's power to judge his enemies even when those enemies are his own people. See comments on 3.12. For the original recipients who lived in a situation of ongoing opposition, this statement may have been a subtle warning to fear God more than they feared their neighbors. A healthy fear of God and the punishment he brings against unbelievers is always an important element in one's faith.[74]

10.32 But remember again the former days, in which, after you were enlightened, you endured a great struggle of sufferings,

The negative warning of verses 26–31 is now followed by positive encouragement, just as in 6.4–12. It is the Biblical method of both rebuking and exhorting in light of teaching from the Scriptures (see 2 Tim 4.2). In his attempt to encourage his readers to remain faithful under pressure from without, the author reminds them that they have done this very thing in the past (*cf.* 6.10). They are, therefore, fully capable of the perseverance that will cause them to avoid the punishment described in verses 26–31. Their own history proves it. They simply must decide to do it. Paul used this same method of appeal in his letters (2 Cor 7.15; Phil 1.3–11). It is not possible to determine the specific event or circumstance that had happened to the readers in their **former days**. It is not even possible to determine how far previous those days had been. The author only gives two general descriptions. First, it was a time of persecution in which the readers **endured a great struggle of sufferings**. The word "struggle" translates the Greek word *athlēsis*, a precursor to our English word "athletic," and denotes a challenge or a contest. By casting the readers' situation in athletic imagery, the author is able to portray them as victors (*cf.* 12.1ff), which contributes to the positive encouragement. The imagery allowed the author to "turn experiences of hardship and deprivation into a noble endeavor. Just as athletes endured much pain and even humiliation on the way to victory, so members of a low-status minority group could regard their suffering and humiliation as a sort of training for an honorable victory."[75] *Cf.* 1 Corinthians 9.24–27. Most important here is the word **endured**, which was

[74] See Amy Peeler, "'A fearful thing to fall into the hands of the living God': A Study of Fear in the Epistle to the Hebrews," *RevExp* 115 (2018): 40–49.

[75] deSilva, *Perseverance in Gratitude*, 362.

the very thing the readers needed to do in their present circumstance and which will be the point of the following exhortation (ch 11). Real faith endures because it looks forward, in hope, to the promised reward.

Second, their former experience of hardship was after they **were enlightened**, which is a way of speaking about receiving the truth from God (John 1.9) and thus becomes a way of speaking about conversion (see Heb 6.4). The text does not tell us how long after their conversion the former persecution had erupted, but it may be fair to assume that it had not been long. If this is correct, the picture that develops is of Christians who, out of zeal in their new faith, had endured persecution, but now, after some time had elapsed, found their faith weaker. The author of Hebrews wrote to encourage them to recapture the steadfastness that characterized their earlier days in the faith. Perhaps many of God's people today also need to recapture the zeal, joy, and courage they had when they first obeyed the gospel.

10.33 partly by being publicly exposed to insults and afflictions, and partly by becoming sharers with those who were treated in such a way.

The author reminds his audience (rhetorically) of just what great faith they had exhibited and hence of which they were capable, and thus uses their own experience as a basis for exhortation. The persecution these Christians had endured in their former days was no small hardship, and their faith was evidenced in the fact that some of them were made objects of **public** scorn. In ancient Greco-Roman society (as today), public honor and respectability were highly prized by most people. Fewer things were worse than to be declared unacceptable in a public way by one's societal peers. Isocrates advised to "Be more careful in guarding against censure than against danger … good men should dread ignominy during life"[76] and, famously, "Guard yourself against accusations, even if they are false; for the multitude are ignorant of the truth and look only to reputation. In all things resolve to act as though the whole world would see what you do."[77] Aristotle said that "vices of character, and the acts resulting from them, … all these are disgraceful, and should make us ashamed. It is also shameful not to have a share in the honorable things which all men ... have a share in."[78] To be well-regarded within society was a long-standing Greek virtue.

---

[76] Isocrates, *To Demonicus* 1.43 (Norlin, LCL)

[77] Isocrates, *To Deminicus* 1.17 (Norlin, LCL).

[78] Aristotle, *Rhetoric* 2.6.11–12 (Freese, LCL).

The readers of Hebrews had been subjected to one of the worst disgraces of their day. The words **publicly exposed** translates the Greek verb *theatrizō* (the verbal form of the word from which the English word "theater" is derived) which, along with the word "fight" in verse 32, helps set up the imagery in 12.1 of the readers engaged in a great struggle with others looking on. The spectacle entertainment that was later so strongly associated with the Roman Coliseum is the picture we are supposed to get here. It has the negative connotation of becoming a public spectacle of shame.[79] An ancient example was that under Nero's persecution in Rome Christians were burned as nightly illumination in the emperor's gardens.[80] We simply do not know if this was the same event being described here.

The scorn came in the form of **insults** and mistreatment (**sufferings**). These terms were part of the ancient vocabulary of shame[81] and this was no small matter to the ancients. Jesus foretold that his followers would be subjected to such disgraces, but that such treatment would put them in the company of some people whose faithful service to God was well-known (Matt 5.10f). The Biblical perspective is that, at least in some cases, the world's scorn is the Christian's honor, and the author of Hebrews was here developing that same kind of point. By reminding his readers of their faithful endurance in hardships, he will show them in chapter 11 that they already shared some significant traits with other people of renowned faith who endured the same things, if not worse.

The ways in which some of these Christians had **become sharers with those who were treated in such a way** is explained in the next verse.

10.34 For you had sympathy for the prisoners[82] and you accepted the plunder of your property with joy, knowing that you have better and lasting property.

---

[79] LSJ 787; *cf.* 1 Cor 4.9.

[80] Tacitus, *Annals* 15.44. Tacitus specifically said this was a "spectacle."

[81] deSilva, *Honor, Patronage, Kinship, and Purity*, 2nd. ed., 18.

[82] A textual variant appears in this verse that requires comment, since it accounts for the different sense of the KJV against other modern English versions. The Greek text underlying the KJV reads *desmois mou* ("my bonds"), but the Nestle-Aland text reads *desmiois*, "prisoners." The Textus Receptus says the author himself had been imprisoned and was visited by some of the people to whom he wrote, the Nestle-Aland text speaks of unnamed prisoners whom the original recipients of Hebrews had visited. The reading of the Nestle-Aland text is more likely the original on the premise that it explains the other reading (Ellingworth, *Epistle to the Hebrews*, 548).

Some of the recipients of Hebrews had (instead? also?) willfully associated with those who were being persecuted. This was an act of **sympathy**, which was also an expression of their loyalty to Christ (Matt 25.36, 40) and to the group founded upon a common faith in him (*cf.* Rom 12.9–13). However, it also publicly identified them with those who were being put to shame (*cf.* Phil 4.14; 2 Tim 1.16; see v 34a below). In the ancient Mediterranean culture, people normally distanced themselves from persons associated with shame, lest they be seen as approving of shameful behavior and they too become tainted with that reputation. Also, fraternizing with people who had been arrested or convicted of a crime was dangerous, because it potentially identified, and thus incriminated, one as a possible collaborator in that crime and made them liable to the same social mistreatment as well. Remember how the disciples of Jesus fled at his arrest (Matt 26.56). Philo relates an illustrative case in the anti-Jewish riots in Alexandria of 38 AD. After many Jews had been killed, "the relations and friends of those who were the real victims, merely because they sympathized with the misery of their relations, were led away to prison, were scourged, were tortured, and after all the ill treatment which their living bodies could endure, found the cross the end of all, and the punishment from which they could not escape."[83] A similar, but later, story during the time of the emperor Trajan is related by John Foxe in his *Book of Martyrs*: "At the martyrdom of Faustines and Jovita, brothers and citizens of Brescia, their torments were so many, and their patience so great that Caloccerius, a pagan, beholding them, was struck with admiration and exclaimed in a kind of ecstasy, 'Great is the God of the Christians!' for which he was apprehended, and suffered a similar fate." Whether the story is true or not, it illustrates the attitude toward people who were sympathetic to those upon whom society heaped its shame.

In addition to insults and mistreatment (v 33), the original recipients of Hebrews had endured the public **plunder of** their **property**. Philo of Alexandria relates how this was done to Jews under the Roman prefect Flaccus in the Alexandrian riots of 38 AD. He records,

> Three of the members of this council of elders, Euodius, and Trypho, and Audro, had been stripped of all their property, being plundered of every-

[83] *Flaccus* 72 (*The Works of Philo: Complete and Unabridged*, trans. Charles Duke Yonge (Peabody, MA: Hendrickson, 1995), 731).

> thing that was in their houses at one onset, and he was well aware that they had been exposed to this treatment, for it had been related to him… ; but nevertheless, though he well knew that they had been deprived of all their property, he scourged them in the very sight of those who had plundered them, that thus they might endure the twofold misery of poverty and personal ill treatment, and that their persecutors might reap the double pleasure of enjoying riches which did in no respect belong to them, and also of feasting their eyes to satiety on the disgrace of those whom they had plundered.[84]

Flaccus later admitted "I consented when they were stripped of their possessions, giving immunity to those who were plundering them."[85] This combination of loss of property plus ill treatment parallels the situation here in verses 33–34. The case of the Jews in Alexandria also shows that illegal mob violence against Jews (which Roman officials often tolerated) could be just as responsible for the loss of property as official action. There is no indication in Hebrews that the persecution these Christians had faced earlier was an official governmental action. Most likely it was ill-treatment from neighbors and fellow townsfolk. Similarly, Eusebius related actions against Christians in Alexandria during the Decian persecution: "Then all with one impulse rushed to the homes of the pious, and they dragged forth whomsoever any one knew as a neighbor, and despoiled and plundered them. They took for themselves the more valuable property; but the poorer articles and those made of wood they scattered about and burned in the streets."[86] Philo gives an example of this as well:

> They drove the Jews entirely out of four quarters, and crammed them all into a very small portion of one; and by reason of their numbers they were dispersed over the seashore, and desert places, and among the tombs, being deprived of all their property; while the populace, overrunning their desolate houses, turned to plunder, and divided the booty among themselves as if they had obtained it in war. And as no one hindered them, they broke open even the workshops of the Jews, which were all shut up because of their mourning for Drusilla, and carried off all that they found

---

[84] *Flaccus* 76–77, 171 (*The Works of Philo*, Yonge, 731, 739).

[85] *Flaccus* 171 (*The Works of Philo*, Yonge, 739).

[86] *Ecclesiastical History* 6.41.5 (*NPNF*^{2} 1:283); see also 4.26.5.

> there, and bore it openly through the middle of the market-place as if they had only been making use of their own property.[87]

Eusebius records a similar action against Roman nobles at a later time: "Domitian, having shown great cruelty toward many, and having unjustly put to death no small number of well-born and notable men at Rome, and having without cause exiled and confiscated the property of a great many other illustrious men."[88] Such an action showed contempt for the ones against whom it was directed. It was in effect a denial of any respect, or honor, to them or their property. Furthermore, it left the victims in poverty,[89] which made the recipients of Hebrews' displays of compassion to others (vv 33f) all the more significant. These Christians had endured this disgrace **with joy**, in the same spirit as others who were mistreated for the name of Jesus (Acts 5.41; Rom 5.3; Jam 1.2; 1 Pet 4.13).

The readers had shown in their past that they possessed the kind of faith, along with the courage and the bond of fellowship it produces, that was necessary in their present situation. The recipients' past example of courage to be counted as a Christian regardless of the social cost stood in sharp contrast to those who were now forsaking the public company of other Christians (v 25). The author therefore produced this reminder for them to eliminate any doubts about their ability to persevere. Included in his reminder is the component of faith that helps prepare for the discussion in chapter 11. They had shown, by their past conduct, that they were people who valued the things of heaven more than the things of this life. Their joyful loss of property manifested their belief that heavenly possessions are **better**, more valuable, and well worth the sacrifice of any or all worldly goods. They had lived the Lord's instruction of Matthew 6.19–21. In fact, their belief in the better nature of heavenly things is described as **knowing**, which serves to emphasize the certainty of true faith. Technically there is a difference between knowing something and believing in something yet unseen, but Biblical faith is so sure that it can be called knowledge (see comments on 11.1). By faith they knew the things yet to be seen are more **lasting** than the things presently visible (*cf.* 2 Cor 4.18). This is the very per-

---

[87] *Flaccus* 55–6 (*Works of Philo*, Yonge, 729–30).

[88] *Ecclesiastical History* 3.17 (*NPNF*[2] 1:147).

[89] Koester, *Hebrews*, 465.

spective to which they needed to return, and it is the perspective that faithful people have always had (as will be illustrated in ch 11).

10.35 Therefore do not throw away your boldness, which has a great recompense.

The readers' previous conduct under trial (vv 32–34) was evidence that they possessed **boldness**, or determination, that had enabled them to persevere (*cf.* Acts 4.13). This boldness was the fruit of the work of Jesus on their behalf (v 19). The way to God that had been closed for so long was now fully open because of the sacrifice of Jesus. With the way standing open, they need not hesitate to go through it, even if the world would hate them for it (and the same consideration still holds true for us today). The author therefore calls upon them **not** to **throw away** the very quality, already in their possession, that would see them through the present distress. As noted in the remarks on verse 19, the author was not encouraging his readers to develop within themselves some worldly sense of self-confidence. Their confidence instead consisted of their access to God in heaven through Jesus. The result of this newly created situation was to impart to them a sense of surety, which lies at the heart of faith, that would enable them to endure to the **great recompense** ahead of them. The word **recompense** literally denotes the payment of wages,[90] but in the NT it is used figuratively because salvation is the *gift* of God (Rom 3.24; Eph 2.8f) and is not earned by what we do. As a figure it simply denotes the prospect of receiving something valuable at the end of one's toil. This teaching of reward for faithfulness, which includes service to others, echoes Jesus' own teaching (*cf.* Matt 5.12; 10.42). The certain prospect of receiving a prize in the future is a legitimate Biblical incentive to motivate faithfulness in the present (Col 3.24; Heb 11.26; 2 John 8).

10.36 For you have need of endurance so that, after you have done God's will, you might receive the promise.

The readers had endured before (v 32), and now they needed to endure again, because that is what people of faith do: they endure, they persevere (6.12). The word here does not denote good-natured tolerance of the faults of others (the Bible calls that longsuffering), but instead means

---

[90] BDAG 653.

endurance, a holding up under pressure and hardship (see Col 1.11; Jam 5.7, 10). It is the opposite of throwing away our boldness, verse 35. People who are convinced that a better thing awaits in heaven (v 34) and who are sure towards God because of what Jesus has made available to them (vv 19, 35) do not quit. Their hope and confidence drive them to reach that upon which they have set their hearts and minds (Matt 6.19ff; Col 3.2). **The will of God** does not refer to a specific commandment, but to the Christian life in general, especially faithfulness through the world's opposition, just as it was God's will for Israel to enter the promised land and not quit because of the hardships of the journey. Jesus accomplished the will of God through his faithful endurance (12.2f; *cf.* John 17.4; Matt 26.39) by which he offered his body in service to God. The readers needed to stand ready to do the same, if necessary, in their service to God's will.

The will of God has been delivered with **the promise** that those who keep the faith will be blessed with eternal glory in heaven (9.15). To Jewish ears, "the promise" is connected inseparably with Abraham. The NT authors affirmed that God's promise to Abraham found its ultimate fulfillment in Jesus and the new order he has created (6.17f; *cf.* Acts 13.32; 26.6f; Rom 4.13ff; Gal 3.14ff; Eph 3.6). There are two ways to understand the phrase **receive the promise**. First, it could mean that God makes a promise to those who do his will. Second, and better I think, it can mean, by metonymy, to receive what is promised (so the NASB, NIV, RSV, *etc.*). The present context's mention of endurance and recompense shows that the latter idea is clearly in view here.

10.37–38 "For yet a very little while longer, and the one who is coming will come, and he will not delay. But my righteous one will live by faith, and if he shrinks back my soul is not pleased with him."

These two verses are a combination of Isaiah 26.20 (the source of the words **for yet a little while**) and Habakkuk 2.3–4.[91] Their combination

[91] There are several differences between the Hebrew and Greek versions in the quotation here. The MT reads: Behold, his soul is puffed up, it is not upright in him (ASV). The Greek reads: And if he shrink back, my soul hath no pleasure in him (ASV). Four of the more significant differences merit discussion. 1) How did "puffed up" become "shrink back"? The MT has *'aphal*, which means "swell up," but the Hebrew word *'alaph* (transposing l and ph) means "swoon." It may be that the LXX translators had a Hebrew text that read *'alaph* instead of *'aphal*. 2) How did "his soul" become "my soul"? Again, the Hebrew word is *naphsho* ("his soul"), the final letter (here a suffixal pronoun) being a *waw*. If the final letter is read as a *yod*, which is quite similar to a *waw*, the word becomes *naphshi* ("my

reflects a normal Jewish technique of combining texts that speak to the same issue (*gezerah shawah*, see Introduction). The phrase from Isaiah actually expands upon, and thus comments on or clarifies, the beginning statement of Habakkuk 2.3: "the vision *is yet (still) for* the appointed time" is thus expanded to Isaiah's "for yet a little while longer." Furthermore, the context in both Isaiah 26 and Habakkuk 2 is one of impending judgment. The author cites these texts here not only because they contain a statement that has been true for God's people of all times, but particularly because the situation of the prophets' days was understood to be paradigmatic of God's people in the messianic age. The combined quotation neatly summarizes the exhortation in verses 26–36.[92]

For yet a very little while (from Isa 26.20; the double use of *hoson* emphasizes the shortness of the duration) is one of the shortest OT quotations in Hebrews, but it is thereby no less significant. Isaiah 26 is sometimes called "the song of the city." It is a messianic text (*cf.* Isa 26.1 "in that day") that speaks of the security and peace of God's people (vv 1–3). It enjoined Israel to "trust in the Lord forever" (v 4) and warned of the coming wrath of God upon sinners (vv 11, 14, 16). The words **a little while** do not indicate for the author of Hebrews the temporal nearness of

---

soul"). Similarly, 3) "the just shall live by his faith" (Hebrew) has become "my just one will live by faith." The pronominal suffix waw at the end of *'emunah* has been read as a *yod* and translated by the LXX as a personal pronoun (Greek *mou*) modifying *dikaios.* 4) How did "not upright" become "hath no pleasure"? This is harder to explain. It may be that the Hebrew text used by the translators of the LXX had a different Hebrew word here, since "upright" and "have pleasure" are distinct words in Hebrew (Bruce, *Epistle to the Hebrews,* 272 fn195; see the critical apparatus for Hab 2.4 in BHS). This is probably best understood as an interpretive alteration, quite common in ancient Jewish citations of the Scriptures. The author of Hebrews apparently did not think that the LXX translation, which he here follows, grossly misrepresented the sense of the original. The text as it stands in the LXX still makes the vital connection between righteousness, faith, and life, and the LXX rendering makes it easier to draw out the messianic, eschatological elements in Habakkuk's words (Bruce, *Epistle to the Hebrews,* 273–74). On the difficulties in this verse, see also P. J. M. Southwell, "A Note on Habakkuk ii.4," *JTS* 19 (1968): 614–17; J. A. Emerton, "The Textual and Linguistic Problems of Habakkuk II.4–5," *JTS* 28 (1977): 1–18; George J. Zemek, Jr., "Interpretive Challenges Relating to Habakkuk 2:4b," *GTJ* 1 (1980): 43–69).

[92] T. W. Lewis ("'and if he shrinks back' (Heb.x.38b)," *NTS* 22 (1975): 88–94) has suggested that some Jewish Christians may have found Isaiah 26.20 to be a justification for their withdrawal from the Christian community. The text says "Come, my people, enter into your rooms and close your doors behind you; hide for a little while until indignation runs its course" (NASB). If the original readers of Hebrews had read this as justification for withdrawing from Christianity until the storm of persecution was past, the author of Hebrews is setting them straight. However, this approach seems strained, since it requires reading much into the combination of verses here.

the coming judgment, but is better understood as expressing the Biblical view that life, even when filled with hardships, is short compared to the eternal existence to come (*cf.* 2 Cor 4.17; 1 Pet 1.6, "for a little while … you have been distressed by various trials"), and thus the endurance required is can be viewed as realistically attainable.

Paul quoted the same verse from Habakkuk to show that a righteous status before God is a matter of faith in Jesus and not membership within ethnic Israel (Rom 1.17; Gal 3.11), but the author of Hebrews draws another (although not unrelated) point from it: the only way to escape the punishment that comes upon the unfaithful is to continue to live by faith. Habakkuk said **the one who is coming will come, and he will not delay**.[93] We must not assume that the author of Hebrews thought this was a reference to the Lord's coming at the end of the world in final judgment, because the language is not restricted to this in the Bible. It is instead the kind of language used whenever God prepares to judge a group of people, and its point is the surety of punishment.

The "**coming**" of the Lord, in Biblical thought, is not limited exclusively to his appearance in judgment at the end of time. The Lord's visitations on ancient nations to punish them for their sins were also "comings" of the Lord (Isa 13.6; 19.1; 26.21; 31.4; 40.10; Mic 1.3; Mal 3.1f; Rev 1.7; *etc.*).[94] In this same way, the Lord was coming against Jerusalem in Habakkuk's day in punishment for the sins of Judah. The situation of the original recipients of Hebrews was broadly parallel to that of Habakkuk's day in that God's people needed to be warned about the consequences of unfaithfulness. The au-

[93] The MT text in Hab 2.3 says "the vision is for an appointed time … and if it tarries, wait for it, because it will certainly come and it will not delay." "Vision" in Hebrew is a masculine noun and is the antecedent for "it" through the rest of the verse. In the LXX, however, "vision" is a feminine noun, and "it" has been translated as masculine, referring not to the vision but to a person who will perform it. The author of Hebrews has supplied a definite article to the LXX phrase *erchomenos hēksei* in Hab 2.3. This has the effect of turning the phrase (an awkward Greek expression, woodenly rendering the original Hebrew infinitive absolute) into a more understandable (in Greek) substantivized participle, and makes the sense of the LXX rendering more explicit. The vision is therefore fulfilled by "the coming one," understood to be Jesus.

[94] Similarly, the idea that the early Christians generally expected the Lord's return in final judgment very soon is a reading of the NT evidence that will not stand under close scrutiny. Jesus taught his followers, and the apostles taught as well, that the "day of the Lord" at the end of the world would come unannounced and without signs to indicate its nearness (Matt 24.43f; 1 Thes 5.2; 2 Pet 3.10).

thor of Hebrews has already warned his readers that the Lord will indeed judge his own people if they become unfaithful (vv 26–31), which truth is vividly proven in the destruction of Jerusalem that was coming from the Lord in Habakkuk's time. The point is not evidence that the destruction of Jerusalem in 70 AD was still ahead at the time Hebrews was written, but that God will, "soon," judge the wicked, and that includes the faithless among his own people. God's judgment upon sinners is certain (see 9.27f). The language is typical apocalyptic talk. God will judge the wicked, and God's people had better make sure they are not among them or they too will be destroyed. Yet God is a fair judge and he will not destroy the **righteous** with the wicked. The righteous—understood here messianically as those who persevere in their faith in Jesus—will be spared from punishment. Thus, the righteous **will live** (survive, escape punishment) **by** their **faith** in, or faithfulness to, the Lord.[95] The life of faithful endurance will be illustrated at length in chapter 11. However, if the righteous **shrink back** (withdraw or fall back; *cf.* "drift away" 2.1; "fall away" 3.12; 6.6; "come short" 4.1; *etc.*) and become unfaithful to the Lord, then the Lord will be displeased with them and they too will be punished as sinners.

10.39 But we are not of those who give up, unto destruction, but we are of those who believe, to the preserving of the soul.

The author now summarizes and paraphrases the Scriptural exhortation in an application to his readers that draws upon the words they just heard from Habakkuk. This is another example of the Jewish technique of applying Scripture known as midrash. His words are positive and encouraging: "**but we** are not this kind of people." *Cf.* 6.9. To **give up** (the Greek word here, *hupostolē,* was used in secular Greek of lowering the sails of a ship, thus not continuing forward) from being faithful is to choose the way that leads to **destruction**. See Matthew 7.13. To **believe**, to live by faith (v 38), is the way that leads **to the preserving of** one's **soul** from God's wrath that comes against sin. Jesus taught that saving the soul from God's wrath is more important than saving the body from mistreatment (Matt 10.28; see also John 5.24). Shrinking back or persevering are the only options. "Hebrews does not allow for a neutral space into which the listeners can retreat."[96]

---

[95] See Zemek, "Interpretive Challenges Relating to Habakkuk 2:4b."

[96] Koester, *Hebrews*, 468.

What it means to **believe**, or to live by faith, will be richly illustrated in chapter 11. We should note here that faith, in the Biblical way of thinking, is not simply an intellectual assent to something. The word can be used that way (for example, when the Bible speaks of believing particular things; *cf.* Matt 9.28; Rom 10.9), but more often the word "faith" is used in a much more general way to refer to that *disposition of trust and commitment to God* that characterizes those who are acceptable to him. It is a relational term.[97] Faith, then, is a term that summarizes everything involved in *man's positive response to God*. This is how, for example, Paul can say that we are saved by faith (Eph 2.8), or how he could tell the Philippian jailer that in order to be saved he needed to believe (Acts 16.31). As a *general term*, faith includes many things: trust (Rom 4.18–20), obedience (John 6.36; Rom 1.5; 16.26; Heb 11.8), good works (Gal 5.6; 1 Thes 1.3; 2 Thes 1.11; Jam 2.14–26), baptism (Col 2.12; Acts 16.31–33), faithfulness, and especially for the exhortation in Hebrews, perseverance (2 Thes 1.4; Heb 11.27).[98] All of these are manifestations or aspects of *a basic orientation and commitment toward God* which the Bible calls faith.

[97] As ably demonstrated by Teresa Morgan, *Roman Faith and Christian Faith*.

[98] See Bultmann, "*pistis*," *TDNT* 6:205–208.

HEBREWS 11

As Melchizedek's priesthood from patriarchal times modelled that of the messianic, so the stories of the faithful patriarchs of old stand as exemplars for those who live "today," in the messianic age. There is an emphasis in this chapter on the faith of those who lived before the generation that perished in the wilderness (whose negative example was held up as a warning by our author in chs 3 and 4). Of forty verses, the first twenty-nine speak of the people of faith up until the exodus, and our author pauses in his list to comment on the faith of the earliest patriarchs (vv 13–16). For the author of Hebrews, Israel's earliest history reveals a prototypical kind of faith.

Example lists were a regular feature of ancient rhetoric. They were used in secular rhetoric,[1] but Jewish exemplars existed as well.[2] What we find here in Hebrews, however, is different in some significant ways. Whereas example lists normally chose great, well-known kings or other such leaders for inclusion, the author of Hebrews has chosen to include people who, by comparison, were obscure or, more importantly, associated with lowliness and rejection in the Biblical narrative. Eisenbaum has referred to this as the author effecting a "paradigm shift" in how he wanted his audience to hear the Biblical story.[3] The picture that emerges from Hebrews 11 is "denationalized," and has been reconfigured to support a new identity for God's people, a people who now found themselves rejected by "national Israel." "Hebrews 11 implicitly functions as a genealogy which legitimates the Christian audience by providing them with

[1] As recommended by Aristotle, *Art of Rhetoric* 2.20.9 (1394a); Cicero, *Rhetoric for Herennius* 4.3.5. See Michael Cosby, *The Rhetorical Composition and Function of Hebrews 11: In Light of Example Lists in Antiquity* (Macon, GA: Mercer University Press, 1988).

[2] Grindheim, *Letter to the Hebrews*, 536–37, citing *Wisd* 10:1–11:14; *Sir* 44:1–50:21; *1 Macc* 2:51–61; *4 Macc* 16:14–23; Philo, *On the Virtues* 198–225; *On Rewards and Punishments* 1–56. However, there is no evidence that the author of Hebrews depended directly on any of them.

[3] Pamela Michelle Eisenbaum, *The Jewish Heroes of Chistian History: Hebrews 11 in Literary Context*, SBL Dissertation Series 156 (Atlanta: Scholars Press, 1997), 14.

a Biblical ancestry. At the same time this ancestry is not identified with the nation of Israel, but forms a trajectory independent of it. That is why this list does not include any priests or kings. All the heroes are outsiders. ... The heroes derive their status from *pistis*, not from any national role or office. *Pistis* allows the author to establish a non-national, salvation-historical trajectory which includes the Hebrews community."[4] The people in Hebrews 11 were people whose existence was determined by a faith that looked forward to the reality made possible by Jesus.[5] Although the Jewish roots of the Christian recipients of Hebrews are preserved by taking stories from the Scriptures, these stories are presented in such a way that emphasized embracing a new and separate identity.[6]

There are several threads that run through these stories. One is a sure belief in what God had said, an ability to "see" what God has promised. Our author will demonstrate that people of faith have always been convicted of the certainty of what God promised. As such, faith is forward-looking, and it manifests itself as absolute commitment to God above all else in life. Another thread that runs through many of the stories is escape from death, survival through a deadly situation, or blessing after death. God's response to man's faith has often been to deliver the faithful from death in its various forms (including suffering and rejection). The list had the suffering of the readers in mind.[7] Another thread is that true faith endures even to the point of death, as faith carries us past this life in expectation of the reward that comes later. People of faith, because of the nature of faith itself, do not quit. Finally, all of these stories implicitly illustrate, and thus lead up to, the faithfulness of the supreme example at the end of the list, Christ himself.[8]

11.1 Now faith is the essence of what is hoped for, the proof of things not seen.

---

[4] Eisenbaum, *The Jewish Heroes of Chistian History*, 187.

[5] Cockerill, *Epistle to the Hebrews*, 517.

[6] See Benjamin Dunning, "The Intersection of Alien Status and Cultic Discourse in the Epistle to the Hebrews," in *Hebrews: Contemporary Methods—New Insights*, ed. Gabriella Gelardini, Biblical Interpretation Series 75 (Atlanta: Society of Biblical Literature, 2005), 177–98.

[7] Grindheim, *Letter to the Hebrews*, 537.

[8] Christopher A. Richardson, *Pioneer and Perfecter of Faith*, WUNT 338 (Tübingen: Mohr Siebeck, 2012), 165–224.

At its most basic root, the faith described in the Bible is *a positive response to God*. Here in Hebrews, this takes on the specific, eschatological focus of *a positive, trusting response to God that endures because it can see what God has placed for his people in the future*. That response involves the heart, the mind, the will, the emotions, obedience, commitment, loyalty, *etc*. It is an inclusive[9] term that covers an entire "package" of things that comprise a positive response to God and his word.

While this verse does not offer a comprehensive definition of Biblical faith, it is, however, a definition[10] for the hortatory purpose of Hebrews, and the author drew attention to particular features of faith that were especially relevant to the situation of his hearers. He has already commended them for their confidence concerning the future (10.34f), and he now wished to strengthen their resolve to endure by concentrating on a particular aspect of faith: Christian **faith** involves a confidence in the better things promised for the future. The author aimed to lift his hearers' attention off their present hardships and refocus it on the great reward that lies ahead (*cf*. 10.36) in order to motivate them to faithful endurance. In due course of the discussion many other traits of Biblical faith come to light as well.

The translation that "faith is the assurance of things hoped for" (NASB, ESV, RSV, NRSV) is questionable. The Greek word *hupostasis* denotes that which "stands under" something, the idea is of what underlies something, what we might call the "basis" of "core" of something. It does not mean "assurance."[11] Morgan suggests that "foundation" best captures the idea here in English.[12] "Reality" or "realization" also gets close to the basic idea of the term.[13] The term denotes what is the **es-**

---

[9] One of the most common mistakes in understanding the Biblical use of the word "faith" (or "believe") is to treat it as if it were always a specific term (such as the mental act of accepting what one is told).

[10] The form of the statement follows classical expressions of definitions. Ellingworth, *Epistle to the Hebrews*, 564; Attridge, *Hebrews*, 307. "Definition is the statement of the fact called in question in appropriate, clear, and concise language." Quintilian, *Institutes of Oratory* 7.3.2 (Butler, LCL).

[11] Hollander, "hupostasis," *EDNT* 3:407. BDAG 1041: "The sense 'confidence', 'assurance' ... favored by Melanchthon and Luther (also Tyndale, NRSV, but not KJV) for Hb 11:1 has enjoyed much favor but must be eliminated, since examples of it cannot be found."

[12] Morgan, *Roman Faith and Christian Faith*, 339.

[13] Robert G. Hoerber, "On the Translation of Hebrews 11:1," *Concordia Journal* 21 (1995): 77–79, at 78: "In faith things hoped for become reality."

sence, the substantial nature or basis that underlies the visible reality of something (as opposed to its outward features or appearance), so that the meaning here is that faith is the core, essence, foundation, or basis of hoping. Philo used the term for the unseen, spiritual world.[14] See comments on 3.14. In legal contexts the word had the sense of "title deed,"[15] so deSilva explains that people of faith "have in their possession, in effect, the title deed to what the person they trust will provide."[16] It is also helpful to remember that the author of Hebrews has presented things from the OT as shadows. Faith, however, is one's connection to the reality, the substance, that produced the shadows.[17]

Faith and **hope** are intimately related (*cf.* Gal 5.5; 1 Pet 1.21). We hope for what we do not yet have or experience. When one hopes for something, beneath that anticipation lies a firm belief or trust that the thing not yet possessed actually exists and that its possession is certainly attainable. When we believe in that for which we hope and are as confident of it as if we already possessed it, then we have true Biblical faith. Faith is by its nature, therefore, forward-looking (*i.e.*, eschatological). True faith is sure, confident, and bold concerning that for which the believer hopes. It is not hesitant or doubtful. Instead, it looks confidently to the future and considers the promises of God as sure as if they were already fulfilled (*cf.* 6.13ff).

Similarly, Biblical faith is a kind of **proof of** the **things** which one has **not** yet **seen**. *Cf.* Romans 8.24, and 2 Corinthians 4.18: "we do not look at the things which are seen, but at the things which are not seen." Given the transcendent nature of faith, the statement implies that people of faith are aware that there is more than the visible, physical universe as the object of perception. That is, people of faith have a view of reality that is broader than the sum of visible things. Christians have not seen what awaits them as a reward for faithfulness (*cf.* 2 Cor 4.18), but they can be just as confident of it (by faith) as if the reality was right in front of them as proof of God's faithfulness. It is in this sense of "confidence" or boldness that our author says that faith is as a kind of proof, and so the newer English versions say, "the conviction of things not seen." The

---

[14] Grindheim, *Letter to the Hebrews*, 92.

[15] BDAG 1041; MM 660.

[16] deSilva, *Perseverance in Gratitude*, 383. Similarly, Johnson (*Hebrews*, 278) sees the statement as expressing the sense of a pledge, down-payment, or initial participation in the things for which one hopes.

[17] Grindheim, *Letter to the Hebrews*, 541–42.

KJV translation of "evidence" can be misleading. The author is not saying that we believe according to the evidence we have. As legitimate as that might be in some contexts, it is not the point here. Instead, he is saying that Biblical faith is a solid confidence in what lies ahead, a confidence so strong as if it had already been proven, even though that proof is presently lacking, and based on the faithfulness of God himself. Confidence in something one has not seen will be a dominant theme through the next several verses. Together the two statements in this verse define faith as something that connects the present and the future, like an anchor extending from the former to the latter (see 6.19). Faith allows believers to participate already, as it were, in what has not yet come.[18] The practical result is that such a faith provides a strong motivation to endure in the present until we fully experience the object of our faith. The examples in the following verses will clarify and further refine this basic definition.

11.2 By this the elders were approved.

This statement is virtually repeated in verse 39 below, forming an inclusio,[19] as well as serving as a kind of thesis statement for the examples to follow. Those who have the kind of faith described in verse 1 ("**this** kind of faith"[20]) are commended by God himself, as history shows.[21] The **elders** were the Biblical Israelite forefathers (1.1 "the fathers") of the Jewish Christians who were now considering the author's exhortation. It has been true throughout all Biblical history that God is pleased by genuine faith in him. Of course, not all the Jews of former generations **were approved**[22] by God, as the author's coverage of the wilderness generation in chapters 3–4 has shown. However, those who *did* obtain God's commen-

---

[18] See S. M. Baugh, "The Cloud of Witnesses in Hebrews 11," *WTJ* 68 (2006): 113–32.

[19] Allen, *Hebrews*, 539.

[20] The demonstrative *houtos* points to what is thematic; see comments on 3.3 (footnote).

[21] "The rhetorical effect" of the long list of examples that follows "is to make this definition seem to represent a statement of timeless truth for which examples can be marshaled from the beginning of human history to the present time: God's people have *always* lived by faith, believing that they would one day receive God's promises which they could not see except through the eyes of faith." Michael R. Cosby, "The Rhetorical Composition of Hebrews 11," *JBL* 107 (1988): 257–73, at 261. Hebrews 11 has features of history, encomium, and biography combined, and was quite normal rhetorically for its time.

[22] The Greek is the passive form of *martureō*, a verb that means "to testify." In the passive, however, it means to give a good report, to approve. Ellingworth, *Epistle to the Hebrews*, 567.

dation did so because they possessed the faith described in verse 1 (*cf.* 3.19, where it was noted that those who did not receive God's approval lacked faith). The connection between faith and God's approval is such that where you find one, the other will be there. In this way, the author can attribute faith to OT characters even when the OT itself did not use that term of them, because their approval before God (which is mentioned) could only be the result of their having had faith.[23] The mention of approval would have been significant to those who lived in a society where being esteemed by others was highly prized. However, the author was trying to convince his hearers that the esteem of God is far more important than, and ultimately relativizes, the esteem of men.[24]

The author, by calling his readers back to their history, was bidding them to live worthy of their heritage which was marked by great examples of the kind of faith described in verse 1. Classical rhetoric sometimes praised figures from the past in order to strengthen the hearer's commitment to the values those figures embodied.[25] Hebrews 11 partakes in this strategy as part of its appeal to remain faithful to Christ. The author will illustrate the general assertion of this verse[26] with several examples in verses 4ff.

11.3 By faith we understand that the world[27] was created by the word of God, so that what is seen did not come from visible things.

Beginning with this verse, the phrase "by faith" becomes the rhetorical refrain of the exhortation. It is drawn from the quotation of Habakkuk 2.4 (at the end of Heb 10, "the righteous will live by faith"), and its repetition through this chapter therefore has the effect of keeping the key phrase from the Habakkuk quotation continually in the ears of his audience. The instrumental dative *pistei* resounds eighteen times in this

---

[23] Morgan, *Roman Faith and Christian Faith*, 335.

[24] deSilva, *The Hope of Glory*, 150, 153.

[25] deSilva, *The Hope of Glory*, 162. See also Cosby, *The Rhetorical Composition and Function of Hebrews 11 in Light of Example-lists in Antiquity*, who cites discussions of the technique in ancient literature.

[26] It was common in ancient times for hortatory speeches to include statements of historical summary. Merland Ray Miller, "What is the Literary Form of Hebrews 11?," *JETS* 29 (1986): 411–17, at 411–12.

[27] Technically the word here is plural ("the worlds"), but this denotes what we call "the universe." Cortez, "Creation in Hebrews," 292.

chapter. The repetition of the same key term reinforces the conceptual theme of the exhortation for the hearers.[28]

The first citation of something accomplished "by faith" is not a story about a person, but a reference to the creation account in Genesis 1–2, which serves a typological function. The way a believer reads that account serves to illustrate how faith operates. Faith causes us to **understand** something we did not see, namely the origin of the universe. Here "understand" has the connotation of "know for certain," and is parallel to assurance and conviction in verse 1. The fact that faith is a confidence in God's promise concerning the future (v 1) implies a more fundamental consideration inherent to the concept: faith is belief in the power of God's word. By our faith in what God says, we have a knowledge about something we did not see, and our faith is of such a nature that we are just as sure of what God tells us as though we ourselves witnessed it. It is important to read this statement correctly. The author does not say that we believe what we understand. In fact, some of the examples below will show that Bible characters were sometimes in a situation of believing what God said even if they did not understand how he would accomplish it or how it fit into his plan (an important point for the original readers who were trying to reconcile the promise of blessing with a life of persecution[29]). Instead, our author is saying that faith, by its nature, gives us an understanding of things we have not personally experienced (or "seen").

Scripture says that **God** brought the universe into existence **by** his **word** ("and God said" occurs eight times in Gen 1.1–27; see also Psa 33.6, 9; 2 Pet 3.5). It is important to note that, in Genesis 1, what God is said to have "made" is the product of his word. God's word has the power within itself to create the situation it dictates (see Isa 55.10f; 42.5f). Thus God said, "Let there be light" and light appeared. God's word is not merely a description of reality, but the power that causes reality to come into existence. When God speaks, things become what God said. The author then carefully reiterates that the creation perfectly illustrates that God, by his word, brings into being things which did not appear before (**what is seen**

[28] Cosby, "The Rhetorical Composition of Hebrews 11," 258 says that "The most highly rhetorical passage in Hebrews is the example list of famous individuals in chap. 11." Relevant facts here are that a discourse of praise was called an *encomium,* the technique of repeating a key term in each example is called *anaphora,* and the call to imitate someone else was called *mimēsis.* See also Richardson, *Pioneer and Perfecter of Faith,* 137–64.

[29] Koester, *Hebrews,* 469.

did not come from visible things). *Cf.* the RSV rendering: "so that what is seen was made out of things which do not appear." That is, all that we now see did not come from pre-existing material, but was originally brought into existence by God's powerful, creative word, and people of faith proceed upon this understanding.

So what did belief in the Biblical creation account have to do with these people and their situation? One answer is that God's role as the creator means that he rules over everything.[30] All things are under his control. Another answer is that the creation account showed that God created a world—a situation, if you will—that did not previously exist and which, in fact, was contrary to the previous situation of chaos, darkness, and "void." Where before there was nothing, God by his word made something. Where there was darkness, God by his word filled it with light, and a lifeless mass was filled with life. Where there was disorder, God brought order and peace. And so, the original recipients of Hebrews were in a situation of distress. Their lives were disordered and chaotic compared to their pre-Christian lives, but God has promised to bring them into his glory (6.18) if they would be faithful. They could not see that glory at present for it was obscured by their trials. Yet the word that created the universe, that brought everything into existence by its sheer power, is that same word of God that promises to bring the faithful to a better place for an inheritance (10.34; 11.16). If one accepts what the Bible says about the power of God's word in creation, one ought to accept God's word concerning the reward of the faithful (10.35; 11.26; Isaiah made a similar argument for the people of his day in Isa 43.15ff). If God's word did not fail at the creation—and a more impressive display of the power and reliability of God's word could hardly be found in Scripture—then God's promise word to glorify the faithful will not fail either. If what did not appear was made to appear by God's word then, so also God will assuredly bring about a new situation of glory even though it is yet unseen because of hardship. That is, the recipients were being encouraged to believe in the coming reality of what God has said (promised), and not concentrate on the visible world of their daily lives.[31]

The author was trying to show his readers that belief in God's word (promise) is wholly justified because God's word is characterized by

---

[30] Cortez, "Creation in Hebrews," 319.

[31] Cockerill, *Epistle to the Hebrews*, 524.

power (as the creation account shows; see also Heb 4.12), and thus it is reliable. They already believed in the power of God as evidenced by their acceptance and understanding of the origin of the universe related through Scripture. They must then continue to believe that God, by the power inherent in his promise word, will bring them to glory, and they must live in accordance with that faith.

11.4 By faith Abel offered a greater sacrifice to God than Cain, through which it was testified that he was righteous (since God was testifying about his gifts), and through it he, although he is dead, still speaks.

The author now launches into a tour of Biblical history to show that the greatest moments of the story of salvation were those that involved God's people living by faith in God's word, people who believed that what God said would come to pass, often in the face of persecution, and always in the face of some form of death.[32] They had the kind of faith that was confident in what God said, and they lived in accordance with that confidence. The list includes examples of both people (vv 4–32) and experiences (vv 33–38) associated with faith. This kind of "example list" to illustrate and recommend a virtue (called an encomium[33]) was common in didactic literature of ancient times.[34] The best-known example of this as a kind of literature is probably Plutarch's series of *Parallel Lives*, in which he presented famous Greek and Roman figures from the past in order to demonstrate the moral virtues they exemplified. Within a discourse, the Roman orator Cicero said "But, in order to persuade those to whom any misfortune has happened that they can and ought to bear it, it is very useful to set before them an enumeration of other persons who have borne similar calamities."[35] The practice also has Biblical roots, as historical lists of examples appear in the OT.[36]

---

[32] Bryan R. Dyer, "'All of These Died in Faith': Hebrews 11 and Faith in the Face of Death," *CBQ* 83 (2021): 638–54.

[33] Hebrews 11 is an encomium on faith. Concerning encomium, "...the primary purpose was that of praise. According to the rhetoricians, suitable subjects for the encomium included persons, cities, things; *i.e.*, any subject an author might select." (Philip L. Shuler, "Encomium," *AYBD* 2:505–06, at 505).

[34] See also Cosby, "The Rhetorical Composition and Function of Hebrews 11"; Koester, *Hebrews*, 470.

[35] *Tusculan Disputations* 4.29 (*Cicero's Tusculan Disputations*, trans. C. D. Yonge (New York: Harper and Brothers, 1877), 154).

[36] Josh 24.2ff; 1 Sam 8.8ff; Neh 9.6ff; Psa 78, 135, 136. Such lists also appear in the in-

The first story of one who obtained approval (v 2) from God is that of **Abel** (Gen 4). Neither the author of Hebrews nor Moses say that Abel's **sacrifice** (offering) was better because it was an animal in contrast to Cain's offering of the produce of the field.[37] We are not told in the Genesis account why each brother chose to offer what he did.[38] In fact, we would wonder where either got the idea that their sacrifice would be acceptable at all if God had not told them so. The narrative does not say that God had demanded an animal, and that Abel consequently complied and Cain did not. In fact, the author of Hebrews has looked at the story in a different way. Given that both men offered sacrifices, that one offering was rejected and the other accepted, and that God did not cite the content of Cain's offering as the problem, it becomes clear that what was wrong with Cain's offering was Cain himself.[39] This is exactly what Genesis says: "the Lord had regard *for Abel* and for his offering ... but *for Cain* and his offering he had no regard" (Gen 4.4f (NASB), emphasis added).[40] The apostle John confirms this as he notes that Cain was an evil man. Cain "was of the evil one and slew his brother. And for what reason did he slay him? Because his deeds were evil, and his brother's were righteous" (1 John 3.12 NASB).[41] What made the sacrifice of Abel acceptable to God, and thus **greater** (*i.e.*, of greater value) than Cain's offering, was not that it was an animal but that it was offered **by faith** on Abel's part. God was pleased with Abel's sacrifice because God was pleased with Abel himself, who lived by faith.[42] Cain, although he offered something to God and was outwardly obedient, was not a man of faith. The problem of presenting sacrifices as external rituals without

---

tertestamental literature (1 Macc 2:51–60, 4 Macc 16;:20ff and 18:11ff) and in the rabbinic literature (Lane, *Hebrews 9–13*, 316–17).

[37] This approach goes back to Philo of Alexandria, in his *On the Sacrifices of Abel and Cain* 27.88–89.

[38] The LXX rendering of the MT narrative actually attempts to offer explanations. See Joel N. Lohr, "Righteous Abel, Wicked Cain: Genesis 4:1–16 in the Masoretic Text, the Septuagint, and the New Testament," *CBQ* 71 (2009): 485–96.

[39] See Bruce K. Waltke, "Cain and His Offering," *WTJ* 48 (1986): 363–72.

[40] Johnson, *Hebrews*, (280–81) takes both positions together: the problem with Cain's offering was both its substance and the one who offered it.

[41] There was apparently a Jewish tradition that read the story in this way, as attested by Josephus (*Ant.* 1.2.1), who referred to Abel as "a lover of righteousness."

[42] Here and in 12.15f, the author interpreted single events in the lives of Biblical characters not as isolated events, but as representations or encapsulations of the entire lives of those characters.

living by faith in God was not uncommon throughout Israel's history (*cf.* 1 Sam 15.22; Isa 1.11; Jer 6.20).

Habakkuk 2.4, which our author quoted in Hebrews 10.37f, linked faith and righteousness ("the righteous will live by faith," itself an echo of Genesis 15.6). Our author has also warned his hearers of having an evil, unbelieving heart in falling away from God (3.12). The heart that lacks faith in God is an evil heart and makes its possessor an evil person, but the heart that believes in God is righteous (just as God counted Abraham righteous because of his faith, Gen 15.6; Noah, Heb 11.7, serves as another example). These same connections appear in the story of Abel's offering. Because he offered his sacrifice accompanied **by faith** in his heart, Abel was counted a **righteous** man by God (see also Matt 23.35). By accepting his offering,[43] God himself was **testifying** (speaking about what he knew) that Abel was a righteous person. That is, God's testimony about the gift was also a testimony about the giver, and so Abel serves as an illustration of one who was approved by his faith (v 2).[44] God's rejection of Cain's offering thus indicated that God saw Cain as a wicked man, and his wickedness lay in his lack of faith. See Proverbs 15.8; 21.27. Cain's lack of faith in God made him an evil person which in turn made his worship unacceptable to God. Abel's faithful worship made him the object of hatred from his wicked brother, and that hatred eventually turned into persecution which cost Abel his life. Abel **still speaks** (*i.e.*, testifies as a witness, Heb 12.1) to those who serve God by faith even though he died long ago. His blood (death) "tells" us that those who draw near to God in full assurance of faith (10.22) will receive God's approval, but they may also receive ill treatment and even death from unbelievers.

The original recipients were undoubtedly likely to see a parallel between Abel and Christ (Heb 12.24). There is also a messianic, eschatological (*i.e.*, forward-looking) aspect to Abel's testimony. In the words **a greater sacrifice** we hear an echo of the discussion in chapters 9 and 10, where it was shown that Jesus in the new covenant has offered the perfect sacrifice for sin. The story of Cain and Abel involves two sacrifices, one **greater** than the other, one that was intimately connected with the **faith**

---

[43] The antecedent of the relative clause "**through which ...**" is best taken as the whole situation of Abel, *i.e.*, his faith and the offering that expressed it.

[44] The word "testifying" in this verse is the same word in the Greek which is translated "approved" in v 2.

that looks ahead and one that was not. Those who worship (or serve; as in 9.1, 6, 9, 14; 10.2) God by faith in Jesus come to God on the basis of a better sacrifice, like Abel. In its own way, therefore, the story of Cain and Abel speaks to the relationship between the sacrifices of the old system, which were not acceptable to take away sins (see comments on 10.1–4, 11), and the new order based on the better, perfect sacrifice of Jesus. Abel thus **still speaks** to later generations about a better sacrifice, which is fulfilled in the work of the faithful Christ (12.24).[45] Yet the original recipients were undoubtedly likely to see a parallel not only between Abel and Christ (Heb 12.24), but also between Abel and themselves. With the story of Cain and Abel began the history of the faithless persecuting the innocent faithful,[46] a history in which the original recipients of Hebrews could find their own identity.[47] Therefore "do not be surprised, brethren, if the world hates you" (1 John 3.13 NASB).

11.5 By faith Enoch was changed so that he would not see death, and he was not found because God changed him; for before his change it was testified that he pleased God.

This verse is another example of one who received approval (v 2) from God, which could only be due to his faith. Yet in contrast to Abel who was killed, we now consider one who never died.[48] The historical details about **Enoch** are sparse but full of significance. Jewish speculation on Enoch was common,[49] but the author of Hebrews has not bought into any of it. Instead, he draws out the clear implication of the Biblical facts, just as he has done with other Biblical data previously (recall 7.1ff). Enoch was a descendant of Seth and was the seventh generation from Adam (see 1 Chron 1.3; *cf.* Jude 14). His story is briefly told in Genesis 5, which some have called "the diary of death." That chapter relates how the curse of Eden (Gen 2.17), resulting from Adam's sin, became a reality for all

---

[45] Baugh, "The Cloud of Witnesses in Hebrews 11," 122–24.

[46] McCruden sees the faithfulness of Jesus as in the foreground here. Kevin B. McCruden, "The Eloquent Blood of Jesus: The Neglected Theme of the Fidelity of Jesus in Hebrews 12:24," *CBQ* 75 (2013): 504–20.

[47] See Tom Thatcher, "Cain and Abel in Early Christian Memory: A Case Study in 'The Use of the Old Testament in the New,'" *CBQ* 72 (2010): 732–51.

[48] Moffatt, *Epistle to the Hebrews*, 162.

[49] See references in Ellingworth, *Epistle to the Hebrews*, 574, Lane, *Hebrews 9–13*, 337, and Moffatt, *Epistle to the Hebrews*, 166.

who followed Adam (*cf.* Rom 5.12). In story after story the end is the same: "and he died" (Gen 5.8, 11, 14, 17, 20). Yet concerning Enoch we are told "and he was not, for God took him" (Gen 5.24 NASB). That is, Enoch did **not** experience (**see**) physical **death**. Why not? The Genesis account tries hard to make the reason clear. Twice in Genesis 5, and only of Enoch, are we told that "he walked with God" (vv 22, 24). The author of Hebrews understood this as the description of a life of faith.

The author emphasizes Enoch's escape from death by piling up the terms "was changed," "would not see death," "was not found," and "God changed him." Because of his faith, Enoch **was not found** because he was taken from the earth. The phrase "was not found" could mean that death did not find him,[50] or it could mean that he could no longer be found anywhere in this world.[51] The words are a quotation of Genesis 5.24. It would appear that Enoch was taken into glory (*cf.* Heb 2.10). The word **changed** renders the Greek word *metatithēmi*, which can denote a change in one's place or in one's condition.[52] Either definition would work here. The author draws upon this change, said in Genesis 5 of Enoch alone, to show that God does indeed reward the faithful (see v 6). After living a life of faith, Enoch was taken to be with God. Those who live by faith transcend, and thus overcome, death. Several of the stories cited in verses 7ff below will make this clear.[53]

As in the previous verse, God's treatment of this person stands as his testimony for all to hear. By taking Enoch into heaven and rescuing him from the world in which sin and death reigned, God was confirming what he had already **testified** about him, that Enoch had pleased him. Enoch is thus another example of the general statement of verse 2. As in other treatments of Scripture by our author, the sequence of the statements of the Biblical text are instructive. The testimony about Enoch comes first ("Enoch walked with God"), then his translation into heaven, so that the former is understood to be the cause of the latter. The author of Hebrews has used the same word for "**pleased**" that is used in the LXX version of the story of Enoch (*euaresteō*) to translate the

[50] Moffatt, *Epistle to the Hebrews*, 165 cites examples of this sense.

[51] Ellingworth, *Epistle to the Hebrews*, 575. In support of this interpretation, the MT simply says that Enoch "was not (there)," *i.e.*, he no longer existed on the earth.

[52] BDAG 642.

[53] See Gareth Lee Cockerill, "The Better Resurrection (Heb. 11:35): A Key to the Structure and Rhetorical Purpose of Hebrews 11," *TynBul* 51 (2000): 215–34.

Hebrew phrase "he walked with God." In the LXX the word is also used in the story of Noah (Gen 6.9) and Abraham (Gen 24.40).

11.6 But without faith it is impossible to please him, for it is necessary for the one who comes to God to believe that he is, and that he is a rewarder of those who seek him out.

The author now briefly pauses from examining the Biblical catalog of faith and provides an addendum to the definition of faith that was offered in verse 1. This additional comment drives home the point he has raised thus far: the stories of Abel and Enoch show that **without faith it is impossible to please** God. As noted in verse 4, God was pleased with Abel, as witnessed by his acceptance of Abel's offering. God was also pleased with Enoch who "walked with God." The case is building that faith is the essential ingredient in those stories of people who pleased God.

The author next spells out two basic components of this God-pleasing faith. Again, this is not meant to be a comprehensive list of faith's features, but is tailored to the specific needs of the original audience in their situation. First, anyone who would come to God and enter into a saving relationship with him **must believe that he is**, that is, that he exists. This takes us back to the "definition" of faith in verse 1. The Biblical God is unseen (John 1.18; 1 Tim 6.16), so the one who approaches him must do so believing firmly that he truly exists. This the hearers of Hebrews had already done. Second, and more importantly for the exhortation here, is something at which the hearers were failing. Those who come to God must believe that he will keep his promises. That is, faith involves more than mental assent on man's part. It also involves a trusting relationship with the living God.[54] If they could believe in an unseen God, they must believe in an unseen reward from that same God as well. One must believe in the ultimate faithfulness of God himself (because he is faithful 10.23) and live accordingly. God has promised to reward (see comments on 10.35) those who are faithful to him (*cf.* 6.18), and anyone who wishes to come to God *must* believe this with the confident, forward-looking faith described in verse 1. The examples that follow will make this clear. The author of Hebrews perceived that his hearers' fault lay in a failure to trust in God's promise of salvation. Many people believe that God exists, yet there is more to pleasing God than this (*cf.* Jam 2.19). One must **seek him out**, a

[54] Lane, *Hebrews 9–13*, 338.

term that expresses effort and diligence. The one who does this commits himself to God and places a right relationship with him above all else.

11.7 By faith Noah, being warned about things not yet seen, reverently prepared an ark unto the saving of his house, through which he condemned the world, and became an heir of the righteousness that is by faith.

The illustrations of true faith now continue. The patriarch **Noah** is a good example of the very kind of faith the author has described thus far and which his hearers needed to develop. Like Enoch, the Bible says that Noah "walked with God" (Gen 6.9; LXX: Noah was well-pleasing to God), and thus like Enoch he was rescued from the death that came upon the world around him by being lifted above it (by the waters of the flood). First, Noah believed God when God **warned** him about something that, in his day, was **not yet seen**, and thus he is a prime example of the faith described in verse 1. Specifically, God warned Noah of the coming destruction of the godless world through a flood of water (Gen 6.13, 17). Even though Noah had never seen such a flood, Noah believed that it would happen exactly as God said. God also told Noah to build an ark whereby he would be spared from the coming destruction. In further and demonstrable trust in God's word, Noah, **reverently prepared** the **ark** according to God's instructions, which resulted in **the saving of** the members of **his** family (**house**; *cf.* 1 Pet 3.20). The mention of Noah's family (**house**) may have been especially significant to the readers of Hebrews who were facing persecution that could possibly end in their deaths. In times of persecution, one would normally fear for the safety of one's family. The story of Noah reassures the faithful that God will care for their families (*cf.* 2.13), and that God will save the people of his own "house" (3.6).

Noah's story stands as an illustration of how faith in God's promise translates into pious or reverent obedience, and results in salvation. It shows how faith is not merely intellectual assent to an idea, but living and acting as if what God has said about the future is absolutely true and reliable and will come to pass without fail. Noah did not simply believe that a flood was coming, he acted like it; he followed God's instructions about what to do to escape destruction in that flood and he was saved from the flood as a result. This is the proper relationship between faith and works; the works are expressions and products of the faith within. If Noah had not believed God, he would not have built the ark. The story further illustrates the endurance that characterizes true faith, since Genesis tells us (and the original readers would have been well-aware of it) that there were 120 years between God's promise to destroy the earth and the fulfillment of it. For all that time, Noah believed in what God had said, and acted like it as he awaited the day when God would perform his word.

Noah's work in building the ark was not only an expression and proof of his faith in God's word, but also served to express his enduring loyalty to God in the midst of a wicked, hostile world.[55] His act of obedience, predicated on his belief in what God had told him about the future, was in effect a scathing condemnation of **the world** of unbelievers around him. His actions, borne of faith, said in effect that the world was wrong for not believing what God said. Noah's conduct spoke volumes of rebuke to the world of his day. The world often understands the rebuke of faithful deeds, and sometimes lashes out against them (*cf.* 1 Pet 4.4). Such a consideration was relevant to the hearers of Hebrews, who were facing hostility from unbelievers for being people of faith in Jesus. The illustration of Noah takes on even more significance in light of the Lord's promise that he will return in judgment for all (9.27f; 10.25). There is a sense in which every child of God today is in the same situation as Noah, living in the shadow of a coming apocalyptic judgment upon the world and trying to live righteously in the hope that God said he will rescue those who prove to trust him (*cf.* 2 Pet 3).

Because of his faith in God's word, Noah **became an heir of the righteousness which is by faith**. While the author of Hebrews does not explicitly say that Noah's faith justified him, that certainly is the idea here. There is an echo of the language of Genesis 15.6 here, hinting at the story of Abraham (next). Because Noah believed what God said concerning the future, and acted and endured in accordance with that word, he was counted as righteous before God, and God has promised to reward the righteous. That Noah later sinned does not annul the didactic value of his conduct before the flood. Moreover, the word **heir** also underscores the forward-looking nature of faith and its reward. Just as an heir is guaranteed to receive his father's wealth but he does not have it now, so believ-

[55] As in v 4, it is best to see the antecedent of the relative clause "**through which ...**" as Noah's conduct as a whole, which resulted in his salvation.

ers (like Noah) have yet to receive the full measure of blessing which God has promised to his faithful children. See comments on 11.39–40.

11.8 By faith Abraham, when he was called, obeyed to go out to a place which he was going to receive as an inheritance; and he went out, not knowing where he was going.

More is said about the patriarch **Abraham** in this chapter than anyone else, and for good reason: he is the Biblical prototype of the person who lives by faith in God. Abraham is remembered more in Scripture for his faith than for anything else.

The first illustration from Abraham's life comes from the beginning of the Scriptural narrative, Genesis 12. There we are told "Now the Lord said to Abram, 'Go forth from your country, and from your relatives and from your father's house, to the land [here, **place**] which I will show you" ... So Abram went forth as the Lord had spoken to him" (vv 1, 4, NASB). God actually gave these instructions to Abraham twice, once in Ur, and once in Haran (see Acts 7.2f). Although moving from one place to another is commonplace in our world, in Abraham's day such a move entailed a nearly complete change in his identity. One's homeland was the place of one's people, the place associated with one's ancestral narrative, the place where one was "at home," the place where they spoke your language, shared your customs, and worshipped the same gods. To leave one's homeland was to leave almost everything that gave a person their identity and to take up a life among foreigners. In ancient times there was a stigma associated with living outside one's homeland. The assumption was that something dishonorable had forced them to leave: "... it is good to live and die in one's own country. Residence abroad brings contempt upon the poor and shame upon the rich as though they had been banished for a crime."[56] Furthermore, people who lived in a place as resident aliens did not have the rights (such as exemptions from certain kinds of service or taxes, voting in public assemblies, or inheritance rights[57]) which the citizens of that place enjoyed. Foreigners could also be viewed

[56] *The Letter of Aristeas* 249; R. J. H. Shutt, "Letter of Aristeas," in *The Old Testament Pseudepigrapha and the New Testament: Expansions of the "Old Testament" and Legends, Wisdom, and Philosophical Literature, Prayers, Psalms and Odes, Fragments of Lost Judeo-Hellenistic Works*, Vol. 2., ed. James H. Charlesworth (New Haven; London: Yale University Press, 1985), 29.

[57] Koester, *Hebrews*, 485.

as a "corrupting" influence on the native culture. Traumas such as famine, war, or enslavement might force one out of one's homeland, but to leave voluntarily would not have been seen as "rational." Furthermore, God told Abraham to leave where he was without any hint in the narrative that Abraham knew where he was going. In effect, God was calling on Abraham to abandon his former identity in order to gain the one God would provide for him. Abraham's response was classic: he got up and left, "**not knowing where he was going**." In other words, his destination was "unseen" to him (recall v 1). This underscores the nature of his faith: he had complete trust in God and his promise. As such his is an example of the confidence and conviction that characterizes true faith in God (v 1). Abraham trusted in God to the point that where he was going did not matter; all that mattered was that God wanted him to go, so he went. Like Noah, he heard what God said and **obeyed** it. Faith will (and must, Jam 2.14ff; Heb 5.9) manifest itself in various ways in one's life, including doing what God has commanded (1 Thes 1.3; 2 Thes 1.11).

We should also keep in mind, as Stephen says, that God "gave him no inheritance in it [the land], not even a foot of ground, and promised to give it to him and to his seed after him when he had no child" (Acts 7.5). This will become important for verses 39f. Abraham inherited the land of Canaan in the limited sense that he lived there for the rest of his life and knew for sure (through faith) that it would belong to his descendants. Otherwise, as the next two verses make clear, Abraham did not consider that his inheritance from God consisted of some earthly plot of land. Again, it is likely that the original recipients of Hebrews could easily identify with Abraham as some of them had made a choice to follow Christ which resulted in the loss of their ancestral associations. In a sense, Christianity involves a radical re-definition of oneself, similar to what Abraham experienced. Such radical change can be difficult to negotiate, and this was undoubtedly part of what the original recipients of Hebrews were thinking.

There is a growing thread as the reader sees the examples of Enoch, Noah, and Abraham. All three, in one sense or another, left the present world behind in order to follow God in faith. Enoch did not follow the ways of the world, but walked with God on this earth and was eventually removed from it. Noah separated himself from the unbelieving world around him with the ark he built through faith in God's word, and Abraham left his ancestral home behind in order to head for a new place of which he had been told by God. The fact that Abraham left his home to follow God made him an even closer example to Christians who had lost their homes and possessions (10.34), and perhaps had been disowned by their families, in order to follow Jesus (*cf.* Matt 19.29). Like Abraham, they too had been **called** by God (Heb 3.1; 9.15; through the gospel, 2 Thes 2.14), which resulted in the loss of many of their ancestral associations, and they left behind an earthly **inheritance** for the sake of a heavenly one that was theirs only in promise (6.12; 1.14).

11.9 By faith he lived in the land of promise as in a foreign land, living in tents with Isaac and Jacob, the fellow-heirs of the same promise,

The word translated **lived** (Greek *paroikeō*) can mean simply to inhabit a place, or it can mean to live in a land that is not one's home country, and thus to live as a resident alien. The latter idea is the one that predominates in the LXX, and is probably intended as the antonym for the other word in this verse translated "living" (see below), and for these reasons this second meaning is preferred here.[58] The land of Canaan did not become Abraham's own possession during his lifetime, but God promised to give it to his descendants (Gen 12.7; 13.15; 15.18; 17.8). Therefore, the land was still the **land of promise** even for Abraham, and although he lived there for the rest of his life, he lived there **as** if it were **a foreign land** to him. Even after he had been living in the land for about sixty years, he told the residents of Hebron "I am a stranger and a sojourner among you" (Gen 23.4 NASB). The fact that he did not possess the land, that is, he did not inherit what God had promised him, is clear from the fact that he lived a nomadic existence there, **living in tents** like the Bedouins still do, in temporary structures characteristic of those who have no permanent settlement or claim to land. The phrase presents the irony of Abraham's situation in somewhat of a contradiction of terms. **Living** here translates the Greek word *katoikeō*, which routinely means to settle down, but the only "settling down" Abraham knew was wandering. Like the tabernacle (ch 9), the fact that Abraham's dwelling was a temporary tent suggested that a better and permanent version was still coming, to be enjoyed ultimately in the messianic time and beyond this world; the temporary pointed to the permanent which far surpassed it in quality. Often in the Bible, the

---

[58] H. Balz, "*paroikeō*," *EDNT* 3:42.

initial fulfillment of a divine promise was only meant to serve as a sample, or type, of the full realization of that promise later (in the Messiah). Something like this was going on in Abraham's situation. He left Ur and lived in Canaan, but he knew that "the land which I will show you" (Gen 12.1) was not ultimately Canaan. His journey to Canaan was a type of the larger, spiritual journey he was on.

God's promise concerning the land was repeated to Isaac (Gen 26.3) and then to Jacob (Gen 28.13; 35.12), so they became **fellow heirs of the same promise**. Esau is not mentioned because he is not a representative of the faith that characterized his father or grandfather (a point will be made about him in 12.16). The statement here that Abraham lived **with** Isaac and Jacob need not be literal (although Abraham knew his grandchildren for the last fifteen years of his life), as if they all lived in the same dwelling or at the same time. It simply means that they lived the same kind of nomadic, sojourning life as he did ("Jacob lived in the land where his father had sojourned," Gen 37.1 NASB). Even when Jacob built a house at Succoth (Gen 33.17), he did not remain there. Our author's statement recalls and summarizes Psalm 105.9–13 and lays the groundwork for the summary in verses 13–16 below. Living as a stranger in the present world was the lifestyle of Israel's founding fathers, and this serves as an example for their Christian descendants.

11.10 for he was awaiting the city that has foundations, the city whose designer and builder is God.

The reason for Abraham's nomadic lifestyle in Canaan, although he lived there for one hundred years, is here given. The fact is that Abraham did not consider any place on this earth to be his true home, and so his lifestyle reflected his view of this world. Instead, he believed that his true home was with God, in a city that he had not yet seen. It is another way of speaking of God's rest (4.1). The heavenly **city** (see comments on v 16 below) stands in stark contrast to the earthly rural areas and tents in which Abraham lived after he had been called by God. In the ancient world, one's citizenship was usually tied to a city, not a country. Citizens of a city were officially and legally "enrolled" there to guarantee their rights and privileges. Being a citizen of a city made one an "insider" there (*cf.* Heb 12.23; Phil 3.20). The idea of **foundations** further underscores the difference between the permanent and solid ("unshakable," 12.28) heavenly dwelling for which Abraham was waiting, and the temporary, foundationless shelters in which he lived on this earth. Psalm 87.1 describes the messianic Zion as having God's foundations (*cf.* also Isa 54.11). Abraham is a prime example of the faith that is the essence of what is hoped for (v 1). The fact that the heavenly city has God as its **designer** (NASB "architect") and **builder** (the two terms were not as conceptually distinct to the ancients as they are to us) suggests that city's perfection, in contrast to the imperfect dwellings made with human hands in this world. In the Greek, this is further communicated by the emphasis (by placing the word at the end of the sentence in Greek) on the word **God.** It is *God* who makes this city, both by his wisdom (he is its designer) and his power (he is its builder).[59] The fact that God is the maker of this city would have communicated to the original recipients of Hebrews that the city reflected God's glory, for an ancient city gained its prestige from its founder and builder.[60]

It is clear from our author's statement here that Abraham knew something about a better life in a better place with God. The extent or clarity of his knowledge is unknown to us, but Abraham's faith ultimately looked to (**he was awaiting**) the messianic time in which the access of all believers to the heavenly city (Heb 12.22) and throne of God (Heb 4.16) would be available.[61] What Abraham only anticipated, Jesus has now reached (12.2), and he has gone there to encourage us to follow him to that same place. Also, Abraham knew (he believed!) enough about the heavenly reward that it affected the way he lived. His lifestyle speaks directly to Christians, who are the ultimate descendants of Abraham (Heb 6.18; *cf.* Rom 4.12f, 16; Gal 3.7). Like our spiritual forefather, we are not to count this world as our home and become attached to it, but instead we must see ourselves as aliens in a world that is not our true home as we anticipate entering that abiding city which God has prepared for those who have faith in him.

---

[59] Lane, *Hebrews 9–13,* 353.

[60] So Augustus' rebuilding of Rome was designed to reflect his own person. See Augustus' *Res Gestae.* Alexandria, Egypt would be another example, trading on the fame of Alexander the Great.

[61] The NT picture is that Christians have entered into the spiritual blessings that are characteristic of heaven itself, but the full measure of our participation in these things awaits us in heaven. The term for this is "inaugurated eschatology." The idea is pervasive in Hebrews. See Mackey, *Eschatology and Exhortation in the Epistle to the Hebrews,* 29–230.

11.11 By faith even Sarah herself, although she was barren,[62] received strength for the deposition of seed, even past the time,[63] since he considered the one who had promised faithful,

This verse is difficult in the Greek because of the awkward idiom it employs, and because the grammatical interpretation of the whole verse depends largely on whether we take Sarah to be the subject of what is said here, or Abraham (in which case, the statement about Sarah is parenthetical), and how to understand the words "Sarah herself." Possible interpretations are:

1) The idiom literally says that he or she "received power for the casting of seed." The word for "casting" (*katabolē*) is used regularly in Greek for sowing seed, that is, planting it in the ground, and this became a metaphor or euphemism for the male part in the procreative act.[64] For this reason it would seem best to take the statement as referring to Abraham, and we would then take the reference to Sarah as a parenthetical remark.[65] Taking Abraham as the subject also fits with the context, in which Abraham is clearly the subject in verses 10 and 12.

2) As soon as we do this, however, we are left with the strange idea that Sarah's barrenness (Gen 11.30 "Sarai was barren") was remedied by making Abraham able to procreate, unless our author intended for us to understand that Sarah's infertility was actually due to a problem on Abraham's part (for which there is no evidence). Most modern English translations, and a host of scholars, have therefore taken **Sarah** as the subject of the sentence (reading the words "Sarah herself" as nominative) and regard the idiom as an otherwise-unattested way of speaking of the woman's conception of a child.[66] The statement would be saying,

---

[62] The Greek text here obviously caused difficulties for some scribes, as the available wordings show. The word "barren" is missing from some ancient manuscripts.

[63] An idiom which means "past the normal time" or "past the proper time" (NASB), in the sense of past the time of strength; the time of older age. BDAG 436.

[64] The second-century Roman physician Galen of Pergamum spoke of "the male seed which is cast into the female mother" (*De Semine* 1); quoted (in Greek) in Ellingworth, *Epistle to the Hebrews*, 586; also Galen's *On the Natural Faculties* 1.6. The idea is also represented in Jewish literature: *Apocalypse of Ezra* 5.12, *cf.* Philo's *On the Creation* 132.

[65] Hofius, *EDNT*, "*katabolē*," 2:256. We could read the phrase as a nominative absolute or *nominativus pendens*.

[66] Some of the rabbis believed that a woman contributed seed to conception as well, so the phrase could possibly refer to a woman's part in procreation. See Friedrich Hauck, *TDNT*, "*katabolē*," 3:621; Attridge, *Hebrews*, 325 fn53. This interpretation seems unlikely to me.

then, that Sarah received power to accept the depositing of seed from Abraham.[67] One advantage of this approach is that the phrase here in Hebrews, **even past the time**, corresponds to the explicit statement made about Sarah in Genesis 18.11: "Sarah was past childbearing" (NASB). The problem, however, is that the statement concerning seed most naturally refers to Abraham. Even more problematic is the fact that Sarah is not depicted in Genesis as **having considered the one who had promised faithful** (*cf.* Gen 18.12). That is attributed to Abraham.

3) Some students of Hebrews (such as Bruce) suggest that we can read the words "Sarah herself" as dative instead of nominative, so that the verse says "By faith he [Abraham] also, *together with [barren] Sarah,* received power..."[68] The problem here is that this is grammatically awkward for an author whose Greek is otherwise polished.[69] It is, however, possibly on the right track, and leads us to consider:

4) The statement is meant to include both Abraham and Sarah, and says that Sarah received the ability for the depositing (lit. "laying down") of seed (*i.e.*, the ability to conceive) because of Abraham's faith.[70] This allows the statement "past the time" to refer to Sarah, and the statements about seed and trusting in God keep Abraham as the primary subject of the sentence. This is the option I have reflected in the translation above.

Faith not only looks past this world to the heavenly city which God has designed and built (v 1), but also trusts that God by his power will overcome any physical obstacles that seem to stand in the way of the fulfillment of his word. Accordingly, God not only promised a land to Abra-

---

[67] Bruce (*Epistle to the Hebrews*, 296 fn100), however, noted that there is a Greek word for "conception" (*sullēpsis*) which the author could have used if that were his meaning here; or he could have said *eis hupodochēn spermatos* (Moffatt, *Epistle to the Hebrews*, 171).

[68] Bruce, *Epistle to the Hebrews*, 296, emphasis added. In uncial Greek letters, with which Hebrews was originally written, down to about the tenth century there was no mark for the iota subscript, so the dative and nominative forms of these words would have looked identical, and context would have determined which form was to be read. See Metzger, *A Textual Commentary on the Greek New Testament, Second Edition*, 602; see Ellingworth, *Epistle to the Hebrews*, 588.

[69] Lane, *Hebrews* 9–13, 345. Also, the scribes who produced the minuscule manuscripts did not read these words as dative, and some have questioned if the expression in the Greek ever used such a dative construction. Koester, *Hebrews*, 488.

[70] Nicholas T. Bott ("'And by faith, because Abraham considered him faithful who had promised, Sarah herself received power to conceive': A Reconsideration of Heb 11:11," *TrinJ* 32 (2011): 205–19.

ham (vv 9–11), but he also promised him life[71]—to make him a great nation, and Abraham had faith in God concerning both promises. Although Abraham had no idea of how God would keep his promise,[72] since the physical situation seemed impossible, still he believed that God would keep his word, and because of that faith God empowered the aged couple to have a child. This empowerment, by which God kept his promise, was God's response to the fact that Abraham considered God, who is **the one who had** made the promise, to be **faithful** (reliable, true to his word; also 10.23). Recall the author's previous treatment of this same topic in 6.13ff, where it was emphasized that Abraham "patiently waited," and thus stands as an example of faith that endures. He stands in contrast to that later generation of his descendants who also "went out" (same verb in 3.16) from their homes in Egypt, but did not endure by faith.

The present point for the readers of Hebrews (including us) is that God uses his power for his people, in keeping with the promises he has made to them, *in response to their faith in him*. Even if their situation seems dire and hopeless from the human standpoint, faith will trust that God can and will act according to his power and prove himself faithful to his word in the end. What God wants to see from his people is that they believe with certainty what he has told them, and that they will endure, or wait for him, to accomplish his promise.

11.12 wherefore there was born from one man, who indeed was as good as dead, a multitude like the stars of heaven in number and like the sand which is by the seashore, innumerable.

The story of Abraham demonstrates that God can do great things for those who trust in his word and faithfully endure until God fulfills it. It is clear from Genesis that Abraham and Sarah had no children when God called the patriarch and told him he would be the father of a great nation of people. Twenty-four years later, when the patriarch was ninety-nine years old (Gen 17.1, 24) God again raised the subject to Abraham, but by this time Abraham's body was **as good as dead** (Rom 4.19) as far as procreation was concerned. The phrase translates a perfect participle, literally "having died," which was used in ancient medical literature of bodily parts that

---

[71] "I will bless you" (Gen 12.2). *Cf.* 2 Tim 1.1. See comments on Heb 6.13–14.

[72] Although Abraham had previously *thought* he had figured out how God was going to keep his promise: through Hagar and Ishmael; but God ruled that out, Gen 15.4.

had ceased to function and thus were impotent.[73] The point is that Abraham might as well have been dead as far as procreation was concerned, because his body was not going to father any children at his age. Paul used the same expression of Abraham in Romans 4.19. Like Paul, the author of Hebrews was drawing attention to the fact that the story of Abraham evidences God's creative power to bring life out of death, and that Abraham believed that God could do this.[74] In this way, Abraham is the prototype of all those who believe in God's ability to raise the dead and who hope in the coming resurrection of the body unto glory. This also has connections to verse 3, because God's bringing life out of death is another way of speaking of his creative power, his ability to bring something out of nothing. We believe that God created the world by the sheer power of his word, just as Abraham believed that God would bring life out of his own "good-as-dead" body as he had promised. Also, like Enoch (v 5) and Noah (v 7), Abraham is an example of a man whose faith enabled him to transcend death (here, the "death" of his body in terms of procreation).

The fact that a great **multitude** (an entire nation of people) came from only **one man** (see Isa 51.2) who by all other considerations would have been considered physically useless for such a purpose is a great testament to the power of God on behalf of those who believe in him. The vast size of the nation of Israel that came from Abraham is communicated by the figurative expressions **like the stars of heaven in number** and **like the sand which is by the seashore**. Those expressions occur in several OT texts.[75]

11.13 All these died in faith, not receiving the things that were promised[76] but seeing and welcoming them from afar, and confessing that they were foreigners and strangers on the earth.

There is another story that illustrates Abraham's belief in God's power to bring life out of death (vv 17–19), but before he moves on to that episode our author expounds upon the forward-looking (*i.e.*, eschatological) nature of the patriarchs' faith, which will also be further illustrated in the specific cases of Isaac, Jacob, and Joseph (vv 20–22).

[73] See references in BDAG 668.

[74] David H. Wenkel ("Abraham's Typological Resurrection from the Dead in Hebrews 11," *CTR* 15 (2018): 51–66) argues that this episode is the root of Biblical thinking about resurrection.

[75] Gen 15.5; 22.17; 26.4; 32.12 Exod 32.13; see also 1 Kngs 4.20, 1 Chron 27.23, and Neh 9.23.

[76] Literally "not receiving the promises." See comments on v 39 below.

Not only did **these** great figures among the patriarchs live by faith, they also **died in faith** as well. That is, their faith endured through the threat of death and they kept their faith until their deaths. If the phrase "**all these**" refers to the people in verses 4–12, then it is understood that Enoch is the exception. Alternately, "all these" might refer only to Abraham and his lineage (discussed in vv 17ff) who lived under God's promise of a "land." The focus of verses 13–16 on the idea of a heavenly place seems to confirm the latter interpretation.[77] Abraham and his immediate lineage lived by faith up until the end of their lives. This is because the object of their faith, the unseen heavenly city (a figure for the messianic time), was not theirs to possess as they lived on this earth. God had promised great things to them, but the fulfillment of these things would come long after their own lifetimes. However, since they were people of genuine faith they were able to "**see**" that fulfillment (recall v 1), they were convinced of the reality of what God had told them, and they believed that God would keep his promises. In this mode of faith, therefore, they were able to **welcome** (greet) the arrival of the promised blessings. Like people who were travelling, but they could see a great city on the horizon (**from afar**) in front of them, these people could see, by their faith, that God's promised blessings were "there" in the future, just as surely as if they had seen them with their physical eyes. This surety allowed them to rejoice in these blessings in their own day almost as if they had experienced them for themselves already. This is what Jesus meant when he told the Jews that "Abraham your father rejoiced to see my day, and he saw it and was glad" (John 8.56).

The patriarchs' forward-looking faith gave them a unique perspective on the world. Like Abraham, these great OT characters considered themselves to be **foreigners and strangers** (the two terms are basically synonymous and stand together in a kind of emphasis) **on** this **earth** (see Psa 119.19). They considered that their true home was with God in another realm, in heaven, and their lives of wandering served as a **confession** of this perspective. We confess our forward-looking faith not only with our words (as in Rom 10.9), but also with our behavior.

It seems clear from this text (vv 13–16, see also v 26) that the patriarchs had some understanding that everything God was promising them would find its fulfillment not in earthly realities, but in spiritual realities

[77] Attridge, *Hebrews*, 329.

that would come in what we now call the messianic time. We may speculate about the clarity of their vision, or their knowledge of the details, but at least this much is true: they understood that God was promising them something far greater than a piece of physical land or a large family of physical descendants. He had ultimately spoken of spiritual, heavenly things, and for this reason they did not consider anything in this world to be the inheritance for which they hoped.

11.14 For those who say such things make it clear that they are seeking their homeland.

This verse is a generic statement, and its rhetorical function is to explain the specific behavior noted in the previous verse. The author explains the specific from the generic often in Hebrews (*cf*. 5.1ff; 6.7f, 16; 7.7, 12; 9.16, 22). People of faith **say such things** as these because they understand that their homeland is not here, and this way of speaking about this present world as a kind of foreign country to them **makes it clear** that they think in this mode. Abraham spoke of the promises in Genesis 24.7, Jacob spoke of them in Genesis 48.21, and Joseph spoke of them in Genesis 50.24. The same sojourner mentality is reflected in passages such as Genesis 23.4, where Abraham called himself a foreigner in the land in which he had been living for over sixty years. David summarized the attitude of the faithful when he said to God, "For we are sojourners before you, and tenants, as all our fathers were" (1 Chron 29.15). The word **homeland** (Greek *patris*) denotes one's fatherland, the place with which a person is originally, and truly, associated. It is more than just seeking "a country" (KJV), but seeking that particular land that one calls home. In ancient times, as well as modern, one's sense of "homeland" was a powerful part of one's own self-understanding and identity. Therefore, those who speak of this world as a strange place to them make it clear that they are not "worldly" people.

11.15 For indeed if they were thinking about that land from which they went out, they would have had opportunity to return.

Lest anyone take the patriarchs' thoughts of their "homeland" (v 14) in strictly nationalistic or physical terms, or lest they might interpret such talk about being strangers and foreigners in the land in which they lived as references to either Ur or Haran, the author makes it clear that these people of faith from the OT meant no such thing when they spoke in these ways. When these patriarchs said such things, our author notes that **they were** not **thinking** of Haran or Ur, both places which could be called Abraham's "home" or the land of his relatives. They were thinking instead of their heavenly homeland.

How did the author know that this is what the patriarchs meant by their talk of being sojourners? He gathered this from the simple fact that if the patriarchs had been talking about either Ur or Haran, they had plenty of **opportunities to return** there during their lifetimes. That is, if Haran was their true home, then all their talk about being away from home and living in a foreign land would have been easily satisfied by going there. However, they never made such a trip. Even when Abraham's servant was sent to find a wife for Isaac, or when Jacob lived in Paddan-aram for several years, there was no indication among them that this was "home," because they left there and continued their nomadic existence in Canaan until their deaths. No, "home" was not Haran, it was someplace else, someplace not in this world.

11.16 But as it is they aspired[78] to a better place, that is, a heavenly one. Therefore, God is not ashamed to be called their God, for he has prepared a city for them.

The patriarchs' homeland was a far better place than any earthly spot, for it is a **heavenly** place. This is why the patriarchs, while they lived on this earth, never spoke as if they had arrived at their true homeland (v 14), or why they never ventured out to some earthly spot which they truly knew as "home" (v 15). The term **better** obviously ties the present discussion to that of chapters 7–10, which discussed the better messianic covenant and its better sacrifice, in a better sanctuary, by a better priest. Those patriarchs who saw the blessings of the messianic age from afar believed that their inheritance lay within this better, heavenly order of things.

Because of their faith which drove them to look past this world to the spiritual, heavenly realities God had promised to them and their de-

[78] The verb here is present tense, therefore some versions translate "they desire" (ASV, NASB, ESV, KJV). It is possible that the subject of this verb is "they who say such things" from verse 14 (which also uses the present tense). However, the present tense is often used in Greek narratives of the past (the so-called "historical present") in order to make the action more prominent in the narrative (see Campbell, *Verbal Aspect, the Indicative Mood, and Narrative*, 74–76; Runge, *Discourse Grammar*, 125–43). I have rendered it here as a past tense in keeping with English usage.

scendants, God **is not** at all **ashamed** of these people. The world may be ashamed of the people of God and treat them as rejects (see 1 Cor 4.13), but in no way does God view them like that. God delights in them because of their faith in him, and he readily accepts being known as **their God**. It is probably hard for many of us to imagine the encouragement these words would have provided to the original audience. In a culture where these people were experiencing the powerful force of social rejection and shame, including from their own families, to know that God was not ashamed of them would have given them a comforting and encouraging sense of belonging with God and his family. In several OT texts God said of the messianic age that "I will be their God, and they will be my people."[79] *Cf.* 2.11, where it was noted that Jesus is not ashamed to call us his brethren.

The connection of the last clause to the verse as a whole hangs on the word "**for**," which often connects a statement to the previous statement and places them in some kind of cause-and-effect relationship. The Greek word here (*gar*) expresses "cause, clarification, or inference,"[80] but even more "introduces offline material that strengthens or supports what precedes."[81] The nuance here is best understood in the sense of "since," indicating a prior action on God's part (he has built a city) that inferentially confirms his present disposition toward them (he is not ashamed of them). That is, since God has built a city for the faithful, it is clear that he is not ashamed of such people, regardless of how the world thinks of them or treats them. He has already planned and prepared to welcome the faithful in heaven. Their faith in God pleases him, and he is eager to bring all such people to himself (see 2.10).

There is no contradiction between heaven as a "land" (v 14) and heaven as a "city" (both already appeared together in vv 9–10). Both suggest the idea of people of the same heritage living together, and in ancient times a city normally controlled the land around it. Similarly, the rabbis spoke of the land of Israel as "Zion." Both images contribute to our understanding of a place that ultimately defies description by human language. In Revelation 21–22, the heavenly city, the New Jerusalem is described with language of both a city (with walls, gates, streets, *etc.*) and a "land"

---

[79] Lev 26.12; Jer 24.7; 31.33—the passage about the new covenant, Heb 8.10; 32.38; Ezek 11.20; 14.11; 37.23, 27; Zech 8.8; often in discussions of transformation.

[80] BDAG 189.

[81] Runge, *Discourse Grammar*, 52.

(with trees, a river, *etc.*). In ancient times, a **city** was a place of safety because it was built with a surrounding fortifying wall (which distinguished it from a village), and a city was usually the center of power of a kingdom (*cf.* Josh 11.10). Correspondingly, God has prepared a safe place in heaven for his faithful people, where their enemies can persecute and harm them no longer, a place where God himself reigns over and protects his own. A city is also a place where people live together (more so than in rural circumstances), and thus the city is also a metaphor for the close fellowship we will enjoy there.[82] This sense of togetherness is a strong part of the encouragement our author here offers. He wants his readers to understand that they are in no way alone as they face persecution and mistreatment from the world (*cf.* 12.1). In fact, they are in a great company of people who did not consider that they fit in with the present world. Furthermore, in the Hellenistic world a city was a place where one had citizenship. To belong to a city thus brought special status and privileges compared to those who were not citizens. See comments on 12.22–23.

11.17 By faith Abraham offered Isaac; being tested he was offering even his only son—the one who had received the promises,

The story of the *Aqedah,* the binding of Isaac, is one of the most well-known Biblical episodes. Jewish rabbinic tradition treated the story in several ways,[83] one of which was as a temptation much like that placed before Job.[84] The rabbis obviously had some problems with this text (especially God's demand for Isaac's life) and did not know exactly what to do with it (*cf.* their problems with the Melchizedek story in the comments on ch 7). One solution was to posit that the test was administered so that all the world could know just how great Abraham was, and Abraham's obedience then acquired a kind of saving power that was available for all Israel. Likewise, some rabbis viewed Isaac as a full-grown man at this point and therefore a willing victim, and thus saw great expiatory power in his actions.[85] While there is much that is enigmatic about that story,

---

[82] See Phil Roberts, "The City of God," in *The Gospel in the Old Testament*, ed. Daniel W. Petty, Florida College Annual Lectures (Temple Terrace, FL: Florida College Bookstore, 2003), 233–51.

[83] See the references in Attridge, *Hebrews*, 333–34.

[84] *b. Sanhedrin* 89b has the incident instigated by Satan.

[85] See Hans Joachim Schoeps, "The Sacrifice of Isaac in Paul's Theology," *JBL* 65 (1946): 385–92.

our author cut to the essence of it as he pointed out the story's value as a paradigmatic episode of Biblical faith.[86]

Abraham had already demonstrated his faith in God's life-giving power to make life (in a situation of death) in the matter of the promise that he and Sarah would have a child (vv 11f). An even greater test of that faith came when God told Abraham to sacrifice Isaac as a burnt offering (Gen 22). After waiting for twenty-five years, God finally gave Abraham and Sarah a child of their own (God had made it clear that Ishmael was not to be counted as the child of promise, Gen 17.19). Then one day, when Isaac was obviously old enough to know what was going on, God demanded that Abraham kill (**offer** as a sacrifice) the child.

While Abraham had already experienced a measure of God's power over death (v 11), thus proving that nothing is impossible with God (Gen 18.14), this was still a significant test of his faith. It is one thing to deal with the death of one's own ability to procreate and to trust that God can remedy that problem, but an altogether different thing when God demands that one kill an innocent child, his **only son**. Whereas the LXX concentrates on the emotional difficulty of this trial by referring to Isaac as Abraham's "beloved" son, our author here instead emphasizes the challenge this test represented to Abraham's faith, since Isaac was the only son of his kind (the MT says "your only son whom you love"). The word **only** (Greek *mongenēs*) does not mean "solitary," but has the sense of unique, one-of-a-kind,[87] and thus denotes prominence. Although Abraham had another son through Hagar, Ishmael was not counted as the "son" of Abraham in terms of the promise of God (Gen 21.12). That designation belonged to **Isaac** alone, so in terms of the promise he was also the "only" (solitary) son. Given Abraham's now-advanced age and God's specific promise concerning him (see the next verse), Isaac was not simply the only son Abraham had, he was the only son Abraham would ever have. That fact is what exacerbated a demand that was already shocking.

While the Genesis text is silent about what Abraham thought about this in response, it is obvious within the narrative that this demand ran counter to all that God had said to Abraham. How could this killing

---

[86] For a history of interpretation, see Robert J. Daly, "The Soteriological Significance of the Sacrifice of Isaac," *CBQ* 39 (1977): 45–75.

[87] BDAG 658.

possibly be justified, and how could God make a great nation out of Abraham with Isaac dead? The demand did not square with **the promises**. The plural **promises** may refer to the repetition of the promise that Abraham would become a great nation of people (Gen 12.2; 13.16; 15.5), or it could refer to all the promises God had made to the patriarch. The point is nearly the same either way, since God's demand for Isaac's life seemingly ran counter to the goodness of those promises. Some of the original readers of Hebrews may have wondered the same kind of thing about their own lives.

Of course, Abraham was not the only person of faith whom God **tested**. In fact, it is quite ordinary for God to test the faith of his people, in order that they might show him the commitment they have in their hearts. The wilderness generation of the Israelites was tested more than once, howbeit with far less impressive results. In this they were not like their forefather.

The fact that the Genesis narrative records no deliberations on Abraham's part only underscores the resolve of his faith. The account simply says, "So Abraham rose early in the morning ... and went to the place of which God had told him" (22.3 NASB). **By** an exercise of his great **faith** (trust) in God, Abraham determined to do exactly what God had ordered. It is in this sense that the NT writers say that Abraham **offered** Isaac (see also Jam 2.21). Although God stopped the sacrifice at the last moment (and never intended for Isaac to die), the deed was already done as far as Abraham was concerned. This great endeavor demonstrated that Abraham was committed to God above any other commitment he had in the world; Abraham was more loyal to God than to his own physical family, a boundary few in the ancient world would have crossed.[88] The repetition of the verb "offered" in the imperfect tense (he **was offering**) has the effect of parading the entire three days of the episode before our eyes and allowing us to see it as more than just a momentary event.[89]

11.18 to whom it had been said that "Your descendants will be called through Isaac"—

This is a quotation from Genesis 21.12. It is quoted to highlight the tremendous tension that was presented to Abraham in this test of his faith

[88] See deSilva, *Honor, Patronage, Kinship, and Purity*, 2nd ed., 176–271.

[89] Campbell, *Verbal Aspect, the Indicative Mood, and Narrative*, 92–93.

in order that we might appreciate the magnitude not only of the test but also of the faith that faced it. The antecedent of the relative clause "**to whom**" is Abraham, as the sense of the quotation demands. God's specification that **Isaac** would carry on Abraham's lineage apparently ruled out the idea that God would give Abraham and Sarah another child to replace Isaac after Abraham offered him. God's demand for Isaac's death therefore seemed irreconcilable with the promise that Isaac was the key to the fulfillment of the promise that Abraham would have a multitude of **descendants**.

11.19 yet considering that God is able even to raise from the dead, from which he received him back figuratively.

Abraham's natural dread of the loss of his child, his former good experience with God, and the promises of God all had to be reconciled with God's command to kill Isaac. According to Romans 4.17, which uses similar language, part of Abraham's thinking involved the fact that God is the creator "who calls into being that which does not exist" (see v 3 above). Another way to think of that is that God is the source of life. If God makes life, and if God demanded the death of Isaac, but Isaac was the key to the promise, then the solution at which Abraham arrived was that after he offered Isaac in obedience to God, God would then **raise** the boy **from the dead** and thus keep his promises (v 18). There was no other alternative.

We do not, however, wish to imply that this became a test of Abraham's intellect, of his ability to figure out how God would accomplish his promised plan. The fact is that God eventually did not do what Abraham thought was going to happen. Isaac was spared, so no literal resurrection from the dead was needed. However, our author concentrates not on God's resolution of the situation, but Abraham's. Abraham resolved the difficulty by his confidence in the trustworthiness of God's word and in God's power. By *faith* he **considered** (reasoned; *cf.* v 3) that there was no way God would fail to do what he had specifically promised in Isaac (Gen 21.12). Therefore, he trusted that God would exercise his power, restore his child to him, and continue with his purposes, which is effectively what God did.

Abraham's conduct here illustrates the confidence attributed to genuine faith in verse 1. All along he had decided to obey with the confidence that God would raise Isaac from the dead. This no doubt explains why he could be represented as so coolly carrying out God's difficult order. In fact, so committed was Abraham to this understanding that, in his mind, Isaac was already dead. When God halted the sacrifice, it was therefore as if (**figuratively**) God was bringing the boy back from the dead. The word "**figuratively**" here translates what literally is "in a parable" in the Greek. This does not mean that the author thought the story of the *Aqedah* was only a parable and not historical. The phrase applies to Isaac's being rescued from certain death.[90] Although it is true that Isaac's rescue from death is a figure of Christ's resurrection and of the resurrection of all believers, that does not seem to be the point in this particular verse.

It is not easy to fathom the depth of Abraham's faith as it is exhibited in this scene, because he stands as such a perfect model of faith at this moment in his life. In a time of great crisis, facing the death of a loved one and being called upon to make great personal, familial sacrifice, Abraham trusted that God could be counted on to make everything alright in the end. His example thus speaks directly to the original readers who were facing opposition, perhaps including loss of families and even the threat of death. The exhortation of their ancestor's example was to trust in God, that he will exercise his power for them, and that what seems for the moment to be contrary to the promises of a good God will, in the end, turn out for salvation. Like Abel, his story continues to speak to people of faith today.

11.20 By faith Isaac blessed Jacob and Esau, even concerning coming things.

This next example of faith refers to the story in Genesis 27, which is otherwise famous as the scene in which Jacob stole the blessing from Esau through a deception foisted upon the aged Isaac. However, that particular feature of the story is not in view here. Regardless of any deception by Jacob, the fact is that **Isaac** exhibited confident faith in "things hoped for" (v 1) as he spoke to his sons about the things God would do in accordance with the promises he had first made to Abraham (**coming things** from the perspective of Isaac's own day, not from our perspective today, *cf.* 2.5; yet their ultimate fulfillment still awaits, vv 39f). To **bless** is to speak well or favorably, and in the scenes of patriarchal blessing it meant to call down

[90] *Cf.* the words of the prodigal's father in Luke 15.32, as he speaks of a son who was "dead"; in Heb 9.9 the author referred to the tabernacle services as a "parable."

God's goodness upon someone. See comments on 7.6f. Like other people of faith, Isaac could see the fulfillment of God's promises "from afar" (v 13) and in this mode he was able to speak of them with surety. As such, Isaac exhibited the kind of forward-looking faith that pleases God.

11.21 By faith Jacob, as he was dying, blessed each of the sons of Joseph and worshipped on the top of his staff.

Although Jacob is often remembered for his deceptive and greedy ways, at times he also exhibited the kind of faith in God our author here wishes to highlight. One such occasion was **as he was dying** (Gen 47.29; *i.e.*, near the end of his life), recorded in Genesis 48, when he passed on God's blessing, which he had experienced in his own life, to Joseph's sons Ephraim and Manasseh. Our author has combined the two stories of Genesis 47.29–31 and Genesis 48.1ff. It is not that he did not know these were two separate incidents, but that he saw the same principle of faith operative in them both, and could thus combine them as making a single point here. Jacob was still speaking about the future God promised even to his last days. He is, therefore, an example of those who "died in faith" (v 13).

In his final days Jacob was thinking about the future (of which God had spoken to him), and in that mode he spoke of the coming goodness for Joseph's children ("he blessed them"). Joseph had two **sons** that were born to him in Egypt, Ephraim and Manasseh. Just as God had designated Isaac over Ishmael, and Jacob over Esau for the lineage of the promise, so here Jacob claimed that Ephraim and Manasseh would be reckoned as Jacob's own children for purposes of the promise (Gen 48.5f). Furthermore, just as the younger had been chosen over the older in the case of Jacob and Esau, so Jacob **blessed** (called God's goodness down upon) the younger Ephraim above the firstborn Manasseh (Gen 48.14–20). As these and other stories illustrate, God does not always fulfill his plans in the way men think he would, but he fulfills them nonetheless. What he wants to see from us as he accomplishes his will is faith.

The statement that Jacob **worshipped** interprets the remark of Genesis 47.31, that the patriarch "bowed" after he made Joseph promise that he would bury him in Canaan (Gen 47.30; which Joseph did, as recorded in Gen 50.7ff). While some have interpreted this as an acknowledgment of Joseph's status (thus fulfilling Gen 37.5ff), our author apparently followed the interpretation that saw this as a gesture of his gratitude to God.[91] It was also an acknowledgment of God's goodness to him throughout his life (Gen 48.15f) and his confidence in the good that God would yet do. In this way he glorified God both by his acknowledgement of God's care of him in the past, and his expression of trust that God would keep his word for this family that was, as promised, growing into a nation. The picture is of an old man, unable to stand (the Genesis account suggests he was basically bedridden at this time) and who either sat on the edge of his bed (*cf.* Gen 49.33) or leaned on his staff to stay upright. The prepositional phrase "**on the top of his staff**" is the LXX translation of Genesis 47.31. The Hebrew text has the word *mittah* (bed), which could also be read as *matteh* (staff). Bowing over a staff was also a gesture of humility.[92] **Faith** anticipates good things that will come beyond one's own lifetime, and Jacob stands as an example to us to believe that God will eventually fulfill his promises to us, and that we can go to our graves trusting in God's word.

11.22 By faith Joseph, when he was dying, mentioned the exodus of the sons of Israel and gave orders concerning his bones.

Joseph is another example of one who went to his grave trusting in God's promises. He learned from his father that the Israelites would one day occupy Canaan (see Gen 48.4, 21), and he too believed that God would keep this promise. Like his father, Joseph's last scene is one that was characterized by the expression of his faith, and he too was confident about God's trustworthiness although he would not personally live to see the fulfillment of the promise. Possessing Canaan according to God's promise would obviously entail leaving the land of Egypt in which they then lived, so Joseph knew that one day there would be an **exodus** of the Israelites from that land. His faith in that future event would also have been bolstered by the fact, of which he surely was aware, that God had rescued Abraham from trouble in Egypt before (Gen 12.10ff), and so he could be counted on to do it again. Therefore, when his life was coming to an end (**he was dying**[93]) he told his brothers that "God will surely ...

[91] *E.g.*, Rabbi Sforno thought it was gratitude for God granting his wish. A. Cohen, ed., *The Soncino Chumush*, Soncino Books of the Bible (New York: Soncino Press, 1977), 297.

[92] Schneider, "*rabdos*," *TDNT* 6:969; *EDNT*, "*rabdos*," 3:206.

[93] There is a different word for "dying" in this verse than the one in v 21. The word used here (*teleutaō*) literally means "ending" but it is used in Greek literature in the sense

bring you up from this land to the land which he promised on oath to Abraham, to Isaac and to Jacob" (Gen 50.25 NASB). Although he would not be alive when it happened, he still wanted to participate in it,[94] so he left **orders** that "you shall carry my **bones** up from here" and bury them in the promised land, which the Israelites did when they finally left Egypt (Exod 13.19). Both Jacob and Joseph insisted on participating, at least symbolically, in the fulfillment of God's promise to bring his people to their homeland.

11.23 By faith Moses, when he was born, was hidden for three months by his parents, because they saw that the child was good and they did not fear the edict of the king.

Verses 23–29 recount in summary the story of Moses and the exodus that he led (which Joseph anticipated). Of course, to Jews, Moses is arguably the second greatest figure in Judaism after Abraham. Our author has already dealt with the status Moses had in the minds of Jews in chapters 1 and 3, where he showed that a greater word from God than the Law of Moses has now come, and that Moses was a servant in God's house whereas Jesus is the Son over God's house. Lest anyone should think that the author, or Christianity, had little use for Moses, he now presents the life of Moses from the perspective of a believer in Jesus. When viewed from this perspective, Moses becomes a great model of faith in Christ.

The story of Moses is the story of a life of faith from its very beginning. It begins not with something Moses himself did, but something that was done for him **by** the **faith** of his **parents. When** Moses **was born**, the Egyptian Pharaoh (**king**) of that time (the Bible does not mention his name), in the attempt to control the Hebrews' population, had ordered the midwives to kill all male Hebrew children at birth. He feared a future slave revolt (Exod 1.10). Not only did the Hebrew midwives refuse to carry out the order, but Moses' own parents decided that there was no way they were going to kill their good child even if the greatest monarch in the world at that time had ordered it. The word here translated **good** (Greek *asteios*) can refer to beauty; beautiful babies and handsome

---

of "death." There is no apparent significance to the change in words, and the author of Hebrews often varied his terminology unless he wished to create emphasis.

[94] The Greek here literally says that Joseph "remembered" the exodus, *i.e.*, he kept it in mind. BDAG 655.

young people were considered as ideal among the ancients, and a handsome appearance was considered a sign of divine favor.[95] However, the word can also mean "refined" (like our English word "classy"), or "well-bred," and in that sense "good."[96] Stephen used the same word of the infant Moses but added "unto God" (Acts 7.20), suggesting a similar sense here, that he was well-pleasing to God. What exactly it refers to about Moses is not specified, but his parents somehow discerned that Moses was a special child. To save his life, they hid him, first apparently at home (Exod 2.2), but eventually putting him in a basket in the reeds that grew along the edge of the Nile (Exod 2.3). Thus, like great people of faith before him (Enoch, Noah, Abraham), Moses was delivered from certain death by an act of faith.

The wording here, as well as the tenor of the story in Exodus, suggests that there was a significant penalty for disobedience to the king's murderous **edict**. However, these godly parents **did not fear** whatever penalty had been assigned, and in defiance of the edict they kept Moses alive. Their actions illustrate further the kind of faith that ultimately trusts that God's power will overcome all threats against the faithful, as well as the boldness and courage that such faith begets.

11.24 By faith Moses, when he had become grown, refused to be called the son of Pharaoh's daughter,

Pharaoh's daughter (her name is not stated in the Biblical record) found Moses in his basket at the edge of the Nile, retrieved him and adopted him as her own son (Exod 2.5–10). Moses was thus raised in the royal Egyptian household, and "was trained in the all the wisdom of the Egyptians, and was a powerful man in words and in deeds" (Acts 7.22). The underlying premise in the Biblical account is that Moses knew he was not an Egyptian, but that he was a Hebrew. It also seems that Moses knew the traditions about Abraham, Isaac, and Jacob and God's dealings with them. When he had **become** a **grown** man (nearly forty years old, Acts 7.23), he decided to renounce his Egyptian identity and to associate himself with his own people (the narrative in Exodus does not mention this decision, but clearly implies it). The Exodus account relates that this did not go well at first, and his fellow-Hebrews did not view

[95] Koester, *Hebrews*, 501. See 1 Sam 16.12.

[96] BDAG 145.

him as one of their own (Exod 2.11ff). Be that as it may, our author concentrates on the decision to renounce one family and embrace another. Like Abraham, he was a man whose identity changed radically. Moses chose to cut his ties with the family that had raised him and to leave the comforts of that life, and to associate himself instead with the despised people of the promise, and in doing so he was demonstrating his **faith** in God. When viewed in this way, Moses' decision involved a reversal of his status, going from "top" to "bottom," from "insider" to despised "outsider" (from the Egyptian point of view). His story may have paralleled that of some of the original readers of Hebrews, especially in terms of perceived status. Some had possibly been rejected by their families upon taking up faith in Jesus, only to find themselves associated with a group that was maligned and rejected. It is probably difficult for us to imagine the social rifts that were caused when some Jews became Christians. Jesus referred to those "who left houses, or brothers, or sisters, or father, or mother, or children, or farms on account of my name" (Matt 19.29) and warned his followers that they would be stepping into a situation where "a man's enemies will be the members of his household" (Matt 10.36). As such Moses is yet another example of one who saw, by faith, things that had not yet been seen (fulfilled, or realized) and who believed that God is a God who keeps his word. Accordingly, he was willing to pay the social price that his faith demanded.

11.25 choosing instead to be mistreated with the people of God rather than to have the temporary enjoyment of sin,

Moses' choice to leave his Egyptian family put him squarely into a life of mistreatment along with the rest of the Hebrew slaves. He forfeited his social standing, his dignity in the eyes of the Egyptians (especially his parents), and the easier life of the royal house. Moses therefore shared in a double stigma: 1) he was one of the slaves (which never had positive connotations in antiquity), and 2) Hebrews were loathsome to Egyptians (Gen 43.32; 46.34).

The author's perspective on Moses' decision also highlights the moral aspect of faith in God. Our author saw an Egyptian life for Moses as **sin**; *i.e.*, at some point it would have been sinful for Moses to continue to live in Pharaoh's house. Exactly how Moses himself saw this decision we are not told (the Exodus narrative is silent about any deliberations he had).

However, it is not hard to imagine the factors that were at work. The Egyptians were polytheistic idolaters, their Pharaoh was considered the son of a god (with a corresponding rejection of the Hebrews' God), he ordered the deaths of newborn babies, Egyptian culture was as materialistic as any other, and they mistreated the Hebrews (see Exod 2.11). Surely it would have been morally difficult for Moses to continue to associate himself with that culture, so several commentators have suggested that the sin was that of being disloyal to his true family, the Hebrews.[97] Or perhaps we could say it was the sin of denying his true calling, the sin of living like an unbeliever when in fact his lot belonged with the Israelites. By whatever understanding he possessed, Moses came to a point where his conscience did not allow him to live in that world any longer, and so he sacrificed the easier life of an Egyptian and took up life with an enslaved people. Another factor involved in his decision was the **temporary** nature of any comfort he could maintain as an Egyptian. As a man of faith, he looked into the future at what God had promised, and there he saw something that was far better and far more enduring than any earthly pleasure. He cherished a relationship with God more than he cherished his relationship with his Egyptian family (*cf.* vv 24f above). The nature of the situation was that he could not do both, and a choice for one **rather than** the other was necessary.[98]

The original readers of Hebrews had likely faced similar mistreatments that manifested social rejection (see 10.32ff), so the example of Moses would have been highly relevant to them. The social sacrifice involved in becoming a Christian put them in the company of one of the greatest figures of their heritage. *Cf.* Matthew 5.10–12.

11.26 regarding the disgrace of Christ as greater wealth than the treasures of Egypt, because he was paying attention to the reward.

The brilliant **treasures**[99] **of Egypt** during the New Kingdom Period[100] were legendary, as modern archaeology has confirmed, and their men-

[97] Moffatt, *Epistle to the Hebrews*, 180; Bruce, *Epistle to the Hebrews*, 319. *cf.* 10.25, 33f.

[98] *Cf.* Matt 6.24; 10.37; 12.30 et par; 1 Kngs 18.21; Gal 1.10; Jam 4.4.

[99] The word (Greek *thēsauros*) denotes a repository, but by metonymy, in the plural (as here), can mean treasures.

[100] Determining the date of the exodus is complicated, but even the so-called late date for the exodus (12th century) falls within Egypt's New Kingdom Period (*c.* 1550–1070). This period was an especially prosperous time for Egypt.

tion here serves to emphasize the magnitude of Moses' choice and the sacrifice it entailed. What made Moses' choice so significant is what he had to lose by making it. His decision to forsake such great **wealth** was made because he believed that he would gain something even **greater**.

To what extent Moses himself understood the messianic significance of his actions is hard to say. The author of Hebrews, however, with Christian hindsight, can see that Moses' choice to leave his Egyptian home and the material wealth that accompanied it was the very kind of choice that would be characteristic of the messianic age. It is in this way that he could refer to Moses' choice as a preference for the **disgrace** (*oneidismos*, insult, reproach, reviling) that was ultimately associated with **Christ** (*cf.* Psa 69.9; 89.50f)—no doubt reflecting the social situation of the original recipients. From the very beginning of the story of Jesus, the call went forth to make a fundamental choice, and the theme of sacrificing in order to follow Christ versus remaining in the comfort of one's prior life is common in the gospels.[101] The original readers of Hebrews had made that choice and had, just like Moses, sacrificed physical pleasure and goods (10.32–34), but they were now growing weary from the rejection and mistreatment that came with it. The example of Moses encouraged them to persevere. In times of hardship and opposition it is difficult to **pay attention** to anything other than the pains of the present, but Moses, by his faith, was able to look past[102] the hardships of the present and see the **reward** (benefit) of following the Lord (see 10.35), one that far outweighed in glory any earthly comfort (2 Cor 4.17), and it was for the sake of that future blessing that he made his famous choice.

11.27 By faith he left Egypt behind, not fearing the wrath of the king, for he persevered in seeing the unseen.

If the author of Hebrews was following a strictly chronological sequence, then this episode would be the one recorded in Exodus 2, when Moses left Egypt after it had been discovered that he had killed an Egyptian in defense of a Hebrew slave. Not only did his fellow-Hebrews not trust him because of his long association with the Egyptians, but now the Pharaoh of Egypt tried to kill him (Exod 2.15). The question arises, though,

[101] See Luke 9.57–62; Matt 4.19f; 19.23f, 29; Luke 14.33; also 1 Tim 6.17.

[102] The Greek word *apoblepō* (translated "pay attention") means to look away from all other objects and to concentrate solely on one thing. LSJ 193.

why would Moses have to **fear the wrath of the** Pharaoh if he was leaving Egypt? It would seem he would only need to fear the king if he had decided to stay. Furthermore, Exodus 2.14 reports that Moses was afraid when his killing of the Egyptian became known, and the account certainly implies that this fear drove him to flee from Egypt.[103] There are a few basic solutions: 1) the author of Hebrews meant that Moses' faith enabled him to overcome his initial fear,[104] or 2) although Moses was afraid, that was not the reason he left Egypt,[105] or 3) the problem can be solved by noting that Moses left Egypt twice in his life, once in Exodus 2 (when he was a fugitive), and again in the exodus of the Israelites. It is possible, then, that the second leaving (the exodus) is in view here. Moses' fear of wrath would have been the concern that the Pharaoh would change his mind about letting the Israelites leave (for he had already proved his obstinacy) and attempt to punish them (which is exactly what he tried to do, Exod 14.5ff).[106] The exodus account leaves the impression that Pharaoh's pursuit of the Israelites did not surprise Moses. Moses' courage (**not fearing**) is then illustrated as he told the Israelites "Do not fear" when they saw the pursuing Egyptian army (Exod 14.13). Because of his trust that the Lord would deliver them all safely, he kept moving onward when those around him were wanting to turn back.

Moses **left** his home **behind** to be with the people of God. In this he was similar to Abraham who left his homeland to live in a different one. The scenario of a man who changed his familial loyalties, and who reaped threats of danger and death for it, also parallels the situation of the early Jewish Christians who, after their conversion to "the Way" (a name that recalls the exodus[107]), were hunted down and persecut-

[103] Both Philo (*Life of Moses* 1.49f) and Josephus (*Ant.* 2.354–6) apparently saw the Biblical account's admission of Moses' fear as a problem (especially for Gentile readers), and they altered the story to make Moses more noble and less afraid.

[104] Lane, *Hebrews 9–13*, 375.

[105] Bruce, *Epistle to the Hebrews*, 322. Similarly, Ellingworth, *Epistle to the Hebrews*, 615: Exod 2.14 does not say that Moses was afraid of Pharaoh, so this fear of the king could refer to something else.

[106] The problem with this solution is that it means the author is not following a strictly chronological presentation (which he otherwise seems to do until v 32). However, this objection is not serious, because the Passover (v 28) was celebrated on the very night the Israelites left Egypt, and the two events were always remembered together. It is a small thing, therefore, if our author mentions the exodus first.

[107] See David Pao, *Acts and the Isaianic New Exodus* (Grand Rapids: Baker Books, 2000), 59–68.

ed (see Acts 9.1ff; 22.4f). Like Pharaoh pursuing Moses and the rebellious Hebrew slaves, Saul of Tarsus, with the official approval of the Jewish leaders, pursued Christians in order to punish their "disobedience." The original readers of Hebrews suffered in a similar kind of trial (10.32ff), even if it was not that specific one. Furthermore, just as fear of reprisal tempted some of the Israelites to question their decision to leave Egypt (Exod 14.10–12), so many Jewish Christians feared the persecution which their decision to join the new exodus brought and were rethinking their commitment to Jesus as a result. The author has already reminded them that they had previously shown a courageous and persevering faith, and he now bid them to show that same fortitude again and imitate Moses. The author has also previously warned his readers about following in the footsteps of the Israelites who did not trust in God (chs 3–4). Moses' faith stood as a stark contrast to the faithlessness of his fellow-Israelites.

What enabled Moses to make such a dangerous choice was that he **persevered**[108] in seeing the unseen. The language of **seeing the unseen** points us back to verse 1 and the nature of Biblical faith, which is the foundation or reality for what we have not yet seen. Moses made his choice not on the basis of anything he had seen,[109] but simply on the basis of what God had promised to his people. Like other great people of faith, Moses could "see" those things from afar (v 13) and valued them more highly than any earthly circumstance. In addition, he kept his spiritual vision focused on the reward God had promised and he did not take his eye (of faith) off that goal. It is the same kind of mental determination that our author will later describe as "fixing our eyes on" the object of our faith (12.2). Not only does true faith cause its possessor to persevere in the demonstration of faith, it also unwaveringly keeps its goal before itself; true faith does not look away (*cf.* Luke 9.62).

---

[108] The regular term for "endure" in Hebrews is *hupomenō*. The word here is *kartereō*, which means to continue doing something without wavering. The participle here is circumstantial. BDAG 510, Lane, *Hebrews 9–13*, 368.

[109] There was a Jewish tradition that Moses had "seen" the inheritance God had planned for him (2 Macc 2.4: Jeremiah "went out to the mountain where Moses had gone up and had seen the inheritance of God"), but no such Biblical statements. The tradition preserved in the statement in 2 Macc essentially removes faith from the patriarch's life after that point.

11.28 By faith he kept the Passover and the application[110] of blood, so that the one who was destroying the firstborn might not touch them.

The **Passover** commemorated the turning-point of Israel's existence. On that night they passed from slavery to freedom. The execution of the tenth plague is consistently attributed to God in the Exodus account; thus he is **the one who was destroying the firstborn** of the Egyptians on that night. The Israelites were spared from the plague by killing the Pascal lamb and displaying (**applying**) its blood on the doorposts of their homes.

The original observance of the Passover required **faith** in at least two ways. First, it required that the Israelites believe that the firstborn were going to die on the appointed night. No such thing had ever happened before, and the account seems to suggest that there were no outward indicators that any such thing was about to happen, so they had to trust that what God said would indeed come to pass (similar in some ways to Noah's situation, v 7). If they had not believed it, they would not have followed God's instructions and they would have died. Second, they had to believe that putting[111] the blood of the Pascal lamb on the doorpost would keep them from being **touched** by death on that night. This was a strange procedure to be sure, for there is no logical connection between putting animal blood on a doorpost and escaping death. It required faith in God's prescribed action.

The Passover feast is one of the greatest messianic institutions of the OT. It was not coincidental that Jesus died at the time of Passover. He is called the "lamb" in the NT (John 1.29; 1 Pet 1.19), Paul exhorted the Corinthians saying, "Christ our Passover has been sacrificed" (1 Cor 5.7), and Jesus himself connected his death (blood) with a spiritual exodus (Matt 26.28). Just as the Israelites trusted that the publicly displayed blood of the lamb would save their lives in a time of death and judgment, so the original readers of Hebrews needed to trust that their identification with the blood of Jesus, and the dedication it represented, was the way to deliverance when there was opposition all around them. And just as Abel, Enoch, Noah, and Abraham all transcended death in some way by their faith, so

---

[110] The Greek word *proschusis* refers to putting liquid on something, and thus can cover the ideas of sprinkling, pouring, spreading, or smearing. BDAG 887. "Sprinkling" (as all the major English versions render it here) may be too specific, since the OT only says that they "put" (Hebrew *natan*) blood on the doorposts (Exod 12.7) with hyssop (v 22).

[111] The Greek word *thinganō* can have a hostile sense: attack, harm, or kill. BDAG 456; LSJ 801.

the Israelites escaped it in the Passover, and persecuted Christians would find their victory over death by faith in the way that is through Jesus.

11.29 By faith they went through the Red Sea as through dry ground, which, when the Egyptians took a try at it, they were swallowed up.

After the Israelites left Egypt, Pharaoh changed his mind and decided to pursue them. God had intentionally led them to a place where they were trapped between the Egyptians and the **Red Sea**. While some of the Israelites panicked and scolded Moses for leading them there, Moses ordered them not to fear and to see how God would deliver them. At God's command he lifted his staff over the waters and they parted by means of a strong east wind that God caused to blow specifically at that time and place. Exodus says that the wind "turned the sea into **dry land** .... The sons of Israel went through the midst of the sea on the dry land" (14.21f NASB). They followed the dry path **through** the Red Sea **by faith**. Surely nothing like this had ever been seen before, and there was no way to be certain (from a human standpoint) that the wind would be sustained long enough for them to cross safely. It took trust in God to step out into that dry seabed. It also required faith that the miracle which allowed them to move onward would not also allow the Egyptians to capture them.

The Egyptians either did not know that God had parted the waters (believing it was a freak occurrence) or simply thought they would take advantage of the miracle themselves, but either way when they too attempted (literally **took a try**) to cross the sea, God slowed their progress and collapsed the walls of water on them before they could get out. Thus, they were **swallowed up**[112] by the sea "and not even one of them remained" (Exod 14.28 NASB). The Israelites saw that they could count on God to deliver them from, and defeat, their enemies.

In 1 Corinthians 10.1ff Paul compared the crossing of the Red Sea to baptism into Christ, and Isaiah spoke of the messianic age as another exodus (see Isa 40.3f, 43.1–3, 44.24–28, 48.2–22). Also, the phrase "dry ground" echoes the creation account. It is not unlikely that the original readers of Hebrews saw the typological, messianic correspondences for themselves. Just as Israel's faith in God led them to cross the waters and

[112] The Greek word *katapinō* literally means to swallow up completely (the compounded preposition *kata* intensifies the meaning of *pinō,* to drink), and is used figuratively of that which overwhelms, overpowers, and thus destroys. BDAG 524.

find deliverance from their enemies, so persecuted Christians, by faith, could rest assured that God would deliver them too, since they had also by faith (Col 2.12) crossed the water of baptism into a new-creational relationship with Jesus. However, on the other side of the Red Sea lay the hard life of the wilderness. Yet the more immediate point of this verse is to further illustrate that faith overcomes any fear we may have because of our earthly circumstances. Moses' faith (and his parents') consists of one example after another of how faith conquered fear, and here the Israelites as a nation joined in that same faith.

11.30 By faith the walls of Jericho fell after having been encircled for seven days.

The author now skips the wilderness period of Israel's history because that period was marked by faithlessness, as chapters 3–4 have already shown. He therefore proceeds from the story of the exodus to the story of the entrance into the land.

The crossing of the Red Sea would not be the only time that God would make a wall (Exod 14.22, 29) fall for Israel's benefit. The story of the fall of **Jericho's walls** is recorded in Joshua 6. Normally, ancient walled cities were taken by a long process of laying siege. The surrounding roads had to be blockaded and the city's water supply had to be shut off (if possible). While the inhabitants of the city slowly consumed their stores of water and food, the attacking army would be building ramps up to the walls and constructing siege towers. When the inhabitants of the city were weakened to the point of starvation, the final attack would commence. The procedure is described in Jeremiah 52. The entire process took months, if not years. The siege of Jerusalem by the Romans in 70 AD took eighteen months, as did the Babylonian siege on that same city in 586 BC. Because of its unique location, Tyre held out against a Babylonian siege for thirteen years, but Alexander conquered it after a siege of "only" seven months. In short, it was simply unheard-of that a walled city could be taken in **seven days** and without using any of the conventional techniques of that time. No one attacked a city by marching around it and blowing trumpets. There was no logical connection between the method and the results, and God used this method because it required that his people act in **faith** in his orders. When his people trusted in his instructions, the walls of Jericho "fell down flat" (Josh 6.20

NASB). Like the defeat of the Egyptian army at the Red Sea, this is another example of how the faith of God's people brought them victory.

11.31 By faith Rahab the prostitute was not destroyed with the unbelievers, having received the spies with peace.

Readers who know the OT narrative might, at this point, be expecting to hear about Joshua. Instead, the author chose to highlight Rahab the harlot. Her inclusion here might have been surprising at first, but she too was a model of the kind of faith the author of Hebrews was trying to emphasize. Before the siege of Jericho, the Israelites had sent spies into the city (Josh 2). Since reconnaissance ultimately proved unnecessary, given the unusual method God had the Israelites use in destroying the city, the mission of the spies had the result of finding a believer in the doomed place. That person was as unlikely as the method of the siege, for she was **Rahab**, a **prostitute**. It has been common to focus on two problems in the narrative: 1) how the Israelite spies wound up with a prostitute, and 2) Rahab's lie to the city's guardians (Josh 2.4f). The first can be explained by positing that Rahab recognized them as Israelites and thus approached them about her safety without any implication of fornication. Apparently the spies had been recognized by others as well (Josh 2.2), and our author here understood that she **received** them **with peace**, that is, not as an enemy, but as one sympathetic to their mission because of their God. The overall picture thus seems to be that she sought them out because of her convictions about their God which she had already formed from the reports she had heard. The second problem may be understood simply as a reflection of Rahab's pagan background. Just because she believed in God's power to take the city, it does not follow that she became morally perfect at that moment. Even people of faith have moments of weakness (*cf.* Abraham's two lies, Gen 12.13 and 20.2) which do not deter them from the overall course of faith which they follow.

However, our author focuses instead on the more significant issue of her **faith** in God. She had heard the reports of the crossing of the Red Sea and that the army of Israel had been unstoppable in Transjordan, and she believed that they would surely conquer Jericho. Specifically, she believed that the God of Israel would be with his people and that there would be no way to win against them. She confessed "I know the Lord has given you the land" (Josh 2.9) and "The Lord your God, He is God in heaven above and on earth beneath" (v 11). In her own way she is an example of one who believed that God "is," and by asking for a promise of safety when the city was taken, she was also an example of one who believed that God would reward her faith (Heb 11.6). She believed what she had been told about God and his power, and she was thus confident that the city, as well as the entire land, would therefore come into Israel's possession. As far as she was concerned, it was a certainty. She is thus another example of the faith that is sure of what has not yet been seen (v 1) and of how faith delivers its possessor from death (she **was not destroyed**, she lived through, and after, a great judgment and destruction by God, and therefore was similar, in some ways to Noah, Moses, and Israel).[113]

Of the inhabitants of Jericho, Rahab alone believed. The rest were **unbelievers**. In this way her faith resembled that of Noah. The Greek word here (*apeithō*, from which we get our English word "apathetic") literally means "unpersuaded" and is the same one used of the Israelites in the wilderness in Hebrews 3.18. It can also mean "disobey" because the person who is unpersuaded of something will not act upon it. Even though the inhabitants of Jericho were afraid of the Israelites and had apparently believed the reports about their unprecedented entrance into that part of the world, they were not persuaded to the point that they were ready to surrender. Their defense of their city demonstrated that they did not believe the city's destruction was inevitable. For their lack of faith in what they had heard, they perished (*cf.* 2.1).

It is possible that what attracted the author of Hebrews to the story of Rahab, in addition to her faith, was the fact that according to Joshua 6.23, when the city was destroyed, "the young men who were spies went in and brought out Rahab and her father and her mother and her brothers and all she had; they also brought out all her relatives and placed them outside the camp of Israel" (NASB). Living "outside the camp" of Israel is exactly what the author of Hebrews will encourage his readers to do in Hebrews 12.13–14. She was an example, then, of someone (like Abraham and Moses) who had to leave her home in her native city to live "outside the camp,"[114] apart from her family and ancestral connections.

---

[113] The subtle implication is that if a pagan prostitute could trust in God, Christians ought to be able to do so as well. Koester, *Hebrews*, 505, 510.

[114] Carl Mosser, "Rahab Outside the Camp," in *The Epistle to the Hebrews and Christian Theology*, ed. Richard Bauckham *et al.* (Grand Rapids: Eerdmans, 2009), 383–404.

11.32 And what further might I say? For time will run out as I relate about Gideon, Barak, Samson, Jephthah, David, and Samuel and the prophets.

At this point the list of examples changes from a list with short narratives to a summary list of names and experiences, a style similar in some ways to a genealogy.[115] One reason that the author could **relate** or describe these stories in detail was because "**time will run out**" if he did so. The phrase was a common rhetorical clue to an audience that the speaker was going to condense the following material,[116] which reflects that Hebrews was read to the congregation, probably in one sitting. But there is another discernible reason for why the example list changes here. It is probably because getting into the land of rest is the assumed goal behind the exhortations in Hebrews (recall chs 3–4), and the example list has now reached that point in Israel's history.

Historically, the great stories of faith tend to be clustered around Israel's earliest history until the death of Joshua. After that, the canonical Biblical narrative increasingly notes how God's people drifted further and further away from him and became more like the nations around them (that is, like unbelievers). This does not mean, however, that there were no bright spots of faith in Israel's history after Joshua. However, the author only mentions six representative names (a similar list already appeared in the OT, 1 Sam 12.11 LXX) plus "the prophets." The fact that the list does not follow chronological order (Barak came before Gideon, Samson came before Jephthah, and Samuel came before David) further suggests that it is meant to be understood as a representative and summary list, not a comprehensive or exclusive catalog of people of faith from the OT. The following verses (vv 33–38) supplement this list with an equally condensed list of things that cumulatively illustrate what faith typically accomplished for these people and others like them.

The names of **Gideon, Barak, Samson, Jephthah**, and **Samuel** have in common that they were all judges of Israel in the pre-monarchy period. These characters are especially appropriate as examples of faith in that none of them were impressive or considered well-qualified to be leaders

---

[115] In fact, a stock part of an *encomium* in ancient rhetorical practice was to include a *genos*, the ancestry of the one being praised. Richardson, *Pioneer and Perfecter of Faith*, 151–54. Here in Hebrews 11, however, we have an ancestry of faith.

[116] Lane, *Hebrews 9–13*, 382–83, Moffatt, *Epistle to the Hebrews*, 184.

by the world's standards. By faith, however, they all accomplished extraordinary things, things that would have been impossible otherwise. Like other people of great faith, they faced extraordinary circumstances and serious personal limitations, and through their faith in God they were empowered to overcome them all.

Gideon was an unlikely leader (judge) of God's people in his day (in fact, all the major judges were). The first time we meet him in the Bible he is hiding from Israel's enemy at that time, the Midianites. Gideon was threshing some wheat in a wine press in order to hide his activity, because the Midianites would raid all Israelite stores of food when they found out about their existence. While "coward" might be too harsh to describe him, he certainly was afraid of the overwhelming enemy (who were "like locusts in number ... innumerable," Jdg 6.5). God called *this* man to lead the army of Israel against the superior force of the enemy. His faith is all the more enhanced when we recall his initial objection that he was a "nobody" within Israel. God's response was "Surely I will be with you, and you shall defeat Midian as one man" (7.16). Gideon's eventual acceptance of the commission (after requesting some reassurances, Jdg 6.17ff) demonstrated his faith that God by his power would indeed give victory to Israel as he had promised. In this regard he is similar to Rahab, the Israelites at Jericho, and Moses. Gideon's faith was also demonstrated in leading a small army into battle against a numerically superior enemy. God reduced his army of 32,000 men to only 300, but Gideon engaged the battle trusting that God would be with them. In defeating overwhelming odds by the exercise of his faith in God, Gideon stands as an example of one who escaped a kind of "death" through his faith (like the patriarchs in Heb 11.4ff).

Like Gideon, **Barak** was also an unlikely leader of God's army. His story is told in Judges 4. He was called to lead God's people against their oppressor, the Canaanites, but he ignobly agreed to do it only if a woman, the prophetess Deborah, would go with him.[117] In the end, the crowning piece of the victory was also due to a woman. In the route of the Canaanites the commander of their army, Sisera, fled the battlefield and took rest in the tent of a woman named Jael, who killed him with a tent stake. To his credit, however, Barak did attack the Canaanite army

---

[117] This embarrassing fact led some rabbis to explain that Barak gave Deborah the more prominent role out of modesty. Moffatt, *Epistle to the Hebrews*, 185.

from Mt. Tabor, and God gave him a tremendous victory on that field. Like Gideon, his faith overcame his fear, and God rewarded him with success. His example is cited as an encouragement for Christians who felt that they too were facing opposition against which they could not possibly stand. His story teaches us that if we will trust in God's power and his promises, he will give us the victory no matter how great the enemy against us is.

Samson's appearance on this list is perhaps one of the most puzzling. He fraternized with the enemy, visited prostitutes and had a weakness for women in general, gave away the secret of his strength, and violated his vow. Like Jacob, his faults were numerous and obvious. Yet also like Jacob, there were times when he exhibited notable faith in God, and especially at the end of his life. He prayed to God for sustenance in Judges 15.17ff, and God brought him water out of a rock (thus providing for him as he had for Israel in the wilderness; Exod 17.6, Num 20.8). In the last scene of his life, he also relied upon God to give him the strength to kill his enemies (Jdg 16.28). This moment of faith thus also illustrates the kind of reliance on God's power that characterizes several of the other names in Hebrews 11. His case is especially significant because he demonstrates what God can do with only one person who has faith. We do not hear of the army of Israel in Samson's time, because Samson was a one-man army of God. However, Samson also introduces another element to the list of characters already presented, namely that some people of faith have lost their lives even as they were acting by faith in God. This does not nullify the fact that God has on several occasions delivered other people of faith out of situations of death. It simply means that some people made the ultimate sacrifice in the demonstration of their faith. Whereas people like Moses sacrificed a family and wealth, and Abraham sacrificed a home, others like Samson sacrificed their lives. In each case, however, the sacrifice was motivated by the same faith in God.

Jephthah is most remembered for his rash vow to offer to God as a burnt offering the first thing that came to meet him out of his tent if God would allow him to return home victorious over the Ammonites (Jdg 11). Jephthah stands as an example of faith to the extent that he was willing to sacrifice dearly for the sake of his trust in God. He also made an unlikely leader of Israel since he was the son of a prostitute and rejected by his brothers (but eventually became the leader of his entire tribe). In this latter aspect he reminds us of Joseph, but like the rest of the judges he was also a classic "nobody." The stories of the judges repeatedly show us that God often works through such nobodies so that it is clear in the end that the power for victory did not lie in the human agent, but in God alone. What made these people useful to God in their time was not their own skills, but their faith. This would have been of great encouragement to early Christians who were rejected from families and synagogues, who were socially marginalized, and who were counted "as the scum of the earth" (1 Cor 4.13). If God could raise and use a man like Jephthah, he could do it with anyone, as long as they are willing to trust him.

David's faith manifested itself on several occasions so that it is easy to see that his whole life was lived by faith. The first is when David faced and defeated the Philistine giant Goliath (1 Sam 17). In that story the young David stands as a giant of faith in contrast to the fear of the rest of the Israelite army. He entered that fight proclaiming "The Lord who delivered me from the paw of the lion and from the paw of the bear, he will deliver me from the hand of this Philistine" (1 Sam 17.37 NASB). David also exhibited faith as he fled from Saul for several months (and refused to kill him when he had the chance, twice—1 Sam 24.1ff and 26.7ff), as he took refuge among Israel's enemies (with the Moabites in 1 Sam 22.3ff, and with the Philistines in 27.1ff), and as he fought against Israel's enemies in establishing his kingdom (the Jebusites, Philistines, Moabites, the people of Hamath, the Edomites, the Ammonites, Zobah and Syria; 2 Sam 5–10). David's many psalms, especially the laments, also testify to his trust in God to deliver him from his enemies.

Samuel was the last judge[118] of Israel (1 Sam 7.6, 15) and is also counted among the prophets (1 Sam 3.20; yet a "non-literary" prophet in that he left behind no book of his preaching). God raised him up in a time of moral and spiritual decline, when Eli and his corrupt sons controlled Israel. Samuel grew up and became the spiritual leader Israel needed. His devotion to God and his trust in God's power prompted him to lead a moral reform in which idols were put away, which further resulted in a crushing defeat of the Philistines (1 Sam 7). His trust in God's protection and his moral courage—both products of his faith in God—led him

[118] He attempted to install his sons as judges, but because of their corruption the people of Israel refused to have them as leaders and demanded the appointment of a king. 1 Sam 8.1ff.

to rebuke Saul over the matter of the sacrifice at Gilgal (1 Sam 13) and again over the matter of the Amalekites (1 Sam 15), at great personal risk to himself, since Saul was becoming increasingly paranoid and ruthless.

The phrase "**the prophets**" covers all those whom God called to deliver his word to his people and their leaders in times of widespread, national unfaithfulness to the covenant. Almost every page of their stories bespeaks their faith, and they are examples of how faith manifests itself in commitment to God, even when that commitment becomes dangerous. The prophets generally worked against opposition from their own people, and they therefore serve as great models to Christians who were experiencing a similar rejection by their own families and fellow countrymen. In the spirit of Hebrews itself, we may offer a representative sample. Nathan rebuked David after his sin with Bathsheba and the subsequent murder of her husband Uriah (2 Sam 12). Rebuking a king was always potentially dangerous work, but Nathan stayed true to his prophetic calling and delivered God's word without regard for the consequences to himself. In doing so he manifested his faith in God. Elijah championed faithfulness to God in the time of Ahab and Jezebel, who tried to eradicate the worship of God from Israel and replace it with the worship of Baal. His famous contest on Mt. Carmel, his slaughter of the prophets of Baal, his rebukes to the king and his wife, and his prayer that it would not rain were all undertaken at great personal risk (Jezebel sought to kill him). He was rejected by his own people and lived a homeless life. At one point he lived outside, by a stream that was drying up, and God fed him by having ravens bring him scraps of food (1 Kngs 17.4–5). Through all of the threats and hardships, he persevered by faith in God, trusting that the God who called him to service would care for him and deliver him from harm. Micaiah had the courage to speak the truth frankly to Ahab when a restrained approach could possibly have saved his life (1 Kngs 22). He was the only prophet in all of Israel, "yet one man" (1 Kngs 22.8), who dared rebuke the king and tell him the truth. The Biblical account implies that he died for his courageous choice that reflected his faith in God. Jeremiah had the unpleasant task of announcing that God was going to empower the Babylonians and use them to destroy Jerusalem. His message sounded like treason to a people who were convinced that the Babylonians could not possibly take God's city, and more than once he was mistreated for his message.

11.33–34 who through faith conquered kingdoms, brought about righteousness, obtained promises, closed the mouths of lions, extinguished the power of fire, eluded the edge of the sword, were strengthened from weakness, became strong in war, and routed foreign armies.

Verses 33–38 comprise a compact list of great accomplishments of faith by past Israelites. The list can be divided into two parts: verses 33–34a, and verses 34b–38. The common theme of the first part of the list is how people escaped death and/or conquered their foes **through faith**. The second part of the list concentrates on the sufferings that people of faith have endured. The author could assume that his Jewish readers would be able to recognize the larger stories to which these kernels referred and the people who accomplished these things. The rapid, staccato presentation without connecting conjunctions has the effect of overwhelming the ear and the mind with examples of faithful endurance in hardship,[119] and creates a sense of proof of the author's main point that faithful, sacrificial endurance based on trust in God is the way to salvation. The multitude of characters these great deeds of faith conjure up leads to the image of a great collection of witnesses in 12.1.

Kingdoms were **conquered** by people like Joshua and David. Although the phrase is generic, it seems here to refer to offensive wars. Successful defensive wars are mentioned later ("routed foreign armies"). Under Joshua Israel defeated enemies that included giants, people who lived in walled, fortified cities, and who made Israel look "like grasshoppers" in comparison (Num 13.33), all because Joshua believed that God would give Israel possession of the land just as he had promised (*cf.* Num 14.7–9; Josh 21.45; 23.14). David and his band of mighty men finished the job and subdued all the nations around Israel (see the list above in comments on v 32) so that Solomon ruled over all the land God had promised to Abraham (see Gen 15.18 and 1 Kngs 4.21). Through leaders who had faith, God gave Israel a kingdom and enlarged it. Conquering another nation was no easy feat, and often in the Biblical stories these conquests came in circumstances that did not favor God's people. The power to succeed was due to their faith in God. In a much greater way

[119] It is a rhetorical technique well-known among the ancients, called asyndeton. The ancient Roman rhetor Quintilian (first cent. AD) said this technique "is useful when we are speaking with special vigour: for it at once impresses the details on the mind and makes them seem more numerous than they really are." (*Institutes of Oratory* 9.3.50 [Butler, LCL]).

God has given us a kingdom (Heb 12.28) that will eventually subdue all other kingdoms, not in an earthly or political sense, but as a kingdom based on God's power and righteousness which will eventually conquer every form of evil (Dan 2.44; Matt 12.28f; 1 Cor 15.24ff; Rom 8.37). It is a kingdom made up of people who trust in God, and in the end they alone will stand victorious and vindicated (Rev 15.2). The image of a wicked world at war with God's saints is common in the NT (see 2 Cor 10.4f; Rom 8.37; 1 Pet 2.11; Rom 13.12; Eph 6.11ff).

The phrase **brought about righteousness** can be understood in several ways: 1) It can mean "worked righteousness" in the sense that those who trusted in God did righteous acts. The sense in this context is that they did these things when all around them was characterized by wickedness, and so their righteous behavior would have been resented and opposed. 2) The phrase could also mean that they brought about righteousness in the sense that they removed wicked practices and established righteous ones in their place. The great reforms of kings such as Asa, Jehoshaphat, Hezekiah, and Josiah,[120] as well as Samuel's reform, would fit well with this sense of the phrase. 3) It could also mean that they brought about justice (the Greek word *dikaiosunē* can have this meaning; so ESV, NET, NIV, RSV), thus creating a picture of standing against and correcting injustices in their day. Many of the prophets preached against social evils such as the neglect of the needy (Jer 5.28), corruption in the courts (Amos 5.12; Hab 1.4), and exploitation of the poor (Isa 3.14f; 10.2; Amos 5.11), and David's reign was a time of righteousness and justice (2 Sam 8.15) as well as Solomon's (1 Kngs 3.28). 4) The ambiguity of the phrase may be intended to cover more than one of its possible senses, so that a combination of the above interpretations is possible. Ezra and Nehemiah come to mind as Biblical characters who did much to right several different kinds of wrongs within Israel in their day.

Because of their faith, these people **obtained promises**. The phrase could mean that God made promises to them, or it could mean that they received what God had promised. We might prefer the former interpretation here on the basis of verse 39 (see comments there), but in several of the OT examples what was promised was also received. Cases in point would be the promises of victory to Barak (Jdg 4.7) and Gideon

[120] For a study of reform movements in ancient Israel, see Walter C. Kaiser, *Quest for Renewal* (Chicago: Moody Press, 1986).

(Jdg 6.16), God's promise to David of victory over the Philistines (2 Sam 5.19), the promise delivered through Isaiah during the Assyrian siege of Jerusalem in Hezekiah's day (2 Kngs 19), the promise of victory delivered through Jahaziel during the Moabite attack in Jehoshaphat's day (2 Chron 20), and the promise of deliverance made through Elisha during the Syrian siege of Samaria (2 Kngs 7).

The story of Daniel is no doubt in mind as exhibiting how faith **closed the mouths of lions**. Daniel was thrown into a den of lions for his refusal to obey an edict that prohibited his prayer to God (Dan 6)—an edict that was passed by his enemies with the goal of eliminating him. His good character was so well-known that the king of Babylon only had the sentence carried out with grief, and he himself told Daniel that "Your God whom you constantly serve will Himself deliver you" (Dan 6.16 NASB). God sent an angel to close the mouths of the lions and Daniel was unharmed. The men who devised the plot against him were thrown to those same lions and were immediately killed. Daniel's story is thus another example of how faith delivers from death.

The reference to faith that involved being afflicted or threatened with **fire** most certainly brings to mind the story of Daniel's three friends and fellow-Hebrews Hananiah, Mishael, and Azariah, otherwise known as Shadrach, Meshach, and Abed-nego. They too refused an order of the king, one that they considered idolatrous. The story is recorded in Daniel 3. Their words of commitment to God are some of the bravest words of any Biblical characters: to the great king of Babylon they said "O Nebuchadnezzar, we do not need to give you an answer concerning this matter. If it be so, our God whom we serve is able to deliver us from the furnace of blazing fire; and he will deliver us out of your hand, O king. But even if he does not, let it be known to you, O king, that we are not going to serve your gods or worship the golden image that you have set up" (Dan 3.16–18 NASB). They were thrown into a great kiln but came out alive and unharmed, "the fire had no effect on the bodies of these men nor was the hair of their head singed, nor were their trousers damaged, nor had the smell of fire even come upon them" (Dan 3.27 NASB). This deadly power had no effect on them because they had stood firm in their commitment to God, that is, in their faith.

The edge of the sword is a common Biblical expression for death inflicted by an army in warfare, although it can refer to death by execution ("the sword" is a common ancient way of speaking of a government's authority over life, see Rom 13.4) or to violence in general (2 Sam 12.10; Nah 3.15; Matt 26.52). The phrase cites a threat of death that God's people often faced. There are several stories in the OT where either a man or the nation was spared from what seemed to be certain destruction, all because either the man or the people had the faith to trust in God to deliver them from the threat. We may think of Elisha's escape from Dothan when the Syrian army had come there to take him (2 Kngs 6), of Jeremiah's life being spared by the Babylonians when hundreds of others in Jerusalem were killed (Jer 39), of God's rescue of the Israelites from the army of Egypt at the Red Sea, of God's rescue of Jerusalem from annihilation by the Assyrian army because of Hezekiah's faith (Isa 37), of God's rescue of Samaria when it was attacked by the Syrians (2 Kngs 7), of God's deliverance of Israel from a combined Moabite-Ammonite army after Jehoshaphat prayed to God (2 Chron 20), of the successful repulsion of the vastly superior Ethiopian force in Asa's day (2 Chron 14, see esp. v 11), or Esther's work that exposed a plot to kill all the Jews in Persia. Jezebel threatened to kill Elijah (1 Kngs 19), and king Jehoram threatened Elisha's life (2 Kngs 6.31). Even in the civil war between Israel and Judah in Abijah's day, "the sons of Judah conquered because they trusted in the Lord, the God of their fathers" (2 Chron 13.18).

People of faith have sometimes found themselves in situations of **weakness** or frailty, either through persecution or simply by the lowly circumstances of their lives. However, it is God's characteristic activity to bring life out of death and **strength** out of weakness (*cf.* 2 Cor 12.10). Just when it seems that the faithful are defeated, God can invigorate them with his power and enable them to stand (*cf.* 2 Cor 4.8–10). Examples are God's care of Elijah, David's strength to kill Goliath, Samson's extraordinary strength (even when he had been captured by the Philistines, Jdg 15.14ff, and blinded, 16.21ff), God's granting of more years to Hezekiah when he was deathly ill and the Assyrians were attacking (2 Kngs 20.1ff), and the ability of barren women (like Sarah, Rebekah, Rachel, Manoah's wife, and Hannah) to bear children. All of these examples involved people of faith who were apparently out of the kinds of resources normally needed to overcome their situations, but God supplied them with the strength they needed. God's use of "nobodies," people who were considered unfit or otherwise inadequate for a task, also demonstrates strength coming out of weakness. The stories of the major judges of Israel, as well as his selection of David to be the king of Israel, fit this mold. On a greater scale, God's creation of the nation of Israel from a couple who were unable to have children, or Israel's ability to conquer Canaan, are other examples of strength coming out of weakness. Psalm 113 is a celebration of God's activity in this way.

People who trusted God **became strong in war** against staggering odds. We have already noted some examples. Joshua led Israel to conquer Canaan, both Gideon and Barak overcame their fear of the enemy, Gideon defeated a huge Midianite army with three hundred men, and Samson became strong (literally) against the Philistines. In this same vein, people of faith were able to **rout** (defeat overwhelmingly) much larger forces and make them flee because they trusted the battle to the Lord. **Foreign armies** that attacked the Israelites but were routed and fled include the Philistines (several times: 1 Sam 7, 17, 19), Arameans (2 Sam 10), Ethiopians (2 Chron 14), Assyrians (Isa 37), and a combined force of Moabites and Ammonites (2 Chron 20).

11.35 Women received their dead by resurrection, but others were tortured, not accepting deliverance in order that they might gain a better resurrection.

There are two OT stories of **women** who literally **received** back **their dead** children **by resurrection**: Elijah raised the son of the widow of Zarephath (1 Kngs 17) and Elisha raised the Shunammite woman's son (2 Kngs 4). Along with Abraham, Sarah received Isaac back figuratively (Heb 11.19).

The verse division would go better if the first line of verse 35 were included with verse 34, since the list of faith's accomplishments clearly shifts at this point away from the triumphs of faith to the sufferings of faith. The point is not to create a sense of fear or dread. It is just the opposite, to create a sense that the great heroes of faith of times past exhibited their faith in contexts of suffering, and unto death. Every trial is an opportunity to demonstrate faith in God, and people of faith in situations of suffering showed exactly what they were made of in those conditions. Their hardships showcased the strength of their faith. The examples are thus adduced as an encouragement to the effect "you can do it too." The list also has the sobering effect of demonstrating that a believer's commitment to God may well cost him his life.

The second list is introduced by the generic statement that some people of faith were **tortured**. The word here (*tumpanizō*, from which we get the name of the kettledrum, the "tympanum") literally means "to beat with a club," possibly while stretched out,[121] but the word acquired the more generic sense of "torture."[122] The word might also denote flogging. Philo describes something like this in his report of the riot in Alexandria, Egypt in the year 38 AD, when he says that some Jews were "scourged, hung up, tortured on the wheel, condemned, and dragged to execution."[123] In ancient times, torture was used to extract information or to punish what were considered the worst offenses against authority (hence Roman crucifixion as punishment for the crime of sedition). Furthermore, it was almost universally recognized as a form of public shame. There are no canonical OT stories of faithful people being tortured, so 1) the author may intend this simply as a generic term that would include a life of hardship imposed by unbelievers as well as direct physical mistreatments. Elijah's difficult life comes to mind, as well as Jeremiah's; or 2) the author here was possibly referring to stories about other martyrs of faith that were well-known among the Jews. This interpretation is bolstered in light of verse 37, which cites a mode of death not mentioned in the OT but is described in noncanonical literature (see below). There is a Jewish tradition that the prophet Amos died after being tortured.[124]

Many students of Hebrews have suggested that the author had in mind a story from the intertestamental period that is recorded in 2 Maccabees 6 and 7.[125] As the story goes, the Syrian king Antiochus Epiphanes, who controlled Palestine at the time, decided to enforce Hellenization upon the Jews, outlawed Torah observances, and rededicated the Jerusalem temple to the Greek god Zeus. Local officials tried to force a man named Eleazar, a scribe, to eat pig meat. When he steadfastly refused, he was put on the "rack" and beaten to death. Seven brothers and their

---

[121] Thayer, *Greek-English Lexicon*, 632.

[122] BDAG 1019; MM 645.

[123] *Flaccus* 85 (*The Works of Philo*, Yonge, 732).

[124] *The Lives of the Prophets* 7.1. The work is dated to the first century. English translation by D. R. A. Hare, in *Old Testament Pseudepigrapha, Vol. 2* , ed. James H. Charlesworth (New York: Doubleday, 1985), 379–99.

[125] 2 Macc has been dated to the first century BC. Its narrative covers the fifteen-year period of 175–160 BC.

mother were subjected to the same pressure. They were "arrested and were being compelled by the king, under torture with whips and cords, to partake of unlawful swine's flesh" (2 Macc 7.1 RSV). When the brothers indicated that they would rather die than eat unclean food, they were tortured to death one at a time, and then their mother. The last words of all eight of the characters are recorded, and the fourth brother said, "One cannot but choose to die at the hands of men and to cherish the hope that God gives of being raised again by him" (7.14 RSV). The account includes mention of how they were offered their lives in exchange for obedience to the king's demands, but all of them refused. This would fit the explanation here that such people did "**not accept deliverance in order that they might gain a better resurrection**."

Is this story what the author of Hebrews had in mind? In favor of this identification is that the story fits the description here in three ways: it is a story about people who were tortured, it includes a refusal of deliverance, and it contains references to faith in a coming resurrection. Jews in NT times knew the Maccabean stories well, and the Maccabean period was remembered as a time of great persecution by unbelievers (specifically, the Hellenistic Syrian monarchs), but also a time of ultimate victory. The suggestion that our author could allude to some of these stories should not bother us. Just because we have no canonical (inspired) record of the intertestamental period does not mean that there were no people of great faith during that time. There is no reason to deny that the story is basically credible.[126] It is not hard to see how it would have been an encouragement to Christians who faced persecution from religious authorities and who were being pressured to deny the faith or blaspheme (*cf.* "punishing them often, I compelled them to blaspheme," Acts 26.11).

11.36 Yet others received a test of scorn and beatings, and even chains and imprisonment.

Everything on the following list has at least one thing in common: they were all expressions of social shame, as well as expressions of hatred and

[126] See Jonathan A. Goldstein, *II Maccabees: A New Translation with Introduction and Commentary*, AYB 41A (New York: Doubleday, 1983), 292, 299. Whether Josephus knew about this account, and alludes to it, has been debated. The fact that Josephus omits the story from his histories is not decisive against its historicity, since Josephus generally wished either to avoid or downplay stories of Jewish mistreatment by foreign monarchs.

rejection. The fact that the sources of these demonstrations were Jews is significant. The sufferings listed below were not inflicted by pagans, but by fellow-Jews who had no regard for God. The original hearers of Hebrews might have identified readily with some of these kinds of experiences at the hands of fellow-Jews. To readers in the first century, both scorn and beating were social demonstrations of social rejection through public shame. In a society where shame was to be avoided and honor bolstered, scorn, reproach, and insults from one's fellow citizens were significant. Elijah was **scorned** (mocked, 2 Kngs 2.23), and Micaiah (1 Kngs 22.8), as were all the prophets of God: "The Lord, the God of their fathers, sent word to them again and again by his messengers, because he had compassion on his people and on his dwelling place; but they continually mocked the messengers of God, despised his words and scoffed at his prophets" (2 Chron 36.15f NASB). People mocked the couriers of Hezekiah who announced that Israel would observe the Passover (2 Chron 30.10), and the foreigners in Judah mocked Nehemiah (Neh 2.19). Jeremiah was beaten at least twice: Jeremiah 20.2 and 37.15. Jehoiakim's destruction of the book containing Jeremiah's preaching (Jer 36) should also be counted as an expression of scorn against the prophet, as well as Jezebel's threat against Elijah's life. Public **beating** was considered not only corporal punishment, but also humiliation.

Chains and imprisonment often went together in the ancient world and were both a mark of degradation and shame (*cf.* 2 Tim 1.16, where Paul says Onesiphorus "was not ashamed of my chain"). Socially, it identified a person as among society's worst. Imprisonment in ancient times was not what it is in our country today. Prisoners were not necessarily fed on a regular basis nor provided basic necessities, and conditions were filthy and full of disease.[127] Samson was chained and imprisoned (Jdg 16). Jeremiah was also both imprisoned (kept in the court of the guard house, Jer 32–33, 38–39; also 37.15) and chained (Jer 40.1–4; the Babylonians eventually released him). The prophet Micaiah was imprisoned by Ahab (2 Chron 18.26), and king Asa imprisoned the prophet Hanani (2 Chron 16.10). Some of the early Christians were bound in the persecution of Saul (Acts 9.2, 21). Recall 10.34.

---

[127] For a good description of imprisonment in Roman times, see Brian Rapske, *Paul in Roman Custody*, vol. 3 of *The Book of Acts in Its First Century Setting* (Grand Rapids: Eerdmans, 1994).

11.37–38 They were stoned, they were sawn in two, they were tested,[128] they died by murder with a sword, they wandered in sheepskins, in hides of goats, they were needy, afflicted, and ill-treated (of whom the world was not worthy), wandering around in deserts and mountains and caves and openings in the earth.

Not only did people of faith suffer (vv 35f), but many of them also eventually died for their faith as well. The author of Hebrews does not sugar-coat the realities of faithful service to God in the midst of a world full of unbelievers. Jesus wanted his followers to know "up front" the consequences of their commitment to him (Luke 8.58; 14.27ff). While faith rescued some people from death, the fact remains that some people of faith lost their lives. *Cf.* the story in Acts 12.1–11.

Zechariah the son of Jehoiada the priest was **stoned** to death inside the temple precincts after he spoke a rebuke by the Spirit of God against the Jews of his day (2 Chron 24.20f), and Jesus charged that the inhabitants of Jerusalem had stoned the messengers God had sent to them (Matt 23.37). Jewish tradition held that Jeremiah was stoned by Jews in Egypt.[129] The reference to someone being **sawn in two** fits the Jewish tradition about the prophet Isaiah, who reportedly met that end under the wicked king Manasseh.[130] **Testing** describes the experiences of many OT figures generally and adds to the overall rhetorical effect of the list. The prophet Uriah, who was a contemporary of Jeremiah, was **murdered by the sword** at the order of king Jehoiakim (Jer 26.20ff). Elijah spoke of how God's prophets had been killed with the sword in his own day (1 Kngs 19.10) and God accused the Jews through Jeremiah saying "In vain I have struck your sons; they accepted no chastening. Your sword has devoured your prophets like a destroying lion" (Jer 2.20 NASB).

Those whose faith did not cost them their lives often faced an existence of extreme hardship. The rough clothing of **sheepskins and hides of goats** were what only the poorest people wore.[131] In ancient times, a prevailing perspective was that fine clothing was not only an indicator

---

[128] The Greek word here (*epeirasthēsan*) is absent from the Nestle text but is likely original. See Peter Malik, "Rid Us (Not) of the Temptation: A Note on the Text of Hebrews 11.37," *JSNT* 44 (2022): 580–89.

[129] *The Lives of the Prophets* 2.1.

[130] *The Lives of the Prophets* 1.1.

[131] Koester, *Hebrews*, 515.

of high social status and respectability (*cf.* Jam 2.2f), but blessing in general was interpreted as one's being pleasing to God. Similarly, poverty and hardships were interpreted as signs of God's displeasure, implying that such people were sinners (*cf.* John 9.1f). By identifying these things with people of faith, the author of Hebrews was inverting the world's perspective and judgment. The world may have judged them as marginal, despised, and useless, but that judgment was wrong. These were people of faith, pleasing to God despite what the world thought of them. This inversion of values would have been a helpful perspective for the original readers of Hebrews who were struggling with the loss of status, honor, and standing within families and their larger cultures. Elijah was noted for his destitute life and wore an animal-skin garment (2 Kngs 1.8). According to Zechariah 13.4, the animal-skin cloak (and the poverty it reflected) was synonymous with a true prophet. The fact that some of God's people wore these was not just an indicator of their poverty (they were **needy**), but even more was a sign of their rejection by the society of their day. The fact that these people were also homeless (they **wandered**; Elijah's rootless life by the Cherith brook comes to mind) bespeaks either their refusal to participate in the materialism of the world around them (like Moses, vv 24f), or their rejection by unbelievers, or both. "Wandering" could have a negative social connotation (see on v 8 above). Their dress and their living conditions reflected their spiritual and moral distance from the world while at the same time they lived in it (*cf.* Matt 11.8). Their lives generally were filled with affliction and ill-treatment of various sorts because their own people refused them. "A prophet is not without honor, except in his homeland and among his relatives and in his family" (Mark 6.4). It is also possible that our author had in mind the Jews who suffered under Antiochus Epiphanes in the Maccabean period. Daniel said they would "will fall by sword and by flame, by captivity and by plunder for many days" (Dan 11.33 NASB).

In the middle of this catalog of suffering, the author parenthetically remarks that **the world was not worthy** of such great people. In Hebrews the **world** (Greek *kosmos*) can be the physical created order, but it can also denote unbelievers (as here and v 7; *cf.* the similar usage in John's writings). It is not as if the people to whom the prophets preached were basically good, upright people who had a few minor problems that needed to be addressed and who deserved, because of their fundamental uprightness, for God to speak to them. They were, generally, wicked and stubborn people who cared nothing about hearing the truth from God and who actively opposed those whom God sent to rebuke and correct them. Such people did not deserve God's patience, they did not deserve that God sent them righteous people in the effort to steer them back to God so that they might avoid the punishment that would come upon them otherwise, nor did they deserve all the sacrifice the prophets went through to preach God's message in their day. These people had already made it clear that they wanted nothing to do with God, but God in his love and mercy sent them the prophets anyway. The irony is that the world judged the prophets to be unworthy of a place among them, and they cast them out. The fact was, however, that it was the world that was unworthy of the company of the prophets. Again, the author of Hebrews inverted the perspective. If the world was not worthy to have God's prophets in it, it is not worthy to have Christians in it either. True Christians are a blessing to any society, but often society sees them as troublemakers (Acts 17.6) and nonconformists who threaten the existing social structure. Their presence in the world is not due to the fact that the world deserves to have them, but to God's mercy in providing the world with people who serve as a light in the darkness (Matt 5.14; Phil 2.15). The presence of godly people in the world, and their violent rejection by the world, only makes the unbelieving world's condemnation all the more obvious.

The last part of the list emphasizes the homeless nature of the heroes of faith. Because this world was not their home (vv 13–16), and because the world had cast them out, many of them literally had no place to live here. They lived wherever they could. Some of them lived in the hot **deserts**, uninhabited places with sparse vegetation and synonymous with hostility to human life. The Israelites lived in deserts after they left Egypt (Isa 48.21, Jer 2.6), and David lived in wildernesses at more than one point in his life.[132] Others lived on the cold **mountains** or found places in **caves** or other natural fissures **in the earth** where they could find some shelter from the elements. All of these have in common that they were away from the rest of the world. **Caves**, like animal-skin clothing, were the homes of the poorest kind of people, or people who were rejected and refused a place among anyone else because they were considered unfit

[132] 1 Sam 23.15, 24, 24.1, 25.1, 2 Sam 15.28; there they had little to eat and none of the comforts of life, 2 Sam 17.27–29; *cf.* Psa 63; 102.6.

for society. David lived in caves as Saul tried to hunt him down (1 Sam 22.1; see Psa 142). Obadiah, an overseer of Ahab's household, hid some prophets of God in a cave and brought them food in the difficult time of Jezebel's fury (1 Kngs 18.4ff), and during that same time Elijah stayed in a cave (1 Kngs 19.9). People of faith may find that their own society (including their own families) rejects them, thus leaving them homeless and poor. The readers of Hebrews may have been facing this very prospect, but if not, these stories of extreme circumstances still served as encouragements. The words of Jesus come to mind, "Blessed are you when people insult you and persecute you, and falsely say all kinds of evil against you because of Me. Rejoice and be glad, for your reward in heaven is great; for in the same way they persecuted the prophets who were before you" (Matt 5.11f). The dispossessed, exposed lives of past heroes of faith are yet another example of the sacrifice that true faith in God is willing to endure for the sake of something much better that God has promised (see vv 9f, 26). The point of rehearsing all these facts (which are difficult to hear) is to show the nobility of these people with respect to their faith.

11.39 And all of these, having been approved through faith, did not obtain what was promised

All of these people lived and died in faith, looking forward to something they had not seen with their eyes but had only heard about through the promises of God. They persevered, they endured. Like true believers, they were just as confident of what God had promised as if they had already experienced it (v 1), and for the sake of that assurance they endured through the difficulties of life in a world that was not their home. During their stay on earth, they **did not obtain** what God had promised, as their nomadic and difficult lives showed. The phrase **obtain what was promised** (a similar expression was used in v 13) literally says "obtained the promise." The phrase can mean either to have a promise given (its literal meaning), or to receive what was promised (its sense by a figure of speech known as metonymy, where one thing is put for another thing that is closely related to it). The context here makes it clear that the latter sense is meant. These people of faith saw past their own day into the messianic time (*cf.* vv 16, 26). How clearly they saw it is hard to say, but all of them were aware that God's promises were not just about earthly families, or an earthly plot of land, *etc.* They knew that these things pointed to an even greater fulfillment that was not ultimately tied to this world.

The fact that **all of these** great people who trusted in God did not get what God had promised to them in this world in no way suggests that there was something deficient about their faith, as if they would have received it had they mustered more faith, much less does it suggest that God failed to keep his promises to them. No, the fact is that they were **approved** by God **through** their **faith** in him and his word (v 6). The word **approved** is the same word from verse 2, so the chapter now comes back to its point that faith—as defined in verse 1 and illustrated in the many cases and traits that have been cited—is what makes a person acceptable to God, as Habakkuk 2.4 (quoted in Heb 10.38) said. So how is it that they were approved and yet not rewarded with what God had promised them? The next verse gives us the answer.

11.40 (God foresaw something better concerning us) in order that they might not be perfected apart from us.

The reason the great heroes of faith (and all others who lived such lives as well) did not receive what God had promised them within their own lifetimes is that God had something far **better** in mind for **them** than any earthly kind of blessings. As enjoyable as they might be, earthly blessings can never be more than temporary, and they can never fulfill the eternal longing of the soul for the things of God. Imagine someone like Abraham leaving their home at the call of God only to find that all God was offering was a piece of earthly real estate. No, the promises of God concern much greater things, spiritual and heavenly things, and it is a great mistake to suppose that the kingdom of God is about physical blessing and pleasure or that it can be defined or measured or conceived by earthly, physical things or standards. "The kingdom of God is not eating and drinking" (Rom 14.17) or any such thing. While God kept his promises perfectly concerning physical or earthly blessings (see Josh 21.45; 23.14; 1 Kngs 8.56), those blessings were always a type, pattern, or illustration of *spiritual* blessings still to come (remember v 15). God always **foresaw** (in the middle voice, as here, the word has the sense "to plan or provide beforehand"[133]) that he would give people of faith something far greater than any earthly blessing, and he has prepared a heavenly city for them (v 16).

---

[133] BDAG 866.

There is another aspect to this larger perspective. God did not plan to reward the patriarchs with one thing and reward Christians with something else. One thing that has been constant throughout all of God's dealings with man, from Adam until the present, is that God wants man to have and to demonstrate faith in him, and the reward for faith is the same for everyone from Adam until now. That is, the reward that the people of faith from the OT will enjoy is *the same reward* that God has promised to us in Christ Jesus. Bockmeuhl notes that "there is therefore a continuous narrative timeline along which God's one pilgrim people undertake the same journey to the same goal by the same faith in the same life-giving God."[134]

The perspective here is interesting. It is not that we will join them, it is that they join us. The fullness of God's promised blessings has always been in the work of the Messiah, Jesus. God promised it to the faithful of former times, and they knew that God was promising them something spiritual (see v 39). By their faith they "saw" it. If God had given them their reward apart from us (*i.e.,* in their own times and under the Law of Moses), then they would have been **perfected** under the old system. Recall that perfection is not moral sinlessness, but the attainment of a goal, the reaching of a state or condition in which things are finished or completed with nothing else lacking. It is here a way of speaking about salvation, for faith finds the fulfillment (the end, or completion) of its hope ultimately in the presence of God. Our author has already demonstrated that no one was going to reach the goal of their faith through the old system under Moses (or that of the earlier patriarchs). "For the Law (having a shadow of the coming good things and not the image itself of those things) can never ...perfect those who draw near" (10.1). So the heroes of faith of former times will join **us** in the reward that God has promised to the faithful of all generations (see 12.23). Just as the prophets understood that the essence of their message was not about their own day but about our times (the messianic time; 1 Pet 1.12), so all the people of faith of former times lived and died in anticipation of a reward that they would not share **apart from us**, a reward enjoyed in a life past this life, which God gives by his power. The result is that they, like us, have yet to possess (in

---

[134] Markus Bockmuehl, "Abraham's Faith in Hebrews 11," in *The Epistle to the Hebrews and Christian Theology*, ed. Richard Bauckham *et al* (Grand Rapids: Eerdmans, 2009), 364–73, at 369.

its final, fullest form) what God has promised. They are heirs (*cf.* v 7), but the inheritance is not in their possession yet. By faith they entered into God's rest in their lifetimes, but not into its fullness (which will be experienced only in heaven). As we live out our time on earth in anticipation of the final reward of faith, they will receive their reward along with us. This sense of togetherness in the faith with those of the past creates the image with which chapter 12 opens.

HEBREWS 12

12.1 Therefore, having such a cloud of witnesses surrounding us, laying aside every hindrance and the sin which easily entangles, through endurance let us also run the race that lies before us,

The great figures of faith from chapter 11 are here collectively referred to as a **cloud** (the word, *nephos,* was used in Greek literature of large crowds[1]) that **surrounds** us. The "spectators" are called **witnesses**. This can be understood in two ways: 1) we can take this to mean that they are witnesses of our behavior. The Roman orator Dio Chrysostom asked, "And who takes greater delight in the works of virtue than he who has all men as spectators and witnesses of his own soul?"[2] The idea of others watching suggests a sense of accountability. Longinus spoke of this effect as an author might imagine past great authors hearing his writings: "For the ordeal is indeed a severe one, if we presuppose such a tribunal and theater for our own utterances, and imagine that we are undergoing a scrutiny of our writings before these great heroes, acting as judges and witnesses."[3] 2) They could also be witnesses in the sense that they testify to us. For this sense the point would be that by faith they "saw" the yet-unseen reward that God has promised to his children (11.13, 26) and they now speak (11.4) about it to us.[4] Aristotle said that examples of actual past facts "have the effect of witnesses giving evidence."[5] The picture would then be like ex-players who are now coaching us as we go through the same struggles in which they once participated, telling us

---

[1] BDAG 670.

[2] *Discourses* 3.11 (Cohoon and Crosby, LCL).

[3] *On the Sublime* 14.2 (*Longinus on the Sublime,* trans. W. Rhys Roberts (London: Cambridge University Press, 1907), 83).

[4] This interpretation is argued in Baugh, "The Cloud of Witnesses in Hebrews 11." Also Bruce, *Epistle to the Hebrews,* 346.

[5] *Rhetoric* 2.20.9 (*The Works of Aristotle, Vol. XI: Rhetorica, De Rhetorica ad Alexandrum, De Poetica,* trans. W. Rhys Roberts (Oxford: Oxford University Press, 1924)).

about the difficulties ahead of us and thus preparing and encouraging us to endure them.[6] This would be in line with ancient practice, where an athlete's father or past athletic victors served as coaches.[7] Either sense, or both, would fit the picture here. Either way, the rhetoric here, with its visual orientation, served to create a sense of solidarity with the heroes of faith mentioned in chapter 11 and allowed the recipients to re-envision and redefine their current situation as one leading to victory and honor.[8]

The imagery of a **race** (Greek *agōn*, an athletic contest[9]; recalling a similar term from 10.32), creates a picture of Christians running the course of faith (Acts 20.24; 2 Tim 4.7) that is ahead of them, with past heroes of the faith in the grandstands cheering them on.[10] The idea of a race with a finish line in the distance **before**, or in front of, **us** suits well the picture of a faith that is forward-looking and that requires determination. Josephus spoke of "those who have a prize before them" and how, when they are zealous about it, they do not stop working for it.[11] Here, the "race" is another way of speaking about the journey that has been described elsewhere in Hebrews (such as chs 3–4) and ending in God's rest. The race metaphor emphasizes perseverance, which is a constant theme in the sermon. Races in Greco-Roman times were held in a public venue called a stadium, of which several ancient examples survive (Olympia, Athens, Rome, Tyre, Laodicea, Pergamum, Ephesus, Priene, Miletus, Aphrodisias, Perge, Sardis, *etc.*). On each side of the racecourse was seating for spectators. The shortest races were about 210 yards, the longest were about 5,000 yards (2.8 miles),[12] so stamina was needed for

---

[6] This latter sense also evidences how the Greek word (*martur*) eventually came to mean a person who suffered for his testimony, hence a martyr. Bruce, *Epistle to the Hebrews*, 347; Attridge, *Hebrews*, 354–5; Lane, *Hebrews 9–13*, 407–8; Moffatt, *Epistle to the Hebrews*, 193.

[7] Stephen J. Instone, "Athletics," *OCD* 206–07.

[8] Scott D. Mackie, "Visually Oriented Rhetoric and Visionary Experience in Hebrews 12.1–4," *CBQ* 79 (2017): 476–97.

[9] Hollinger suggests that the phrase here should be translated "let us undergo the struggle." Zoe Hollinger, "Rethinking the Translation of *trechōmen ton … agōna* in Hebrews 12.1 in Light of Ancient Graeco-Roman Literature," *The Bible Translator* 70 (2019): 94–111.

[10] *Cf.* 4 Macc 17.11–14: "Truly the contest in which they were engaged was divine, for on that day virtue gave the awards and tested them for their endurance. The prize was immortality in endless life. Eleazar was the first contestant, the mother of the seven sons entered the competition, and the brothers contended. The tyrant was the antagonist, and the world and the human race were the spectators." (NRSV).

[11] *Ant.* 8.302.

[12] Instone, "Athletics."

any one of them. The point of the imagery here is not about speed, nor who crosses first, but about **endurance** and running in the best possible way so as to finish what was started. From this perspective, the winner is the one who finishes, and the loser is the one who drops out before the end (*cf.* 1 Cor 9.24ff). An athletic contest is characterized by prolonged strenuous effort and thus requires strength over time, or perseverance, and the cheering crowd imparts encouragement to the athlete to put forth his best effort and finish in victory. The thrust of the entire catalog of chapter 11, then, is that the examples of the heroes of faith continue to encourage us today (Rom 15.4) to retain our confidence (Heb 10.35) and to endure to the saving of our souls (Heb 10.39).

Like serious runners, we must **lay aside** (put off from ourselves, rid ourselves of) anything that might interfere with our successful completion of the course of faith ahead of us. This includes any and **every** kind of **hindrance**. The word (Greek *ogkos*) denotes bulk, size, or mass[13] and thus suggests that which is an impediment to a runner. No runner wants to be laden with an unnecessary load (like excess body weight) or something that will **entangle** (wrap itself around) him and restrict his stride (like a bulky cloak). Such things would only sap his strength, impede his progress, and jeopardize his ability to finish the race. For a spiritual race, the hindrance consists of **sin**. Any sin is an entanglement, although Hebrews has foremost in mind the specific sin of faithlessness (quitting). We must sacrifice anything and everything that would keep us from crossing the finish line in the end (*cf.* Matt 5.29f). For the original readers of Hebrews this may have included things like family ties, but in this context the idea leans toward discouragement and distrust of God (see vv 12f).

12.2 fixing our eyes on Jesus, the founder and finisher of faith, who, because of[14] the joy that lay before him endured the cross, disregarding its shame, has been seated at the right hand of the throne of God.

---

[13] LSJ 1197.

[14] The Greek word *anti* can mean "because of, for the sake of" or it can mean "instead of." If we take the former meaning, the verse says that Jesus endured the cross for the sake of a heavenly joy beyond it. If we take the latter meaning, the verse says that he endured the cross instead of choosing to enjoy the pleasures of his heavenly life. The former meaning fits the forward-looking context best here. For a defense of the latter view, see Lane, *Hebrews 9–13*, 413.

Successful running requires a fixation on the goal, not on the difficulties along the way.[15] It is for this reason that we are to **fix our eyes upon** Jesus. The term (Greek *aphoraō*) literally means to *look away* from other things which would distract us (such as our hardships) and look solely at one thing. We might have expected our author to encourage us to fix our eyes upon heaven, but we need more than to know about the goal. We also need to know how to reach that goal successfully. For this reason, then, the author bids us to look to Jesus and follow his example of perseverance. When we do that, we will arrive where he has already gone (John 12.26; 14.3; 17.24) in the way that he did it.

Jesus is the greatest example of faithful endurance in all of Biblical history, and he stands here as the capstone of the list of chapter 11. He is here called by the name he wore as a man on earth, thus connecting him with suffering. Because of his faithful endurance in the days of his flesh (5.7), Jesus has now become the founder and finisher of faith. Many English translations read "the founder and finisher of *our* faith." The idea of possession does not always need to be explicitly stated in Greek if the context makes that idea clear enough. The question, therefore, is whether this context demands it. While it is true that we look to Jesus from beginning to end with regard to our faith, and that he is the one who made our faith possible and who will bring our faith to its goal, this may not be the primary point in this context. The author is speaking about Jesus' own accomplishment of faith (he endured the cross and took his seat in glory). For this reason, it is better to translate the phrase without inserting the word "our," while recognizing that what Jesus did serves as an example for us. The word **founder** is the same word from 2.10 (see comments there). He is the founder of faith not in the sense that he was the first person to have faith in God, but that he was the first one to finish the course of faith all the way to heaven itself and to receive his heavenly reward. In this way, then, he is both founder and **finisher** (a word which describes someone who brings something to its fullest development, and in this sense to its perfection[16]). He has blazed the full

---

[15] *Cf.* Aristotle, *Rhetoric* 3.9: "runners, just when they have reached the goal, lose their breath and strength, whereas before, when the end is in sight, they show no signs of fatigue" (Freese, LCL).

[16] N. Clayton Croy, "A Note on Hebrews 12:2," *JBL* 114 (1995): 117–19. Whereas in "normal" human experience one person begins a thing, and then another person perfects it later, in the case of genuine faith in God Jesus is both the prototype and the paragon.

length of the trail before us, showing us the way to reach that same goal ourselves (*cf.* 2.10). His faith in the Father, with its core components of trust and endurance, has become the example for our faith so that we too might finish what we have started (*cf.* Heb 3.14).

Jesus' success in faithfully enduring the hardships of life, which culminated in the shameful mode of his death at the hands of wicked people, and his success in receiving faith's reward, is attributed to his determination to reach the reward God had promised him. This is described in two complementary ways. First, he looked to the **joy that** was **before him**, a delight that consisted of heavenly glory with the Father (see John 17.5). Second, he **disregarded** the shame of the cross. This word (Greek *kataphroneō*) is translated "despised" in several of the English versions. However, in Greek, to despise does not necessarily carry with it the strong negative connotations of hatred or contempt that the word has in modern English usage. It normally has the milder sense of "to disregard" or "to think little or nothing" of something. It is as when we say that something is "no big deal." This is the attitude that Jesus had toward the shame and rejection that reached its apex in his death on the cross. He did not consider it something that should hinder him or cause him to live otherwise, nor should his followers.

Like us (v 1), Jesus had a "prize" (reward, or blessing from efforts) set **before him**. However, whereas the people mentioned in chapter 11 only "saw" (by faith) the finish line and the reward for completion in the future, ahead of them, Jesus has actually crossed the finish line and has reached the heavenly goal itself. There he remains out of our sight (*cf.* 1 Pet 1.8), so we too must look to him with the vision of faith. Our author returns to the language of Psalm 110, which has served as the core of the sermon's exhortation. Here he reminds his readers that Jesus now sits **at the right hand of God's throne** in heaven, in fulfillment of Psalm 110.1 (see comments on 8.1). The fact that he is sitting (**seated**) indicates the finished nature of Jesus' work (recall 10.12) as well as the typical portrayal of a monarch (in fulfillment of Psa 2). Not only has he gone there to serve as our sympathetic high priest (4.14; 7.26; 8.1), but also to enter into his glorious reign. There is no indication that the doctrine of Jesus' exaltation was being either questioned or rejected by the readers. Instead, our author here cites it for them to demonstrate the greatness of Jesus' accomplishment and its value for them.

Specifically, the example of Jesus is that he **endured**, which has been the thrust of the sermon's exhortation. And what he endured was not minor: he endured the torturous death of a Roman **cross**. From a physical point of view, crucifixion was surely one of the most excruciating ways to die ever invented.[17] However, as noted in the remarks on 6.6 and 11.35f, public physical abuse in the ancient world was not only designed to be painful, but humiliating and full of **shame**. In ancient culture, recipients of punitive justice, and especially victims of crucifixion, were branded with a lasting stigma. While we often focus on the pain Jesus endured, perhaps we do not appreciate enough the shame that was associated with the story of the gospel and how difficult it was in the ancient world to proclaim a message about a man who had died shamefully. Christians were associated with a story of shame. It was not an honorable thing, in the eyes of first-century society, to be a Christian (*cf.* Acts 28.22, "concerning this sect, ... it is spoken against everywhere"). The original readers had already experienced some of society's shame in their own experiences (10.32ff). For them, therefore, the example of Jesus was especially pertinent.

12.3 For consider the one who has endured such hostility by sinners against himself, in order that you might not become weary, exhausted in your souls.

Jesus is not just another example of faithful endurance for the readers to **consider** (*i.e.*, think about carefully; the word can mean "calculate" or weigh in comparison[18]). He is *the* example by which their own conduct is to be measured and evaluated. The conjunction **for** can have the effect in the Greek of marking a strong affirmative command.[19] The author has already demonstrated that Jesus participated fully in humanity when he was on this earth (2.9, 14f). This not only qualified him to be a merciful high priest (2.17), but also made him the example for us to follow. Since he participated in human existence, his followers need to be "partakers of Christ" (3.13; *cf.* 3.1).

Like the readers of Hebrews, Jesus experienced the **hostility**, scorn, reproaches, and rejection of **sinners** (*i.e.*, unbelievers). Their attitude to-

---

[17] See John Granger Cook, *Crucifixion in the Mediterranean World*, WUNT 327 (Tübingen: Mohr Siebeck, 2014).

[18] LSJ 111.

[19] Lane, *Hebrews 9–13*, 400.

ward him was not just that they chose not to listen, but they hated him and wanted him dead (see comments on 6.6; *cf.* also Luke 4.29; John 5.18; 7.1). Yet all throughout the ordeal which he suffered at their hands, Jesus **endured**. When confronted about his behavior and his identity, he confessed his loyalty to God (1 Tim 6.13; Matt 26.63–65) even when it meant his life. He never allowed threats (Luke 13.31f), friends (Matt 16.21–23) or whatever weariness or exasperation he felt (*cf.* John 14.9) to deter him from his course. His conduct stands as a towering example of the kind of determination, dedication, and courage the readers of Hebrews needed. If they did not consider the example of Jesus but instead became caught up in their own fears, the author was concerned that they would become worn out, fatigued, discouraged, and spiritually **exhausted**, and eventually quit the "race." The heart that does not fill itself with the example of Jesus will eventually lose strength (because there is no strength for perseverance otherwise; 2 Thes 2.16f; 3.3; 1 Pet 5.10) and will become an evil heart of unbelief (3.12) that falls away from its commitment to the Lord.

12.4 For in your struggling against sin you have not yet resisted to the point of bloodshed,

In the previous verse the author demanded that his readers compare their situation with that of Jesus. The specific point of comparison is now spelled out: comparing their own situation to Jesus' ordeal (v 3) would certainly reveal that theirs was the lighter burden. While the readers were certainly facing something that had discouraged them, the fact is that this was not as bad as they might have made it out to be in their own minds (we tend to think of our troubles as worse than they really are). Unlike Jesus, they had not yet come **to the point of bloodshed** (death; the word can denote being murdered) as they stood in their faith (**resisted**) against the hostility of unbelievers. This observation was intended to put their dilemma into the proper perspective. Given the right understanding of their problem, it might even prove to be easier to handle than they thought it would be. Enduring jeers, cursing, and rejection is relatively easy compared to giving up one's life!

The faithfulness of the readers is here called a **struggling**. In the Greek it is a verbal form of the same word that appeared in verse 1 (Greek *agōn*) and was translated "race." The word here is a compounded verbal form and means to be engaged in a contest against something, which requires strength and endurance. The footrace was but one aspect of ancient athletics. Other events included wrestling, boxing, and equestrian skills. Since all of these sports were commonly grouped together as the "games," it is not unusual for the imagery here to shift from one sport to another (Paul did the same thing in 1 Cor 9.26). So here the author shifted from the "race" of verses 1–3 to "fighting" in verse 4. Of course, the imagery is not intended to trivialize the hardships of being a Christian as if they were no more than parts of some kind of "game." Instead, it emphasizes the strenuous nature of the undertaking for the sake of a reward at the end. Death from boxing matches in ancient times was not uncommon.[20] The opposition coming from the readers' unnamed enemies is characterized as **sin** just as it was in the case of those who killed Jesus, because their persecution of God's people is fundamentally a rejection of God himself (Luke 10.16).

This verse's statement of the social condition of the recipients is too vague to give us any definite clue about their location. If they were the Christians in the area of Jerusalem, the author could mean that none of that particular generation had yet been called upon to die for the Lord (although some disciples from the first generation of believers had paid such a price for their faith, namely Stephen and James). If the recipients were in Rome (which is a common view; see the Introduction), then this verse could mean that the famous persecution against Christians under Nero in 64 AD, which resulted in many of their deaths, had not yet happened. But we know so little about the original recipients of Hebrews, therefore we cannot understand the statement precisely. The phrase could apply to first-century Christians just about anywhere before that time, and still in many places after it.

12.5 and you have completely forgotten the exhortation which addresses you as sons: "My son, do not esteem the training of the Lord lightly, nor become weary when being scrutinized by him.

The author now adds another important perspective to the athletic imagery ("struggling"), informed from Scripture. In saying[21] that the read-

---

[20] See Robert Brophy and Mary Brophy, "Deaths in the Pan-Hellenic Games II: All Combative Sports," *AJP* 106 (1985): 171–98.

[21] The statement could also be punctuated as a rhetorical question: "And have you completely forgotten ...?" Johnson, *Hebrews*, 320.

ers had **completely forgotten**, the author perhaps spoke with a touch of rhetorical hyperbole in order to emphasize just how little attention they were giving to the words of Scripture as they faced their hardships. Scripture provides us with an **exhortation**; the word (*paraklēsis*) denotes a challenging appeal, but it can also suggest that which is comforting. The Christian who attempts to stand against evil without consulting Scripture is like a soldier who goes into battle without a weapon (Matt 4.3ff; Eph 6.12–17).

The quotation, extending down through verse 6, is from Proverbs 3.11f LXX. The main point of the quotation is to introduce the concept of the Lord's **training** into the readers' perspective on their situation. The thematic Greek word here, *paideia,* had a similar meaning to our word "education." It could denote discipline in the sense of punishment designed to correct a flaw, but this was not its primary signification, nor is it the primary sense here. There is nothing to suggest that the ongoing opposition the recipients of Hebrews were facing was supposed to be viewed as corrective punishment from God. Our word "training" comes closer to capturing the idea of *paideia,* which can include instruction and preparation, or subjection to difficulty or challenge in order to produce and demonstrate strength, or the result of these things. Furthermore, while the instruction that was collectively denoted by the word *paideia* included things such as the knowledge of elementary subjects (reading, writing, *etc.*), it by no means was limited to or exhausted by these things (*cf.* Heb 6.1ff). For the ancients, it included personal moral training and the development of character.[22] Things like physical training in athletics[23] (*cf.* vv 1ff, with their metaphors of running; recall also 5.14, which spoke of being "exercised") and learning music were part of it. Hellenistic education also encompassed instruction in the values of Hellenistic culture with its mythology, customs, laws (*cf.* how Paul uses the verb in

---

[22] Plutarch said its goal was make their lives good. *The Education of Children* 1. See Werner Jaeger, *Paideia: The Ideals of Greek Culture,* 3 vols. (Oxford: Blackwell, 1944–46).

[23] Herodian, *History* 5.7: "But his mother Mamaea kept Alexander from taking part in activities so disgraceful and unworthy of an emperor. Privately, she summoned teachers of every subject and had her son trained in the lessons of self-discipline; since he devoted himself to wrestling and to physical exercise as well, he was, by his mother's efforts, educated according to both the Greek and the Roman systems." (*Herodian of Antioch's History of the Roman Empire,* trans. Edward C. Echols (Berkeley: University of California Press, 1961), 149–50).

Acts 22.3), history,[24] philosophy[25] and general worldview (*cf.* Acts 7.22), and training in rhetoric for use in public service. It was the cultivation of the whole man considered as connected to his society, and the goal was to produce a person whose life avoided evil.[26] The ancients understood that improper training only leads to the retention of bad practices and ultimately to failure. For the author to say that the readers' hardships were God's *paideia*, then, was to say that it was part of God's process of education of the whole person so that they might mature properly and fulfill their role in his kingdom (see Acts 14.22; 2 Thes 1.4f; Psa 119.67–71). However, the Greco-Roman concept of *paideia* is not the only concept at work here. It has been modified by its association with the biblical picture of Israel's wilderness experience.[27] The statement in Proverbs itself echoes the language of Deuteronomy 8.5, and therefore proffers advice to a later generation on the basis of Israel's time in the wilderness, much like Psalm 95 (quoted in Hebrews 3 and 4) warns a later generation on that same basis as well. Through these connections, the theme of Israel in the wilderness (as discussed in Hebrews 3–4) is never far behind. That is, *paideia* here comes from God. Also, *paideia* was, among some, an element of identity in the ancient world.[28] What *kind* of education one had was a matter of rivalry and served to distinguish people, and groups, from

---

[24] This may help us gain added appreciation for the history recounted in Heb 11. It is part of the education that all Christians need, an instruction in the nature of the faith well past the basics (the "milk," Heb 5.12f).

[25] Isocrates, *Antidosis* 15.181–82: "In light of this, some of our ancestors long ago saw that although many arts existed for other matters, none had been established for the body and soul, and when they had invented two disciplines, they handed them down to us: physical training for the body, of which gymnastic is a part, and philosophy for the soul, which I shall be discussing. These two disciplines are complementary, interconnected, and consistent with each other, and through them those who have mastered them make the soul more intelligent and the body more useful. They do not separate these two kinds of education but use similar methods of instruction, exercise, and other kinds of practice." (*Isocrates I*, vol. 4 of *The Oratory of Classical Greece*, trans. David C. Mirhady and Yun Lee Too (Austin: University of Texas Press, 2000), 239).

[26] Georg Bertram, *"paideuō ktl,"* *TDNT* 5.596–603; *"paideuō ktl,"* *NIDNTTE* 3.584–90.

[27] See Matthew Thiessen, "Hebrews 12.5–13, the Wilderness Period, and Israel's Discipline," *NTS* 55 (2009): 366–79; Patrick Pouchelle, "The Septuagintal *Paideia* and the Construction of a Jewish Identity during the Late Hellenistic and Early Roman Period," *CBQ* 81 (2019): 33–45.

[28] *E.g.*, Isocrates defined Greek identity partly in terms of education (Panegyricus 50: " 'Hellenes' suggests no longer a race but an intelligence, and that the title 'Hellenes' is applied rather to those who share our culture than to those who share a common blood." (Norlin, LCL)).

each other.[29] Here, *paideia* serves to mark off God's people as having received a distinctive, divine education.

The Proverbs quotation offers the proper way to view one's hardships as a child of the heavenly Father (see 2.10, 13) and even corrects (**addresses**[30]) our misunderstandings about it. The first words of the quotation, wherein God speaks to the sufferer as **my son**, hold one of the keys to the picture. The term **sons** here[31] is meant as a term of both endearment (see v 6) and status (see v 8). Moreover, it is yet another example of how the author of Hebrews read the OT messianically. He understood the "son" addressed in the proverb ultimately as a child of God in the messianic age. Because of the new covenant which we have entered with God through Jesus, we are now his children, his **sons** (Heb 2.10). Seeing ourselves as sons in a Father-son relationship gives us the proper perspective by which we are to understand the hardships that he allows us to suffer; the training is part of a loving relationship on God's part.[32]

The command is **not** to **esteem the Lord's training lightly**, which means not to think ill or disparagingly of it. The phrase stands in parallel with **become weary**, and the two terms express the idea of psychologically distancing oneself from the experience. We rarely relish the prospect

---

[29] See Jason von Ehrenkrook, "Christians, Pagans, and the Politics of *Paideia* in Late Antiquity," in *Second Temple Jewish Paideia in Context*, ed. Jason M. Zurawski and Gabriele Boccaccini, BZNW 228 (Berlin: De Gruyter, 2017), 255–65. The Jews also used *paideia* as a way of crafting their identity, but exactly what form it should take was debated. See Jason M. Zurawski, "Jewish Education and Identity: Towards an Understanding of Second Temple *Paideia*," in *Second Temple Jewish Paideia in Context*, ed. Jason M. Zurawski and Gabriele Boccaccini, BZNW 228 (Berlin: De Gruyter, 2017), 267–78; Tyler A. Stewart, "Jewish *Paideia*: Greek Education in the Letter of Aristeas and 2 Maccabees," *JSJ* 48 (2017): 182–202.

[30] The Greek word *dialegomai* can mean to inform or to discuss, but also to argue and dispute. BDAG 232.

[31] For various uses of the word "son" in the Bible, see comments on 1.2.

[32] "In Heb 12, the paradigm of fatherly divine discipline encourages the audience to endure by viewing their situation as a natural, though painful, feature of sonship, but at the same time this implies the need for ongoing submission to God in an educational process that ultimately develops the very virtue expected of the audience elsewhere in the book." (Phillip A. Davis, Jr., *The Place of Paideia in Hebrews' Moral Thought*, WUNT 475 (Tübingen: Mohr Siebeck, 2018), 3). In contrast, pagan religion offered no such comfort. The Roman historian Tacitus complained, in speaking about a tumultuous time in Roman history, that "Never surely did more terrible calamities of the Roman People, or evidence more conclusive, prove that the gods take no thought for our happiness, but only for our punishment" (*Histories* 1.3; *The History of Tacitus*, trans. Alfred John Church and William Jackson Brodribb (Cambridge: MacMillan, 1864), 3).

of hardship. However, God's educational dealings with us are not meant to drive us away from him, but to draw us closer to him. Accordingly, we should not give up our faith in him when trials and hardships come along (as they do in every life). They are to be understood as God's training of our character, and we should appreciate the concern they reflect (v 9).

The concept of *paideia* is given a more specific focus in this passage by the parallel with the term **scrutinized** (often translated "reproved"), which means to examine carefully,[33] then to illuminate in the sense of pointing something out or exposing something as bad. God's training in holiness includes open scrutiny of our hearts and lives (*cf.* Heb 4.12). He tests us to bring to light what is deficient about us. The challenges he allows us to face reveal our weaknesses so that we might address them (*cf.* the imagery in 1 Pet 1.7), or else they give us an opportunity to demonstrate the strength of our faith (like Abraham in Gen 22).

12.6 For whom the Lord loves, he trains, and he scourges every son he receives."

The quotation from Proverbs 3 continues, now from verse 12, and gives the reason why God's children should not become bitter when their Father subjects them to training. We are not told what the readers had been thinking or saying about the new round of persecution which had arisen, but it is possible that they, like many who have suffered, began to question God's goodness. Such a conclusion, however, would be totally unwarranted, for the fact is that their hardships were actually evidence of God's love and care for them. Only a father who does not care about how his children turn out, or who does not care about how well-equipped they are to face tests and trials, would withhold training from them. A loving father, because he is concerned about his children's well-being and wants them to know the joy and stability that can come only from a properly developed character, **trains** them in the best ways to think and act, even when it is challenging for the child (and even sometimes involving correction). It should not surprise us, then, when God trains us, for our good (see Rom 5.3f), and that this training can be challenging at times. The **scourging**[34] here is poetic hyperbole, to be understood in the

[33] Greek *elegchō*; BDAG 315.

[34] The MT says, "For whom the Lord loves he reproves, even as a father corrects the son in whom he delights" (NASB). The Hebrew *ke' ab* ("even as a father") was read by the

parallelism with "train."[35] It makes the point that the Lord will sometimes subject his children to a harsh regimen. Accordingly, the author wanted them to view their sufferings as training in virtue and an opportunity for improvement,[36] to demonstrate endurance instead of withdrawal. It is a proof of his loving concern for us and of the fact that he has indeed accepted, acknowledged and welcomed (Greek *paradechomai*; **received**) us as his own children. God truly **loves** his children and does not want to see them developing bad habits, nor does he ignore any weaknesses or deficiencies he sees in them. The nature of God's love (Greek *agapē*) is that it desires the best for others, even if the attainment of it requires some things that are temporarily unpleasant.

12.7 It is for training that you endure, as God treats you like sons. For what son is there whom a father does not train?

Challenges, as manifestations of God's program of **training** for his children, are to be **endured for** the sake of, or with a view to, the education they impart to us. They are God's way of testing us and of exposing our weaknesses so that we can give them proper attention, as well as teaching us what we need to know to live correctly. As such they are designed to improve both our character and our faith (Rom 5.3f; Jam 1.2–4). The person who withdraws from God's training and only learns to resent its difficulty is acting foolishly in so doing. The wilderness generation of the Israelites experienced God's training in faith[37] (Deut 8.5) through multiple challenges (bitter water, no water, no meat, strong enemies, *etc.*), but their reaction was to rebel and complain. Instead of submitting and learning for their improvement, they became weary and faithless, and they died for it. Recall Hebrews 3, 4. Rather than become upset with God, we should view his training as the demonstration of his fatherly care for our spiritual well-being.

LXX translator as *ka'ab*, which in the Hiphil means "to cause pain." Koester, *Hebrews*, 536; Attridge, *Hebrews*, 361.

[35] The verb *paideuō*, which here means "train," can be used of corporal punishment, and could include scourging (Luke 23.16) that is administered for the purpose of "teaching someone a lesson."

[36] See N. Clayton Croy, *Endurance in Suffering: Hebrews 12:1–13 in Its Rhetorical, Religious, and Philosophical Context*, SNTSMS 98 (Cambridge: Cambridge University Press, 1998), 218–19.

[37] See Theissen, "Hebrews 12.5–13, the Wilderness Period, and Israel's Discipline."

The fact is that God trains those who are indeed his own children, and he is simply **treating them like** a father should treat his **sons**. *Cf.* Deuteronomy 8.5. In Hellenistic culture, fathers oversaw the education of sons once they came of age.[38] God was doing what any responsible father was expected to do. That this should come as no surprise, and even be expected, is reinforced by a rhetorical question (**For what son is there...?**) which emphasizes just how normal it is for a father to do this. In fact, it would be quite unusual if God did nothing to train his children and educate them in the way they should be and live. A lack of such attention would indicate that something was wrong with the relationship, as the next verse illustrates. Furthermore, the author has already pointed out that God perfected his Son through suffering (2.10), so it should not surprise us that the rest of his sons should be required to follow the same path to the father.[39]

12.8 But if you are without training, of which you all have become sharers, then you are illegitimate children and not sons.

While it might be nice to imagine a relationship with God in which he never subjected his children to testing or gave them difficult lessons to learn, the fact is that such inaction on God's part would be more characteristic of how a father would think toward those who are not truly his children. In times of hardship, it becomes easy to question one's status with God. It was common in the ancient world (as even today), and especially among the Jews, to equate a life of ease with divine favor, and hardships with divine displeasure. However, the situation is more complicated than that (see John 9.1–3), and such a simplistic view, when forced to fit every situation, may actually lead to wrong conclusions. The fact is that some of our suffering is due to the fact that a loving God is treating us like legitimate children whom he wishes to educate and form after his own character. Our hardships, then, can be proof of our relationship and our good standing with him. The author therefore reassured his readers that their sufferings in no way meant that God had cast them off as sons. **All** of them had **shared** in the training God had provided, and this was to be understood as meaning that their status with God as sons was intact.

[38] Plutarch, *The Education of Children* 5B–C.

[39] Johnson, *Hebrews*, 321.

Our author certainly is not suggesting anything base about God by bringing up an illustration involving illegitimate children. He is simply drawing on a legal distinction that was well-known to the original recipients. In ancient times, the identification of legitimate children was directly connected to the inheritance of an estate, and only a man's legitimate children were considered his heirs. Under Greek law, **illegitimate children** (*i.e.*, children born outside of a citizen union) had no claim on their father's estate.[40] A father would thus spend his educational efforts on the children who were truly his **sons**, who would continue the family and receive his wealth. They are the ones whom he would work to form into good people and who would carry on his name. Any other children were, in a sense, rejected (at least from a standpoint of inheritance). They were not the objects of the same kind of concern and they were not given the same attention because they lacked the status of legitimate sons. A similar distinction appears in Galatians 4.22ff, where Ishmael, Abraham's child from the slave woman Hagar, is not counted as an heir along with Isaac, his child from the free woman Sarah. Plutarch also noted that illegitimacy carried a stigma in the ancient world and was practically synonymous with bad behavior.[41] Whereas the author has encouraged his readers not to worry about rejection by the world (v 2), here he bid them to be very concerned about being rejected by God (see comments on v 17 below).

12.9 Furthermore, all of us had human fathers as teachers, and we respected them. Will we not much more subject ourselves to the father of spirits and live?

It is possible that the more strenuously the NT authors argued an issue, the more controversial or hard-to-accept it was for the original readers. The present extended discussion of how we can accept hardships as beneficial education from a loving God may be a case in point. The concept of willfully accepting hardships as training from a gracious God can be a hard one to accept, especially when the hardships are already upon us. The best time for such reflection would probably be when life is at relative peace. However, even then we often do not like to dwell on the

[40] James C. Walters and Jerry L. Sumney, "Paul, Adoption, and Inheritance," in *Paul in the Greco-Roman World: A Handbook*, ed. J. Paul Sampley, rev. ed., (London; Oxford; New York: Bloomsbury; Bloomsbury T&T Clark, 2016), 1.33–67, at 39.

[41] *The Education of Children* 2.

subject of suffering. Since it is a difficult subject to fathom, the author provides yet another consideration, in the form of an argument from the lesser to the greater, to "prove" his main point that the readers' sufferings were actually a good thing.

We come to have **respect** and admiration for our **human fathers** (the word in the plural can mean "parents," as in 11.23) who were our moral and spiritual **teachers**. Their instruction, although often difficult (as most education is) was administered in a spirit of love, and therefore we continued to accept their guidance, trusting that their intentions were good. The challenges they gave us did not make us rebellious people but imparted valuable insights. Although when we were young we might not have understood much about why our parents trained us as they did, we grew to the point that we could see why the course they chose was necessary and we are now glad that our parents loved us enough to teach us to live as we do. If we are perceptive enough, we will see that the education and training in life that they gave us actually spared us from pain and misery later in our lives.

If we can see these kinds of benefits from the training we received from our earthly parents, and we thankfully respect them for it, then how **much more** should we be able to see these same kinds of things in our relationship with our heavenly father and respect him and **subject ourselves** to his loving concern? Our physical parents were human, and thus subject to all the limitations that come with being human. Nevertheless, in spite of that, they were able to provide a good service to us through the education they gave us. God is our spiritual father (**the father of** our **spirits**; Num 16.22; 27.16). He created us and endowed each of us with an eternal spirit that is after his own image (Gen 1.27; in contrast to the physical procreation of our human fathers) and he is perfect in holiness, righteousness, and love. God is a greater parent to us, his children, than we are to our own children (Matt 7.11). As a greater being than our human parents, his education is much more beneficial to us than what we received from them by virtue of the fact that his training is given with a far greater wisdom. Refusal to accept his regimen for us signals that we are rebellious and that we intend to pursue a life that leads to spiritual death. It is better, therefore, to accept God's instruction, to willingly subject ourselves to his good care **and live** (*cf.* 2 Cor 7.10) than to refuse it and die like the Israelites who came out of Egypt (Psa 95 and

Heb 3–4). "**Live**" echoes Deuteronomy 8.1–5, continuing the author's association of his exhortation with Israel's time in the wilderness.[42]

Of course, throughout the analogy the author assumes the model of good, loving parents who actively engage in the business of raising their children and training their minds and hearts in a way that is balanced and beneficial (*cf.* Eph 6.4). Even though such godly parents will make occasional mistakes in molding the lives of their children, their efforts are always controlled by love. God, however, fulfills that model to perfection.

12.10 For they administered training for a few days according to what seemed good to them, but he trains us for what is profitable in order that we might share his holiness.

The analogy with human fathers continues in another argument from the lesser to the greater. The previous argument (v 9) reasoned that God is a far better father than any earthly parent, and so we can be assured that the intention of his training is only good even though it might be difficult. The argument of this verse concentrates on the outcome of that training. The education we received from our human parents was characterized by limitation. It only lasted **for a few days**, comparatively speaking, and it was administered on the basis of human judgment (as it **seemed good to them**), which is also limited. God's education, however, has no such imperfections associated with it. It is truly **profitable** (useful, advantageous, in our interest; *cf.* 1 Tim 4.8) and its result is that we come to **share** in **his holiness**. The NT picture of Christians is that they are children who share in their Father's qualities. They love as he loves (Eph 4.32–5.1), they partake of his nature (2 Pet 1.4), and they become holy as he is holy (1 Pet 1.15f). One of the ways that we learn to become unlike the world and more like our Father is through the regimen of preparation and testing that he gives to us. In this sense our increasing in holiness through discipline is a perfecting of ourselves (Jam 1.2–4). Holiness, or sanctification, is a key idea in Hebrews, given the imagery of a journey that ends in the presence of God. Only holy people can be in God's presence. *Cf.* verse 14 below.

Like many other things in Hebrews, the present topic also has future and eternal (*i.e.*, eschatological) dimensions. Holiness characterizes the nature of God, and so sharing in his holiness ultimately means that

[42] Albert J. Coetsee, "Hebrews 12:9 Revisited: The Background of the Phrase 'and live'," *HvTSt* 76 (2020). https://doi.org/ 10.4102/hts.v76i1.5863

we come to be in his holy presence in heaven itself. See Hebrews 9.24; Colossians 1.22. Whereas our parents taught us with temporal limitation (for a few days), God's education prepares us for eternity. The contrast between earthly, temporary things and heavenly, eternal things has appeared elsewhere at key points in the author's exhortation (*cf.* 7.26ff; 8.1ff; 9.1ff, 12ff, 21ff; 11.13ff), so it is not surprising that he returns to this basic perspective to encourage his readers to see their sufferings correctly.

12.11 All training, for the present, does not seem to be joyous but painful, but it later repays the peaceful fruit of righteousness to those who have been exercised through it.

The last remark on the subject builds on the contrast between the temporary and the eternal from the previous verse, as the author bids the readers to take up the eschatological perspective and not look at the **present**, but to the future. This is also consistent with the forward-looking nature of faith which the author paraded before the hearers in chapter 11. God's training of his children (if they will accept it) has a future reward. This was a lesson that the Israelites who came out of Egypt never learned, and their fixation on their present circumstances caused them to forfeit their inheritance in the land of Canaan. Similarly, the difficult and challenging nature of the **training** that we receive from God ought not be the focus of our attention, and it certainly ought not distract us from reaching the heavenly city (11.13–16; 12.12ff). That training is designed to discipline us, to help us perfect our faith and reach our goal, not divert us from it. The perspective from which we see it makes all the difference.

This, of course, is easier to describe than to practice because hardships have a way of claiming all of our attention at the moment. It is difficult to see the good in the pain when the pain is upon us. Therein, however, lies a subtle deception. Our immediate inclination is to think that no suffering could have good results, but this is not true. The hardship of an education is like **exercise**. At the moment it is strenuous, even **painful**, and requires endurance. Or, to use the botanical imagery, training is like planting a seed that bears **fruit**. Aristotle said that the roots of education were bitter, but the fruit was sweet.[43] The difficulty of the training **repays** improvement **later**. For this reason, we willingly engage in it because we

[43] Diogenes Laertius, *The Lives and Opinions of Eminent Philosophers*, 5.18 (Hicks, LCL). The saying was apparently a common one.

know that the present challenge produces future good. In the same way, God's training results in a "fruit" that consists of a **righteousness** that is also **peaceful**, not fretful (*cf.* Jam 3.18). Peace and righteousness are often combined in statements about the messianic age,[44] so these qualities characterize God's children through the Messiah (2 Tim 2.22). They are the product of a refined faith that has learned to trust in God no matter what. The good result of God's strenuous training encourages us to accept it with subjection and gratitude for the blessing it is.

12.12–13 Therefore strengthen the drooping hands and the weakened knees, and make straight tracks for your feet so that the disabled limb might not be dislocated but instead be restored.

The author now continues the imagery from the previous verses. Whether we consider it from the metaphor of an athlete who is exhausted, or from the metaphor of a son who is tired from the demanding training his father has given him, the point is the same. The image of one with **drooping hands and weak knees** conveys weariness and fatigue, or discouragement (Jer 6.24). The expression is taken from Isaiah 35.3 (see also Zeph 3.16). Philo of Alexandria used this same imagery: "For the invisible trial and proofs of the soul are in laboring and in enduring bitterness; for then it is hard to know which way it will incline; for many men are very speedily fatigued and fall away, thinking labor a terrible adversary, and they let their hands fall out of weakness, like tired wrestlers, determining to return to Egypt to the indulgence of their passions."[45] The readers needed to collect their strength and renew their resolve to endure. Like an athlete who squeezes more energy from his body although he is already tired (think of a boxer in the final rounds of a fight, or a runner in the last section of a race), they needed to press on.

The **tracks** to which our author refers are the ruts in the ground left by chariots and wagons (still visible in places where old Roman roads survive). Repeated wear had the effect of creating a path that a wheeled vehicle would naturally and easily follow. In Biblical thought, the phrase **make straight tracks** became an image of following what was right and leading a good moral life. *Cf.* Proverbs 3.6; 4.26. It has the sense of following the path that leads straight to the goal, without taking any deviation

[44] Psa 72.3, 7; 85.10; Isa 9.7; 32.17; 60.17; Rom 14.17.

[45] *On Mating with the Preliminary Studies* 164 (*The Works of Philo*, Yonge, 319).

from it.[46] In this context it takes on the specific sense of faithfulness to God. In Proverbs 9.15 the sinner wanders from the straight path as he heeds the call of worldly pleasure, so that the person who strays from obedience to God is like a fornicator (see v 16 below). A fear of persecution in the original readers of Hebrews reflected a weakness in their faith which was like a traveler who had gone off the road and was heading in the wrong direction. They needed to get "back on track," as the saying goes, back on the course of faith. *Cf.* Matthew 7.13f.

It was time for the readers of Hebrews to decide that they were going to continue in the faith and endure whatever hardships it entailed. They stood at a spiritual and moral crossroads and needed to decide that they would straighten out the things that were wrong with themselves (things such as a lack of trust in God, fear of hardships, anxiety over social rejection, *etc.*) rather than quit. The word that is here translated **restore** (Greek *iaomai*) was a medical term that meant "heal" or "cure." It came to be used figuratively of deliverance from any kind of problem and thus meant "restore" or "recover."[47] Their present situation is compared to a person with a paralyzed or **disabled** limb. Their experiences of hardship in the past created within them a reluctance to persevere in the face of renewed opposition. A part of them had stopped working, as it were. This fear and lack of trust in God was like an injury that threatened their entire spiritual well-being. Prolonged inattention to God would turn it into an "incurable wound" (Jer 30.12; Mic 1.9). They could choose to ignore their problem, which would result in further damage with the "limb" becoming **dislocated** (out of joint) and eventually becoming useless, or they could turn to the Lord for healing so that it could return to full use (*cf.* Psa 41.4; 107.20; 147.3; Prov 3.7f; Jer 3.22; Hos 6.1). The choice was theirs. It is unclear if the imagery means that the group is like a body and that some of its members were spiritually disabled,[48] or whether it means that each individual Christian was to examine himself for personal spiritual defects. The plural imperative could cover both.

The imagery of the exodus generation of the Israelites is not far in the background here. As they headed into the wilderness and faced God's tests there, God warned them that they needed to show faith in him. If

---

[46] Herbert Preisker, "*orthos ktl*," *TDNT* 5:449–50.

[47] BDAG 465.

[48] So Lane, *Hebrews 9–13*, 428; Bruce, *Epistle to the Hebrews*, 364.

they did not, God would smite them with the same kinds of plagues with which he had afflicted the Egyptians. Avoidance of punishment depended on continual obedience to God, as he reminded them that "I, the Lord, am your healer" (Exod 15.26). The readers of Hebrews needed to remember the warning and the example of chapters 3–4, based on Psalm 95, and not repeat the mistakes of that former generation. The author encouraged them to pick up their weakened resolve and give attention to the attitude of their hearts (3.8, 10, 12) that was causing them to pause in their faith, lest it turn into something worse (see vv 15–17 below). He has already indicated what can happen to the person who does not go forward in his faith (6.1–6).

12.14 Pursue peace with everyone and the holiness without which no one will see the Lord,

Here, in summary, lay their program for healing. Psalm 34.12–22 is possibly in the background. The admonition to **pursue peace** with others could imply that Christians were the objects of scorn or mistreatment. Rather than retaliate in kind, God's people are to react to mistreatment in a peaceful way. See Romans 12.17–21; 1 Peter 2.21–23. While it runs counter to the impulses of the flesh to act in this way, returning peace for abuse is an exercise and demonstration of our faith in God's will. We react with peace because we believe that God's way is the best for us. Rather than take justice into our own hands (Rom 12.17–19), by faith we leave it for God to deal with, and we trust that he will (1 Pet 2.23). However, there is ultimately more than just external behavior in view. Jesus teaches us that not only must we say and do peaceable things to others, but that we must be peaceable people in heart and in character. Beyond restraining ourselves from hitting back, we are to become people who do not wish evil upon anyone (even when they have inflicted harm upon us). Matthew 5.38ff. Pursuing peace with others, then, is a matter of the heart as well as conduct.

Similarly, Christians are to pursue holiness in all they do and speak. As God's training allows us to share in his holiness (v 10), the exhortation to pursue this holiness therefore becomes an encouragement to persevere on the journey that ends in God's presence (see on v 10 above). The root idea of **holiness** is separation (see 1 Chron 23.13), but not separation simply for the sake of being different. Instead, what is holy is set apart from normal or common use and reserved for, or dedicated to, God alone. In particular, only holy things, or holy people, can be in God's presence. If the recipients hoped to **see the Lord** one day as the reward for their faithfulness, then they needed to maintain their holiness (*cf.* Matt 5.8). The opposite of holiness is defilement, or being "common" (profane). In Hebrews, the author primarily had the sin of unfaithfulness in mind as that which would defile his readers and cost them to miss out on finally and fully being in God's presence in the end. Also, in a context of behavior in the face of opposition, things like retaliation, returning insults, or becoming hateful of those who reproach and oppose would be additional examples of defilement that would ruin one's holiness and prevent them from seeing God. Holy people do not act like the defiled world around them but live in such a way that reflects their dedication to God and their trust in his word.

12.15 looking out[49] that no one misses out on the grace of God, that no root of bitterness springing up causes trouble and through it many become defiled,

If anyone (the phrase **no one** is just as generic in the Greek as it is in English) of the readers does not decide to renew his dedication and continue in faith, he runs the real risk of **missing out** (same word as in 4.1) on what God has to offer. The Greek verb *hustereō* means to arrive too late, to miss an appointment, and thus to be excluded from what was available and end up in a situation of lack.[50] In a context of missing out, there are two possible senses to the phrase **the grace of God** here:

1) It can refer to the present outpouring of God's grace that provides us with the opportunity to hear and obey the gospel and become children of God. See Titus 2.11. This opportunity will not last forever. The window of opportunity closes either when one dies (and response to the gospel

[49] This is a participle in the Greek. It can be understood as an adverbial participle modifying the main verb "pursue" in v 14 (so ASV), but a participle can have an imperatival force as well, which is how many modern vss. have translated it here. See Travis Williams, "The Imperatival Participle in the New Testament" (paper read at the Southwestern Regional Meeting of the Evangelical Theological Society, 24 March 2006, <http://bible.org/article/imperatival-participle-new-testament>). This usage has been attributed to Semitic influence. See also Philip Kanjuparambil, "Imperatival Participles in Rom 12 9–21," *JBL* 102 (1983): 285–88.

[50] LSJ 1905–06.

is no longer possible) or when the Lord returns. With this interpretation, the exhortation is that if the readers procrastinated in deciding to remain faithful, they ran the risk that the opportunity to respond to God's gracious offer may end before they planned. We must act as long as it is still "Today," the time when entering into God's rest is possible (Heb 3.13). *Cf.* the parable in Matt 25.1ff.

2) The term can refer, by metonymy, to the product or result of God's grace, *viz.*, salvation in the end. *Cf.* 1 Peter 1.13, "the grace that is to be brought to you at the revelation of Jesus Christ." In this interpretation, the phrase refers to the reward that God has promised to the faithful, and the exhortation is that unfaithfulness now will result in denial of one's inheritance later. The two interpretations are closely related, since the grace of God not only opens up a present relationship with God but also bids us to look to the future at the fuller measure of that relationship in heaven (Tit 2.11–13). The present and the future cannot be easily separated in NT ethics. Of the two, however, the latter interpretation is preferable given the eschatological (forward-looking) nature of the context and of the book in general. See comments on 4.1.

Those with stronger faith are to help those with weaker faith (Heb 3.13; Rom 15.1ff; Gal 6.2; 1 Thes 5.14). It is in this sense that they **look out** for (Greek *episkopeō*; used elsewhere of "overseeing") the spiritual welfare of others. One person in whom there is bitterness can negatively influence **many** others with his pessimistic lack of trust in God. "A little leaven leavens the whole lump of dough" (1 Cor 5.6). The phrase **root of bitterness** simply means "a bitter root" or a root that produces bitter fruit (the word **root** (Greek *hriza*) can also denote what comes from a root, hence a shoot). The bitter root is a metaphor for a person who does not have the right relationship with God. *Cf.* Acts 8.23, where Simon was said to be "in the gall of bitterness." Here it depicts a person who does not trust God's way and, like the ancient Israelites, only becomes angry at God when that way becomes difficult. If such an attitude is not corrected and replaced with the proper perspective (the one commended in vv 4–13), his bitterness will **spring up** like a noxious plant and **cause trouble** (interfere, annoy) by spreading its faithlessness to others. Pessimism can be highly contagious. See Deuteronomy 29.18.

Again, the exodus generation of Israel is the backdrop here. The Israelites who came out of Egypt constantly wanted to turn back because of the testing they encountered in the wilderness. They complained that the life of the wilderness was too hard, forgetting about the good life in Canaan that lay ahead of them. When they were on the verge of entering the land, the spies who had surveyed it brought back a pessimistic report that the rest of the group quickly believed (Num 13.27–33), which resulted in that generation being denied entrance into (missing out on) the land. The application here was straightforward. The readers needed to make sure that no one of them harbored resentment against God either for the challenges that they had experienced or for those which they could see on the horizon ahead of them. They needed to check any faithless attitudes before discouragement spread and brought many to spiritual ruin.

12.16 that there is no fornicator or worldly person like Esau, who for one meal gave away his own birthright.

In contrast to the heroes of faith of chapter 11, who looked ahead to the future reward and sacrificed earthly pleasure for it, stands Esau, who valued physical comfort above future good. In the context, another way to say that would be that the heroes of faith in Hebrews 11 accepted God's training, but Esau did not. The mention of fornication at first seems surprising, since the author has been discussing the need for spiritual endurance. However, this particular sin is cited in a kind of metonymy as an example in the context of a wider warning and based on the Biblical story of Esau. The author of Hebrews was not saying that Esau literally was a **fornicator**. He meant that Esau was a **worldly person**, and a fornicator is often, in the Bible, the prime example of a worldly person. Fornication encapsulates the fleshly, worldly life.[51] Such a person follows the desires and dictates of the flesh rather than following the way of God (Gal 5.16ff; Eph 2.1–3; Rom 8.5–8), he loves worldly things rather than the heavenly, spiritual things of God (1 John 2.15f). Esau was like the person in Proverbs 9.15 (see v 13 above) who deviates from the straight path to blessing for the sake of fleshly gratification. It is possible, however, that there may have been some problem with (literal) fornication among the original readers (see 13.4), a sign that they were concentrating on the physical and not the spiritual.

The particular episode the author cites is from Genesis 25.27–34, where Esau traded his birthright in the family for a meal. A **birthright** (Hebrew *bekorah*) was the special *status* that belonged by right to the firstborn son.

[51] See Matt 15.19; Acts 15.20; 1 Cor 6.9; *cf.* "evil and adulterous" in Matt 12.29.

It meant that, upon the father's death, he received a double portion of the father's inheritance.[52] It also meant that he retained the official claim to become the family's patriarch, so it was also a position of status and "reign" above that of other family members[53] (so the figurative use in Col 1.15; Exod 4.22; *etc.*). The firstborn son could relinquish the position if he did not want it, but apparently it could not be traded back and forth. Once surrendered it could not be recovered. In an act of foolishness, for nothing more than to satisfy momentary hunger pangs, Esau **gave** this privilege and status **away** to his younger brother Jacob. He traded a long-term future spiritual benefit for **one meal** that provided physical gratification for a little while. In this sense he was like a fornicator.[54] As such he stands as an example of a worldly person who valued physical comfort above all else, and who sacrificed a greater, lasting, and more valuable thing for something temporary. He is like the Christian who dissociates himself from the faith, from his covenant relationship with the Lord, and from the Lord's people in order to avoid the momentary hardship it brings (*cf.* Gal 6.12). Such a person foolishly values the comfort of his flesh more than the future promised reward that awaits the faithful. The author of Hebrews implies that his original readers were on the verge of doing the very thing Esau had done, but with even greater loss at stake. Esau's story thus stands as a firm warning not to throw away what they had attained in Jesus (10.35), specifically their status as true children of God (see vv 5–8 above, and v 23 below). Those who relinquish their place with God find that they lose his blessing in the end.

12.17 For you know that, as he was later wishing to inherit the blessing, he was rejected, for he found no place for a change of mind although he sought it with tears.

The author now recalls for his readers the sad ending of Esau's story, which illustrates the significant consequences of his rash decision. The story is recorded in Genesis 27. Isaac was old and his eyesight was dim. Esau's brother, Jacob, took advantage of this fact (with his mother's

---

[52] M. Tsevat, "*bekor, bkr, bekorah, bikkurim*," *TDOT* 2:121–7. See Gen 48.22; Deut 21.17.

[53] J. Wilson and R. K. Harrison, "Birthright," *ISBE*, rev. ed. 1:515–16.

[54] This interpretation seems preferable to those which see Esau literally as a fornicator, or as an idolater ("fornication" could have this figurative sense in Jewish contexts), or which understand "fornicator" to mean "apostate." There is no OT evidence that Esau was any of these.

help), dressed himself so that his father thought he was Esau, and received the blessing by trickery. When Esau later approached Isaac in order to be blessed (not knowing what had happened), he then discovered that Jacob had stolen the blessing.

The blessing was not the same thing as the birthright, as the stories of both Esau and Joseph[55] illustrate. The blessing made its recipient the one through whom God continued his promise, and with it came prosperity and protection. Although Esau did not care if he got a double portion of Isaac's inheritance, he certainly still expected to receive his father's blessing, and Isaac intended to give it to him (Gen 27.4). The author of Hebrews did not get the two stories of Genesis 25 and 27 confused, as some have suggested. Instead, he connected the rejection of the birthright with the loss of the blessing; he read the former as the cause of the latter. The underlying premise of the author's reading of these two stories seems to be that Esau's relinquishing of his birthright was not a singular event, but represented the kind of person he regularly was. His status with God was simply not of great concern to him. Therefore, when the blessing was stolen, rather than restoring it to Esau, Isaac refused to right the wrong that had been done because Esau had never demonstrated that he cared for it anyway. Those familiar with the Biblical story (as the author of Hebrews certainly was) also know that God had foretold this reversal of status between the twins (Gen 25.23). It may be that Isaac saw the hand of God in the treachery of Jacob, and that this was an added reason for not restoring the blessing to Esau. The author of Hebrews used the story of Esau to illustrate that the person who rejects and discards his status with the father (vv 5ff above; see also v 23) for the sake of physical comfort will miss out on blessing in the end, and warned his hearers not to become such people, because their thoughts about quitting Christianity to relieve the ongoing stress of opposition was, as he saw it, the same kind of behavior.[56] The idea of a coming, valuable inheritance from God is an important theme in Hebrews (1.14; 6.12; 9.15; 11.8).

---

[55] *Cf.* 1 Chron 5.1f. Jacob gave the birthright to Joseph's sons instead of his own firstborn son Reuben (because of Reuben's sin in Gen 35.22). However, in Gen 49, the patriarch split his blessing between Judah and Joseph.

[56] Cockerill, *Epistle to the Hebrews,* 640: "The godless and profane way in which he rejected the promise of God that was his birthright foreshadowed the way in which the pastor's hearers were in danger of definitively and publicly spurning the fulfillment of that promise in Christ."

When Esau found out that Jacob had received the blessing instead, he pleaded with his father to bless him also, but it was too late, and he was **rejected** because he was unable to **find** any **place** (opportunity[57]) **for a change of mind** (repentance). The mention of "repentance" recalls the discussion of Hebrews 6.4–6. Esau is an example of the kind of person discussed there. Two things make this text difficult: 1) One must decide on the sense of the Greek word *metanoia* ("repentance") in this context. The word literally denotes a change of mind, but in the NT it often has the more religious sense of repentance from sin and can thus take on the sense of "regret" and, by extension, a change of conduct. An opinion about which of these ideas is operative in this context will determine how one interprets the larger scene. So, did Esau not find an opportunity to change his mind? Or does it mean that he could not find an opportunity to change the situation (*i.e.*, reverse the past[58])? And 2) Who rejected Esau? Isaac, or God? Some possibilities are:

1) Esau found no opportunity to repent of his former decision in the sense that God would not allow him to repent. While this interpretation is commonly touted in commentaries, it is highly questionable that the Scriptures actually teach that God does not allow some people to repent. Some appeal to Acts 5.31; 11.18, and 2 Timothy 2.25, which speak of God granting repentance and argue that there is the possibility that he does not grant it to some people. However, God grants repentance in the same way he grants forgiveness (Act 5.31), by making an opportunity for it, by making it possible, by offering the privilege. Nothing in Genesis suggests that God did not allow Esau an opportunity to change his own mind.[59]

2) Esau found no opportunity to repent of his former decision in the sense that it was now too late (by God's doing) to change his mind with any good results. That is, he could find no way to reverse the consequences of his former decision.[60] In this way he was like a person who does not want to attend a baseball game and therefore sells his ticket to someone

---

[57] The word "place" is used in the sense of "opportunity" in Acts 25.16.

[58] H. Merklein, "*metanoia*," *EDNT* 2:415–19, at 418.

[59] Closer examination of the wording in the Greek bears this out. The expression "place of repentance" appears in *Wisd* 12.10, *1 Clement* 7.5, *Baruch* 85.12, and *4 Ezra* 9.12, which speak of God giving an opportunity for someone else to repent. The converse would be not finding an opportunity. The phrase thus suggests that either God or Isaac was not giving Esau any opportunity to change the situation, not that Esau could not change within himself.

[60] Moffatt, *Epistle to the Hebrews*, 212.

else. Then, right before the game begins, he decides that he wants to attend the game after all, only to find out that the game is sold out. This, however, would be an unusual use of the word "repentance."

3) Esau found no place for repentance within himself. He had become so hard-hearted by this point in his life that he had no desire to repent or change himself. He still wanted the blessing, but he had no intention of changing his heart.

4) Esau found no change of mind within Isaac, or on Isaac's part. Isaac's reply was "Now as for you then, what can I do, my son?" (Gen 27.27 NASB).

The last three of these interpretations are related, and it may be that the author of Hebrews saw that elements from each of them were in play in the Biblical narrative. The interpretation of the "change of mind" is related to another difficulty in this verse, namely the antecedent of the word **it**. What was "it" that Esau **sought**? The two basic options are:

1) "It" refers to repentance. That is, Esau wanted to repent, but it was too late. A door had been shut and it could not be opened again, as when the Israelites refused to enter Canaan and had to face the consequences of death in the wilderness. The problem with this interpretation is that it requires a questionable meaning for the word "repent."

2) "It" refers to the blessing which Esau sought from his father but was now unavailable. This seems to fit better with the context both in Genesis and here in Hebrews, which emphasizes the future reward and warns against losing it. Esau begged his father to call down God's goodness on (bless) him as well, but instead Isaac pronounced that Esau would live the more difficult life, deprived of blessing and goodness and subject to hardship and violence (Gen 27.39f). Comparing the blessing that Jacob got (Gen 27.28f) with Isaac's words about Esau reveals that Esau basically received the opposite of the good things promised to Jacob. In this sense, then, he was cursed (*cf.* Heb 6.8). Since the blessing and Isaac's bestowal of it were closely related, the "**it**" may be inclusive of both. The overall picture is that Esau's earlier decision (which was probably an indicator of his habitual mindset) had put him in a situation which—by the hand of God and by his own doing at the same time—he could not change. Esau protested loudly **with tears** because of what had happened. "He cried out with an exceedingly great and bitter cry" (Gen 27.34 NASB) and "he raised his voice and wept" (v 38). He was weeping over a situation that

was now beyond his control (*cf.* Matt 8.12; 13.42, 50). Esau stands as an example of one who got himself into a bad situation from which he could not get out, all because he made a rash decision based on the temporary comfort of his flesh. Because he did not value his status with his father, he lost the blessing later. His story becomes a warning to Christians who would despise and forfeit the divine gift of eternal, heavenly blessing for momentary, worldly comfort (*i.e.*, relief from opposition), and find out that they have lost it forever. See 2.3; 4.1f; 6.4–8, and 10.26–31. It is the nature of our relationship with God that sometimes we are called upon to choose between the two (like Moses, 11.25f).

12.18 For you have not come to that which can be touched, and to a burning fire, and to darkness and gloom and storm,

The final, climactic exhortation provides a reason (**for**) why the readers must persevere in pursuing sanctification (v 14). The author takes a familiar tact as he returns, one more time, to the imagery of a journey. That journey ends in the heavenly presence of God, made possible by the fact that Jesus our high priest has opened up the way. Here the imagery is used to construct a final comparison of the old and the new in order to show the surpassing greatness of the new, and especially concerning its end. In this way, one of the main themes of the sermon (that the new is better) now becomes an exhortation to consider the goal of the Christian life, which provides the ultimate incentive for endurance in faith. Some have argued that verses 18–24 are a summary of the entire sermon.[61]

The comparison centers on the contrast between Mt. Sinai (vv 12–21) and the messianic Mt. Zion (vv 22–24),[62] both of which lay at the end

[61] Kiwoong Son has suggested that Heb 12.18–24 is the "hermeneutical key to the epistle" (*Zion Symbolism in Hebrews: Hebrews 12:18–24 as a Hermeneutical Key to the Epistle* (Milton Keynes: Paternoster, 2005)); Beale says that Heb 12.24 is the climax of the entire epistle (Beale, *A New Testament Biblical Theology*, 321; following Ellingworth, *Epistle to the Hebrews*, 681).

[62] One might wonder why the author compared Sinai and the heavenly Jerusalem, instead of the earthly Jerusalem and the heavenly Jerusalem. Several answers are possible. First, the author of Hebrews has concentrated, in the sermon, on the original exodus generation of Israel. That generation never got to Jerusalem (Mt. Moriah). Sinai was their only mountain experience with God. Second, Mt. Sinai was never intended to be Israel's only mountain experience with God. They were supposed to press on and reach Mt. Moriah, but they did not. Therefore, the contrast between Sinai and Zion becomes a contrast between a mountain that was a temporary stopping place versus a mountain that is the eternal home of God's people. Third, both mountains have in common that God spoke from each of them. Just as God spoke from the top of Sinai, God has spoken now from

of an exodus journey. The former mountain, to which Israel came under the leadership of Moses (recall Heb 3.1–6), was characterized by fear and no access to God's presence, whereas the latter one, to which Jesus brings us, is characterized by welcome and full entrance into the fellowship of God. The sermon began with a contrast between the word delivered through angels on Sinai and the word delivered through the Son in "these last days" (ch 1). The exhortation thus, in a sense, comes full circle back to the revelation of Sinai, but this time with an emphasis on the fear and dread of that former scene contrasted with the full, glorious scope of what we have available in Jesus. The general sense of forbidding depicted in the exodus narrative of God's descent on Mt. Sinai (Exod 19) reflects that same quality of the Law in general (*cf.* Deut 5.22). Like Mt. Sinai itself, the Law was physical, earthly, and fearful. And like the mountain, the Levitical system that came from that place did not allow access to the presence of God.

The pair of expressions "**you have not come to** … but you have come to…" both use the same verb and in the same tense, the Greek perfect, which "semantically encodes imperfective aspect with the spatial value of heightened proximity."[63] The depiction is from the point of view of one watching an unfolding scene from a close vantage-point. While the word translated "come to" (Greek *proserchomai*) is a compounded form of the normal Greek verb for coming to a place, it can also be used to indicate "coming," or entering, into a situation[64] or a relationship.[65] This is the sense of "you have come" in this context, since we have not yet literally come to most of the things in verses 22–24 except by faith (see also 13.14).[66] See further on verse 22 below. The sense of the passage is that we have arrived not at the kind of situation that the Israelites encountered at Sinai (vv 18–21; *cf.* Deut 4.11), but at a new and better state of affairs made possible by Jesus (vv 22–24; 7.25; 10.22). Chapters 7–10 explained how this better situation came about, so it is natural that our author would now take us to the next step, *viz.* the results of this new situation. In the same way, the things on the list are meant to be

heaven, here depicted as a mountaintop city, through his exalted Son who is enthroned there (Heb 2.3–4; 12.25).

[63] Campbell, *Basics of Verbal Aspect in Biblical Greek*, 51, 104.

[64] See Gal 3.25; Eph 5.6; 1 Thes 5.2; 2 Thes 2.3; esp. Phil 1.12; 1 Tim 2.4; 6.3; 2 Tim 3.7.

[65] Attridge, *Hebrews*, 372; *cf.* Heb 4.16; 7.25; 10.22; 11.6.

[66] Koester, *Hebrews*, 550.

viewed not individually, but as complementary parts of a whole. It is the entire "package" and its nature that the author wished to set before his readers. Even though we have not yet fully experienced all this new situation has to offer, we have come to the point that it is offered, it is in view like never before, and we have begun to taste its joys. The language conjures up the image of a traveler who is close to his destination city with its features in full view (although the last, short part of the journey must still be completed), and thus recalls the journey of faith in 11.13ff. The exhortation of this passage is to appreciate the new situation that confronts us and to resolve to avail ourselves, by persevering faith, of the new opportunity that opens up before us.

That which can be touched designates that which is physical and the object of sense perception (it is the same word used in Luke 24.39 and 1 John 1.1 of touching Jesus). Although it refers specifically to Mt. Sinai in the comparison here, there is no word for "mountain" in the Greek. This is because the emphasis is not on one mountain versus another, but on the qualities of those mountains as symbols for the characteristics of the two covenants. The phrase thus stands as a kind of summary description of the nature of the old system under Moses with its earthly sanctuary, animal sacrifices, and mortal priests. Paul made a similar comparison of the qualities of the two covenants in his comparison of Hagar and Sarah in Galatians 4 and said that they correspond to Mt. Sinai and "the Jerusalem that is above" respectively. Recall also from Hebrews 9, that the earthly is, by nature, inferior to the heavenly.

The rest of the terms in this verse describe the terrifying theophany of Exodus 19. **Burning fire** is mentioned in Exodus 19.18 and Deuteronomy 4.11 as the mode in which God descended. The **darkness** and the **storm** are mentioned in Moses' recollection of the event in Deuteronomy 4.11 and 5.22 (LXX). The Exodus account says that it was morning when God descended on the mountain, but that the appearance of the mountain included not only a thick cloud but also smoke from the fire of God's appearance (Exod 19.18), which would create the sense of darkness the author here mentions. The **gloom** perhaps refers to what the OT account says was a thick cloud on the mountain (Exod 19.16) but is otherwise the author's own term to summarize the scene.

The phenomena mentioned in this verse have in common not only that they were aspects of God's descent that could be seen with the eyes, but they were also things associated, in the ancient ways of thinking, with fear. Nothing in the scene was visually inviting. In fact, every visible indication said otherwise. What the Israelites saw on that day was frightening and was meant to instill within them a healthy fear of their God out of respect for his power. Fear of terrible retribution from such a powerful God played a large part in the covenant between God and Israel (*cf.* Deut 28, the curses of the Law).

12.19 and to the sound of a trumpet and to the sound of words, which those who heard them begged that no further word be added to them,

God's descent on Sinai was also accompanied by phenomena addressed to the ear. There was **the sound of a trumpet** blast that was initially "very loud" (Exod 19.16) and "grew louder and louder" as God came nearer (v 19). In the OT, a *shofar* was often used to call an assembly and that was the purpose here as well. God had already instructed them that they were to approach the mountain "when the ram's horn sounds a long blast" (v 13).[67] God was calling his people to assemble around the mountain and hear the terms of the covenant that he was entering with them, but again, it is fear that dominates the scene. The combination of the sights and the sounds was already overwhelming, and then God began to speak to the assembled nation. He spoke the ten commandments in the hearing of them all, and when he was finished the people **begged** Moses to go up on the mountain and relay the rest of God's instructions to them, because the sound of God's voice was so terrifying that the people feared that hearing it any longer would kill them (Exod 20.19).

There are two different Greek words for **sound** in this verse: the sound (*hēkos*) of the trumpet and the sound (*phōnē*) of God's voice. Both words are fairly generic terms and no contrast seems to be in view.[68] What is emphasized, however, is not the content of what they heard, but the nature of the sound. This is especially true in the phrase **the sound of** God's **words** (the phrase is from Deut 4.12 LXX). The particulars of what God said are not in view, but the terrifying character of the sound of God's voice on that day. However, the terrifying sound reflected a terrifying

---

[67] Similarly, the gathering of the saints at the last day will be signaled with a trumpet sound (1 Thes 4.16).

[68] The LXX of Exod 19.16 uses the verbal form of *hēkos* along with the word *phonē:* "the voice of the trumpet sounded greatly."

message. The fearful nature of God's word delivered at Sinai has already been suggested in Hebrews 10.28, which mentioned that the Law had no provisions of mercy for those who transgressed it willfully. The Law itself was "hard to hear" in the sense that it made difficult demands on the hearers (*cf.* Acts 15.10; Gal 5.1).

12.20 for they could not bear that which had been commanded: "If even a beast should touch the mountain, it shall be stoned."

The reference here is to Exodus 19.12f, which is quoted in a highly abbreviated form. The Israelites' fear of being so close to God was also reflected in the orders which God had given before he descended on Sinai, which forbade any man or beast from getting any closer than the appointed boundaries around the mountain. Any living thing that passed the boundaries was to be killed at a distance, either by **stoning** or being shot through. The comment that Israel **could not bear** this commandment does not mean that Israel could not find a way to obey it. Instead, it means that the command was onerous and threatening past anything they had experienced about God. Everything about the scene of Mt. Sinai, from the sights to the sounds to the orders concerning their approach to it, said "Stay away!" and generally ordered death for those who did not. God did not allow anyone to get close to him except Moses and a select few leaders (Exod 24.9–11). The average Israelite had to keep his distance from God, otherwise it would cost him his life. This same exclusion was built into the plan of the tabernacle (recall Heb 9.6–8), so the mountain experience symbolized the nature of the religious system that came from it.

And so it was with the Law that came from Sinai. The average Israelite was not permitted to approach God. Only a select group (the priests) could enter God's tent, and only the high priest could enter the sanctuary, the Most Holy Place, and then only once per year on the Day of Atonement. Access to God was thus extremely limited, and the Law kept God's people at a distance from him. See comments on 9.8.

12.21 and (so fearful was the sight) Moses said, "I am terrified and trembling."

As a final testament to the fearful nature of that scene, the author climactically notes that **Moses** was frightened at the sights and sounds of

Sinai. The point is not just that the Sinai display was frightening, but the point lies in who was frightened. It was one thing for the Israelites to be afraid at what they saw and heard, because their long years in Egypt had not afforded them any close encounters with God. *Any* appearance of God was likely to be frightening to them. Moses, however, was accustomed to talking with God, "face to face" (Exod 33.11; *cf.* Exod 3.6; Acts 7.32). God had even spoken to Moses in anger before (Exod 4.14), but what he saw and heard at Sinai overwhelmed even him. It was far beyond any display, or voice, that he had ever experienced from God before. For *Moses* to be afraid and trembling, the scene must have been extraordinarily violent.

The quotation here appears to be a paraphrase of Deuteronomy 9.19, where Moses was recalling his fear of what God would do to the Israelites when they sinned in the matter of the golden calf. The verse says, "I was afraid of the anger and hot displeasure with which the Lord was wrathful against you in order to destroy you" (NASB). Although Moses spoke these words in the specific context of God's angry reaction to the golden calf, the author of Hebrews seems to have interpreted it as characteristic of the overall Sinai experience (because Israel was still at Sinai when they made the calf), and thus was able to attribute Moses' fear to the whole episode in general.[69]

12.22 But you have come to Mt. Zion, even to the city of the living God, the heavenly Jerusalem, and to myriads of angels in festal gathering,

Arriving at God's presence on his mountain is a familiar Biblical motif (*cf.* Psa 24.3; 48.1; 68.16; Isa 2.2; 56.7; 66.20), but it is also reminiscent of Eden, which was on a mountain (Ezek 28.14). Here, in Hebrews 12, this is undoubtedly the backdrop. To come to the heavenly mountain is to return to Eden, to come completely out of Adamic exile and to return fully to the presence of God (like Adam originally experienced). Jesus the high priest brings us here, to God's mountain, and fully "in," into the presence of God himself. The contrast between the old system (the Law and the Aaronic priesthood, represented by the scene at Sinai) and the new system is now laid out in a list of seven things (*cf.* the list of seven attributes of the Son in ch 1). The purpose of this list is threefold:

[69] See the discussion in Lane, *Hebrews 9–13*, 464. Jewish tradition (logically) asserted that Moses was afraid at the scene in Exod 19 (*b. Shabb.* 88b).

1) It forms a stark contrast to the situation described in verses 18–21. As with other comparisons and contrasts in Hebrews, the point is not necessarily to denigrate the old system but to show just how much better the new order of things in Jesus is. 2) It is meant to impress us with the positive greatness of what we have been offered through Jesus, which in turn is designed to encourage us to persevere in our faith so as to attain it,[70] and 3) It is meant to create a serious hesitation in those who are contemplating quitting the faith.

Part of what drives the picture here, and the exhortation that comes from it, is the ancient value system of honor and shame. In Hellenistic culture, the dynamics of honor and shame were a powerful force in most relationships.[71] When someone (especially a patron) provided another person with a great gift (which was called "grace"),[72] the recipient was obligated to act in such a way that clearly demonstrated his gratitude (see v 28). This usually meant that the recipient of the gift was *indebted* to respond with loyalty, to provide some kind of service for the giver (if possible), and to enhance the giver's public honor. While there were no written laws that governed the relationship, reciprocity was expected. Failure to demonstrate gratitude for a gift was considered a breach of fidelity, was the worst kind of offense, and ultimately hurt the recipient himself in that it meant he would receive no more gifts from the giver (or anyone else) in the future (*cf.* 10.26). The absolute worst response would be to insult the giver (see Heb 10.29; *cf.* the parable in Matt 21.33ff). These dynamics are at work in the exhortation here. The risk of insulting God and incurring his wrath is exactly where this exhortation is headed (see vv 25–29). The author not only describes the wonderful blessings which are set before us, but he also reminds his readers that God is judge (v 23). Before the original readers decided to quit, they needed to consider just how great a gift they were being offered, and the consequences of turning their backs on it.

Note that the author did not say "you will come" (future tense) or "you may come" (subjunctive mood). He says, "**you have come**," perfect

---

[70] Although the presentation is in the present ("you have come"), the entire picture partakes of an apocalyptic quality in which the glorious end of God's people is set before the reader as already in view, similar in some ways to Rev 21–22.

[71] See deSilva, *The Hope of Glory* 1–33, 144–77, and *idem, Honor, Patronage, Kinship, and Purity, 2nd ed.*, 38–71.

[72] deSilva, *Honor, Patronage, Kinship, and Purity, 2nd ed.*, 107–8.

tense.[73] It is a picture of having arrived at a wonderful, transcendent, eschatological situation, even if the fullness of that situation still lies ahead. The author's choice of verb here is *proserchomai*, which in the LXX is always used of approaching God, and which the author of Hebrews has used repeatedly to mean "draw near" (4.16; 7.25; 10.1, 22; 11.6). It is the situation of finally drawing near to God, by faith.[74] This creates the ironic situation that Israel came to a mountain which they could see, but they could not approach, whereas we come to a mountain that we cannot see (recall Heb 11.1), but we can approach it freely.

1) First, the new order is represented by **Zion**. This is an alternate name for Jerusalem in OT texts and is especially associated with David's conquest of that site (2 Sam 5.7).[75] Technically Zion is the mountain on which the city was built, but the two are nearly inseparable in biblical thought (see Zech 8.3). The term often has messianic significance, it is the name for the city of the Messiah and his people. Zion is the spiritual counterpart to the earthly Jerusalem and represents the spiritual fulfillment and perfection of all that the earthly city symbolized. Jerusalem was, of course, the city of God, the place where God made his name (his presence) dwell among his own people (Deut 12.11) in a permanent kind of way (relatively speaking, compared to the tabernacle). The building of the temple in Jerusalem was also understood as God's commitment and closeness to his people and was a symbol of the covenant relationship between God and Israel. There was a kind of tension, however, built into the temple's presence in Jerusalem. While in one sense it symbolized the closeness of God to his people, the fact remains that God's Law denied entrance into his house for everyone except the priests, and exclusion from God's presence for everyone except the high priest, once per year. The closeness of the temple thus stood in tension with the exclusion from God's presence. Among other things, the covenant promised that God would protect his people, and so Jerusalem came to be thought of as not only the place where God and his people live together, but also as the place which God defended (Joel 3.16; but not unconditionally, *cf.* Jer 7). *Cf.* Psalm 69.35–36, which combines the ideas of closeness and safety in

---

[73] See on v 18 above.

[74] See David H. Wenkel, "Sensory Experience and the Contrast Between the Covenants in Hebrews 12," *BibSac* 173 (2016): 219–34.

[75] See J. J. M. Roberts, "The Davidic Origin of the Zion Tradition," *JBL* 92 (1973): 329–44.

a vision of the messianic age. Zion is the substance for which Jerusalem was the shadow. Zion is not an earthly place, but a heavenly place. It is the city which Abraham was looking forward to entering (Heb 11.16) and the goal of all the faithful of all ages (Heb 11.40). In Zion the closeness of God does not stand in tension with his distance from his people because there God's people are brought to him by the Son (Heb 2.10; ultimately by the resurrection of the dead), and they all live in his presence. "They will see his face" (Rev 22.4), or to use the terminology of Hebrews, there they "enter in." In Zion there is no temple, because God's people live in God's immediate presence (Rev 21.22).

Zion is the **heavenly Jerusalem** (*cf.* Gal 4.26),[76] **the city of the living God**. It is described to the extent that words can describe it in Revelation 21–22. The picture there is that this place has already been prepared for us, and it awaits our arrival. Although it is described as a beautiful and perfect place, its main attraction for Christians is that **God** is there. Like everything else in the new order of things opened up by Jesus, the city that awaits us and that we contemplate is heavenly, which is also to say that it is eternal and better than anything the old, earthly system could offer. **City** recalls the eternal home envisioned by past heroes of faith in 11.16, and also suggests a place of belonging. In the ancient world, a person's home city was the place where he had his citizenship. See comments on verse 23 below. God is here called the **living** God, a phrase which sets him above and apart from idols. "Living" can emphasize the ideas of "true" and "only" (Jer 10.10). Also, because God himself is living he can impart life to his children so that they can live with him eternally (John 5.26). However, the phrase is also used in contexts that denote God in his power, his judgment, or his terrifying nature,[77] and in texts where the surety of God's will and his faithfulness to his word are emphasized (echoing the language of an oath; recall 3.12).

The connection between Zion and Jerusalem finds an interesting interplay in the events of Acts 2, where the prophecies about Zion began their fulfillment. Note the following chart which compares and contrasts Sinai with the events of "Zion" in Acts 2:

---

[76] Given the regular identification of Zion with the city of God in the OT (Psa 48.2; 60.14; Zech 8.3), we here take the Greek word *kai* as adverbial ("even") or explicative, and not connective.

[77] Heb 3.12; 10.31; see also Deut 5.26; Dan 6.26.

At Sinai (Exodus)	At Zion (Acts 2)
Fire on the mountain (19.16–18)	Tongues of fire (2.3)
Loud sound (19.19)	Loud sound (2.2)
The Law given (chs 20–31)	The gospel given (2.22–36)
A false god worshipped (32.1–6)	Jesus acknowledged as Lord (2.36)
God's anger proclaimed (32.10)	God's love proclaimed (2.39)
Covenant broken (32.19)	Covenant entered (2.41a)
3000 died (32.28)	3000 saved (2.41b)

This does not mean that the events of Acts 2 exhausted the prophecies about Zion, but that Acts 2 was when "these last days" (Heb 1.2) began. From that day forward a new situation began to exist, and a better kind of relationship with God became possible.

2) Our relationship with Jesus has not only brought us to the prospect of living in the heavenly city of Zion but has also brought us to a grand gathering of **myriads** (a myriad in Greek is 10,000) **of angels**. To be among angels is to have transcended the earthly, to have entered the heavenly realm. The throne of God in heaven is depicted as being surrounded by angels and other spiritual beings (Rev 5.11) who make up his royal court, and our author has already noted that the role of angels in the messianic order of things is to serve the interests of those who will inherit salvation (1.14). They are interested in what God has done to save us (1 Pet 1.12; although they do not seem to know any more about it than we do, Mark 13.32), and they watch our progress (1 Cor 4.9; Luke 15.10). The picture seems to be that they are eager for our final arrival in heaven, as they are depicted as a great **festal gathering** (Greek *panēguris*),[78] which

[78] It is possible to understand this word as a separate item on the list. However, it is not separated by "and" (Greek *kai)* and thus is best understood either as appositional to "myriads of angels" or as a descriptive dative (as the dative "heavenly" describes "Jerusalem" in this same verse). For this same reason, it is probably not best to treat it as parallel to the word "assembly" *(ekklēsia)*, as some English versions have done ("to the general assembly and church ..."). Heinrich Seesemann, *"panēguris," TDNT* 5:722; Attridge, *Hebrews*, 375.

in secular literature denoted a celebratory assembly in honor of a god and then came to denote a joyful gathering of any kind.[79] The term perhaps faintly recalls the Israelites standing on the far shore of the Red Sea, singing the victory Song of Moses (Exod 15), and now depicts Christian saints as having achieved that same kind of victory. *Cf.* also Isaiah 25.6–9. Instead of the picture of an assembly gripped by fear at the prospect of being in God's presence, as at Sinai (v 19), and of a bare mountain inhabited by no one (at God's command), the picture here is one of a joyous company of heavenly beings. The scene is meant to be inviting, and thus encourages us to join them by enduring in our faith.

12.23 and to the church of the firstborn who are enrolled in heaven, and to God who is the judge of all, and to the spirits of perfected righteous people,

3) In Christ we have also come to the **church** of the firstborn ones. The Greek word for the official assembly of citizens (*ekklēsia*) is the word the NT authors used for God's group in Jesus, the church, and that seems to be the group in view here as well. The church consists of that group of people who share a relationship with God through Jesus by means of the forgiveness available through his blood. They are the "brethren" whom Jesus is bringing to God (2.10, 12). We must be careful, however, that we catch the cosmic nuance of the term in this context. In connection with the heavenly Jerusalem and angels, and in keeping with the contrast between the earthly and the heavenly in this context (vv 18ff), the author is not thinking so much about the earthly aspect of the church, or the local churches of which the original readers were members, as he is its heavenly aspect and nature. The church is God's people whose identity and life (Col 3.3) are viewed by God himself as spiritual, not physical. Our author's emphasis is that we have come into (joined) a spiritual assembly of God's people, heaven's citizens (see 2.12, with Jesus; our present, earthly location notwithstanding). Such a view encourages us to transcend our earthly perspective and see ourselves as part of something much more grand, much more glorious, and much more significant than any earthly relationship (some of the readers may have been ostracized from syna-

---

For a defense of connecting it with "church," see W. J. Dumbrell, "The Spirits of Just Men Made Perfect," *EvQ* 48 (1976): 154–59.

[79] LSJ 1297.

gogues or their families). That perspective in turn encourages us to persevere, for God has brought his people together in the church partially for their own encouragement (see 10.24f).

The church is the same people who are called **the firstborn.** This was God's term for Israel (Exod 4.22f), so the comparison with Israel of old persists. Furthermore, the word here is plural: these are God's firstborn ones (and thus does not refer to Jesus here). This is an interesting use of the word, since in a family there is normally only one firstborn son. We must remember, however, that the term is primarily a designation of honor and status, and that is how it is used when applied either to Jesus (Rom 8.29; Heb 1.6) or to God's people in the NT. In this sense, then, all of God's children are firstborn to him, all of them have a special and high status with the Father. Also, the firstborn have a special portion of inheritance in store for them (see comments on 12.16).

These children of God are also **enrolled** in heaven. The word "enrolled" (from the verb *apographō*) was a term used of taking a census and writing down the names of people who were officially acknowledged (the term is used in Luke 2.1–5). They were thus registered and their existence and status were officially recognized. Enrollment was an important aspect of ancient social life, since having one's name on the official registers meant that one was a citizen. In the Hellenistic world one's citizenship was usually in a city, not a country, and if one was a citizen, he then had all the privileges and rights that went with it (such as voting in the assembly of citizens, exemption from certain taxes, *etc.*). Being put on the list of citizens required either some kind of proof of ancestry or the granting of that privilege by a monarch, and exclusion from the city register of citizens meant that one was an alien and not reckoned as an equal, so enrollment and citizenship also became expressions of status in the ancient world.[80] In short, to be enrolled was to be an "insider" whose life and identity were bound up with that city. This is, no doubt, the sense here, especially since it is used along with other indicators of status ("city," "assembly," and "firstborn"). The point of this description of God's people is that as partakers of Christ we have come to be officially recognized as God's people, citizens of his heavenly city and thus possessors of rights and promises that are unavailable to those who have not joined themselves to

[80] *Cf.* Josephus' attempts to convince the Romans that Jews were full citizens of the cities in which they lived. *Ant.* 14.185–267; 19.281.

Jesus. The author was inverting the earthly reality of his original readers. While many Christians were rejected by their earthly society, he wanted them to know that they had status in the heavenly city (where it really counts) where unbelievers had no part. Passages such as Exodus 32.32, Philippians 4.3, and Revelation 3.5 speak of a book of names kept by God, a literary figure to convey that God knows, personally and individually, the identities of those who belong to him (2 Tim 2.19). This is intended to give believers a sense of confidence and security. Our God does not treat us as a nameless, faceless multitude, but knows each one who belongs to him and is ready to welcome each one into his presence.

4) The terms of verses 22–24 proceed to a climax. The picture is of one who has left the world behind and enters the heavenly city, who has come into a great throng of joyous spiritual beings (angels and brethren), and then into the presence of **God** himself. As such it echoes the journey of faith described in 11.13–16, but with the difference that we have come to God in an access that was unavailable before (recall vv 18ff; Heb 4.16; 7.25; 10.22; *cf.* Eph 3.12). Since it is possible for us to come closer to God than anyone before us could come, it would be foolish to turn around and quit. In this way, this picture of unprecedented access to God, with its future prospect of standing directly in his presence later, was meant to encourage the readers of Hebrews to persevere. While we might expect the procession to have come next to a temple, the scene here is like that of Revelation 21.22 where it is explained that God himself is the dwelling place of his people.

The Biblical view of God's love and kindness is supplemented by the view of God as the **judge of all**. In the Hellenistic world, every city had a judge (see Luke 18.2), and God's city is no exception.[81] It must be remembered that the verb "judge" in Greek often had the sense of condemnation associated with it, so a judge was a person who held the power of life and death over others. In the ideal city, the judge was the guardian of fairness and justice, and a protector of those who were victimized by people who abused their power (Deut 1.16–18). The present context is one of joyous anticipation, so it seems unlikely that the description of God as judge was here meant to instill a sense of fear. God's role as judge is a comfort to those who have been faithful in that he will vindicate them against all untruthful charges (Rom 8.33) and condemn their unrighteous enemies (see also 1 John 2.28; 4.17).

---

[81] Koester, *Hebrews*, 545.

5) The next thing encountered on this heavenly procession is **the spirits of perfected righteous people.** Since each of the separate items on this list are delimited by the word "and," this would therefore appear to be a different group from the church mentioned in the earlier part of the verse (the fact that the two groups are separated by putting God between them is another indicator). These are no doubt the spirits of people of faith from the past, people like those in Hebrews 11. The phrase "spirits of the righteous" is used in extra-Biblical Jewish literature of the godly dead.[82] Their faith is what made them **righteous** (Heb 10.38, quoting Hab 2.4) and so they too have a place in God's kingdom (see Matt 8.11). They are the "great cloud of witnesses" of 12.1, and they are depicted as standing in heaven cheering us on and ready to enjoy our company. *Cf.* Revelation 6.9–12. They are **perfected** in the sense that they have faithfully endured and they have received the reward for which they hoped (recall Heb 11.40). See comments on 2.10; also 12.2. The fact that they are depicted as so close to the presence of God himself seems significant and is consistent with the picture in Revelation 21.22. It might suggest that they share in his reign and victory over evil (2 Tim 2.12), although that concept does not appear in Hebrews. Being with God, in his presence, which is the goal of every believer, is the idea here. We must remember that the author here is describing a situation, an opportunity to which we have come, yet one that is still to be fully consummated. That situation includes ultimately being with all the faithful people of God in heaven. The depiction here is anticipatory, and thus does not contradict 11.39f or those passages which speak of a resurrection and a final judgment after which the faithful enter into heaven (Matt 25.31ff; 1 Thes 4.13ff). We have come to the prospect of joining, in heaven, those who have gone on before us in faith. Joyous participation in that (future) assembly is part of the entire "package" we have been offered and for which we must now choose. In this connection, then, we probably should not make too much of the fact that they are here identified as **spirits** (as if they have not received their resurrection bodies). It is the character of these people, not the mode of their existence, that the author wants us to see.

12.24 and to the mediator of the new covenant, Jesus, and to sprinkled blood which speaks better than that of Abel.

---

[82] Lane, *Hebrews 9–13*, 470.

6) In the company of God is **Jesus**. Our author has repeatedly called attention to Psalm 110.1 and its fulfillment in our Lord. That psalm depicts him as seated at the right hand of God, and such is the general picture here as well. In this way the author has also returned to the theme of the greatness of God's Son, the topic with which the sermon began (see 1.14). His role as **mediator of the new**[83] **covenant** is here brought to the forefront again (recall 8.6 and 9.15) and calls us to remember that Jesus also fulfills Psalm 110.4, which declares him to be our Melchizedekian priest who has also fulfilled the prophecy of Jeremiah 31 (Heb 7–10). Jesus in his priesthood is the reason we have come to the prospect of Zion and its heavenly glory. Of course, the death that ratified the new covenant and the blood that was shed to make atonement in the heavenly sanctuary are associated with the work of our Lord as a human, and so his human name (**Jesus**) appears here even though he is depicted as in heaven.[84] The mention of Jesus perhaps reminds us of the underlying sense of warning that pervades this joyous scene. To reject God's offer is to reject Jesus, and it will eventually lead a person to become the same kind of enemy as those who killed him (recall 6.4–6).

7) The last item on the list is the **blood** of Jesus, which lies at the center of his high priestly work and which makes the completion of our journey possible. In the OT, the **sprinkling** of blood purified and consecrated both things and people (Exod 24.8; 20.21; Heb 9.13, 21). It was especially part of the sacrificial rituals, including that of the Day of Atonement (Lev 16.14f, 19). In keeping with the Day of Atonement imagery of Hebrews 9–10, to come to the sprinkled blood means to come into the presence of God himself. This is the end of the journey. Our author takes us back to the language of chapters 9–10 to remember the significance of what our great high priest has done for us. Jesus' blood has cleansed (sprinkled) our consciences and made us holy people (Heb 10.29; 1 Pet 1.2) in a way that the animal blood of the OT sacrifices never could. Whereas the old covenant was marked by distance and exclusion, the new covenant, because of Jesus' blood, is characterized by reconciliation and welcome.[85]

---

[83] The word for "new" in the phrase "new covenant" is normally *kainē* (which can indicate new in kind, new in nature), but here (only) it is *nea* (which can mean new in time). The question here is whether this change in words is significant or if it is simply rhetorical variation (since the two words are often used synonymously). Most scholars take the latter view.

[84] Lane, *Hebrews 9–13*, 472.

[85] Moffatt, *Epistle to the Hebrews*, 218.

The blood of Jesus[86] is here said to **speak**, like **Abel's** (undoubtedly referring to Gen 4.10, which depicts Abel's blood as crying out from the ground), but in a much **better** way. See comments on 11.4. Abel's blood (death) testified to the fact that those who approach God in faith will suffer persecution. He came to God "by faith" (or faithfulness) and it cost him his life at the hands of a wicked man. Jesus fulfills (*i.e.*, fills up) the pattern that was established in the story of Cain and Abel, and more. Just as Abel offered his sacrifice out of fidelity to God, so Jesus, even more, has offered a better sacrifice (himself) out of unwavering faithfulness to God.[87] Both Abel and Jesus were innocent of wrongdoing but suffered death in connection with their offerings, but Jesus' sufferings were greater (he suffered the shame of the cross, Heb 12.2), and the results of his death were greater (his sacrificial death cleanses the conscience of sinners, Heb 9.14). Abel's offering was the first in the Bible, but Jesus' is the last ("once and for all"; Heb 7.27; 9.12; 10.10) because it has a final, eternal quality. Abel's blood is depicted as crying out, even throughout the ages, for retributive justice, but the blood of Christ effects reconciliation.[88] Some have suggested, however, that since Cain was not required to pay for his murder with his life (which would have been the usual Biblical punishment), that perhaps Abel was crying out for mercy.[89] If that is the case, then the blood of Jesus does not just cry out for mercy, but actually provides it. In these ways, then, Jesus' blood "speaks" better than Abel's. The message his blood speaks is that we come to God by faithfully enduring opposition from the wicked, which is part of God's training for us (12.4ff).

12.25 See to it that you do not refuse the one who is speaking. If those people who refused the one who warned on earth did not escape,

---

[86] Alternately, the last part of the verse could be translated "to Jesus, mediator of a new covenant, and to blood of sprinkling, to one who speaks better than Abel," taking the adjectival participle as referring to Jesus and not to "blood." The participle could be either masculine or neuter, so theoretically it could refer to either. For a defense of this reading, see Gene Smillie, "'The One Who is Speaking' in Hebrews 12:25," *TynBul* 55 (2004): 275–94.

[87] See McCruden, "The Eloquent Blood of Jesus."

[88] John Byron, "Abel's Blood and the Ongoing Cry for Vengeance," *CBQ* 73 (2011): 743–56.

[89] R. Walter L. Moberly, "Exemplars of Faith in Hebrews 11: Abel," in *The Epistle to the Hebrews and Christian Theology*, ed. Richard Bauckham *et al* (Grand Rapids: Eerdmans, 2009), 353–63, at 360; Attridge, *Hebrews*, 317.

how much more will we not escape who repudiate the one who warns from heaven?

God's[90] **speaking** and man's hearing has been a theme throughout the sermon.[91] The book began with the fact that God has now spoken in a final way through his Son (1.2), followed by an exhortation to pay closer attention to what we have heard (2.1–4), reinforced by the appeal of Psalm 95 to hear God's voice in the time of "Today," and supplemented with an encouragement to hear with faith (4.1). The rest of the sermon has been, in effect, an appeal to hear (in the Biblical sense of "receive" and "accept") and not **refuse** God and his word. "Speaking" also recalls the blood of Jesus which speaks (v 24). Through the gospel about Jesus Christ (2 Thes 2.14), God is issuing a call (invitation) to come to him and receive the blessings he has in store for those who trust him. In this way he is still **speaking** to men today. The verb **warn** (Greek *chrēmatizō*) means "to impart a divine message"[92] and thus is roughly synonymous with God's speaking. The context of indebtedness and judgment suggests that there is a negative sense to it here, and so it is commonly translated "warn" in this passage. The statement echoes Psalm 95 and the divine warning that issues to those who live "Today," in the messianic age (see chs 3 and 4). Further indication of the connection is that the same imperative (**see to it**) appears in the exposition of Psalm 95 (in Heb 3.12).[93]

It is a mistake to think that God is only offering salvation (rescue) from the punishment that is coming to sinners. Beyond that (1 Thes 1.10), God is offering us a blessed and life-giving relationship with himself, a relationship that begins here and will last throughout eternity in heaven. Therefore, to **refuse** God's offer is to refuse God himself. Furthermore, his summons is accompanied by the sacrifice of Jesus and his installment as high priest (in fulfillment of Psa 110.1, 4) which are God's gifts that make our coming to him possible. God has therefore both opened up the way to himself and issued the invitation for us to follow it. As noted in the comments on verse 22 (see also on 6.4), the original readers of Hebrews

[90] God is both the one who warned from earth and the one who warns from heaven. The interpretation that sees two speakers here, *viz.* Moses and Jesus, makes nonsense out of v 26.

[91] 1.1f; 2.1, 3.7, 16; 4.2; 5.11; as well as the testimony of witnesses, 2.4, 6; 10.15; 11.4; 12.24.

[92] BDAG 1089.

[93] Attridge, *Hebrews*, 379.

lived in a culture in which the dynamics of the patron-client relationship were a powerful social force for right behavior. Having just reviewed the greatness of what God offers in verses 22–24, it is only fitting that he should now explicitly warn them of the consequences of refusing their great benefactor and thus incurring his wrath. It is sad that (in my opinion) our culture is increasingly losing its sense of indebtedness to God, but Christians can afford no such attitude. As this verse makes clear, in light of the great cost on God's part and its nature as an act of pure grace, there is no way to politely refuse God and his offer.

As we have seen elsewhere, the author of Hebrews likes to impress the force of his point with an argument from the lesser to the greater (2.2f; 3.2–6; 7.4–10; 9.14; 10.29; 12.9), sometimes coupled with a rhetorical question (as in 2.3). **Those**[94] people are the Israelites of the exodus generation who were gathered at Sinai.[95] They begged that God not speak to them anymore (Exod 19.21), but that betrayed a much more deep-rooted reluctance on their part to hear anything God said, as was borne out in their subsequent behaviors (as recalled by Psa 95, in Heb 3–4). Their initial reluctance eventually became wholesale rejection of God's word to them, for which they perished. They **refused**[96] him; we must not. Once God's verdict on their faithlessness was pronounced against them (Num 14.28ff), they **could not escape** it and they died in the wilderness (see Heb 4.17). Like Esau (v 17), their failure to see (by faith) the value of God's future blessing resulted in their losing it permanently with no way to get it back. More importantly, they failed to enter into God's rest to which they had been invited (see Heb 4.18).

There are two words for rejection in this verse, and most English versions attempt to indicate something of the difference. The Israelites refused God, but the readers of Hebrews contemplated **repudiating** (Greek *apostrephō*, turning away from,[97] turning one's back on[98]) him. The for-

[94] The demonstrative pronoun functions as personal pronoun here. Whereas *houtos* (this, these) points to what is thematic in a context, *ekeinos* (that, those) refers to something that was previously mentioned but is non-thematic in the context (Levinshon, "Towards a Unified Linguistic Description of *houtos* and *ekeinos*"). Christians are thematic in this text.

[95] See Michael Kibbe, "Requesting and Rejecting: *Paraiteomai* in Heb 12, 18–29," *Bib* 96 (2015): 282–86.

[96] The verb *paraiteomai* had a wide semantic range. It could mean "request" (as in v 19), but can also mean to refuse or reject (as here). See Kibbe, "Requesting and Rejecting," 283.

[97] BDAG 122–23.

[98] LSJ 220.

mer term can have a mild sense (it can mean "beg off" or "excuse"), but the latter is a stronger term and is the same willful renunciation of trust in God and refusal of his guidance that the author has elsewhere called "falling away" (3.12; 4.11; 6.6).

Like most everything else in the old system under Moses, God's warning to the Israelites was associated with a place **on** the **earth**, Mt. Sinai. However, the author has shown that the earthly nature of the old system has been eclipsed by the heavenly and eternal nature of the new (9.1ff). What is heavenly is, by its nature, greater than what is earthly. God is no longer speaking from a place on the earth, but now speaks **from heaven** through the gospel (1 Pet 1.12; *cf.* Rev 14.6) which **warns** us to repent and not to give up following God in faith (Luke 12.5; 1 Thes 4.6; *cf.* Heb 11.7). So if God warned them from earth in such a way that refusal to listen produced condemnation from which they could not escape, then much more it is the case that those who refuse the better, heavenly warning of the eternal gospel will be unable to escape God's wrath if they refuse him.

12.26 Whose voice shook the earth then, but now has promised saying "Once more I will shake not only the earth but also heaven."

The author now proceeds to another argument from the lesser to the greater, presented as a **then**-versus-**now** statement, corresponding to the them-versus-us scenario in the previous verse. The operative notion is that what happened before is only a pale imitation of the greater event to which it points. The comparison is built around the idea of shaking. Psalm 96.9–10 is likely in the background,[99] but the quotation comes from Haggai 2.6. Shaking is a violent, even destructive action. In 2 Samuel 22.8 (= Psa 18.7) and Isaiah 13.13; 24.19 the shaking of the earth is associated with God's anger, which corresponds to the depiction of the frightful scene at Sinai in Hebrews 12.18–21. In Nehemiah 5.13, shaking is a symbol of judgment. God's frightening (v 19) **voice** at Sinai **shook the earth**, which is probably a reference to Exodus 19.18 or Psalm 68.8, or else is our author's own summary of that scene (since the verb "shake" does not appear in the Exodus account). God's voice is described as a powerful force in Psalm 29.8; Ezekiel 1.24; 10.5; it was mistaken for thunder in John 12.29. So powerful is God's voice that in Deuteronomy 4.33 and 5.26 there

[99] Lane, *Hebrews 9–13,* 479; Joshua Caleb Hutchens, "Christian Worship in Hebrews 12:28 as Ethical and Exclusive," *JETS* 59 (2016): 507–22, at 512.

is amazement that the Israelites lived to tell about hearing it. This in turn is taken as a type of another time when God will destroy the universe; the partial shaking then foreshadows the complete "shaking to pieces"[100] (destruction) that is to come. The surety of that time is guaranteed by the fact that God has **promised** it, and he is always faithful to his word. The mention of "promise" here provides a verbal echo with Psalm 95 and the entrance into God's rest (see 4.1).[101]

The prophet Haggai looked to the time when God, in an apocalyptic event,[102] would **shake** the universe (dry land, seas, **earth**, **heavens**, and nations), thus loosing his captive people, and they would come out to be gathered to his house (Hag 2.7; a similar picture appears in Amos 9.9–11). The "nations" of Haggai 2.7 are, as typical in the OT, Gentiles, or unbelievers. Haggai preached in the days when the first group of Jews had returned from Babylonian captivity under Zerubabbel's leadership. They had begun work on the temple but were interrupted, and it lay unfinished for fifteen years. Haggai, along with Zechariah, encouraged the people to resume the building and finish it. In that context God promised that more of his people would return, and "the latter glory of this house will be greater than the former" (Hag 2.9 NASB). Thus the "shaking" is the prelude to glory;[103] the destruction of unbelievers would leave only the faithful as survivors.[104] The return from Babylonian captivity was but an illustration of the greater fulfillment of this prophecy that was to come in the messianic age; it was *a* fulfillment of Haggai's words, but not *the* fulfillment (*cf.* on 1.5 and the quotation from 2 Sam 7.14). The author of

---

[100] Bruce, *Epistle to the Hebrews*, 383.

[101] Koester, *Hebrews*, 547.

[102] See Jihye Lee, "The Unshakable Kingdom through the Shaking of Heaven and Earth in Heb 12:26–29," *NovT* 62 (2020): 257–72.

[103] Lane, *Hebrews 9–13*, 479.

[104] It is also tempting to think that the author of Hebrews understood the prophecy, according to his Messianic perspective on the OT, as referring ultimately to the resurrection of God's people and his gathering them to heaven, the ultimate dwelling-place of believers (see v 23 above). The shaking of the heavens and the earth (*cf.* 2 Pet 3.7, 10) that looses God's people brings them from the land and the sea or beyond (Rev 20.13), as well as out of the nations in which they live (see 1 Cor 15.52ff), and sets them all free from their slavery to the flesh and to death (see Rom 8.21; *cf.* this symbolism in the event of Acts 16.26). In the NT, the resurrection and gathering of the people of God is not just an event at the end of time but is a process that begins when they hear the gospel (John 5.25–29). However, the final event is in view here. In the process of this shaking, the created order that once held God's people is destroyed.

Hebrews thus saw in Haggai's prophecy a threat of coming final judgment in which the faithless will be destroyed and God's people would enjoy the ultimate measure of freedom from exile. This was an important consideration for Christians who were contemplating quitting the faith.

It is sometimes objected that it is hard to see how the prophecy of Haggai could mean this (the same objection is raised against many NT quotations of the OT). The key lies not so much in the historical context of the original prophecy but in the new perspective which the early Christians brought to the text as a result of their belief that Jesus and his work was the fulfillment of everything to which the OT pointed. It is about patterns.[105] What was new about this was not that they saw the OT as pointing to realities beyond itself in the messianic age—the Jews already had such a perspective (demonstrated in their method of *midrash,* which contemporized the ancient text; see Introduction). The Jews already believed that OT historical events and statements were, in a sense, promises of something yet to come. What was new was that the early Christians believed that *Jesus* and the situation he created by his death and resurrection was the fulfillment of the patterns that had been previously revealed in those Scriptures. That perspective enabled the Christians to see the OT not only in a fuller way, but as speaking directly to them. Furthermore, there are usually verbal clues within a text that encourage such a treatment (recall the phrase "son of man" in Psa 8, Heb 2.6). A feature of Haggai's prophecy that points toward an eschatological interpretation is the opening phrase **once more,** which has the sense of "one last time."[106] Given the Christian worldview, this must refer to the end of time.

12.27 The phrase[107] "Yet once more" indicates a removal of the things which can be shaken, as of things that have been made, in order that the things which cannot be shaken might remain.

As our author has frequently done before, he now takes his readers to a specific part of the OT quotation to expound upon its meaning and significance (see Heb 4.15; 4.3, 5, 7). It is his careful method at work. Often

---

[105] See Neusner, "Paradigmatic Thinking Versus Historical Thinking."

[106] BDAG 97. The expression appears in the LXX of Gen 18.32 and Jdg 6.39.

[107] The word "phrase" attempts to translate a Greek construction (the first words of the quotation have been substantivized with a neuter singular definite article functioning demonstratively) that has no English equivalent.

the author of Hebrews focused on specific words for their implications (see Heb 4.4f; 7.4, 7; 8.13; *etc.*), and that is what he does here as well. The phrase **yet once more** ("one last time") implies finality. After the shaking of which Haggai spoke, there will be no more (for nothing will be left to shake after this). This means that the "shaking" will be so complete that all that is physical and temporal (*i.e.*, everything that **can be shaken**, which is a way of speaking about the created order, the universe of material, physical **things that have been made** by God) will be destroyed (**removed**), and the only things that will be left from this process are those **things** which are eternal (that **which cannot be shaken**; see also Isa 54.10). The author noted in the opening chapter that the Son has the power to roll the heavens up like a cloak (1.10–12), and the author now ends with that theme here.[108]

12.28 Wherefore, since we are receiving an unshakable kingdom, let us have gratitude through which we might serve God in an acceptable way with reverence and awe,

The eternal (**unshakable**, indestructible) thing that will remain after the destruction (shaking apart) of the universe and all rival powers (Hag 2.21f; 1 Cor 15.25) will be the kingdom of God (see Dan 2.44; 7.14). The book began with a reference to the Son's kingdom (1.8), and so it ends with one as well. On the idea of a kingdom, see comments on 1.8. **Kingdom** carries with it the idea of power, since a kingdom exists by virtue of the power of its king.[109] God's kingdom endures forever because God himself is omnipotent. However, "kingdom" also suggests relationship, for a kingdom is made up of those who have submitted to the authority (power) of the king. The faithful are said to be "unshakable" in the OT (Psa 16.8; 21.7; 62.6). God's kingdom is made up of those who have entered into the new covenant with him (see Isa 54.10), those who enter his rest (Heb 3–4). In this sense **we are receiving** the kingdom; we are presently in a relationship with the Almighty king himself, a relationship that will never be broken by death or any other thing (*cf.* Rom 8.35–39). "Kingdom" can also suggest a location, and there is something of that

[108] Moffatt, *Epistle to the Hebrews*, 222.

[109] The phrase "receive a kingdom" can also mean "receive kingship" (*cf.* Luke 19.12), but that does not seem to be the sense here. The context here is about submission to God, not reigning with him.

here as well. The author has spoken of going to God's city and homeland and to the new Jerusalem, and this context contrasts earthly and heavenly locations from which God speaks. In this aspect, we are receiving a place in which to live that is secure from the "shaking" of the universe.[110]

There is a sense in which citizenship in God's great messianic kingdom summarizes all that God has provided for us in Jesus, so that the expression here summarizes verses 22–24. Every spiritual blessing, every plan, and every act of God was designed to create and to bring us into his kingdom and to make life within it wonderful. The eternal nature of this kingdom sets the temporary hardships of life into proper perspective. The rejection and persecution Christians receive from the world lasts only for a moment compared to the eternity we will enjoy in heaven (2 Cor 4.17). This perspective is designed to encourage us to set our priorities right (2 Pet 3.11f), to persevere (see 2 Pet 1.10f), and to look, by faith, at what is not yet seen with our eyes (Heb 11.1; 2 Cor 4.18). Like Moses, we are called to sacrifice the lesser earthly things for the greater heavenly things (Heb 11.26). Family ties were very strong in ancient Jewish culture, and no doubt many Jewish Christians found it hard to persist in the faith when their families did not support them in it. Jesus himself spoke about the difficulty this would create (Matt 10.35–37; 19.29). The author of Hebrews bids us to think about a greater family to which we belong (the kingdom of God), and to secure our place in it above all else.

The magnitude of God's offer to us is designed to evoke within us a sense of profound **gratitude** (Col 2.7). Anything less reflects scorn for God and the great, sacrificial lengths to which he has gone to bring us to himself (see John 3.16). Within Hellenistic culture and the pervasive ethics of the patron-client relationship (see comments on v 22 above and 6.4–6), the necessity of showing gratitude toward a benefactor was obvious. Recipients of a gift from a benefactor were indebted to **serve** him as he might require. In an even greater way, we are indebted to serve God with our lives, our minds, and all that is in us in response to the wonderful things he has provided for us. The kind of reciprocal service that is **acceptable** to God is that spiritual service that his people give him in lives of dedication (see Rom 12.1). The word "**serve**" here (Greek *latreuō*) is the word regularly used of the work of priests as they performed the worship of God (used in Heb 8.5; 13.10; and in the LXX). The language here is

[110] Ellingworth, *Epistle to the Hebrews*, 689–90.

metaphorical. While God's people in the Messiah are described with the language of priests, the priestly service they offer to God is in the form of personal purity, faithful endurance, praise, and deeds of love, as chapter 13 will spell out.[111] Any response to divine grace that is less than this service displays ingratitude and insults the giver, which results in loss of blessings and wrath. Nor should we serve God simply out of a cold sense of duty, as if such service were onerous and bothersome to us. Only the person who does not appreciate the gifts of God, and who values worldly pursuits above the things of heaven, would think in such a way. Instead, we are to serve him gladly, out of a deep sense of **reverence and awe**. These two terms are nearly synonymous. **Reverence** denotes a godly fear that issues in piety. The word can have the sense of "caution."[112] **Awe** also communicates the idea of fear in the presence of greatness, with a corresponding sense of respect. Both terms indicate that we may not trifle in our view of, or service to, God.

12.29 for our God is a consuming fire.

The last words of the last major exhortation are calculated and stern. Here the sermon reaches its formal conclusion. **For** connects this statement with the ideas of fearful respect in verse 28 and gives the reason such respect is necessary in dealing with God. After this statement the main part of the sermon effectively ends, and the words that are left ringing in the hearer's ears are **our God is a consuming**, destroying **fire**. The author wants his readers to be fully aware of the consequences if they should decide to quit the faith and become unbelievers again. The words are probably a quotation from Deuteronomy 4.24, although it is also possible to understand that these words summarize succinctly the message of many OT passages. In the context of Deuteronomy 4, Moses warned the new generation of Israelites "So watch yourselves, lest you forget the covenant of the Lord your God" (v 23 NASB). Unfaithfulness to the covenant manifests apathetic ingratitude to the one who has done so much to save us, and brings the destructive, fiery wrath of God. God referred to himself as "a consuming fire" also in Deuteronomy 9.3, where he spoke of how he would destroy the inhabitants of Canaan before the Israelites. In fact, the image of God as a **consuming fire** that burns all

[111] See Hutchens, "Christian Worship in Hebrews 12:28."

[112] LSJ 720.

in its path is quite common in the OT.[113] In ancient times, fires in a city or in the fields, once started, were almost impossible to extinguish.[114] In light of the background of this statement, it does not seem likely that this is primarily a reference to hell.[115] Instead, the imagery is of a cleansing fire, like when farmers burn a field. Complementary to the imagery of "shaking" in verses 26–28 above, it is an image of a coming (apocalyptic) destruction that results in renewal, one in which the unfaithful will not have a part. *Cf.* 2 Peter 3.12f.

[113] God as a consuming fire appears in Exod 24.17; Isa 29.6; 30.27, 30. See also Gen 19.24; Josh 7.25; Isa 5.24; 10.16ff; 26.11; 29.6; 30.27, 30; 66.15f; Jer 4.4; 21.14; Lam 4.11; Ezek 15.7; 20.47; 22.31; Amos 5.6; 7.4; Zeph 3.8.

[114] As an illustration, the famous fire in Rome in 64 AD burned for about a week. Of the city's fourteen districts, three were completely destroyed and seven more were mostly destroyed. Tacitus, *Annals* 15.40. There were also fires in Rome in 15, 27, 31, 36, 38, 53, 69, and 80 AD.

[115] Charles C. Bing, "Does Fire in Hebrews Refer to Hell?," *BibSac* 167 (2010): 342–57.

HEBREWS 13

Some commentators treat chapter 13 as a kind of appendix, thus implying that it has only secondary importance. However, far from being an unconnected and jumbled assortment of various exhortations and ideas, the chapter called the readers back to some of the main ideas of the sermon[1] and provided them with considerations for how they could manage the present crisis. In short, it provided them with a guide to how they could maintain their faith and their sanctification in times of trial.

The sermon proper ended in 12.29. Chapter 13 may be thought of as "concluding remarks," related to the sermon's exhortation but not strictly part of it. Before the author closed his remarks to his readers/hearers, he left them with some particular matters to consider and one last encouragement that draws on their connection with Jesus (vv 10–16). Although the things he commanded them in verses 1–9, 17–19 might at first seem to be unrelated, they have in common at least four things: 1) they are things they have demonstrated before (and therefore they have proven they can do them),[2] 2) they are things that express their sense of togetherness and their commitment to each other rather than a withdrawal from the group,[3] 3) that they are things that will help them to endure the hardships they were facing, either by way of things to pursue or things to avoid, and 4) they are things that people who are considered to be social "outsiders" typically have to be aware of as they are constantly viewed critically by the dominant, "insider" culture.[4] Even though the formal close of the sermon was on a frightening and negative note (12.29), the address ends on a more positive note.

---

[1] See Pavel Paluchník, "Let us Go Outside the Camp: Hebrews 13:13 and the Purpose of the Epistle," *Communio Viatorum* 63 (2021): 185–208.

[2] Lane, *Hebrews 9–13*, 509. Love, hospitality, association with prisoners, lack of concern for material possessions, and confidence all appear in their past behavior as described in 10.32–34, and listening to the word of their teachers was mentioned in 2.1ff.

[3] Lane, *Hebrews 9–13*, 515.

[4] See James W. Thompson, "Insider Ethics for Outsiders: Ethics for Aliens in Hebrews," *ResQ* 53 (2011): 207–19.

13.1 Let brotherly love continue.

It is often true that, whenever a NT author presents a list, the first thing on the list is the key item and serves as a summary of all the others. That seems to be true of the list of exhortations here as well, as brotherly love pervades every other consideration. *Cf.* Romans 13.8–10; 1 Thessalonians 4.9ff. The idea is also related to the overall presentation of the book. Jesus, our older brother in the family of God, loved us, so we ought to love him and the rest of God's family as well.[5] It is probably useless to try to differentiate sharply between the **brotherly love** of this verse and the love taught elsewhere in the NT.[6] The fact that a different word is used (here: *philadelphia*, also used in Rom 12.10; 1 Thes 4.9; 1 Pet 1.22; 2 Pet 1.7; otherwise *agapē*) matters little.[7] The choice of words here may have been dictated by the context's emphasis on mutual care (as opposed to general philanthropism). We learn the nature of this kind of love from Jesus himself, who left us an example of genuine care and concern, as well as sacrifice, for the good of others. True Christian love is an attitude we have towards each other, an undefeatable good will toward each other that prioritizes others over self and includes the manifestation of that attitude in word and in deed (1 John 3.17f; Jam 2.15).

The exhortation to love recalls 10.24. In times of hardship, the strength and encouragement of the group is needed all the more. The emotional strain of hardship can cause people to become bitter towards others in general, or at least make them aloof (Heb 10.24f). Such may have been the circumstances behind this exhortation, but exhortations to brotherly love are always timely. Genuine Christian love is not conditioned on our mood at the moment, the dangers of a situation, *etc.* We are to love each other when times are good and when times are hard, when it is easy to do so and when it is hard to do so. That is, it must **continue** the same regardless of the circumstances in which we find ourselves. True brotherly love encourages us to remain in God's family.

---

[5] Gray, "Brotherly Love and the High Priest Christology of Hebrews."

[6] See John 13.34; 15.12, 17; 1 Cor 14.1; Gal 5.13; Phil 2.2; Col 2.2; *etc.*

[7] In my opinion, the differences between the various Greek words for love have been greatly exaggerated in expositions of the NT teaching on this subject. In the overall context of the NT's presentation of divine love, the semantics remain the same regardless of the individual terms used.

13.2 Do not overlook hospitality, for some, without knowing it, have taken in angels.

One expression of brotherly love is kindness to fellow-Christians, even if we do not know them personally. The author's exhortation (**do not overlook**) does not necessarily imply that they had overlooked this important matter. It is simply a reminder that it must be part of their lives as Christians. **Hospitality** (Greek *philoxenia,* literally "friendship to strangers") was a special form of brotherly kindness (Rom 12.13) and was considered a virtue in Hellenistic society.[8] The Greeks long believed that the gods tested them by visiting them in the form of humans, and so kind treatment toward strangers pleased the gods (which in turn kept them from bringing disaster upon a place). The practice of showing kindness to strangers was specifically recommended by Greek and Roman philosophers and moralists. Although there were inns, they were normally not the kind of place where most people would have wanted to stay.[9] In such a culture, it was even more important for Christians, who were bound together by brotherly love, to make sure that they did not fail to demonstrate that love by **taking in** strangers[10] who needed their help. As with love (v 1), the focus here is on others (especially fellow-Christians).

Although it is clear what hospitality is, the identity of the strangers here is not so clear, nor is the reference to **some** people. Does "some" refer to past examples in the lives of people of faith, like Abraham who apparently hosted angels in Genesis 18? Or does "some" refer to Christians of the first century, whose cases were known to the author personally? Nothing in the immediate context helps us answer this question, but most commentators take the former view.

Concerning the strangers, they are called *angeloi,* but the precise meaning of that term here is the problem. There are two basic possibilities:

1) The word refers to those heavenly beings we call **angels**. This is the more common usage of the word in the NT. We have a few OT examples of people taking in angels as guests. Most think that Genesis 18 is primarily in view here, but see also Genesis 19 and Judges 6.11ff;

---

[8] See Donald Wayne Riddle, "Early Christian Hospitality: A Factor in the Gospel Transmission," *JBL* 57 (1938): 141–54, at 143.

[9] Moffatt, *Epistle to the Hebrews,* 224–25.

[10] The verb here (*zenizō*) is verbal form of the Greek word for "stranger" or "alien" (*zenos*) and means to receive a stranger into one's home.

13.2ff. This interpretation raises the question of why God would send angels to his people. There may be some suggestion that they are sent to comfort God's people (see Matt 4.11) or to render some kind of special aid.[11] Beyond this we can only speculate. The overall effect of the verse, if we adopt "angels" as the translation, would be that our hospitality sometimes does more good than we could possibly realize at the time. The verse does not say that God sends them as a test of his people's kindness or faithfulness.

2) The Greek word *angelos* generically means "messenger." Accordingly, some have noted that while angels are often messengers, they are not the only ones who are called messengers in the Bible.[12] Many early Christians went about preaching the word in an early persecution (Acts 8.4), and some Jewish Christians had been forced out of Rome under Claudius (Acts 18.2). In verse 23, the author sends greetings from some fellow-Christians who are "from Italy," possibly suggesting that they had left Italy. Some Christians probably had to leave their homes not knowing where they would stay from one night to the next. As such, like Abraham, they were strangers, exiles, and wanderers on the earth because of their faith in God. Similarly, Jesus said that taking in a fellow-Christian as a stranger is considered personal service to himself (Matt 25.35–40). For this reason, it has been suggested that the term should be translated "messengers" here, suggesting that Christians were likely to take other Christians into their homes without always knowing it.

13.3 As fellow prisoners, remember the prisoners who are being mistreated, as you yourselves also are in the body.

Some Christians were in prison at the time the letter was delivered. Whether the recipients of Hebrews knew these **prisoners** personally, or whether they simply knew of them, we do not know, nor do we know the author's relationship with them. Although the statement is vague, it would seem fit the conditions we know later in the first century. Imprisonment of Christians apparently became more common as their reputation for being troublemakers spread. How they were being **mistreated** is not stated, but imprisonment itself could be ill treatment enough. See on 10.34. When Christians were imprisoned, they especially counted

[11] Heb 1.14; see also Num 20.16; 2 Chron 32.21; Dan 3.28; 6.22; Acts 12.7ff.

[12] See Mal 3.1 = Matt 11.10; Luke 7.24; 9.52; Jam 2.25; Mal 2.7.

on the brotherly love of other Christians to provide things for them in such miserable places (*cf.* 2 Tim 1.16; 4.13).[13] Moreover, imprisonment was not a form of punishment in the Roman legal system. Prisons were for people who were awaiting trial, or who were awaiting execution. The author called upon his readers to put themselves in their brethren's place, as it were, and consider themselves **as fellow-prisoners**. The idea is not so much to imagine what prison life was like for their incarcerated brethren, but to cultivate that sense of spiritual solidarity in which what affects one affects all (Rom 12.15). Exactly how they were to **remember** these fellow-Christians is not stated. It could mean that they were to keep them in their prayers (see Col 4.18), or it could mean to visit them and care for them (Matt 25.36; 2 Tim 1.16; *cf.* Gal 2.10, where "remember" = "provide for"). Either of these would be manifestations of brotherly love. The phrase could also mean to think about their imprisonment and the faith it exhibited as something that would give courage (2 Tim 2.8; see v 7 below).

The last phrase of the verse, **as** (or since) **you yourselves also are in the body**, can be understood in two ways. The "body" could be a reference to the church (Eph 5.23; Col 1.18, 24), in which case the exhortation is that the members of the body are to have the same care for one another (*cf.* 1 Cor 12.25–27). The "body" could, however, refer to the flesh, to have a human body, with the sense that the readers knew from their own personal experience just what it was like to be mistreated by unbelievers since they too suffered ill-treatment against their bodies (*cf.* 10.32). This latter interpretation is more consistent with how the phrase is used in the Greek (*en sōmati*, 2 Cor 12.2f).

13.4 Marriage is to be respected by all,[14] and the bed is to be undefiled, for God will judge fornicators and adulterers.

The exhortations now move from those which bid us to look to others (vv 1–3), to those which warn us to keep ourselves from fleshly lusts (vv 4–6). A desire to please the flesh was what doomed the Israelites

[13] There are notices in ancient literature of Christians visiting their imprisoned brethren. Lucian, *Death of Peregrinus* 12; Aristides *Apology* 15; Tertullian, *To the Martyrs* 1–2; *Apology* 39.

[14] The Greek phrase (*en pasin*) can also mean "in all things" (*pasin* could be either masculine or neuter).

who came out of Egypt. The incident at Baal-peor (Num 25.1–3) is possibly in the background of the author's mind here. Those Israelites were more concerned about their immediate physical comfort than they were about their coming inheritance and rest with God. The author therefore mentions the kinds of things that are typical manifestations of the worldly, fleshly spirit that will eventually pull a person away from the faith. See Gal 5.16ff.

There are numerous warnings in the NT against fornication which are directed toward Christians.[15] It is the sin in which fleshly people typically engage. How much of a problem this was among the readers of Hebrews is impossible to say. It may well be that there was no problem at all and that the author is simply reminding them of what their conduct must continue to be. God has designed that the sexual union (here called **the bed**) of a man and woman is for the **marriage** relationship (1 Cor 7.2; Matt 5.32; 19.4–9). God himself created this relationship in the beginning, and it is just as much a part of God's design for the world as the sun and moon (Gen 2.24). Outside of that relationship, sexual union is fornication (generally) and adultery (when it involves a married person). The reference to marriage here makes it clear that the author was not referring to idolatry or worldliness in general, which is figuratively called fornication or adultery in the Bible (Matt 12.29; Mark 8.38; Jam 4.4; 2 Pet 2.14). Sexual infidelity was common in the ancient world, possibly more so among Greeks than Romans. In ancient Greek culture, it was assumed that a man would have both a wife (for bearing children) and a mistress (for sexual pleasure). Augustus outlawed adultery among Romans,[16] but this probably only had the effect of making the practice more discreet. However, even some pagans bemoaned the loss of morality that adultery signaled.[17] Christians ought to be known as people who neither condone nor practice fornication (Eph 5.3).

Respect (high regard and honor) for the sanctity of marriage keeps the sexual union pure (undefiled). This includes respect for one's own marriage as well as the marriage of others. Each husband is to love his

---

[15] See Acts 15.20; 1 Cor 5.1ff; 6.9, 13, 18; Gal 5.19ff; Eph 5.3, 5; Col 3.5; 1 Thes 4.3.

[16] In the *Julian Laws*, 18–17 BC.

[17] *Cf.* Horace *Odes* 3.6: "Our age, fertile in its wickedness, has first defiled the marriage bed, our offspring, and homes: disaster's stream has flowed from this source through the people and the fatherland." (A. S. Kline, "Horace: The Odes," 2003, <https://www.poetryintranslation.com/PITBR/Latin/Horacehome.php>).

own wife, and no one is to share "the bed" with another man's wife (1 Cor 7.2; Eph 5.28, 33); brotherly love demands no less. Fornication and adultery are not just sins against one's flesh (1 Cor 6.18), they are also the manifestation of a worldly and fleshly mind and heart (Matt 15.19) that really cares nothing for what God says. A lack of respect for God's design for marriage betrays a preference for the gratification of the flesh rather than pleasing God and is a step toward complete renunciation of Jesus. Conversely, having the proper attitude toward marriage is part of having a mind that is set on the things of God (Rom 8.6f).

As often in the NT, the word **judge** here has the sense of "condemn." Fornicators and adulterers demonstrate, by these sins, their true characters as people who live by the dictates of the flesh, people who are morally defiled and thus demonstrate their unholy characters (see 12.14). God, however, calls us to crucify the flesh to ourselves (Gal 5.24) and live instead according to his word. Those who reject God's word and make the flesh their master will lose their inheritance (see 12.16f) and receive God's condemnation. The fact that God will condemn fornicators and adulterers shows that the problem is not simply the social disruption that is caused when sexual infidelity is discovered.[18] It is immoral, and God will condemn those who practice it whether they ever get "caught" in this life or not.

13.5 Your way of life must not be greedy; be[19] content with what you have. For he has said: "In no way will I abandon you nor forsake you,"

Compared to modern America, the supply of goods was more limited in the ancient world. The original recipients of Hebrews may have been experiencing denials of material goods because of their Christian faith, causing them to feel marginalized and envious of those who had access to such goods, and possibly discouraging them from sharing whatever goods they had with others. If the opposition faced by the recipients of Hebrews included denial of goods, it is easy to see how greed could be fostered in these conditions. **Greed** is another characteristic that is typical of worldly people, and it is often mentioned in the same context with fornication (see Eph 5.3; Col 3.5; *cf.* 1 Cor 5.11) because it is a manifestation of the same desire for selfish pleasure and fleshly indulgence (see Eph 4.19).

---

[18] Koester, *Hebrews*, 566.

[19] The participle here is imperatival. Ellingworth, *Epistle to the Hebrews*, 699.

It is, in a sense, the opposite of love because greed is fueled by selfishness, and it can easily lead a person to reject God (1 Tim 6.10). "The man greedy for gain curses and renounces the Lord" (Psa 10.3 RSV). Greed is also mentioned as a reason the Israelites in the wilderness did not have faith (Num 11.4), and those people perished before reaching Canaan. It is not just a problem that rich people have. It can be just as much a problem among people who have lost their possessions (10.34) and who hope to regain the (false) sense of stability and security that comes with them. Also, greed can be divisive, since it is often accompanied by jealousy or coveting. Brotherly love instead demands that we use our goods to help others (see Eph 4.28), as the original readers had already done (10.33f).

As with fornication, the way to overcome greed is to change one's heart and mind, teaching it from the Scriptures to value God's way above the way of the flesh. In this particular case, there are two things the author puts before God's people. First, the mind must learn the virtue of contentment. The heart set on selfish acquisition is greedy, but the person who sees worldly things as temporary and corruptible at best, and therefore who does not value them so highly, will be **content with what** he **has**. Recall the example of Moses in 11.16; see also 1 Timothy 6.6–10. The temporary nature of worldly goods should keep us from setting our hopes and values on them (recall Heb 1.11; Luke 12.15ff). Second, we must trust the divine promise of care. The words "**In no way will I abandon you nor forsake you**" is not from a specific OT text but is a condensed and paraphrased version of a divine promise that is made several times in the OT (Deut 31.6, 8; Josh 1.5; *cf.* Gen 28.15; 1 Chron 28.20). It is possible that our author understood the speaker of these words (**he has said**) to be Jesus (see Matt 28.20; Acts 18.10), but in Hebrews it is more common for God to be the author of promises. The greedy person basically believes that his future welfare is up to himself; he does not believe that God will take care of him. The presence of greed among God's people thus betrays a concern for the physical over the spiritual and a refusal to trust in God's promises.

13.6 so that, being confident, it is possible for us to say, "The Lord is my helper, I will not be frightened; what can man do to me?"

The author adds another quotation that has to do not only with trust in God's promise of care, but also with the matter of fear. The words come from Psalm 118.6 and summarize the attitude of the person who relies on the Lord, unlike the greedy man who relies on himself. Like greed, **fear** of suffering at the hands of unbelievers is another manifestation of lack of faith in the divine promise of care. It is not clear if **the Lord** refers to Jesus (v 8) or God (v 4; the Son is called "Lord" in 1.10). The quotation works either way. On the one hand, Jesus is on our side, both as the one who is leading us to God (Heb 2.10) and as our sympathetic and merciful high priest who atones for our sins. On the other hand, Paul paraphrases the same verse in a similar context in Romans 8.31, where he emphasizes the unfailing nature of God's love for his people as grounds for confidence in our salvation. Either way, deity is our **helper**, and this should give us **confidence** that others will not be able to harm us.

Of course, our author is fully aware of the fact that some of God's people had suffered in their stand for God (Heb 11.35–38), and others would suffer as well. In this light, it is not likely that the author presented the words of the Psalm as if they were some kind of promise of immunity from all hardship. The Psalm speaks to a higher perspective, *viz.* that the rejection and abuse of the world cannot rob us of what God has promised. *Cf.* Romans 8.31–39. The contrast in the quotation is between the power of God and the relative powerlessness of other human beings (**man**). In the end, all that men can do is kill the body (Matt 10.28), but for a Christian who knows that God will raise the faithful dead and give them glory, the death of the body is not the ultimate concern. A classic example of the kind of confidence and courage described in this verse appears in the story of Daniel's friends, Daniel 3.16–18.

13.7 Remember your leaders, who spoke the word of God to you, and as you consider the outcome of their way of life, imitate their faith.

It is not possible to identify who these **leaders** were. The Greek word here (the verbal form of *hēgemōn*) is generic, so it is not possible to tell if they were apostles, elders, or evangelists.[20] Any of these could have **spoken God's word to** them. It is possible that they are the same people mentioned in 2.3–4, who were eyewitnesses of Jesus and who worked miracles among them. This would suggest that the leaders were apostles and could also possibly suggest that the Jewish Christians in or near

[20] *Cf. The Letter of Aristeas* 310, which mentions "the priests, and the elders of the translators and the Jewish community, and the leaders of the people."

Jerusalem were the original recipients of the letter (see Introduction). However, we know very little about the movements of most of the apostles, so it is possible that the language here could just as easily describe Jewish Christians in other places. At any rate, leadership in the church belongs to those who handle the word (see Eph 4.11f). Some think that the language about **the outcome of their lives** implies that these leaders were not only dead when the epistle was written, but that they had been martyred. While this is possible, the verse falls short of a clear implication to this effect. In the context it could mean that the readers are urged to consider past examples of people known to them whose lives constituted clear examples of God's faithfulness to his promise of care (v 6). In the context (with vv 17 and 24), however, there is a general sense that the leaders referred to in this verse were gone.

Whatever had happened to their leaders, it is their example of **faith** that the author wished them to **consider** with care and to **imitate**. In the context of Hebrews, their faith must first mean their endurance because of their trust in God. Any, or all, of these things are expressions of one's basic trust in God and his word. Their leaders, then, had also become part of the "great cloud of witnesses" who stand to encourage them to persevere. Whatever the specific outcome of their lives was, the author seems to suggest that they were worthy examples of what it means to live "by faith," and they stood as additional proof that those who remain faithful to God will inherit the blessings God has promised to his people.

This verse touches on what is the essence of the Biblical model of leadership. Leaders of God's people need to be persons who are filled up with God's word, who have Jesus living in them, and who are therefore able not only to teach the way of Christ to others but also to demonstrate, by their way of life, what it means to be a Christian. For a true leader, teaching in word is of little use without the proper life to accompany it. A leader is to be a person for whom it is obvious that his faith in God and Jesus determines all else about him (1 Tim 4.12), one to whom others can look and imitate his faith (1 Cor 11.1; 2 Thes 3.9; *cf.* 1 Thes 1.6f; 2.14). Other skills, as valuable as they might be in inter-human relationships, can never take the place of such spiritual qualities. A man is fit to lead God's people only to the extent that he is personally full of God's word in his mind, heart, character, and will.

13.8 Jesus Christ is the same yesterday, today, and forever.

This statement might at first seem random, if not out of place, in this context. However, it is anything but random. The author has just mentioned the outcome of the lives of their faithful leaders. The statement here presents Jesus as the crowning example of such faithful leadership (much like 12.1–3 crowns chapter 11), as well as provides the assurance, or guarantee, for that outcome. "**The same**" is another way of speaking about the unwavering faithfulness of Christ (*cf.* 10.23), especially to his people. In proclaiming and living the "word of God" (v 7), their former leaders were demonstrating their well-placed faith in Jesus, and the readers needed to do likewise.[21] The statement also provides another connection with the sermon's opening, where Jesus was acknowledged to be **the same** in 1.12 (quoting Psa 102). This kind of language is used of God elsewhere in the Bible. See Malachi 3.6; James 1.17; Revelation 4.8. In this way, then, Jesus is again presented as sharing in divine attributes (in this case, immutability). The use of both his human name (**Jesus**) and his exalted title (**Christ**) recalls that he is the one who came to earth (Heb 2, quoting Psa 8) and then took his place at God's right hand in fulfillment of Psalm 110, to intercede for us. There he stands perpetually (recall Psa 110.4 "the Lord has sworn and will not change his mind") as a faithful high priest of God on our behalf. With such constantly-available access to God, we should resolve not to be distracted by the cares of life and to draw close to God (see 4.14–16). Also, the unchangeable nature of our Lord Jesus Christ gives us confidence in God's faithfulness to his promises. All that God has done for man is summed up in him (Eph 1.10). The unchanging nature of Jesus thus demonstrates the reliability of God and the promise of joining him in glory.

13.9 Do not be carried away by various and strange teachings, for it is good for the heart to be strengthened by grace, not by foods by which those who walk in them have not been benefited.

In contrast to the examples of faithfulness they knew in their leaders and in Jesus, there was the threat of false teachings that would **carry** them **away**. The openness to others that characterizes Christian love must be tempered with a watchful spirit, lest we become receptive to

---

[21] Cockerill, *Epistle to the Hebrews*, 690–91.

things that are false.[22] The word (Greek *parapherō*) is used literally of clouds that are blown by the wind, of things that are moved by the force of water, or things that turned in the wrong direction. When used figuratively (as here), the word means to be misled, to be led astray.[23] *Cf.* "drift away" in 2.1. The NT warns about false teaching.[24] While the idea of a religious idea being "false" is not agreeable to modern tastes, the view of the NT is that there is one truth of the gospel, one faith (Eph 4.5) in which Christians must remain.[25] Other (**various**; the word *poikilos* can have the sense of "ambiguous, crafty, sly, deceitful"[26]) **teachings** are not the truth but only inferior, powerless, **strange** (foreign, coming from outside), and counterfeit (compared to the truth of the gospel). Of course, the assumption that makes this exhortation work is that Christians know what the gospel is in the first place. People who do not know the truth are hardly in a position to judge whether or not they have been carried away from it (recall the warning of Heb 5.11–14). For this reason, it behooves all Christians to learn and understand the teaching of the NT as accurately as possible.

It is not possible to identify with precision the false teachings the author may have had in mind here. From the generic tone of his language, some have suggested that no specific opponent or threat was in mind.[27] Cockerill suggests that they were teachings that "persisted in denying the obsolescence of the old despite the coming of Christ."[28] The context of Hebrews itself could suggest that the doctrines the author had in mind here were teachings that reinforced the idea that salvation was possible only when the recipients of Hebrews renounced Christianity and remained loyal to non-Christian Jewish beliefs and practices. It seems clear that the teachings are related to the food mentioned below. "It is most likely, therefore, that the author is warning the audience against attaching saving significance to observation of the Mosaic law. On this interpretation, 'food' does not refer to any specific laws or practices but, by

---

[22] *Cf.* 2 John 10f, where false teachers had apparently learned to take unfair advantage of Christian hospitality in order to spread their doctrines.

[23] BDAG 772; LSJ 1329.

[24] See Eph 4.14; Col 2.22; 1 Tim 1.3; 4.1; 6.3; 2 Tim 4.3ff; 2 Pet 2.1.

[25] Acts 6.7; 14.22; 1 Cor 16.13; Phil 1.27; Col 1.23; 1 Tim 4.1; 6.10, 21; Tit 1.13 Jude 3; *etc.*

[26] BDAG 842.

[27] Grindheim, *Letter to the Hebrews*, 678–79.

[28] Cockerill, *Epistle to the Hebrews*, 693.

synecdoche, to the law as a whole."[29] We could possibly advance this one step further and suggest that the "teachings" could have been repeated appeals by Jewish friends and family to the effect that Christians can be saved only when they maintained their former (non-Christian) way of life that included fellowship meals with other Jews.

All false teaching has at least this much in common, that it is designed to cater to human desires or human ideas of what is right and wrong. Even those teachings that impose stricter regulations on a Christian's life than the gospel itself are designed to satisfy the inventors' ideas of what a good religion ought to be, to make the gospel conform to their notions of what is right. Such doctrines are often driven by people who only want a sense of control over others (2 Cor 11.20). Of course, most false teaching looses what God has bound and attempts to make indulgence of the flesh or physical comfort acceptable (see Gal 6.12; 2 Pet 2.18f). Paul warned the Christians in Rome concerning those who did not follow sound doctrine because they were "slaves, not of our Lord Christ but of their own appetites" (Rom 16.18). In this way, then, the warning about false teachings is in the same class as the warning about fornication (v 4) and greed (v 5). All of them have in common that they exhibit a desire to please the flesh rather than trust in God.

The reference to **food** here can be taken in a few different ways:

1) If taken literally, then some kind of doctrine involving food is possibly in view. There were disputes over "eating meat" in churches where Jewish and Gentile Christians met together (Rom 14; 1 Cor 8). We mostly hear about the issue of food in Paul's writings, since his work among the Gentiles tended to provoke it. However, it does not seem likely that such doctrines would have been troublesome to a group of Jewish Christians like the readers of Hebrews who, as far as we know, would have continued to follow their traditional (cultural) dietary practices. It has been suggested that there may have been some kind of ascetic teaching that prohibited eating as an indulgence of the flesh,[30] but this too seems unlikely since Jews already followed a diet that excluded the eating of certain things.[31] Some have suggested that the text here addressed a temptation to partic-

[29] Grindheim, *Letter to the Hebrews*, 677.

[30] We are told enough about such doctrines in NT times to inform us that they existed, but we know little about their actual content. See 1 Tim 4.3; Col 2.16; 1 Cor 8.8.

[31] Helmut Koester, "'Outside the Camp': Hebrews 13.9–14," *HTR* 55 (1962): 299–315, at 304.

ipate in pagan meals,[32] but it is hard to imagine how a Jew would have been convinced that such meals could strengthen the heart. There may have been some other doctrine about food of which we simply have no knowledge, but this direction seems unlikely to shed light on this passage.

2) Koester thinks that the expression is parallel to the statement about various doctrines in the first part of the verse. In this way, then, strange doctrines themselves are "food" that does not nourish or benefit those who walk in them.[33] Accordingly, Koester does not limit the doctrines here to Jewish views. The author spoke of receiving Christian teachings in terms of "eating" in 5.11–14, and the author uses it again in verses 10ff below, so the imagery is not foreign to Hebrews. Similarly, Jesus spoke of the "leaven" of the scribes and Pharisees, meaning their teaching (Matt 16.6–12).

3) Thompson interprets the food as a reference to what is fleshly and worldly (*cf.* 9.10, and also 12.16, where Esau was distracted by "food"). The point, as he sees it, is that "the church will not find its stability in any earthly assurances."[34]

4) Some connect the "food" of this verse with ancient social notions of inclusion and exclusion in verses 10–14. Talk of insiders and outsiders, or inclusion and rejection, suggests the teachings in question here are specifically Jewish. The difference between those who identified themselves with God's people through the Law and those who did not was maintained, in part, through control of the company with which one ate. Jews appealed to Psalm 104.14f to declare all meals as a means of fellowship with God.[35] Thus meals in Judaism served to indicate who was accepted and who was not; they ate with each other[36] but not with "outsiders."[37]

---

[32] Such as Michael Wade Martin and Jason A. Whitlark, "Strengthened by Grace and Not by Foods: Reconsidering the Literary, Theological, and Social Context of Hebrews 13:7–14," *NovT* 65 (2012): 350–80; Moffatt, *Epistle to the Hebrews*, 233.

[33] Koester, *Hebrews*, 560, 567–68.

[34] James W. Thompson, "Outside the Camp: A Study of Heb 13:9–14," *CBQ* 40 (1978): 53–63, at 58.

[35] As reflected in the regular benediction pronounced before meals (*m. Berakhot* 6.1–3), taken from the language of Psa 104.14f. Lane, *Hebrews 9–13*, 534; see also Koester, *Hebrews*, 561.

[36] Josephus attests that this was common throughout the Roman world, *Antiquities* 14.214.

[37] Note Peter's practice, in Gal 2.11–13, of not eating with those whom he (mistakenly) thought were not in his fellowship. Jesus was often criticized for the company he kept at meals. Matt 9.11; Mark 14.18; Luke 15.2; *cf.* 1 Cor 5.11. See also Lane, *Hebrews 9–13*, 534.

In this approach, the statement about "**walking**" in "**food**" is understood as a general reference to those who followed the regulations of the Law of Moses (the reference to the "tabernacle" in v 10 seems to confirm this) in the belief that it kept them within the group of God's chosen people, and in particular refers to the practice of table fellowship. On this view, then, the recipients of Hebrews, because of their faith in Jesus, were being excluded from meals with other (unbelieving) Jews. This exclusion was troubling to them, because it meant that they were being rejected from the only culture they had ever known, the culture that gave them their sense of identity.[38] This was probably a more powerful force in the ancient Mediterranean world than it is in ours today. The author has already noted that the Mosaical system was characterized by "food and drink and various washings, regulations for the body" (9.10), so he could say here that those who participated in them are **not benefited** by those things (*cf.* 4.2). In this context, it takes on the added sense that such things do not identify them as the true people of God.

If this fourth interpretation is the correct approach (and I think it is), then the "strange teachings" are probably assertions concerning the true effectiveness of the Mosaical system in general, coupled with an exclusion from meals for those who did not accept them (*i.e.*, Christians). As noted in the Introduction, the recipients of Hebrews were not Jews who had left Judaism and were contemplating "returning," but were Jews who had learned to place a different value, or interpretation, on the things of Judaism in light of the work of Jesus of Nazareth, whom they believed to be the Messiah of Israel. However, the rejection which this brought, along with the sense of disorientation it brought (and probably other factors as well), was causing some of the readers to rethink their loyalty toward Christ for the social cost they had paid and were still paying.

For Christians, there are some things that are spiritually beneficial and some things that clearly are not. Here, teachings that reinforced one's pre-Christian social ties and a sense of belonging seem especially in view as fitting in the latter category. Those who follow (**walk in**) such strange teachings are **not benefited** by them even if those teachings provide them with a valuable sense of identity and acceptance. Indeed, they are usually seriously harmed (1 Tim 1.18–20; 6.21; 2 Tim 2.18; 2 Pet

[38] There are some verbal parallels with Psa 69. Adam W. Day, "Bearing the Reproach of Christ: The Background of Psalm 68 (LXX) in Hebrews 13:9–16," *Presb* 44 (2018): 126–41.

2.1–3) because false teaching, by its nature, demands that one deny the one faith of Jesus Christ. The reference here to the **heart** recalls again the warning of Psalm 95 and the Israelites who always went astray in their hearts, and the warning of Hebrews 4.12 to make sure that an evil, unbelieving heart does not form within a Christian. While indulgence in the values and activities of unbelievers may give some a cherished sense of belonging and being "in," these things do nothing to **strengthen** the heart of a Christian toward God. Often, instead, they only weaken a Christian's heart and encourage him or her to turn away from God and find comfort in acceptance by unbelievers. Only the truth of God, delivered by his **grace** and which promises us good things to come, can establish or **strengthen** the heart toward God as it ought to be (2 Thes 2.16f). Implicit in the author's words here is the idea that a Christian must make a fundamental choice as to where he or she will find their identity: with the people of God, or outside of them.

13.10 We have an altar from which those who serve the tabernacle have no right to eat.

The metaphor of eating in the previous verse gives rise to the sermon's last comparison between the old and the new (13.10–16[39]) and reaffirms the perspective of a people whose true home does not lie within any earthly society, but in heaven. In chapters 9–10 the author contrasted the old, Mosaical sacrificial system with the perfect sacrifice for sin in the new system. If we understand the "doctrines" of verse 9 to be specifically Jewish teachings tied to table fellowship, then the roots of what would eventually become known as "the divide" between Judaism and Christianity can be seen here. This passage is written from the perspective of Jewish Christians who had been shunned and rejected by their earthly families and friends because they were Christians, and who felt the pain of such dissociation. Family ties were strong in ancient Jewish culture, and rejection by one's own family was a difficult burden to bear. A sense of belonging to a legitimate group was important in ancient culture. The author gave his readers a way to think about it that inverted it. Rather than seeing themselves negatively as "outsiders" from their families and their culture, the author gave them a way to see themselves as insiders of

[39] The section is further identified as a unit by its inverse parallel structure. See Lane, *Hebrews 9–13*, 503.

the new order, and to see unbelievers as the outsiders. However, the perspective of being an "outsider" to the world is still useful for Christians, and our author expounds upon it as well in verses 11–14.

Nothing in the context suggests or warrants that the language of "eating" refers to the Lord's Supper, much less any kind of sacramental interpretation of the Lord's Supper which says that it is the means by which we receive the forgiveness of sins by grace. In fact, such an interpretation runs counter to what this passage says, with its denial of the idea that food can strengthen the heart. The imagery comes instead from the tabernacle and its sacrifices. Our author uses the word **tabernacle** here, as he has throughout the sermon, as a metaphor for the rituals of Judaism under the "first covenant" (Heb 8.7). He spoke of this "tabernacle" in the present tense (the priests **who serve the tabernacle**), but this does not necessarily imply that the Jerusalem temple had not yet been destroyed. Instead, the present tense, as elsewhere in Hebrews, simply describes what is normally true from the perspective of the "tabernacle."

Generally, in the OT sacrifices except the burnt offering, part of the sacrificial animal was given to God on the **altar** of sacrifice, and other parts were for the priests.[40] Laymen generally could not participate in the holy meals (Exod 29.32f; Lev 22.7, 10–13); only the holy priests were allowed **to eat from** the **altar**. It is also important to remember that the meal represented the fellowship of God with his people. The author of Hebrews saw in the sacrificial procedure a type of the distinction that would exist in the Messianic age between believers and unbelievers. He inverted the OT distinction between priests and laymen, between insiders and outsiders, to the advantage of his readers. If anyone is currently shut out from "eating" and its benefits, it is unbelievers. It is Christians who are the true insiders. In this way, then, Christians become the priests of the new covenant (see v 15 below), and they alone have the **right**[41] of fellowship with God. Those who do not believe in Jesus have no access to nor fellowship with God, for that comes through Jesus alone. He himself, his own body, was the sacrifice that was offered for our sins, and in a spiritual sense every Christian partakes of him. See John 6.53ff (again, this is not a reference to the Lord's Supper). He was offered on a different

---

[40] In the case of the peace offering, the meat that did not go to God was split between the priest and the offeror.

[41] The same Greek word (*exousia*) can mean "authority" or "power."

"altar"—whether it was a heavenly altar, or the cross, the author does not say. Those who refuse to come to that altar by refusing to accept Jesus cannot partake of the fellowship (**the right to eat**) with God which it provides. As in chapter 12, the author was trying here to adjust the perspective by which they were viewing their lives. These Christians were being excluded from meals with family and other Jews, making them feel rejected and identifying them as outsiders. The author of Hebrews was saying, in effect, "It is not you who are the outsiders, but them. It is not that you cannot 'eat' with them, but they cannot 'eat' with you."

13.11 As for the animals whose blood is brought as a sacrifice for sin into the most holy place by the high priest, the bodies of these animals are burned outside the camp.

The inversion of the priest-laymen exclusion in the previous verse might be of spiritual comfort, but it did not change the fact that many Jewish Christians were rejected by their families and friends, or by the world at large, when they took up faith in Jesus. To this our author notes that such is the way of Jesus Christ, who fulfills the pattern of the OT **sin** offering (**a sacrifice for sin**). The mention of the **most holy place** and the **high priest** here signals that the author had the Day of Atonement procedure in mind (as he usually does throughout the sermon). The priest sprinkled the animal's blood in front of the ark of the covenant (Lev 16.15). Then the sweetest and innermost parts of the victim were burned on the altar, and the rest of the body was taken outside the camp and burned (Lev 16.25, 27).

The sin offering was the one used on the Day of Atonement (Lev 16.27), and the sacrifice of Jesus was implicitly compared to this sin offering in Hebrews 9–10. Here that comparison is made more explicit. The vertical dimension of the work of Christ in chapters 9–10 also has implications on the horizontal level in the lives of the original readers.[42] As in chapters 9–10, the author of Hebrews saw that Jesus was the fulfillment of the ritual of the Day of Atonement. The fact that the **bodies** of these sacrificial animals were **burned** has no direct counterpart to how Jesus' body was treated after his death. It is the removal of the

---

[42] Peter Walker, "Jerusalem in Hebrews 13:9–14 and the Dating of the Epistle," *TynBul* 45 (1994): 39–71, at 42 (although I do not agree with his conclusion that this text necessarily dates Hebrews to before 70 AD).

sacrificial goat to **outside the camp** that is the focus here. The author of Hebrews was specifically picking up on the explicit language of "outside" in Leviticus 16.27 and reading it as a typological pattern that now operated in the situation of his readers.

13.12 Wherefore also Jesus, that he might sanctify the people through his own blood, suffered outside the gate.

As in chapters 9–10, our author saw the work of **Jesus** in this ritual. However, whereas there the focus was on Jesus the priest and the sacrificial victim, here the focus is on Jesus the rejected one whose body was taken outside the city. The comparison lies in the fact that the dead body of a sacrificial animal of a sin offering could not abide within the camp of God's people. Our author saw in this ritual a preview of the rejection of Jesus. In his work of bearing the sins of God's people as the perfect and final sacrificial victim, he was sent out of the camp as it were, rejected by unbelievers who wanted nothing to do with him and gave him no place in their city (*cf.* Matt 21.38f *et par*). Just as the sin offering was taken outside the camp, so the sacrificial body of Jesus was taken outside the city gates (v 12).[43] While Jesus literally **suffered** and died on the cross **outside the** city **gate** of Jerusalem (John 19.20), it is the sociological significance of that fact that is in view here, as the repeated term "outside" suggests rejection.[44] It is worth noting that if Jesus had not really, historically died outside of the city of Jerusalem, the author's argument here would be wholly fallacious. It is the historicity of the death of Jesus, and the fact that it happened outside the city, that makes the typology work.

Those who press the typology too far will quickly become confused. Technically, the animals used on the Day of Atonement died inside the camp, and their dead bodies were then taken outside after the ritual was

---

[43] The Jews saw the walls of Jerusalem as serving the same function as the boundaries of the mobile camp of Israel in the wilderness. Both delineated holy space from defiled space. See references in Lane, *Hebrews 9–13*, 542. Therefore, the author of Hebrews can switch easily from "the camp" to the city; both represent the same thing.

[44] The author is not necessarily saying that crucifixion was done outside of the city for this reason. The Romans crucified criminals along public roads or in designated places outside of a city because there the public "message" conveyed by crucifixion would have the most exposure (Quintilian *Declamations* 274; Josephus *Jewish War* 5.289). The city of Rome had such a place, called the Sessorium (see Tacitus, *Annals* 15.60.1). Also, in Jerusalem (as in most ancient cities), dead bodies were not allowed inside the city, so executions were performed outside the walls. See Koester, *Hebrews*, 570.

finished. However, the typology does not lie in the sequence, but in the connections, in the correspondences. It is the fact that the sacrificial animal ended up outside the camp that is significant. The sanctification (forgiveness, which restored their holiness) of Israel on the Day of Atonement required the blood of an animal whose body was taken outside the camp. In the same way, Jesus suffered the rejection of his fellow-countrymen in his work of sanctifying God's **people through his own blood** (see comments on 9.12). On sanctification, see on 12.10, 14.

13.13 So let us go out to him outside the camp, bearing his reproach.

Joining Jesus, being with him, in heaven has been an important theme in the sermon (2.10; 6.20; 10.22; 12.2). That same logic is now applied to the earthly lives of the first readers: their rightful place is where he "is" in terms of social location. Like Abraham who "went out" (11.8), we are called to leave behind, if necessary, the things that once defined us in order to grab hold of a new identity that is bound up with the savior we follow, and that includes taking on the **reproach** (insult, disgrace; thus rejection) he bore. Recall that death by crucifixion was not just painful, it was shameful, so the call to bear his reproach is essentially the call to take up one's own cross. Some have suggested that the incident of the golden calf may also be in the background here. On that occasion Israel had rejected God in favor of something else (of their own making), and God's presence then moved "outside the camp" (Exod 33.7f). This suggests that unbelieving Jews who had rejected Jesus had repeated their forefathers' mistake of rejecting God, and now God was not to be found with them, but in a "place" outside of their gatherings.[45]

We get a sense here of the stigma that was associated with the gospel in the first century. Jesus died the death that was reserved for the worst criminals and was socially rejected by both the Romans and his own people. The call to follow Jesus thus sounded like a call to follow a condemned criminal who was deemed unworthy to be part of his own society.[46] We should also

---

[45] Lane, *Hebrews 9–13*, 543–44; Bruce, *Epistle to the Hebrews*, 403; Ellingworth, *Epistle to the Hebrews*, 714.

[46] The charge appears in Minucius Felix, *Octavius* 29; Cyril, *On the Words Crucified and Buried* 4; Origen, *Contra Celsus* 2.44; the Roman historian Tacitus felt compelled to mention that Jesus had been executed, *Annals* 15.44.3. It should be noted, however, that this would have typically been the view of the elite, but members of lower social classes might not necessarily have thought this way. Some philosophers even acknowledged that the best

realize that, to the ancients, religion and society went hand-in-hand. Each society or culture had its own distinctive religion that had developed over hundreds of years. Christians, however, appeared to have violated this ancient social bond, which only made them look more like rebels.[47] Furthermore, by the middle of the first century, Christians had a general reputation for being troublemakers (Acts 17.6; 28.22). From these facts we begin to understand how hard it must have been for some Christians to maintain their loyalty to (their confession of) Jesus, because it entailed sharing the scorn, contempt, and **reproach** that was associated with Jesus himself. The author offered no apologies for this. The social reality for Christians is bound up in the fact that the world knew neither God nor the truth (1 Cor 1–2), and so it should not surprise us that the world cannot abide someone like Jesus or those who follow him. Rather than explain the innocence of Jesus or take any other such course, the author simply exhorts us to follow Jesus **outside the camp. Camp** here has the same symbolic connotation as "food" in verse 9 and "tabernacle" in verse 10—all of these terms suggest the temporary, earthly, and socio-cultural nature of what Judaism had to offer. Alternately, it suggests the unbelieving, rebellious world in general.[48] Leaving it behind meant sharing in the social rejection Jesus suffered. "All who desire to live godly in Christ Jesus will be persecuted" (2 Tim 3.12). Jesus said that his followers would need to take up their crosses and follow him (Matt 16.24), and following him will lead us out of the world's favor. As people of faith, however, we will gladly leave the world behind (like Abraham and Moses) in order to gain a better home.

If a specifically Jewish teaching, coupled with exclusion from meals, was the problem, then the author, in giving this instruction, was basically telling his Jewish Christian readers that a break from Judaism was probably inevitable[49] as long as unbelieving Jews were making belief in the

---

people suffer as if they were wicked, because they are not appreciated by others. For example, Plato opined that "They will tell you that the just man who is thought unjust will be scourged, racked, bound—will have his eyes burnt out; and, at last, after suffering every kind of evil, he will be impaled" (*Republic* 2.5 (=361e), *The Republic of Plato Translated into English*, trans. Benjamin Jowett, 3rd ed. (Oxford: Oxford University Press, 1927)). See also Chapman, *Ancient Jewish and Christian Perceptions of Crucifixion*, 213–28.

[47] Robert Louis Wilken, *The Christians as the Romans Saw Them*, 2nd ed. (New Haven: Yale University Press, 1984), 124–25.

[48] Koester, *Hebrews*, 571.

[49] Walker, "Jerusalem in Hebrews 13:9–14 and the Dating of the Epistle," 42; Young, " 'Bearing His Reproach' (Heb 13.9–14)," 255–60.

Levitical sacrifices a condition for inclusion within the culture. However, the scenario could also be interpreted as the same kind of "leaving the world behind" as was exemplified in Abraham and Moses.[50] Either way, while Christianity can exist within almost any culture, it is not compatible with any or all religious beliefs that a culture may hold as part of its collective identity. If a Christian is forced to decide between maintaining a respectable place within one's culture and compromising his faith in Jesus on the one hand, or turning his back on his culture to remain true to Jesus on the other hand, his faith compels him or her to take a stand with Jesus. This seems to be the situation that faced the original readers of Hebrews.

13.14 For we do not have here an abiding city, but we seek the city that is coming.

To leave one's place entails going to another, and that logic brings the author to note that going "outside" of the social acceptance of the world means that we have gone to find our place somewhere else, somewhere not of this world. C. S. Lewis famously said, "If we find ourselves with a desire that nothing in this world can satisfy, the most probable explanation is that we were made for another world."[51] We might modify that to fit the context here: "If we find that we have no acceptance in this world, it means that our true home lies in another world." Leaving the temporary camp will bring one to the eternal city. As with everything else in Hebrews, the picture is that we have left the earthly in favor of that which is better and heavenly. Because their faith enables them to "see" what God has prepared for the faithful (Heb 11.13, 16; 12.22), because they trust God's faithfulness to his promises, and because they value heavenly and eternal (abiding) things more than physical comfort, Christians are perfectly willing to sacrifice company and approval here, in this world, for a place in a lasting city that is coming, the heavenly Jerusalem (12.22) whose gates we are approaching. The fact that it is "coming" means that we must wait for its arrival with the eagerness[52] and perseverance that characterizes true faith.

---

[50] Koester, *Hebrews*, 571.

[51] C. S. Lewis, *Mere Christianity* (1952, repr., New York: HarperCollins, 2001), 136–37.

[52] This is the sense of the word "seek" (Greek *epizēteō*) in this verse. We do not seek for heaven in the sense that we do not know where it is, but in the sense that we are eagerly "looking" ahead for its appearing and that we have a strong desire for it. BDAG 371.

For the significance of "**city**," see comments on 12.23. Christians may be excluded from the rolls of earthly associations, but they belong to a higher order, and their citizenship lies in a superior city. This realization is meant to put into proper perspective the readers' rejection from earthly relationships because of their faith in Jesus, and to renew the encouragement to see themselves as strangers and foreigners in this world, like people of faith in times past (Heb 11). In this light, the loss of earthly relationships and acceptance (the very thing they lamented, and which constituted their "reproach") turns out to be a good thing, for it brings them to something better.

It is tempting to see in this verse evidence that the epistle was addressed to Jewish Christians in the vicinity of Jerusalem, for Jerusalem was *the* city of Judaism, and in no place would a sense of alienation for Christians have been stronger than there. Jewish Christians who felt unwelcome in Jerusalem because of their faith in Jesus would have identified strongly with this verse's talk of not having an earthly city, *i.e.* not having status in it. They would have been treated like heretics and apostates from Judaism, like foreigners.[53] Besides, Jerusalem was the place where Jesus died "outside the city gate" (v 12). However, the verse probably falls short of providing such evidence. The fact is that Jewish Christians would have felt like castaways in just about any city in which there were unbelieving Jews who refused their company. Jews who lived abroad (*i.e.*, in the *diaspora*) still identified Jerusalem as their ancestral home city, so the imagery would have been powerful to them as well.

13.15 Through him, then, let us offer up continually a sacrifice of praise to God, that is, the fruit of lips that confess[54] his name,

---

[53] Young, " 'Bearing His Reproach' (Heb 13.9–14)," 257–58.

[54] Many English translations have "give thanks to his name." The Greek word here (*homologeō*) normally means to acknowledge, to agree. It can mean "to praise" in the extended sense that we acknowledge God's goodness. A compound form of this word, *exomologeō*, is frequently used in the Psalms and means "praise." Some think that *homologeō* here means "praise" as well, because of the context, the Greek construction, and because the language of the verse is drawn generally from the psalms (Lane, *Hebrews 9–13*, 551). However, since "confession" is such an important idea in Hebrews (3.1; 4.14; 10.23; 11.13), it is possible that the author chose this term deliberately instead of *exomologeō*, although it still calls to mind the similar term from the psalms.

Verses 15–16 stand in parallel to each other.[55] The author has hinted before that every believer in Jesus is like a priest in the new covenant (see also 1 Pet 2.5) and can **offer up** sacrifice to God (see comments on 12.28). We do not offer our priestly service to God independently, however, but **through him** (Jesus, from v 12), the high priest who, although rejected by men, has opened the way for our access to the Father. The sacrifice which Christians offer is not something external to them or earthly (like an animal), but the **praise** that comes from their hearts. The scene recalls 2.12, where Jesus joins his brethren in praise to God. It is here called **the fruit of lips**, since worship is not just something we think or feel within us but is also something that we express outwardly. There is an echo of Psalm 63.5 here.[56] The praises that we offer to God in prayers and in songs in public worship assemblies (Eph 5.19; Col 3.16) are included in this, but individual expressions of praise are certainly part of it as well (Acts 16.25 "hymns of praise"). Of course, true Biblical praise is a combination of both the inward and the outward elements. Simply singing or saying words to God out of a sense of duty or ritual is not what the author, or any Biblical writer, has in mind concerning true worship. The praise that comes out of the lips must reflect gratitude and love within the heart, else the worship is meaningless (Matt 15.8).

When we praise God, we **confess his name**. A **name** in Biblical thought is not simply the tag by which we distinguish one person from another but represents the person himself. Biblical names often summarized or described the people who wore them (see comments on 1.4). This is even more true of God, whose names reveal and describe who he is (Exod 3.15; 6.3; 15.3; Isa 42.8; Jer 16.21; *etc.*). **Confessing** includes affirming our belief in him, but all expressions of praise, by their nature, are open acknowledgements of God and his greatness and articulations of commitment (see 3.1). See Acts 2.47. Holding on to our confession is, in a sense, the exhortation of Hebrews (4.14; 10.23; *cf.* 11.13).

The point of the verse is the same as 4.14–16 and 10.19–25. Since we belong to a better system in which we can get closer to God than was possible before, we ought to spend our time doing that very thing, approaching God **continually** with our spiritual sacrifices and enjoying the fellow-

[55] That the verses are meant to be read together is indicated by their inverse parallel structure: sacrifice ... fruit of lips ... doing good and sharing ... sacrifices. Lane, *Hebrews 9–13*, 504.

[56] *Cf.* also Hos 14.3 LXX; Psa 40.9; 50.14, 23; 51.15; 107.22.

ship we can have with him. Our gathering together for public worship is part of this continual expression of praise, but in no way exhausts it.

13.16 but do not overlook doing good and sharing, for God is pleased by such sacrifices.

Another way in which we praise God and confess (acknowledge) our association with him, and offer him priestly service, is by well-doing and sharing. The term **doing good** sometimes appears in contexts of helping others (Acts 10.38; Gal 6.9). That is, it is not general goodness that is in view, but expressions of Christian love in giving ourselves and possessions to help others (v 1). The term's appearance along with **sharing**, and in a context of making sacrifices, confirms that this is the meaning here as well. Sharing can mean "fellowship" in a spiritual, religious sense (sharing a common faith), or sharing in someone's experiences (10.33), but the term is also used of sharing material things (Rom 15.26; 2 Cor 8.4; 9.13; Phil 1.5). In the case of Christians, sharing our goods with brethren who are in need is an outward reflection of the sharing in the faith that we continually experience. See Romans 15.27. A willingness to share our material goods with each other is important because it is a manifestation of a selfless, loving spirit of generosity and concern for others (see Phil 4.17). It is a sign of our commitment to God's family (*cf.* 10.24f), and when we sacrifice for our brethren, we sacrifice to God. Times of persecution produced hardships for many Christians (see 10.32–34). Some were forced out of their homes and out of the cities in which they lived, and this exposed some of them to hunger and destitution. The author thus bid the readers to carry on the loving spirit that characterized Christians from the beginning (Acts 2.45; 4.32–37). It is not only a demonstration of our love for each other, but also of our fellowship with God (2 Cor 8.3–5) in that generosity with our goods demonstrates that we truly are children of our Father, and that we have taken on his characteristic of love. Like the worship we give to God from our hearts and lips (v 15 above), sharing with others is something that comes from inside us, from a loving, giving heart. When they are done in this way, the **sacrifices** we make of physical things for others are also **pleasing** to our **God**.

13.17 Obey your leaders and submit to them, for they look after your souls as those who must give an account, in order that they might do this with joy and not sighing; this would be unprofitable for you.

As with verse 7, it is not possible to determine exactly who these **leaders** are (the same generic term is used here). The noun form of the term is used in the NT of secular governmental authorities, but that is clearly not the sense here. Nor is it likely that the term refers here to apostles, since it is hard to imagine that the readers would need to be exhorted to submit to them if they had apostles in their number. Their authority in the early church was generally respected, even far outside Jerusalem. The term therefore probably refers either to elders or to prophets (Acts 15.22, 32; the same word is used there), although the generic term "leaders" in this verse may indicate that more than elders were in view in the author's mind.[57] That the term refers to elders is the better guess, since the leaders are further described as those who **look after** the readers' **souls**. The word translated **look after** (Greek *agrupneō*) is not otherwise used of elders in the NT, but surely it is synonymous with the work of overseeing and shepherding that is attributed to elders in Acts 20.28 and 1 Peter 5.1f. The fact that verses 8–16 are framed (vv 7, 17) by an exhortation to follow their leaders (both past examples and present ones) suggests that much of their work at the time was keeping the flock from being swept away by the problems discussed in verses 10–16. Jewish Christians, as part of their experience in the social fabric of Judaism, were accustomed to having older men who were leaders of the community.

The verse addresses both the work of leaders and the responsibility of the local group toward them. The work of these men is to watch out[58] for those things that are spiritually harmful to the group, like shepherds who watch for predators that would harm the flock. This would include addressing discouragement (13.12) and exhorting the members to maintain their association with the group (10.24f, as manifesting faith and perseverance) in times of persecution. Their abilities to teach the truth and to encourage and exhort their brethren are to be employed in this work. Their job is not to make rules for others simply because they are leaders (which the Bible calls "lording it over the flock," 1 Pet 5.3; Jesus made it clear that his church was not a place for worldly notions of superiority and power, Matt 20.25–28). They are to lead primarily by virtue of their spiritual maturity which is exhibited in their lives, for it is their own spir-

---

[57] Timothy M. Willis, "'Obey your leaders': Hebrews 13 and Leadership in the Church," *ResQ* 36 (1994): 316–26, at 319.

[58] This is the basic meaning of *agrupneō*. See Luke 21.36 and Eph 6.18.

itual maturity that makes them fit to lead others and that will encourage others to follow them.[59] They are fit to lead to the extent that they are filled up with the word of God and its effects upon their minds and hearts. The grave nature of the task is indicated by the fact that these men **must give an account** to the Lord for how they have cared for the flock among them. The assumption is that these men had taken on their roles, probably that of overseers, out of a serious sense of what was at stake. The author of Hebrews possibly knew these leaders personally, and thus may have been vouching for the purity of their motives.

The responsibility of the local church is to **obey** its rightful leaders. "Obey" here is the same term that is translated "trust" in 2.13 and "persuaded" in 6.9 and 13.18, and thus denotes confidence and trust in someone to the point of being willing to follow them.[60] Again, this is not to be understood from the perspective that elders are men who make rules for people to obey; it is not authority for its own sake. Instead, the picture is more like a shepherd who, because of his experience, knows where the sheep ought to go, and he exhorts and encourages them to go there. It is not his personal whim that determines where the sheep should go, but his experience with what is good and right (hence the qualifications in 1 Tim and Titus). Obedience to the elders is therefore necessary for at least two reasons. First, these leaders were serving voluntarily out of a sense of concern for the group and knowing that they would be accountable to the Lord himself for how they handled this important work. For this reason, they ought to be respected and accorded all cooperation so that their work is not a constant source of **sighing** (groaning, indicating difficulty and exasperation) but **joy**. The local church ought to trust the judgments of properly qualified elders even when another course might be appealing. Such is the nature of **submission** (the word in the Greek, *hupeikō*, means to yield or to give way). Second, it is in the sheep's best interest to follow the shepherd's leading. To refuse to follow **would be unprofitable for** the sheep. The sense of this last statement is that a refusal to trust and follow the guidance of spiritually mature leaders can only result in harm for oneself. They have the good of the church at heart, and so it would be foolish to refuse to follow their leading.

---

[59] See Willis "'Obey your leaders'," 319–23.

[60] The negative form of the word is used in 3.18, in parallel with "unbelief" in 3.19.

While the author urges his readers to obey their leaders, we should not necessarily take this as an indicator that some of them were disobeying their leaders. It may be that the reminder was timely simply because of the persecution which would try their faith. Hardship often creates a sense of panic or disorientation in some people, or causes some people to withdraw. It is especially important in times of difficulty not only to have good leaders among God's people, but for Christians to follow their lead. Such leaders can help Christians avoid improper responses to hardship, and they can offer and represent the kind of strength that others need.

13.18 Pray for us, for we are persuaded that we have a good conscience, wishing to behave well in all things.

As he closes his address, the author (a rhetorical **us**;[61] "I" in the next verse) asks for the prayers of his audience (v 18), just as he also prays for them (vv 20f). There is arguably nothing that we may do for each other that is greater than praying for one another. Praying to God and asking him to take care of another person expresses our own care for them and calls on the greatest power in the world on their behalf. Prayer "moves the arm that moves and governs the universe."[62] The fact that the author solicits their prayers indicates that he still wants to be thought of as one who is within their fellowship. He has not written them off but considers them good brethren whose prayers, and thus whose fellowship, are valuable to him. They are in his concern, and he wants to be in theirs as well.

That the author was worthy of their prayers is indicated by the sincerity in which he did **all things**. There may be a hint here that there was some displeasure, if not accusation, against him on the part of the readers (*cf.* 2 Cor 1.11f).[63] To the contrary, the author claims that he had a **good conscience**, *i.e.*, he was not aware of any sin in his life which would hinder prayers on his behalf. On the conscience, see on 9.9. Not only was the author's conscience clear of any wrong, but he also testified that his motives were equally good. His goal was **to behave** (conduct) himself **well** in everything. This too is measured by the standard of God's word.

---

[61] Lane, (*Hebrews 9–13*, 556) thinks that the author was identifying himself as one of their rightful leaders mentioned in v 17.

[62] Robert Milligan, *The Scheme of Redemption* (1869, repr., St. Louis: Bethany Press, 1957), 372.

[63] Lane, *Hebrews 9–13*, 556; Bruce, *Epistle to the Hebrews*, 409; Ellingworth, *Epistle to the Hebrews*, 725.

It is possible that this verse also expresses, at a deeper level, the author's own view of the exhortation he has just given them (*i.e.*, the entire address). He has not written to them in order to upbraid them or castigate them, and in this sense his conscience is also clear. His motive in writing was nothing but good, to effect the encouragement of brethren who were showing signs of wanting to quit. Because he has spoken to them only what is good and right (including the frightening prospects of judgment if they quit), he has wronged them in no way and thus has the boldness to ask for their prayers.

13.19 But I exhort you to do this all the more, that I might be restored to you more quickly.

We simply do not know why the author and his readers were separated. Whatever the reason, he obviously knew them well and longed to be with them again, so he asked for the prayers of his readers to that end. So convinced was he of the power and effectiveness of prayer, that he expressed his confidence that their prayers would get him to them **more quickly** than if they left the reunion up to the fortunes of ordinary time and opportunity. He believed that God would providentially arrange the way to them sooner if they would participate in asking for it. The term **restored** simply denotes a return. The author and his readers certainly knew each other, but it does not necessarily imply that the author was originally one of their own number.

The fact that the author hoped to see his audience in person speaks to his personal concern over their spiritual situation, and thus his deep Christian love for them. It was not enough, in his estimation, simply to write a letter and hope that they read it and follow its instructions. Exhorting and encouraging is not simply the impartation of the right information. The NT example is that it is to be done in the context of a relationship between people, a relationship built on love and friendship. Encouragement in the faith is not meant to be something that is done simply by a book, but by another person. For this reason, the Lord's church will always need evangelists, elders, and teachers (Eph 4.11) even though it already has God's word. The personal encouragement and presence of a beloved fellow-Christian makes the exhortation even stronger.

13.20–21 Now may the God of peace who by the blood of the eternal covenant brought up from the dead the great shepherd of the sheep,

our Lord Jesus, prepare you in every good thing to do his will, doing in us that which is pleasing in his sight through Jesus Christ, to whom be the glory forever, amen.

The author's prayer for them reflects his great love for them. He has already expressed his confidence that they will decide to persevere (Heb 6.9), but now he prays to that end as well. It is common in the NT documents that their openings and closings summarize their major themes. Here, the author's prayer contains key terms and concepts which recall the overall argument of the sermon and brings them all together in a prayer that the readers will follow the sermon's exhortation and become "perfect" themselves.

The basis upon which the author prayed reminded his readers of some things that were of vital importance for them in facing ongoing opposition. First, his prayer for them went out to the **God of peace,**[64] who would be able to comfort them and ease their fears. The reference probably derives from Ezekiel 34.25 and 37.26 (see below; *cf.* also Ezek 38.14). In the Roman world, peace also carried with it the idea of conquest, since peace was not the absence of war, but the result of war.[65] Peace was what happened when an enemy was defeated (see Rom 16.20). If that is the operative idea here, the prayer would be that God would relieve their suffering by defeating those who persecuted them. We have already seen several examples in chapter 11 of how God rescued from peril or death those who trusted in him. If God did it for them, he will do it for us as well. In a Jewish context, peace is not simply the absence of strife, but denotes wholeness and well-being. This is a large part of the intended meaning here as well, since he asks God that they might be perfected or made whole in every way (see below).

God's power to deliver his people from their hardships is demonstrated in the fact that he **brought up Jesus Christ, the great shepherd of God's sheep, from the dead**. There is possibly an echo of Isaiah 63.11 here (*cf.* also Isa 40.11); the call for the restoration of God's people has been answered. If God has rescued Jesus, he will rescue those who are joined with Jesus as well (*cf.* 1 Thes 4.14); where the shepherd has gone,

---

[64] The phrase "God of peace" is typically Pauline, so this may be an indicator of the author's acquaintance with Paul and his writings. See Introduction.

[65] See Klaus Wengst, *Pax Romana and the Peace of Jesus Christ,* trans. John Bowden (Philadelphia: Fortress, 1987).

the sheep will go. This also reminds the readers of God's determination to bring his people to himself (2.10). But perhaps even stronger is the allusion to Ezekiel 37, where the same verb **bring up** (in the LXX version of Ezekiel, Greek *anagō*) appears three times.[66] The theme of shepherds is also prominent in Ezekiel 34 and 37. Resurrection and shepherding are restoration language. If this allusion is correct, then the reference is not just to Jesus, but to Jesus as the leader of the great resurrection and restoration of God's people depicted in Ezekiel. The return from Babylon was another exodus,[67] as it were, and eschatologically and messianically ends in the presence of God (Ezekiel's book ends with a vision of a new temple). The readers of Hebrews, then, were subtly encouraged to see themselves as these returnees, following in the path of their shepherd, Jesus.

God's people now have unprecedented access to him because of what **Jesus**, the Messiah (**Christ**) did. The use of both of his names suggests that both his earthly work and his heavenly work are for the same purpose of bringing God's people home. Jesus faithfully obeyed the Father's will and thereby provided the final, perfect sacrifice for sins that makes our access possible. That obedience cost Jesus his life, but God then raised him (**brought** him **up**) from the dead and fulfilled Psalm 110, which spoke of how God would seat him at his right hand and make him high priest over God's people. The normal verb used for the resurrection in the NT is *egeirō*, but the author here has used *anagō*, a compounded form of the verb used in 2.10, echoing Ezekiel 37 (see above). The point is not so much God's act of raising Jesus, but of God's bringing Jesus to himself (thus implying exaltation[68]). This corresponds with the word **great**, which formerly was used of Jesus as high priest (4.14); the high priest is our shepherd in that he brings us to God. The picture, then, is that when God brought Jesus to himself, Jesus in turn brought us with him to God. In this way we see both his complete humanity (in his suffering and death) and his complete deity (in his sharing the throne of God). As the pioneer of our salvation and as our high priest, Jesus has opened up the way to God. He is now bringing us

---

[66] Justin Harrison Duff, "Allusions to Ezekiel and Bodily Resurrection in Hebrews," *CBQ* 84 (2022): 627–41.

[67] The language of shepherding is "exodus language": Psa 77.20; 78.52. Significantly, shepherding imagery also recalls Psalm 95 (v 7), which was the foundation for the exhortation in Heb 3–4.

[68] Johnson, *Hebrews*, 355.

to God (2.10) through his continuing, perpetual intercession as our high priest and by the encouragement of his own example (12.2).

The resurrection of Jesus was the capstone of a life on earth that culminated in his death. God brought Jesus back into life **by**, or through,[69] the route of death, which death involved the shedding of his **blood** in order to ratify the new, **eternal covenant** of which Jeremiah spoke (Jer 31; quoted in Heb 8; see also Zech 9.11; Isa 55.3; 61.8).[70] The mention of the covenant here minds the readers of their better relationship with God, with its better promises (8.6), a covenant in which God is (as always) utterly faithful (10.23).

In bringing us to God, Jesus truly is the great shepherd of God's sheep, who leads them to heavenly pasture in the presence of God himself (see John 10.16; 1 Pet 2.25; Isa 40.11; Jer 31.10; Psa 23). The point is that everything God has done, he has done with the purpose of bringing his people to himself in glory. Having accomplished so much for them already, and having promised (and sworn) to his people (since Abraham's time) that he would bring them to a heavenly city where they truly belonged, there is no way that God will fail to bring his people all the way home to himself in heaven. The basis of the author's prayer is thus meant to encourage the readers that their salvation is sure *unless they decide to refuse it*.

The request of the prayer is that God will **prepare** them. The Greek word here (*katartizō*) means to put in order, to restore, to put in proper condition, and thus can also mean to equip.[71] It is closely related to the idea of "perfecting" (bringing to completion) which is so common in Hebrews. The prayer is that God will strengthen them and supply them to be complete **in every good thing** so that they might accomplish (**do**) **his will** for them (see Phil 2.13). The phrase **every good thing** also appears in Philemon 6, where it likewise denotes the product of a relationship with God and Christ. Whatever good we possess, it is there from God, and it is to be used for doing his will, and to this end we must

[69] The Greek preposition *en* (often translated "in") can mean "through," BDAG 329; Lane, *Hebrews 9–13*, 559, who cites Zerwick, *Biblical Greek* §119. The phrase here ("in the blood …") is unique in the NT and difficult to interpret. See Ellingworth, *Epistle to the Hebrews*, 727–28.

[70] "New" and "eternal" go together in the thought of Hebrews (9.12–15). Consequently, this is not a reference to a supposed covenant that God made with man before the creation. See Richard L. Mayhue, "Heb 13:20: Covenant of Grace or New Covenant? An Exegetical Note," *TMSJ* 7 (1996): 251–57.

[71] BDAG 526.

allow God to fill us with all his goodness. See Romans 15.14; Galatians 5.22; Ephesians 5.9. God's **will** involves us both in the present and in the future. For the present, it entails God using us as his instruments in this world. Our lives are not for us, but we exist for the purpose of God. In accomplishing his plans and purposes in this world, God typically uses people whom he empowers, and that means that we must be willing to be used in this way, which in turns means that we must persevere. See 2 Corinthians 12.9–10. God uses his own people to help each other (Rom 15.14) and to spread his kingdom (Matt 5.13ff). For the future, God's will is that we come home to him in heaven. See Philippians 1.6. God wants his children to be with him, but he will not drag anyone into heaven against their will. So, whether their need was for the removal of fear, more knowledge, greater trust, or greater perseverance, the author expressed his desire that God would "fix" whatever was lacking in them so that they too might cross the finish line of faith's course and enjoy the victor's reward.

Of course, God will do this in the way that he, as a loving father (12.4ff), knows is best for us. He will **do in us that which is pleasing in his sight**. The entire phrase is adverbial in function and further describes how God will "complete" the readers. We can only be complete and perfect (whole) for God's will and purpose if we allow him to transform and change us according to his will. Like clay in the hands of the potter (Isa 64.8), we must be willing to accept his design for us, whatever it might entail. In the end, what is important is that he is pleased with the result. Our part of that is to be flexible and submissive in his hands, conforming to his will. The prepositional phrase **in us** can be understood in at least two ways:

1) It could mean that God does what he wills within us, inside us, making our hearts and minds what they ought to be and filling them with every good thing. In this way God completes and perfects us for his use. God may do this by subjecting us to additional training, he may allow us to be tested so that our faith is exercised and made stronger (see Rom 5.3f), or he may provide opportunities for greater growth in his word. We are God's workmanship, the product of his creative activity through his powerful word (Eph 2.10; 4.24) which fixes us from the inside out.

2) The phrase could also be understood in an instrumental sense, so that it means that God will do what pleases him by means of us. When understood in this way, the point is that once we have been made

complete for service, the purpose of our lives is to be the instruments through which God works his will in the world.

Either of these interpretations complement the prayer that God would complete the readers for the doing of his will. Of course, if it pleases God then we may rest assured that it is in no way harmful to us (although it might be difficult for us for a little while).

God will do his work in us **through Jesus Christ**, that is, through our relationship with him—the very relationship that was in question for the original readers of the epistle. His earthly life (summarized in his earthly name, **Jesus**) and his heavenly, exalted status (summarized in his title, **Christ**) both work for our benefit. Together they remind us that he is the perfecter of faith (12.2), the one who has gone before us and opened up the way to God. We will join him if we follow his example of trust and endurance.

The ascription of **glory forever** could belong either to God or to Jesus; either could be the antecedent of the relative pronoun (**to whom**), and the NT ascribes eternal glory to both.[72] It is more commonly said of God (who is the subject of this sentence), but Jesus is the nearer noun in the sentence.

13.22 I exhort you, brethren, bear with this word of exhortation, for I have written to you briefly.

Within its original Hellenistic Jewish setting, the "book" of Hebrews was **written** primarily (like most ancient literature) that it might be heard as it was read out loud to an assembly (see Col 4.16; 1 Thes 5.27; 1 Tim 4.13; Rev 1.3).[73] The phrase **word of exhortation** is used of a synagogue address in Acts 13.15 (see Introduction). In the Jewish synagogue there was Scripture reading followed by a Biblically-based address. Likewise, in the early churches there was Scripture reading and exhortation (1 Tim 4.13). Hebrews would have been read to a church in lieu of the author's personal presence.

The term **bear with** can mean "listen patiently" when used of messages (2 Tim 4.3), and thus comes close to meaning "consider" and eventually "hear." There is a subtle, almost playful reference here to the idea of

---

[72] God: Neh 9.5; Psa 72.19; 86.12; Rom 11.36; 16.27; Eph 3.21; Phil 4.20; 1 Tim 1.17; 1 Pet 4.11; Jude 25; Jesus: 2 Tim 4.18 and Rev 1.6.

[73] For an overview on this point, see Rosalind Thomas, *Literacy and Orality in Ancient Greece*, Key Themes in Ancient History (Cambridge: Cambridge University Press, 1992).

endurance/perseverance that is central to the sermon. To repeated calls for endurance in the Christian life is added a call to endure the author's sermon. The call for enduring the address is based on the idea that the sermon might seem lengthy to some of its hearers. The author downplays this when he adds that he has written **briefly**. While it is possible that he meant this in a mildly sarcastic way, we must be careful of using modern tastes to judge an ancient work. Modern people are less accustomed to listening to speeches than the ancients were, and probably even less than people were just two or three generations ago. At a pace of 130 words per minute (which is at the low end of the rate of normal speech), Hebrews would only take about forty minutes to read out loud (4,953 words in the Greek NT[74]); modern audio recordings of Hebrews are about forty-one minutes long. Romans and 1 Corinthians are longer. It is also possible that the call for endurance subtly acknowledged that the message of Hebrews was difficult. Its purpose was to exhort the hearers to draw near to Jesus instead of distancing themselves from him, and that involved rebuke and warning along with encouragement. The teaching of the NT can be "hard to hear" in the sense that its demands are not always pleasant nor easy. See 2 Corinthians 11.1–4. The message can also be difficult for Christians who are not as receptive as they ought to be (see Heb 5.11).

13.23 Know that our brother Timothy has been released, with whom, if he comes soon, I will see you.

One final example of endurance is someone they know, **Timothy**. It seems likely that this is the same Timothy who was often Paul's companion and fellow-worker (Acts 16.1–3; Rom 16.21; 1 Cor 4.17). Paul cited Timothy to the Philippians as an example of commitment and sacrifice (Phil 2.19–24). There is no other NT reference to Timothy's imprisonment, so the information here does not allow us to establish the date of Hebrews. We do not know why Timothy had been in prison, for how long, or where. The fact that Timothy had worked with churches all over the ancient Roman world likewise does not help us to discover the location of the original recipients of Hebrews. It is possible that

[74] By comparison, a random sample of Cicero's speeches and epistles yields an average of 8,762 words per address. By contrast, Pickard's English translation of Demosthenes' speech *On the Embassy* is close to 37,000 words; his speech *Against Neaira* (a written speech that was read in the public courts) is over 14,000 words in DeWitt's English translation.

Timothy had been imprisoned with Paul (see Col 1.1; although Paul only mentions himself as a prisoner in Phlm 1), but Timothy was not in prison when Paul was imprisoned for the last time. Whatever the circumstances had been, the author communicated this news to his readers for two reasons: 1) it would no doubt have been a bit of good news, an encouragement in an otherwise difficult situation, and 2) the author himself intended to join Timothy in a visit to the "Hebrews."

Timothy was an example of the kind of endurance in the faith that the hearers of Hebrews themselves needed to have. The recipients of Hebrews were not the only Christians who were suffering, and they needed to remember that (recall 13.3). It may be that Timothy's recent release is also intended as an encouragement for the readers to the effect that whatever hardship was facing them, it would not be a permanent condition for them. If God was caring for his servant Timothy and delivering him from unbelievers, the hearers of Hebrews could take courage that God would do the same for them. Timothy himself could testify to that when he came with the author for a visit. We hope that the visit materialized and that the results were good.

13.24 Greet all your leaders and all the saints. Those who are from Italy greet you.

How well the author of Hebrews knew the leaders among his addressees is not known. The fact that he singled them out for separate greeting could mean that he knew them personally, but it could equally mean that he did not know them but was acknowledging their leadership in order to affirm their status among the recipients. In Philippians, Paul singled out the elders and deacons for special greeting (Phil 1.1), suggesting not only that Paul supported the work they did, but also that a significant part of the burden of the present situation was theirs as well. It is possible that the same intention is reflected here.

As for **those who are from Italy**, we know nothing about them other than the implication that they were fellow-Christians. The words do not necessarily mean that the author was in Italy, although it would seem to suggest that these friends were Italians. The phrase could easily mean that some Christians from Italy who were known to the recipients were with the author when he wrote Hebrews (wherever he was), or it could mean that the author had recently had some contact with these Italian

Christians (in another place, or even by a letter) and that he was simply forwarding their "hello," in which case the author and these Christians could have been anywhere in the ancient Roman empire, even in separate places. Were these Italian Christians still in Italy? The preposition **from** (Greek *apo*) can be just as ambiguous in Greek as it is in English. It could mean that Italy was their homeland and that is where they lived,[75] or it could mean that they had left Italy and were now somewhere else.[76] Whatever the details, this verse is further evidence to the network of relationships that existed among the early Christians across the Roman empire in the first century. *Cf.* Romans 16, where Paul greeted many people he knew, even though he had not yet visited the church in Rome. That network was no doubt a great source of encouragement, as it was meant to be. The author of Hebrews thus, in this simple forwarding of greetings, reminds his readers that other Christians were aware of their situation, and that they should not feel alone in this world.

13.25 Grace be with all of you.

Whereas Hellenistic letters often ended with "be well" (the Greek word *errōsthe*; Acts 15.29),[77] Christian correspondence modified this in such a way that reflected their relationship with God, so that a common closing is to wish God's **grace**, or kindness, upon the recipients. This should not be thought of as a casual statement, a matter of mere convention. Generally speaking, the NT documents were written to address problems among their original readers. In facing such problems, the readers would need plenty of God's grace that would supply them with the solutions. Hebrews was no different. By his grace God has given us Jesus (2.9) and the opportunity to escape the divine wrath (12.15), and the author had already encouraged them to go to the throne of grace for help (4.16). He thus closes with the expressed wish that the same divine grace would sustain them in their present difficulty.

---

[75] Deissmann, *Light from the Ancient East*, 200.

[76] BDF §437.

[77] See examples in John L. White, *Light from Ancient Letters*.

APPENDIX

Candidates for the Author of Hebrews

Paul, Barnabas, Apollos, Luke, Priscilla and Aquila, Silas (Silvanus), Philip, Peter, Jude, Mary, Epaphras, and Clement of Rome have all been suggested as possible authors.[1] There is no hard evidence that proves any one candidate to be more probable than the others, and there is much that we do not know about each of them. Furthermore, pinpointing the authorship is not absolutely necessary, although if we knew the author, and if we had other works from his hand, it would possibly help clarify some interpretational questions along the way. However, we know so little about so many Biblical characters that knowing the name of the author of Hebrews might not shed much light on the background or interpretation of the book anyway. It certainly is not something about which anyone should be dogmatic.

It is quite amazing, therefore, just how much time and effort has gone into the question of the authorship of this "epistle." However, this question has not always been pursued merely out of curiosity, but because it was thought to have some bearing on the authority, and therefore the canonicity, of the document. False teachers wrote letters and circulated doctrines contrary to those taught by the apostles (*cf.* 2 Thes 2.2). Thus, for several years after the close of the NT period the canonical status of the book of Hebrews was a legitimate concern, and it was believed that one way to settle the matter was to determine who wrote it. Today, however, the matter of which writings properly belong in the NT canon has been settled for a long time.

---

[1] Simon Kistemaker, "The Authorship of Hebrews," *Faith and Mission* 18 (2001): 57–69, at 59. For an extensive survey, see Allen, *Hebrews*, 29–61.

Paul?[2]

It is no doubt out of a concern to endow the document with respectable credentials that some (in both ancient and modern times) have attributed it to the apostle Paul. Thus, in the King James Version the title of the book reads "The Epistle of Paul the Apostle to the Hebrews." It must be understood, however, that the titles of the books were not part of the original documents. Furthermore, the oldest manuscripts that contain copies of Hebrews simply titled the book "To the Hebrews" (which itself may have been a guess about the recipients). All the more amazing is the subscription in the King James Version, "Written to the Hebrews from Italy by Timothy." At the other end of the spectrum, the current canonical arrangement of the books of the NT reflects the belief that Paul did not write Hebrews—or that if he did, this is not certain. The letters of Paul appear in our Bibles generally in order from longest to shortest, and from those addressed to churches to those addressed to individuals. After the collection of Paul's letters comes the collection of non-Pauline works, grouped generally by length and author. The fact that the longer book of Hebrews (written to a church or churches) comes after the shortest letter of Paul that was written to an individual indicates that, in the classification scheme used to compile the canon, Hebrews was not considered to be one of Paul's letters and that a new sub-collection of writings in the canon begins with Hebrews (or at least that Hebrews' correct place in the order of books is ambiguous).[3] However, the earliest codex that contains a copy of Hebrews (P^{46}, dated to about 200 AD) places it after Romans, and Hebrews comes between 2 Thessalonians and 1 Timothy in Codex Sinaiticus (4th cent. AD). This, of course, proves nothing about who the author of Hebrews was or was not. It simply shows that some, even at a very early time,[4] have treated the book as Paul's and others have not. While attributing the book to Paul might be an easy way to settle the question of the book's authority and canonicity, we must not jump to conclusions.

---

[2] See David Allen Black, "On the Pauline Authorship of Hebrews," *Faith and Mission* 16 (1999): 32–51 and 78–86, and *idem*, "Who Wrote Hebrews? The Internal and External Evidence Reexamined," *Faith and Mission* 18 (2001): 3–26; *idem*, *The Authorship of Hebrews: The Case for Paul* (Gonzalez, FL: Energion Publications, 2013).

[3] James W. Thompson, "The Epistle to the Hebrews and the Pauline Legacy," *ResQ* 47 (2005): 197–206, at 198.

[4] See the argument in Charles P. Anderson, "The Epistle to the Hebrews and the Pauline Letter Collection," *HTR* 59 (1966): 429–39.

While it is theoretically possible that Paul could have been the author of Hebrews, a fairly good case can be made against such an idea. First, the known letters of Paul all begin with him identifying himself as the author, but this characteristic feature is absent from Hebrews. Some, following the lead of Clement of Alexandria, have tried to explain this by postulating that Paul was writing to Jewish Christians in Palestine where he was regarded as somewhat of a maverick (*cf.* Acts 21.20–21). In such a situation, we are told, the teachings of this letter would have been better received if it did not have Paul's name attached to it. Eusebius related Clement's opinion thusly:

> But he [Clement] says that the words, 'Paul the Apostle,' were probably not prefixed, because, in sending it to the Hebrews, who were prejudiced and suspicious of him, he wisely did not wish to repel them at the very beginning by giving his name. Farther on he says: "But now, as the blessed presbyter said, since the Lord being the apostle of the Almighty, was sent to the Hebrews, Paul, as sent to the Gentiles, on account of his modesty did not subscribe himself an apostle of the Hebrews, through respect for the Lord, and because being a herald and apostle of the Gentiles he wrote to the Hebrews out of his superabundance."[5]

This explanation was pure conjecture and has at least three difficulties. First, it could be argued just as well that Paul would have identified himself, and defended his apostleship, to such a hostile audience, as he did in 2 Corinthians. Second, Hebrews 13 seems to imply that the author and his audience knew each other well and that they were on friendly terms. Third, that Paul, the self-acknowledged apostle to the Gentiles, ever wrote to a church made up mostly of Jewish Christians is nothing but an assumption.[6]

A second problem with ascribing Hebrews to Paul is that the literary style of Hebrews is obviously different from Paul's letters. If one reads both Paul and Hebrews in the original Greek, the difference is clear. While we must acknowledge that appeals to stylistic differences are not conclusive in terms of authorship, nevertheless the stylistic differences between Hebrews and the extant letters of Paul are significant. The language of Hebrews is more elegant, more polished, smoother, much more in the literary

---

[5] *Ecclesiastical History* 6.14 (*NPNF*[2] 1:261).

[6] Lünemann, *Epistle to the Hebrews*, 348. See pages 6ff on recipients.

style, and less vernacular, than the known letters of Paul.[7] In fact, Hebrews is generally acknowledged to be the "best" Greek (that is, most approximating Classical literary ideals) in the NT and more than just a step above Paul's. For example, the transitions between one section and the next are smoother in Hebrews than in Paul's epistles,[8] the author of Hebrews was generally careful to write in periods (a period in Greek literature was similar to what we would call a "complete paragraph" in English[9]) while Paul was not, and this author was much more careful to avoid hiatus (an abrupt stop in the flow of the language) than Paul.[10] Origen, in the early third century AD, noted the heightened style of Hebrews when he said "the verbal style of the epistle entitled 'To the Hebrews,' is not rude like the language of the apostle, who acknowledged himself 'rude in speech,' that is, in expression; but that its diction is purer Greek, anyone who has the power to discern differences of phraseology will acknowledge."[11]

In addition to this, Hebrews is more than just a well-written document. It comes the closest in the NT to being a piece of rhetoric.[12] Rhetoric is the art of using words to persuade, and in ancient times skill in rhetoric was acquired through special training. Although many scholars have recently argued that there are rhetorical techniques at work in Paul's letters, Paul says that he consciously and explicitly distanced himself from such things (*cf.* 1 Cor 2.1, 4; 2 Cor 10.10; 11.6). While Paul certainly argued and persuaded in his letters, the author of Hebrews showed a greater skill at it, or at least did so more explicitly. Also, Paul sometimes allowed himself to wander off his present topic, but the writer of Hebrews never did.

Against this observation, some point out that Paul's letters were aimed at churches that were predominantly Gentile in their make-up, and it may be that Paul wrote Hebrews differently because it was written to a group that consisted mostly, if not completely, of Jewish Christians. While there

---

[7] See James Hope Moulton and Nigel Turner, *A Grammar of New Testament Greek, Vol. 4: Style* (Edinburgh: T&T Clark, 1976), 106–13; Robertson, *Grammar*, 132–33.

[8] *Cf.* BDF §463.

[9] See Aristotle, *Rhetoric* 3.9. A good discussion of the Greek period is found in Cortez, "From the Holy to the Most Holy Place," 529–34. See also BDF §464; S. M. Baugh, "Greek Periods in the Book of Hebrews," *NovT* 60 (2018): 24–44.

[10] BDF §486. Yet see Daniel A. Penick, "Paul's Epistles Compared with One Another and with the Epistle to the Hebrews," *American Journal of Philology* 42 (1921): 58–72.

[11] Quoted in Eusebius, *Ecclesiastical History* 6.25 (*NPNF*² 1:273).

[12] See Walters, "The Rhetorical Arrangement of Hebrews," 59–70. Cockerill lists the rhetorical features of Hebrews (Cockerill, *Epistle to the Hebrews*, 11).

is some evidence that Paul *slightly* modified his literary style for different audiences,[13] it remains an assumption, however, that a different audience could adequately account for such sweeping changes in an author's diction and mode as we see between Hebrews and Paul's letters—on top of the unwarranted assumption noted above, that Paul ever wrote to a predominantly Jewish church. At best, the suggestion that Paul deliberately changed his style for writing Hebrews is only a guess and is insufficient grounds for arguing for Pauline authorship. Even if we could grant some plausibility to this suggestion, we still would agree with Godet that it would be "strange indeed that he should have written in polished Greek to the Hebrews, while all his life he had been writing to the Hellenes in a style abounding with rugged and barbarous Hebraisms."[14]

Third, and closely related to the matter of style, is what seems to be a fundamental difference in vocabulary. Some of Paul's favorite words and expressions find little or no usage in Hebrews, and some words appear in Hebrews that never appear in Paul. However, as we noted concerning style, arguments based on vocabulary cannot be conclusive because vocabulary choices are partly determined by the subject matter, and the different subject of Hebrews would naturally call for different terminology. But even among the words that are common to Paul and Hebrews, there are differences in the way those words are used. A good example of this is how Paul referred to Jesus. Paul seldom referred to him simply as "Jesus," and most often used "Christ Jesus." Hebrews, however, often uses "Jesus" alone and *never* refers to him as "Christ Jesus." Also, Hebrews often refers to Jesus simply as "the Son" (without any qualifiers such as "of God"), but Paul almost never did. Now, again, it has been argued that Paul could have changed his vocabulary and usage on occasion if he desired. But while it is a theoretical possibility, it is not likely a practical one. It would be unusual and difficult for someone to change their vocabulary and usage so drastically, Paul included. While things like the choice of

---

[13] Compare, for example, the difference in style (in Greek) between 2 Cor and a letter like Gal. For a specific grammatical example, see Fuller, "The 'Genitive Absolute'," 142–67, where she notes that Paul uses this construction more in letters that went to Rome and Achaia, and less in letters that went to Macedonia and Asia Minor. However, there may have been several factors that influenced Paul's "style" for any given epistolary project, including his choice of amanuensis (secretary). Dogmatic judgments about which style *must* belong to a particular author are not possible.

[14] Frédéric Louis Godet, *Studies on the Epistles of St. Paul,* trans. Annie Harwood Holmden (New York: Hodder and Stoughton, 1889), 332.

names used in referring to Jesus may seem to be a trivial matter on which to base a judgment about authorship, the fact is that such things would accurately reflect the personal preferences and literary habits of the author. Such things become literary signatures. It would be one thing for an author to change his tone, or to alter his style with regards to grammar or sentence structure, but widescale changes in one's vocabulary and preferences for certain terms would be another thing altogether.

Fourth, there is what we may call a different mindset or way of thinking.[15] The author of Hebrews had a different set of key concepts and a different emphasis in formulating arguments and exhortations than did Paul. For example, although both Paul and the author of Hebrews used the exodus of Israel as a warning (1 Cor 10.1–5 and Hebrews 3–4), Paul did not use the concept of entering into God's rest. While both Paul and Hebrews criticized the old Law, each presented that critique differently (compare, for example, Heb 7.18 with Rom 3.20). The phrase "in Christ," Paul's most-used expression, appears nowhere in Hebrews.[16] Other well-known Pauline themes, such as conflict between flesh and spirit, are also absent from Hebrews. Such differences strongly suggest that someone other than Paul wrote Hebrews. If changing one's style on the level of grammar and vocabulary would be a difficult task, change on the conceptual level might be even more difficult and unlikely. The easiest reading of the conceptual differences between Hebrews and Paul is that a mind and personality other than Paul's was behind Hebrews.

It is too easy, however, to make too much of such differences. There are legitimate points of similarity between Paul and Hebrews (see below), and differences between Paul and Hebrews are sometimes overstated. For example, it is often claimed that Paul emphasizes the redemptive work of Christ while Hebrews emphasizes the sanctifying work of Christ, but these distinctions are more vivid in the theological biases and presuppositions of commentators than they are in the NT. Even more objectionable are the suggestions that there are competing theologies in the NT,

---

[15] "Paul and the author of Hebrews are not in conflict, but there is a different 'feel' to Hebrews when compared to the Pauline Epistles." (Allen, *Hebrews*, 40). He then cites Wright, who said "Entering the world of the letter to the Hebrews after a close study of Paul is a bit like listening to Monteverdi after listening to Bach" (Wright, *The New Testament and the People of God*, 409).

[16] Although the *idea* is there: "partakers of Christ" (Heb 3.14). See Ribbens, "Partakers of Christ."

specifically that Paul and the author of Hebrews had some fundamental disagreements about certain things. Hebrews does not contradict anything else in the NT, but it does offer some things that are unique. While the uniqueness of the thought of Hebrews leads us to doubt a Pauline origin, that uniqueness never becomes dissent. We agree with Origen when he said, "that the thoughts of the epistle are admirable, and not inferior to the acknowledged apostolic writings, anyone who carefully examines the apostolic text will admit."[17]

Fifth, there is a difference in presentation between the letters of Paul and Hebrews. Paul typically started with a "doctrinal" section, followed by a "practical" section (I use the terms with caution; we must not let such a description lead us to think that doctrine and practice are unrelated!). Also, Paul generally liked to finish his argument before he discussed its practical ramifications. Hebrews, however, has doctrine and exhortation interwoven in five main sections (see the outline of the book, below).

Finally, there is a difference between Hebrews and Paul in the way the OT was quoted. Paul normally introduced an OT passage using a form of the verb "to write" (Greek *graphein*), such as in the phrase "it is written." The author of Hebrews, however, introduced OT quotations with a form of the verb "to say" (usually the Greek verb *legein*), as in the phrases "it says" or "he says." While this is by no means decisive, it is suggestive. Additionally, the quotations in Hebrews are generally longer than they are in Paul.

Some have responded to all of these observations by proposing that the Holy Spirit could change a writer's style as he saw fit. In this way, it is argued, Paul could still be the author even though Hebrews is remarkably dissimilar from anything else he wrote. But this is needless speculation and is an appeal to the miraculous to avoid the obvious. The fact that individual NT writers such as John, Luke, and Paul show a uniqueness and consistency of style across several of their writings most naturally means that the Spirit used human penmen in such a way that incorporated their own individual styles. All of John's writings, for example, have the same distinct style, which is markedly different from both Paul and Luke. While it is not impossible that the Spirit could have overtaken Paul so as to cause him to write in a style completely different from what was normal for him, the evidence of the NT itself speaks against such an idea.

---

[17] Quoted in Eusebius, *Ecclesiastical History* 6.25 (*NPNF*[2] 1:273).

Perhaps the conclusive indicator against Pauline authorship comes from Hebrews 2.1–4. There the author grouped himself with those who had received their knowledge of the truth from human teachers. He said, "we ought to give the more earnest heed to the things which we have heard" (v 1), and he speaks of how the word which was first spoken through the Lord "was confirmed to us by those who heard him (Jesus)" (v 3). The author's statement implies that he himself had not heard Jesus but had received the gospel from eyewitnesses. Paul, however, was quick to deny that he had received his knowledge of the gospel from another human person. Paul took special delight in the fact that he received what he knew directly from the Lord. Paul strongly asserted that "the gospel which was preached by me is not according to man. For I neither received it from man, nor was I taught it, but I received it through a revelation of Jesus Christ" (Gal 1.11–12). The author's own testimony concerning himself should carry great weight in any deliberation on the matter of authorship, and this seems to rule Paul out as the author. It has been offered, in response, that the "we" and "us" in Hebrews 2.1–4 may simply be a rhetorical device in which the author included himself with his readers. While the author of Hebrews certainly did this in some places, "on such a vital matter as the source of his message he would scarcely have failed to give his personal testimony, had he any to give."[18] While no one of the factors discussed above may, by itself, eliminate Paul as the author of Hebrews, together they make a strong presumptive case against Pauline authorship.[19]

There are features of Hebrews, however, that align with Paul and his letters. As for the authors, the author of Hebrews was well-acquainted with the OT and its institutions, and Paul had received rabbinical training from the best teachers of his day (Acts 22.3). Among the documents, the allegory of Sarah and Hagar in Galatians 4.21–31, involving two mountains, is broadly similar to the comparison of Sinai and Zion in Hebrews 12.18–29. Also, both Galatians and Hebrews seem to use the Greek word *diathēkē* in the sense of "testament."[20] The distinction between the milk

---

[18] Ellingworth, *The Epistle to the Hebrews*, 7.

[19] Cockerill, *Epistle to the Hebrews*, 7: "These many ways, therefore, in which Hebrews differs from the Pauline letters in style, vocabulary, and content all but rule out Pauline authorship."

[20] Ben Witherington III, "The Influence of Galatians on Hebrews," *NTS* 37 (1991): 146–52; at 147.

and the solid food of the word in Hebrews 5 finds a parallel in 1 Corinthians 3. Both authors spoke of Christians participating in Christ's heavenly existence (Heb 10.19 and Eph 2.6). Only Hebrews and Paul quoted from the book of Habakkuk, and both quoted the same passage (Hab 2.3–4, in Gal 3.11, Rom 1.17, and Heb 10.38). Several of the exhortations in Hebrews 13 sound familiar to students of Paul, and Timothy, who is often mentioned in Paul's letters, is mentioned in Hebrews 13.23.[21]

How are we to make sense of these two sets of facts, that Hebrews is both similar and dissimilar to the writings of Paul? Undoubtedly, the answer lies in the fact that there were many truths that were held in common among Christians in all places, including a high view of the exalted Jesus, a difference between the "old" and the "new," the use of exodus typology to describe the effects of Christ's work, the exemplary nature of Abraham's faith, *etc.* It should not surprise us that Paul and the author of Hebrews "overlapped" as they drew upon this common set of beliefs, and most, if not all, of the similarities between Hebrews and Paul can be accounted for in this way.[22] Hebrews 13.24 indicates that the author of Hebrews was someone within Paul's circle of friends, but there is no proof that he borrowed ideas specifically from Paul.[23] The author of Hebrews was his own thinker.

Which of Paul's associates could have written Hebrews?[24] Of the remaining candidates that have been suggested, we can rule out Clement of Rome because there is no evidence that any inspired writings came from him. We may just as easily dismiss the suggestions that Jude, Stephen,

---

[21] For other similarities, see Grindheim, *Letter to the Hebrews,* 7–10. Bates suggested that 2 Peter 3.15 proves that Paul wrote Hebrews (William H. Bates, "The Authorship of the Epistle to the Hebrews Again," *BibSac* 79 (1922): 93–96), but this "evidence" depends on too many other assumptions to be a serious argument for the Pauline authorship of Hebrews.

[22] See Hurst, *The Epistle to the Hebrews: Its Background of Thought,* 124: "... there is evidence that in Hebrews one finds a similar development of some central themes of Pauline theology. In some cases this is seen in the same ideas being expressed by a different deployment of the same terms; in other cases these ideas are expressed in different language and imagery. Such unity and diversity are what one would expect if both writers are engaging in a deep interaction with the same traditions."

[23] Thompson, "The Epistle to the Hebrews and the Pauline Legacy," 206: "the relationship between Hebrews and the Pauline tradition is minimal."

[24] I do not believe that Hebrews was written as a deliberate pseudepigraphical attempt to pass it off as Paul's. Such is the proposal of Clare K. Rothschild, *Hebrews as Pseudepigraphon,* WUNT 2.235 (Tübingen: Mohr Siebeck, 2009). For a response, see Bryan R. Dyer, "The Epistle to the Hebrews in Recent Research: Studies on the Author's Identity, His Use of the Old Testament, and Theology," *JGRChJ* 9 (2013): 104–31, at 109–11.

Peter, Philip, Ariston (the supposed author of Mark 16.9–20), Priscilla and Aquila, Epaphras, Nicodemus, Timothy, or Mary the mother of Jesus wrote Hebrews. None of these guesses have any real merit to them.

Apollos?[25]

Apollos has long been an attractive candidate because of what we are told about him in Acts 18.24: "And a certain Jew named Apollos, born at Alexandria, an eloquent man, and mighty in the Scriptures, came to Ephesus." To say that he was "eloquent" meant that he had training in rhetoric, and the author of Hebrews certainly knew rhetoric. Also, Alexandria, Egypt was a great center of learning and culture in NT times. The city was home to a sizable Jewish population and advanced studies in Judaism could be pursued there (Philo, who was roughly contemporary with Paul and who produced several allegorical treatments of Biblical texts, lived in Alexandria). This, it has been argued, would account for Apollos' eloquence and knowledge of the Scriptures, and it certainly seems that Hebrews was written by exactly such a person. Apollos was also within "the Pauline circle" of coworkers, and likely knew Timothy (thus possibly explaining Heb 13.23). Furthermore, the Greek translation of the OT (the Septuagint, hereafter LXX) was produced in Apollos' hometown of Alexandria, and as noted above, the author of Hebrews used the LXX when he quoted the OT.

However attractive the suggestion that Apollos wrote Hebrews may be, we must stop just short of it for a few important reasons. First, the early Alexandrian church fathers thought that Paul wrote Hebrews. If Apollos were in fact the real author, their insistence on Pauline authorship at such an early date becomes hard to explain.[26] Second, we have no known writings of Apollos with which to compare Hebrews. Without a basis of comparison, we cannot be sure that Apollos wrote Hebrews no matter how well he may fit other criteria. Third, while Acts 18.24 makes Apollos a candidate, it does not make him the only candidate. The same words probably could have described any number of Christians in the first century, for it is not likely that Apollos was the only educated Hellenistic Jew in the early church. Fourth, no one in ancient times attributed Hebrews

[25] See George H. Guthrie, "The Case for Apollos as the Author of Hebrews," *Faith and Mission* 18 (2001): 41–56. Johnson also inclines towards identifying Apollos as the author (*Hebrews*, 42–44), as does Grindheim (*Letter to the Hebrews*, 17): "as far as guesses go, Apollos is the best."

[26] Bruce, *Epistle to the Hebrews*, 12.

to Apollos. Although this objection is not conclusive (the church fathers were either wrong or uninformed about some things), it does raise the question of why a letter by Apollos was not recognized as such in Alexandria. If Hebrews was the work of the Alexandrian Apollos, we might expect Clement to have known this. But, as noted above, Clement of Alexandria, writing *c.* 200 AD, cited Paul as the author, possibly to connect it with the orthodoxy represented in that apostle's name.[27] This likely means that Clement did not know who wrote Hebrews, and specifically that he did not know that Apollos wrote it. And the argument from the origin of the LXX in Alexandria proves nothing, as the LXX was used widely.

Luke?[28]

Luke certainly could have written the elegant lines of Hebrews. After Hebrews, the writings of Luke are the most literary in the NT. Both authors exhibit literary skill, and there is one particular trait that seems to stand out in common in the writings of Luke and in Hebrews: the technique of foreshadowing. Both authors were fond of introducing a feature in their discussion ahead of the place in the discussion where that feature becomes prominent. The fact that Luke was closely associated with Paul could explain the similarities between Paul and Hebrews, and this, along with the fact that Luke wrote a gospel, could also account for why the early church accepted Hebrews as Scripture. None of these considerations by themselves prove anything, but together they show that Luke is a viable candidate for the author of Hebrews. In addition to these points, there is some ancient opinion that Luke had a part in writing Hebrews. Clement of Alexandria thought that Paul wrote the document in Hebrew (or Aramaic) and that Luke translated it into Greek. Eusebius reports

> He [Clement] says that the Epistle to the Hebrews is the work of Paul, and that it was written to the Hebrews in the Hebrew language; but that Luke translated it carefully and published it for the Greeks, and hence the same style of expression is found in this epistle and in the Acts.[29]

---

[27] In Eusebius, *Ecclesiastical History* 6.14 (*NPNF*^{2} 1:261).

[28] See David L. Allen, "The Authorship of Hebrews: The Lukan Proposal," *Faith and Mission* 18 (2001): 27–40; *idem,* "The Authorship of Hebrews: Historical Survey of the Lukan Theory," *CTR* 8 (2011): 3–18; *idem, Hebrews,* 47–61; *idem, Lukan Authorship of Hebrews* (Nashville, TN: B&H Academic, 2010).

[29] *Ecclesiastical History* 6.14 (*NPNF*^{2} 1:261).

But Clement was clearly speculating. Hebrews does not read like a translation (at least in the modern sense of the term) and shows every sign of having been originally composed in Greek. There are compound Greek words which would have no analogues in Hebrew, its arguments are sometimes based on verbatim quotations from the LXX, the author paused to explain a Hebrew name in 7.2, and there are ample occurrences of rhythm, assonance, and alliteration[30] which would not have been present in a supposed Hebrew or Aramaic original. As noted above, Clement probably associated Hebrews with Paul to preserve the letter's canonicity, and his statement about Luke being the translator was probably his attempt to explain why Hebrews was written in such a different style than Paul's, or why a "letter to Hebrews" was preserved in Greek.

While Clement's explanation is unlikely, Luke remains a candidate for the author of Hebrews on stylistic grounds. Yet, as already noted, stylistic grounds alone are not an adequate basis for such a conclusion, and, as already noted, there must have been other Christians of that time who were educated enough to write in good literary style. Furthermore, while the style of Hebrews is more similar to Luke's writings than to Paul's, there are also differences between the styles of Luke and Hebrews. If differences between the styles of Hebrews and Paul tend to speak against a Pauline authorship, then differences between the styles of Hebrews and Luke would tend to speak against a Lukan authorship as well. Also, anyone who adopts the Lukan theory would have to wrestle with why Luke's presentation of Jesus in his gospel is so different from that of Hebrews. That is, if Luke presented Jesus as the new high priest in Hebrews, then why did he not say anything about this in his gospel? Perhaps the biggest problem is that Luke was most likely of a Gentile background (Col 4.11, 14), but the author of Hebrews seems to have been of a Jewish background.[31] The best we could say is that the Lukan authorship of Hebrews is not impossible, but neither is it founded in any facts.

Silas?

What about Silas? Silas was associated with Timothy, which would fit well with Hebrews 13.23. Silas certainly was a long-time companion of Paul and may have been the amanuensis for 1 Peter (see 1 Pet 5.12). Given

---

[30] See in Moffatt, *Epistle to the Hebrews*, lvi–lxii.

[31] Lünemann. *Epistle to the Hebrews*, 363.

the similarities between Hebrews and 1 Peter (for example, both speak of Jesus as the shepherd, both speak of the sacrificial blood of Christ, sprinkling, inheritance, *etc.*), Silas is a possible candidate for the author of Hebrews. But the similarities between 1 Peter and Hebrews can be explained quite adequately on the basis of common OT motifs from which both documents drew heavily and leaves unexplained the many differences between the two. There is much that we do not know about Silas, and any attribution of Hebrews to him is, again, only a guess.

Barnabas?

The only name that has been suggested that possibly has more merit than the others (with the exception of Apollos) would be Barnabas. That Barnabas wrote Hebrews was suggested as early as the late second century AD by Tertullian. He said

> I wish, however, redundantly to superadd the testimony likewise of one particular comrade of the apostles,—(a testimony) aptly suited for confirming, by most proximate right, the discipline of his masters. For there is extant withal an Epistle to the Hebrews under the name of Barnabas—a man sufficiently accredited by God, as being one whom Paul has stationed next to himself in the uninterrupted observance of abstinence: "Or else, I alone and Barnabas, have not we the power of working?" And, of course, the Epistle of Barnabas is more generally received among the Churches than that apocryphal "Shepherd" of adulterers.[32]

Barnabas was a Levite (Acts 4.36), which means he presumably would have had special training in Judaism. It certainly means that he would have been closely familiar with the Jewish sacrificial system and the ritual on the Day of Atonement, both of which figure prominently in Hebrews. It has also been suggested that since part of the job of the Levites was to sing chants from the Psalms in the temple services,[33] authorship by a known Levite would account for why most of the OT quotations in Hebrews are from the Psalms. Furthermore, Barnabas was known as "the encourager," which would fit well with the spirit of Hebrews and may be echoed in 13.22, where the author says, "But I urge you, brethren, bear

---

[32] *On Modesty* 20 (*ANF* 4:97).

[33] Alfred Edersheim, *The Temple: Its Ministry and Services as They Were at the Time of Christ* (Grand Rapids: Eerdmans, 1980), 172.

with this word of exhortation, for I have written to you briefly." Lane observes that the author "appears to have been a charismatic leader who led by force of mind and personality rather than by virtue of an office or title,"[34] which could be an apt description of Barnabas. That Barnabas was from Cyprus (Acts 4.36) suggests that he would have received a good Hellenistic education, something that the author of Hebrews apparently possessed. Barnabas was certainly well-known to Paul and to the Christians in Palestine and he was one of those called an apostle in Acts 14.14, which means that he had a considerable reputation as a leader and an authoritative teacher in early Christianity.

Again, however, we must acknowledge that while Barnabas is an attractive candidate, we cannot attribute Hebrews to him with certainty. Some think that Hebrews 2.3 may not be a fitting description of Barnabas (but this objection is not a serious obstacle). More problematic is the fact that if Barnabas did write an "epistle," his name certainly had enough weight to warrant attaching it to the work, and if it ever was attached to the document it would be hard to explain how his name later became dissociated from it. The fact that no author's name was attached to this document even in ancient times may well mean that no prominent figure in early Christianity wrote it. Tertullian's identification of Barnabas as the author is likewise problematic. Since he called Hebrews the epistle of Barnabas, he may have confused the Biblical book with the later apocryphal work entitled *The Epistle of Barnabas,* to which it is somewhat similar.[35] Alternately, his theological concerns of the moment may have led him to make an uncritical statement. In the passage quoted above, Tertullian was arguing against what he believed was a false doctrine (specifically the idea that adulterers could repent and come back into the church), and he appealed to Hebrews because Hebrews "says" what he wanted to say against his opponents (*i.e.,* that some people cannot repent, Heb 6.6). However, in order for this to work, he needed to connect Hebrews with some authoritative name. By connecting Hebrews with Barnabas, Tertullian could discredit the document known as "the Shepherd of Hermas," an apocryphal work which his opponents used on their side of the debate. It was to say, in effect, "I have good authority for my position, but you do not." The point is that his zeal to make his argument work com-

[34] Lane, *Hebrews 1–8,* li.

[35] Ellingworth, *Epistle to the Hebrews,* 14.

promised his statement that Barnabas wrote Hebrews. Another problem, as noted in the commentary, is that Hebrews was not concerned with the temple, but with the tabernacle, which had vanished well over a thousand years prior to the writing of Hebrews. The connection with a Levite in the *first* century is thus relativized and this reduces the significance of Barnabas' supposed expertise in the affairs of the temple. In a similar vein, tracing the frequency of psalm citations back to an author who was a Levite is pure speculation, first because Levites surely had no monopoly on familiarity with the psalms, and second because it ignores the (better) possibility that the *content* of the psalms that are cited in Hebrews is what prompted their citation.

Before we leave the discussion of authorship, we may note that there are some connections between Hebrews and Stephen's speech in Acts 7. While this does not mean that Stephen wrote Hebrews, it could suggest that the author may have belonged to a group of Hellenistic Jewish Christians that had the boldness to criticize Judaism in light of the work of Jesus. Hurst, building on the earlier work of Manson, has noted six strong connections between Hebrews and the speech of Stephen: 1) a similar attitude toward the Law, 2) an emphasis on the life of the faithful as a life of wandering, 3) God's word is called "living," 4) reference to Joshua and the "rest" of God's people, 5) mention of the Law delivered through angels, and 6) in the NT, only Hebrews and Stephen quote Exodus 25.40.[36] The affinities between Hebrews and what is known about early Hellenistic Jewish Christianity are interesting, but gaps in our knowledge must prevent us from connecting the two with certainty.[37]

Conclusion

In the end we may paraphrase the words of the ancient observation of Origen: who wrote Hebrews, God only knows.[38] We also agree with

---

[36] Hurst, *The Epistle to the Hebrews: Its Background of Thought*, 94–106. See also Lane, *Hebrews 1–8*, cxliv–cl.

[37] See Oskar Skarsaune, *In the Shadow of the Temple: Jewish Influences on Early Christianity* (Downers Grove, IL: InterVarsity Press, 2002), 152–55, who rightly points out that the opposition to Stephen (Acts 7–8) and Paul (Acts 9) was a matter of the audience, not necessarily the message: "What was new about Stephen was not the message he proclaimed, but the audience he proclaimed it to. ... Stephen was not persecuted because he introduced a new theology, but because he encountered a new group of adversaries ...." (154).

[38] In Eusebius, *Ecclesiastical History* 6.25 (*NPNF*[2] 1:273). Black has argued that since Origen spoke as if he thought the letter originated with Paul (he constantly introduces

Westcott, who said, "plausible conjectures unsupported by evidence cannot remove our ignorance even if they satisfy our curiosity."[39] The best guess is that a Hellenistic Jewish Christian, who was well-known to the recipients and whose exhortation they would have respected, wrote the document. Our inability to know who wrote Hebrews should not, however, weaken our confidence that it is inspired Scripture, just as our concern for having only inspired Scripture in our Bibles should not lead us to conclude that Paul must have written it. The matters of authorship and inspiration are two different issues. Hebrews presents the same high view of Jesus, the same hope, the same ethics, and the same gospel as the rest of the NT. The early Christians recognized it, at an early time, as having come from an inspired author, and it is by these things that we are assured that it is inspired Scripture. It is Scripture regardless of whom God used to write it. The message of the book, not speculations about the author, must be our primary focus.[40]

---

references to the letter by saying "Paul says" or similar words), his famous, often-quoted statement actually means that he did not know who the penman was who put the words on paper as Paul's assistant ("Who Wrote Hebrews", 20), but this interpretation is not likely (Cockerill, *Epistle to the Hebrews*, 8).

[39] Westcott, *Epistle to the Hebrews*, xliv.

[40] *Cf.* Kistemaker, "The Authorship of Hebrews," 57–69.

BIBLIOGRAPHY

Alford, Henry. *Alford's Greek Testament: An Exegetical and Critical Commentary*. Grand Rapids: Guardian Press, 1976.

Allen, David L. "The Authorship of Hebrews: The Lukan Proposal." *Faith and Mission* 18 (2001): 27–40.

———. "More Than Just Numbers: Deuteronomic Influence in Hebrews 3:7–4:11." *TynBul* 58 (2007): 129–49.

———. *Hebrews*. NAC. Nashville, TN: B & H Publishing Group, 2010.

———. *Lukan Authorship of Hebrews*. Nashville, TN: B&H Academic, 2010.

———. "The Authorship of Hebrews: Historical Survey of the Lukan Theory." *CTR* 8 (2011): 3–18.

Anderson, Charles P. "The Epistle to the Hebrews and the Pauline Letter Collection." *HTR* 59 (1966): 429–39.

Aristotle. *The "Art" of Rhetoric*. Translated by John Henry Freese. LCL. London: William Heinemann, 1926.

———. *The Works of Aristotle, Vol. XI: Rhetorica, De Rhetorica ad Alexandrum, De Poetica*. Translated by W. Rhys Roberts. Oxford: Oxford University Press, 1924.

Aschim, Anders. "Melchizedek and Jesus: 11QMelchizedek and the Epistle to the Hebrews" Pages 131–47 in *The Jewish Roots of Christological Monotheism*. Edited by Carey C. Newman, James R. Davila, and Gladys S. Lewis. JSJSup 63. Leiden: Brill, 1999.

Attridge, Harold W. "'Heard Because of His Reverence' (Heb 5:7)." *JBL* 98 (1979): 90–93.

———. *The Epistle to the Hebrews: A Commentary on the Epistle to the Hebrews*. Hermeneia. Philadelphia: Fortress Press, 1989.

Aune, David E. *Prophecy in Early Christianity and the Ancient Mediterranean World*. Grand Rapids: Eerdmans, 1983.

__________. *Revelation 17–22*. WBC 52C. Dallas: Word, Incorporated, 1998.

Balz, Horst Robert, and Gerhard Schneider, eds. *Exegetical Dictionary of the New Testament*. 3 vols. Grand Rapids: Eerdmans, 1990.

Barclay, John M. G. "Mirror-reading a Polemical Letter: Galatians as a Test Case." *JSNT* 31 (1987): 73–93.

__________. *Paul and the Gift*. Grand Rapids: Eerdmans, 2015.

Barton, George A. "The Date of the Epistle to the Hebrews." *JBL* 57 (1938): 195–207.

Basta, Pasquale. "Only the One Who Works Enters into Rest: The Homiletic Logic of Heb 3,7–4,11." *Bib* 99 (2018): 567–91.

Bateman, IV, Herbert W. "Psalm 110:1 and the New Testament." *BibSac* 149 (1992): 438–53.

__________. "Two First-Century Messianic Uses of the OT: Heb 1:5–13 and *4QFlor* 1.1–19." *JETS* 38 (1995): 11–27.

__________. "Psalm 45:6–7 and Its Christological Contributions to Hebrews." *TrinJ* 22 (2001): 3–21.

Bates, William H. "The Authorship of the Epistle to the Hebrews Again." *BibSac* 79 (1922): 93–96.

Bauckham, Richard. "Monotheism and Christology in Hebrews 1." Pages 167–85 in *Early Jewish and Christian Monotheism*. Edited by Loren T. Stuckenbruck and Wendy E. S. North. London; New York: T&T Clark, 2004.

__________. "The Parting of the Ways: What Happened and Why." Pages 175–92 in *The Jewish World around the New Testament: Collected Essays I*. Edited by Jörg Frey. WUNT 233. Tübingen: Mohr Siebeck, 2008.

__________. *Jesus and the God of Israel: God Crucified and Other Essays on the New Testament's Christology of Divine Identity*. Grand Rapids: Eerdmans, 2008.

__________. "The Divinity of Jesus Christ in the Epistle to the Hebrews," Pages 15–36 in *The Epistle to the Hebrews and Christian Theology*. Edited by Richard Bauckham *et al*. Grand Rapids: Eerdmans, 2009.

Baugh, S. M. "The Cloud of Witnesses in Hebrews 11." *WTJ* 68 (2006): 113–32.

———. "Greek Periods in the Book of Hebrews." *NovT* 60 (2018): 24–44.

Beale, G. K. *The Temple and the Church's Mission: A Biblical Theology of the Dwelling Place of God*. NSBT 17. Downers Grove, IL: InterVarsity Press, 2004.

———. *A New Testament Biblical Theology: The Unfolding of the Old Testament in the New*. Grand Rapids: Baker Academic, 2011.

Beale, G. K., and Mitchell Kim. *God Dwells among Us: A Biblical Theology of the Temple*. ESBT. Downers Grove, IL: IVP Academic, 2021.

Beard, Mary, *et al. Literacy in the Roman World*. JRASup 3. Ann Arbor: University of Michigan Press, 1991.

Beasley-Murray, George R. *Baptism in the New Testament*. Grand Rapids: Eerdmans, 1962.

Becker, Adam H., and Annette Yoshiko Reed, eds. *The Ways That Never Parted: Jews and Christians in Late Antiquity and the Early Middle Ages*. Philadelphia: Fortress, 2007.

Bendoraitis, Kristian A. *"Behold, the Angels Came and Served Him": A Compositional Analysis of Angels in Matthew*. LNTS 523. London: Bloomsbury T&T Clark, 2015.

Bertolet, Timothy. "Hebrews 5:7 as the Cry of the Davidic Sufferer." *IDS* 51 (2017). https://doi.org/10.4102/ids.v51i1.2286.

Bing, Charles C. "Does Fire in Hebrews Refer to Hell?" *BibSac* 167 (2010): 342–57.

Black, David Alan. "The Problem of the Literary Structure of Hebrews: An Evaluation and a Proposal." *GTJ* 7 (1986): 163–77.

———. "Hebrews 1:1–4: A Study in Discourse Analysis." *WTJ* 49 (1987): 175–94.

———. "On the Pauline Authorship of Hebrews." *Faith and Mission* 16 (1999): 32–51, 78–86.

———. "Who Wrote Hebrews? The Internal and External Evidence Reexamined." *Faith and Mission* 18 (2001): 3–26.

———. *The Authorship of Hebrews: The Case for Paul*. Gonzalez, FL: Energion Publications, 2013.

Blass, Friedrich, Albert Debrunner, and Robert Walter Funk. *A Greek Grammar of the New Testament and Other Early Christian Literature*. Chicago: University of Chicago Press, 1961.

Bligh, John. *Chiastic Analysis of the Epistle to the Hebrews*. Oxon: Athenaeum Press, 1966.

Blomberg, Craig. "The Structure of 2 Corinthians 1–7." *CTR* 4 (1989): 3–20.

Bockmuehl, Markus. "Abraham's Faith in Hebrews 11." Pages 364–73 in *The Epistle to the Hebrews and Christian Theology*. Edited by Richard Bauckham *et al*. Grand Rapids: Eerdmans, 2009.

Bott, Nicholas T. "'And by faith, because Abraham considered him faithful who had promised, Sarah herself received power to conceive': A Reconsideration of Heb 11:11." *TrinJ* 32 (2011): 205–19.

Botterweck, G. Johannes, Helmer Ringgren, and Heinz-Josef Fabry, eds. *Theological Dictionary of the Old Testament*. 15 vols. Grand Rapids; Cambridge, U.K.: Eerdmans, 1977–2012.

Boyarin, Daniel. "Midrash in Hebrews / Hebrews as Midrash." Pages 15–30 in *Hebrews in Contexts*. Edited by Gabriella Gelardini and Harold W. Attridge. Ancient Judaism and Early Christianity 91. Leiden: Brill, 2016.

Briggs, Charles Augustus. *Messianic Prophecy*. New York: Charles Scribner's Sons, 1886.

Bromiley, Geoffrey W., ed. *The International Standard Bible Encyclopedia, Revised*. Grand Rapids: Eerdmans, 1979–1988.

Brophy, Robert, and Mary Brophy. "Deaths in the Pan-Hellenic Games II: All Combative Sports." *AJP* 106 (1985): 171–98.

Brown, Colin, ed. *New International Dictionary of New Testament Theology*. 4 vols. Grand Rapids: Zondervan, 1975–1985.

Brown, Francis, Samuel Rolles Driver, and Charles Augustus Briggs. *Enhanced Brown-Driver-Briggs Hebrew and English Lexicon*. Oxford: Clarendon Press, 1977.

Brown, Raymond E. "Does the New Testament Call Jesus God?" *TS* 26 (1965): 545–73.

Bruce, F. F. *New Testament History*. New York: Doubleday, 1969.

———. *The Epistle to the Hebrews*. Rev. ed. NICNT. Grand Rapids: Eerdmans, 1990.

Burns, Lanier. "Hermeneutical Issues and Principles in Hebrews as Exemplified in the Second Chapter." *JETS* 39 (1996): 587–607.

Byron, John. "Abel's Blood and the Ongoing Cry for Vengeance." *CBQ* 73 (2011): 743–56.

Cadwallader, Alan H. "The Correction of the Text of Hebrews Towards the LXX." *NovT* 34 (1992): 257–92.

Caird, George B. "The Exegetical Method of the Epistle to the Hebrews." *CJT* 5 (1959): 44–51.

Calaway, Jared C. *The Sabbath and the Sanctuary: Access to God in the Letter to the Hebrews and Its Priestly Context*. WUNT 349. Tübingen: Mohr Siebeck, 2013.

Camacho, Harold S. "The Altar of Incense in Hebrews 9:3–4." *AUSS* 24 (1986): 5–12.

Campbell, Constantine R. *Verbal Aspect, the Indicative Mood, and Narrative*. New York: Peter Lang, 2007.

____________. *Verbal Aspect and Non-Indicative Verbs: Further Soundings in the Greek New Testament*. Studies in Biblical Greek 15. New York: Peter Lang 2008.

____________. *Basics of Verbal Aspect in Biblical Greek*. Grand Rapids: Zondervan, 2008.

Caneday, Ardel B. "The Eschatological World Already Subjected to the Son: The *oikoumenē* of Hebrews 1:6 and the Son's Enthronement." Pages 28–39 in *A Cloud of Witnesses: The Theology of Hebrews in Its Ancient Contexts*. Edited by Richard Bauckham *et al*. LNTS 387. London: T&T Clark, 2008.

Capes, David B. *Old Testament Yahweh Texts in Paul's Christology*. Tübingen: Mohr Siebeck, 1992. Repr. Waco, TX: Baylor University Press, 2017.

____________. "YHWH Texts and Monotheism in Paul's Christology." Pages 120–37 in *Early Jewish and Christian Monotheism*. Edited by Loren T. Stuckenbruck and Wendy E. S. North. London; New York: T&T Clark, 2004.

Cathcart, Kevin, Michael Maher, and Martin McNamara, eds. *The Aramaic Bible: The Isaiah Targum*. Vol. 11. Translated by Bruce D. Chilton. Collegeville, MN: The Liturgical Press, 1990.

Cathcart, Kevin, Michael Maher, and Martin McNamara, eds. *The Aramaic Bible: The Targum of Psalms*. Vol. 16. Translated by David M. Stec. Collegeville, MN: Liturgical Press, 2004.

Chapman, David W. *Ancient Jewish and Christian Perceptions of Crucifixion*. WUNT 244. Tübingen: Mohr Siebeck, 2008.

Charles, J. Daryl. "The Angels, Sonship and Birthright in the Letter to the Hebrews." *JETS* 33 (1990): 171–78.

Charlesworth, James H., ed. *The Old Testament Pseudepigrapha and the New Testament: Expansions of the "Old Testament" and Legends, Wisdom, and Philosophical Literature, Prayers, Psalms and Odes, Fragments of Lost Judeo-Hellenistic Works*. Vol. 2. New Haven; London: Yale University Press, 1985.

Chernick, Michael "Internal Restraints on Gezerah Shawah's Application." *JQR* 80 (1990): 253–82.

Chilton, Bruce, and Jacob Neusner. *Judaism in the New Testament: Practices and Beliefs*. New York: Routledge, 1995.

Church, Philip. "Hebrews 1:10–12 and the Renewal of the Cosmos." *TynBul* 67 (2016): 269–86.

__________. "The Punctuation of Hebrews 10:2 and Its Significance for the Date of Hebrews." *TynBul* 71 (2020): 281–92.

__________. "Turning Away from the Living God (Heb. 3:12): The Growth and Decline of the Relapse Theory for the Setting of Hebrews." *EvQ* 94 (2023): 1–25.

Cicero, Marcus Tullius. *Cicero's Tusculan Disputations*. Translated by C. D. Yonge. New York: Harper and Brothers, 1877.

Clark, David J. "Criteria for Identifying Chiasm." *LB* 35 (1975): 63–72.

Clements, Ronald E. "The Use of the Old Testament in Hebrews." *SWJT* 28 (1985): 36–45.

Cockerill, Gareth Lee Cockerill. "Hebrews 1:6: Source and Significance." *BBR* 9 (1999): 51–64.

__________. "The Better Resurrection (Heb. 11:35): A Key to the Structure and Rhetorical Purpose of Hebrews 11." *TynBul* 51 (2000): 215–34.

__________. "A Wesleyan Arminian View." Pages in 257–92 in *Four Views on the Warning Passages in Hebrews*. Edited by Herbert W. Bateman IV. Grand Rapids: Kregel, 2007.

__________. "A Wesleyan Arminian Response to a Moderate Reformed View." Pages 415–29 in *Four Views on the Warning Passages in Hebrews*. Edited by Herbert W. Bateman IV. Grand Rapids: Kregel, 2007.

———. *The Epistle to the Hebrews*. NICNT. Grand Rapids: Eerdmans, 2012.

Coetsee, Albert J. "Hebrews 12:9 Revisited: The Background of the Phrase 'and live'." *HvTSt* 76 (2020). https://doi.org/ 10.4102/hts.v76i1.5863

Cohen, A., ed. *The Soncino* Chumash. Soncino Books of the Bible. New York: Soncino Press, 1977.

Cohn-Sherbok, Dan. "Paul and Rabbinic Exegesis." *SJT* 35 (1982): 117–32.

Colijn, Brenda B. "'Let Us Approach': Soteriology in the Epistle to the Hebrews." *JETS* 39 (1996): 571–86.

Collins, John J. "Messianism in the Maccabean Period." Pages 97–109 in *Judaisms and their Messiahs at the Turn of the Christian Era*. Edited by Jacob Neusner, Williams S. Green, and Ernest Frerichs. Cambridge: Cambridge University Press, 1987.

———. "Introduction: Towards the Morphology of a Genre." *Semeia* 14 (2003): 1–29.

Compton, Jared. "The Origin of *soma* in Heb 10:5, Another Look at a Recent Proposal." *TrinJ* 32 (2011): 19–29.

———. *Psalm 110 and the Logic of Hebrews*. LNTS 537. London: Bloomsbury T&T Clark, 2015.

Cook, John Granger. *Crucifixion in the Mediterranean World*. WUNT 327. Tübingen: Mohr Siebeck, 2014.

Cortez, Felix H. "From the Holy to the Most Holy Place: The Period of Hebrews 9:6–10 and the Day of Atonement as a Metaphor of Transition." *JBL* 125 (2006): 527–47.

———. "Creation in Hebrews." *AUSS* 53 (2105): 279–320.

Cosby, Michael. *The Rhetorical Composition and Function of Hebrews 11: In Light of Example Lists in Antiquity*. Macon, GA: Mercer University Press, 1988.

———. "The Rhetorical Composition of Hebrews 11." *JBL* 107 (1988): 257–73.

Costly, Angela. "A New Look at Hebrews 4:12–13." *PIBA* 40 (2017): 23–42.

Craigie, Peter C. *Psalms 1–50*. 2nd ed. WBC 19. Nashville: Nelson, 2004.

Croy, N. Clayton. *Endurance in Suffering: Hebrews 12:1–13 in Its Rhetorical, Religious, and Philosophical Context.* SNTSMS 98. Cambridge: Cambridge University Press, 1998.

Crowe, Brandon D. "Son and Priest, Then and Now: Christology and Redemptive History in Hebrews in Light of the History of Interpretation." *WTJ* 84 (2022): 19–39.

Dahms, John V. "The First Readers of Hebrews." *JETS* 20 (1977): 365–75.

Daly, Robert J. "The Soteriological Significance of the Sacrifice of Isaac." *CBQ* 39 (1977): 45–75.

Daniel, Jerry L. "Anti-Semitism in the Hellenistic-Roman Period." *JBL* 98 (1979): 45–65.

Danker, Frederick W., Walter Bauer, William F. Arndt, and F. Wilbur Gingrich. *Greek-English Lexicon of the New Testament and Other Early Christian Literature.* 3rd ed. Chicago: University of Chicago Press, 2000.

Das, A. Andrew. *Solving the Romans Debate*. Minneapolis: Fortress, 2007.

Davis, Barry C. "Is Psalm 110 a Messianic Psalm?" *BibSac* 157 (2000): 160–73.

Davis, Jr., Phillip A. *The Place of Paideia in Hebrews' Moral Thought*. WUNT 475. Tübingen: Mohr Siebeck, 2018.

Day, Adam W. "Bearing the Reproach of Christ: The Background of Psalm 68 (LXX) in Hebrews 13:9–16." *Presb* 44 (2018): 126–41.

Decker, Rodney J. "The Original Readers of Hebrews." *Journal of Ministry and Theology* 3 (1999): 20–49.

deClaissé-Walford, Nancy, Rolf A. Jacobson, and Beth LaNeel Tanner. *The Book of Psalms*. NICOT. Grand Rapids: Eerdmans, 2014.

Deissmann, Gustav Adolf. *Bible Studies: Contributions Chiefly from Papyri and Inscriptions to the History of the Language, the Literature and the Religion of Hellenistic Judaism and Primitive Christianity*. Translated by Alexander Grieve. 1901. Repr., Winona Lake, IN: Alpha Publications, 1979.

Delitzsch, Franz. *Commentary on the Epistle to the Hebrews*. Clark's Foreign Theological Library. Edinburgh: T&T Clark, 1874.

Demarest, Bruce A. "Hebrews 7:3: A *Crux Interpretum* Historically Considered." *EvQ* 49 (1977): 141–62.

deSilva, David A. "Despising Shame: A Cultural-Anthropological Investigation of the Epistle to the Hebrews." *JBL* 113 (1994): 439–61.

———. "The Epistle to the Hebrews in Social-Scientific Perspective." *ResQ* 36 (1994): 1–21.

———. "Exchanging Favor for Wrath: Apostasy in Hebrews and Patron-Client Relationships." *JBL* 115 (1996): 91–116.

———. "Hebrews 6:4–8: A Socio-Rhetorical Investigation (Part 1)." *TynBul* 50 (1999): 33–57.

———. *The Hope of Glory: Honor Discourse and New Testament Interpretation*. Collegeville, MN: Liturgical Press, 1999.

———. *Perseverance in Gratitude: A Social-Rhetorical Commentary on the Epistle 'to the Hebrews.'* Grand Rapids: Eerdmans, 2000.

———. *The Letter to the Hebrews in Social-Scientific Perspective*. Cascade Companion 15. Eugene, OR: Cascade Books, 2012.

———. *Honor, Patronage, Kinship, and Purity: Unlocking New Testament Culture*. 2nd ed. Downers Grove, IL: IVP Academic, 2022.

Dio Chrysostom. *Discourses*. Translated by J. W. Cohoon and H. Lamar Crosby. 5 vols. LCL. London: William Heinemann, 1922.

Diogenes Laertius. *Lives of Eminent Philosophers*. Translated by R. D. Hicks. 2 vols. LCL. Cambridge: Harvard University press, 1959.

Dodd, C. H. *According to the Scriptures: The Substructure of New Testament Theology*. London: Fontana Books 1965.

Dods, Marcus. *The Epistle to the Hebrews*. Vol. 4 of *The Expositor's Greek Testament*. Edited by W. Robertson Nicoll. Repr., Grand Rapids: Eerdmans, 1979.

Donfried, Karl P., and Peter Richardson, eds. *Judaism and Christianity in First-Century Rome*. Grand Rapids: Eerdmans, 1998.

Doran, Robert. "The Persuasive Arguments at Play in Heb 2:11 and 7:12." *NovT* 60 (2018): 45–54.

du Toit, Andrie. "*ta pros ton theon* in Romans and Hebrews: Towards Understanding an Enigmatic Phrase." *ZNW* 101 (2010): 241–51.

Duff, Justin Harrison. "The Blood of Goats and Calves … and Bulls? An Allusion to Isaiah 1:11 LXX in Hebrews 10:4." *JBL* 137 (2018): 765–83.

__________. "Allusions to Ezekiel and Bodily Resurrection in Hebrews." *CBQ* 84 (2022): 627–41.

Dumbrell, W. J. "The Spirits of Just Men Made Perfect." *EvQ* 48 (1976): 154–59.

Dunn, James D. G. *The Partings of the Ways: Between Christianity and Judaism and Their Significance for the Character of Christianity*, 2nd ed. London: SCM Press, 2006.

Dunn, James D. G., ed. *Jews and Christians: The Parting of the Ways A.D. 70 to 135*. Grand Rapids: Eerdmans, 1999.

Dunning, Benjamin. "The Intersection of Alien Status and Cultic Discourse in the Epistle to the Hebrews." Pages 177–98 in *Hebrews: Contemporary Methods—New Insights*. Edited by Gabriella Gelardini. Biblical Interpretation Series 75. Atlanta: Society of Biblical Literature, 2005.

Dyer, Bryan R. "The Epistle to the Hebrews in Recent Research: Studies on the Author's Identity, His Use of the Old Testament, and Theology." *JGRChJ* 9 (2013): 104–31.

__________. "'All of These Died in Faith': Hebrews 11 and Faith in the Face of Death." *CBQ* 83 (2021): 638–54.

__________. "'In the Midst of the Assembly I Will Praise You': Hebrews 2.12 and Its Contribution to the Argument of the Epistle." *JSNT* 43 (2021): 523–38.

__________. "The Wordplay *mathein-pathein* in Hebrews 5:8." *NovT* 63 (2021): 489–504.

Ebert, Daniel J. "The Chiastic Structure of the Prologue to Hebrews." *TrinJ* 13 (1992): 163–79.

Edersheim, Alfred. *The Temple: Its Ministry and Services as They Were at the Time of Christ*. Grand Rapids: Eerdmans, 1980.

Ehorn, Seth M. *Exodus in the New Testament*. LNTS 663. New York: T&T Clark, 2022.

Ehrenkrook, Jason von. "Christians, Pagans, and the Politics of *Paideia* in Late Antiquity." Pages 255–65 in *Second Temple Jewish Paideia in Context*. Edited by Jason M. Zurawski and Gabriele Boccaccini. BZNW 228. Berlin: De Gruyter, 2017.

Eisenbaum, Pamela M. *The Jewish Heroes of Chistian History: Hebrews 11 in Literary Context*. SBL Dissertation Series 156. Atlanta: Scholars Press, 1997.

———. "Locating Hebrews Within the Literary Landscape of Christian Origins." Pages 213–37 in *Hebrews: Contemporary Methods—New Insights*. Edited by Gabriella Gelardini. Atlanta: Society of Biblical Literature, 2005.

Ellingworth, Paul. *The Epistle to the Hebrews: A Commentary on the Greek Text*. NIGTC. Grand Rapids: Eerdmans, 1993.

Ellis, E. Earle. "Biblical Interpretation in the New Testament Church." Pages 691–725 in *Mikra: Text, Translation, Reading and Interpretation of the Hebrew Bible in Ancient Judaism and Early Christianity*. Edited by Martin Jan Mulder. CRINT 2.1. Philadelphia: Fortress, 1988.

———. *The Old Testament in Early Christianity*. Grand Rapids: Baker Books, 1991.

Emadi, Matthew H. *The Royal Priest: Psalm 110 in Biblical Theology*. NSBT 60. Downers Grove, IL: IVP Academic, 2022.

Emerton, J. A. "The Textual and Linguistic Problems of Habakkuk II.4–5." *JTS* 28 (1977): 1–18.

Emmrich, Martin. "*Pneuma* in Hebrews: Prophet and Interpreter." *WTJ* 63 (2002): 55–71.

———. "Hebrews 6:4–6—Again!" *WTJ* 65 (2003): 83–95.

Enns, Peter E. "Creation and Re-Creation: Psalm 95 and Its Interpretation in Hebrews 3:1–4:13." *WTJ* 55 (1993): 255–80.

Erickson, Millard J. *Christian Theology*. 3rd ed. Grand Rapids: Baker Academic, 2013.

Estelle, Bryan D. *Echoes of Exodus: Tracing a Biblical Motif*. Downers Grove, IL: IVP Academic, 2018.

Eusebius of Caesarea. *Eusebius: Church History, Life of Constantine the Great, and Oration in Praise of Constantine*. In Vol. 1 of *The Nicene and Post-Nicene Fathers*, Series 2. Edited by Philip Schaff. 1886–1889. 14 vols. Repr., Peabody, MA: Hendrickson, 1994.

Evans, Craig A., "Jesus and the Continuing Exile of Israel." Pages 77–100 in *Jesus and the Restoration of Israel: A Critical Assessment of N. T. Wright's Jesus and the Victory of God*. Edited by Carey C. Newman. Downers Grove, IL: IVP Academic, 1999.

Fairhurst, Alan M. "Hellenistic Influence in the Epistle to the Hebrews." *TynBul* 7–8 (1961): 17–27.

Fanning, Buist M. *Verbal Aspect in New Testament Greek*. Oxford: Clarendon, 1990.

Fee, Gordon D. *Pauline Christology: An Exegetical-Theological Study*. Peabody, MA: Hendrickson, 2007.

Ferch, Arthur J. *The Son of Man in Daniel Seven*. Andrews University Seminary Doctoral Dissertation Series 6. Berrien Springs: Andrews University Press, 1979.

Filson, Floyd V. "The Epistle to the Hebrews." *JBR* 22 (1954): 20–26.

Finegan, Jack. *Handbook of Biblical Chronology*. Rev. ed. Peabody, MA: Hendrickson, 1998.

Fitzmyer, Jospeh A. "'Now This Melchizedek…' (Heb 7,1)." *CBQ* 25 (1963) 305–21.

__________. "Further Light on Melchizedek from Qumran Cave 11." *JBL* 86 (1967): 25–41.

Fletcher-Louis, Crispin. *Jesus Monotheism: Christological Origins: The Emerging Consensus and Beyond*. Vol. 1. Eugene, OR: Whymanity Publishing, 2019.

Flusser, David. "Today If You Will Listen to His Voice: Creative Jewish Exegesis in Hebrews 3–4." Pages 55–61 in *Creative Biblical Exegesis: Christian and Jewish Hermeneutics through the Centuries*. Edited by Benjamin Uffenheimer and Henning Graf Reventlow. JSOTSup 59. Sheffield: JSOT Press, 1988.

Fox, Michael R. ed. *Reverberations of the Exodus in Scripture*. Eugene, OR: Pickwick Publications, 2014.

France, R. T. "The Writer of Hebrews as a Biblical Expositor." *TynBul* 47 (1996): 245–76.

Freeman, Hobart E. "The Problem of the Efficacy of the Old Testament Sacrifices." *Bulletin of the Evangelical Theological Society* 5 (1962): 73–79.

Freedman, David Noel *et al*, eds. *The Anchor Yale Bible Dictionary*. New York: Doubleday, 1992.

Fuller, Lois K. "The 'Genitive Absolute' in New Testament/Hellenistic Greek: A Proposal for Clearer Understanding." *JGRChJ* 3 (2006): 142–67.

Gambetti, Sandra. The Alexandrian Riots of 38 C.E. and the Persecution of the Jews: A Historical Reconstruction. JSJSup 135. Leiden: Brill, 2009.

Gamble, J. "Symbol and Reality in the Epistle to the Hebrews." *JBL* 45 (1926): 162–70.

Garrett, Susan R. *No Ordinary Angel: Celestial Spirits and Christian Claims about Jesus*. New Haven; London: Yale University Press, 2008.

Gieschen, Charles A. *Angelomorphic Christology: Antecedents and Early Evidence*. AGJU 42. Leiden: Brill, 1998.

Gelardini, Gabriella. "Hebrews, An Ancient Synagogue Homily for *Tisha Be-Av*: Its Function, Its Basis, Its Theological Interpretation." Pages 107–27 in *Hebrews: Contemporary Methods—New Insights*. Edited by Gabriella Gelardini. Atlanta: Society of Biblical Literature 2005.

______. *Verhartet eure Herzen nicht: Der Hebraer, eine Synagogenhomilie zu Tischa be-Aw*. Leiden: Brill, 2006.

______. "From 'Linguistic Turn' and Hebrews Scholarship to *Anadiplosis Iterata*: The Enigma of a Structure." *HTR* 102 (2009): 51–73.

______. "The Inauguration of Yom Kippur according to the LXX and Its Cessation or Perpetuation according to the Book of Hebrews: A Systematic Comparison." Pages 225–54 in *The Day of Atonement: Its Interpretations in Early Jewish and Christian Traditions*. Edited by Thomas Hieke and Tobias Nicklas. Leiden: Brill, 2012.

______. "Faith in Hebrews and Its Relationship to Soteriology: An Interpretation in the Context of the Concept of Fides in Roman Culture." Pages 249–56 in *So Great a Salvation: A Dialogue on the Atonement in Hebrews*. Edited by Jon C. Laansma, George H. Guthrie, Cynthia Long Westfall, and Chris Keith. LNTS 516. London; New York; Oxford; New Delhi; Sydney: T&T Clark, 2019.

Gabriella Gelardini and Harold W. Attridge, eds. *Hebrews in Contexts*. Ancient Judaism and Early Christianity 91. Leiden: Brill, 2016

Girdwood, James, and Peter Verkruyse. *Hebrews*. College Press NIV Commentary. Joplin: College Press, 1997.

Gleason, Randall C. "The Old Testament Background of the Warning in Hebrews 6:4–8." *BibSac* 155 (1998): 62–91.

______. "The Old Testament Background of Rest in Hebrews 3:7–4:11." *BibSac* 157 (2000): 281–303.

______. "Angels and the Eschatology of Heb 1–2." *NTS* 49 (2003): 90–107.

Gleaves, G. Scott. *Did Jesus Speak Greek?: The Emerging Evidence of Greek Dominance in First-Century Palestine*. Eugene, OR: Pickwick, 2015.

Godet, Frédéric Louis. *Studies on the Epistles of St. Paul*. Translated by Annie Harwood Holmden. New York: Hodder and Stoughton, 1889.

Goldstein, Jonathan A. *II Maccabees: A New Translation with Introduction and Commentary*. AYB 41A. New York: Doubleday, 1983.

Goppelt, Leonhard. *Typos: The Typological Interpretation of the Old Testament in the New*. Translated by Donald H. Madvig. Grand Rapids: Eerdmans, 1982.

Gorman, Michael. *Apostle of the Crucified Lord: A Theological Introduction to Paul and His Letters, 2nd ed.* Grand Rapids: Eerdmans, 2017.

Gräbe, Peter. "The New Covenant and Christian Identity in Hebrews." Pages 118–27 in *A Cloud of Witnesses: The Theology of Hebrews in Its Ancient Contexts*. Edited by Richard Bauckham *et al*. LNTS 387. London: T&T Clark, 2008.

Granerød, Gard. "Melchizedek in Hebrews 7." *Bib* 90 (2009): 188–202.

Gray, Patrick. "Brotherly Love and the High Priest Christology of Hebrews." *JBL* 122 (2003): 335–51.

Griffith, Sheila. "The Epistle to the Hebrews in Modern Interpretation." *RevExp* 102 (2005): 235–54.

Grillmeier, Aloys. *Christ in Christian Tradition, Vol. 1: From the Apostolic Age to Chalcedon (451)*. 2nd rev. ed. Translated by John Bowden. Atlanta: John Knox Press, 1975.

Grindheim, Sigurd. "Direct Dependence on Philo in the Epistle to the Hebrews." *NovT* 65 (2023): 517–43.

———. *The Letter to the Hebrews*. PNTC. Grand Rapids: Eerdmans, 2023.

Gunton, Colin E. *The Actuality of Atonement: A Study of Metaphor, Rationality, and the Christian Tradition*. London; New York: T&T Clark, 2003.

Gurdorf, Michael E. "Through a Classical Lens: Hebrews 2:16." *JBL* 119 (2000): 105–108.

Gurtner, Daniel M. "LXX Syntax and the Identity of the NT Veil." *NovT* 47 (2005): 344–53.

Guthrie, George H. *The Structure of Hebrews: A Text-Linguistic Analysis*. Biblical Studies Library. Grand Rapids: Baker Books, 1998.

———. "Hebrews' Eschatology in Hermeneutical Perspective." Paper read at the Annual Meeting of the Evangelical Theological Society, Danvers, MA, 1999.

———. "The Case for Apollos as the Author of Hebrews." *Faith and Mission* 18 (2001): 41–56.

———. "Hebrews' Use of the Old Testament: Recent Trends in Research." *CurBR* 1 (2003): 271–94.

Guthrie, George H., and Russell D. Quinn, "A Discourse Analysis of the Use of Psalm 8:4–6 in Hebrews 2:5–9." *JETS* 49 (2006): 235–46.

Hagner, Donald A. *Hebrews*. NIBCNT. Peabody, MA: Hendrickson, 1990.

———. *Hebrews*. Understanding the Bible Commentary Series. Grand Rapids: Baker Books, 2011.

Hahn, Scott W. "A Broken Covenant and the Curse of Death: A Study of Hebrews 9:15–22." *CBQ* 66 (2004): 416–36.

Hamm, Dennis. "Praying 'Regularly' (not 'Constantly'): A Note on the Cultic Background of *dia pantos* at Luke 24:53, Acts 10:2, and Hebrews 9:6, 13:15." *ExpTim* 116 (2004): 50–52.

Hanson, Paul D. *The Dawn of Apocalyptic: The Historical and Sociological Roots of Jewish Apocalyptic Eschatology*. Rev. ed. Philadelphia: Fortress, 1979.

Harland, Philip A. *Associations, Synagogues, and Congregations: Claiming a Place in Ancient Mediterranean Society*. Minneapolis: Augsburg Fortress, 2003.

Harriman, K. R. "Through Whom He Made the Ages." *NovT* 61 (2019): 423–39.

Harris, Murray J. "The Translation and Significance of '*ho theos*' in Hebrews 1:8–9." *TynBul* 36 (1985): 129–62.

———. *Jesus as God: The New Testament Use of* Theos *in Reference to Jesus*. Grand Rapids: Baker Books, 1992.

Harris, R. Laird, Gleason L. Archer Jr., and Bruce K. Waltke, eds. *Theological Wordbook of the Old Testament*. Chicago: Moody Press, 1999.

Harris, William V. *Ancient Literacy*. Cambridge: Harvard University Press, 1989.

Harrisville, Roy. "The Concept of Newness in the New Testament." *JBL* 74 (1955): 69–79.

Hasel, Gerhard F. "Sabbath. " *AYBD* 5:849–56.

Hay, David M. *Glory at the Right Hand*. SBLMS 18. Atlanta: Society of Biblical Literature, 1989.

Hays, Richard B. *Echoes of Scripture in the Letters of Paul*. New Haven: Yale University Press, 1989.

———. "'Here We Have No Lasting City': New Covenantalism in Hebrews." Pages 151–73 in *The Epistle to the Hebrews and Christian Theology*. Edited by Richard Bauckham *et al*. Grand Rapids: Eerdmans, 2009.

Heath, David M. "Chiastic Structures in Hebrews: With a Focus on 1:7–14 and 12:26–29." *Neot* 46 (2012): 61–82.

Hengel, Martin. *Judaism and Hellenism: Studies in Their Encounter in Palestine during the Early Hellenistic Period*. Translated by John Bowden. Vols. 1 & 2. Philadelphia: Fortress, 1974.

Herodian. *Herodian of Antioch's History of the Roman Empire*. Translated by Edward C. Echols. Berkeley: University of California Press, 1961.

Hill, Craig Allen. "The Use of Perfection Language in Hebrews 5:14 and 6:1 and the Contextual Interpretation of 5:11–6:3." *JETS* 57 (2014): 727–42.

Hill, Craig C. *Hellenists and Hebrews*. Minneapolis: Augsburg Fortress, 1992.

Hinson, David Francis. *Theology of the Old Testament*. London: SPCK, 2001.

Hoerber, Robert G. "On the Translation of Hebrews 11:1." *Concordia Journal* 21 (1995): 77–79.

Hollinger, Zoe. "Rethinking the Translation of *trechōmen ton … agōna* in Hebrews 12.1 in Light of Ancient Graeco-Roman Literature." *The Bible Translator* 70 (2019): 94–111.

Holmgren, Fredrick. *The Old Testament and the Significance of Jesus*. Grand Rapids: Eerdmans, 1999.

Horace (Quintus Horatius Flaccus). "Horace: The Odes." Translated by A. S. Kline, 2003. <https://www.poetryintranslation.com/PITBR/Latin/Horacehome.php>

Horbury, W. "The Aaronic Priesthood in the Epistle to the Hebrews." *JSNT* 19 (1983): 43–71.

Hornblower, Simon, and Antony Spawforth, eds. *Oxford Classical Dictionary*. Edited by 3rd ed. Oxford: Oxford University Press, 2003.

Horton, Jr., Fred L. *The Melchizedek Tradition: A Critical examination of the Sources to the Fifth Century A.D. and in the Epistle to the Hebrews*. Cambridge: Cambridge University Press, 1976.

Howard, George. "Hebrews and the OT Quotations." *NovT* 10 (1968): 208–16.

Hutchens, Joshua Caleb. "Christian Worship in Hebrews 12:28 as Ethical and Exclusive." *JETS* 59 (2016): 507–22.

Hughes, John J. "Hebrews IX 15ff and Galatians III 15ff: A Study in Covenant Practice and Procedure." *NovT* 21 (1979): 27–96.

Hughes, Philip Edgcumbe. "Hebrews 6:4–6 and the Peril of Apostasy." *WTJ* 35 (1973): 137–55.

———. "The Blood of Jesus and His Heavenly Priesthood in Hebrews. Part I, The Significance of the Blood of Jesus," *BibSac* 130 (1973): 99–109.

———. "The Blood of Jesus and His Heavenly Priesthood in Hebrews. Part II, The High-Priestly Sacrifice of Christ." *BibSac* 130 (1973): 195–212.

———. "The Blood of Jesus and His Heavenly Priesthood in Hebrews. Part III, The Meaning of 'the true tent' and 'the greater and more perfect tent'." *BibSac* 130 (1973): 305–14.

———. *A Commentary on the Epistle to the Hebrews*. NICNT. Grand Rapids: Eerdmans, 1977.

Hurst, L. D. "How 'Platonic' are Heb. viii.5 and ix.23f?" *JTS* 34 (1983): 156–68.

———. *The Epistle to the Hebrews: Its Background of Thought*. SNTSMS 65. Cambridge: Cambridge University Press, 1990.

Isocrates. *Isocrates I*. Vol. 4 of *The Oratory of Classical Greece*. Translated by David C. Mirhady and Yun Lee Too. Austin: University of Texas Press, 2000.

———. *Isocrates*. Translated by George Norlin. 3 vols. LCL. London: William Heinemann, 1928.

Jaeger, Werner. *Paideia: The Ideals of Greek Culture*. 3 vols. Oxford: Blackwell, 1944–46.

Jaki, Stanley L. "The Sabbath-Rest of the Maker of All." *Asbury Theological Journal* 50 (1995): 37–49.

Jamieson, R. B. "When and Where Did Jesus Offer Himself? A Taxonomy of Recent Scholarship on Hebrews." *CurBR* 15 (2017): 338–68.

Jennings, Mark A. "The Veil and the High Priestly Robes of the Incarnation: Understanding the Context of Heb 10:20." *PRSt* 37 (2010): 85–97.

Jobes, Karen H. "Rhetorical Achievement in the Hebrews 10 'Misquote' of Psalm 40." *Bib* 72 (1991): 387–96.

____________. "The Function of Paranomasia in Hebrews 10:5–7." *TrinJ* 13 (1997): 181–91.

Johnson, Luke Timothy. *Hebrews: A Commentary*. NTL. Louisville: Westminster John Knox, 2012.

Johnson, Richard W. *Going Outside the Camp: The Sociological Function of the Levitical Critique in the Epistle to the Hebrews*. JSNTSup 209. Sheffield: Sheffield Academic, 2001.

Johnson, S. Lewis. "Some Important Mistranslations in Hebrews." *BibSac* 110 (1953): 25–31.

____________. *The Old Testament in the New: An Argument for Biblical Inspiration*. Grand Rapids: Zondervan, 1980.

Johnsson, William G. "The Pilgrimage Motif in the Book of Hebrews." *JBL* 97 (1978): 239–51.

Josephus, Flavius, and William Whiston. *The Works of Josephus: Complete and Unabridged*. Peabody: Hendrickson, 1987.

Joslin, Barry C. "Can Hebrews Be Structured? An Assessment of Eight Approaches." *CurBR* 6 (2007): 99–129.

Kaiser, Jr., Walter C. "The Promise Theme and the Theology of Rest." *BibSac* 130 (1973): 135–50.

____________. *Toward an Old Testament Theology*. Grand Rapids: Zondervan, 1978.

____________. *Toward Old Testament Ethics*. Grand Rapids: Academie Books, 1983.

____________. *The Uses of the Old Testament in the New*. Chicago: Moody Press, 1985.

____________. *Quest for Renewal*. Chicago: Moody Press, 1986.

Kaminsky, Joel S. "Corporate Personality." Pages 285–87 in *Eerdmans Dictionary of the Bible*. Edited by David Noel Freedman. Grand Rapids: Eerdmans, 2000.

Kanjuparambil, Philip. "Imperatival Participles in Rom 12 9–21." *JBL* 102 (1983): 285–88.

Katz, Peter. "The Quotations from Deuteronomy in Hebrews." *ZNW* 49 (1958): 213–23.

Kautzsch, Emil, ed. *Gesenius' Hebrew Grammar*. Translated by Arther E. Cowley. 2nd ed. Oxford: Clarendon, 1910.

Kees, Jason P. "Having Our Hearts Sprinkled Clean: The Influence of Ezekiel 36:25–26 on Hebrews 10:22." *WTJ* 83 (2021): 237–50.

Keil, Carl Friedrich, and Franz Delitzsch. *Biblical Commentary on the Old Testament*. Translated by James Martin *et al*. 25 vols. Edinburgh, 1857–1878. Repr., 10 vols., Grand Rapids: Eerdmans, 1949.

Kempson, Wayne R. "Hebrews 6:1–8." *RevExp* 91 (1994): 567–73.

Kibbe, Michael. "Requesting and Rejecting: *Paraiteomai* in Heb 12, 18–29." *Bib* 96 (2015): 282–86.

Kiley, Mark. "A Note on Hebrews 5:14." *CBQ* 42 (1980): 501–503.

Kim, Daniel E. "Jewish and Christian Theology from the Hebrew Bible: The Concept of Rest and Temple in the Targummim, Hebrews, and the Old Testament." Pages 31–46 in *Hebrews in Contexts*. Edited by Gabriella Gelardini and Harold W. Attridge. Ancient Judaism and Early Christianity 91. Leiden: Brill, 2016.

Kissi, Seth, and Ernest van Eck. "An Appeal to Personality in Hebrews; A Social-Scientific Study." *Neot* 51 (2017): 315–35.

Kistemaker, Simon. *The Psalm Citations in the Epistle to the Hebrews*. Amsterdam: Van Soest, 1961.

____________. *Exposition of the Epistle to the Hebrews*. NTC. Grand Rapids: Baker Books, 1984.

____________. "The Authorship of Hebrews." *Faith and Mission* 18 (2001): 57–69.

Kittel, Gerhard, and Gerhard Friedrich, eds. *Theological Dictionary of the New Testament*. Translated by Geoffrey W. Bromiley. 10 vols. Grand Rapids: Eerdmans, 1964–1976.

Klauck, Hans-Josef. *Ancient Letters and the New Testament: A Guide to Context and Exegesis*. Waco, TX: Baylor University Press, 2006.

Kline, Meredith. *Treaty of the Great King*. Grand Rapids: Eerdmans, 1963.

Kloppenborg, John S. *Christ's Associations: Connecting and Belonging in the Ancient City*. New Haven: Yale University Press, 2019.

Koehler, Ludwig, Walter Baumgartner, M. E. J. Richardson, and Johann Jakob Stamm. *The Hebrew and Aramaic Lexicon of the Old Testament*. 4 vols. Leiden: E.J. Brill, 1994–2000.

Koester, Craig R. "Hebrews, Rhetoric, and the Future of Humanity." *CBQ* 64 (2002): 103–23.

__________. *Hebrews: A New Translation with Introduction and Commentary*. AYB 36. New Haven: Yale University Press, 2008.

Koester, Helmut. "'Outside the Camp': Hebrews 13.9–14." *HTR* 55 (1962): 299–315.

Laansma, Jon. *'I Will Give You Rest.' The Rest Motif in the New Testament with Special Reference to Mt 11 and Heb 3–4*. WUNT 98. Tübingen: Mohr Siebeck, 1997.

Ladd, George Eldon. *Jesus and the Kingdom*. Waco, TX: Word Books, 1964.

Landgraf, Paul David. "The Structure of Hebrews; A Word of Exhortation in Light of the Day of Atonement." Pages 19–27 in *A Cloud of Witnesses: The Theology of Hebrews in its Ancients Contexts*. Edited by Richard Bauckham *et al*. LNTS 387. London: T&T Clark, 2008.

Lane, William L. "Hebrews: A Sermon in Search of a Setting." *SWJT* 28 (1985): 13–18.

__________. *Hebrews 1–8*. WBC 47A. Dallas: Word, 1991.

__________. *Hebrews 9–13*. WBC 47B. Dallas: Word, 1991.

Layton, Scott C. "Christ Over His House (Hebrews 3.6) and Hebrew *asher al-habayit*'." *NTS* 37 (1991): 473–77.

Lee, E. Kenneth. "Words Denoting 'Pattern' in the New Testament." *NTS* 8 (1962): 166–73.

Lee, Jihye. "The Unshakable Kingdom through the Shaking of Heaven and Earth in Heb 12:26–29." *NovT* 62 (2020): 257–72.

Lee, John A. L. "Hebrews 5:14 and *hexis*: A History of Misunderstanding." *NovT* 39 (1997): 151–76.

Levinsohn, Stephen H. "The definite article with proper names for referring to people in the Greek of Acts." *Work Papers of the Summer Institute of Linguistics, University of North Dakota Session* 35 (1991): 91–102.

__________. "Towards a Unified Linguistic Description of *houtos* and *ekeinos*" Pages 204–16 in *The Linguist as Pedagogue: Trends in the Teaching and Linguistic*

Analysis of the Greek New Testament. Edited by Stanley E. Porter and Matthew Brook O'Donnell. Sheffield: Sheffield Phoenix Press, 2009.

Lewis, C. S. *Mere Christianity*. 1952. Repr., New York: HarperCollins, 2001.

Lewis, T. W. "'and if he shrinks back' (Heb.x.38b)." *NTS* 22 (1975): 88–94.

Liddell, Henry George, Robert Scott, Henry Stuart Jones, and Roderick McKenzie. *A Greek-English Lexicon*. 9th ed. with Supplement. Oxford: Clarendon Press, 1996.

Lightfoot, Neil R. "The Saving of the Savior." *ResQ* 16 (1973): 166–73.

Lincoln, Andrew. T. "Sabbath, Rest, and Eschatology in the New Testament." Pages 197–217 in *From Sabbath to Lord's Day*. Edited by Donald A. Carson. Grand Rapids: Zondervan, 1982.

Lindars, Barnabas. "The Rhetorical Structure of Hebrews." *NTS* 35 (1989): 382–406.

Lindsay, Dennis R. "*Pistis* and *'Emunah*: The Nature of Faith in the Epistle to the Hebrews." Pages 158–69 in *A Cloud of Witnesses: The Theology of Hebrews in Its Ancient Contexts*. Edited by Richard Bauckham *et al*. LNTS 387. London: T&T Clark, 2008.

Loader, William. "Revisiting High Priesthood Christology in Hebrews." *ZNW* 109 (1018): 235–83.

Lohr, Joel N. "Righteous Abel, Wicked Cain: Genesis 4:1–16 in the Masoretic Text, the Septuagint, and the New Testament." *CBQ* 71 (2009): 485–96.

Loke, Andrew Ter Ern. *The Origin of Divine Christology*. SNTSMS 169. Cambridge: Cambridge University Press, 2017.

Longenecker, Bruce W. *Rhetoric at the Boundaries: The Art and Theology of New Testament Chain-Link Transitions*. Waco, TX: Baylor University Press, 2005.

Longenecker, Richard N. *Biblical Exegesis in the Apostolic Period*. Grand Rapids: Eerdmans, 1975.

Longinus. *Longinus on the Sublime*. Translated by W. Rhys Roberts. London: Cambridge University Press, 1907.

López, René A. "Identifying 'The Angel of the Lord' in the Book of Judges: A Model for Reconsidering the Referent in Other Old Testament Loci." *BBR* 20 (2010): 1–18.

Louw, Johannes P., and Eugene Albert Nida. *Greek-English Lexicon of the New Testament: Based on Semantic Domains*. New York: United Bible Societies, 1996.

Lünemann, Gottlieb. *Critical and Exegetical Handbook to the Epistle to the Hebrews*. Translated by Maurice J. Evans. Critical and Exegetical Commentary on the New Testament. Edinburgh: T&T Clark, 1882.

MacDonald, William Graham. "Christology and 'The Angel of the Lord.'" Pages 324–35 in *Current Issues in Biblical and Patristic Interpretation: Studies in Honor of Merrill C. Tenney Presented by His Former Students*. Edited by Gerald F. Hawthorne. Grand Rapids: Eerdmans, 1975.

Mackie, Scott D. *Eschatology and Exhortation in the Epistle to the Hebrews*. WUNT 223. Tübingen: Mohr Siebeck, 2007.

———. "Confession of the Son of God in Hebrews." *NTS* 53 (2007): 114–29.

———. "Early Christian Eschatological Experience in the Warnings and Exhortations of the Epistle to the Hebrews." *TynBul* 63 (2012): 93–114.

———. "Visually Oriented Rhetoric and Visionary Experience in Hebrews 12.1–4." *CBQ* 79 (2017): 476–97.

MacLeod, David J. "The Literary Structure of the Book of Hebrews." *BibSac* 146 (1989): 185–97.

———. "The Cleansing of the True Tabernacle." *BibSac* 152 (1995): 60–71.

Malik, Peter. "Rid Us (Not) of the Temptation: A Note on the Text of Hebrews 11.37." *JSNT* 44 (2022): 580–89.

Malone, Andrew S. *God's Mediators: A Biblical Theology of Priesthood*. NSBT 43. Downers Grove, IL: InterVarsity Press, 2017.

Marohl, Matthew. "Letter Writing and Social Identity." Pages 93–104 in *T&T Clark Handbook to Social Identity in the New Testament*. Edited by J. Brian Tucker and Coleman A. Baker. London: Bloomsbury T&T Clark, 2014.

Marshall, I. Howard. *Kept by the Power of God*. Minneapolis: Bethany Fellowship, 1969.

Martin, Michael W. "Is Hebrews 5:11–6:20 Really a Digression?" *NovT* 57 (2015): 295–310.

Mayhue, Richard L. "Heb 13:20: Covenant of Grace or New Covenant? An Exegetical Note." *TMSJ* 7 (1996): 251–57.

Michael Wade Martin and Jason A. Whitlark. "Strengthened by Grace and Not by Foods: Reconsidering the Literary, Theological, and Social Context of Hebrews 13:7–14." *NovT* 65 (2012): 350–80.

Maston, Jason. "'What is Man?' An Argument for the Christological Reading of Psalm 8 in Hebrews 2." *ZNW* 112 (2021): 89–104.

____________. "The Son and Scripture in Hebrews 1–2." *JSNT* 44 (2022): 496–515.

Mathewson, Dave. "Reading Heb 6:4–6 in Light of the Old Testament." *WTJ* 61 (1999): 209–25.

McAfee, Matthew. "Covenant and the Warnings of Hebrews: The Blessing and the Curse." *JETS* 57 (2014): 537–53.

McClister, David. *Relationships in the Messianic Time: A Commentary on Philemon.* Tampa: DeWard Publishing Company, Ltd., 2022.

McCruden, Kevin B. "The Eloquent Blood of Jesus: The Neglected Theme of the Fidelity of Jesus in Hebrews 12:24." *CBQ* 75 (2013): 504–20.

McCullough, J. Cecil. "The Impossibility of a Second Repentance in Hebrews." *BTB* 24 (1974) 1–7.

____________. "The Old Testament Quotations in Hebrews." *NTS* 26 (1980): 363–79.

____________. "Isaiah in Hebrews." Pages 159–73 in *Isaiah in the New Testament.* Edited by Steve Moyise and Maaten J. J. Menken. London: T&T Clark, 2005.

McKnight, Scot. "The Warning Passages of Hebrews: A Formal Analysis and Theological Conclusions." *TrinJ* 13 (1992): 21–59.

McNamara, Martin. "Melchizedek: Gen 14,17–20 in the Targums, in Rabbinic and Early Christian Literature." *Bib* 81 (2000): 1–31.

Merrill, Eugene H. "Royal Priesthood: An Old Testament Messianic Motif." *BibSac* 150 (1993): 50–61.

Metzger, Bruce M. "The Formulas Introducing Quotations of Scripture in the NT and the Mishnah." *JBL* 70 (1951): 297–307.

____________. *A Textual Commentary on the Greek New Testament, Second Edition, A Companion Volume to the United Bible Societies' Greek New Testament*. 4th rev. ed. London; New York: United Bible Societies, 1994.

Miller, Merland Ray. "What is the Literary Form of Hebrews 11?" *JETS* 29 (1986): 411–17.

Milligan, Robert. *The Scheme of Redemption*. 1869. Repr., St. Louis: Bethany Press, 1957.

———. *A Commentary on the Epistle to the Hebrews*. Nashville: Gospel Advocate Company, 1973.

Moberly, R. Walter L. "Exemplars of Faith in Hebrews 11: Abel." Pages 353–63 in *The Epistle to the Hebrews and Christian Theology*. Edited by Richard Bauckham *et al*. Grand Rapids: Eerdmans, 2009.

Moffatt, James. *A Critical and Exegetical Commentary on the Epistle to the Hebrews*. ICC. Edinburgh: T&T Clark, 1924.

Moffitt, David M. *Atonement and the Logic of Resurrection in the Epistle to the Hebrews*. NovTSup 141. Leiden: Brill, 2011.

———. "Exodus in Hebrews." Pages 146–63 in *Exodus in the New Testament*. Edited by Seth M. Ehorn. LNTS 663. London: T&T Clark, 2022.

Montanari, Franco. *The Brill Dictionary of Ancient Greek*. Leiden: Brill, 2015.

Moore, Nicholas J. *Repetition in Hebrews*. WUNT 388. Tübingen: Mohr Siebeck, 2015.

Morales, Michael L. *Who Shall Ascend the Mountain of the Lord?: A Biblical Theology of the Book of Leviticus*. NSBT 37. Downers Grove, IL: InterVarsity Press, 2015.

———. *Exodus Old and New: A Biblical Theology of Redemption*. The Essential Studies in Biblical Theology. Downers Grove, IL: IVP Academic, 2020.

Morgan, Teresa. *Roman Faith and Christian Faith:* Pistis *and* Fides *in the Early Roman Empire and Early Churches*. Oxford: Oxford University Press, 2015.

Morris, Leon. *The Cross in the New Testament*. Grand Rapids: Eerdmans, 1965.

———. *Hebrews*. The Expositor's Bible Commentary. Grand Rapids: Zondervan, 1996.

Mosser, Carl. "No Lasting City: Rome, Jerusalem and the Place of Hebrews in the History of Earliest 'Christianity.'" PhD diss., St. Mary's College, University of St. Andrews, 2004.

———. "Rahab Outside the Camp." Pages 383–404 in *The Epistle to the Hebrews and Christian Theology*. Edited by Richard Bauckham at al. Grand Rapids: Eerdmans, 2009.

Motyer, Stephen. "The Psalm Quotations of Hebrews 1: A Hermeneutic-Free Zone?" *TynBul* 50 (1999): 3–22.

Moulton, James Hope, and George Milligan. *The Vocabulary of the Greek Testament*. London: Hodder and Stoughton, 1930.

Moulton, James Hope and Nigel Turner. *A Grammar of New Testament Greek: Syntax*. Vol. 3. Edinburgh: T&T Clark, 1963.

____________. *A Grammar of New Testament Greek: Style*. Vol. 4. Edinburgh: T&T Clark, 1976.

Murphy-O'Connor, Jerome. "Lots of God-Fearers? '*theosebeis*' in the Aphrodisias Inscription." *RB* 99 (1992): 418–24.

Nardoni, Enrique. "Partakers in Christ (Hebrews 3.14)." *NTS* 37 (1991): 456–72.

Neusner, Jacob. *The Mishnah: A New Translation*. New Haven: Yale University Press, 1988.

____________. *Writing with Scripture*. Minneapolis: Fortress, 1989.

____________. "Paradigmatic Thinking Versus Historical Thinking: The Case of Rabbinic Judaism." Pages 163–92 in *Approaches to Ancient Judaism Vol 11*. Edited by Jacob Neusner. Atlanta: Scholars Press 1997.

Neusner, Jacob, Alan J. Avery-Peck, and William Scott Green, eds. *EJud*. 2nd ed. 5 vols. Leiden: Brill, 2005.

Neyrey, Jerome H. "'Without Beginning of Days or End of Life' (Hebrews 7:3): Topos for a True Deity." *CBQ* 53 (1991): 439–55.

____________. "Group Orientation." Pages 88–91 in *Biblical Social Values and Their Meaning: A Handbook*. 3rd ed. Edited by John J. Pilch and Bruce J. Malina. Matrix: The Bible in Mediterranean Context 10. Eugene, OR: Cascade Books, 2016.

____________. *Honor and Shame in the Gospel of Matthew*. Louisville: Westminster John Knox Press, 1998.

Nicole, Roger. "The New Testament Use of the Old Testament." Pages 135–51 in *Revelation and the Bible*. Edited by Carl Henry. Grand Rapids: Baker Books, 1958.

Nongbri, Brent. "A Touch of Condemnation in a Word of Exhortation: Apocalyptic Language and Graeco-Roman Rhetoric in Hebrews 6:4–12." *NovT* 45 (2003): 265–79.

Orfali, Moisés. "*Conversos* in Medieval Spain." *EJud* 4:1676–90.

Paluchník, Pavel. "Let us Go Outside the Camp: Hebrews 13:13 and the Purpose of the Epistle." *Communio Viatorum* 63 (2021): 185–208.

Pao, David. *Acts and the Isaianic New Exodus*. Grand Rapids: Baker Books, 2000.

Pate, Brian. "Who is Speaking? The Use of Isaiah 8:17–18 in Hebrews 2:13 as a Case Study for Applying the Speech of Key OT Figures to Christ." *JETS* 59 (2016): 731–45.

Paul, M. J. "The Order of Melchizedek (Ps 110:4 and Heb 7:3)." *WTJ* 49 (1987): 195–211.

Pickering, P. E. "Did the Greek Ear Detect 'Careless Verbal Repetitions'?" *Classical Quarterly* 53 (2003): 490–99.

Peeler, Amy. " 'A fearful thing to fall into the hands of the living God': A Study of Fear in the Epistle to the Hebrews." *RevExp* 115 (2018): 40–49.

Penick, Daniel A. "Paul's Epistles Compared with One Another and with the Epistle to the Hebrews." *American Journal of Philology* 42 (1921): 58–72.

Peters, Ronald D. *The Greek Article: A Functional Grammar of ho-items in the Greek New Testament with Special Emphasis on the Greek Article*. Linguistic Biblical Studies 9. Leiden: Brill, 2014.

Peterson, David G. *Hebrews: An Introduction and Commentary*. TNTC 15. Downers Grove, IL: InterVarsity Press, 2020.

Philo of Alexandria. *The Works of Philo: Complete and Unabridged*. Translated by Charles Duke Yonge. Peabody, MA: Hendrickson, 1995.

Pickup, Martin. "'According to the Order of Melchizedek': The Use of Psalm 110 in Hebrews 7." Pages 112–35 in *A Tribute to Melvin D. Curry, Jr.* Edited by Ferrell Jenkins. Temple Terrace: Florida College, 1997.

__________. "New Testament Interpretation of the Old Testament: The Theological Rationale of Midrashic Exegesis." *JETS* 51 (2008): 353–81.

Pierce, Madison N. *Divine Discourse in the Epistle to the Hebrews: The Recontextualization of Spoken Quotations of Scripture*. SNTSMS 178. Cambridge: Cambridge University Press, 2020.

Piotrowski, Nicholas G. "The Concept of Exile in Late Second Temple Judaism: A Review of Recent Scholarship," *CurBR* 15 (2017): 214–47.

Plato. *The Republic of Plato Translated into English*. Translated by Benjamin Jowett. 3rd ed. Oxford: Oxford University Press, 1927.

Porter, Stanley E. "Two Myths: Corporate Personality and Language/Mentality Determinism." *SJT* 43 (1990): 289–307.

———. *Verbal Aspect in the Greek of the New Testament with Reference to Tense and Mood.* Studies in Biblical Greek 1. New York: Peter Lang, 2010.

Postell, Seth D. "A Literary, Compositional, and Intertextual Analysis of Psalm 45." *BibSac* 176 (2019): 146–63.

Poteat, Hubert McNeill. "Rome and the Christians," *Classical Journal* 33 (1937): 134–44.

Pouchelle, Patrick. "The Septuagintal *Paideia* and the Construction of a Jewish Identity during the Late Hellenistic and Early Roman Period." *CBQ* 81 (2019): 33–45.

Poythress, Vern. *The Shadow of Christ in the Law of Moses*. Brentwood, TN: Wolgemuth & Hyatt, 1991.

Proctor, John. "Judgement or Vindication? Deuteronomy 32 in Hebrews 10:30." *TynBul* 55 (2004): 65–80.

Quintillian. *Quintilian, With an English Translation.* Edited by Harold Edgeworth Butler. Cambridge: Harvard University Press, 1920.

———. *Quintillian.* Translated by H. E. Butler. 4 vols. LCL. London: William Heinemann, 1922.

Rapske, Brian. *Paul in Roman Custody*. Vol. 3 of *The Book of Acts in Its First Century Setting,* Grand Rapids: Eerdmans, 1994.

Reed, Jeffrey T. "The Epistle." Pages 171–93 in *Handbook of Classical Rhetoric in the Hellenistic Period (330 B.C.–A.D. 400).* Edited by Stanley E. Porter. Leiden: Brill, 1997.

Rhee, Victor. "Christology and the Concept of Faith in Hebrews 1:1–2:4." *BibSac* 157 (2000): 174–89.

———. "The Role of Chiasm for Understanding Christology in Hebrews 1:1–14." *JBL* 131 (2012): 341–62.

Ribbens, Benjamin J. "The Sacrifice God Desired: Psalm 40:6–8 in Hebrews 10." *NTS* 67 (2021): 284–304.

———. "Partakers of Christ: Union with Christ in Hebrews." *Pro Ecclesia* 31 (2022): 282–301.

Rice, George E. "The Chiastic Structure of the Central Section of the Epistle to the Hebrews." *AUSS* 19 (1981): 243–46.

Richardson, Christopher. "Apostasy as a Motif and its Effect on the Structure of Hebrews." *AUSS* 23 (1985): 29–35.

__________. "The Passion: Reconsidering Hebrews 5:7–8." Pages 51–67 in *A Cloud of Witnesses: The Theology of Hebrews in Its Ancient Contexts*. Edited by Richard Bauckham *et al*. LNTS 387. London: T&T Clark, 2008.

__________. *Pioneer and Perfecter of Faith*. WUNT 338. Tübingen: Mohr Siebeck, 2012.

Riddle, Donald Wayne. "Hebrews, First Clement, and the Persecution of Domitian." *JBL* 43 (1924): 329–48.

__________. "Early Christian Hospitality: A Factor in the Gospel Transmission." *JBL* 57 (1938): 141–54.

Roberts, Alastair, and Andrew Wilson. *Echoes of Exodus: Tracing Themes of Redemption through Scripture*. Wheaton, IL: Crossway, 2018.

Roberts, Alexander, and James Donaldson, eds. *The Ante-Nicene Fathers*. 1885–1887. 10 vols. Repr., Peabody, MA: Hendrickson, 1994.

Roberts, J. J. M. "The Davidic Origin of the Zion Tradition." *JBL* 92 (1973): 329–44.

Roberts, Phil. "The Story of the Tabernacle." Pages 65–83 in *Hebrews for Every Man: Florida College Annual Lectures 1988*. Edited by Melvin D. Curry. Temple Terrace: Florida College, 1988.

__________. "The City of God." Pages 233–51 in *The Gospel in the Old Testament*. Edited by Daniel W. Petty. Florida College Annual Lectures. Temple Terrace, FL: Florida College Bookstore, 2003.

Robertson, A. T. *A Grammar of the Greek New Testament in the Light of Historical Research*. 4th ed. New York: Doran, 1923.

Robinson, Gnana. "The Idea of Rest in the Old Testament and the Search for the Basic Character of Sabbath." *ZAW* 92 (1980): 32–42.

Rogerson, J. W. "The Hebrew Conception of Corporate Personality: A Re-examination." *JTS* 21 (1970): 1–16.

Rohrbaugh, Richard L. "Honor." Pages 63–78 in *The Ancient Mediterranean Social World: A Sourcebook*. Edited by Zeba A. Crook. Grand Rapids: Eerdmans, 2020.

Rosenberg, Joel. "Jeremiah and Ezekiel." Pages 184–206 in *The Literary Guide to the Bible*. Edited by Robert Alter and Frank Kermode. Cambridge: Harvard University Press, 1987.

Rowell, J. B. "Exposition of Hebrews Six: "An Age-Long Battleground." *BibSac* 94 (1937): 321–42.

Runge, Steven E. *Discourse Grammar of the Greek New Testament: A Practical Introduction for Teaching and Exegesis*. Bellingham, WA: Lexham Press, 2010.

Ryken, Leland *et al. Dictionary of Biblical Imagery*. Downers Grove, IL: InterVarsity Press, 2000.

Sakenfeld, Katharine Doob, ed. *The New Interpreter's Dictionary of the Bible*. 5 vols. Nashville: Abingdon, 2006–2009.

Saltz, Jared W. "Parting the Waves, Parting the Ways: The Identity of Christ and Christianity in the Early Church." Pages 28–57 in *Studies in Church History: Essays in Honor of Daniel W. Petty*. Edited by David McClister. Temple Terrace: Florida College Press, 2020.

Sanders, E. P. *Paul and Palestinian Judaism: A Comparison of Patterns of Religion*. Philadelphia: Fortress, 1977.

Scandrett, Joel, and William G. Witt. *Mapping Atonement: The Doctrine of Reconciliation in Christian History and Theology*. Grand Rapids: Baker Academic, 2022.

Schaff, Philip, ed. *The Nicene and Post-Nicene Fathers*, Series 1. Edited by Philip Schaff. 1886–1889. 14 vols. Repr., Peabody, MA: Hendrickson, 1994.

———. *The Nicene and Post-Nicene Fathers*, Series 2. Edited by Philip Schaff. 1886–1889. 14 vols. Repr., Peabody, MA: Hendrickson, 1994.

Schenck, Kenneth L. "A Celebration of the Enthroned Son: The Catena of Hebrews 1." *JBL* 120 (2001): 469–85.

Schmidt, Thomas E. "Moral Lethargy and the Epistle to the Hebrews." *WTJ* 54 (1992): 167–73.

Schnittjer, Gary Edward. "A Comparison of the Use of the Scripture in the NT and Early Rabbinic Traditions." Paper presented at the Annual Meeting of the Evangelical Theological Society. Nashville, TN, 15 November 2000.

Schoeps, Hans Joachim. "The Sacrifice of Isaac in Paul's Theology." *JBL* 65 (1946): 385–92.

Schreiner Thomas R. *Hebrews*. Evangelical Biblical Theology Commentary. Bellingham, WA: Lexham Press, 2021.

Scott, Brett R. "Jesus' Superiority Over Moses in Hebrews 3:1–6." *BibSac* 155 (1998): 201–10.

Scott, E. "The Epistle to the Hebrews and Roman Christianity." *HTR* 13 (1920): 205–19.

Scott, Jr., J. Julius. "*Archegos* in the Salvation History of the Epistle to the Hebrews." *JETS* 29 (1986): 47–54.

Scott, James M., ed. *Exile: Old Testament, Jewish, and Christian Conceptions*. JSJSupp 56. Leiden: Brill, 1997.

__________. ed. *Exile: A Conversation with N. T. Wright*. Downers Grove, IL: IVP Academic, 2017.

Selby, Gary S. "The Meaning and Function of *suneidēsis* in Hebrews 9 and 10." *ResQ* 28 (1985–6): 145–54.

Shuler, Philip L. "Encomium." *AYBD* 2:505–06.

Silva, Moises. "Perfection and Eschatology in Hebrews." *WTJ* 39 (1976): 60–71.

Silva, Moises, ed. *New International Dictionary of New Testament Theology and Exegesis*. 5 vols. Grand Rapids: Zondervan, 2014.

Simmers, Gary. "Who is 'The Angel of the Lord'?" *Faith and Mission* 17 (2000): 3–16.

Skarsaune, Oskar. *In the Shadow of the Temple: Jewish Influences on Early Christianity*. Downers Grove, IL: InterVarsity Press, 2002.

__________. "Does the Letter to the Hebrews Articulate a Supersessionist Theology? A Response to Richard Hays." Pages 174–82 in *The Epistle to the Hebrews and Christian Theology*. Edited by Richard Bauckham *et al*. Grand Rapids: Eerdmans, 2009.

Sklar, Jay. *Sin, Impurity, Sacrifice, Atonement: The Priestly Conceptions*. Hebrew Bible Monographs 2. Sheffield: Sheffield Phoenix Press, 2015.

Slingerland, H. Dixon. *Claudian Policymaking and the Early Imperial Repression of Judaism at Rome*. USF Studies in the History of Judaism 160. Atlanta: Scholars Press, 1997.

Smallwood, E. Mary. "Domitian's Attitude towards Jews and Judaism." *Classical Philology* 51 (1956): 1–13.

Smillie, Gene R. "'The One Who is Speaking' in Hebrews 12:25." *TynBul* 55 (2004): 275–94.

____________. "Contrast or Continuity in Hebrews 1.1–2?" *NTS* 51 (2005): 543–60.

____________. "'The Other *logos*' at the End of Heb 4:13." *NovT* 47 (2005): 19–25.

Smyth, Herbert Weir. *Greek Grammar*. Rev. ed. Cambridge: Harvard University Press, 1956.

Son, Kiwoong. *Zion Symbolism in Hebrews: Hebrews 12:18–24 as a Hermeneutical Key to the Epistle*. Milton Keynes: Paternoster, 2005.

Songer, Harold S., "A Superior Priesthood: Hebrews 4:14–7:28." *RevExp* 82 (1985): 345–59.

Southwell, P. J. M. "A Note on Habakkuk ii.4." *JTS* 19 (1968): 614–17.

Sproule, John A. "*Parapesontas* in Hebrews 6:6." *GTJ* 2 (1981): 327–32.

Stanley, Christopher D. "'Pearls Before Swine': Did Paul's Audiences Understand His Biblical Quotations?" *NovT* 41 (1999): 124–44.

Stanley, Steve. "Hebrews 9:6–10: The 'Parable' of the Tabernacle." *NovT* 37 (1995): 385–99.

Stauffer, Ethelbert. *New Testament Theology*. New York: Macmillan, 1955.

Stern, Menahem, ed., *Greek and Latin Authors on Jews and Judaism*. Jerusalem: Israel Academy of Sciences and Humanities, 1984.

Stevens, Daniel. "Is It Valid? A Case for the Repunctuation of Hebrews 9:17." *JBL* 137 (2018): 1019–1025.

Steyn, Gert. "Addressing an Angelomorphic Christological Myth in Hebrews?" *HTS* 59 (2003): 1107–28.

____________. "Hebrews' Angelology in the Light of early Jewish Apocalyptic Imagery." *Journal of Early Christian History* 1 (2011): 143–64.

Still, Todd D. "*Christos* as *Pistos*: The Faith(fulness) of Jesus in the Epistle to the Hebrews." *CBQ* 69 (2007): 746–55.

Stock, Augustine. "Chiastic Awareness and Education in Antiquity." *BTB* 14 (1984): 23–27.

Stowers, Stanley K. *Letter-Writing in Greco-Roman Antiquity*. LEC. Philadelphia: Westminster, 1986.

Strack, Hermann L., and Paul Billerbeck. *A Commentary on the New Testament from the Talmud & Midrash*. Edited by Jacob N. Cerone. Translated by Andrew Bowden and Joseph Longarino. 3 vols. Bellingham, WA: Lexham Press, 2021–2022.

Stewart, Tyler A. "Jewish *Paideia*: Greek Education in the Letter of Aristeas and 2 Maccabees." *JSJ* 48 (2017): 182–202.

Stuckenbruck, Loren T. *Angel Veneration and Christology: A Study in Early Judaism and in the Christology of the Apocalypse of John*. WUNT 70. Tübingen: Mohr Siebeck, 1995.

———. "'Angels' and 'God': Exploring the Limits of Early Jewish Monotheism." Pages 45–70 in *Early Jewish and Christian Monotheism*. Edited by Loren T. Stuckenbruck and Wendy E. S. North. London; New York: T&T Clark, 2004.

Sulc, Kevin. "The Gospel of the Kingdom: Jesus and the Kingdom of God." Pages 97–109 in *Jesus for a New Millennium: Florida College Annual Lectures 2001*. Edited by Ferrell Jenkins. Temple Terrace: Florida College, 2001.

Swetnam, James. "'The Greater and More Perfect Tent': A Contribution to the Discussion of Hebrews 9,11." *Bib* 47 (1966): 91–106.

———. "On the Literary Genre of the 'Epistle' to the Hebrews." *NovT* 11 (1969): 261–69.

———. "Hebrews 9,2 and The Uses of Consistency." *CBQ* 32 (1970): 205–21.

———. "Jesus as *Logos* in Hebrews 4,12–13." *Bib* 62 (1981): 214–24.

———. "The Crux at Hebrews 5,7–8." *Bib* 81 (2000): 347–61.

———. "*ex henos* in Hebrews 2,11." *Bib* 88 (2007): 517–25.

———. "*ho apostolos* in Hebrews 3.1" *Bib* 89 (2008): 252–62.

Swinson, L. Timothy. "'Wind' and 'Fire' in Hebrews 1:7: A Reflection upon the Use of Psalm 104 (103)." *TrinJ* 28 (2007): 215–28.

Tacitus, Publius Cornelius. *The Annals of Tacitus*. Translated by Alfred John Church and William Jackson Brodribb. New York: MacMillan, 1906.

———. *The History of Tacitus*. Translated by Alfred John Church and William Jackson Brodribb. Cambridge: MacMillan and Co., 1864.

Tenney, Merrill C. "A New Approach to the Book of Hebrews." *BibSac* 123 (1966): 230–36.

Thatcher, Tom. "Cain and Abel in Early Christian Memory: A Case Study in 'The Use of the Old Testament in the New.'" *CBQ* 72 (2010): 732–51.

Thayer, Joseph Henry. *A Greek-English Lexicon of the New Testament*. New York: Harper & Brothers, 1889.

Thiessen, Matthew. "Hebrews and the End of the Exodus." *NovT* 49 (2007): 353–69.

———. "Hebrews 12.5–13, the Wilderness Period, and Israel's Discipline." *NTS* 55 (2009): 366–79.

Theophilus, Michael P. "The Numismatic Background of *charactēr* in Hebrews 1:3." *ABR* 64 (2016): 69–80.

Thomas, Rosalind. *Literacy and Orality in Ancient Greece*. Key Themes in Ancient History. Cambridge: Cambridge University Press, 1992.

Thompson, James W. "The Underlying Unity of Hebrews." *ResQ* 18 (1975): 129–36.

———. "The Conceptual Background and Purpose of the Midrash in Hebrews vii." *NovT* 19 (1977): 209–23.

———. "Outside the Camp: A Study of Heb 13:9–14." *CBQ* 40 (1978): 53–63.

———. "Hebrews 9 and Hellenistic Concepts of Sacrifice." *JBL* 98 (1979): 567–78.

———. "The Hermeneutics of the Epistle to the Hebrews." *ResQ* 38 (1996): 229–37.

———. "The Epistle to the Hebrews and the Pauline Legacy." *ResQ* 47 (2005): 197–206.

———. "*EPHAPAX*: The One and the Many in Hebrews," *NTS* 53 (2007): 566–81.

———. *Hebrews*. Paideia. Grand Rapids: Baker Academic, 2008.

———. "Insider Ethics for Outsiders: Ethics for Aliens in Hebrews." *ResQ* 53 (2011): 207–19.

———. *Strangers on the Earth: Philosophy and Rhetoric in Hebrews*. Eugene, OR: Cascade Books, 2020.

Thompson, Leonard. "A Sociological Analysis of Tribulation in the Apocalypse of John." *Semeia* 36 (1986): 147–74.

———. *The Book of Revelation: Apocalypse and Empire*. Oxford: Oxford University Press, 1990.

Tönges, Elke. "The Epistle to the Hebrews as a 'Jesus Midrash'." Pages 89–105 in *Hebrews: Contemporary Methods—New Insights*. Edited by Gabriella Gelardini. Biblical Interpretation Series Volume 75. Atlanta: Society of Biblical Literature, 2005.

Trench, Richard Chenevix. *Synonyms of the New Testament*. London: Macmillan and Co., 1880.

VanGemeren, Willem, ed. *New International Dictionary of Old Testament Theology & Exegesis*. 5 vols. Grand Rapids: Zondervan, 1997.

Vanhoye, Albert. *A Structured Translation of the Epistle to the Hebrews*. Translated by James Swetnam. Rome: Pontifical Biblical Institute, 1964.

Walker, Peter "Jerusalem in Hebrews 13:9–14 and the Dating of the Epistle." *TynBul* 45 (1994): 39–71.

Wallace, Daniel B. *Greek Grammar beyond the Basics: An Exegetical Syntax of the New Testament*. Grand Rapids: Zondervan, 1996.

———. "Hebrews 2:3–4 and the Sign Gifts." < https://bible.org/article/hebrews-23-4-and-sign-gifts>

Wallace, David. "The Use of Psalms in the Shaping of a Text: Psalm 2:7 and Psalm 110:1 in Hebrews 1." *ResQ* 45 (2003): 41–50.

Wallace, Howard N. "Genesis 2:1–3—Creation and Sabbath." *Pacifica* 1 (1980): 235–50.

Wallis, Wilber B. "The Use of Psalms 8 and 110 in I Corinthians 15:25–27 and in Hebrews 1 and 2." *JETS* 15 (1972): 25–29.

Walsh, Matthew L. *Angels Associated with Israel in the Dead Sea Scrolls*. WUNT 509. Tübingen: Mohr Siebeck, 2019.

Walters, James C., and Jerry L. Sumney. "Paul, Adoption, and Inheritance." Pages 33–67 in *Paul in the Greco-Roman World: A Handbook*, Vol. 1. Edited by J. Paul Sampley. Rev. ed. London; Oxford; New York: Bloomsbury; Bloomsbury T&T Clark, 2016.

Walters, John R. "The Rhetorical Arrangement of Hebrews." *ATJ* 51 (1996): 59–70.

Waltke, Bruce K. "Cain and His Offering." *WTJ* 48 (1986): 363–72.

Warden, Duane. "Imperial Persecution and the Dating of 1 Peter and Revelation." *JETS* 34 (1991): 203–12.

Weiser, Artur. *The Psalms*. OTL. Philadelphia: Fortress, 1962.

Weiss, Herold. "*Sabbatismos* in the Epistle to the Hebrews," *CBQ* 58 (1996): 674–89.

Wengst, Klaus. *Pax Romana and the Peace of Jesus Christ*. Translated by John Bowden. Philadelphia: Fortress, 1987.

Wenkel, David H. "Gezerah Shawah as Analogy in the Epistle to the Hebrews." *BTB* 37 (2007): 62–68.

———. "Sensory Experience and the Contrast Between the Covenants in Hebrews 12." *BibSac* 173 (2016): 219–34.

———. "Abraham's Typological Resurrection from the Dead in Hebrews 11." *CTR* 15 (2018): 51–66.

Westcott, Brooke Foss. *The Epistle to the Hebrews: The Greek Text with Notes and Essays*. 3rd ed. London: Macmillan, 1903.

Westfall, Cynthia Long. A Discourse Analysis of the Letter to the Hebrews: The Relationship between Form and Meaning. LNTS 297. London: T&T Clark, 2005.

White, John L. *Light from Ancient Letters*. Philadelphia: Fortress, 1986.

White, Stephen L. "Angel of the Lord: Messenger or Euphemism?" *TynBul* 50 (1999): 299–305.

Whitfield, Bryan J. *Joshua Traditions and the Argument of Hebrews 3 and 4*. BZNW 194. Berlin: DeGruyter, 2013.

Whitlark, Jason A. "Funerary Anchors of Hope and Hebrews: A Reappraisal of the Origins of the Anchor Iconography in the Catacombs of Rome." *PRSt* 48 (2021): 219–41.

Wilken, Robert Louis. *The Christians as the Romans Saw Them*. 2nd ed. New Haven: Yale University Press, 1984.

Williams, Travis. "The Imperatival Participle in the New Testament." Paper read at the Southwestern Regional Meeting of the Evangelical Theological Society, 24 March 24, 2006. <http://bible.org/article/imperatival-participle-new-testament>.

Williamson, Ronald. *Philo and the Epistle to the Hebrews*. ALGHJ 4. Leiden: Brill, 1970.

Willis, Timothy M. "'Obey your leaders': Hebrews 13 and Leadership in the Church" *ResQ* 36 (1994): 316–26.

Wills, L. "The Form of the Sermon in Hellenistic Judaism and early Christianity." *HTR* 77 (1984): 277–99.

Wilson, J., and R. K. Harrison. "Birthright." *ISBE*, rev. ed. 1:515–16.

Wise, Michael O., Martin G. Abegg Jr., and Edward M. Cook. *The Dead Sea Scrolls: A New Translation*. New York: HarperOne, 2005.

Witherington III, Ben. "The Influence of Galatians on Hebrews." *NTS* 37 (1991): 146–52.

Worley, David R. "Fleeing to Two Immutable Things, God's Oath-Taking and Oath-Witnessing: The Use of Litigant Oath in Hebrews 6:12–20." *ResQ* 36 (1994): 223–36.

Wright, Brian J. "Ancient Literacy in New Testament Research: Incorporating a Few More Lines of Inquiry." *TrinJ* 36 (2015): 161–89.

Wright, N. T. *The New Testament and the People of God*. London: SPCK, 1992.

———. *Paul: Fresh Perspectives*. London: SPCK, 2005.

———. *Paul and the Faithfulness of God*. Vol. 4 of *Christian Origins and the Question of God*. Minneapolis: Fortress, 2013.

Young, Norman H. "*tout' estin tēs sarkos autou* (Heb, x.20): Apposition, Dependent or Explicative?" *NTS* 20 (1973): 100–104.

———. "The Gospel According to Hebrews 9." *NTS* 27 (1981): 198–210.

———. "'Bearing His Reproach' (Heb 13.9–14)." *NTS* 48 (2002): 243–61.

Young, Richard A. *Intermediate New Testament Greek: A Linguistic and Exegetical Approach*. Nashville: Broadman & Holman, 1994.

Yuh, Jason N. "Abandonment and Absenteeism in the Letter to the Hebrews and Greco-Roman Associations." *JBL* 138 (2019): 863–82.

Zemek, Jr., George J. "Interpretive Challenges Relating to Habakkuk 2:4b." *GTJ* 1 (1980): 43–69.

Zurawski, Jason M. "Jewish Education and Identity: Towards an Understanding of Second Temple *Paideia*." Pages 267–78 in *Second Temple Jewish Paideia in Context*. Edited by Jason M. Zurawski and Gabriele Boccaccini. BZNW 228. Berlin: De Gruyter, 2017.

Relationships in the Messianic Time

A Commentary on Philemon

This commentary attempts to show that the usual questions about Onesimus are not the focus of the text itself. Instead, Paul was concerned about Philemon's acceptance of Onesimus as a brother in the Lord. This acceptance, made possible by the transforming work of Christ in both men and by Paul's modelling of Christian love, respected the socio-cultural positions of each man but at the same time acknowledged that these positions were now reconfigured by their Christian identity.

Walk Worthily

A Commentary on Ephesians

Walk Worthily is an exegetical commentary on the Greek text of Ephesians that aims to highlight the particular circumstances addressed by the letter, namely Gentile Christians seeking to be a part of a body that started out as wholly Jewish. Paul's letter was both an assurance to Gentile Christians of their place in God's scheme and God's house, and also an exhortation to these Gentiles to walk worthily of their calling such that the unity of the body of Christ might be practical and not merely theoretical.

Christ Revealed

A Commentary on Matthew

This volume is the second edition of Kenneth "Tack" Chumbley's commentary on Matthew. It has been thoroughly revised and expanded from the first edition.

MORE BIBLE COMMENTARIES BY DEWARD PUBLISHING

Exposition of Genesis (volumes 1 and 2), H.C. Leupold

The Growth of the Seed: Notes on the Book of Genesis, Nathan Ward

Thinking Through Job, L.A. Mott

Searching for the Meaning of Life: Studies in the Book of Ecclesiastes, Paul Earnhart

Thinking Through Jeremiah, L.A. Mott

Let Us Search Our Ways: A Commentary on Lamentations, Evan and Marie Blackmore

Invitation to a Spiritual Revolution: Studies in the Sermon on the Mount, Paul Earnhart

Original Commentary on Acts, J.W. McGarvey

Uncommon Sense: The Wisdom of James for Dispossessed Believers, James T. South

The Lamb, The Woman, and the Dragon: Studies in the Revelation of St. John, Albertus Pieters

For a full listing of DeWard Publishing Company books, visit our website:

www.deward.com

www.ingramcontent.com/pod-product-compliance
Lightning Source LLC
Chambersburg PA
CBHW020340100426
42812CB00029B/3196/J
* 9 7 8 1 9 4 7 9 2 9 3 4 0 *